All the King's Men

All the King's Men

The British Soldier from the Restoration to Waterloo

SAUL DAVID

VIKING

an imprint of

PENGUIN BOOKS

VIKING

Published by the Penguin Group

Penguin Books Ltd, 80 Strand, London WC2R ORL, England

Penguin Group (USA) Inc., 375 Hudson Street, New York, New York 10014, USA

Penguin Group (Canada), 90 Eglinton Avenue East, Suite 700, Toronto, Ontario, Canada M4P 2Y3
(a division of Pearson Penguin Canada Inc.)

Penguin Ireland, 25 St Stephen's Green, Dublin 2, Ireland (a division of Penguin Books Ltd)

Penguin Group (Australia), 250 Camberwell Road,
Camberwell, Victoria 3124, Australia (a division of Pearson Australia Group Pty Ltd)

Penguin Books India Pvt Ltd, 11 Community Centre,
Panchsheel Park, New Delhi – 110 017, India

Penguin Group (NZ), 67 Apollo Drive, Rosedale, Auckland 0632, New Zealand
(a division of Pearson New Zealand Ltd)

Penguin Books (South Africa) (Pty) Ltd, 24 Sturdee Avenue,
Rosebank, Johannesburg 2196, South Africa

Penguin Books Ltd, Registered Offices: 80 Strand, London WC2R ORL, England

www.penguin.com

First published 2012

I

Set in 12/14.75 pt Bembo Book MT Std
Typeset by Jouve (UK), Milton Keynes
Printed in Great Britain by Clays Ltd, St Ives plc

A CIP catalogue record for this book is available from the British Library

ISBN: 978-0-670-91663-4

www.gre

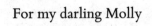

For my darling Molly

Contents

Illustrations

Section One

1. 'Fifteenth, or the Yorkshire East Riding Regiment 1685', hand-coloured print by C. H. Hodges, after Edward Dayes

2. 'Captain Robert Parker, The Royal Regiment of Ireland, *c.* 1720', oil on canvas by Alexis Simon Belle

3. 'Marlborough in Armour', hand-coloured copper engraving by John Bowles, 1722.

4. 'Glorious Battle of Blenheim, August 13th 1704', hand-coloured engraving by G. Scotin after Antoine Benoist

5. 'Blow Your Match', from *The Granadiers Exercise of the Granade*, by Bernard Lens, 1735

6. 'Throw Your Granade', from *The Granadiers Exercise of the Granade*

7. 'The March of the Guards towards Scotland in the year 1745', coloured engraving by Luke Sullivan after William Hogarth, 1750

8. 'The Battle of Culloden, 16 April 1746', coloured engraving by R. Sayer and J. Bennett, *c.* 1780

9. William, Duke of Cumberland, oil on canvas by David Morier, *c.* 1750

10. 'A View of the Taking of Quebec, 13 September 1759', hand-coloured engraving by Carrington Bowles, 1795

11. 'Death of General Wolfe', oil on canvas by Benjamin West

12. 'British Grenadier and Country Girl, *c.* 1760', colour plate by Seymour Lucas, 1790

Section Two

41. 'View of the Village of Waterloo, the Day after the Battle, 19 June 1815', coloured aquatint by Thomas Sutherland after 'A. M. S.' (unidentified artist), 1816

42. 'The Chelsea Pensioners Reading the Waterloo Dispatch', oil on wood by David Wilkie, 1822

Illustration Acknowledgements

The author and publishers are grateful to the following for permission to reproduce the following illustrations:

National Army Museum for nos. 1, 2, 5, 6, 7, 8, 9, 13, 14, 21–4, 27, 28, 29, 31–3; Anne S. K. Brown Military Collection for nos. 3, 4, 10, 12, 15, 17, 19, 20, 26, 30, 34–41; Library of Congress for nos. 16, 18; private collection/ Phillips, Fine Art Auctioneers, New York, USA/ The Bridgeman Art Library for no. 11; Apsley House, The Wellington Museum/Bridgeman Art Library for no. 42; The Trustees of the Victoria and Albert Museum for no. 25

Maps

Author's Note

Much of the history of Britain's rise to greatness in the eighteenth century has been written from the perspective of the Royal Navy. I wanted to redress the balance by focusing on the British Army, and in particular on the lives of its generals and soldiers. To do this I deliberately set out to find diarists and letter writers who were not officers so that I could tell the story from the bottom up as well as top down. Private soldiers were mostly illiterate during this period, but some remarkable first-hand accounts were written and survive: notably one by John Deane of the 1st Foot Guards, which is the only known record of Marlborough's wars by a British private; another by Private Richard Humphrys of the 28th Foot, who fought at Quebec and went on to become an officer; and also that of Private John Timewell of the 43rd Light Infantry, who served with Wellington in the Peninsula.

The book is as much a social history of the British soldier as it is a chronicle of their many successes (and occasional failures) in battle. It explains who they were, why they joined up and how they lived in peacetime and at war. It also tells the story of the soldiers' families – women *and* children – many of whom followed their menfolk to war, were on the army strength (and therefore drew rations) and shared their hardships and danger – quite literally in the sense that they were eyewitnesses to many battles, looted the dead and, occasionally, became casualties themselves.

The British Army owed much of its battlefield success during this period to a roll call of brilliant commanders, some of the greatest in its history, including Marlborough, Wolfe, Moore, Wellington and even that great reformer the Duke of York. But they were only as good as the material they had to work with and it was fortunate for them that the ordinary British soldier was so formidable: disciplined and unflinching with the perfect tactic of 'fire and steel' – a close-range volley followed by a bayonet charge – that would sweep all (or almost all) before it.

If I had to choose the single greatest feat by British soldiers during this period it would be Wolfe's amphibious night landing on the shore below Quebec, the arduous climb up a near-vertical cliff face, followed by a battle on the heights above against a much fresher French army. Wolfe was killed at the moment of victory, but the battle secured Canada for the British. And if I could have been present at one of the battles I write about it would be Waterloo. It must have been an amazing if gory spectacle: 200,000 men fighting over two square miles of ground, a ridge on either side and a wonderful bird's eye view for the commanders, Wellington and Napoleon. The noise, smell and sight of battle must have been unforgettable: last-ditch defences, cavalry charges, infantry in squares, massed artillery, the final doomed advance of the undefeated Imperial Guard – it had it all.

I chose 1815 as the end-point for the book because Wellington's defeat of Napoleon at Waterloo (with a little help from his Dutch, Belgian and Prussian allies) marked the glorious conclusion to 150 years of fighting and usually beating the French, and was the point at which Britain and its army's stock had never stood higher. Ever since that date, British soldiers have fought in major wars with, rather than against, their French counterparts (Vichy troops excepted), though Lord Raglan's constant referral of the enemy as 'the French' during the Crimean War shows that old habits died hard. Their efforts, moreover, have not always been successful: the highpoints include the Alma, the '100 Days' campaign of 1918, El Alamein, D-Day, Slim's successes in Burma, and the Falklands; but there have been just as many lows, with the Retreat from Kabul, Isandlwana, Spion Kop, Kut, Singapore, Tobruk and, mostly recently, Iraq among the more notable setbacks. Certainly Waterloo marked the end of a century-long period when the British soldier could rightfully claim to be the best in the world.

Completing this book has taken six years (with one or two minor distractions) and I have many people to thank: Tom Weldon and Venetia Butterfield, boss of Penguin UK and Publishing Director of Viking respectively, for initiating and keeping faith with such a long-running project; Henry van Moyland, the late fifth Lord Raglan's nephew, for sending me a transcript of, and letting me quote from, the Duke of Wellington's letter to his brother William, written the morning after Waterloo; Simon Sebag Montefiore; General Sir Frank Kitson; James Lester; Rupert and Chiggy Little; Tim and Daisy Woodhead; Colin and Alison Busby; Mick Crumplin; and Matthew Jackson.

I was given excellent assistance by the staffs of the following institutions: British Library, London Library, National Archives, National Army Museum, National Museums of Liverpool, Prince Consort's Library, Royal Artillery Museum (Firepower!), Royal Greenjackets Museum, Royal Scots Dragoon Guards Museum, 1st Queen's Dragoon Guards Museum, and Royal Welch Fusiliers Museum. I would particularly like to thank Lieutenant-Colonel Robin Binks, Karen O'Rourke, Paul Evans, Richard Kemp, Matthew Buck, Dr Alasdair Massie, Christine Pullen, Tim Ward and Anne Pedley.

To my editor at Penguin, Eleo Gordon, I owe a special debt of gratitude for steering this book to publication. She was assisted by a first-class team: Ben Brusey, Jeff Edwards (wonderful maps), Lisa Simmonds, Keith Taylor, Douglas Matthews, Caroline Craig and Donna Poppy.

My agent Peter Robinson and publicist Richard Foreman have provided invaluable support and advice, as always, as has my wonderful wife Lou. My daughters Nell, Tamar and Natasha, on the other hand, still can't quite see the point of a father who does nothing but write about war.

Prologue

In the early hours of 6 July 1685, as the Earl of Feversham's royal army slept in its camp on the field of Sedgemoor in Somerset, a large rebel force crept ever closer, determined to murder the king's soldiers in their tents. The rebels – most of whom were solid West Country dissenters – were led by the handsome and staunchly Protestant Duke of Monmouth, the 36-year-old illegitimate son of the late King Charles II and his mistress Lucy Walter. An experienced soldier who had served with distinction in the Third Anglo-Dutch War of 1672–4, Monmouth had long maintained that his parents were married at the time of his birth, making him and not his uncle, the openly Catholic James II, the rightful heir to the throne.

But his father had failed to support his claim, causing Monmouth to throw in his lot with the ultra-Protestant Rye House plotters who had tried, in 1683, to assassinate both royal brothers and make him king. They failed and Monmouth was banished to Holland, remaining there until his father's death on 6 February 1685. Determined to seize the throne, he landed at Lyme Regis on 11 June with barely 150 followers, proclaiming his uncle a Catholic usurper. West Country puritans rallied to his cause and at one point his army numbered 6,000 men. But after he had failed to take Bristol, and with his support ebbing away, he decided to risk all in the attack on the royal camp at Sedgemoor.

Though his force had shrunk to just 600 cavalry and 3,000 infantry (in five colour-coded regiments), it still outnumbered the Earl of Feversham's royal army of 750 horse, 1,900 infantry and 200 artillerymen sent to oppose it.* But in every other respect Monmouth's force was inferior: it had fewer cannon, four to the royalists' twenty-six; it

---

* Feversham had a further 1,500 militiamen in nearby villages; they did not take part in the battle.

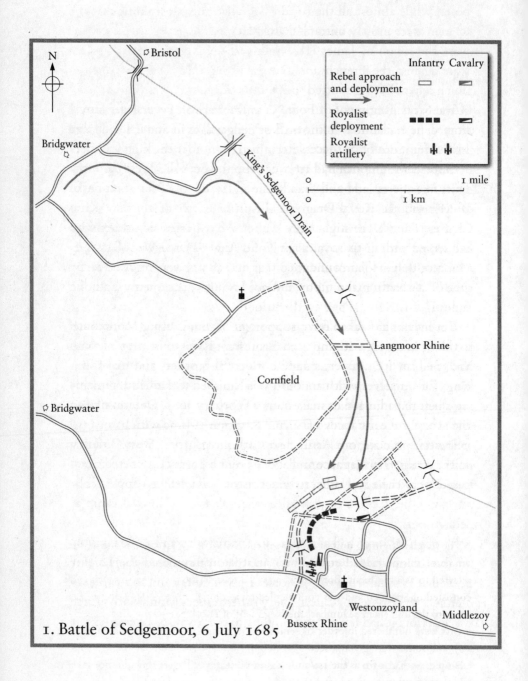

N

♦ Bristol

Bridgwater

King's Sedgemoor Drain

	Infantry	Cavalry
Rebel approach and deployment		
Royalist deployment		
Royalist artillery		

0   1 mile
0   1 km

Bridgwater

Cornfield

Langmoor Rhine

Westonzoyland   Middlezoy

1. Battle of Sedgemoor, 6 July 1685   Bussex Rhine

was poorly armed with matchlock muskets and scythes on eight-foot poles, while almost all the royal troops had the latest flintlocks; and its men were mostly untrained amateurs, while Feversham's soldiers were the cream of James II's standing army, veterans of the recent wars against the French and Dutch. Monmouth acknowledged as much when, having spotted the colours of Dumbarton's (later the 1st Royal Scots) Regiment of Foot,* a unit that had served under him in France, he exclaimed: 'I know these men will fight and if I had them I would not doubt of success.'[1]

Instead Monmouth had to overcome the Scots – and other crack units like the 1st and 2nd Foot Guards, the Royal Horse Guards (or Blues†) and the Royal Dragoons – and he knew his only hope was surprise. Hence the night attack on the royal camp at Sedgemoor, which, according to royal gunner Edward Dummer, was a strong position 'bequirt [surrounded] with a dry (but in some places mirey) ditch . . . fronting the moor; a place copious and commodious for fighting'.[2]

Feversham had taken few precautions, beyond posting sentries and cavalry pickets. No attempt had been made to fortify the royal camp and, recorded Dummer, a supine mood and 'a preposterous confidence of ourselves, with an understanding of the Rebells that many days before had made us make such tedious marches, had put us into the worst circumstances of surprise: Our Horse in quarters, some near, some remote; our Artillery distant, and in a separate post to that of the camp – neither accomodable to generall resistance'.[3] So unprepared were the royal officers, according to a member of the Blues,

---

* The standard fighting unit of infantry in the British Army is (and was during the whole of this period) a battalion, but, due to the regimental system, it is often referred to as a regiment. Both terms are used to describe the same-sized unit. It consisted of 800 men and was commanded by a colonel who, until 1750, gave his name to the unit (hence Dumbarton's Regiment of Foot). After 1747 the foot regiments were numbered in order of seniority (the former Dumbarton's became the 1st), and some were given a second battalion (the two battalions of the 20th, for example, were known as the 1st/20th and 2nd/20th).
† The regiment was named after the colour of its uniform, Oxford Blue.

that most of them were 'drunk and had no matter of apprehension of the enemy'.[4]

Initially fortune smiled on Monmouth. A thick mist helped to obscure his march from Bridgwater, and as he moved down the east side of the moor he slipped between two royal patrols and would certainly have been discovered by a third at the Langmoor Rhine, a drainage ditch directly in his path, had it not recently been removed. Having reached the Langmoor, Monmouth gave his final orders. The cavalry, under Lord Grey, would use a ford to cross the final obstacle, a ditch called the Bussex Rhine, before entering the village of Westonzoyland, where they would kill and capture the royal horsemen in their beds; this done, they would attack the royal foot in their tents and attempt to capture the artillery. Meanwhile Monmouth, having formed the rebel foot and artillery into a single line, would sweep across the Bussex Rhine and take the panicked royal infantry from the rear. Or, as the royalist Reverend Paschall put it: 'Their first orders were to fire and run over the ditch within which the camp was, it being presumed that the Lord Grey with his 500 Horse would have drawn the army in the camp into the town, by the alarm designed to be given from hence.'[5] To succeed, Monmouth's plan depended upon absolute surprise and thus far his luck had held. But as his men crossed the Langmoor Rhine in the misty twilight, a pistol shot rang out. A lone trooper of the Blues had spotted the rebels and, having raised the alarm, rode north to warn the commander of his patrol, Lieutenant-Colonel Sir Francis Compton. On hearing the news, Compton sent a trooper to warn the camp and followed with the rest of his 150-strong patrol, colliding with the tail end of the rebel horse as it rode towards the Bussex Rhine. During the brief skirmish, Compton was shot in the chest and the royal horse withdrew. But the delay was compounded when Lord Grey, at the head of the column, missed the ford in the dark and instead led his horsemen along the north bank of the Bussex Rhine, effectively cut off from his objective by an obstacle that was impassable for riders. Meanwhile the alarm had been raised in the royal camp – with the trooper shouting 'Beat your drums, the enemy is come; for the Lord's sake, the enemy is come' – and the six battalions of redcoated infantry were forming up between their tents and the Bussex Rhine.[6] Only one, Dumbarton's, was armed with the older matchlock and its location was clearly marked by the glow of match-cord as the corporals, whose job it was, lit their men's matches. It was the rebels' particular misfortune that, with Feversham still asleep in quarters nearby, the senior royal officer in camp at this moment was 35-year-old Major-General Lord Churchill, a talented soldier who had fought under Monmouth in France and who, as the Duke of Marlborough, would go on to win some of Britain's greatest battlefield victories. The official account of Sedgemoor records Churchill 'having command of the foot and seeing every man at his post doing his duty'.[7] Dumbarton's Regiment was on the right of the redcoats' line and it was across its front that the rebel horse first rode. But, fooled by the rebels' cries that they were loyal militia horse, the Scotsmen held their fire; not so the men of the next two units in line, both battalions of the 1st Foot Guards (commanded by Monmouth's illegitimate half-brother, the Duke of Grafton), who shot at Grey's horse, as did part of the neighbouring battalion of the 2nd Foot Guards. Raked in the flank, Grey's men fled back up the moor, colliding as they went with the two rearmost rebel infantry regiments, the Blue and White, who had just crossed the Langmoor Rhine. By now Monmouth's foremost regiments – the Red, Yellow and Green – had reached the Bussex Rhine, where, supported by three light cannon manned by Dutch artillerymen, they opened fire on the right of the royal army's line, barely 100 yards distant. Nathaniel Wade, commanding the Red Regiment, explained what happened:

> I advanced within 30 or 40 paces of the ditch being opposite to the Scotch batalion of the King's [Dumbarton's], as I learnt since, and there was forced to make a full stop to put the Batalion in some order, the Duke having caused them to march so exceeding swift after he saw his Horse runn, that they were all in confusion. By that time I had putt them in some order and was preparing to pass the ditch (not intending to fire until I had advanced these to our enemyes). Col. Matthews [commanding the Yellow Regiment] was come up and began to fire at distance, upon which the Batalion I commanded fired likewise and after that I could not gett them to advance.[8]

In battle for the first time, many of the rebel musketeers fired high; but the Dutch gunners were more accurate and their case-shot – similar to the effect of a shotgun – tore great holes in the royal battalions opposite, particularly Dumbarton's, which lost all but four of its officers.

Aware that his line was overlapped on the right by the rebel left, Churchill sent two troops of Royal Dragoons to support Dumbarton's, and another to the lower of the two fords over the Bussex Rhine, ready to advance when required. He also ordered six light cannon to be brought from the artillery park nearby, though the panicked flight of the Ordnance Board's civilian drivers with their teams meant that others horses had to be found. One account has the Bishop of Winchester, a royalist captain during the Civil War, using his carriage horses to tug at least one cannon into position. Once there, the guns soon silenced the rebel cannon and began to engage their infantry, supported by the steady volleys from Churchill's disciplined foot.

The time was ripe for a counter-attack. But Feversham, at last on the scene, was fearful of friendly-fire incidents and refused to order his men forward until daybreak. As a half-measure, however, he divided his horse and sent it across both fords of the Bussex Rhine to threaten the rebel flanks. The group on the right got ahead of itself until, badly mauled by both the remnants of Grey's horse and a regiment of foot, it withdrew out of range.

Churchill, meanwhile, had moved his two leftmost battalions, Kirke's and Trelawney's, to the right, where the fire was hottest. They had barely reached their new position when dawn broke, revealing part of the rebel army already in retreat. Feversham at once ordered his cavalry to charge and, as they did so, Churchill sent his elite grenadier companies across the Bussex Rhine in support. They scrambled over the ditch with a yell, wrote James II later, 'which the Rebels seeing, ran before they came to bandy blows'.[9] With their cannon quickly overrun, the rebel retreat became a panicked flight. 'They stood near an hour and a halfe with great shouting, briskly fyring,' recorded Edward Dummer, 'and then, throwing down their armes, fell into rout and confusion.'[10]

Their leader, Monmouth, had long since fled the field, leaving his banner (with the motto 'Fear nothing but GOD') to be recovered by Dumbarton's grenadiers. James II wrote of his nephew's flight with obvious delight:

> Some time after his Horse were all gone, and that Williams a servant of his told him he might see the King's Horse on their flanks, going as he believed to encompass them, he put off his arms, and took one hundred guineas from his servant, left his Foott still fighting, and went away with Ld Grey (who came to him after his Horse were all disperst or gone), one a Brandenburger and one or two more, and went up the hill which overlooks the moor as you go towards Bristol, and from thence looked about and could see his Foott still firing, and continued on his way to the top of the Mendip hills.[11]

At first the royal troops gave no quarter and the Tangiers veterans of Kirke's (later the Queen's 2nd) Regiment of Foot were particularly merciless during the pursuit, a brutality that earned them the ironic nickname of Kirke's Lambs (after their paschal lamb emblem). Locals buried 1,384 rebel bodies, and, according to a royal militiaman, 'many more they did believe lay dead unfound in the corn'.[12] Of those captured, 333 were sentenced to death and a further 814 to transportation by Judge George Jeffreys, the lord chief justice, during his notorious 'Bloody Assizes'. Total rebel casualties, therefore, were more than 70 per cent of the force engaged, a figure almost unprecedented in modern warfare. Royal losses, by contrast, were 80 killed and 200 wounded, mostly from artillery fire.[13]

Having cravenly abandoned his men, Monmouth got his comeuppance two days later when he was captured, disguised as a shepherd, in a ditch near Blandford Forum. Taken before the king, he begged for his life; but James II was in no mood for mercy, declaring that he 'did not behave himself so well as I expected nor as one ought to have expected from one who had taken upon him to be King'.[14] He was beheaded at Tower Hill on 15 July, the executioner using a knife to sever his head after five blows of the axe had failed to get the job done, much to the fury of the watching crowd.[15]

Churchill was considered by many to have saved the royal army from destruction. Certainly he managed the crucial opening phase of the fight with great skill, and handed over command to his superior, the Earl of Feversham, only when the battle was won. 'As Major General in command of the infantry,' writes John Tincey in *Sedgemoor 1685*, the best account of the battle,

> Churchill deserves the credit for the alertness of the Royal camp and the efficiency and discipline of the soldiers . . . The ability of the Royal infantry to form line of battle, in the dark and within minutes, removed the Rebels' advantage of surprise . . . By the time Feversham arrived the battle was won and he had little to do but, with the dawn, to organise the pursuit of a beaten enemy . . . Sedgemoor may not have been John Churchill's most spectacular victory, but it must rightfully be considered to be his first.[16]

Of even greater significance, however, is the fact that Sedgemoor was the last set-piece battle fought on English soil, and the last time the redcoats of the standing army – formed barely a quarter of a century earlier by the restored Charles II – were prepared to uphold the authority of an unpopular monarch. Three years later, when called upon to repel a second Protestant invader in the shape of William of Orange, many soldiers refused to fight and James II was forced into exile. A relieved Parliament offered the throne jointly to William of Orange and his wife, Mary, James II's Protestant daughter; and in return they agreed to a Declaration of Rights that reaffirmed existing limits on a monarch's power.

For the redcoats of the army, the 'Glorious Revolution' was a major turning point. Henceforth they would no longer serve as the coercive power of an individual monarch or monarchs (though they would continue to be known as royal troops, and their officers would still receive their commissions from the sovereign), but rather as the constitutionally established security force of the English – and later the British – people, or at least of their representatives in Parliament.

There would, of course, be challenges to this new Protestant Supremacy – chiefly from the Jacobite supporters of James II and his descendants – which the army would have to meet and overcome. But most of its victories during the next century and a quarter would be won abroad, as the British redcoat played a key role in his country's rise to greatness. Hitherto most of the credit for this extraordinary period of martial success and imperial expansion has gone to the sailors of the Royal Navy, who protected sea-lanes, helped to launch amphibious attacks and opened up new areas of trade. Yet only a land force as professional, flexible and effective as the British Army could have won no fewer than three great conflicts against France – the War of the Spanish Succession, the Seven Years War and Napoleonic Wars – in just over a hundred years. In each case, the key battleground was not in the colonies or on the seas but on the Continent, where Britain's primary foreign-policy objective was to prevent a single power – France – from dominating Europe – the same objective that had prevailed in Elizabethan times, when Spain was the chief threat, and would again in the twentieth century, as first Germany and then Russia sought European hegemony. 'As to armies on the continent,' writes N. A. M. Rodger, our finest naval historian, 'it is unquestionable that a Continental victory requires a Continental commitment'[17] – and by that he meant British redcoats. Without their contribution to the seminal victories at Blenheim, Ramillies, Dettingen, Minden, Salamanca, Vitoria and, finally, the Allies' crushing triumph over Napoleon at Waterloo, Britain could not have become, by 1815, the paramount imperial and industrial power in the world.

Not that the British redcoat was always triumphant. He emerged from the War of the Austrian Succession of 1740–48 with his reputation barely intact; and, though he won many battles, he lost the war against the American colonists in 1775–83 (the only time the modern British soldier has lost a major conflict). But in both cases he learned from his setbacks, as did his generals, and emerged from the next war as the victor. His greatest attribute was to make the best of a bad lot. Whenever and wherever he served – from the rolling plains of Flanders to the wilderness of North America, from the baking heat of India to the mountains of the Iberian Peninsula – he put his difficulties to one side and trusted in his sword, musket and bayonet to make him master of the battlefield.

This, then, is the story of the redcoats' golden age from the Glorious Revolution to Waterloo. It is a tale that encompasses military, political and social history; and it explains how and why men from the opposite ends of the social spectrum became soldiers, fought together and died together. The central figures are those giants of British military history who played their leading roles to perfection – William of Orange, Marlborough, Wolfe, Moore and Wellington – and one or two lesser mortals like Cumberland and Howe who, more often than not, fluffed their lines. But the bit players, the ordinary soldiers who make up the backbone of any army, are no less significant; and it is their view of soldiering in peacetime and war that makes this story so compelling.

1. The Restoration Soldier

John Churchill – the soldier who would play the key role in the Battle of Sedgemoor and the 'Glorious Revolution' three years later – was born on 26 May 1650, just sixteen months after the execution of King Charles I and the abolition of the monarchy. The republican government would last, in various forms, just eleven years; but during that time the Churchill family suffered the financial cost of choosing the wrong side in the English Civil War of 1642–6 between the king and Parliament. For young John's father, Winston, a well-to-do Dorset gentleman, had fought for King Charles as a captain of horse, and in 1649 was charged by Parliament with 'delinquency' and fined £464. For a man worth just £160 a year, it was a crippling blow and for most of the 1650s he and his family were forced to live under the roof of his Parliamentarian mother-in-law, Lady Drake.

Even after the Restoration of Charles II in 1660 – when Winston was rewarded for his loyal service with a knighthood, an appointment at court and rooms in the royal palace of Whitehall – the Churchills could not afford the £200 needed to purchase John a junior officer's commission in the 1st Foot Guards. That John became a soldier was entirely due to the influence of his elder sister, Arabella, who, in 1665, was appointed a maid of honour to the wife of the king's brother, James, Duke of York. She soon became York's *maîtresse-en-titre*, bearing him four illegitimate children (including the Duke of Berwick, who would find fame as a soldier in the service of the French), and was able to use her influence to wangle her brother the position of page in the duke's household. It was the duke who procured for John, in 1667, a commission that did not have to be paid for.[1]

John's regiment, the 1st Foot Guards, had been in existence for just six years, and was part of the 4,000-strong permanent royal bodyguard that Charles II had raised in 1661 to prevent him suffering the

same fate as his father. The significance of this tiny standing army –
comprised of the 1st and 2nd Foot Guards, Life Guards, Blues and a
number of non-regimented garrison companies – is that it was the
first time a British monarch had maintained field regiments in peacetime, though it was always referred to as 'the Guards and garrisons'
rather than the 'army' to make it seem less of a political threat.

The royal army's first commander was the first Duke of Albemarle,
who, as plain General George Monck, had made the Restoration possible by marching on London with his Scottish troops in January 1660
to reinstate the authority of Parliament. Monck's crossing of the
Tweed at Coldstream was a point of no return, and one every bit
as significant as Julius Caesar's famous crossing of the Rubicon in
46 BC. Both incursions would ultimately result in the replacement of
a republican system of government with a monarchy. But there the
similarities end because, unlike Caesar, Monck had no personal political ambition. 'His main concerns were . . . to counter the drift
towards anarchy,' wrote Austin Woolrych, 'and to set his country
back on course towards ordered and acceptable government. He
was widely misunderstood and it suited his purpose to keep people
guessing about his intentions, but behind his bull-like appearance, his
blunt speech, his coarse humour and rough temper – behind his whole
cultivation of the persona of a plain, tobacco-chewing, aleswilling,
professional soldier – lay a shrewdness, a seriousness of purpose and
a sense of honour that have often been underrated.'[2]

When Charles landed at Dover on 25 May 1660, he was embraced
by Monck 'with all imaginable love and respect', according to the
diarist Samuel Pepys, who was rowed ashore with the 'King's favourite dog'.[3] Monck's reward for restoring parliamentary rule – and
ultimately the monarchy – was a veritable flood of honours and
appointments: he was raised to the peerage as the Duke of Albemarle;
given land and houses worth £7,000 a year and an annual pension of
£700; and appointed to the king's Privy Council and confirmed as
commander-in-chief – or lord general – for life.

What type of army the new duke would command, and its size
and composition, were for a time undecided. Charles II's preference
had long been for a permanent royal force that would owe its alle-

giance to him alone. Parliament was opposed to the idea, on the grounds of cost and the danger that Charles would attempt to rule by force. But a spate of republican plots in late 1660, centred on ex-officers of Parliament's recently disbanded New Model Army, enabled Charles to have his way. To provide security a regiment of 1,200 foot – the 1st Foot Guards – was formed in late November under the command of Colonel John Russell, a staunch royalist. It was joined in January 1661 by three more regiments: the Life Guards, the 2nd Foot Guards and the Blues (all partly or wholly raised from former units in Monck's Scottish garrison).* The chief role of this new standing army was as a 'ceremonial, household army of royal guards' based on the French model. It would protect the king's person, appear on state occasions, carry out police duties (if necessary) and act as a trained cadre that could be expanded rapidly in time of war.[4] What it was designed not to do, according to its creator Monck, was involve itself in politics. 'It is a dangerous thing,' wrote Monck in his 1640s treatise *Observations upon Military & Political Affairs*, 'for a General to make himself chief in perswading a Prince, or State to any weighty and important resolution, so that the counsel whereof be wholly imputed to him, which belongs to many.'[5] Of course Monck did not stay out of politics. If he had, then the history of England – and Britain – would have been very different. But his decision to use his troops as a political instrument – and only after all other options had failed – was for the common good, as he saw it. He preferred to serve a civil, representative government; had this not been the case, he might have taken power for himself in 1660. Yet the legacy of his involvement of the army in politics, not to mention Cromwell's military rule of the 1650s, was a strong distrust of standing armies (and

---

* The 2nd Foot Guards, formed from Monck's Regiment of Foot, were later known as the 2nd (Coldstream) Guards, or Coldstreamers, in memory of the town they garrisoned before Monck's momentous decision to cross the Tweed and restore civil government in 1660. The regiment's motto, *Nulli Secundus* – 'Second to None' – refers to its heritage as the oldest unit with continuous service in the British Army, though the 1st (Grenadier) Guards would argue that its seniority is underpinned by the, albeit temporary, disbandment of the Coldstreamers in 1661.

the high taxes needed to pay for them), military government and overtly 'political' generals, which was to remain a factor in British political life until the nineteenth century.

When John Churchill joined the royal army as a seventeen-year-old ensign in 1667, he was one of many officers from a similar background. Typically they were the younger sons of the nobility and the landed gentry, and came from the opposite end of the social spectrum to that of the ordinary soldiers (the exceptions being the gentleman-privates of the Life Guards and, to a lesser extent, the Blues). They tended to be royalists who had followed the king into exile, or the sons of those who had fought for Charles I in the Civil Wars.

Pay was fairly generous, though it depended on the regiment: an ensign of foot or foot guards (like Churchill) received £54 and his colonel £363* a year (or 3s. and 20s. a day respectively); but the equivalent ranks in the Life Guards (cornet and captain of the King's Troop) were given £236 and £546. All compare reasonably favourably with the salaries of contemporary lawyers and 'eminent clergy' – the only other acceptable professions for gentlemen – who earned an average of £154 and £72.[6]

Unlike Churchill – who took advantage of his sister's relationship with the king's brother – most officers had to purchase their commissions, thereby ensuring they were men of wealth and property who had a vested interest in the status quo. Purchase provided a career structure and a rudimentary pension system, but it also precluded many with talent but no money, and encouraged some officers to regard their commissions as business opportunities. Lord Gerard, Captain of the King's Troop of Life Guards (and therefore the senior officer in the regiment), used to invest his men's pay and pass it on to them only when it had earned him sufficient interest. The matter came to a head in 1667, when Gerard's intermediary, a crooked army agent called William Carr, fled to France with £1,630 of the soldiers' money. With his position untenable, Gerard sold his captaincy to the

---

* This was made up of £218 for the colonelcy and another £145 for his dual role as captain of a company.

then nineteen-year-old Duke of Monmouth for the exorbitant sum of £12,000. Various attempts were made to fix the prices at which commissions changed hands, but there was no official tariff until George I set one in 1720, and even then it was often ignored: for some, the payment of a premium was still a route to promotion within exclusive regiments.[7]

Another drawback of the system was that many officers did not see why, having paid for their rank, they needed to take soldiering seriously. This particularly applied to officers in the horse and foot guards' regiments, many of whom appointed deputies to undertake their duties. They tended to be present only for major escorts or parades, and otherwise spent their time at leisure, court or Parliament. Almost half of the 188 officers who served in the four guards' regiments in the 1660s held seats in the House of Commons, while a further 61 were peers.

And yet the weaknesses of the purchase system need to be qualified. Purchase operated only at regimental level – below the rank of lieutenant-colonel – so that patronage, moderated by seniority, was the key to advancement to the senior ranks. Even in the lower officer ranks the effect of purchase has been exaggerated: 'vacancies created by death were not filled by purchase, and in wartime in particular purchase played proportionately little part in sustaining the upward mobility in the army.'[8]

The world inhabited by the ordinary British redcoat, however, could not have been more different. 'He was unmarried,' writes John Childs, 'could not be a householder, could not run a tavern, had no permanent home being continually on the move from quarter to quarter, and carried all he possessed on his back. If he swore or drank he could be cashiered, and if he wished to leave the service then he had to seek the approval of his commanding officer, which was rarely ever given.'[9] Given such harsh conditions of service – and the fact all soldiers enlisted for life, with very occasional discharges granted for sickness or disability – it was perhaps inevitable that most recruits volunteered out of desperation. Typically they were 'discontented agricultural workers, vagrants, unemployed apprentices and journeymen'. Criminals avoiding arrest and debtors also saw the military as a safe haven.[10]

The troopers in the regiments of horse guards, on the other hand, were recruited from the poorer gentry and even from old royalist officers who had been unable to get commissions in the new army. The Life Guards, in particular, was a stepping-stone to greater things, a school 'for young gentlemen of very considerable Families, who are there made fit for Military Commands'.[11] Not all made the transition. John Gwyn had been a captain in the Civil War, a lieutenant in the royalist army in Flanders before the Restoration, and was still serving as a lowly gentleman-trooper in the King's Troop of Life Guards when he wrote his memoirs in the early 1680s. Even then he still hoped for promotion, writing to Charles II in the preface that '[I have] served you immutably, from youth to old age' and 'faithfully spent my prime years in your service'.[12]

There were many John Gwyns in the Life Guards, a unit that in social composition and military experience was not unlike Louis XIV's famous Mousquetaires.* Because of this, Life Guardsmen held two ranks: their regimental position and their army rank. In 1666 the system was formalized by a royal warrant giving the regiment precedence over all others in the army, and their officers superiority over equivalent ranks in other units. The practice continued until 1788, when the Life Guards became part of the regular army.[13]

Recruits in dragoon regiments tended to come from sturdy yeoman stock, and were neither gentlemen nor paupers. When in the field with their mounts, they were counted as a regiment of horse with precedence over all foot soldiers; when in barracks, they were considered infantry. This ambivalence was ended in the early eighteenth century, when all dragoons became fully fledged cavalry.[14]

---

* Created in 1622 as a junior unit of the royal bodyguard, or Maison du Roi, the Mousquetaires de la Garde (Musketeers of the Guard) fought in battle both on foot and on horseback, and were similar to British dragoons. Because of its junior status, the unit attracted the minor nobility, who served in all ranks. They were tough, determined soldiers whose only hope of career and social advancement was by excelling in war.

Pay was roughly analogous to the social status of the recruit. Foot soldiers, therefore, were not well remunerated. A line infantryman received 8*d*. per day, two pennies less than a foot guardsman. From this was deducted daily 'off-reckonings' of 2*d*. to meet the cost of his uniform, accoutrements and sword. This left subsistence money for food and lodgings, which was further reduced by various stoppages, including the 'poundage' (a shilling from every pound of army pay) due to the paymaster-general. A soldier was lucky if he cleared 5*d*. a day. It was not enough to live on, except on campaign, when accommodation and bread were provided (though the latter cost 1¼*d*.).[15]

Cavalrymen were better paid, with privates in the dragoons and the Blues receiving 1*s*.4*d*. and 2*s*.6*d*. a day respectively. But out of this sum they had to pay for their mounts as well as themselves, and were also subject to off-reckonings.[16] Only the Life Guards private gentlemen were considered well off with 4*s*. a day, a reflection of their higher social status. Yet some had paid up to £100 to enter the regiment – the only time in the history of the British Army that the rank of private was purchased, albeit unofficially – and once in they had to supply and feed their own horses, provide their own ornate saddlery and uniforms, and buy their own weapons. The cost could be exorbitant. As well as front and back armour they wore a 'pot' helmet under a wide-brimmed felt hat (decorated with feathers specially imported from France), redcoats richly decorated with gold lace facings, and breeches and boots of soft, buff-coloured leather. They also carried the long and straight regulation cavalry sword, two 14-inch pistols and a carbine mounted on a belt with a swivel hook. All firearms were modern flintlocks, rather than the more cumbersome matchlocks, and were issued centrally from the Ordnance.[17]

The uniform worn by foot soldiers was far less splendid, with the 1st Foot Guards clothed in redcoats faced with light blue, blue breeches and stockings, and white waist sashes fringed with blue (the 2nd Foot Guards wore a similar garb, but with green facings, breeches and stockings). At the beginning of Charles II's reign the fashion was for short coats and high-crowned hats, but by 1680 the influence of the French had brought in long coats, baggy breeches, wigs and an abundance of lace. A regimental officer of the time would have worn a broad-brimmed, low-crowned black hat, and a white linen shirt and cravat. His coat was cassock-shaped and buttoned at the front as far as the waist, with coloured ribbons at each shoulder and a silk sash around the waist. His legs and feet were clad in voluminous breeches that ended just below the knee, worsted stockings and high-heeled shoes with buckles. Dress for ordinary soldiers was similar in style, but less ornate.[18]

Provision for soldiers maimed in battle was made from the official army establishment, but there was nothing for those who lost their place through age, illness, or under pressure from 'better men'. It was to cater for 'the succor and relief of veterans broken by war and age' that Charles II founded the Royal Hospital at Chelsea in 1681; yet, when the hospital finally opened its doors in 1692, its maximum capacity of 476 veterans was only a fraction of the number of soldiers who qualified for assistance. As a temporary expedient, therefore, James II introduced a scheme in 1685 for pensions to be given to privates and NCOs who had been either disabled on active service or had served for a minimum of twenty years. The gratuities ranged from 5d. a day for a private foot soldier to 1s.6d. a day for an ex-trooper of the Life Guards, and would be paid until the Royal Hospital was able to accommodate them. Inevitably the scheme had to be continued after the completion of the hospital to give relief to those who qualified but could not be accommodated. But there was still nothing for those who fell ill or were dismissed before they had served twenty years.[19]

With little or no spare cash, soldiers were often unruly, refused to pay for their quarters and behaved little better than armed thugs. Many officers failed to act, partly because they sympathized with their soldiers' predicament, and partly because they lacked the disciplinary power to punish them effectively until the passing of the Mutiny Act in 1689. Impecunious troops also took civilian jobs on the side, working at their original trades or as labourers in the cities and towns, and helping with the harvest in the countryside. Some even ran taverns, their moonlighting made easier by the practice of billeting troops in small groups.

There were some barracks in England, mostly in fortresses like

Berwick and Hull, but they were generally occupied by independent companies, and were moreover in a lamentable condition. Colonel John Hutchinson wrote of Sandown Castle in Kent:

> He found it a lamentable old ruined place, almost a mile distant from the town, the rooms all out of repair, not weather proof, no kind of accommodation for lodging or diet, or any convenience of life. Before he came, there were not half a dozen soldiers in it, and a poor lieutenant with his wife and children, and two or three cannoniers [artillerymen], and a few guns almost dismounted, upon rotten carriages; but at the colonel's coming thither, a company of foot besides were sent up from Dover to help to guard the place, pitiful weak fellows, half-starved and eaten up with vermin, whom the Governor of Dover cheated of half their pay, and the other half they spent in drink.[20]

Most soldiers, as a result, were billeted with private householders who often struggled to make their impoverished guests pay what they owed, with civil–military relations suffering as a result. Billeting also broke up regiments and had a detrimental effect on discipline and morale. One solution, proposed in 1697, was to build a network of barracks across the country; but it was rejected on the grounds of expense. Small wonder, then, that soldiers at the turn of the eighteenth century were regarded by society at large 'as public blights and private rogues and wastrels to be avoided whenever possible'.[21] It was an attitude that would not alter much during the next 150 years.

The Restoration Army was, therefore, thanks to its lack of resources and administrative machinery, very much a work in progress:

> Soldiers worked and lived as civilians [writes John Childs] whilst their officers were entrusted with the task of running the army for the State in return for a host of semi-legal frauds and perquisites. Effectively the army was rented to its officers, who undertook to recruit, clothe, train, and pay their men on behalf of the State. The *quid pro quo* was that the State interfered as little as possible in the army's internal financial affairs allowing the officers to turn the army into a profitable business. There was supposed to be a British standing army in this period; *de facto* it was a territorial force.[22]

One potential civilizing influence on soldiers was the presence of women. This was the belief of Sir James Turner, a former soldier, whose *Pallas Armata: Military Essayes of the Ancient Grecian, Roman and Modern Art of War* was published in 1683. 'As a woman was created to be a helpmate to man,' he wrote, 'so women are great helpers to armies, to their husbands, especially those of the lower conditions.' They should be tolerated in small numbers, he argued, to 'provide, buy and dress their husbands meat when their husbands are on duty, or newly come from it', and to 'bring fewel for fire, and wash their linens, and in such manner of employments a Souldiers wife may be helpful to her husband and her self'.[23]

The military authorities agreed, but in an effort to restrict the number of wives they ruled in 1685 that a soldier could marry only with the permission of his commanding officer (a restriction that still applies today). This was rarely given unless the applicant had a spotless record of long service, and his bride was thought to be of good character. There was no official quota, but most colonels restricted the number of wives to six per company (of a hundred soldiers). They were allowed to sleep in quarters, as were their children, to share the company's rations, to undertake regimental duties like cooking, cleaning and laundry (thus earning them extra money), and to accompany their husbands on campaign. They were often joined by a similar number of 'unofficial' wives and girlfriends who were 'off the strength' and had to fend for themselves.[24]

2. The 'First' Churchill

In 1667, tasked with protecting the monarch, Ensign John Churchill's regiment was quartered in and around London, a metropolis of 300,000 souls that was mainly confined to the north bank of the Thames. At its heart was the Palace of Whitehall, the monarch's principal residence, a veritable rabbit warren of gardens, galleries, apartments and larger buildings that ran for half a mile along the river, close to the modern Embankment. On the north side of the palace was a cavalry guardhouse, known as Horse Guards, which contained quarters for fifty private gentlemen of the Life Guards. These troopers monitored access to the neighbouring St James's Park, where Charles II was wont to walk his dogs, and passes for entrance to the park were highly coveted.

Churchill knew the palace well, having first moved in with his parents in 1661. More recently he had, in his capacity as a royal page, spent much time in the apartments of the Duke of York in the southwest corner of the palace. Situated conveniently nearby was the lodging of his second cousin Barbara Castlemaine, twenty-seven, the wife of a lawyer and the king's favourite mistress. Though ten years Churchill's senior, the sexually voracious lady was attracted to the handsome young guards officer and in due course would bear him a daughter, also called Barbara. But at this point – according to Winston S. Churchill, biographer of his illustrious forebear – their relationship was strictly platonic:

> Very likely she had known him from his childhood. Naturally she was nice to him, and extended her powerful protection to her young and sprightly relation. Naturally, too, she aroused his schoolboy's admiration. There is not . . . the slightest ground for suggesting that the beginning of their affection was not perfectly innocent.[1]

Innocent or not, Churchill's habit of spending hours in his cousin's lodgings, eating sweets and chatting, was enough to ruffle royal feathers and may explain his posting in 1668 to the garrison of Tangiers (a North African colony that had been, along with Bombay in India, part of the marriage contract between Charles II and his Portuguese wife Catherine of Braganza). 'The jealousy of one of the royal brothers,' wrote a contemporary, 'was the cause of his temporary banishment.'[2]

Churchill left no record of this period, but we know from other sources that his time in the colony would not have been easy. Tangiers lies to the west of the Pillar of Hercules, on the stormy Atlantic coast, and is dominated by high ground that enabled the Moorish factions who controlled Morocco in the seventeenth century to overlook the town. Despite improving the outer defences by building two rings of forts (1663–9), the English were under constant attack and conditions within the garrison were grim: pay was intermittent, food was poor and disease was rife. Mutinies were frequent, and some soldiers even deserted to the Moors, where slavery awaited them.[3]

Frequent were the skirmishes below the city walls, and it was probably here that Churchill received his baptism of fire. A fellow officer wrote: '[The Moors] lodge their ambushes within our very lines, and sometimes they killed our men as they passed to discover, which they continually do without any other danger than hazarding a few shots, whilst they leap over the lines and run into the fields of their own country. This insecurity makes men all the more shy in passing about the fields.'[4]

Samuel Pepys visited the colony as part of a Royal Commission in 1683, and was appalled by the lack of discipline:

> To show how little [Colonel Sir Percy Kirke, the garrison commander] makes of drunkenness . . . I have seen, as he has been walking with me in the street, a soldier reel on him as drunk as a dog . . . He hath only laughed at him and cried 'The fellow hath got a good morning's draft already!' . . . [He is said] to have got his wife's sister with child . . . And that while he is with his whores at his little bathing-house which he has furnished with jade a-purpose there, his wife, whom he

keeps by in awe, sends for her gallants and plays the jade by herself at home.[5]

The colony was finally abandoned the following year as a direct result of the Royal Commission's recommendation that it would require the staggering sum of £4.8 million to make it defensible.

Churchill, meanwhile, had gained more valuable combat experience and a number of steps in rank. In 1673, during the Third Anglo-Dutch War, he fought alongside the French in the Netherlands, taking part in the assault on a key outwork of Maastricht that prompted the Dutch to capitulate. Fighting with him that day was the Duke of Monmouth – the man he would defeat at Sedgemoor – and the Comte d'Artagnan, commanding a company of Louis XIV's Mousquetaires Gris (and the inspiration for Alexandre Dumas's novel *The Three Musketeers*). An eye-witness recorded:

> We marched with our swords in our hands to the barricade of the enemy's, where only one man could pass at a time. There was Monsieur d'Artagnan with his musketeers who did very bravely. This gentleman was one of the greatest reputation in the army, and he would have persuaded the duke not to have passed that place, but that being not to be done, this gentleman would go along with him, but in passing that narrow place was killed with a shot in his head . . . The soldiers at this took heart, the duke twice leading them on with great courage; when his grace found the enemy begin to retire, he was prevailed with to retire to the trench, the better to give his commands.[6]

Churchill also performed prodigies that day and was later credited by Monmouth 'as the brave man who saved my life'.[7] A year later, commanding a regiment in the British Brigade, Churchill won the admiration of the great Marshal Henri Turenne, one of the finest soldiers of his age, for the part he played in the French defeat of the Austrians at Ensheim. 'I durst not brag too much of our victory,' wrote Churchill, 'but it is certain that they left the field as soon as we. We have three of their cannon, several of their colours and some prisoners.'[8]

Shortly before his promotion to full colonel in 1678, Churchill married Sarah Jennings, eighteen, whose once wealthy father had died ten years earlier. Requiring a patron, Sarah had followed her sister into the service of the Duke of York's second wife, Mary of Modena – his first, Anne Hyde, had died in 1671 – which is how she met her husband. It was also during her time in the York household that Sarah became friendly with Princess Anne, the duke's younger daughter by his first wife. 'We used to play together when she was a child,' recalled Sarah, 'and even then she expressed a particular fondness for me.'[9] It was a relationship that would become increasingly intense, and have, in turn, happy and disastrous consequences for Churchill's military career.

In the short to medium term, however, his wife's close association with Anne – culminating in Sarah's appointment as lady-in-waiting to the young princess in 1683 – was wholly beneficial for Churchill. When the Duke of York became James II on the death of his brother in February 1685, John was raised to the English peerage as Baron Churchill.[10] It was later that year that he played the key role in the suppression of the Monmouth Rebellion. His stock had never been higher and, in recognition of this, he was promoted to major-general.

Why then, just three years later, did he – along with other senior military figures – abandon his long-time patron and monarch? The answer lies in James II's faith: Roman Catholicism. Unlike his brother Charles, who converted only on his deathbed, James had long professed himself a Catholic. So worried had one powerful clique of Protestant 'Country Party' MPs become that from 1678 to 1681 they had repeatedly tried and failed to pass a bill that would have excluded him from the succession on account of his religion (a political upheaval known as the 'Exclusion Crisis'). Their worst fears were soon realized.

No sooner was he crowned than James II began to remove the obstacles that prevented Catholics from participating in local and national government, and becoming officers in the army. First he dissolved Parliament and used his royal prerogative to excuse Catholics from the Test Act of 1673 (which obliged all public servants to take an oath of allegiance to the Church of England). This enabled him to appoint Catholics to magistracies and town councils, and to commission more Catholic officers for the permanent army, which, in response to the Monmouth Rebellion, had rapidly expanded from 9,000 to 20,000 men, including six new regiments of horse, two of dragoons and nine of infantry.[11]

The recruitment of Catholics was part of a wider process by which James was attempting to ensure the personal loyalty of his army by replacing politically suspect gentlemen with 'members of the new breed of professional careerists who depended upon their sword for their livelihood'. His plan was to turn the army into the sort of political instrument, separate from civil society, that Monck had feared, and that would enable him to establish an absolutist and centralized form of government.[12]

But ultimately James could not rely on all his soldiers. Even his 'professional' officers – among them his protégé Lord Churchill – were opposed to Catholic toleration; nor could they forgive his habit of sacking officers who voiced a dislike of his religious policies, or opposed him politically, on the grounds that 'any threat to the ownership of a commission was an attack on the property of the individual.'[13] Their discontent was heightened by the gradual Catholicization of the Irish Army under the Earl of Tyrconnell, James's lieutenant-general and, from 1687, his lord lieutenant. In the summer of 1688, anticipating a similar purge in the English Army, a number of officers at Hounslow camp joined the Association of Protestant Officers that began to plot James's overthrow. Their most senior adherent was Churchill himself.

'Like most of the professional soldiers involved in [the plot],' writes Richard Holmes, 'Churchill relied primarily upon his army pay, and so the much-feared purge of the English army after the Irish model would strike at his fundamental interests.' He was, moreover, 'sincere in his commitment to Anglicanism' and was convinced that James's religious policies would end in disaster.[14]

He was joined in this belief by a number of prominent civilians, including the Earl of Devonshire, Henry Sidney, the Bishop of London and Prince George of Denmark, husband of Princess Anne. Their conspiracy was galvanized by the birth, on 10 June 1688, of James II's son and heir, Prince James. The king's daughters Mary and

Anne, by his first wife Anne Hyde, had been raised as Protestants. But the new prince's mother, Mary of Modena, was a Catholic and there was no doubt he would follow that faith. His birth had, at a stroke, disinherited his elder sisters and ensured James's Catholic policies would not be reversed by his successor.

On 30 June seven of the civilian conspirators – the 'Immortal Seven' – wrote a secret letter to Prince William of Orange, husband of James's eldest daughter, Mary, promising him support from 'nineteen parts of twenty of the people' if he invaded the country.[15] Crucially they added that many of James's senior officers were 'so discontented' they would desert to the Prince's cause.[16]

Dutch propaganda would later depict William of Orange's invasion as a crusade to liberate the British Isles from popery and arbitrary government. It was anything but. His true motives were to secure his wife's accession to the throne and, more importantly, to prevent England 'from being dragged into the circle of alliances drawn by France and to secure her financial, commercial, colonial, naval, and military power for the Protestant forces of western Europe in their fight against the imperialism of Louis XIV'.[17] For the merchants of Amsterdam, the real power brokers in the United Provinces (a loose confederation of seven states also known as the Dutch Republic), a compliant England would help to break the economic stranglehold that France had placed on Dutch trade.

Irrespective of motives, William was certainly the right man for the job of usurping James II and achieving a political and religious settlement that would satisfy England's ruling elite. The son of Charles I's eldest daughter, Mary, with his own valid claim to the English and Scottish thrones, he had held the dual appointments of stadtholder and captain-general of the United Provinces since the age of twenty-one. Now thirty-eight, he had proved himself an astute politician and a no less determined and skilful military commander during the long war against France in the 1670s, capturing Bonn and forcing Louis to evacuate all occupied territory. His looks and constitution, however, belied his ability. 'Of fair height but slight build,' wrote a chronicler of the early British Army, '[he was] sickly-looking both in face and figure, rather sallow of complexion.

Small-pox, asthma, and weakness of the lungs had somewhat stooped his shoulders, and prematurely drawn the lines of his face; but the peculiarly expressive features compensated for the lack of regal presence.'[18]

Assisted by a favourable 'Protestant Wind' that prevented James II's navy from intercepting his huge armada of 49 warships and over 400 transports, William of Orange landed at Torbay in Devon on 5 November 1688. He brought with him a polyglot force of 20,000 troops – including Dutch, English, Scots, Irish, French Huguenots, Germans and Swedes – that was significantly outnumbered by James's army of 40,000 regulars.

If James had been determined to fight, he might still have saved his crown. The actual number of military conspirators was relatively small, and few of his ordinary soldiers were minded to disobey a direct order. But the king was not a well man: he was suffering from a persistent nosebleed – a disorder that afflicted the Stuarts in time of stress – and a spate of early defections by prominent officers knocked his confidence. On 23 November he ordered the bulk of his army to withdraw from Salisbury Plain to London. This only encouraged more officers and men to desert – Lord Churchill among them – and by mid-December barely 4,000 soldiers were still loyal to James in camps near Windsor and Uxbridge. On 21 December, preferring flight to political humiliation, James followed his wife and son into exile in France.

A Convention Parliament met in early 1689 and, after much debate, offered the crown jointly to William and Mary, with succession going after both their deaths to their children (if they had any), and then to Princess Anne and her children. At the same time the joint monarchs were presented with a Declaration of Rights that, as an Act of Parliament, would serve as the new constitutional settlement. It has long been claimed that the declaration imposed new limits on the monarch's power, and that William was forced to accept it in return for the throne. But, in truth, this so-called 'Glorious Revolution' simply reaffirmed existing laws and much of it was retrospective, 'denouncing the perceived excess of James II's rule'.[19]

In its final form the declaration affirmed the illegality of the royal prerogative and the levying of money without parliamentary consent.

It asserted the right of petitioning, the need for the free election of MPs, the privileges of freedom of speech and debate in Parliament, and the need for regular Parliaments. It also criticized the manipulation of the judiciary, in particular the imposition of excessive bail and the infliction of cruel and unusual punishments. The only truly novel restriction that it trumpeted was the illegality of keeping a standing army without parliamentary consent.

Recent scholarship suggests that the constitutional importance of the Declaration of Rights has been exaggerated. 'Overall,' argues Edward Vallance, 'they expressed a bipartisan agreement that English monarchs were obliged to act within the rule of law and reign in cooperation with Parliament. Yet there were no safeguards, even after the Declaration had been enshrined in law as the Bill of Rights, to ensure that its demands would be observed.'[20]

In much the same way the new coronation oath – which required a promise to govern 'according to the statutes in parliament agreed on, and the laws and customs of the same' – was more symbolic than legally enforceable. 'By 1689, then,' observes Vallance, 'the only thing that had been established with any sort of permanency was the Protestant succession.'[21]

In fact, the 'Glorious Revolution' had one other lasting achievement, and that was to remove control of the army from the monarch and hand it to Parliament. This was confirmed by the passing of the first annual Mutiny Act,* a piece of legislation that recognized the existence of both the standing army and its courts martial, and permitted the latter to pass sentences of corporal and capital punishment. The Act enabled Parliament to regulate army business on an annual basis, and therefore established political control over the military without giving permanent sanction to the existence of a standing army in peacetime; nor did it specifically make the Articles of War –

---

* So called because it was initially designed to deal with a mutiny at Ipswich among troops bound for Flanders. The Act recognized that a specific system of justice was required for the army, but only in cases of mutiny, sedition or desertion; and it authorized the crown or its generals to try these crimes by court martial and to impose in the most serious cases the death penalty.

the army's internal code of discipline, first issued in 1663 – into a recognized legal code.

Thus, for the first time since its creation in 1661, the army was properly subordinated to Parliament. This did not make it popular, as many Britons continued to regard a standing army as unnecessarily expensive and a possible threat to their civil liberties; but it did make it less likely that it could ever be used as a tool of political coercion. The Duke of Albemarle's hope that the army would stay aloof from politics was close to being realized.

3. William's Wars

The 'Glorious Revolution' gave Parliament a statutory control over the army that continues to this day; but it also left the army of 1689 – or what remained of it after the mass desertions and the order to disband – in a state of chaos. Leaderless, unpaid and without orders, bands of unruly soldiers wandered the land. The obvious solution would have been to dissolve the army entirely and start again, as Charles II had done in 1660. But William III did not have that luxury. With a new war brewing against France in the Low Countries, and Jacobite rebellions in Scotland and Ireland (the latter led by James II himself), he was forced to throw the hastily reorganized English and Scottish armies straight into the fray.

His key adviser in carrying out this restructuring was John Churchill, newly promoted in the peerage to the earldom of Marlborough and the senior surviving officer of James's army. Churchill knew the first vital task was to purge the old officer corps, and to this end he suggested names for appointment and promotion, most of which William would confirm. 'Churchill and the king were pushing in the same direction,' wrote John Childs. 'William desired a professional and loyal officer corps, while Churchill wanted to build up his own circle of clientage by drawing on his contacts among the professionals.'[1]

All Catholics, Jacobites and those considered to be politically unreliable were stripped of their commissions. Many of those who remained were 'professionals' who had fought for France, the Dutch Republic, Spain and the Holy Roman Empire before bringing their 'technical expertise and the attitudes of the international military brotherhood' to James's expanded army.[2] In all, about a third of James's officers would serve under William; another third retired from military life, 'unable to compromise their oaths of allegiance and yet unwilling to act treasonably; whilst the remainder took up arms for their old master in Scotland and Ireland'.[3] For William, who was naturally suspicious of those like Churchill who had switched horse in mid-stream, it was a question of needs must. He 'felt keenly that no English politician or soldier was to be fully trusted but he did not possess enough Dutchmen or Germans to officer all the new regiments of the English army'.[4]

William felt the same way about the civilian administrators of the army, such as Secretary at War William Blathwayt. Since the death of the Duke of Albemarle and the abolition of the post of lord general in 1670, the army had been administered by two civilian secretaries of state. Its day-to-day running, however, was the responsibility of more junior civilian officials and staff officers, the most important of whom was the secretary at war. At first the secretaries were little more than clerks to the commander-in-chief, with the issue of marching orders their chief priority. But under Blathwayt, who purchased the position in 1683, the functions of the office were extended to include all aspects of routine administration (barring finance): movement orders, the registration of commissions, billeting instructions, regimental precedence and standing orders. In effect, Blathwayt established the War Office as a department of government, though he remained subordinate to the secretaries of state.

William III, however, was keen to have someone running the War Office that he could trust. But no one knew the army like Blathwayt, and in late January 1689, after a six-week gap – during which time William's personal secretary, Constantijn Huygens, had been the acting secretary at war – he resumed control of military administration. William could now concentrate on bringing the army back to operational effectiveness, and he did this by disbanding all Catholic soldiers (and transporting four Irish regiments to the Isle of Wight from where many escaped to France and Ireland), removing all English soldiers from duty in London and replacing them with Dutch and German troops, establishing regimental depots for recruitment and administration, offering rewards of up to 5s. for 'recovered' weapons and ensuring regular pay.

There were still outbreaks of indiscipline. Some of the units earmarked for foreign service in the Low Countries experienced mass desertions – including two battalions of the 2nd Foot Guards – while one, the 1st Foot, went further by expelling most of its officers and heading home to Scotland. Intercepted en route by three Dutch cavalry regiments, the mutinous Scots got off lightly: one captain was executed; the rest were simply shipped overseas. But, overall, William's hasty reorganization bore fruit, with 8,000 British troops in Flanders by the end of May 1689, and a further twelve regiments in Ireland by late summer.

It was not a moment too soon, because, by then, William was facing threats at home and abroad. His chief foe was France, whose rise to pre-eminence owed much to a succession of able politicians – Cardinals Mazarin and Richelieu, and then King Louis XIV himself – and their creation of the first truly centralized European state. Part of this process was a remodelling of the French Army: a single war minister was given responsibility for food supply, quartering, artillery and fortifications; the officer corps became more meritocratic and professional, with colonels no longer able to buy and sell their regiments like private businesses; and a new model infantry regiment, the Régiment du Roi, was raised and trained by a Colonel Jean Martinet, whose name today is the synonym for a disciplinarian. Thanks to these reforms the French Army – all 115 regiments of it by 1688 – became the most feared in Europe, winning a string of victories over Dutch, Imperial and Spanish forces and acquiring for France large tracts of territory in the Spanish Netherlands and on the Rhine in the 1670s and 1680s. These victories were due in no small part to a succession of brilliant generals – including the Prince de Condé, the Vicomte de Turenne, the Duc de Vendôme and the Duc de Luxembourg – who made the French all but unbeatable in open battle.

In the spring of 1689, in response to yet more French gains on the Rhine the previous autumn, a Grand Alliance of powers united against Louis XIV with the aim of depriving him of all his new territory. William's United Provinces declared war first, swiftly followed by the Holy Roman Empire, Spain and England (though not officially until September 1689). William knew that a resurgent France – easily the most powerful state in Europe with its 20 million people, efficient administration and excellent network of roads and canals – posed a mortal danger to his Dutch homeland, and that England might just tip the balance. Yet, by committing troops to the Continent, he revived debates between two schools of grand strategy that stretched back to Elizabeth I's reign. The 'Continental' school believed that no one power could be allowed to dominate the continent of Europe as France was attempting to do (and Spain had before her), and that the only way to prevent this was to defeat her armies in the field using a combination of military force, money and diplomacy. Sea operations against enemy trade and colonies could only be an adjunct to the main effort.

The 'maritime' school, on the other hand, preferred to concentrate on amphibious operations and peripheral campaigns – an option that B. H. Liddell Hart, the twentieth-century military theorist, would describe as 'The British Way in Warfare' – on the grounds that a British land force as part of a Continental coalition was less effective than a similar-sized force transported by sea to exposed coastlines, ports and colonies. In William III's time, the 'Continental' argument had the upper hand – not least because he was also the sovereign of a Continental power, the United Provinces – but the debate would continue to rage until the twentieth century, with first one school gaining ascendancy, and then the other, with the result that British troops were often ill-prepared for the type of wars they were expected to fight.

In 1689, however, William was distracted by the additional problem of the Jacobite rebellions and so appointed the elderly Prince of Waldeck as commander of the Dutch forces in Flanders, with the Earl of Marlborough in charge of the 8,000-strong British Contingent.

Waldeck, however, was not impressed with the quality of Marlborough's troops. 'The English suffer,' he noted, 'from sickness, temperament, nonchallance, wretched clothing and the worst of shoes.'[5]

Yet they performed well in action, and much of the credit must go to Marlborough. For three months, before battle was joined, he drilled his men tirelessly, and spared no effort to secure adequate uniforms, arms and equipment. Waldeck acknowledged the transformation, informing William in July that he could not 'sufficiently praise the English', and that 'Monsieur Milord Marlbrouck and the Colonels have shown that their application has had a good effect.'[6]

At the Battle of Walcourt, in late August, Marlborough's men demonstrated their worth. His infantry took the brunt of the French attack, before Marlborough personally led the Life Guards and Blues in a spirited counter-charge that won the day. Though Waldeck would fail to capitalize on this victory, he was generous in his praise of the 'English' troops in general and Marlborough in particular, reporting to William that the 39-year-old had, 'in spite of his youth', displayed in this one campaign greater military aptitude than most generals achieve in a lifetime.[7] William told Marlborough: 'It is to you that this advantage is principally owing,' and rewarded him with the colonelcy of a regiment that would become the Royal Fusiliers.[8]

In Scotland, meanwhile, the variability of William's British troops was dramatically underlined at the Battle of Killiecrankie, on 27 July, when General Hugh Mackay's 4,000-strong army was routed as it attempted to raise the siege of Blair Atholl Castle by a smaller Jacobite force under Viscount 'Bonnie' Dundee. A Scotsman serving in Mackay's army described the Highlanders' charge:

> The sun going down caused the Highlandmen to advance on us like madmen, without shoe or stocking, covering themselves from our fire with their targets [light shields]; at last they cast away their musquets, drew their broadswords, and advanced furiously upon us, and were in the middle of us before we could fire three shots apiece, broke us and obliged us to retreat.[9]

Unfortunately for the Jacobites, it was a hollow victory. They lost a third of their men, including Dundee, their charismatic leader, who was killed by one of the last Williamite volleys. Most of the Highlander casualties were shot at a range of between 50 to 100 yards, and the effectiveness of their typically bold but desperate charge would diminish as muskets got lighter, more accurate and more reliable, and the plug bayonet was replaced by the socket variety, which could be fixed before firing (see p. 42). Even in 1689 the one-dimensional rush tactic of the Highlanders did not always work. Three weeks after their victory at Killiecrankie, bereft of their leader, they were badly defeated at Dunkeld by a single regiment of foot – the Earl of Angus's* – that fired from walls and houses to negate the effect of the Highlanders' mass charge. In Scotland, at least, the Jacobite rebellion was all but over.

This was not the case in Ireland. Within a month of landing at Kinsale, in March 1689, James II had taken control of virtually the whole island, bar a few pockets of resistance in Ulster at Enniskillen and Londonderry. The siege of the latter – costing the defenders, many of whom were Apprentice Boys, 8,000 lives – lasted 105 days and was finally raised by a force under General Percy Kirke on 10 August. Three days later, the Duke of Schomberg landed near Bangor with William's main army of 14,000 Dutch, English and Danish troops. The weakness of this hastily assembled force, however, was clear for all to see. 'Although there were regiments of men,' noted a historian of the early British Army, 'there was no army. There was no organization, no field-administration, in fact none of that fitness for immediate active service to be found even at that time in continental armies . . . Many of the regiments consisted of recruits so raw that they were not even in uniform, while some had not yet been furnished with their arms.'[10]

Fortunately Schomberg's Dutch and Danish regiments were of better quality, and in the first month he managed to capture Carrickfergus, Belfast and Dundalk. But a combination of bad weather, inadequate supplies and sickness caused him to suspend hostilities for the winter. By February 1690, 5,600 of his soldiers, most of them English, had died of dysentery or fever.

The opportunity was there for James to sweep the ailing Protestants out of Ireland. But, if anything, the Catholic army was in an even worse condition. Even after the arrival of 6,000 French troops in March 1690, bringing his total numbers up to 35,000, James was woefully underequipped. His commander Tyrconnell complained that the army was short of 20,000 firearms and that two thirds of the men

---

* Later known as the 26th (Cameronians).

had never fired a shot because of insufficient powder. The English Jacobite John Stevens noted the men had 'neither beds nor so much straw to lie on',

> or any thing to cover them during the whole winter, and even their clothes were worn to rags, inasmuch that many could scarce hide their nakedness in the daytime, and abundance of them were barefoot or at least so near it that their wretched shoes and stockings could scarce be made to hang on their feet and legs . . . To add to their suffering the allowance of meat and corn was so small that men rather starved than live upon it.[11]

Yet the arrival of French troops raised the stakes for William, and in June 1690, convinced that 'nothing worthwhile would be done' unless he was there to do it, he arrived in Ireland to take personal control of his army, leaving the government in the hands of Mary and a council of nine, one of whom was the Earl of Marlborough, back from Flanders and now commander-in-chief in England.[12] William still did not entirely trust Marlborough – despite his recent success in Flanders – and was unsure how he would perform if he were to face his former patron in the field. One of James's senior commanders, moreover, was the Duke of Berwick, his illegitimate son by Marlborough's sister.

According to a contemporary account, William joined his army of 37,000 in camp at Loughbrickland on 22 June, a 'dry and Windy' day 'which made the Dust very Troublesome', and at once inspected each regiment. 'This pleased the Soldiers mightily, and the King never lay out of the Camp during his stay in Ireland.' Like all good commanders, William was quick to form a bond of trust and mutual respect with his soldiers so that they were always willing to do his bidding, no matter how hard or how dangerous the task he set them. He also knew the vital importance of reconnaissance, and lost no time sending out 'Major General Scravenmore with Five Hundred Horse, to discover the Ways, and observe the Enemy'.[13]

William himself went out scouting the following day, and on his return to camp refused to sign a paper for the purchase of wine and other produce for his mess because 'he was dissatisfied that all things for his Soldiers were not ready as desired, *And with some heat protested, that he would rather drink Water than his Men should want.*' He was constantly in the saddle, 'observed the Country as he Rid along, and ordered the manner of Encamping himself'.[14] This attention to detail is almost a prerequisite for a successful general, and a trait shared by many of Britain's best commanders.

Harried by William's superior force, James withdrew his smaller Catholic army of 25,000 men back over the River Boyne, the only effective line of defence before Dublin, 'the old Rubicon of the Pale, and the frontier of the corn country'.[15] His French allies wanted him to burn Dublin and retreat behind the Shannon, but James thought the Boyne a formidable barrier and was determined 'not to be walked out of Ireland without having at least one blow for it'.[16] Yet his army was heavily outnumbered and poor in quality. A quarter of his infantry carried pikes and the rest outdated matchlocks; William's regiments were mostly armed with the latest flintlocks and plug bayonets. On the other hand, the 7,000 French infantry under James's command were of excellent quality, as were his 5,000 horsemen.

When William reached the Boyne on 30 June, he found James's men defending the bridge at Drogheda and the position 'not only difficult but almost impracticable'.[17] Yet he knew from local spies that the Boyne was tidal and could be forded upstream of Drogheda at certain times and places. While reconnoitring the main ford at Oldbridge, in the afternoon of 30 June, he and his escort of Dutch Guards were fired on by a Jacobite cannon. The first shot killed two horses and a rider; the second, according to an eyewitness, 'grazed the Bank of the River, and in the rising slanted upon the King's Right Shoulder, took out a piece of his Coat and tore the Skin and Flesh'.[18] The eyewitness added:

> My Lord Congingsby seeing his Majesty struck, Rid up and put his Handkerchief upon the place; his Majesty took very little notice of it, but rid on about Forty Yards farther, return'd the way he came, the Enemies Cannon firing on us all the while, killed two of his Guards and several Horses, which made the King give Order for his Horse to draw a little backwards.

Having changed his coat and had his wound dressed, William called a council of war, where it was 'resolved to pass the River the next Day'. The only dissenting voice was the experienced Duke of Schomberg, but William's determination to fight won him over.

The plan was for a three-pronged assault: a right flanking move over the ford at Rosnaree, followed by simultaneous attacks across the fords between Oldbridge and Drybridge. The Rosnaree assault was launched first, at 6 a.m. on 1 July, and drew a disproportionate response from James, who dispatched two thirds of his army to meet it. William, in turn, sent reinforcements to this sector, leaving just half his army for the frontal attack. He need not have worried. So difficult was the terrain in the western sector – intersected by bogs, ditches and ravines – that few of the combatants actually came to grips. The battle would be decided around Oldbridge, where 8,000 Jacobites were up against twice that number of Williamites.

At 10 a.m., after English artillery had softened up the Jacobite defenders, William's elite Dutch Guards stormed the ford and took the village of Oldbridge. Irish infantry counter-attacked, but were beaten back by platoon volleys from flintlock muskets. Meanwhile Huguenot regiments – Protestant refugees from Louis XIV's religious persecution – had crossed 100 yards to the left of the Dutch Guards. As the two forces moved forward they were attacked by Jacobite cavalry, who emerged from dead ground as if by magic. Attacking with 'unspeakable bravery', the Irishmen broke through the Huguenots, who lacked bayonets, killing the Duke of Schomberg in the process. But the Dutch held firm. Rowland Davies, chaplain to one of William's cavalry regiments, recalled:

> At the first push the front rank only fired and then fell on their faces, loading their muskets again as they lay on the ground; at the next charge they fired a volley of three ranks; then, at the next, . . . the two rear ranks drew up in two platoons and flanked the enemy across, and the rest, screwing their swords into their muskets, received the charge with all imaginable bravery and in a minute dismounted them all.[19]

By now, more of William's infantry had crossed further downstream, as had the king himself with 2,000 cavalry on the extreme left of his front. Having struggled with difficulty through mud left by the receding tide – which bogged down his horse and forced him to dismount – William led his cavalry in a charge up Donore Hill. But it was met by Jacobite cavalry and his lead regiment, the Inniskilling Horse, 'deserted him at the first charge, and carried with them a Dutch regiment that sustained them'. Eventually William rallied his Blue Troop of Dutch Guards, and 'with them he charged in person and routed the enemy'.[20]

Facing imminent defeat, James proposed a last-ditch attack by the main body of his troops on the force that had crossed at Rosnaree. But the ground was unfavourable and soon the Jacobite army had begun a panicked retreat towards Duleek, where the Dublin road crosses the River Nanny. 'Our foot being unable to march as they did,' recorded Davies, 'we could not come up to fight again, but, on the night coming on, we were forced to let them go; but had we engaged half an hour sooner, or the day held half an hour longer, we had certainly destroyed that army.'[21]

In truth the pursuit was half-hearted in the face of a disciplined French rearguard, and more damage was caused to James II's army by panic-stricken cavalry trampling their own infantry at the Duleek bottleneck than by enemy action. Even so, more than 1,000 Jacobites were killed, many shot 'like hares amongst the corn', with a further 2,000 wounded; William's army lost 500 killed and a similar number wounded.[22]

In contrast to William's inspirational, if tactically questionable, leadership at the forefront of his troops, James was conspicuous by his absence from the fighting. Nor was he generous in defeat, complaining to Lady Tyrconnell in Dublin that his Irish troops had run away. 'I see,' she replied acerbically, 'you have preceded them yourself, your Majesty.'[23]

By the time William entered Dublin in triumph on 6 July, James was already back in France, never to return. Yet William's failure to prevent the escape of three quarters of the Catholic army from the Boyne meant the war dragged on for another year. It began with a setback for William when an attempt to storm the stronghold of Limerick was bloodily repulsed in late August. Matters improved in

the autumn, however, when Marlborough led a successful amphibious expedition – his first independent command – that captured the
key Jacobite ports of Cork and Kinsale. But Jacobite resistance in
Ireland continued on into 1691 and ended only with defeat at the battle of Aughrim on 12 July, the capitulation of Galway in the same
month and the final surrender of Limerick on 3 October. Though
less well known than the Boyne, Aughrim was a much more decisive
battle, with the numerically superior Jacobites suffering more than
7,000 fatalities, 'lying most of them by the Ditches where they were
shot, and the rest . . . like a great flock of sheep scattered up and down
the country for almost four miles round'.[24]

Though not present at Aughrim, Marlborough had hoped that
his earlier successes at Cork and Kinsale would be rewarded with the
office of master-general of the Ordnance, left vacant by Schomberg's
death. But it went instead to the civilian Henry Sidney and Marlborough was to receive no other tangible recognition for his services.
Instead he was sent back to the Low Countries in May 1691 to command the British Contingent in the war against the French, a campaign
that ended badly in September when the Allied rearguard was badly
mauled near Grammont before Marlborough could intervene.

William III won his victories in Ireland during a period of significant
military change. For much of Charles II's reign, the standard infantry
weapon had been the smoothbore, muzzle-loading matchlock musket.
It used a spring-operated firing system so that when the trigger was
pressed the cock holding the burning match was allowed to fall on thus
a pan of priming powder, thus igniting the charge. But the matchlock
had a number of drawbacks. It was slow to load, clumsy to operate and
at the mercy of the elements; between shots, moreover, the musketeer
was vulnerable to cavalry attack unless protected by pikemen.

The solution to the first problem was the introduction of a new,
lighter musket with a more robust firing system – the flintlock – that
produced sparks by striking a flint against a steel plate above the pan.
A form of flintlock had been available since the early seventeenth
century; but it was more expensive than the matchlock and, by the
time of the English Civil War, had been issued only to elite troops

like the Life Guards or those fusilier regiments (named after *fusil*, the French word for the flintlock mechanism) whose job it was to protect powder stores and artillery trains.

All this changed in the mid-1670s, when a new type of soldier – the grenadier – was introduced to the English Army. Armed with flintlock muskets and an early form of hand grenade – its name derived from the Spanish for 'pomegranate', the fruit it resembled – the grenadiers were originally a select band in each company, though they were soon given a company of their own and would stand in battle on the right of the regiment's line. They wore crownless mitre caps, instead of wide-brimmed tricorne hats, enabling them to sling their muskets across their backs, and leaving both hands free to light and throw their grenades. They were especially effective during assaults on fortifications, as described by the famous military song 'The British Grenadiers':

> When'er we are commanded to storm the palisades
> Our leaders march with fuses and we with hand grenades
> We throw them from the glacis, about our enemies' ears
> Sing tow row, row, row, row, the British Grenadiers[25]

Inevitably there were accidents. During the siege of Maastricht, a Private Donald McBane was in the act of throwing his grenade when it exploded in his hands, 'killing several about me, and blew me over the palisades; burnt my clothes so that the skin came off me'. He fell among 'Murray's Company of Grenadiers, flayed like an old dead horse from head to foot', and had to be 'cast into the water to put out the fire about me'.[26]

But overall these new troops were a great success, and the raising of the first grenadier companies coincided with the introduction of a weapon that, with the flintlock, would complete the transformation of the musketeer from a lumbering, vulnerable and ineffective soldier to something resembling the all-purpose infantryman that still exists in the British Army today. The weapon was the bayonet,*

---

* So called after the French town of Bayonne, where it was said to have been invented.

a removable spearhead that instantly converted the musketeer into a pikeman and enabled him to defend himself when his musket was unloaded. The first version, issued exclusively to grenadiers, was the 'plug' bayonet, which attached inside the muzzle and made firing impossible. But it was replaced in the early 1690s by the 'socket' bayonet, which allowed the gun to fire by fitting around the muzzle. At the same time the use of the bayonet spread from the elite grenadiers to the other line companies, so that by 1697 the proportion of pikes to muskets had fallen from 1:3 to 1:4, with the majority of musketeers carrying the socket bayonet. The pike disappeared altogether during the War of the Spanish Succession (1701–14), and thereafter all foot soldiers were equipped with the flintlock musket and socket bayonet. A modified version of the flintlock – dubbed the 'Brown Bess' after the colour of its stock – would become the British Army's standard infantry musket until it was superseded by first the percussion musket, then the rifle, in the mid-nineteenth century.[27]

The performance of the flintlock was further improved in the early 1690s by the replacement of bandoliers and powder horns with made-up paper cartridges, and by reducing the size of the musket-ball from 12 balls to a pound of lead, to 16 smaller ones. Prior to this a musket was loaded by pouring a finely calculated charge of powder into the barrel from a flask, followed by the heavy lead ball or shot, and finally the wad to keep the ball in place; the contents were then firmly rammed home with a rod. All this took time, and few infantrymen could fire more than one shot a minute. The new cartridges – containing powder and one-ounce ball – and a simplified loading drill made it possible to more than double the rate of fire (with a good infantryman managing two to three shots a minute). What they could not do, however, was appreciably alter the effective range of a musket, which remained at 75–100 yards.[28]

Nevertheless, the improvements made possible a drastic change in infantry tactics. Before them a typical infantry battalion – the largest permanent tactical and administrative formation that existed – was made up of seven companies of a hundred men, with each company consisting of two thirds musketeers and one third pikemen. In battle they formed a line with the pikemen in the centre, five ranks deep, and six ranks of musketeers on either flank. The pikemen gave protection against cavalry attack, while the musketeers were more offensively minded and fired volleys by rank. Such tactics had changed little since the heyday of the great Swedish general King Gustavus Adolphus in the 1630s.[29] But with the improvement in their weapons making them less vulnerable to cavalry attack, the English infantry were able to fight three ranks deep, the first rank kneeling, with only a gap of a few paces between battalions or regiments so the line was almost continuous. Volleys were delivered not by ranks but by platoons of thirty to forty men (or three to a company), with a battalion line subdivided into eighteen equal platoons, and half the elite grenadier company on each flank. The platoons were assigned to separate 'firings' of six platoons each, spread equally along the line, so that the effect was a constant, rolling fire.

A battalion would advance until it was within 100 yards of its foe, and preferably closer. On the colonel's order 'First Firing, Take Care!', the six platoons of the first firing and the whole of the first rank would prepare to fire. The first rank knelt while the remaining two ranks of the first-firing platoons manoeuvred into close order and 'locked'. This meant they pointed their left shoulder towards their target, and placed their left foot close behind the rear-facing right foot of the man in front. That way all three ranks had a clear field of fire and friendly-fire accidents were avoided – something that could not be said for the French Army, whose soldiers lined up one behind the other, forcing the middle rank to stoop when a battalion volley was ordered.

On a further order, all six platoons of the first firing discharged their weapons simultaneously. Immediately after, these platoons would open order and start to reload, while the second and third firings were brought into play. The third firing was the most destructive, as the fire of the last six platoons was augmented by the two halves of the grenadier company. A well-trained battalion could deliver two shots per man – or six firings – a minute.

The advantages of platoon volleys were twofold: the enemy was exposed to continuous fire against every part of his line; and at any one time a third of a battalion would be reloaded and ready for any eventuality. For the first time in history – thanks to these technological and tactical improvements – the foot soldier became the dominant factor on the battlefield. 'Firearms and not cold steel now decide battles,' wrote a noted French military theorist.[30]

But as firepower increased, so did casualties. At the Battle of Steenkirk in 1692, fought between the Allies and the French, each side suffered 4,000 casualties out of a combined total of 90,000 actually engaged (or just under 9 per cent). Twelve years later at Blenheim, by which time most European armies were equipped with flintlocks,* the vanquished French and Bavarian casualties were 40 per cent of the total engaged, and that did not include prisoners.[31]

The proportion of infantry to cavalry inevitably grew, most notably in the French Army, where it rose from 1:2 during Turenne's early campaigns to 3:1 at his death in 1677. Yet horsemen of all European armies – the famed 'armes blanches' – retained both their social prestige and their usefulness. They could scout, escort convoys, protect camps, conduct raids, set ambushes, harry a defeated enemy and, of course, charge in battle.

Not that all countries agreed on the best way to employ cavalry in battle. The French thought it valuable chiefly as mobile firepower, rather than as an instrument of shock, and tended to advance their cavalry on a narrow front with each formation discharging its pistols before wheeling to the rear to reload. The English preferred shock-action over a broad front. 'Probably, they deployed in three ranks,' writes John Childs, 'but charged at the trot in two ranks. The cavalry were armed with pistols and sabres whilst the dragoons also carried carbines.'[32]

In fact, some of the early dragoons did not even carry swords. Hay's Dragoons (later the Scots Greys), for example, were mounted on sturdy farm ponies and armed with the shorter-barrelled picklock

---

* The exceptions were the Russian and Ottoman armies, which clung to the matchlock for a little longer.

carbine (though twelve per troop used pistols and 7-foot-long halberds, a combination of axe and spear). Their specialities were guard and escort duties, cordon and search operations, and other forms of internal security, though in battle they could more than hold their own: it was a regiment of dragoons that had put Charles I's Life Guards to flight at Naseby in 1645.[33] They would eventually become cavalry proper, and fight chiefly with the sabre, but for much of the Stuart period they retained their tactical flexibility. The *Military Dictionary* of 1702 described them as:

> Musketeers mounted, who sometimes serve a-foot, and sometimes a-horseback, being always ready upon anything that requires expedition, as being able to keep pace with the horse, and do the service of foot. In battle, or attacks, they are commonly the *Enfants Perdus*, or Forlorn [Hope], being the first that fall on.[34]

The third major weapon that a commander could use in battle was artillery. There were two basic types: siege artillery – heavy guns (36- to 60-pounders*), howitzers and mortars – to create breaches in fortifications; and field artillery – medium and light guns, varying in size from 1½- to 24-pounders – to support infantry and cavalry. Both types were moved in vast artillery trains that included engineers, pioneers and supply services as well as gunners, and that, because of their slowness, determined the speed at which an army could march. In William III's Low Countries campaign of 1692, for example, his artillery train was comprised of 38 brass cannon of varying sizes and at least 240 four-horse wagons of munitions and ordnance stores (not to mention the many baggage and supply wagons). Sixteen years later, the Duke of Marlborough's 'Great Convoy' required 16,000 horses to draw 80 heavy guns, 20 siege mortars and 3,000 assorted munitions' and stores' wagons, and covered 30 miles of road.[35]

Even field guns were difficult to move. 'With guns weighing at least three tons each,' writes one British expert on the era's warfare, 'drawn by long strings of horses harnessed in tandem, and with difficult

---

* The calibre was set at the weight of the cannonball, though this was far from exact.

civilian drivers to contend with, it is amazing that they made any
progress at all.'[36] Part of the problem was the fact that the Board of
Ordnance, which controlled the artillery and engineers, was virtually an independent organ of state and not under army control. Many
of its employees, moreover, were civilians and quasi-military, and
this inevitably produced friction with the 'fighting' officers, who had
been drawn from the line-infantry regiments. This anomaly would
not be removed until separate permanent corps of gunners and engineers were founded in 1716 and formally incorporated into the British
Army (though even then the Board of Ordnance retained its independent status).

Yet Marlborough was able to improve mobility during the War
of the Spanish Succession by using a light, two-wheeled cart with
springs for much of the train transport. It was drawn by two horses
and much speedier than the huge six-wheeled, eight-horse 'tum-
brills' used by many of his allies and opponents. Marshal Camille
Tallard, his opponent at Blenheim, would need eight days to move
the 6,000 wagons of his artillery train through the relatively short
passes of the Black Forest in July 1704. Marlborough's 'Great Convoy' of 1708, on the other hand, was able to cover 12 miles in a single
day.[37]

On the battlefield, artillery was grouped in batteries of six or eight
pieces. Marlborough, in particular, took great care in siting his guns
because he knew their effect could be decisive – in both a defensive
and an offensive capacity – and that they were virtually impossible to
recover if a battle went badly. He was also prepared to move them to
gain a tactical advantage during a battle, and made good use of the
new English practice (introduced during William's reign from earlier
Swedish examples) of attaching two light 1½- or 3-pounder guns to
each battalion for close-fire support. But, given that the effective
range of all field guns was between 450–600 yards, even the batteries
had to be stationed dangerously close to the firing line.

Of the three main types of artillery ammunition, the most prevalent was a solid cast-iron ball known as round-shot, which could be
used either as an all-purpose projectile against men and horses, or
in larger calibres for breaching fortifications. Fired from a gun at

point-blank range, the shot would fly for a couple of hundred yards at the height of a man before striking the ground and bouncing the same distance again. If directed against massed targets, a single shot could kill ten or more men.

The other ammunition used by field artillery was canister or case-shot, a cylindrical tin packed with lead balls that had the effect of a large shotgun, and was used chiefly as an anti-personnel weapon at short ranges. Lastly there was the common shell, a hollow cast-iron sphere packed with gunpowder and fitted with a fuse, which was fired at higher elevations by stubbier guns known as howitzers. The fuse – little more than a wooden plug containing a train of gunpowder – was ignited by the flash of hot gases from the main charge, and could be adjusted in length so that the shell would explode in mid-air, hurling pieces of its casing into the enemy.

The performance of William III's English troops in the Grand Alliance's Nine Years War against France (1688–97) was mixed. They did well under Marlborough at Walcourt, as we have seen, and also fought stubbornly under William himself in an action fought chiefly between the English and French vanguards at Steenkirk in 1692, and again during the defeat at Landen in 1693. Yet the only decisive victory won by the English during the war was fought not on land but at sea in May/ June 1692, when a combined Anglo-Dutch fleet defeated a smaller French force off Cap Barfleur in the Cherbourg Peninsula, and then a few days later used fireships to destroy the surviving French ships in the bay of Saint-Vaast-la-Hougue. The victory ensured English and Dutch naval domination of the Channel and effectively ended Louis XIV's plan to invade England and restore James II.

For much of the war on the Continent, however, the French had the upper hand: securing a number of key fortresses (including Namur and Heidelberg) and winning resounding victories over the Allies at Fleurus in the Spanish Netherlands in 1690, Marsaglia in northern Italy in 1693 and at Torroella in Catalonia in 1694. But none of these successes was decisive and by 1695 – the year the Allies regained Namur and death deprived Louis XIV of his best commander, Marshal François Luxembourg – the balance of military power was turning against the French. A peace was eventually signed at Rijswijk in September 1697, its terms largely confirming the pre-war status quo. Louis XIV was allowed to keep Alsace and the western third of the Caribbean island of Hispaniola (modern Haiti); but had to hand back Lorraine and all his recent territorial gains on the right bank of the Rhine. In addition he was forced to withdraw from the Spanish Netherlands and Catalonia, to grant the Dutch a highly favourable commercial treaty, and to recognize William III as King of England and undertake not to support the candidature of James II's Catholic son, James Stuart (the 'Old Pretender').

The war had thus ended satisfactorily for William III. His soldiers had made only a minor contribution to the Allied war effort, however – far less than his sailors, for example – and would have to wait for the War of the Spanish Succession (1702–14), and the extraordinary exploits of arguably the greatest general this island has produced, to establish a reputation as the finest of their era.

4.   The War of the Spanish Succession

In 1692 the Earl of Marlborough's late-flourishing career was brought to a sudden, grinding halt when he was dismissed from all his military and court appointments and imprisoned briefly in the Tower of London. The official reason for Marlborough's sacking was his outspoken criticism of William's preference for Dutch rather than English generals. His imprisonment, however, was on a far more serious charge: that he was actively plotting the restoration of James II.

Given the key role that Marlborough had played in James's downfall, it seems extraordinary that such a charge could even have been levelled; and, as it happened, it took only a month for the documentary evidence to be declared a forgery and Marlborough released on bail. But he was lucky because, unbeknown to William's agents, he had long hedged his bets by remaining in secret contact with the exiled court of James II, and would continue to do so for the rest of his life, though it is doubtful that he ever provided the Jacobites with any really useful intelligence.

Even so, Marlborough's conduct was treasonable and, had it become public knowledge, would have cost him his life. Fortunately for him *and* his country, it never did and just five years after his disgrace he was able to resume his military career. His rehabilitation owed much to four timely deaths: first those of three senior British generals – Mackay, Sir John Lanier and Thomas Tollemache – who were all killed in battle at a time when William III was under political pressure to replace Dutch or 'foreign' generals with Britons; and then, at the close of 1694, that of Queen Mary II herself from smallpox, thus restoring her sister Princess Anne to favour as heir apparent. Given the closeness of Anne's relationship with Marlborough's wife, Sarah, this was a development that was bound to benefit the earl in the long run.

Though William forgave Marlborough publicly by allowing him

to kiss hands in March 1695, a further three years would elapse before he felt able to entrust the earl with the prestigious and lucrative post of governor to Anne's seven-year-old son, the Duke of Gloucester. Soon after, Marlborough was restored to his army rank and his place in the Privy Council; and when William left for Holland in the summer of 1698, he was one of the lords justice left in charge of the country. He would have to wait another three years before he was given an office of state, yet in the interim William regularly consulted him on military and political matters. It was as if William, unconvinced that Louis XIV would keep the recent peace, was looking ahead to the next inevitable war and, with his health failing, had identified Marlborough as the man to continue the fight against France.

William's suspicions of Louis XIV were soon justified. Louis had long dreamed of uniting the crowns of France and Spain and, though he had formally renounced any claim to the Spanish throne in 1659 on marrying the *infanta* Maria Teresa, he later used the pretext that the marriage dowry had not been paid to declare the agreement void. Meanwhile the deformed and half imbecile Charles II ('the Sufferer') became King of Spain and Louis put his plans into abeyance. But when Charles died in November 1700, his will named his great-nephew Philip of Anjou, Louis's grandson, as his sole heir (and only if Anjou and his younger brother, the Duc de Berry, refused the inheritance was it to be offered to the king's nephew, Archduke Charles, the younger son of the Holy Roman Emperor). The sole condition was that the crowns of Spain and France should never be united.

The will was in direct contravention to a partition treaty, signed in 1699 by England and France, which stated that the Spanish Empire (then the greatest in the world) was to be divided between Archduke Charles, who would receive the lion's share including Spain, the Spanish Netherlands and the huge Spanish Empire beyond Europe, and Louis, 'Le Grand Dauphin' of France (Charles II's nephew and father of Philip of Anjou), who would rule Naples, Sardinia and Lorraine. All eyes turned to Louis XIV's magnificent palace at Versailles. It was in the French king's power to uphold the treaty by forbidding his grandson to accept the proffered crown. But he did the opposite –

introducing Philip of Anjou to a room full of waiting courtiers and ambassadors with the words, 'Gentlemen, here is the king of Spain'[1] – and war was inevitable.

It took almost a year for William to bring the English Parliament and people round to the idea of another costly war. But he managed it thanks, once again, to the political ineptitude of Louis XIV, who, on the death of the exiled James II in September 1701, at once proclaimed the now thirteen-year-old Prince James Stuart as the rightful King of England ('James III'). That same month, in The Hague, the Allies signed a Treaty of Grand Alliance, which bound Austria (in the person of the Holy Roman Emperor, Leopold I), the Dutch and the English to support the partition of the Spanish Empire with 'satisfactory compensation' for the Habsburgs, and gains for the maritime powers in the Caribbean.* The man who conducted these negotiations for William was the Earl of Marlborough, who, earlier that year, had been appointed commander of all English troops in Holland and Ambassador-Extraordinary and Plenipotentiary, with the right to 'conceive treaties without reference, if need be, to King or Parliament'.[2] His rehabilitation was complete.

William III would not enjoy this diplomatic coup for long. On 8 March 1702, two weeks after sustaining a broken collarbone in a fall from his horse, he died at Kensington Palace. His successor Queen Anne at once appointed Marlborough, her favourite's husband, as captain-general of her army and master-general of the Ordnance (with direct control over the infantry, the cavalry *and* the artillery, an important factor in the campaigns to come). He was also confirmed in his ambassadorial role to the United Provinces, and soon after appointed deputy commander of the Dutch Army. No general since Cromwell had enjoyed such a combination of diplomatic and military authority. His 'responsibilities', writes his most recent biographer, 'immeasurably outweighed those exercised by British commanders-in-chief in the great wars of the twentieth century, for he did not simply execute

* An interesting codicil to the treaty was Leopold's recognition of the Elector of Brandenburg as the King of Prussia in return for his military support against France. Thus was Prussia's – and later Germany's – rise as a great power initiated.

strategy but helped to determine it. In the context of 1944, for example, he would have been Eisenhower, Montgomery and Brooke rolled into one.'[3]

It helped, of course, that Marlborough had the unique talents that such wide-ranging responsibility required, and would prove not only a brilliant battlefield tactician and campaign strategist, a superb trainer of men and master of logistics, but also a natural diplomatist as deft at handling the often recalcitrant Dutch politicians as he was other Allied generals. He possessed, moreover, a 'shamanistic quality' that, according to Richard Holmes, enables great generals to 'get straight to the hearts of the soldiers they command'.[4]

All of these talents might have counted for nothing had a recent revolution in public finances not provided him with the funds to fight a war that would last for more than a decade. In the early 1690s, with the cost of war outstripping revenue and virtually no long-term system of borrowing, the government had introduced the land tax, exchequer bills and the concept of National Debt, and in 1694 Charles Montagu (later Lord Halifax) set up the Bank of England. Two years later Montagu carried out a total recoinage, disposing of clipped and counterfeit coins, and reducing the value of a guinea from 30s. to 21s. Exchequer bills alone – secured by future tax revenues from the national exchequer and paying 10 per cent interest – would allow the government to spend more than £42 million during the Nine Years War (also known as the War of the League of Augsburg). It expanded the army to 90,000 men and the navy from 109 ships in 1690 to 176 ten years later. 'The modern English state had arrived,' writes Arthur Herman, 'with powerful fiscal and military instruments at its disposal. These would be the powerhouse of modern Great Britain.'[5]

Marlborough, as a result, would not be starved of resources. Yet, at the outset of the war, he would have to contend with the ruthless defence cuts that Parliament had made since 1697, notably the reduction of the army to a peacetime establishment of 7,000 in England and 12,000 in Ireland. For those discharged, the future was bleak. Despite a number of emergency measures, such as opening up all trades to ex-officers and soldiers without the need for an apprenticeship (an expedient that had worked well in 1660), many demobbed soldiers turned to crime, particularly ex-cavalrymen who were allowed to keep their horses and became highwaymen. So bad did it become in London that a line of guardhouses was built on the road from the City to Kensington to protect travellers from ex-soldiers.[6] Never popular at the best of times, soldiers were now feared and despised in equal measure.

Many of these vagrant ex-soldiers were only too happy to return to the colours when the army doubled in size to provide troops to fight in Flanders and elsewhere in 1702. But as the war dragged on and more troops were required – 150,000 were serving Queen Anne in the field by 1709, though only half of them were British – it became increasingly difficult to find new recruits.[7] One expedient was to sentence minor criminals to service in the army, and to release others if they volunteered. Another was for professional recruiters, or 'crimpers', to kidnap men from the streets and then sell them to recruiting parties (a practice akin to the naval press-gang). So unwilling were many such 'volunteers' that they were locked in gaols prior to being sent abroad.

Less heavy-handed tactics after Blenheim included recruiting parties using Marlborough's fame to attract volunteers – one recruiting ditty, sung to the tune of 'Waltzing Matilda', included the refrain 'who'll come a-soldiering with Marlborough and me?' Nonetheless, many of these parties had to resort to the type of tricks and machinations that Captain Plume and Sergeant Kite used in George Farquhar's contemporary play *The Recruiting Officer* (1706). Farquhar himself had been a recruiting lieutenant for the Earl of Orrery's Regiment of Foot, and the following speech, which he gives to Kite, has the ring of authenticity:

> If any gentleman soldiers, or others, have a mind to serve Her Majesty, and pull down the French king; if any prentices have severe masters, any children have undutiful parents; if any servants have too little wages, or any husband too much wife; let them repair to the noble Sergeant Kite, at the Sign of the Raven, in this good town of Shrewsbury, and they shall receive present relief and entertainment.[8]

Even such oratory as this left the quotas unfilled, forcing the government to increase the already generous bounty from £2 a head in 1703 to £5 in 1708, and to pass no fewer than nine recruiting statutes during the course of the twelve-year struggle.[9] Clearly military life remained deeply unpopular with society at large, an attitude summed up by the author Daniel Defoe when he noted (in descending order of preference): 'In winter, the poor starve, thieve or turn soldier.'[10] A contemporary newspaper, the London *Spy*, was even more derogatory when it noted the soldier was 'generally beloved of two sorts of companion, in whores and lice, for both these Vermin are great admirers'.[11]

When the Earl of Marlborough arrived in the Low Countries to take command of English and Dutch troops in July 1702, he was already fifty-two years old (six years older than the Duke of Wellington and Napoleon at Waterloo) and keen to establish the military reputation denied him in his prime. He would face the same problem that confronts all commanders of polyglot forces: how to get his allies, in particular the Dutch, to agree to his strategy. This was no easy task for two interlinked reasons: the complicated nature of the United Provinces' political system; and the fact that its political representatives liked to keep a close eye on military affairs.

Since breaking away from Spanish control in the early seventeenth century, the United Provinces had been governed by an elected estate headed by an official known as a pensionary. These estates in turn sent delegates to the States-General, the national parliament, where each province had a single vote. It was left to Holland, the largest and richest province, to provide the 'grand pensionary', the republic's equivalent of a chief executive. He had day-to-day control of foreign affairs and also presided over the Council of State.

In 1702 the grand pensionary was (and had been for the previous fourteen years) Anthonie Heinsius, a sixty-year-old bachelor of ascetic tastes who lived for his work. His lifestyle could not have contrasted more with that of the Marlboroughs, who, now that they were high in the queen's favour, were enjoying huge financial rewards.* Yet he

---

* On Queen Anne's accession, Marlborough's wife, Sarah, had become Lady of the Bedchamber and Keeper of the Privy Purse. Marlborough himself held appointments and perquisites worth an astonishing £60,000 a year (or £6 million in today's money).

appreciated Marlborough's seriousness when it came to professional matters, and the close personal relationship they forged during the treaty negotiations would be one of the cornerstones of the Grand Alliance. Even Heinsius, however, had to defer all-important decisions to the States-General, where opinions were rarely united; and Marlborough's hands would be further tied by the fact that each provincial estate elected deputies to accompany Dutch armies in the field. Though they held no military rank, their influence was immense and no Dutch general would fight if the field deputies did not want him to, regardless of the wishes of an Allied commander-in-chief.

The strategic situation in July 1702, moreover, was far from satisfactory. A year earlier the French had forced the Dutch to relinquish the barrier towns in the Spanish Netherlands – including Luxembourg, Mons, Namur and Oudenaarde – granted to them by the Treaty of Rijswijk, and on which the Dutch had pinned their long-term hopes of security. Louis XIV had followed this up in the late spring of 1702 by dispatching the able Marshal Louis Boufflers and 60,000 veteran troops to invade Holland itself. Boufflers had easily outmanoeuvred the Allied commander, Godard van Reede Ginckel, Earl of Athlone (ennobled by William III for his service in Ireland), and driven him back towards Nijmegen on the lower Rhine. Such was the parlous state of affairs when Marlborough took personal command of the now reinforced Allied Army at Nijmegen in the summer of 1702. It was comprised of 60,000 troops, only a quarter of whom were British; the remainder were Dutch (the largest contingent, though their regiments included many Scots and Swiss), Germans and Danes.

Marlborough at once sought to knock the French off balance by crossing the River Maas (Meuse in French) below Graves and threatening Boufflers's lines of communication back to the Spanish Netherlands. He hoped that Prince Louis of Baden's Imperial forces on the upper Rhine would put pressure on the French right. But before this plan of action could be agreed, Louis XIV ordered Boufflers to send a strong detachment to the upper Rhine, giving Marlborough a distinct numerical advantage. Even then the Dutch hesitated, so fearful were they of losing Nijmegen, causing Marlborough to write a forceful letter to

Heinsius that concluded: 'Till we act offensively, all things must go ill.'[12]

The letter had the desired effect, and on 22 July, with Dutch permission, Marlborough crossed the Maas and struck south-west towards Liège. A British sergeant recalled:

> At night there was orders for the quartermaster general [William Cadogan, Marlborough's principal staff officer], the vanguard and camp colour men to parade on the right of the front line by four o'clock in the morning and the General to beat at 5.00. Which orders were all punctually obeyed and the army decamped accordingly and that day passed the Maas and advanced about two and a half leagues [7½ miles] and there encamped. Whereupon the enemy decamped also.[13]

The sergeant describes a typical move for an early-eighteenth-century army. First the engineers would have bridged the Maas with pontoons for the troops to cross, while the guns, carts and heavy baggage crossed the existing bridge in Graves. The vanguard was led by Cadogan with a small cavalry escort, followed by units in order of seniority. Camp colourmen were guides from each battalion who carried flags to enable the commanding officers to identify their allocated campsite at the end of each day's march.

Boufflers responded by crossing the Maas at Roermond, but in hurrying to get ahead of the Allied march he exposed his flank to a dawn attack. 'Lord Marlborough had his men under arms,' recalled Lieutenant Robert Parker, a Protestant from Kilkenny who had risen from the ranks in the Royal Regiment of Ireland (later the 18th Foot), 'and just ready to march, when the Field-Deputies came to him, and prayed him to desist. This greatly surprised him, as they had agreed to his scheme the night before: but being a man of great temper and prudence, and being determined not to do anything this first campaign without their approbation, at their earnest treaty he desisted.'[14]

It would not be the last time the field deputies thwarted Marlborough's plans. He had, nonetheless, achieved his broader objective – to force Boufflers to evacuate Dutch territory – and was now able to concentrate on retaking a number of key French-held towns, including

Venlo and Liège (which fell by storm on 23 September and 23 October respectively). At the citadel of Liège, showing more courage than sense, the French commander had refused Marlborough's terms of surrender and his soldiers paid the price. Parker confessed: 'Our men gave no quarter for some time, so that the greater part of the garrison was cut to pieces.'[15]

Leaving part of his army to besiege the fortress of Rheinberg, Marlborough returned to England in triumph (though not without hazard, as the boat in which he was travelling down the Maas was stopped by French troops from Guelders and he was allowed to proceed only when his clerk produced an out-of-date passport). In barely three months he had removed the threat to Holland and cleared the Maas as far as Liège. His reward was a dukedom, yet the Tory majority in the House of Commons refused to grant him a suitable pension (on the grounds of cost) and insisted on twinning his congratulatory address with one saluting the navy's successful action at Vigo Bay that had led to the capture of the Spanish treasure fleet. 'By commending naval commanders alongside Marlborough,' writes the duke's biographer, 'the Tories were making clear their preference for the "traditional" British strategy based on seapower, rather than on a Continental commitment.'[16] It was a debate that would trouble Marlborough for many years to come as the government attempted to conduct Continental and maritime campaigns simultaneously – in Flanders and Spain – with the inevitable dispersal of military force that such a compromise strategy entailed.

5. The March to the Danube

The freshly minted Duke of Marlborough was still on leave in London, basking in the warm glow of public acclaim, when word reached him in mid-February 1703 that his only son, John, Marquess of Blandford, a sixteen-year-old undergraduate at Cambridge, was dangerously ill with smallpox. His wife rushed to her son's bedside, but Marlborough saw no sense in both of them risking infection and sent physicians in his stead. 'I am so troubled at the sad condition this poor child seems to be in,' he wrote soon after to the duchess, 'that I know not what to do. I pray God to give you some comfort in this great affliction. If you think my coming can be of the least use let me know it.'[1]

For thirty-six hours, Marlborough waited anxiously for news of his son's recovery. But it never came and, fearing the worst, he travelled to Cambridge and was at the bedside when Blandford died in the morning of 20 February 1703. A grief-stricken Marlborough threw himself with even more energy than usual into the new campaigning season, and by the autumn of 1703 had captured Bonn, Huy and Limburg. But other, more ambitious plans had come to naught, thanks to a combination of Dutch caution, incompetence and infighting: notably his 'Great Design' to seize the port of Antwerp; and his attempts to pierce the incomplete French defensive system known as the Lines of Brabant so that he could engage Boufflers and his colleague, Marshal François Villeroi, in open battle. Meanwhile, further south, his ally Emperor Leopold I of Austria was under threat from two directions: from Hungary, recently wrested from Turkish rule, where unpopular Austrian taxation had provoked an uprising; and from Bavaria, the most powerful state in southern Germany, which had switched sides to join France at the start of the year. What made this betrayal doubly shocking was that Bavaria's ruler, the Elector Maximilian, was the emperor's son-in-law and had served him as governor-general of the Spanish Netherlands during the previous war. A ruthlessly ambitious man, Maximilian hoped to replace Leopold as Holy Roman Emperor and saw an alliance with France as the means. His first act was to capture the free city of Ulm on the Danube, thus threatening Vienna and opening up a new front deep in Germany that the French were quick to support. By the end of the year the Franco-Bavarian forces had overwhelmed a smaller Imperial army at Höchstädt, and had taken the fortresses of Ratisbon on the Danube, Augsburg on the Lech and Landau near the Rhine.

With Austria in danger of being knocked out of the war, Count Wratislaw, the emperor's ambassador in London, spent the winter of 1703/4 pleading with Marlborough to march an army south from Holland to relieve the pressure. Mindful of the logistical difficulties and the inevitable Dutch opposition, his initial response was non-committal. But at last he relented, telling Wratislaw that it was his intention 'to induce the Estates-General to decide upon a siege of Landau, or a diversion on the Moselle', and that if he was successful in taking Landau he would supply Prince Louis of Baden, the Imperial commander on the upper Rhine, 'with as many troops as possible to enable him to overthrow the Elector of Bavaria'.[2]

In the event, both Prince Louis and the Dutch preferred to limit the offensive to the Moselle Valley and a simultaneous assault on Landau, whereas Marlborough and Prince Eugène of Savoy,* the most talented and aggressive Imperial commander (and a man who had won important victories over the French in Italy in the first year of war, 1701), favoured a march all the way to the Danube. Mindful of the need to tread carefully, it was not until 18 April that Marlborough outlined his strategy, and his plan to overcome Dutch opposition, in a letter to his close friend Lord Godolphin, the first lord of the Treasury:[†]

---

* Born in Paris, the great-nephew of Cardinal Mazarin, Eugène had left France at the age of twenty because Louis XIV refused to let him become a soldier. After a fifty-year military career, chiefly in the service of France's enemies, Napoleon Bonaparte would judge him one of the seven greatest captains in history.

[†] A post equivalent to prime minister, though the term did not yet exist.

My intentions are to march all the English to Koblenz, and to declare
here that I intend to command on the Moselle; but when I come there
to write to the States[-General], that I think it absolutely necessary
for saving the Empire to march with the troops under my command
to join those in Germany that are in her Majesty's and Dutch pay, in
order to take the measure with Prince Louis for the speedy reducing
of the Elector of Bavaria. The army I propose there would consist of
upwards of 40,000 men. If I should act in any other manner . . . my
design would immediately be known to the French, and these people
[the Dutch] would never consent to let so many troops go so far from
their frontiers.[3]

Only Heinsius and Lieutenant-General Johan van Goor, the Dutch
commander who had lately been serving under Prince Louis, were
told the truth. With good reason, because Marlborough's secret plan
was extremely hazardous. It required a flank march along the eastern
borders of France, with an ever-lengthening line of communication that would be vulnerable to a French counter-attack. It meant
crossing great rivers, many of them unbridged, and marching across
250 miles of wooded, hilly and poorly tracked country. And all the
while Marlborough would have to feed, water, shelter and move an
army of 40,000 soldiers – a third more than the population of Bristol,
then the largest city in England after London – with its size growing
to 60,000 after other contingents had joined the line of march.

It helped that his quartermaster-general, William Cadogan, was a
man of outstanding ability whose roles included master logistician,
chief of intelligence and commander of the advance guard. And
never were his talents put to better use than during the march to
Bavaria when he and his staff had to help Marlborough 'plot the line
of march, and select suitable places for nightly camps; arrange for the
baking of bread, the army's staple ration; set up depots along the line
of march to be stocked ahead of the army's arrival with food and
other supplies – even fresh shoes to replace those worn out by marching'. They also had to hire the army's transport of 1,700 wagons and
4,000 draught animals, collect boats to move heavy supplies up the
Rhine, and arrange sufficient fodder for 19,000 horses, all the draught

animals and the beef ration on the hoof. The fodder alone amounted to 100 tons of oats a day.[4] To pay for all this, and to ensure his men received their wages in full and on time (and were, as a result, less inclined to loot), Marlborough would take with him closely guarded coffers of gold, known collectively as the Military Chest. The coffers were 'guarantors of good will and fine order during a manoeuvre that, by its nature, promised extreme fatigue and continuous stress'.[5]

Finally, after much frantic preparation, the epic march began at Bedburg, west of Cologne, at first light on 20 May 1704.

Marlborough took with him an army of 21,000 men (more than 14,000 of whom were British and Irish, many recently recruited), and was joined by a further 5,000 Prussians and Hanoverians when he reached Coblenz, on the confluence of the Moselle and the Rhine, on the 26th. It was here that the French, and indeed most of his own soldiers, expected him to turn along the northern bank of the Moselle towards France. But instead, after a two-day halt, and 'to the surprise of all', according to one of his officers, 'we crossed the Moselle and Rhine both at this place, and marched through the country of Hesse-Cassell, where we were joined by the Hereditary Prince of that country with a body of Hessians, which completed the Duke's army to about 40,000.'[6]

Thus far Marlborough's march had been shadowed to the west by a French army under Marshal Villeroi. When the Allies did not follow the Moselle, but instead crossed the Rhine, Louis XIV and his advisers assumed their true objective was to recross further south at Philippsburg – where another bridge-of-boats was, on Marlborough's orders, in the process of being constructed – so that he could recapture Landau and invade Alsace. To prevent this, Louis ordered Villeroi to continue his march south to Landau, where he would link up with a separate French army from Strasbourg under Marshal Tallard. But the bridge-of-boats at Philippsburg was a ruse and the French would not discover Marlborough's true intention until he crossed the River Main on 3 June. By then it was too late for either marshal to prevent him from linking up with Louis of Baden.

And all the while, thanks to Cadogan's brilliant organization, the march went like clockwork. To save time, Marlborough had left his

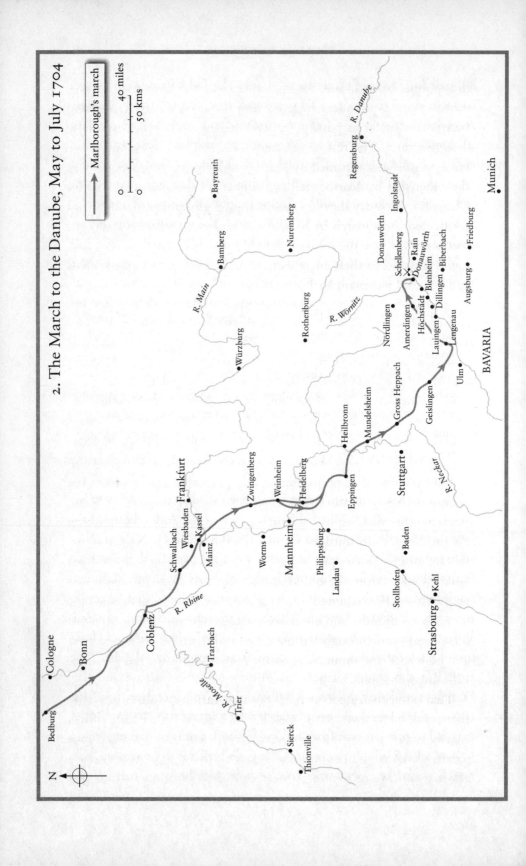

2. The March to the Danube, May to July 1704

→ Marlborough's march

40 miles
50 kms

N

Bedburg
Cologne
Bonn
Coblenz
R. Rhine
R. Moselle
Trarbach
Trier
Sierck
Thionville

Schwalbach
Wiesbaden
Frankfurt
Kassel
Mainz
Worms
Mannheim
Philippsburg
Landau
Baden
Stollhofen
Kehl
Strasbourg

Zwingenberg
Weinheim
Heidelberg
Eppingen
Stuttgart
R. Neckar

Würzburg
Rothenburg
R. Main
Bamberg
Nuremberg
Bayreuth

Heilbronn
Mundelsheim
Gross Heppach
Geislingen
Ulm
Lengenau

R. Wörnitz
Nördlingen
Amerdingen
Hochstädt
Lauingen
Dillingen
Biberbach
Augsburg
Friedburg

Donauwörth
Schellenberg
Rain
Donauwörth
Blenheim

BAVARIA

Regensburg
Ingolstadt
R. Danube
Munich

heavy guns behind, and all vital stores and the remaining guns – mostly 3- and 6-pounders, supported by mortars and howitzers – were transported as far as possible in river barges, and then in specially designed carts. The rest of the army marched in two columns: the horse in one, accompanied by Marlborough himself; the infantry in the other, led by Marlborough's younger brother, General Charles Churchill. Each day they left their camping grounds at first light and completed their march by nine in the morning, before the sun got too hot. This way the soldiers were able to cover 12–14 miles a day, but also conserve their energies, and those of their draught animals and horses. Lieutenant Parker wrote:

> We frequently marched three, sometimes four days, successively, and halted a day . . . As we marched through the countries of our Allies, commissaries were appointed to furnish us with all manner of necessaries for men or horse; these were brought to the ground before we arrived, and the soldiers had nothing to do, but pitch their tents, boil their kettles, and lie down to rest. Surely never was such a march carried on with more order and regularity, and with less fatigue to both man and horse.[7]

But no amount of preparation could protect the troops from the unseasonal rainy weather that, according to Sergeant John Wilson, rendered the roads 'so bad that there was no possibility of moveing the [artillery] train' until the roads had been repaired by working parties and double horses put on each gun.[8] John Deane of the 1st Foot Guards, who wrote the only known record of Marlborough's wars by a British private, noted in his journal that the rain continued for more than a month, 'and miserable marches we have had for deep and dirty roads and through tedious woods and wildernesses and over cast high rock and mountains, that it may easily be judged what our little army endured'.[9]

That fewer than 1,000 men fell out sick during the inclement weather was largely down to the measured tempo of the advance – with Marlborough urging his brother in one letter 'not to press your marches as to prejudice your men or horses'[10] – and the fact that every effort was made to minimize the men's discomfort. On 8 June, for example, the duke found the time in his hectic schedule to write to his brother about how best to replace the infantry's worn-out shoes:

> Col. Rowe [commanding an infantry brigade] . . . writes that the foot may soon be in want of shoes; that they are to be had at Francfort at reasonable rates, and that the contractors will send them forward to Nuremberg: therefore I desire you will call the commanding officers together that you may know the number they will want, and there-upon order Col. Rowe to write to Francfort that they may be hastened to Nuremberg, where we can send for them or order them to come forward to us.[11]

Marlborough also established two transit hospitals at Kassel and Heidenheim, using medical equipment moved by river and road convoy. Towards the end of the march he directed his brother to send 'your sick men' to the latter hospital, which was further south, 'in carts with an able [surgeon] and a mate or two to look after them, and such commission and non-commission officers as you shall think fit, giving them at the same time money for their subsistence'.[12] It was yet another example of the tireless attention to logistical detail and soldierly welfare that prompted Marlborough's men to give him the grateful soubriquet of 'Corporal John'. Marshal Tallard's French army, by contrast, had lost a third of its effectives to illness, desertion and stragglers during the march to Ulm in May.

On 12 June, Marlborough met the two Imperial commanders, Princes Louis of Baden and Eugène, at the Inn of the Golden Fleece at Gross Heppach near Stuttgart to coordinate strategy. Forty years old, coarse-featured, badly dressed, a harsh disciplinarian and allegedly homosexual, Eugène's personal appearance and character could not have contrasted more with Marlborough's. Yet the two would get along famously, not least because both were risk-taking generals who preferred the lottery of the battlefield to the boredom of sieges. The fifty-year-old Louis was more cautious in approach and, as the nominal senior of the three in experience and rank, a tricky obstacle for Marlborough to overcome. He managed this by charm and tact, agreeing that he and Louis should sign orders on alternate days as if they were exercising a joint command; whereas, in reality, the emperor had acknowledged Marlborough's superiority and made plans for Prince Louis's supersession should he prove obstructive.

The plan agreed by the trio at Gross Heppach was that Eugène would return with 30,000 men to the Lines of Stollhofen, a defensive position on the Rhine, to keep an eye on Tallard, while Marlborough and Louis joined forces to seek out the Franco-Bavarian army under Marshal Ferdinand Marsin and Elector Maximilian. Marlborough would have preferred to work closely with Eugène, with Louis sent to the Rhine. But the Prince of Baden refused to be sidelined, and Eugène had to go in his place.

For their part, the French were slowly waking up to the threat that Marlborough posed to their Vienna campaign, and Tallard in particular was urging Louis XIV to act. But it was not until 27 June that the French king authorized his advance through the Black Forest into Bavaria with forty battalions and fifty squadrons; meanwhile Villeroi, with a slightly stronger army, was to march south to Stollhofen and join Tallard only if the Allies moved all their forces towards the Danube.

On 30 June, after a feint attack on the Lines of Stollhofen to confuse Eugène about his true intentions, Tallard finally left Strasbourg. His progress would be torturously slow – thanks to an outbreak of sickness among his horses, the lumbering size of his huge wagon train and an unsuccessful siege of the small town of Villingen – and he would not rendezvous with Marshal Marsin and Elector Maximilian in Bavaria until early August.[13]

Meanwhile Marlborough and Louis, with a combined force of 60,000 men, had reached the Danube Valley, where they found the smaller Franco-Bavarian army of 40,000 men in a fortified camp at Dillingen on the left bank of the river. Unwilling to attack without heavy artillery, Marlborough bypassed Dillingen and set up his own camp to the north-east at Amerdingen. His plan was to draw the enemy out of their strong defensive position by invading Bavaria. But first he had to secure a town on the Danube that would serve as his forward base. The obvious choice was Donauwörth, 20 miles downstream from Dillingen, at the confluence of the Wörnitz and Danube rivers. To secure Donauwörth, however, he would have to take the

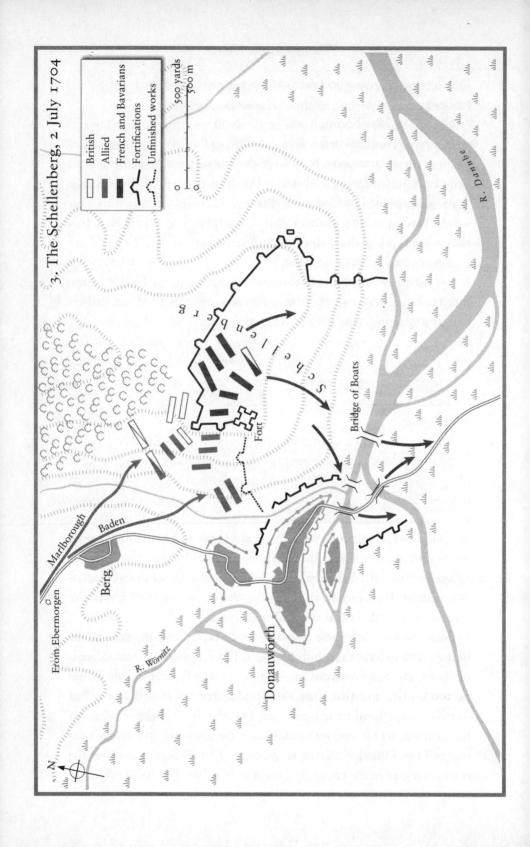

3. The Schellenberg, 2 July 1704

British
Allied
French and Bavarians
Fortifications
Unfinished works

500 yards
500 m

N

From Ebermorgen

Marlborough

Baden

Berg

R. Wörnitz

Donauwörth

Fort

Schellenberg

Bridge of Boats

R. Danube

hill to the east, rising 100 yards above the river, known as the Schellenberg.

On 1 July, Marlborough was in his quarters at Amerdingen when he received information from a local peasant that 'about 13,000 of the enemy were encamped upon the Schellenberg, and that they were very busy in fortifying and entrenching themselves'. Confirmation was soon provided by Cadogan and an escort of 400 horse, who 'perceived several of the enemy's battalions lying encamped, and that they were working hard upon their intrenchments'.[14]

Among the French defenders that day was Lieutenant-Colonel Jean-Martin de la Colonie of the Grenadiers Rouge, an infantry regiment in Bavarian service composed largely of roving French soldiers and deserters from the Imperial Army. He remembered:

> The [Schellenberg] height is oval in plan, with a gentle slope on the southern side, which affords easy communication with [Donauwörth]; whilst on the northern the country is covered with very thick woods and undergrowth, reaching close up to the old entrenchments. The two extremities of the entrenchment were practically safe from an assault, and the attack on this height could only be made on one of the two flanks; a choice had to be made between the two, owing to the lack of good communication. Both flanks had precipitous contours, leading to flat country of a considerable area.[15]

Yet because the approach to the western flank was partly covered by fire from the town walls, Marshal Jean-Baptiste d'Arco, the Bavarian commander of the Schellenberg, chose to concentrate his entrenching work on the east flank, 'whilst the entrenchment of the opposite side was postponed until this was completed'.[16]

Armed with Cadogan's reconnaissance report, Marlborough was determined to attack the hill as soon as possible. True to form, Louis of Baden tried to dissuade him – arguing that a frontal assault would be too costly, and that they should wait for heavy artillery – but Marlborough stood his ground, insisting that it was his turn to command the army the following day, and that Donauwörth was a 'post of great consequence'. His only concession to Louis was to order the medical commissary to set up a field hospital at nearby Nördlingen, and for the apothecaries and surgeons to make ready. 'He then gave orders,' recalled his chaplain, Dr Francis Hare, 'that a detachment of 130 men out of each battalion of the left wing (whereof ten were to be grenadiers), and likewise 35 squadrons of horse, should be ready to march at two o'clock in the morning, with three regiments of Imperial grenadiers, furnished by Prince Lewis [*sic*].'[17]

Among the cavalry designated for the assault were two squadrons of Hay's Dragoons, mounted on sturdy grey horses, and armed with pistols and muskets but no swords. 'They are all stout broad-shouldered fellows,' states a regimental history, 'each wearing a long square-skirted scarlet coat (the grey having by this time been discarded), fastened at the throat and falling away on either side, burned back with blue, over a blue undercoat or waistcoat, the cuffs being ornamented with buttons. The hair is worn long; and two broad brown leather belts cross the chest . . . The men carry their muskets with butt or stock resting in a "bucket", the barrel projecting under the soldier's right arm.'[18]

This vanguard – augmented by 5,850 British and Dutch infantrymen under the command of the Dutch Lieutenant-General Johan van Goor – duly left camp in two columns at 3 a.m. on 2 July, followed two hours later by the rest of the army. Van Goor's men made slow but steady progress – thanks to the tireless efforts of the pioneers who had preceded them to 'level the ways' – and by midday reached the Wörnitz River, where engineers had constructed a pontoon bridge.[19]

Already outlying pickets had warned Marshal d'Arco of the army's approach. His panicked response, according to Colonel de la Colonie, was to 'send off a courier to the Elector with a request for support, and set his infantry to work with picks and shovels to improve the defenceless flank upon which the enemy was advancing'. De la Colonie added:

> The time left to us was too short to complete this satisfactorily; we could only place fascines [bundles of brushwood] one on the other, sparsely covered with earth, so as to form something of the nature of a parapet, which, moreover, was neither high enough nor wide enough to be of much use. As to the ditch on the enemy's side, from which

works of this sort derive their chief strength, the Imperial force gave us no time to even begin it.[20]

He noted, in particular, a stretch of slope between the hill and the town that had received little attention because it was felt the narrow line of approach was too exposed to fire from the town walls. De la Colonie was right to be worried.

While all this frantic work was going on, Marlborough and his senior generals rode into view on a final reconnaissance. 'They were now so near the enemy,' recorded Dr Hare, 'that they were exposed to their great shot, which began to pour upon them plentifully from several of their works. However this did not prevent the generals from informing themselves more particularly with respect to the nature of the ground and of the intrenchments they were going to force.'[21] In particular, Marlborough noticed that the enemy was busy marking out a camp on the far side of the Danube, opposite Donau-wörth, and rightly concluded that it would soon be filled by Maximilian's army. Though it would be some hours before his troops were in a position to attack, he knew that day might be his last oppor-tunity to capture Donauwörth and he was determined to take it.

His plan of attack was hampered by the terrain: the wood to the north of the Schellenberg made it difficult to outflank the position from the east; while the town walls and a stream known as the Kai-bach seemed to protect the hill's western approaches. Marlborough's only option, therefore, was to advance from the north-west and make a frontal assault along the side of the wood where the hill was at its steepest.

What he could not know, but must have suspected, was that Mar-shal d'Arco, his opponent, had anticipated just such a move by concentrating the bulk of his defenders – three battalions of whom were the elector's own elite Guards – along the parapet in this sector, supported by a battery of eight guns. Even d'Arco's reserve, de la Colonie's Grenadiers Rouge, was close at hand on rising ground 50 yards to the rear of the parapet, with orders for their colonel 'to lead the regiment to whichever point I thought fit when the assault was made'. Yet such a concentration of troops left just a single battalion from the regiment of Nectancourt, and that 'much spread out', to occupy the largely unfinished defences between the top of the Schellenberg and the town, which d'Arco assumed would be covered by fire from the town wall.[22]

By 4 p.m. Goor's vanguard was in sight of the Schellenberg and Marlborough was anxious to start. He had judged it 'absolutely necessary to attack the enemy without giving them time to make their intrenchments yet stronger', and had 'just then received intelligence, by an adjutant-general from Prince Eugene' that French reinforcements were being sent through the Black Forest.[23]

But first, to soften up the defenders, he ordered two batteries of guns to open fire from marshy ground between the outlying village of Berg and the foot of the Schellenberg. Their first salvos cleared the parapet and tore into the visible ranks of the Grenadiers Rouge beyond. 'They concentrated this fire on us,' recalled Colonel de la Colonie, 'and with their first discharge carried off Count de la Bastide, the lieutenant of my own company with whom at the moment I was speaking, and twelve grenadiers, who fell side by side in the ranks, so that my coat was covered in brains and blood. So accurate was the fire that each discharge of the cannons stretched some of my men on the ground.' His battalion lost five officers and eighty men killed before it had fired a single shot.[24]

By now Marlborough had personally formed up the assaulting columns of foot and horse on the ground below the Schellenberg. Having seen the strength of the defences, he had decided to bolster the storm detachment with eight more battalions who, 'in case the detachment could not sufficiently extend itself, or take up ground enough when they came to attack', were to support them on their right. A further eight battalions would provide close support, bringing the number of infantry committed to the assault to 18,000.[25] With the preparations complete, Marlborough withdrew with his staff to a small hill near Berg from where he could observe the battle. Dr Hare recalled:

> It was near six o'clock, and his Grace ordered . . . Goor to begin the attack. Accordingly the detachment moved in six lines (viz. four of foot and two of horse) up the rising ground, the English being the left

of all, and close by the wood. The fascines being brought from hence by the horse, every officer and soldier took one, and they were ordered to carry them till they could throw them down in the enemy's intrenchments [to enable them to cross], and to move on closely and slowly, forbearing to fire till they came thither.[26]

As the attackers began to climb the hill, their left flank resting on the side of the wood, the defenders replied with a storm of artillery fire from the battery on the Schellenberg, and from another on the town walls, the round-shot tearing great holes in the British and Dutch ranks. Still the foot 'advanced with great calmness and resolution to within eighty paces of the intrenchments, the horse and dragoons sustaining them as gallantly'. At this point the defenders' guns switched from round-shot to case-shot — a hollow shell filled with bullets, designed for use at close range — and the first salvo did 'very great execution', claiming among others General van Goor, who was hit in the eye and killed instantly.[27]

The attack wavered, but not for long, as the surviving generals rallied their men and drove them on. Within twenty-five paces of the entrenchment they came across a dry stream that some mistakenly assumed was part of the defensive system and so threw in the fascines they were carrying. They had, as a result, nothing with which to bridge the ditch in front of the earth and wooden parapet. Not that it was easy to reach it, for musket fire and grenades 'came so thick as was by no means to be withstood, insomuch that some of our men began to double in the rear and to give way'.

Convinced the attack had failed, many of the Bavarian defenders fixed bayonets and leaped over the parapet to pursue their beaten foe. But they were quickly stopped in their tracks by volleys from British infantry, especially the 1st Foot Guards, which had provided the Forlorn Hope* of an officer and eighty men, and 'which always kept its ground, though most of the commanding officers were at this time either killed or wounded'.[28]

---

* From the Dutch *verloren hoop*, 'lost unit', a term used for the vanguard of an attacking force.

Led by dismounted generals, a second assault was made on the entrenchment. Colonel de la Colonie, who by this time had rushed his men forward to the parapet, recalled:

> The enemy broke into the charge, and rushed at full speed shouting at the top of their voices, to throw themselves into our entrench-ments . . . The English infantry led this attack with the greatest intrepidity, right up to our parapet, but there they were opposed with a courage at least as equal as their own . . . We were all fighting hand to hand, hurling them back as they clutched at the parapet; men were slaying, or tearing at the muzzles of guns and the bayonets which pierced their entrails; crushing under their feet their own wounded comrades, and even gouging out their opponents eyes with their nails, when the grip was so close that neither could make use of their weapons . . . At last the enemy . . . were obliged to relax their hold, and they fell back for shelter to the dip of the slope where we could not harm them.[29]

Twice repulsed, the British infantry 'was inclinable to retire' down the hill, but it was dissuaded from doing so by an advance of the first line of horse and dragoons, which, in turn, took heavy casualties, including its commander, Major-General Wood, who was killed by a musket-ball. 'But for all this,' noted Dr Hare, 'both the lines of horse continued firm, and encouraged the infantry to keep their ground and to press the attack with renewed vigour.'[30]

Still the Bavarians held on and, with time running out and casualties mounting, Marlborough needed a miracle to prevent a costly defeat. He got one. Back came a report that some of the attackers, edging away from the heaviest fire to the right, had discovered that the defensive line between the hill and town was only partially completed and thinly held, and that there was little enfilade fire from the town's outer defences. De la Colonie would later insist that the town commandant, du Bourdet, had withdrawn men from the outer defences into the town proper.[31] Dr Hare, on the other hand, blamed Count d'Arco for denuding this part of the line to bolster his main position on top of the hill.[32] Either way, the western flank of the Schellenberg was dangerously exposed.

Before one of Marlborough's staff officers could confirm this, however, Prince Louis of Baden received similar intelligence and at once sent his three battalions of Imperial grenadiers, waiting patiently in the Kaibach Valley, to take advantage. Dr Hare watched them advance:

> The Imperialists, finding little opposition, advanced to the enemy's intrenchments without firing a shot, and throwing their fascines into the ditch, passed over with little loss. The greatest opposition they met with was from the enemy's horse, which charged them very briskly, but was as bravely repulsed . . . Upon this the Imperial foot immediately inclined to the left, and took the enemy in flank to favour and facilitate the attack of the English and Dutch.[33]

De la Colonie saw them coming and assumed they were reinforcements from the town. When he realized his error, it was too late. The grenadiers drew up into a line and fired volley after volley into the flank of the French and Bavarian defenders, causing them to reel back in confusion. As they did so, a charge by dismounted dragoons of Lord John Hay's Regiment finally breached the main defences, and was quickly supported by mounted troopers of the Queen's Horse. Assailed from two sides, the defenders broke and fled down the hill, to where a bridge-of-boats offered refuge over the Danube. Hundreds were cut down en route by the ruthless cavalry and dragoon pursuit ordered by Marlborough, who, having climbed the hill, chose to keep his battered infantry in hand.

'A cruel slaughter was made of them,' recalled Kit Davies, a woman who for ten years had successfully masqueraded as a male trooper in Hay's Dragoons, 'and the bridge over the Danube breaking down, a great number were drowned, or taken prisoners. In the second attack, I received a ball in my hip, which is so lodged between the bones that it can never be extracted. Captain Young who, poor gentleman, was soon after killed, desired me to get off; but, upon my refusal, he ordered two of my comrades to take me up, and they set me at the foot of the tree.'[34]

Among the few senior Bavarian and French officers to escape were Marshal d'Arco, who gained refuge in the town, and Colonel de la

Colonie, whose deliverance was particularly dramatic. Struck in the jaw and temporarily stunned by an Imperialist musket-ball, he rose to conduct a heroic fighting retreat along the top of the hill that only dissolved into headlong flight once his men had crossed the entrenchments on the east flank of the Schellenberg. So he, too, ran for his life through fields of standing corn, stopping for just a moment to ask a tearful soldier's wife – no longer safe in the rear of the battlefield – to remove his tall, tightly fitting riding boots, before plunging into the Danube. 'Finally,' he wrote, 'after a very long and hard swim, I was lucky enough to reach the other bank, in spite of the strength of the stream.'[35]

Of the original garrison of 12,000, fewer than 3,000 French and Bavarians rejoined the elector's main army at Dillingen.[36] D'Arco had lost many of the best Bavarian regiments, not to mention 200 tons of gunpowder, 3,000 sacks of flour and the whole of the Bavarian engineer train, including all its pontoon bridges. And now that the Allies had secured both a base and a crossing point on the Danube, Maximilian and Marsin were forced to withdraw south from their outflanked position at Dillingen to Augsburg on the River Lech, leaving only Colonel de la Colonie and a small force to garrison the small town of Rain, 8 miles to the east of Donauwörth on the edge of the Bavarian lowlands. (Rain would fall to the Allies, after a week-long assault, on 16 July.) Now the only town on the Danube that the Franco-Bavarians still possessed was Ingolstadt, 25 miles downstream from Donauwörth.

The close-run victory had been shockingly costly for the Allies too. Their 5,000 casualties – 1,342 killed and 3,699 wounded – included 16 generals and 375 other officers. The worst-hit British units were the 1st Foot Guards (12 officers and 217 men), the two battalions of Orkney's Regiment★ (30 officers and 418 men) and a battalion of Ingoldsby's Regiment (16 officers and 228 men).[37] Only 700 Allied soldiers were killed on the field of battle; the rest died soon after of their wounds, either near the battlefield or on their way to the base hospital at Nördlingen. 'The moment this action was ended,' recalled Marlborough's chaplain, 'it grew dark, and rained violently. This proved very fatal to the wounded.'[38]

★ Later the Royal Scots and the Royal Hampshire Regiment.

Medical care for those wounded in battle at this time was basic and often counter-productive. There was no ambulance train and casualties were ferried to hospitals, often miles from the battlefield, in wagons and on stretchers. The ordeal, over rough roads, could be excruciating. Once at the basic hospital, all casualties were bled in the hope that it would ward off fever and help to dry the moisture round the injury. In practice, of course, it simply incurred further blood loss and cost many their lives. Those who survived were given bread, soup and wine to fortify them for the ordeal of surgery.

In common with their civilian counterparts, medical officers had limited scientific knowledge. Although they knew, thanks to William Harvey's discoveries, that blood was pumped round the body by the heart, many still relied on medieval remedies and so-called 'miracle cures'. It did not help that a military surgeon was generally of low calibre, and likely to be a man 'who would have buried his talents and his industry in a situation where obscurity, poverty, and neglect, spread all their horrors before him'.[39]

They tended to amputate damaged limbs without anaesthetic as quickly as they could, convinced it gave the patients a much better chance of survival (which it often did); and most surgeons understood the importance of cleaning a wound. Spirit vinegar was used as an antiseptic, while burns were treated with an ointment made from one part salt to eight parts onion juice. Charlatans were inevitable, and none was more successful than John Colbatch, whose 'Vulnerary Powder'* was supposedly a cure for any injury.

Many of those killed at the Schellenberg left widows and children, some of whom were accompanying the army. At the time there was no official scheme to provide for them, though Marlborough had offered relief to dead officers' sons by arranging commissions for them in their father's battalion (though the number of 'orphan' officers was limited to two per battalion). He had also encouraged officers to subscribe to schemes for the support of widows. Ordinary soldiers, of course, could not afford such schemes; so, after the carnage of the Schellenberg, Marlborough decreed that some of the widows

---

* 'Vulnerary' is from the Latin *vulnus*, or 'wound'.

should be added to the ration roll as nurses, and the balance sent home with their passages paid for.[40]

Marlborough acknowledged the price of victory at the Schellenberg when he wrote to his wife on 3 July: 'We have ruined the best of the Elector's foot,' yet the English infantry had 'suffered a good deal' in the process.[41]

Was it worth it? Private Deane of the 1st Foot Guards thought so, describing it as a 'glorious action' in which 'both English and Dutch behaved themselves to admiration'.[42] The Imperial court agreed, rejoicing in a victory that seemed to guarantee Vienna's safety now that Marlborough had interposed himself between it and the elector's army. But at least one of Marlborough's men, a British cavalry lieutenant who had had his horse shot under him during the attack, thought it 'a considerable advantage purchased at a dear rate'.[43]

Certainly the battle was not one of Marlborough's finer tactical victories, for the simple reason that time constraints and the terrain had narrowed his options to an unsubtle frontal assault. His discovery of the enemy's weak spot, moreover, was lucky in the extreme. His swift and conclusive reaction was not, and is evidence that Marlborough possessed that quality most prized in a military commander: *coup d'œil*, literally 'stroke of eye', or comprehensive glance, the ability to recognize the decisive moment in a fight and to act accordingly. It would be displayed to even greater effect in the next major engagement of the war.

6. Blenheim

Three days after the hard-fought victory at the Schellenberg, Marl-borough's heavy losses were more than compensated for by the arrival of the Danish Contingent of seven infantry battalions and twenty-one squadrons of cavalry. Yet the duke still lacked heavy artillery, and without it knew that he would struggle to take either Augsburg, where the elector had established his new defensive position, or the Bavarian capital of Munich. So instead he opened negotiations with Maximilian in the hope of persuading him to return to his Imperial allegiance. For a time the ploy looked like working, and on 14 July, egged on by his wife, Maximilian agreed to switch sides and pro-vide the Allies with 12,000 troops in return for an annual subsidy of 200,000 crowns. But as he was about to put pen to paper, Maximilian received word that Marshal Tallard was marching to his rescue with 35,000 men, and at once suspended the talks.

On 23 July, in exasperation, Marlborough unleashed his cavalry in the hope that its depredations would force Maximilian either to fight in the open or to make peace. 'If he does not,' he told his wife, 'he may be sure . . . we will destroy [his country] before we leave. You will, I hope, believe that my nature suffers, when I see so many fine palaces burnt.'[1]

Three thousand cavalrymen were sent as far as the gates of Munich with orders to burn and pillage. Kit Davies, freshly discharged from hospital, was among them. 'We spared nothing,' she recalled, 'kill-ing, burning or otherwise destroying whatever we could [not] carry off. The bells of the churches we broke to pieces, that we might bring them away with us.'[2] The elector, though, would only respond to this provocation by sending out detachments totalling 15,000 men to protect his own far-flung estates. He himself remained inactive at Biberbach, near Augsburg, while no fewer than 400 Bavarian villages were put to the torch. On 6 August he was joined there by Tallard and, with a combined army of 56,000 and more on their way as Maximilian ordered in his detachments, it seemed as if the balance had once more tipped the Franco-Bavarians' way. Tallard certainly thought so, and at once sought to take the initiative by marching north to the Danube in the hope of cutting Marlborough's lines of communication.

Fortunately for Marlborough, help was at hand. When Tallard had begun his move through the Black Forest in late June, Eugène set off in pursuit with 17,000 men, leaving the rest of his army to pin Marshal Villeroi to the Lines of Stollhofen. Louis XIV's reaction, when he heard that Eugène was on the move, was to order Villeroi to follow Tallard. If the marshal had obeyed this order, Marlborough would have been heavily outnumbered in Bavaria, even with Eugène's reinforcements, and left with no option but to withdraw to the Rhine. The history of the war – and of the British Army's role in it – might have been very different. But Villeroi did not obey because he was taken in by Eugène's clever feint to the north while leaving a cavalry screen to shadow Tallard. Assuming that Eugène was returning to Stollhofen with the bulk of his troops, Villeroi decided on his own initiative to remain where he was in case the Allies invaded Alsace. It was a miscalculation that would prove extremely costly for his fellow marshals and his Bavarian ally.

En route to Bavaria, Eugène had written to Marlborough, urging him either to take Munich by storm or to cut the elector's supply lines. Much to Eugène's frustration, neither had been accomplished by the time he reached Höchstädt on the north bank of the Danube in the first week in August. Eugène suspected that General Van Goor's death had much to do with Marlborough's uncharacteristic hesitation – and he was right. 'Since [the Schellenberg],' wrote the duke to his wife, 'I have hardly had time to sleep, for Lieutenant-General Goor helped me in a great many things, which I am now forced to do myself.' But just as significant were Prince Louis of Baden's staunch opposition to any bold move, particularly an assault on Munich, and the fact that Marlborough, weighed down by the strain of his onerous responsibilities and the losses he had already incurred, was suffering from severe migraines.[3]

On 7 August, Eugène met Marlborough and Prince Louis at Schrobenhausen, south of Donauwörth. Their agreed strategy was for Prince Louis to besiege Ingolstadt with 15,000 men, a move that if successful would provide them with an alternative means of crossing the Danube in case Donauwörth fell to the Franco-Bavarians. Marlborough and Eugène, meanwhile, would cover the siege in case Tallard tried to intervene. One historian, while acknowledging that the plan was Prince Louis's, has suggested that Marlborough and Eugène 'plainly felt it worthwhile to have the cautious and obstructive Margrave out of the way during the series of bold operations about to commence'.[4] There may be some truth in this. Certainly Marlborough saw the strategic sense of a siege that would, he assured Heinsius, enable Prince Louis 'to do whatever he pleases with his horse in the country of Bavaria', while the duke himself would link up with Eugène the moment he heard that the Franco-Bavarians had crossed the Danube. And, he added, if the enemy offered a battle he would certainly take it, 'our troops being full of courage and desiring nothing more'.[5]

Late on 10 August, Marlborough received an urgent message from Eugène that he was withdrawing from the plain of Höchstädt to Donauwörth. 'The enemy have marched,' wrote the Imperial marshal. 'It is almost certain that the whole army is crossing the Danube at Lauingen . . . The plain of Dillingen is crowded with troops. I have held on all day here; but with 18 battalions I dare not risk staying the night . . . Everything, milord, consists in speed and that you put yourself forthwith in movement to join me tomorrow, without which I fear it will be too late.'[6]

Marlborough's response was immediate. That evening, he sent a strong force of Imperial cavalry to support Eugène, while his brother was ordered to follow with 20 battalions of infantry in the early hours of the 11th. Marlborough himself led the rest of the army at daybreak, crossing the Danube at Donauwörth and linking up with Eugène between the River Kessel and the Schellenberg at dusk. His plan was to reoccupy Eugène's camp at Höchstädt the following day, once the artillery train had arrived. But when he and his staff moved forward to reconnoitre in the morning, escorted by a huge force of cavalry, they discovered that Tallard was already *in situ*, having captured the fort at Höchstädt the day before. To get a better view of the Franco-Bavarian position, they used 'spy glasses' from the church tower in Tapfheim, a village 5 miles to the north-east of Höchstädt . From there they were delighted to see the French and Bavarian quartermasters marking out a camp site in the plain north of Höchstädt, between the villages of Lutzingen and Blenheim – or Blindheim, as the Germans call it – where the ground was flat and dry, and perfect for the deployment of cavalry. 'Here was a fine plain,' wrote Lieutenant Parker, 'without a hedge or ditch, for the cavalry on both sides to show their bravery.'[7]

They were encouraged, too, by the unusual layout of the enemy front, not that of a single army but of two armies side by side: Tallard's on the right, Marsin and the elector's on the left. So instead of the traditional deployment of infantry in the centre and cavalry on both wings, the Franco-Bavarian force was drawn up with a double block of cavalry at its centre, which was, both Marlborough and Eugène knew, an obvious point of weakness if attacked by foot *and* horse.

For all that, the position was not without merit: on raised ground, its left flank was screened by thick woodland, and its right by the 300-foot-wide Danube. Across its four-mile front ran a boggy tributary of the Danube, the Nebel Stream, which was 'thought unpassable, as it afterwards was found in several places'.[8] While a string of villages – from left to right, Lutzingen, Oberglau and Blenheim – acted as strongpoints in the defensive system.

Marlborough knew, too – thanks to his excellent intelligence service – that the Franco-Bavarians had 60,000 men and 100 cannon to his own combined force of 56,000 men and 60 guns;[9] that Marshal Villeroi, aware at last that Eugène had given him the slip, was threatening their lines of communication to the north; and that it was against all conventional military wisdom to attack an enemy superior in numbers. And yet, as he wrote later, 'we resolved to attack them' the following day.[10]

The stakes could not have been higher for Marlborough. He had undertaken the campaign on his own initiative, and without the sanction of either his own Parliament or the Dutch Estates-General. Many of his enemies in both Houses – disgruntled Whigs and displaced Tories alike – felt he had at last overreached himself and were savouring the prospect of his downfall, with one claiming that if Marlborough failed 'we will break him up as the hounds do a hare'.[11] And, quite apart from personal ambition, the duke knew that he had to defeat the Franco-Bavarians in the field if he was to save both Vienna and the Grand Alliance. He knew, too, that with 14 battalions of Bavarian reinforcements converging on Höchstädt, this might be his last chance. It was all or nothing.

That evening, as they bivouacked between the villages of Tapfheim and Münster, within easy striking distance of the unsuspecting Franco-Bavarians, Marlborough and Eugène's troops were given their battle orders. 'No body can express the courage and joy which both officers and soldiers showed,' recalled Marlborough's chaplain, 'when they thought they should come to an engagement.'[12] Incredibly his opponents were still oblivious of the danger, though French cavalry patrols had been beaten back by British infantry that day when they tried to investigate reports that Marlborough's pioneers were improving tracks through the woods near Tapfheim. They simply could not conceive that an inferior force would dare to attack them, and as a result had failed to secure the vital narrow gap around the village of Schwenningen, 2 miles north of Blenheim, where the wooded hills and marshy meadows of the Danube came close together. Had they held this gap, they would have reduced the distance they needed to defend to just a mile. Instead, and without firing a shot, Marlborough took possession of Schwenningen during the evening of the 12th, thus giving him access to the plain of Höchstädt and increasing the frontage of his attack to 4 miles. It was a tactical coup that did much to decide the outcome of the battle.

Having left their campsite in darkness, the eight columns of Marlborough's army reached Schwenningen at six in the morning. There they paused while the Allied commanders, in consultation with a Prussian general who had been wounded in the defeat at Höchstädt the previous year and knew the ground well, made their final preparations:

Marlborough with 36,000 men – fewer than a third of whom were British – would attack Tallard's equal-sized army on the left, with the village of Blenheim as his key objective; while Eugène, with just 16,000 men – chiefly Danes and Prussians – was up against Marsin and the elector's combined army of 24,000 troops on the right. Not only was Eugène outnumbered, he would also have to perform a dangerous flank march in the face of the enemy to reach his start position. The battle proper, as a result, would not begin until 12.30 p.m.

Among the first of the Franco-Bavarians to witness the approach of Marlborough's army was the Comte de Mérode-Westerloo, a Walloon nobleman commanding a wing of Tallard's army. Billeted in a barn near Blenheim, he was woken at six by his head groom. 'This fellow, Lefranc, shook me awake and blurted out that the enemy were there,' recalled the comte. 'Thinking to mock him, I asked, "Where? There?" and he at once replied, "Yes – there – there!", flinging wide as he spoke the door of the barn and drawing my bed-curtains. The door opened straight on to the fine, sunlit plain beyond – and the whole area appeared to be covered by enemy squadrons.'[13]

Pausing only to dress and down his morning cup of chocolate, Mérode-Westerloo rushed to warn Tallard of the enemy's approach. At first the short-sighted 52-year-old marshal, a former French ambassador to London and victor at Speyerbach nine months earlier, refused to believe a battle was imminent. The strong display of enemy cavalry was, he thought, merely a smokescreen to enable the rest of Marlborough's army to escape to the north. Only when subsequent reports confirmed that Marlborough and Eugène's combined army was advancing on his position did he accept the truth and summon the other commanders – Marsin and the elector – to a war council in Blenheim. Yet still Tallard laboured under the misapprehension that Marlborough had been reinforced by Prince Louis of Baden's army, and therefore possessed a significant numerical advantage. It was for this reason that he persuaded his fellow commanders, when they climbed Blenheim's church tower at 9 a.m., to fight a defensive battle in which the flanks of the Franco-Bavarian line had to be held at all costs. Blenheim, a medium-sized village of 300 dwellings nestled close to the Danube, gained by this calculation an exaggerated importance that would downgrade other sectors and materially affect the outcome of the battle. Nine battalions, the cream of the French infantry, were assigned to its defence, with twelve squadrons of dismounted dragoons holding the gap between the village and the Danube. A further eighteen infantry battalions were in reserve, a few hundred yards to the left rear. All were under the command of the Marquis of Clérambault.

Tallard also advised the elector and Marsin to garrison Oberglau with eight battalions, and to mass the rest of their twenty-one infantry battalions – including the elite units of 'Wild Geese' (Irish mercenaries who had left their homeland after William III's victories in the 1690s) – close to Oberglau and Lutzingen on the extreme left flank. Tallard's concentration of the best infantry units in and around the three villages left him with just nine battalions of inexperienced infantry in the centre of his line; they were bolstered by sixty-four squadrons of French and Bavarian cavalry that at the critical moment would, Tallard hoped, charge downhill and drive the Allies into the Nebel. The Blenheim and Oberglau garrisons, having first provided supporting fire, would join in the slaughter with fixed bayonets. It was an optimistic plan and one that the elector tried to modify by arguing that if the cavalry were sent too late the enemy might prove impossible to dislodge. The alternatives were obvious: either hold the line of the Nebel, or attack as the enemy was in the act of crossing. But Tallard – fearful that such tactics would cause a premature retreat and cheat him of a decisive victory – would not be overruled.

Marlborough, meanwhile, had not failed to notice the flaws in Tallard's dispositions, particularly the fact that his two separate armies would make it difficult for one to support the other. He was also aware of the danger of Tallard's chosen 'killing-ground' in the centre of the line, but was convinced that if the garrisons of Blenheim and Oberglau could be contained in their defences, the French centre would be vulnerable. Had Marlborough worked out a detailed plan of battle? That is doubtful and even he did not make that claim. Rather he was prepared to put pressure on various key points of the enemy line in the hope that they would either buckle or draw troops from elsewhere so that he could switch his point of attack to the newly vulnerable area. In particular he hoped that Eugène's attack would fix the troops under the elector and Marsin to their position between Lutzingen and Oberglau, while he engaged and destroyed Tallard's army. It was all a matter of timing.

Mérode-Westerloo recalled the lull before the storm: 'It would be impossible to imagine a more magnificent spectacle. The two armies in full battle array were so close to one another that they exchanged fanfares of trumpet-calls and rolls of kettle-drums. When ours stopped, their music struck up again. This went on until the deployment of their right flank was completed, their left preparing to attack the village. The brightest imaginable sun shone down on the two armies drawn up in the plain. You could even distinguish the uniforms of each successive unit; a number of generals and aides-de-camp galloped here and there: all in all, it was an almost indescribably stirring sight.'[14]

The first shots had been fired at 7 a.m. by French artillery batteries in Blenheim. 'As soon as ever the enemy got sight of us,' recorded Private Deane of the 1st Foot Guards, 'they fired their great guns upon us, but we played none at them till toward 9 a clock in the morning.'[15] This was to give Marlborough time to site his cannon. 'His Grace ordered Colonel Blood to plant several counter batteries upon the most advantageous parts of the ground,' wrote Marlborough's chaplain, 'and his Grace visited each battery, and stood by to observe the range of the guns and the effect of their fire.'[16] The most effective of the counter-batteries was posted on high ground above the village of Unterglau, close to the Nebel Stream, which the French had set on fire. But it could do little to assist Prince Eugène's men, who, thanks to the length and difficulty of their march, had to form up without the benefit of artillery cover, and suffered many casualties as a result. 'We marched up within shot of the enemy,' recalled Private Donald McBane of Orkney's Regiment in the centre of Marlborough's line, 'and halted there upon our arms, until Prince Eugène came through the woods.'[17]

It was not until noon that William Cadogan brought Marlborough the welcome news that Eugène was ready to attack. He at once 'called for his horse, and sent the young Prince of Hesse with orders to Lord

Cutts to begin the attack upon Blenheim. At the same time he ordered all the lines to move forward and to pass the rivulet [the Nebel] over the pontoon bridges which he had caused to be laid.'[18]

Blenheim was a particularly tough objective, surrounded as it was 'by hedges, fences and other obstacles, enclosed gardens and meadows'.[19] Private Deane explained: '[The] village they had fortified and made so vastly strong and barackaded so fast with trees, planks, coffers, chests, wagons, carts and palisades that it was almost an impossibility to think which way to get into it.'[20] The first assault was made by the five British battalions of Rowe's brigade, among them Deane's 1st Foot Guards, who had been ordered by their commander to hold their fire until he struck the village palisade with his sword. He managed this, but was mortally wounded soon after, as was the second-in-command of his regiment (later the 21st Foot). One in three of Rowe's force was killed or wounded before the survivors fell back in confusion, harried by three squadrons of the crack French Gens d'Armes – the equivalent of the English Household Cavalry – who captured Rowe's regimental colour. But the horsemen were rebuffed in turn by the supporting Allied brigade of Hessians, who recaptured the colour and returned it to their British allies.

Cutts, however, could see the threat that French cavalry posed to his advance on Blenheim and requested some horsemen to cover his flank. Five squadrons of Wyndham's Horse duly crossed the Nebel, and were at once spotted by General Zurlauben, Tallard's Swiss-born cavalry commander, who led forward all eight squadrons of the Gens d'Armes to repulse them. The clash epitomized the different tactical uses to which the French and British put their cavalry, with fortune favouring the brave. 'Those of the enemy gave their fire at a little distance,' recalled Marlborough's chaplain, 'but the English squadrons charged up to them sword in hand, and broke and put them to flight.'[21]

Unfortunately the victorious horsemen did not stop there – a perennial failing of British cavalry from Prince Rupert at Edgehill to the Union Brigade at Waterloo – and many saddles were emptied by fire from Blenheim before they withdrew out of range. Nonetheless, the psychological effect of their minor success was felt throughout the battlefield. 'What!' exclaimed the elector on witnessing the action. 'There is the *Gendarmerie* running away? Is it possible?'[22]

With his flank now secure, Cutts launched a second furious assault on Blenheim with his Hessian brigade but it, too, was driven back with heavy loss. So shaken was the Marquis de Clérambault by the ferocity of these attacks, however, and so convinced was he that the next might succeed, that he panicked and ordered the dismounted dragoons and all eighteen battalions of Tallard's infantry reserve into the village. 'The men were so crowded in upon one another that they couldn't even fire,' recalled Mérode-Westerloo, watching from the cavalry lines, 'let alone receive or carry out any orders. Not a single shot of the enemy missed its mark, whilst only those of our men at the front could return fire.'[23]

By 2 p.m., thanks to de Clérambault's blunder, sixteen Allied battalions were containing a French force of almost twice their number in Blenheim. From his vantage point in a windmill behind the Nebel, Marlborough noticed this and at once ordered Cutts, who was on the point of leading his Hanoverian troops in a third assault, to cease his attacks and stand on the defensive. Cutts did so, and even sent some of his force to reinforce the rest of the Allied line that, by this time, was under considerable pressure.

The greatest setback was on the far right of the Allied line, in the area of Lutzingen, where Eugène's eighteen infantry battalions and ninety-two cavalry squadrons had been driven back behind the Nebel by a Bavarian counter-attack, his Prussian battalions losing many men and ten regimental colours in the process. At Oberglau, too, an initial cavalry attack was repulsed, as was the follow-up by ten of Marlborough's Hanoverian battalions under the Prince of Holstein-Beck. The prince and two battalions were attacked by the Wild Geese as they crossed the Nebel. At the same time a separate force of French cavalry, having broken through the Allied horsemen, then threatened Holstein-Beck's battalions from the right. Aware of the danger, the prince sent a galloper to request the urgent assistance of General Graf von Fugger's brigade of Imperial Cuirassiers, the nearest source of aid. But Fugger would not move without Eugène's permission, and in the ensuing pincer-attack the two battalions were cut to pieces and Holstein-Beck taken prisoner with severe wounds. His force was now leaderless and in danger of disintegrating. 'At this moment,' recalled Tallard, 'I saw the hope of victory.'[24]

But the centre of the Allied line held, just, thanks to Marlborough's personal intervention. Riding forward from his post near the burning village of Unterglau, he personally led three of Holstein-Beck's reserve battalions of Hanoverians, under Brigadier-General Bernsdorff, across the Nebel to plug the gap left by the prince's reverse. He also called forward Colonel Holcroft Blood's battery of cannon over the pontoon bridges and sited it to cover both the infantry and the right flank of the Allied cavalry. The movement of guns over marshy ground was slow and hazardous, but once in position their first salvos forced the Wild Geese and their French allies to retire out of range. The threat now was from Marsin's cavalry, but Marlborough countered it by repeating Holstein-Beck's request for support from Fugger's heavy cavalry. Eugène at once complied, though he himself was sorely pressed, and Fugger's breast-plated horsemen arrived in time to take Marsin's charging cavalry in the flank, deflecting their attack away from Marlborough's vulnerable centre. Once again Holstein-Beck's men advanced and, supported by Blood's battery, 'made a great slaughter of the enemy', driving the Franco-Irish battalions back into Oberglau.[25]

It was now three o'clock and for the next hour a comparative lull fell over the centre of the battlefield while Marlborough's remaining force, under his brother Charles Churchill, advanced beyond the Nebel in four lines: the first made up of seven battalions of infantry; the next two of seventy-two squadrons of cavalry; and lastly an infantry reserve of eleven battalions. Sergeant Millner of the Royal Irish was amazed by Tallard's failure to oppose the crossing: 'The enemy gave us all the time we wanted for that purpose, and kept very quiet on the hill they were possessed of, without descending to the meadow towards the rivulet; insomuch that even our second line of horse had time to form themselves.'[26]

By 4 p.m. Churchill's formidable force was poised to attack, and all Tallard had to oppose it were sixty-four squadrons of cavalry, many of whom had already been in action. In desperation he called for infantry support, but the only units available were the nine battalions of raw recruits. Marsin and the elector refused to release any of their infantry because they were needed to check a fresh assault by Eugène's men, who, rejuvenated after the earlier setbacks, were trying to work round the Lutzingen flank. Meanwhile, the main body of Tallard's infantry reserve was still cooped up in Blenheim. Even the personal intervention of the Comte de Mérode-Westerloo had failed to secure their release. 'I rode over to Blenheim,' he recorded, 'wanting to bring out a dozen battalions (which they certainly did not need there) to form a line on the edge of the stream supported by the cannons and the debris of my squadrons. The brigades of Saint-Ségond and Monfort were setting out to follow them when M. de Clérambault in person countermanded the move, and shouting and swearing drove them back into the village.'[27]

Without enough infantry to fight defensively, Tallard tried one last roll of the dice by ordering his cavalry to charge the two lines of Allied horsemen who, by now, had advanced beyond their own foot soldiers. The gamble almost paid off. 'All our Brigades charged briskly,' recalled one of Tallard's generals, 'and made all the Squadrons they attacked give way.'[28] But Marlborough had planned for just such an emergency by supporting his horse with both foot and cannon. 'By this time,' recalled Lord Orkney, commanding the first line of infantry, 'I had got over about nine battalions of foot which were left with me, and marched to sustain the horse, whom I found repulsed, calling out for foot, being pushed by the gendarmerie. I went to the head of several squadrons and got 'em to rally and form upon my right and left, and brought up four pieces of cannon, and then charged both foot and horse. The [enemy] horse were put to flight.'[29]

Tallard pushed forward his remaining nine infantry battalions to stem the tide; but close-range cannon and musket fire cut great swathes in their line. 'They stood firm for a time,' recorded Dr Hare, 'closing their ranks as fast as they were broken, till being much weakened, they were at last thrown into disorder, when our squadrons falling upon them, they were cut down in entire ranks, and were seen so lying after the battle.'[30]

With the battle as good as lost, Tallard tried desperately to save what was left of his army. 'At this time,' recalled Sergeant Millner, 'Count Tallard rallied his broken cavalry behind some tents that were all this time standing in his camp, and then seeing things were in this desperate condition, resolved to draw off his dragoons and foot out of Blenheim, and sent orders by one of his Aide de Camps to Marshal Marsin at [Oberglau] to face the enemy with some troops on the right of the said village, to keep them in play, and favour the retreat of his infantry that was in Blenheim.'[31] But it was too late: word came back from the Blenheim garrison that it 'could neither help him or themselves' as they were pinned down by infantry fire; while Marsin reported he had 'too much work on his own hands'.[32]

Marlborough knew the decisive moment was at hand and, with just thirteen battered squadrons of cavalry holding the centre of Tallard's line, ordered his horsemen to charge. At the sound of the trumpets, two lines of horsemen advanced at the full trot, knee to knee, swords at the ready. It was 5 p.m. Hare wrote: 'Those of the enemy presented their fusils at some small distance and fired, but they had no sooner done so than they immediately wheeled about, broke one another, and betook themselves to flight. The gens-d'armes fled towards Hochstet (which was about 2 miles in the rear) and the others towards the village of Sonderheim, which was nearer, and upon the bank of the Danube.'[33] Mérode-Westerloo was in the latter group, and so 'tight was the press' that his horse 'was carried along some three hundred paces without putting hoof to the ground, right to the edge of a deep ravine', down which it plunged, trapping its rider beneath it. The comte eventually extricated himself and, having killed a British horse grenadier who tried to take him prisoner, made it to the far side of Höchstädt, where he rallied the remnants of the French cavalry and made his escape.[34]

Mérode-Westerloo was lucky. Most of the horsemen who made for Sonderheim were driven into the Danube where they drowned. Anxious to avoid their fate, Marshal Tallard and two of his senior officers tried to flee up the riverbank towards Höchstädt. But they were captured en route by Hessian cavalry and taken before Marlborough, who, still on horseback, chivalrously offered them the use of his coach. 'I congratulate you, Sir,' said Tallard, 'on beating the best soldiers in the world.'

'Your lordship, I presume,' replied the duke, 'excepts those who had the honour to beat them.'[35]

Marlborough then called for paper and, still mounted (as he had been for most of this long, hot day), wrote to his wife one of the most celebrated field dispatches in British history:

> August 13 1704. I have not time to say more, but to beg you will give my duty to the queen, and let her know her army has had a glorious victory. M. Tallard and two other generals are in my coach, and I am following the rest. The bearer, my aide-de-camp, Colonel Parke, will give her an account of what has passed. I shall do it in a day or two, by another more at large. Marlborough.[36]

Now, in an attempt to turn the victory into a rout, Marlborough led a number of cavalry squadrons against the open right flank of the Elector of Bavaria and Marshal Marsin's army, which, thanks to Eugène's persistent attacks, had been gradually forced back from its original position on the extreme left. This combined pressure, and the knowledge that Tallard's centre and left wing had disintegrated, caused the elector and Marsin to order an immediate withdrawal to Lauingen, upstream of Höchstädt, where there was a good crossing point. 'They instantly, and with great dexterity and expedition,' recalled Lieutenant Parker, 'formed their troops into three columns, and marched off with the greatest dispatch possible.'[37] Both Marlborough and Eugène ordered a cavalry pursuit, but their respective horsemen mistook each other for the enemy and were halted to prevent being taken in the flank. 'As it was now growing too dark to distinguish clearly the several corps,' wrote Hare, 'the retreat of the enemy was not further impeded in this direction. There was also a wood hard by, which greatly favoured it.'[38]

The last point of French resistance was at Blenheim, where the garrison had long been surrounded by British infantry. Aware that the French might try to break out at night, Marlborough ordered Cutts and Churchill to take the village by storm. Attacks were duly launched from two directions, 'but being unable to make a front

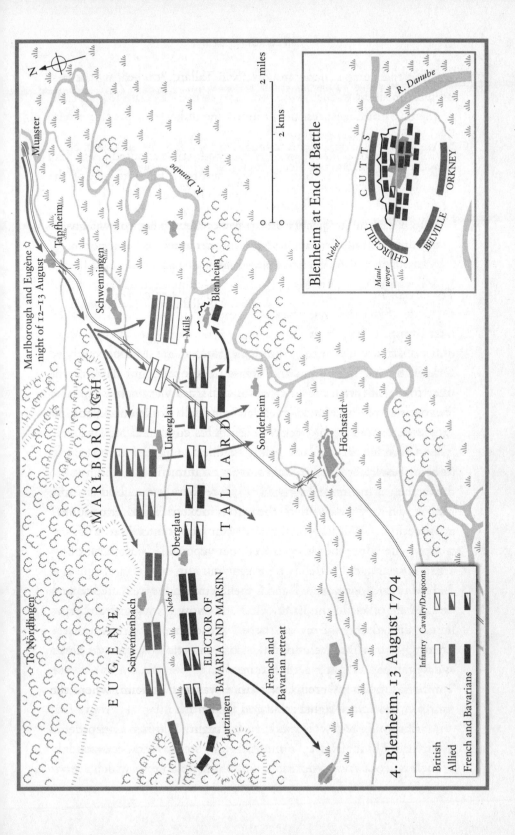

Blenheim at End of Battle

R. Danube

C U T T S

CHURCHILL

ORKNEY

BELVILLE

Nebel

Maul-
ueyer

N

2 miles

2 kms

Munster

Tapfheim

Marlborough and Eugène
night of 12–13 August

Schwenningen

R. Danube

Mills

Blenheim

MARLBOROUGH

Unterglau

Sonderheim

Höchstädt

To Nördlingen

E U G È N E

Schwennenbach

Oberglau

Nebel

T A L L A R D

ELECTOR OF
BAVARIA AND MARSIN

Lutzingen

French and
Bavarian retreat

Infantry   Cavalry/Dragoons

British

Allied

French and Bavarians

4. Blenheim, 13 August 1704

equal to that of the enemy, especially in the churchyard, which had high walls round it, they were forced to retire'.[39] Private John Deane of the 1st Foot Guards recalled the chaos:

> We according to our command fought our way into the village which was all of a fire, and our men fought in and through the fire and pursued others through it, until many on both sides were burnt to death. At length the enemy making all the force they could upon us forced us to retreat and to quit the village having lost a great many of our men, but we rallied again, having received some fresh ammunition, resolving to give the enemy another salute.[40]

To prevent further bloodshed, Lord Orkney called on the French to surrender. Since the disappearance of de Clérambault – who, it would later transpire, had drowned trying to cross the Danube – the Marquis de Blanzac had taken command. He and his subordinates met Orkney amidst the bodies and debris of the shattered village, and were told that further resistance was useless: Tallard was a prisoner and the rest of the Franco-Bavarian army had broken and fled. 'As they were discussing the terms of the capitulation,' recalled Dr Hare, 'Gen. Churchill arrived, and telling them that he had no time to lose (it being now past seven in the evening), and that if they did not lay down their arms immediately, he must renew the attack, they submitted, and they were with all the troops in Blenheim made prisoners at discretion.'[41] With this final capitulation of 11,000 of France's finest troops – including the vaunted Régiment du Roi, and those of Navarre and Languedoc – the battle was over.

That night, Marlborough and Eugène's exhausted men bivouacked on the field of battle amidst the dead and dying, though several regiments availed themselves of the enemy's tents, 'which were left standing, and which were found to contain great quantities of herbs and vegetables'. Private Deane remembered the ground as covered 'for three English miles' with the 'dead bodies of both armies so that from any more such sights good god deliver me'.[42]

Marlborough had won a victory as decisive as it was unexpected, given his slight inferiority in numbers and the 'advantageous nature' of the Franco-Bavarian position, notably the 'obstacles which everywhere obstructed the approaches to it'.[43] He had taken more than 14,000 prisoners (including 40 generals and 1,100 officers), 300 colours and standards, 60 cannon and the entire contents of the enemy's camp. The Franco-Bavarians, in addition, had lost a further 20,000 killed and wounded, giving a total casualty rate of well over 57 per cent of the troops engaged. The Allies, too, had suffered badly. Of their 13,000 casualties (4,500 of whom were killed), more than 8,500 were from Marlborough's army. And of these, the largest proportion – 2,234 out of their 10,786 combatants, or more than one in five – was British. Some of the battalions that had attacked Blenheim – notably Rowe's, Ingoldsby's and Howe's – lost two thirds of their officers.[44]

Among the wounded who lay out that night was Private Donald McBane of Orkney's Regiment, hit in the final attack on Blenheim. 'About the middle of the night,' he remembered, 'the Dutch of our army came a plundering, and stripped me of all except my shirt; a little after another came and took the shirt also. I besought him to leave me it, but he gave me a stroke with the butt of his gun.' It was not until the 15th, two days after the battle, that McBane was found by his friends and taken to a surgeon.[45]

It was undoubtedly an Allied victory: Dutch, Hanoverian, Hessian, Prussian and Danish soldiers all played their part, as did Prince Eugène, praised by Marlborough for his 'good conduct and the bravery of his men'.[46] But British soldiers did more than their share of the fighting – as evidenced by their casualties – and the battle was won not by Eugène's generalship but Marlborough's: 'the bold night advance, his firm, flexible control of the battle at its different stages, his personal intervention at the places of crisis, and his proven ability to wield a multi-national army into an integrated weapon of high morale and single-minded purpose, contrasted most markedly with Tallard's muddled leadership and weak authority.'[47]

Blenheim had far-reaching consequences for the European balance of power. It saved Vienna and, with the elector and Marsin withdrawing the battered remnants of their army to Strasbourg, enabled the Allies to take Ulm, Ingolstadt and the rest of Bavaria, thus binding many wavering German princes to the Imperial cause. It established Marlborough's reputation as the finest general in Europe: he would enjoy many more victories over the French in the coming years – notably Ramillies in 1706, Oudenaarde in 1708, Malplaquet in 1709 and piercing the 'Ne Plus Ultra' Lines in 1711 – but none was as significant as Blenheim. No such decisive victory had been won in Europe by any general, not even Condé, Turenne or Luxembourg, since the successes of the Swedish king Gustavus Adolphus at Breitenfeld and Lützen in the Thirty Years War (with Gustavus paying for the second triumph with his life). It was, moreover, the first major defeat suffered by the armies of the Sun King, who, for the previous forty years, had swept all before them. The Duc de Saint-Simon, courtier and diarist, recorded the feelings of 'general consternation' when the news reached Paris: 'It can be guessed . . . what was the predicament of the ministry of finance and the ministry of war at having to make good the loss of an entire army; and what was the anguish of the King, who had held the Emperor's fate in his hands, and who, with this ignominy and loss, saw himself reduced to defending his own lands.'[48] It was a low point from which the French would never fully recover. The prestige of their army was in tatters.

Britain was quick to claim the victory as its own: cannon thundered, church bells pealed and bonfires blazed as the country greeted the news with an outpouring of national rejoicing that had not been seen since the defeat of the Armada in 1588 (and not for a victory on the Continent since Agincourt in 1415). Colonel Parke, the bringer of such welcome tidings, was rewarded with a miniature portrait of the queen and 1,000 guineas. Marlborough – though his political enemies tried to take some of the lustre off his victory by bracketing it with Admiral Rooke's capture and defence of Gibraltar in 1704 – received from Anne the prestigious and lucrative post of Colonel of the 1st Foot Guards, a grant of £5,000 a year to him and his heirs in perpetuity, and, in 1705, the gift of the Royal Manor and Park of Woodstock so that he could build a home suitable for a hero. Parliament agreed to foot the bill, and voted the colossal sum of £240,000. But even this was not enough to keep pace with the escalating costs – deemed unacceptable by the Tory administration that took control in 1710, and by a monarch who had fallen out of love with her former favourites – and the duke would not live to see the completion of the magnificent Blenheim Palace, designed by Sir John Vanbrugh in the Baroque style, and still the largest private house in the country.

And yet no one benefited more by the victory at Blenheim, not even Marlborough himself, than the British Army. 'The strategic-logistical brilliance of the march to the Danube,' writes one recent chronicler, 'the tactical daring of the night approach to contact, the unorthodoxy of the infantry-cavalry deployments, the all-arms coordination, and the sheer aggressive use of infantry in particular – all these set the standard for British troops to measure themselves against in the future.'[49] Brigadier-General Emmanuel Howe, present at the battle, summed up the scale of Marlborough's achievement: 'Certainly such a victory was never gained before over an army equal in number and composed of old and disciplined troops.'[50] From 1704, as a direct result of Blenheim, the most feared soldier on the battlefield was no longer a Frenchman but a Briton.

By the end of 1708, following two more stunning successes by Marl-borough in the Low Countries – victory over Marshal Louis Vendôme at the encounter-battle of Oudenaarde on 11 July and, five months later, the capture of the fortress-city of Lille – France's fortunes were at their lowest ebb. The harvest had failed and the winter would be one of the bitterest in history: more than half of France's livestock perished, there were bread riots in Paris, and the coinage was depreci-ated by 30 per cent. Shaken by yet more military setbacks and the prospect of economic ruin, Louis was at last ready for peace. He was even prepared to concede the Allies' principal war aim: that the Span-ish throne should go to the Habsburg claimant without compensation for his grandson, Philip V.

Nothing, it seemed, could prevent the Grand Alliance from win-ning the war – apart from itself. Convinced they had France on the run, the Allies hardened their stance by insisting that Louis XIV guar-anteed, by force of arms if necessary, the unconditional acceptance of their terms by Philip V. They also demanded some of France's frontier fortresses as a pledge of good faith. Not surprisingly, Louis refused to agree to these humiliating terms and, on the advice of his foreign minister, instead made them public. This produced an unprecedented display of patriotic sentiment from the outraged populace – with nobles and prelates offering their plate to the treasury, and peasants volunteering for the army in their thousands – that enabled Louis to continue the fight, with varying fortunes, for a further four years.

The high point of that effort, and a battle that recouped for the French Army some of the honour forfeited at Blenheim, was Marshal Claude Villars's narrow loss to Marlborough at Malplaquet in September 1709. It was, in many ways, a mirror of Blenheim, with wave after wave of Allied attacks foundering against a strong defensive position, until, late in the day, Marlborough finally broke through the French centre and forced a general retreat. This time it was a retreat in good order and, when the butcher's bill was totted up, it showed more Allied casualties than French: 18,000 to 11,000 (with only 500 of the latter taken as prisoners). Veterans like Colonel Blackader of Ferguson's (formerly the Earl of Angus's) Regiment had never seen 'the dead bodies lie so thick as they were in some places about the retrenchments particularly at the battery where the Dutch Guards attacked'.[51] The duke himself described it to Godolphin as a 'very murdering battle', and even three weeks later was still badly affected by the losses.[52]

It was in many ways a hollow victory. Marlborough confessed he had never seen the French fight better, and if anything the battle stiffened Louis's resolve to fight on. In England and the Netherlands, on the other hand, the appalling losses and lack of a decisive result were seized upon by pro-peace Tory members of the Opposition as evidence that the war could never be won on the battlefield. Queen Anne, no longer in thrall to the Duchess of Marlborough, had also grown tired of the war and the inflexible attitude of her government, known as the Whig Junto, which insisted on fighting to the finish. Marlborough, too, was seen as pro-war, and his weakening political position was made even more precarious when, just a month after Malplaquet, he asked to be made captain-general for life. It was an ill-judged request that was not only refused by Queen Anne, but that also brought forth the Tory accusation that he was seeking to become a dictator.

There was still time for one more glorious victory in the summer of 1711, when Marlborough pierced the supposedly impenetrable 'Ne Plus Ultra' defensive lines, which ran 160 miles from the Channel to the Ardennes, after a rapid night march that left Marshal Villars, who had proved such an obdurate opponent at Malplaquet, trailing in his wake. Robert Parker, one of his own soldiers, considered this final campaign Marlborough's crowning achievement:

> The noble scheme he formed for passing Villars's lines: the infinite arts and stratagems he used to deceive him: his passing the lines without the loss of a man; his insulting Villars afterwards, and daring him, by marching with an inferior force at mid-day along the front of his army, and within cannon-shot of him: his passing the Scheldt unmolested in the face of his army, and taking the fortress of Bouchain, the key and inlet into the kingdom of France, while Villars stood looking on, advantageously posted, and with a superior force, yet not daring to interfere: all this is stupendous, and inimitably great . . . Had not I been an eyewitness of these things, I should hardly have believed them.[53]

But it was not enough to win the war or save his career. A year earlier, after the collapse of yet more peace negotiations, Queen Anne had dismissed the Whig Junto (including Marlborough's old friend and ally Lord Godolphin) and the Tories under Robert Harley swept to power at the subsequent general election. They at once opened secret peace negotiations with France – in breach of the original treaty of alliance – and these talks were given added urgency when Archduke Charles unexpectedly succeeded to the Austrian throne on the death of his brother Joseph I in April 1711, thus raising the spectre of a new Habsburg Empire under Charles VI – which seemed even less palatable to the Tories than the Franco-Spanish connection under Philip V. In December 1711, at the opening of Parliament, the queen was able to announce, 'notwithstanding the arts of those who delight in war, both time and place are appointed for opening the treaty of a general peace.'[54] Apart from Austria, all of Britain's allies followed suit. A month later, with his martial services no longer required, the queen relieved Marlborough of all his posts while Parliament investigated his alleged misappropriation of army funds (a charge never proved in court, but one a recent biographer felt was partly justified, describing the duke as 'unquestionably avaricious in an avaricious age').[55]

After tortuous negotiations – during which the new British captain-general, Lord Ormonde, was ordered not to attack the French, much to the fury of his troops – the Treaty of Utrecht was finally signed in April 1713. If more palatable to France than the diktat of 1709, the treaty still conceded much to Britain. Louis XIV confirmed his grandson Philip V of Spain's renunciation of his French rights (thus removing the nightmare of a Franco-Spanish Empire), and recognized the Hanoverian Succession in Britain after the death of the childless Queen Anne, agreeing in the process to expel James Stuart, the 'Old Pretender'. Louis also surrendered France's 'favoured nation' status in terms of Spanish trade, agreed to the permanent demilitarization of Dunkirk, and ceded the colonial possessions of St Kitts, Hudson Bay, Nova Scotia and Newfoundland to Britain. In return the British recognized Philip V of Spain, and agreed to abandon the Catalan rebels they had, until recently, been supporting. In a subsidiary treaty with Spain, signed in July, Britain also received limited trading rights in the Americas and was confirmed in possession of Gibraltar and Minorca (retaining the former to this day).

Only Austria continued the fight, but after the loss of Landau and Freiburg to Marshal Villars it, too, sued for peace. By the terms of the Treaty of Baden (signed in September 1714), the Emperor Charles VI received Milan, Sardinia, Naples, Mantua and the Spanish Netherlands; but he was forced to relinquish to France all territory on the west bank of the Rhine, and to agree to the full reinstatement of the Elector of Bavaria.

The country that benefited most from the war was Britain. With the United Provinces in terminal decline, it emerged from the war as the world's greatest maritime power, with a seaborne empire – including colonies in North America, the Caribbean and India – whose trade in slaves and sugar would soon dominate the world's commerce. It had also assumed, for the first time since Agincourt, the military leadership of Europe.

The Royal Navy had played its part, not least by protecting the

expansion of British trade during the war. Yet by far the most significant theatre of conflict was not at sea but on the Continent, where
the armies of France – the superpower of the day – were met and
repeatedly defeated by Marlborough's polyglot forces. But for the
duke's inspired generalship, and the increasingly impressive performance of his British troops, Louis XIV's France would have gained
mastery over mainland Europe, the Channel coast and, ultimately,
the British Isles. It was to prevent such a political and military catas-
trophe that the British government knew it had to send troops to the
Continent in 1702, and would do so again when similar threats
loomed in 1759, 1808, 1914, 1939 and 1944. Not to have done so would,
in all probability, have reduced Britain to the status of a third-rate
power, if not a satellite of France, a far cry from the imperial and
trading leviathan it was about to become. That much was at stake.

7. The Two Georges

At six in the evening on 18 September 1714, a short, thickset, sullen-looking man of fifty-four stepped off a Royal Navy frigate at Greenwich in Kent to an enthusiastic reception from the waiting crowd and the richly attired horsemen of the Life Guards and Horse Grenadiers. Six weeks earlier, as Georg Ludwig, Elector of Hanover, he was just another ruler of a medium-sized German principality. But since the death of Queen Anne on 1 August, he had become King George I of Great Britain and Ireland. It was an accession that would prove highly beneficial to the British soldier.

The sequence of events that brought this minor German prince to the throne of Europe's foremost trading and naval power began in July 1700 with the death from smallpox of eleven-year-old Prince William Henry, Duke of Gloucester, the only one of Princess (later Queen) Anne's children to survive infancy. With William III and the late Queen Mary also childless, it became necessary to nominate a new heir apparent to guarantee the Protestant Succession and exclude James II's Catholic son, James Stuart. Only one claimant had the right religious and royal credentials: the seventy-year-old Electress Sophia of Hanover, daughter of Frederick V of the Palatine and Princess Elizabeth of England, and granddaughter of King James I. So in June 1701, Parliament passed the Act of Settlement, naming Sophia and her progeny as heirs to the throne. In the event, Sophia predeceased Anne by six weeks, and it was her son Georg Ludwig who became the first Hanoverian monarch of Great Britain.

On 19 September, George gave his first royal reception at the Queen's House in Greenwich Park. It was notable for the friendliness with which he received the Whig lords in attendance, and his marked hostility towards their Tory rivals. Some might have imagined from his simple, taciturn demeanour – he spoke only a few words of English and preferred to converse either in his native German or in

French – that he would be easily led. The truth could not have been more different. For George, despite his unimpressive appearance, was a wily political operator. What he prized above all else was loyalty, and in particular loyalty to the Hanoverian succession, a quality not always displayed by Tory politicians, who, despite their recent support for his accession, had long been sympathetic to the Jacobite cause. It was therefore inevitable that he would entrust his first government chiefly to Whig ministers, a preference confirmed by the electorate when it returned a sizeable Whig majority at the subsequent general election. This in turn gave George the opportunity to press for the impeachment of those leading Tories – Robert Harley, the Earl of Oxford among them – whom he had never forgiven for making a separate peace with France in 1713, leaving Hanover and the Austrian Empire to fight on alone.

In military affairs, too, George was determined to take the lead. An experienced soldier and former commander of both the Hanoverian and Imperial armies, George quickly made clear his determination to take personal control of the British Army. The very first state paper he signed was the reappointment of the Duke of Marlborough to all his former offices, including that of captain-general. Given the duke's advancing years and long-suspected links to the Jacobites, it seems at first glance an odd appointment. However, Marlborough was no Jacobite and had worked hard since his fall from power to ensure the Hanoverian succession was as bloodless as possible. The captain-generalcy was his reward, though never again would he command armies in the field. Instead, before his powers of concentration were destroyed by the first of a series of strokes in 1716, he confined himself to remodelling an army that, since the signing of the Peace of Utrecht, had been cut by thirteen cavalry and twenty-two infantry units to just 22,000 men in 1714, of which two thirds were stationed in the colonies and Flanders.[1]

This savage retrenchment was temporarily halted in the autumn of 1715 when the Earl of Mar raised the flag of Jacobite rebellion at Braemar in the Scottish Highlands on behalf of the Catholic Pretender, James Stuart. Marlborough responded by sending north all available troops – including a number of regiments that were earmarked for disbandment – and by asking his former Dutch allies for reinforcements, and they were happy to oblige. But it was Marlborough's protégés, the Duke of Argyll and William Cadogan, who actually commanded the royal army in the field, holding off the numerically superior Jacobites at the inconclusive Battle of Sheriffmuir on 13 November, and then beating a second rebel army at Preston a day later. The Jacobites' spirits were raised in mid-December by the belated arrival from France of the 'Old Pretender', who duly set up court at Scone, near Perth, and did his best to rally Mar's troops. But he was soon afflicted by the same bouts of melancholy and indecision that had crippled his father in 1688, and early the following year he returned to France, advising his followers to 'shift' for themselves.

The rebellion was over before it had properly begun, though discontent would rumble on for many years. To prevent another full-scale rising in the Highlands, the government passed the Disarming Act (banning all Highlanders from owning, manufacturing or carrying arms), built forts and barracks linked by military arteries known as the 'Wade Roads' (after Major-General George Wade) and, in 1725, formed six independent companies of Highlanders to police the unruly districts, units that became known, on account of their dark 'government-approved' tartans, as the Black Watch. (It was not until 1739 that these six companies were augmented by four more and formed into a single-battalion regiment, the 43rd – later the 42nd – Highlanders.[2])

Marlborough did not live to see the formation of the Black Watch, the first of many Highland units that would distinguish themselves in the service of the British Army. He died in 1722, at the ripe age of seventy-two, prompting even his former political enemies to acknowledge his outstanding talent. Viscount Bolingbroke described him as 'the greatest general, and the greatest minister that our country, or perhaps any other has produced'.[3] The final word, however, should rest with one of his soldiers. In the ten campaigns that Marlborough fought against the French, wrote Robert Parker, 'it cannot be said that he ever slipped an opportunity of fighting, when there was any probability of coming at his enemy: and upon all occasions he concerted matters with so much judgement and forecast, that he never fought a battle, which he did not gain, nor laid siege to a town which he did not take.'[4]

By the time of Marlborough's death, however, his once formidable army had shrunk to just 18,000 men (with a further 12,000 on the Irish establishment), a figure that would not start to rise until the outbreak of the next major war in 1739. In the meantime, George I, and later his son George II (1727–60), would do their best to maintain and even improve standards in a force that, by dint of almost continual campaigning between 1689 and 1713, had become highly proficient in battle. George I tried to introduce German methods of regimental organization, economy and tactics – but with mixed success. On the one hand, stoppages from pay were regulated by warrant, a standard arms-drill was introduced for the whole army, and all regiments at home were annually inspected and the report sent to the king; on the other, tactical drill depended on the choice made by the individual colonel from the available manuals, and standard drill in the movement of formed bodies of troops would have to wait until the 1790s.

More successful was the introduction of a beefed-up code of discipline, known as the Articles of War, in 1718. There had always been the provision for severe physical punishment in the army, but it was only during William III's campaigns that its use became widespread. But now, even in peacetime, specific military crimes like treachery, disobedience and mutiny were general court-martial offences punishable by death, as were desertion, persuasion to desert, breaking out of prison, abandoning your post and plundering. Even regimental courts martial could cashier officers (for being drunk on duty) and sentence men to a range of corporal punishments including flogging, whipping, running the gauntlet, the wooden horse and the 'strappado', where a man was hoisted with his arms and legs behind his back, and then dropped with a jerk.[5] One private in the 1st Dragoons who deserted during peacetime avoided the death penalty but was instead sentenced to three lashes for every soldier in his regiment, roughly 1,200 strokes of the cat. He survived.[6]

George I also held strong opinions on the importance of experience, merit and length of service as criteria for promotion, and the evils of buying and selling commissions and of patronage. The first step to creating a disciplined and centralized officer corps was, he felt, the abolition of the purchase system. But he was thwarted in the attempt – the cost was too great and the political opposition too entrenched – and had to settle instead for regulation. In February 1719 a royal warrant established a definite tariff of prices for each regiment – a lieutenant-colonelcy in the Horse Grenadier Guards, for example, was fixed at £3,600 and the adjutancy at £270 – and decreed that commissions could be bought only by the rank below. It also stipulated that lieutenants could become captains solely on the condition that they had served for ten years with the lesser rank.[7] Prior to this, many promotions within the infantry and cavalry regiments had been based upon private financial arrangements between the officers themselves. The new regulations formally acknowledged purchase as a viable means of promotion, but simultaneously established the crown as the collector and disburser of purchase money.

In addition, the two Georges established the principle that officers held their commissions not simply because of their wealth, but also because of their education and abilities (with George II keeping a notebook of individual officers' talents and appointments). Many of their officers were the sons of professionals, and some were even ex-rankers. To them pay mattered, and George I recognized this by extending the provisions of the half-pay system – introduced in 1697 to prevent the dispersal of the officer corps at a time of savage cuts – so that it not only kept officers in reserve but also provided pensions for those disabled in action or anxious to retire. The Scots, in particular, were drawn to the army as an outlet for their ambition, and between 1714 and 1763 more than a quarter of all officers were from north of the border, a figure far in excess of their national proportion. The Georges were also keen to reward length of service and martial achievement: of the 290 regimental colonels appointed between 1714 and 1763, over 20 had served for more than 45 years, over 60 had served between 35 and 45 years, and 90 had served more than fifteen years. Thanks to the first two Georges, the eighteenth century saw the rapid expansion of military families, with sons following their fathers into the army.[8]

Not that George II, who had had a horse killed under him at

Oudenaarde, was content merely to consolidate his father's reforms. In 1729 he made attempts to improve and standardize the quality of recruits, horses and uniforms. Soldiers in the Blues, for example, were given 'a new cloth coat well lined with serge, a new waistcoat, a new laced hat, a pair of new large buff gloves with stiff tops' every two years and new boots and saddles 'as they shall be wanting'. Horses were to be between 15.1 and 15.2 hands, 'not exceeding', with recruits not less than 5 feet 10 inches 'in stockings'.[9] He also championed the first Royal Military Academy that opened at Woolwich in 1741 to teach gunnery and engineering to officer cadets. (Two separate permanent corps of engineers and artillery had been formed at Marlborough's prompting in 1716, with the gunners becoming the Royal Regiment of Artillery six years later, and the Sappers the Corps of Royal Engineers in 1757.) But George II's chief claim to military fame is that he was the last British monarch to lead an army in battle: at Dettingen, in Bavaria, during the War of the Austrian Succession (1740–48).

The war was sparked by the death of Emperor Charles VI in 1740. The right of his daughter and heir, Maria Theresa, to inherit all his domains – Austria, Hungary, Croatia, Bohemia, the Austrian Netherlands and extensive territory in Italy – had been guaranteed by all the great powers at the end of the War of the Spanish Succession. But when the time came, three of those powers – Prussia, Bavaria and France – chose to ignore the agreement known as the Pragmatic Sanction, citing Salic Law, which forbade a woman to succeed to a throne. Their true motive, of course, was self-aggrandizement: seeing Maria Theresa as young and inexperienced, and judging her kingdom to be on the decline, they set about dismembering it.

King Frederick II – later 'the Great' – of Prussia (1740–86) was the first to strike, invading Silesia without warning in December 1740. His forces quickly overran the province and the following April, at the Battle of Mollwitz, met an Austrian relief army under Field Marshal Wilhelm von Neipperg. It was the Prussian king's first test as a military commander and almost ended in disaster. Successive Austrian cavalry charges routed the Prussian horse and, with the battle seemingly lost, Frederick was advised by his deputy, Field Marshal

Kurt von Schwerin, to flee the field. It was left to Schwerin to rally the excellent Prussian infantry and eventually win the battle.

The victory reverberated round Europe and gave warning of a rising new power whose army was, quite literally, a state within a state. Frederick II's father, Frederick William I (the 'Soldier King', 1713–40), had begun the process by increasing the size of the army from 30,000 to 80,000, a huge figure for a country with a population of just two and a quarter million and a revenue of just £1 million. Compulsory military service had been introduced in 1733, requiring four fifths of the state budget to pay for the expanded army; and even with conscription, anything up to two thirds of the army was made up of mercenaries from other German states. The strength of the army was its officer corps, chiefly drawn from the hardy and dutiful sons of Prussian landowners (*Junkers*) who were handsomely rewarded in terms of pay and prestige, and who were promoted by seniority and merit, not by money and influence.

These highly professional officers were complemented by some of the finest infantry in Europe, their tactics and organization the brainchild of Prince Leopold of Anhalt-Dessau ('the Old Dessauer'), who had fought under Marlborough at Blenheim. Leopold demanded rapid fire and aggression in attack. To facilitate this he replaced breakable wooden ramrods with iron – one of the most significant military innovations of the period – trimmed off full-skirted clothing so that ranks could stand closer, and introduced individual firearms drills that raised the Prussian rate of fire to three or four shots a minute. Allied to a system of universal drill that enabled a regiment to change front, direction or formation as if it were a single being, he made the Prussian infantryman all but unbeatable. Mollwitz was proof of that.

Inspired by Frederick's 'victory', King Louis XV of France and the Elector Charles of Bavaria entered the fray: the former looking to conquer the Austrian Netherlands and the latter hoping to win the Imperial crown (as his predecessor had tried to do, without success, in the War of the Spanish Succession). This in turn prompted Britain – already at war with Bourbon Spain over trading rights in the Caribbean, and fearful of French designs on the Low Countries and Hanover, not to mention the obvious threat to the European balance of power – to enter the conflict on the side of the Austrians.

As in 1702, this meant raising a field army virtually from scratch and sending it to the Continent. But to do so would take time – the estimates of 1742, for example, called for an increased British establishment of 62,000 men – and the 16,000-strong army that the Earl of Stair assembled in Flanders in the autumn of 1742 was poorly trained and inexperienced. It suffered, moreover, from the lack of any common procedures for manoeuvring regiments either on the march or in battle; this was left to the choice of individual colonels. Also infantry tactics had developed little since Marlborough's day, and relied heavily on the improved firepower of the .753-calibre flintlock musket, introduced in the 1720s, known as the Brown Bess. Fire was now strictly controlled in rolling volleys that were ordered by officers only when it seemed likely that every shot would find its mark.[10]

But, for all the reforms instituted by the two Georges, the reality of life for the average British soldier of the mid-1740s was still 'dirty, depraved and despised', according to the Scottish historian John Prebble:

> All men preyed on the soldier, and in his turn he robbed and bullied them. He stood on a no-man's land outside the law, its victim and its guardian. When called to support it during civil riots he risked death by shooting if he refused, and trial for murder by the civil power if he obeyed . . . Flogging was monotonously commonplace. Almost every day's entry in the Order Books contains the names of one, two or three men sentenced to the lash, receiving anything from the minimum of twenty-five strokes to the maximum of three thousand . . . Battle came almost as a relief.[11]

A typical soldier was a minimum of 5 feet 5 inches, and tended to enlist out of economic necessity for a term of three years and a bounty of £4, 'most of which was drunk for him by the recruiting sergeant on the day of his enlistment'. He was frequently literate, or at least able to write his own name, and wore a 'wide-skirted coat of heavy scarlet, well-buttoned and piped, and cuffed and faced with the regimental colour', and a long-flapped waistcoat. Breeches were also scarlet, and covered to mid-thigh by white or grey gaiters. Beneath his black tricorne hat, the soldier's head was held upright by a tight leather stock, forcing him to look to his front. Over his left shoulder he wore a wide leather belt, stiffened with pipeclay made from one part yellow ochre to four parts of whiting; from this belt hung his cartridge pouch of 24 rounds. On his left hip, attached to a waist-belt, was a 16-inch bayonet of fluted steel. A grey canvas haver-sack, when he carried it, had enough room for two shirts, two leather neck-stocks, two pairs of stockings, a pair of breeches, a pair of buckled shoes, brushes, blacking and pipeclay, and enough bread for six days.[12]

His Brown Bess flintlock musket – made either at the Minories in London or bought from abroad – weighed 11 lb. 2 oz. and carried a barrel 3½ feet long. It had a .753 bore and fired a ball weighing 1⅓ oz. Cartridges consisted of the ball and 4½ drams of black powder, wrapped in paper. To load, the soldier tore the top off the cartridge with his teeth and, having sprinkled a small amount of powder into the priming pan, poured the rest down the barrel, followed by the ball and remaining paper, all rammed home with an iron rod. But it remained a clumsy weapon that could be rendered ineffective by wind and rain, either of which might prevent the ignition of the powder in the pan. Nor could it, even in the best conditions, be loaded quickly or fired accurately. Most men could manage a firing rate of no more than two or three shots a minute; and though it could kill at 300 yards, it was really effective only at much closer distances and in skilled hands. When the bayonet, more than a foot long and weighing 1lb., was fixed it became almost impossible to use the ramrod to reload, while the overbalanced barrel was harder to aim. Its true value lay in the controlled firepower of 100 or more in one discharge. 'A regiment that stood its ground under assault,' wrote Prebble, 'biting the cartridge, priming the pan, ramming home the ball, firing at the beat of the drum and loading again, a regiment thus engaged could not, in theory, be overrun . . . Like most arguments in theory it was frequently confounded in practice.'[13]

The first proper opportunity since 1713 for these effective but far from unbeatable soldiers to prove themselves in battle against a major military power – once again the French – was at Dettingen on 27 June 1743. A year earlier, having won a second victory over the Austrians at the Battle of Chotusitz, Frederick II of Prussia had withdrawn from the war, with Silesia as his prize; but Austria was still being threatened by French and Bavarian armies along the Danube, and it was to relieve that pressure that the British Contingent in Flanders linked up with Hanoverian and Austrian forces on the lower Rhine. Their initial commander was the Earl of Stair, a vastly experienced general who had been present at all of Marlborough's major victories. He was superseded, however, in mid-June 1743 when the soldier-king George II arrived to take personal command of the 44,000-strong Allied force.

Ignoring Stair's advice, George posted his army on the north bank of the River Main at Aschaffenburg, 30 miles upstream from Frankfurt, in an attempt to intercept a retreating French army. But he was outmanoeuvred by his French opponent, the Duc de Noailles, who sent part of his army to block George's retreat, thus trapping him in the narrow gap between the wooded Spessart Hills and the River Main. The king's only hope of escape was to fight his way through the 28,000-strong blocking army that de Noailles had placed around the village of Dettingen.

George's men began their march on the morning of 27 June and soon came under heavy enfilade fire from French artillery batteries south of the Main. 'The enemy began to cannonade us very hot before we could bring our Cannons to bear,' recalled a gunner in the Royal Artillery. 'They play'd upon us 3 hours . . . [until] we at last came to a convenient ground where we fixed [several] Batteries, and play'd upon them with success, with round shott. When we had cannonaded a considerable time, our horse & foot engaged with loud huzzas.'[14]

On a plain to the east of Dettingen, George deployed them for battle in three lines – with the infantry in the centre and the cavalry on the wings – and was extremely fortunate that the French commander at Dettingen, Noailles's nephew the Duc de Gramont, chose to leave his fortified position and fight in the open. De Gramont's fatal error was to assume that the main Allied army had somehow eluded him, and that the force before him was no more than a rear-guard.

But even with a numerical advantage, the battle did not begin well for the Allies and, scared by the first ineffective exchange of musket fire, George's horse bolted to the rear. He rejoined the battle on foot, but by then Stair had assumed tactical control and the superior British musketry was taking its toll. An officer of the 23rd Welsh (later Royal Welch) Fusiliers, one of the units retained after Utrecht, recalled:

> We attack'd the Regiment of Navarre, one of their prime Regiments. Our people imitated their predecessors in the last War gloriously, marching in close order, as firm as a wall, and did not fire till we came within 60 paces, and still kept advancing; so that we had soon closed with the enemy, if they had not retreated: for when the smoak blew off a little, instead of being among their living, we found the dead in heaps by us: and the second fire turn'd them to the right about, and upon a long trot. We engaged two other Regiments afterwards, one after the other, who stood but one fire each: and their Blue French Foot Guards made the best of their way without firing a shot.[15]

The 23rd suffered 'no more than 50 killed and wounded', according to this officer, who put their preservation down to 'keeping close order' and holding fire until the last minute. He added: 'Several that popp'd at 100 paces lost more of their men, and did less execution: for the French will stand fire at a distance, tho' 'tis plain they cannot look men in the face.'[16]

The struggle continued for some hours, with the Scots Greys and the 3rd (King's) Dragoons charging with distinction, but it was the British and Allied infantry that, after a shaky start, decided the battle in George's favour. They were like a wall of brass, wrote de Noailles, 'from which there issued so brisk and well sustained a fire that the oldest officers owned that they had never seen anything like it, incomparably superior to our own'.[17] Outgunned, the French fled the field, losing many of their 6,000 casualties in the waters of the Main. The Allied losses were 2,500.

George II was rightly proud of his unlikely victory, as were his subjects back home. 'The British troops and all the Allied army, who were engaged in this action,' trumpeted the *London Gazette*, 'behaved with the utmost resolution, bravery and intrepidity.'[18] But in truth George had done little to influence the outcome, and his inexperienced soldiers had benefited from the enemy's blunders. Next time they would not be so lucky.

8.   James Wolfe

If the hard-fought victory at Dettingen proved anything, it was that George II was no Marlborough. Yet also present that hot summer's day was a young officer who, but for his untimely death sixteen years later, might have stood the comparison. James Wolfe, born in Kent in 1727 into a family of professional soldiers, will forever be associated with the victory at Quebec in 1759 that cost him his life – and decided the fate of North America. Incredibly, Wolfe was just thirty-two years old when he was killed in Canada, but he had already achieved more during his short career – particularly in the fields of training and battlefield tactics – than many officers do in a lifetime.

Wolfe's father, grandfather and great-grandfather had all worn the redcoat of the British soldier and there was never a doubt he would follow in their footsteps. The first unit he joined as a thirteen-year-old officer-cadet in 1740 was a new battalion of marines, technically part of the Royal Navy, which his father had raised the previous year for service in the Caribbean against the Spanish. He was too sick to board the transports, and it was just as well because the expedition, racked by sickness and inter-service rivalry, was not a success. Instead, in March 1742, Wolfe exchanged from the marines into Duroure's (later the 12th) Regiment of Foot* with the rank of ensign. A month later his regiment was ordered to Flanders as part of the British expeditionary force sent to assist Austria.

Wolfe spent almost a year in Ghent learning the basics of his profession, and was evidently a quick learner because, shortly before the British Contingent marched south into Germany, he was appointed acting adjutant at the age of just sixteen. The adjutant was, in effect, the commanding officer's right-hand man, with responsibility for

* Until 1747 regiments were named after their colonels; after that date they were numbered in order of seniority.

regimental administration, discipline and training. If anything under-lines Wolfe's natural aptitude for soldiering it was this key appointment at such a young age.

Nor did Wolfe disappoint. At Dettingen – as he related to his father in a letter – he and the regiment's acting commander 'were employed in begging and ordering the men not to fire at too great a distance, but to keep it until the enemy should come near us, but to little purpose'. Wolfe added:

> The whole fired when they thought they could reach them, which had like to have ruined us. We did very little execution with it. As soon as the French saw we presented they all fell down, and when we had fired they all got up, and marched close to us in tolerable good order, and gave us a brisk fire, which put us into some disorder and made us give way a little, particularly ours and two or three more regiments, who were in the hottest of it. However we soon rallied again, and attacked them with great fury, which gained us a complete victory, and forced the enemy to retire in great haste.[1]

Despite having a horse shot from under him, Wolfe showed remark-able composure and maturity for one so young; this was noticed by the king's 22-year-old son, William, Duke of Cumberland, who spoke to Wolfe 'several times' as the battle raged. The admiration was mutual. 'He gave his orders with a great deal of calmness,' recalled Wolfe, 'and seemed quite unconcerned. The soldiers were in a high delight to have him so near them.' Though he was carried off the field with a musket-ball in the calf, Cumberland never forgot the brave young adjutant and, thereafter, Wolfe's meteoric rise owed as much to royal patronage as it did to his undoubted talents.[2]

Within weeks of Dettingen, he had been confirmed as adjutant and promoted to lieutenant. A year later, still only seventeen, he trans-ferred to Barrell's (later the 4th) Regiment of Foot as a captain and served for a year in Flanders under the aged and ineffective Field Marshal George Wade. The replacement of Wade by the Duke of Cumberland in early 1745 augured well for Wolfe. He was fortunate, too, that his battalion was on garrison duty at Ghent when the duke rashly attacked a well-dug-in French army under Marshal Maurice de

Saxe at Fontenoy, near Tournai, on 11 May. As ever the redoubtable British infantry performed well and, despite enfilade fire from a redoubt to their right, managed to storm the French entrenchments and even enter the camp behind. But the Dutch in the centre and the Austrians on the right had less success and, unsupported, the British withdrew with heavy losses and the retreat became general. Cumberland's overconfidence had cost the Allies 10,000 men, with Wolfe's old battalion, the 12th, particularly badly hit and sent to garrison Ostend while it recovered.

Within days, Barrell's had reinforced the remnants of Cumberland's army at Lessines, and thereby avoided capture when Ghent fell to the French a few weeks later. Wolfe's good fortune continued in June, when he was promoted by Cumberland to brevet-major of brigade,* a key staff appointment he would hold for the next three years. At eighteen, he had secured three promotions in as many years – circumventing, in the process, the requirement to spend at least ten years as a lieutenant before he could be considered for promotion to captain – and was the youngest major in the British Army. His next experience of battle, however, was not against the French but his own countrymen, and the defeat at Fontenoy was partly to blame because it gave Prince Charles Edward ('Bonnie Prince Charlie'), son of the Old Pretender and grandson of James II, the courage to launch the final Jacobite rebellion known as the Forty-Five.

It was almost over before it had begun when a British warship intercepted the tiny French convoy carrying the prince and 700 Irish volunteers as they approached Scotland in early July. The ship carrying the bulk of the troops was damaged in the action and forced to turn back, leaving the prince to land on the isle of Eriskay in the Outer Hebrides with only a handful of men. From there he sailed to the mainland and in mid-August, at Glenfinnan on Loch Shiel, he raised his standard and was at once joined by 1,200 men from the local clans. They came not out of any particular loyalty to the Stuarts (though they thought them preferable to the Hanoverians), nor because they

---

* A brevet was a nominal promotion that gave the holder the authority of the more senior rank but not the pay.

were desperate to free Scotland from the English yoke; but rather because their clan chiefs told them to, and because brigandage and fighting was a way of life. Duncan Forbes, Lord President of the Scottish Court of Sessions in 1745, described the Highlands as 'that large tract of mountainous Ground

> to the Northwest of the Tay, where the natives speak the Irish language. The inhabitants stick close to their ancient and idle way of life; retain their barbarous customs and maxims; depend generally on their Chiefs as their Sovereign Lords and masters; and being accustomed to the use of Arms, and inured to hard living, are dangerous to the public peace; and must continue to be so until being deprived of Arms for some years, they forget the use of them.[3]

Forbes put the number of armed Highlanders at 32,000, a fighting force so formidable that in former times the crown 'was obliged to put Sheriffships and other Jurisdictions in the hands of powerful families in the Highlands, who by their respective Clans and following could give execution to the Laws within their several territories, and frequently did so at considerable bloodshed'.[4] Fortunately for George II, the clans were never united. 'Religion, feuds, the political ambitions of chiefs, the natural jealousies of men who live remote and primitive lives,' wrote John Prebble, 'made common cause impossible. Each clan was enough to itself, and the world ended beyond the glen, or with the sea that locked in the islands.'[5]

So it was during the Forty-Five, when most of the clans stayed aloof from the rebellion and, as a result, Bonnie Prince Charlie's army never numbered more than 8,000 men. Yet these rebels were all hardy raw-boned men, clad in loose togas of woollen plaid (from which the kilt was developed), and armed with muskets, small target shields and the fearsome claymore sword. They were particularly effective at close quarters, as they proved at Prestonpans, near Edinburgh, on 21 September, when fewer than 2,500 Highlanders surprised and routed a slightly smaller government force under Sir John Cope. Unable to stand the Highlanders' battle charge, Cope's men broke and fled, though fewer than 200 got away. The remaining 2,000 or so were killed or taken prisoner, at a cost to the Jacobites of just 100 men.

News of the defeat caused panic in London, and the government's immediate response was to recall eight battalions from Flanders and send them by ship to Newcastle-upon-Tyne. Among the reinforcement officers was Major James Wolfe, who reached the north-east in early November. Assigned to the staff of his old chief, 72-year-old Field Marshal George Wade, Wolfe was optimistic that the Jacobites would soon be crushed, informing his mother on 14 November that it was the 'opinion of most men that these rebels won't stand the King's troops'.[6]

Wolfe, however, had not bargained on Wade's caution; nor on the intrepidity of Bonnie Prince Charlie and his 6,000 men, who, having invaded England by the western route, captured Carlisle on 16 November. That same day Wade marched his troops through snow to Carlisle's assistance; but when he received word on the 17th that the town had fallen, he 'turned round in his tracks back to Newcastle, leaving the insurgents to do as they please'. An early Wolfe biographer commented: 'How sick the Brigade-major of nineteen must have been at Marshal Wade's method of waging war! – a capital illustration of how not to do it.'[7]

The prince continued his march south, entering Preston on 26 November. By now Wade had set off in pursuit, while the Duke of Cumberland, just back from Flanders with yet more reinforcements, had gathered a force of 8,000 in the Midlands. The duke's plan was to crush the Jacobites between his hammer and Wade's anvil; but he was outwitted by Lord George Murray, the prince's military commander, who used a feint towards Wales to disguise his real target: London. The duke took the bait, leaving the road open to Derby, where the Jacobites arrived on 4 December. The only troops that now lay between the fast-marching Highlanders and London was a scratch force, consisting chiefly of militia, that was being assembled north of the city at Finchley.

If Bonnie Prince Charlie had continued his march he might – just might – have regained the throne for his father. He himself was keen to advance. But his advisers were depressed by the lack of visible support for the Jacobite cause and urged him to retreat, saying he might defeat one of the three English armies that were hunting for him –

Cumberland's, Wade's and the Finchley force – but not all three. With extreme reluctance, and after a long day of argument, the prince bowed to his council's advice and the retreat began on 6 December.

It was a knife-edge decision. 'When the Highlanders, by a most incredible march,' wrote the novelist and magistrate Henry Fielding, 'got between the Duke's army and the metropolis, they struck a terror into it scarce to be credited.' So severe was the run on the Bank of England that it was reduced to paying out sixpences to stave off bankruptcy. Only when the news reached London of the Scots' withdrawal did the panic subside.[8]

True to form, Wade failed to intercept the retreating Jacobites, who, having fought a successful rearguard action against Cumberland's cavalry near Penrith (the last skirmish on English soil), crossed back into Scotland in late December. With Wade plainly unequal to the task, and Cumberland required down south to meet a possible French invasion, the general sent in pursuit of the Jacobites was Henry 'Hangman' Hawley, a hard-drinking martinet who, according to one observer, 'if not a good soldier, studies to be thought so, by his severity of manners, and strictness of discipline'.[9] Wolfe and Barrell's Regiment were part of Hawley's force of 8,000.

By the time Hawley reached Edinburgh in early January 1746, the Jacobites had invested Stirling Castle, the gateway to the Highlands. Hawley at once set off to relieve it – as King Edward II, the commander of another English army, had tried to do more than four centuries earlier, and with a similar outcome. Having contributed to the collapse of the Jacobite left wing at Sheriffmuir in 1715, Hawley was convinced he could counteract the Highlanders' dreaded charge with disciplined, close-range musketry. He ordered his men, therefore, to hold their fire until the Jacobites were within ten or twelve paces. But timing was everything. 'If the fire is given at a distance,' he warned, 'you probably will be broke for you never get time to load a second cartridge, and if you give way you may give your foot for dead, for they [the Highlanders] being without a firelock or any load, no man with his arms, accoutrements etc can escape them, and they give no quarters.'[10]

At Falkirk, Hawley established a strong camp while he considered his next move. So certain was he that the camp was safe from attack that he left it in the morning of 16 January to breakfast in nearby Callendar House, the home of the staunchly Jacobite Lady Kilmarnock. He was still there at 11 a.m. when outposts at the camp spotted the Highlanders' approach. At first his deputy ordered the men to arms, but then changed his mind when it was reported that the Jacobites had halted and lit their fires. Unconcerned by the contradictory reports, Hawley continued with his breakfast. It was only when a third message warned that the enemy was nearing Falkirk Moor, which dominated the royal camp, that Hawley realized the danger and called for his horse.

Arriving back in camp hatless and sweating, he sent his dragoons up the steep slope of the moor in a desperate race for the high ground, with the slower-moving infantry and artillery toiling behind. The guns got stuck in a bog, but the infantry trudged onwards in the teeth of an icy gale. 'As we march'd, all the way up hill,' wrote General James Cholmondeley, Hawley's second-in-command, 'and over very uneven ground, our men were greatly blown.'[11]

They were also too late, the lightly equipped Jacobites having reached the summit before them, forcing Hawley to form his troops up on slightly lower ground. So wild was the storm that it was 'difficult to see or hear', recalled the government commander.[12] Undeterred, he ordered his cavalry to charge the right wing of an army that, at 9,000-strong, was marginally superior to his own. Nor was it any less disciplined, the Highlanders unleashing a devastating close-range volley that emptied many saddles and, after a brief mêlée, caused the surviving horsemen to flee the field, taking an indignant Hawley with them. Abandoned by their cavalry, exhausted from the climb and with many of their cartridges soaked and useless, most of the demoralized government foot soldiers put up an equally feeble resistance. They 'gave a feint fire', wrote Cholmondeley, 'and then faced to the right about, as regularly as if they had the word of command, and could not be rallied, 'till they got a considerable distance'.[13]

Only on the right of the government line did a handful of battalions, protected by a ravine, hold their ground and stop the Highland charge in its tracks. Barrell's Regiment was among them, as was

Ligonier's and Cholmondeley's (later the 59th and 34th Foot respectively). Commanded by Cholmondeley and Brigadier-General John
Huske, they prevented a rout by covering the army's retreat to Lin-
lithgow, themselves departing the battlefield to the beat of drums
and with flying colours. It is likely that Wolfe himself was serving
with Barrell's that day, and if so he would have shared in the praise
that Cholmondeley lavished upon the officers of Barrell's and Ligonier's 'for the spirit they shew'd'; without their example, the army
would have been 'cut to pieces'.[14] And yet Hawley's casualties of
650 killed, wounded and missing were almost five times greater than
the Jacobite losses, and he had lost his camp and two cannon. Once
again, some of King George's redcoats had fled before a Highland
charge, and Cholmondeley was right to dub the battle a 'scandalous
affair'.[15] Hawley put the blame squarely on his troops, accusing both
officers and men of cowardice, and underlining this with a spate of
courts martial that cashiered some and hanged others. Only partly
convinced by this explanation, George II was quick to demote Hawley
to cavalry commander and make his own son, the Duke of Cumberland, the new commander-in-chief.

Cumberland joined the army at Edinburgh on 30 January 1746, by
which time Wolfe, much to his disgust, had been appointed one of
Hawley's aides-de-camp. Wolfe wrote later of the loser of Falkirk:
'The troops dread his severity, hate the man, and hold his military
knowledge in contempt.'[16] Cumberland, by contrast, was a welcome
relief. No tactical genius – as he showed at Fontenoy – he was nevertheless hard-working, dogged and fearless. The troops loved him and
he them. On 31 January he marched on Stirling with 7,800 men,
causing Bonnie Prince Charlie to raise the siege and withdraw to
Inverness. Cumberland followed as far as Perth, but then paused to
await the arrival of 5,000 Hessian troops, needed to guard the rivers
Tay and Forth.

Once the Hessians were in position, Cumberland continued on to
Aberdeen, entering the Granite City on 28 February. Again he halted,
this time for six weeks, while his army replenished its supplies, clothing and equipment – much of which had been lost at Falkirk – from
ships sent from England. He also took the opportunity to drill his

foot soldiers in a new bayonet exercise that, he hoped, would combat the threat of the Highlanders' claymore. Each soldier was ordered to thrust his bayonet not at the man immediately opposite him, but at the exposed underarm of the clansman attacking his comrade on the right, and to trust that his comrade on the left would do the same for him. That way the enemy would not be able to use their target shields to protect themselves.

Wolfe, meanwhile, was worried about the redcoats' morale. 'I know their discipline to be bad and their valour precarious,' he wrote, presumably with Falkirk in mind. 'They are easily put into disorder and hard to recover out of it. They frequently kill their officers through fear, and murder one another in confusion.'[17]

While the men were drilled, Cumberland and Hawley enjoyed the comforts of two large requisitioned houses in Aberdeen. The owner of Hawley's quarters, a Mrs Gordon, later accused Wolfe of failing to keep his promise that 'everything would be restored' to her after they departed.[18] In the event, Hawley had most of her movable possessions – including china, bed and table linen, books, clocks, clothes – packed up and sent in his name to Edinburgh. According to Mrs Gordon, Hawley also consumed large quantities of her tea, sugar, chocolate, beef, pork, hams, sweetmeats, honey, 'with many things 'tis impossible to mention'.[19] Looting on such a scale was not unusual, particularly from civilians who were known to be Jacobite supporters (as Mrs Gordon was); and it may be that Wolfe wanted to keep his word but was overruled by his superior. Even so, it was not an episode that reflects much credit on Wolfe.

On 8 April, Cumberland finally left Aberdeen with 6,400 foot and 2,400 horse, pausing a week later to celebrate his twenty-fifth birthday at Nairn on the coast. That night, Bonnie Prince Charlie's smaller army of 6,000 attempted a surprise attack on the English camp, confident that Cumberland's soldiers would still be drunk after toasting their commander's birthday with an extra issue of grog. But the 12-mile march from Inverness took longer than expected as the men toiled in the dark across a broken and waterlogged terrain; and, once it became clear they would not reach their destination before dawn, the attack was called off amidst scenes of recrimination and bickering. The exhausted and hungry Highlanders fell back to the boggy expanse of Culloden Moor, 4 miles east of Inverness, where they would make their stand.

At dawn on 16 April, Cumberland's men approached the moor in three columns of infantry, each of five battalions, flanked by a column of artillery and one of horse, the latter comprising three regiments led by Hawley and his staff (Wolfe among them). The infantry marched to the beat of the drum, each battalion led by its grenadier company in their mitre caps, and preceded by two junior officers called ensigns whose job it was to carry the battalion's unfurled colours: the King's Colour, or Union Flag; and the Regimental Colour, which was blue, yellow, green or buff to match the facings on the redcoats' uniforms (the facings of Barrell's, for example, were blue). Threaded on the colours in silk, or painted, were the devices of each battalion: a lion for Barrell's, a thistle or saltire for the Scots' regiments, and the King's cipher for those that were 'Royal'.

Following the columns were the bat-wagons, bread-wagons, sutler-wagons (carrying provisions and liquor) and the carriages of the senior officers. Seated on or marching beside the bat-wagons, with their skirts hitched to their knees, were soldiers' wives and doxies, a motley crew liable to be whipped if they moved ahead of the transport. They were subject to the same harsh discipline that applied to the men: one woman convicted of petty theft in 1745 had 'her tail immediately turned up before the door of the house, where the robbery was committed, and the Drummer of the Regiment tickled her with 100 very good lashes'.[20]

Among the foot soldiers marching through the damp heather that day, at the regulation 75 paces a minute, was Private Alexander Taylor of the Royals (later the 1st Foot). 'It was a very cold, rainy morning,' he recalled, 'and nothing to buy to comfort us. But we had the ammunition loaf, thank God, but not a dram of brandy or spirits had you given a crown for a gill; nor nothing but the loaf and water.' Another private, Edward Linn of Campbell's (later the 21st Foot), had the Divine Presence on his mind for a very different reason, and would later write to his 'beloved spouse' asking her to 'give praise to Almighty God' that he had emerged from the battle unscathed.[21]

By late morning, scouts reported that the Highlanders were forming in line across the spine of Culloden Moor. 'We marched on a mile
or two,' recalled Private Michael Hughes of Bligh's (later the 20th
Foot), 'before we could discern the terrible boasting Highlanders,
and upon first sight of them we formed into line of action, which was
done with great beauty of discipline and order.'[22]

But seeing no forward movement from the enemy, Cumberland
advanced once more. 'We marched up to our knees in water,' wrote
Hughes, 'over a bog that brought us to the perfect sight of them. We
kept advancing with drums beating and colours flying, with fixed
bayonets till we came within gunshot.'[23] There Cumberland arranged
his troops into three lines of infantry – the first two of six battalions,
the third a reserve of three – with cavalry on either flank and two
3-pounder guns between each of the front-line battalions. Their left
flank rested on the corner of a stone-wall enclosure that extended the
length of the 600-yard battlefield; their right on a marshy bog. Facing
them across the gently sloping moorside, laced with dead heather
and pocked by bog-holes, were two lines of Jacobites, the Highland
clans mostly in the first line, protected by three four-gun batteries.

With battle imminent, Cumberland rode before his men to
embolden them with a final address. He was immensely fat, yet sat his
charger well. His scarlet frock coat had lapels and cuffs of blue edged
with gold, and on his left breast twinkled the distinctive star of the
Order of the Garter. His face, framed by the white curls of his wig,
was bloated and red, his eyes dark and protruding. Adonis he was
not, yet his men knew him to be a capable commander, personally
brave and not prone to panic. A general, in short, they could trust.

'If there is any man,' he cried, tricorne hat in hand, 'who, from
disinclination to the cause from having relations in the rebel army,
would now prefer to retire I beg him in God's name to do so, as
I would rather face the Highlanders with 1,000 determined men at
my back than have 10,000 with a tithe of them lukewarm.'[24]

The redcoats' response was unanimous. 'Flanders! Flanders!' they
roared, hats on bayonets in salute of the British infantry's valour at
Fontenoy. 'We'll follow you!'[25]

The first shot was fired by Jacobite artillery, 4- and 6-pounders poorly served by inexperienced Highlanders. It was badly aimed and whistled over the heads of the leading battalions, killing a soldier in the rear. The Jacobite gunnery would not improve. Cumberland's artillerymen, on the other hand, were veterans of Dettingen and Fontenoy, and their first salvo of round-shot scythed through the front rank of Highlanders with deadly effect. Some guns targeted Bonnie Prince Charlie himself, killing his groom, wounding his horse and forcing the Young Pretender to move to the left of the Jacobite rear. For thirty minutes this unequal dual continued, until, able to stand it no longer, the clans in the centre and right of the Jacobite front line broke ranks and charged.

By now Cumberland had reinforced his front line with two extra battalions, one on each flank, and sent his loyalist Campbell militia and five squadrons of dragoons into the stone enclosure on the left flank. As the charging Highlanders came within range – a blood-curdling sight that one soldier likened to a horde of 'hungry wolves'[26] – the kneeling front rank and flanking grenadiers of each infantry company fired first, followed by the second rank and then the third. In this way the rolling fire from six battalions was almost continuous. 'We kept up a continual closs [storm of fire],' remembered Edward Linn of Campbell's, 'firing upon them with our small-arms . . . We gave them a closs with grape-shot which galled them very much.'[27]

Most of the Jacobite officers were killed before they got within 20 yards of Cumberland's first line. A few of their men broke through, but were shot or bayoneted by the second line. The only serious contest took place on the left, where the right wing of the Jacobite army – composed of the Atholl, Cameron and Stewart clans – closed with the three regiments near the corner of the stone enclosure, Munro's (later the 37th Foot), Barrell's and Wolfe's★ (later the 8th Foot). Wolfe's – assisted by flanking fire from the Campbell militia-men, who, by this time, were lining the stone wall that ran the length of the battlefield – stopped the Atholl men in their tracks. But to their right rear the fight, for a brief moment, was in the balance.

★ So-called because Wolfe's father, Edward, was its colonel, and not to be confused with the regiment in which James Wolfe held his commission, Barrell's.

Only the left platoons of Munro's were attacked, yet still they lost 19 killed and 63 wounded in a matter of minutes. 'Our lads fought more like devils than men,' remembered their grenadier captain.[28]

It was fortunate, then, that the heaviest blow fell on the battalion that had fought so well at Falkirk: Barrell's. Wolfe wrote the following day:

> They were attacked by the Camerons (the bravest clan among them), and 'twas for some time a dispute between the swords and bayonets; but the latter was found by far the most destructable weapon. The regiment behaved with uncommon resolution, killing some say almost their own number . . . They were, however, surrounded by superiority, and would have been all destroyed had not Col. Martin with his regiment [later the 25th Scottish Borderers] mov'd forward to their assistance, prevented mischief, and by a well-timed fire destroyed a great number of them and obliged them to run off.[29]

Barrell's lost more than a third of its 350 men, including its captain of grenadiers and commanding officer (the latter losing his hand and sword to a cut from a broadsword). Some of the platoons fell back in the face of the Camerons' ferocious onslaught, only to re-form on the flank of the Border Scots. 'There was scarce a soldier or officer of Barrell's,' wrote one of them, 'and of that part of Munro's which engaged, who did not kill one or two men each with their bayonets and spontoons. Not a bayonet but was bent or bloody and stained with blood to the muzzles of their muskets.'[30]

As the survivors of the right and centre of the Jacobite front line withdrew, taking their supports with them, the left wing made its own ill-timed and half-hearted assault. They were Macdonalds, sore at having been deprived of their usual post of honour on the right of the line, and had the furthest distance to cover. 'They came down . . . several times within a hundred yards,' recalled Cumberland, 'firing their pistols and brandishing their swords, but the Royals and Pulteney's [later the 13th Foot] hardly took their firelocks from their shoulders.'[31]

Their honour satisfied, if not their bloodlust, the Macdonalds joined the rest of the Jacobite infantry in flight. 'What a spectacle of horror!' wrote one their officers. 'The same Highlanders who had advanced to the charge like lions, with bold and determined countenance, were in an instant seen flying like trembling cowards in the greatest disorder.'[32] He joined them.

Wolfe himself, meanwhile, was with Hawley's cavalry on the left. 'As soon as the Rebels began to give way and the fire of the Foot slackened,' he wrote a day later, '[Hawley] ordered Genl Bland to charge the rest of them with three squadrons, and Cobham to support him with the two. It was done with wonderful spirit and completed the victory with great slaughter. We have taken 22 pieces of brass cannon or near it, a number of colours, and near 700 prisoners . . .'[33]

What Wolfe failed to mention, however, was that the cavalry could and should have played a decisive role much earlier in the battle. But, having outflanked the first two Jacobite lines, and with just a shallow ravine, a weak battalion and a tiny force of rebel horse between him and the rebel rear, Hawley chose to stay his 500 riders until victory was certain. Their chief contribution to the battle, therefore, was in the pursuit. They 'cleared all the country for three miles before them', noted their proud commander, 'and . . . made great slaughter every way'.[34]

A famous anecdote, written many years after the battle, is that Wolfe stayed aloof from the slaughter, refusing Cumberland's order to shoot a wounded Jacobite officer with the words: 'I never can consent to become an executioner.'[35] But there is no reliable evidence for such an exchange, and it flies in the face of Wolfe's admiration for the duke's conduct at Culloden ('a great and gallant General')[36] and his belief that the butchery was justified. 'Orders were publicly given in the rebel army, the day before the action,' he wrote to his uncle, 'that no quarter should be given to our troops. We had an opportunity of avenging ourselves, and I assure you as few prisoners were taken of the Highlanders as possible.'[37]

According to Wolfe, the government suffered 320 killed and wounded at Culloden, while Jacobite fatalities alone were 'nearly 1,500'.[38] Many more would die in the brutal occupation of the Highlands by Cumberland's troops as they searched for the Young Pretender and his supporters. In theory only those found with arms were to be executed and their property confiscated or destroyed. But such niceties were often ignored as the innocent suffered with the guilty in a spate of beatings, rapes and murders that earned for the duke the soubriquet of 'Butcher'. Wolfe played his part, informing a captain of dragoons on 19 May that Hawley 'approves of everything you have done, and desires you will continue that assiduity in apprehending such as have been in open rebellion or are known abettors, and that you will be careful to collect all proofs and accusations against them'.[39] In a subsequent letter, he told the captain that the duke was happy for him to dispose of a suspected rebel's property, and that the soldiers involved would receive a share of the proceeds in proportion to their pay.[40] This principle of dividing up loot according to rank would continue well into the nineteenth century.

What was not acceptable to Cumberland was freelance pillaging by ordinary soldiers. 'No plundering on any account,' read his Orders of the Day, 'except by order and in presence of an officer.' The punishment for transgressors was a flogging, but even that horrific experience was not a deterrent for all. In early May, a soldier of the 8th Foot was given 1,200 lashes 'for morauding and steeling', 240 a day for five days. Soon after, another soldier in the same battalion received 2,000 strokes in batches of 200 for stealing fifteen sheep, and was ordered to pay 3s.9d. for the meat he had consumed before arrest. The fine added insult to injury.[41]

A flogging was a grim ritual. The battalion formed a three-sided hollow square, with the men facing inwards towards the whipping-post, a triangle made from the halberds of four sergeants, three forming the legs and the fourth a steadying crossbar. The prisoner was marched into the square by the provost guard to hear his sentence read by the adjutant. He was then stripped to the waist and, after a brief examination by the surgeon, strapped to the halberds by the drum-major. The strokes were given by relays of drummers, twenty-five each, using the dreaded cat-o'-nine-tails (comprised of a foot-long wooden handle and nine lengths of knotted whipcord). The cat fell to the tap of a drum and, as a rule, a maximum of 300 strokes were given per punishment. If the man's sentence was for more, he was paraded every morning until it was complete. Incredibly, few men died from such an ordeal, though their lacerated backs, marked with a bloody *X*, would take weeks to heal. Not that this prevented most from returning to duty, with pack and musket slung, within two days of the flogging.[42]

Wolfe remained in the Highlands until November 1746, by which time Cumberland and Hawley had long since returned as heroes to London, the duke receiving from a grateful Parliament an increase in his allowance from £15,000 to £40,000 a year. Bonnie Prince Charlie had also left Scotland, boarding a French ship near Arisaig on the west coast in mid-September after more than five months on the run, an odyssey that took in the Hebridean islands of Benbecula, Scalpay, Lewis and Skye (his escape to the last island assisted by the redoubtable Flora Macdonald). He never returned to Scotland, and died in Rome without issue in 1788, a century after his grandfather James II had lost his throne. The Jacobite cause would finally end with the death of Charles Stuart's childless younger brother Henry, the Cardinal Bishop of Ostia, in 1807.

After Culloden, many in government felt their response to the previous rebellion had been too lenient. So they put in place a series of draconian laws and measures designed to prevent a fresh outbreak, including the Abolition of Heritable Jurisdictions Act of 1747, which ended the hereditary right of Scottish landowners to dispense justice on their estates through barony courts; the confiscation of estates from those lords and clan chiefs who had supported the rebellion; the permanent stationing of royal troops in the Highlands at strongholds such as the new Fort George near Inverness; and the passing of the Highland Dress Act in 1746, which banned the wearing of tartan in Scotland except by members of the British Army. Though bitterly resented, these measures must have worked because never again would the Highlands rise for the Stuarts.

But, while Cumberland's victory at Culloden – the last full-scale battle fought on British soil – ended the internal threat to Hanoverian rule, it did nothing to neutralize the external danger from France in the ongoing War of the Austrian Succession. If anything, it increased it by removing British troops from Flanders at a vital moment, thus enabling Marshal de Saxe to make further inroads into the Austrian Netherlands by seizing Brussels in February 1746 and the fortresses of Mons and Namur in the summer. By the end of the campaigning season, after yet another victory over an Allied army at Rocoux in October, de Saxe was poised to invade the Dutch Republic.

The time was ripe for the Duke of Cumberland, his victory laurels still fresh from Culloden, to re-enter the fray and gain revenge for Fontenoy. In early 1747 he returned to the Low Countries to resume command of the Allied Army, and was joined there by his protégé James Wolfe, who, refreshed by six weeks' leave in London, was keen to return to active service. Cumberland's priority was to protect the fortress city of Maastricht, long considered the key to Holland's defence, and in mid-June, on hearing of de Saxe's approach, he concentrated his army there. The clash, when it took place on 2 July, was for possession of the hamlet of Lauffeldt, just 3 miles to the west of the citadel. At first, according to his aide-de-camp George Townshend, Cumberland failed to appreciate the hamlet's importance, and 'it was once ordered to be *burnt* and twice to be *evacuated* and *repossessed*.'[43] Only at the last minute was it garrisoned by British and Hanoverian troops – among them Wolfe, who was serving as brigade-major to Sir John Mordaunt – part of a multinational army of 126,000 that also included Dutch, Hessian, Bavarian and Austrian troops. It was the British and Hanoverians at Lauffeldt on the left of the Allied line, however, who shouldered the bulk of the fighting when the French attacked at 10 a.m. on 2 July.

For five hours the battle raged, with both sides feeding yet more brigades into the meat-grinder of Lauffeldt, until the French, alone, had committed almost fifty battalions. Only after the fifth assault did the surviving defenders withdraw, but not before they had shot off the last of their cartridges and evacuated their wounded. The latter included Wolfe, shot through the body by a musket-ball. His most vivid memory was of his servant Roland coming to his assistance 'at the hazard of his life' with a fresh horse. '[He] would have continued close by me,' wrote Wolfe, 'had I not ordered him to retire. I believe he was slightly wounded just at that time, and the horse he held was shot likewise.'[44]

Meanwhile, desperate to relieve the pressure, Cumberland had ordered the Dutch and Austrians on his right to advance. But when a force of Dutch cavalry panicked and fled, trampling two British battalions (the 21st and 23rd Foot) in the process, the army was cut in two. It was saved from annihilation by a suicidal cavalry charge of Irish and Scots dragoons led by Sir John Ligonier that checked the French advance long enough for the retreating Allies to reach the safety of the walls of Maastricht. Ligonier was captured – and later exchanged – and most of his men either killed or wounded.

It was, for de Saxe, an unsatisfactory win. Having suffered more casualties than his opponent – 10,000 to the Allies' 6,000 (with the Anglo-Hanoverians accounting for the vast majority) – he was no longer strong enough to take Maastricht and so withdrew. Cumberland congratulated his soldiers 'for their bravery and good conduct', and asked his commanding officers to recommend those deserving promotion. But not all had fought well. Three days after the battle, Captain Robert Cholmondely of the 3rd (Scots) Foot Guards was cashiered for 'quitting his platoon in the action'. Not long after, a private of the 21st Scots Fusiliers was 'tryed and condemned for leaving his party on the day of action and presenting his firelock at Lieutenant Levison when he ordered him to return'. He was hanged.[45]

British troops were not present when the Dutch fortress of Bergen-op-Zoom was stormed and sacked by the French in September 1747, but the implications were clear. If the rest of Holland fell, France would have a stranglehold on British trade. Determined to prevent that from happening, the government joined the Dutch Republic in peace negotiations with the French in March 1748, signing the Treaty of Aix-la-Chapelle on 30 April. Its terms restored all conquests made during the war and seem, at first glance, remarkably favourable to the Allies, given the recent French successes on the Continent. They had, however, been counterbalanced by significant British victories at sea and in North America, notably the capture of the French fortress of Louisbourg, at the entrance to the St Lawrence River in Canada, by Massachusetts volunteers in June 1745, and two naval victories off Cape Finisterre in May and October 1747. The French, on the other hand, had taken the British trading post of

Madras on the east coast of India in September 1746. It would now be swapped for Louisbourg (much to the fury of the American colonists, who had played such a prominent role in its capture). The French, in addition, had agreed to recognize the Hanoverians as Great Britain's legitimate rulers, and to expel Bonnie Prince Charlie. The big loser of the treaty was the Empress Maria Theresa of Austria, who, like her predecessor Leopold, had been abandoned by her allies in mid-war. She would receive back from the French the Austrian Netherlands, but not Silesia (Frederick II of Prussia having signed a separate peace), and never forgave Britain for its betrayal. When global war flared again, just eight years later, she would side with France against Britain and Prussia.

James Wolfe, meanwhile, was sufficiently recovered from his wound at Lauffeldt to celebrate his twenty-first birthday in London and resume his military career. In just eight years' service he had served through six campaigns and four pitched battles. Two were defeats, it is true, but Wolfe was acute enough to realize that the 'more a soldier thinks of the false steps of those that are gone before, the more likely he is to avoid them'. Nor should, he believed, 'the examples worthiest of imitation' ever be lost sight of, 'as they will be the best and truest guides in every undertaking'.[46]

Peace, on the other hand, promised boredom and slow promotion, and it was for this reason, as much as a desire to widen his horizons, that Wolfe applied in the summer of 1748 for extended leave from his regiment so that he could travel. The request was denied by Cumberland, though he sweetened the pill in January 1749 by arranging Wolfe's promotion to major and acting commander of the 20th (formerly Bligh's) Regiment of Foot, then stationed in Scotland. He was still just twenty-two, and to a stranger must have seemed an unlikely commanding officer. His one advantage was his height – at 6 feet he was exceptionally tall for the time – and his scrawny physique made him look loftier still. The effect was rather spoiled, however, by his pasty, freckled complexion, red hair and long nose, not to mention his backward-sloping forehead and weak chin, which made his profile look like a tilted triangle.

But Wolfe's unmartial appearance was deceptive. He had already proved himself to be a first-rate company commander and staff officer, quick to learn and physically brave, and the command of a battalion would give him the opportunity to put his many tactical theories into practice. His first priority, however, was to get to know his men. In February 1749, soon after arriving at Stirling, he wrote in the regimental orders:

> The major desires to be acquainted in writing with the men and the companies they belong to, and as soon as possible with their charac-ters, that he may know the proper objects to encourage and those over whom it will be necessary to keep a strict hand. The officers are enjoined to visit the soldiers' quarters frequently; now and then to go round between nine and eleven o'clock at night, and not to trust to sergeants' reports. They are also requested to watch the looks of the privates and observe whether any of them were paler than usual, and that the reason might be inquired into and proper means used to restore them to their former vigour. And subalterns are told that 'a younger officer should not think he does too much.'[47]

Such attention to detail was typical of Wolfe – and, indeed, of other ambitious and talented officers who took their profession seriously – and its effect was to impress upon his men that he was hard but fair, a commanding officer whose chief concern was for their welfare.*

In March 1750, again thanks to Cumberland's patronage, Wolfe was promoted to lieutenant-colonel. He was just twenty-three, half the age at which his father had held the same rank. For most of the next five years – bar a seven-month period of leave in 1752/3 that he spent mostly in Ireland and France, visiting Versailles and meeting Louis XV's infamous mistress Madame de Pompadour – he was ever present with his battalion, transforming it into one of the most effi-cient in the service. Part of this process was to discourage his men from marrying, because, as he told his officers in 1751, 'the Service suffers by the multitude of women already in the Regiment.' Any

---

* A compilation of his regimental orders would later be posthumously published in 1768 as *General Wolfe's Instructions to Young Officers*.

who married without sanction, he warned his men, could expect 'to be proceeded against with the utmost Rigour'.[48]

In January 1755, with tension rising between British and French colonials in North America, and a full-scale war with France ever more likely, he issued a barrage of orders intended to prepare the battalion, and in particular its newest recruits, for the challenges that lay ahead. Deserters, he warned ominously, would be regarded as cowards and traitors, and could expect no mercy; yet he hoped his men would instead demonstrate courage and fidelity. To help ensure this, officers were to spare no pains with recruits' training and welfare, supervising their target practice and bayonet drill, their diet and even the company they kept.[49]

More groundbreaking, however, was the change he made to their firing drill. Since Marlborough's day, a battalion had been divided into eighteen fire units, or platoons, each one numbered and grouped into three larger 'firings'. In action the platoons fired in various choreographed patterns designed to ensure that no part of the line was left unloaded and vulnerable to attack (see p. 43). That was the theory. Wolfe's own experience of battle – particularly at Dettingen and Lauffeldt – had shown him that this system invariably broke down under pressure into an undisciplined free-for-all. He felt, moreover, that it undermined the company structure of a battalion, with soldiers commanded by unfamiliar officers and NCOs. So he ordered his men to adopt the much simpler 'alternate-fire' system, based on the Prussian model, whereby each of the ten companies now constituted a fire unit that could, if necessary, be split into two platoons or doubled up into 'grand divisions'. As the new system was 'the most simple, plain, and easy, and used by the best-disciplined troops in Europe', explained Wolfe, 'we are at all times to imitate them in that respect.'[50]

At the same time he also revised the bayonet drill – still mired in the outdated pike-handling techniques of the seventeenth century – by ordering his men to present their weapons not at the shoulder but at the hip, in the Prussian manner, so that they could be carried and used in a charge. By so doing, he converted the bayonet from an essentially defensive weapon to one that was now largely offensive, a minor tactical change that when generally adopted would make the British redcoat as feared as he had been in Marlborough's day.

A few months later – by which time news had reached Britain of the defeat of General Edward Braddock's army of regulars and colonials by a smaller force of French and their Indian allies at Monongahela in Ohio, and the south coast was gripped by fear of a French invasion – Wolfe refined his battle tactics still further. 'A cool, well leveled fire, with the pieces carefully loaded' was, he assured his men, 'far deadlier than the quickest fire in confusion'. When defending a fortified position, they were to open fire when the enemy came within effective range – about 200 yards – and to keep that up until the attackers reached the parapet, when they were to fix bayonets and 'make a bloody resistance'. In the open, they should fire 'a few rounds' and then 'charge them with their bayonets'.[51]

Wolfe had also noticed the French tendency to attack in column, rather than in line, and if that happened the wings of his battalion were to angle their fire obliquely while the centre companies kept their powder dry, having loaded their muskets with one or two extra balls. Only when the enemy was within 20 yards were they to 'fire with a good aim'. This heavy, close-range volley would, he believed, 'necessarily stop them a little', and if the fight continued it was to be finished with the bayonet. Thus did Wolfe preach in 1755 the same creed of controlled aggression – or, as his most recent biographer puts it, a 'fusion of fire and steel' – that Wellington would use to such good effect in the Peninsular and at Waterloo half a century later.[52]

Some senior generals were quick to see the worth of Wolfe's innovations, and in 1757, while training on the Isle of Wight for the ill-fated expedition to Rochefort, Sir John Mordaunt insisted that all ten of his infantry battalions adopt the 20th's alternate-fire system. 'This is truly great,' wrote the Duke of Richmond, one of Wolfe's protégés, to his brother, 'and you have no idea how much it has improved the other regiments.' But when the Duke of Cumberland, then commanding troops in Germany, got to hear of the innovations he was not impressed, telling the secretary at war that he was surprised his orders should be 'changed according to the whim and supposed improvements of every fertile genius'. Henceforth, he insisted, *all* generals were to conform exactly to Standing Orders. The 'fertile genius' he was referring to so caustically was not Mordaunt but Wolfe, his former protégé.[53]

For the humble redcoat, the brief interlude of peace in the 1750s was a welcome relief from the dangers and hardship of war. One of the best portraits of this period is the remarkable journal of Corporal William Todd of the 30th Foot. The son of a farm labourer, Todd was baptized 'Willi' in the parish of Holderness near Hull on 4 February 1724 (his exact date of birth is unknown). Few boys of similar origins would have been literate enough to keep a diary. Todd was lucky. A local benefactor had left £200 in his will for a schoolmaster 'to teach the poor Children' of Holderness, and Todd took full advantage. He became a voracious reader, good with numbers and – though not overtly religious – possessed of a strong moral compass.[54]

Todd began his military service as a volunteer with the East Riding militia during the Jacobite Rebellion of 1745–6, and continued in the regular army until 1763. For most of this period he kept a detailed and fluently written journal that gives an extraordinary insight into eighteenth-century regimental life. Of his first recruitment in early October 1745, shortly after the government's shock defeat at Prestonpans, he writes:

> Captain Grimston of Kilnwick who is raising a Company of Blues at Beverly [*sic*] came past me as I was sitting at Sutton Salts and he seeing that I was young & likely for Service ask'd me if I would inlist to which I told him I had no inclination. He told me as the rebellion was broke out so strong he greatly question'd but every one must as able to bear arms & he desired me to consider of it & enter with him.

Todd did reconsider and, two days later, enlisted at Beverley. 'We receiv'd five shillings entrance and one shilling a day, & I was quarter'd at John Tongues at the Cross Keys [inn] & we paid sixpence a day for our quarters & we receiv'd a blue coat faced with red, a cockade, hat and haversack etc.'[55] A few weeks later Bonnie Prince Charlie invaded England and it seemed that Todd and his comrades would have to fight. But the danger passed with the Jacobites' retreat from Derby, and Todd was discharged in February 1746.

Soon after, having enjoyed his brief taste of military service, he enlisted in the regular army. The date is uncertain because for the next three years he made no journal entries. When it resumes, in June 1749, he is a corporal in the 30th Foot, stationed in Kilkenny in the west of Ireland (a city, according to Todd, 'remarkable for its coals having no smoak', a 'fine fresh' river 'with plenty of salmon trouts in it', and its streets 'paved with marble').[56] Todd's early years in Ireland were relatively uneventful as the 30th was moved from one garrison town to another. But violence erupted within the regiment in November 1751 when one soldier killed another in a fight – probably over a woman – and was later hanged by the civil authorities. A year later Todd was sent back to Yorkshire with a recruiting party and told to 'hire a drummer at Hull & to recruit every market day at each place'. He eventually returned to his regiment with the new soldiers the following March.[57]

The first real excitement for Todd was in November 1753, when he and a small party of soldiers cooperated with the Royal Navy to capture a notorious smuggler who had murdered a Customs Officer, 'where by £500 was offered for the apprehending & takeing him dead or alive'. Todd recorded:

> We sailed all day along the shore till about 11 o clock at night we run into a small break betwixt two large mountains. Our guide order'd us to land & we march'd very silent about 3 miles until we came to some small cabins or huts where our guide shew'd us his hut. Our officer immediately ordere'd us to surround it & every man upon his guard & to fire at any one who should attempt to break out of the house . . . His wife & other two women hearing our guns & being very much frighten'd came out & begged their lives, which was granted them, he being in the house with four or five men more. They fired & wounded two of our men out of the windows with blunderbusses, but we set his house on fire over their heads. The men rushed out, we fired & killed two of them. Himself came out last with a loaded blunderbuss & it missing fire we shot him dead at his door & we got into the

house . . . Each man received £4.12s.* for his share. The rest the officers, guides & informers got divided amongst them.[58]

With war looming in 1755, the 30th Foot returned to England to prepare for active service by bringing its companies up to their war
establishment of five NCOs, two drummers and 70 privates. A year
later, by which time the 30th was part of a brigade camp at Chatham,
a deserter from the marines was 'shot in front of the encampment,
our whole line being under arms & each man marched singly by him
as he lay to strike a terror in the rest'. Even more brutal was the sentence given to a drummer of Todd's corps who had slit his wife's
throat with a razor for sleeping with a sergeant of the same company.
'The next day he was sent to Gaol to Rochester where he was hanged
and gibbeted.' As shocking, in its own way, was the punishment in
1757 of a private who stole a silver tankard from his billet: seven
years' transportation.[59]

* Almost three months' pay for a private soldier and a huge windfall for
Todd and his lucky companions.

9. The Seven Years War

Despite the reversal at Monongahela in Ohio, Britain did not formally declare war on France – the start of a much wider global conflict that came to be known as the Seven Years War – until 18 May 1756. The immediate cause was France's unprovoked assault a month earlier on Minorca, the Balearic isle captured by Britain in 1708 and since established as the Royal Navy's key Mediterranean possession. With the vital harbour and fortress of Port Mahon under siege from the landward side, the navy sent a squadron of ships under Vice-Admiral John Byng to defeat the French support fleet and so sever the besiegers' line of supply. But the ensuing action on 20 May was inconclusive, with neither side prepared to come to close quarters, and after it Byng made the fatal decision to withdraw to Gibraltar to refit, leaving the four battalions of the Minorca garrison to their fate. They duly surrendered on 28 June, but only after a stubborn resistance, and having gained terms that enabled them to march out of the battered fortress with drums beating and colours flying, before taking ship to Gibraltar. The loss of the island was seen as a national calamity and Byng took the blame. Court-martialled and sentenced to death, he was shot on the quarterdeck of his flagship on 14 March 1757. The reason, in Voltaire's immortal phrase: *Dans ce pays-ci, il est bon de tuer de temps en temps un amiral pour encourager les autres* ('In England, it is good, from time to time, to kill an admiral, to encourage the others').

The conflict might have been confined to trade routes and colonies but for two factors: Britain's need to protect Hanover and her government's fear that France would prove too powerful an opponent if she was allowed to concentrate solely on the maritime and colonial struggle. The solution to both problems was an alliance with at least one other major Continental power and, with Austria still smarting from Britain's betrayal in 1748, the only viable option was Frederick II's Prussia. A treaty with the Prussians was signed by the

Duke of Newcastle's government in January 1756, prompting the outraged French to make a pact of their own with the Austrians, their former enemies, who were desperate to recover Silesia. This suited Britain, as it meant the Austrian Netherlands – and therefore the Low Countries in general – was safe from French attack. Less palatable was Russia's subsequent entry into the war on the Franco-Austrian side.

Britain's preparations for war had long preceded the actual declaration, with Chelsea Pensioners called up for garrison duty in the autumn of 1755 so that fitter troops were available for field service. In December 1755 ten new regiments of infantry were raised and the following March, after another invasion scare, a Press Act was passed for the forced conscription of the unemployed poor. That same year all cavalry regiments received an extra fifteen men per troop, and an additional light troop for reconnaissance, skirmishing and outpost duty. This was part of a general move by European armies to recruit light horsemen or hussars,* and in Britain would lead to the formation of eleven regiments of light dragoons.

Units of light infantry were also being raised across the Continent. As the tactics of the volley-firing infantry of the line became ever more rigid, there was a need for more lightly equipped, faster-moving troops to get ahead of the main line and take advantage of the terrain, delay attacks and fire accurately at individual targets. Hence the Austrians recruited light regiments from the rugged frontier provinces of Hungary and Croatia, German states formed companies of Jäger (hunters skilled in the use of rifles), and the French raised Chasseurs on foot and horse. The British had had light troops of a sort at Fontenoy in the shape of the lightly equipped and agile Highlanders of the Black Watch – and would recruit two more Highland regiments in 1757 – but the first specialist unit of light infantry was raised in Pennsylvania in 1756 as a response to the defeat of regular British troops in the wilderness of Monongahela. Composed largely of German and Swiss immigrants, it was known as the Royal American Regiment (later the 60th Rifles).

* Derived from the Hungarian word *Huszar*, meaning 'freebooter' or 'raider', the name given to irregular light horsemen since the fifteenth century.

A further expansion of the British Army took place in September 1756, when fifteen regiments were authorized to raise second battalions that, two years later, became regiments in their own right as the 61st to 75th Foot.

Despite these preparations, however, public anger at the loss of Minorca and fresh disasters in India and North America – notably the loss of Calcutta to the Indian Nawab of Bengal,* and the surrender of the important outpost of Oswego on Lake Ontario to the French – eventually forced the Duke of Newcastle's government from office in November 1756. It was replaced by one headed by the Duke of Devonshire, but the new ministry's real leader was William Pitt the Elder, secretary of state for the Southern Department, whose brief included North America. Arrogant and aloof, with an imposing physical presence and the powerful voice of an actor, Pitt was a consummate politician who knew by instinct that one must 'look like the innocent flower but be the serpent under't'.[1] If he had had his way, Britain would have concentrated its war effort in the West Indies, the centre of the sugar industry. In 1775 sugar would account for more than a fifth of the value of British imports and was worth five times Britain's tobacco trade. Pitt was well aware of its importance at the heart of the Atlantic trading system – cheap trade goods to Africa, slaves to the Americas, and sugar and tobacco back to Britain – that underpinned his nation's prosperity, and once described the French sugar island of Guadeloupe as worth more than the whole of Canada, and the West Indies worth more than North America. He had a point. Even as late as 1773 the value of British imports from Jamaica was five times that produced by *all* the American colonies.

For all that, George II was never going to allow him to ignore North America's security, let alone Hanover's, and on taking office Pitt at once announced extra troops for both America and the Continent, with the Duke of Cumberland given command of the latter. The only ray of sunshine for the new regime, however, was in India,

---

* A defeat that resulted in the deaths of scores of European prisoners after they were crammed into the small and airless room used as the base's gaol, an atrocity known thereafter as the Black Hole of Calcutta.

where Robert Clive, a young employee of the Honourable East India Company, retook Calcutta and then defeated the vastly superior army of the Nawab of Bengal at Plassey on 23 June 1757, a victory that won for the Company the right to tax the indigenous population, and thus paved the way for Britain's Indian Empire and the army's long association with the Subcontinent.

Elsewhere the outlook was grim. Five days before Plassey, the seemingly invincible Prussians under Frederick the Great were defeated by the Austrians at Kolin, near Prague, leaving Cumberland to fend off the marauding French alone. He failed, and defeat at Hastenbeck in late July was followed by the Convention of Klosterzeven, which allowed for the evacuation of his army – including the Hanoverian Contingent to Denmark – and left the rest of Hanover at the mercy of the French. George II was apoplectic at this 'betrayal' and at once recalled his second son and former favourite, replacing him as commander-in-chief with Sir John Ligonier (who was ennobled as Viscount Ligonier). The disgraced Cumberland never served again.

In America, too, there were setbacks with the loss to the French of Fort William Henry, at the head of Lake George on the route from New York to Montreal, and the failure of Lord Loudoun, the commander of British forces, to retake Louisbourg thanks to the presence of superior French naval forces. Closer to home, Sir John Mordaunt's ambitious attempt to land an army that included Wolfe's 20th Foot at Rochefort on the west coast of France in September 1757 – an operation designed to relieve the pressure on America and Hanover – was called off when its hesitant commander received conflicting reports of the strength of coastal defences. Corporal Todd, whose 30th Foot was also part of the expedition, recorded: 'Our landing seems now to be quite given over, and we have a great talk of returning to England as the country here being all alarmed, & all up in arms, & we have quite demolished the Island de Aix of all its batteries, stores etc and brought off every thing that was found in it worth notice. I should be very glad orders would come for to go on board of the Thetis, man of war, again, for we are so very thick stowed here in the transport ships, & also such short allowance of provisions . . . that all our men is very uneasy.' They weighed anchor the following day.[2]

Wolfe was furious, blaming senior officers in the army and navy alike for a collective loss of nerve. 'If they would even blunder on and fight a little,' he informed his uncle, 'making some amends to their public by their courage for their want of skill; but this excessive degree of caution . . . leaves exceeding bad impressions among the troops, who, to do them justice, upon this occasion showed all the signs of spirit and good will.'[3]

Not all the troops were so forgiving. 'We certainly cut but a poor figure on our return,' wrote Private James Miller of the 15th Foot, 'and were frequently insulted in our quarters by the vulgar, as if soldiers were answerable for the conduct of their superiors. I was now pretty well cured of the romantic notions imbibed in youth.'[4] Mordaunt was eventually held to account when he was court-martialled for disobeying orders. He argued that his orders gave him scope for discretion and the court agreed, finding him not guilty. But George II made his displeasure at the verdict known when he snubbed Mordaunt at court and dropped him from his personal staff.

Though Wolfe gave evidence at the trial, he reserved his most acerbic comments for his private correspondence, describing Mordaunt and the naval leaders as 'dilatory, ignorant, irresolute'. He was, however, not sorry to have accompanied the expedition, noting that 'one may always pick up something useful from amongst the most fatal errors.' In particular that an admiral 'should anchor the transport ships and frigates as close as he can to land; that he should reconnoitre and observe it as quick as possible, and lose no time in getting the troops on shore'; and, above all, that 'pushing on smartly is the road to success.'[5] It was a tactic prescribed by all the great captains of war – from Alexander the Great onwards – but not one that Wolfe would practise in the lead-up to the operation that sealed his fame. Yet, in the short term, his involvement with the Rochefort operation did nothing to harm his career, as shown by his promotion soon after to colonel of the newly raised 2nd Battalion of the 20th Foot (2/20th).

Amidst the military disasters of the year, the reshuffled Pitt–Newcastle government passed the Militia Act in June, after much fierce debate. An attempt to ease the burden on regular troops by putting local defence on a more stable footing, it abolished the system that had been in place since the Restoration – whereby property-owners supplied men, equipment and horses at a rate equivalent to their wealth – and replaced it with one based on local taxation. Each county was to select a fixed quota of men by compulsory ballot and pay for them out of the rates. Command was given to the lord-lieutenant, a royal appointment, but was balanced by deputy lieutenants or colonels appointed from local landowners with incomes of £444 a year, or heirs of men worth double; the remaining officers owned smaller estates. Foot soldiers were aged between fifteen and fifty, but substitutes were allowed if those balloted could afford to pay them. It was this compromise of the principle of universal personal obligation that caused a wave of anti-Militia Act riots in the summer of 1757, tying down regular troops desperately needed elsewhere.

In serious danger of losing the war, Britain was rejuvenated by two of the greatest battlefield victories of the era: Rossbach and Leuthen. The architect of both was Frederick the Great, who, since his defeat at Kolin in June, had withdrawn his troops into Prussia proper, pursued by armies from Austria, France and Russia. His demise seemed certain, particularly after Austro-Hungarian troops raided his capital of Berlin in mid-October, plundering the prosperous homes on the Unter den Linden and forcing his court to flee to nearby Spandau. Yet a narrow victory over the Russians in East Prussia by one of his subordinates had given him a little breathing space, and he took full advantage. Force-marching his 21,000 men a distance of 170 miles in two weeks, he met a Franco-Imperial army of 40,000 near the village of Rossbach in Thuringia on 5 November. The over-confident French commander, the Prince of Soubise, assumed he had only to outflank Frederick to force him to withdraw. That, too, was Frederick's first instinct as the French advanced in dense columns, with no advanced guard, round the left, or southern, flank of the Prussian position. Yet instead of outflanking the Prussians, the French simply exposed their own flanks to attack, an invitation that Frederick's cavalry commander, General Friedrich von Seydlitz, was not about to refuse. As the rest of the Prussian army changed front, he charged the leading Franco-Imperial columns, stopping them in their tracks. Soon after Frederick brought the Prussian artillery and infantry into action, their combined fire shattering the enemy columns. A final charge by von Seydlitz's horse completed the rout, with at least three Franconian regiments throwing away their arms as they ran. The survivors were scattered over 40 miles of country. At a cost of just 500 casualties, Frederick had killed and wounded 5,000 of the enemy, and taken prisoner a similar number.

He had, moreover, saved Germany from French domination, and Voltaire, no less, would describe Rossbach as 'the most unimaginable and most complete rout in history . . . The defeats of Agincourt, Crécy and Poitiers were not as humiliating.'[6] When the news reached Britain, Pitt's government at once voted more subsidies for Prussia and authorized Duke Ferdinand of Brunswick, a former Prussian general who had had some success against the French, to take command of the Hanoverian army.

Frederick the Great, meanwhile, was still faced with the Austrians, who, since their victory at Kolin, had overrun half of Silesia and captured Breslau. Pausing for a week to refit, he set out from Leipzig with 13,000 men on 13 November and, with his army again displaying superhuman traits of endurance and organization, marched a further 170 miles in two weeks, with just one day's rest. His eve-of-battle address to his officers at Parchwitz in Silesia was reminiscent of Cumberland's at Culloden. 'We must beat the enemy,' he told them, 'or bury ourselves before his guns . . . If there is one or other of you who is frightened to share these dangers with me, he can take his leave without suffering the slightest reproach.'[7]

Frederick's rapid advance caught the Austrians by surprise: they had assumed that after Rossbach he would go into winter quarters. Instead, reinforced by local troops to a total strength of 39,000 men, he made straight for the Austrian position near the village of Leuthen, where 66,000 men were drawn up in a defensive formation that stretched for 5½ miles. It was the perfect opportunity for him to use his 'oblique order' of attack. He explained: 'You refuse one wing to the enemy and strengthen the one that is to attack. With the latter you do your utmost against one wing of the enemy, which you take in the flank. An Army of 100,000 men taken in flank may be beaten by 30,000 in a very short time.'[8]

So it proved at Leuthen. At dawn on 5 December, Frederick's advance guard drove an Austrian infantry force out of the village of Borne and captured 800 men. From the village Frederick could see the whole of the enemy. Sending some cavalry in pursuit of the beaten Austrian infantry, he wheeled the main body of his army to the right under cover of a rise in the ground. One observer wrote: 'It is impossible to witness a more beautiful sight; all the heads of the columns were parallel to each other, and in exact distances to form line, and the divisions marched with such precision, that they seemed to be at a review, ready to wheel into line in a moment.'[9]

As Frederick's army vanished from sight, the Austrian general assumed he was in full retreat. A little after noon, however, the head of the Prussian army reappeared in front of the Austrian left wing, which had earlier been weakened to strengthen the threatened Austrian right. The officer in command of the left sent an urgent request for reinforcements. But it was too late. At 1 p.m. Frederick's vanguard attacked with infantry, cavalry and artillery, and within half an hour the Austrian left wing had been routed. Frederick now took the Austrian centre in the flank, capturing Leuthen after a hard fight.

At 4 p.m., with the light failing, the Austrian general ordered his cavalry to charge the flank of the Prussian infantry. But in attempting to do so the Austrian horse was surprised by a concealed force of Prussian cavalry and driven from the field. The cavalry then wheeled to the right and charged the Austrian infantry from the rear, while infantry attacked their left flank from Leuthen. The Austrian line collapsed and the defeat became a rout.

The Austrians suffered 10,000 casualties, with a further 21,000 men, 116 guns, 51 colours and 4,000 wagons captured. Prussian casualties were 6,000 killed and wounded. The battle resulted in the recapture of Silesia and the establishment of Prussia as the most formidable military power in Europe. It also sealed Frederick the Great's reputation as one of the finest battlefield commanders in history.

Inspired by Prussia's victories, Ferdinand of Brunswick went on the offensive in Hanover, surprising the French, who had expected him to enter winter quarters. By January 1758 he had liberated the principality and driven the invaders back across the Rhine. Six weeks later he followed, inflicting more defeats on the French and tying up 80,000 troops – twice the size of his own army – who might have tipped the balance elsewhere. Thanks to Frederick and Brunswick's superb generalship, Pitt's strategy of keeping the French occupied on the Continent was working. And at relatively little cost to the military effort elsewhere: it was not until September 1758, for example, that Brunswick's German army (including, of course, mercenaries in British pay) was reinforced by a British Contingent of five regiments of foot and fourteen squadrons of horse.

By this time the situation in North America had taken a decided turn for the better thanks to the efforts of Pitt and the new commander-in-chief of the British Army, Lord Ligonier. Pitt's chief contribution was to rally the American colonies for a new offensive against the French by mingling appeals to patriotism with the promise of financial reimbursement. But it was Ligonier who devised the new strategy of simultaneous attacks by land and sea, using a mixture of regular and colonial troops, against the three centres of French power: Fort Duquesne, Montreal and Quebec. And though the theatre commander was the unexceptional General James Abercromby, the 51-year-old successor to Lord Loudoun, three of his four senior officers were relatively young and of proven ability: Major-General Jeffery Amherst, forty-two; Brigadier-General Viscount Howe, thirty-two; and Brigadier-General James Wolfe, thirty-one. The exception was John Forbes, the third brigadier-general, who was fifty and had served as Cumberland's quartermaster-general. Wolfe's protégé Richmond applauded these 'extraordinary rises', which enabled 'people of merit' to exercise command 'in the prime of their age'.[10] It is ironic, however, that the architect of this meritocracy, Ligonier, was a septuagenarian field marshal, albeit a sprightly bachelor whose four mistresses had a combined age of just fifty-eight.

The success of the operations led by these young tyros in 1758 was mixed. Amherst, ably supported by Wolfe and a naval squadron under Vice-Admiral Edward Boscawen, did indeed capture Louisbourg in July after a risky amphibious landing in which Private James Miller of the 15th Foot received the baptism of fire denied him at

Rochefort. The concealed defenders 'preserved their fire', he recalled, 'until our boats got near the shore, when such a tremendous one commenced from their great guns, and small arms, as I have never since beheld'.[11] Fortunately a group of light infantry got ashore on a narrow strand and, observing this from his cutter, Wolfe followed them with the rest of his 3,000-strong assault brigade made up of grenadiers, light infantry, Highlanders and New England irregulars known as 'Rangers'. The fortress fell after a six-week siege, with one officer praising Wolfe's role as 'general, soldier, and engineer'. He added: 'He commanded, fought and built batteries and I need not add has acquir'd all the glory of our expedition.'[12] The rank and file was no less admiring of Wolfe. 'Oh, he was a noble fellow!' wrote a grenadier sergeant in Fraser's Highlanders. 'And he was so kind and attentive to the men, that they would have gone through fire and water to have served him.'[13]

Wolfe himself was far too modest to take all the credit, instead ascribing the victory to inter-service cooperation. 'For the first time,' he wrote on 28 July, 'the fleet and army have agreed to work together. The Admiral has given us all possible aid of marines, sailors, boats, cannon, ammunition, and every thing that was ask'd or requir'd: and I do believe that if the enterprise had been four times as difficult, our union would have carried it thro.'[14] There the cooperation ended. Wolfe was all for continuing on up the St Lawrence River; but Boscawen would go no further, insisting it was too late in the year to attempt an assault on Quebec.

The other expeditions did not fare so well. Abercromby was in charge of the main land invasion force, and by June had assembled an army of 15,000 British and colonial troops at the head of Lake George, part of the long inland waterway that connected New York to Montreal via the Hudson River. Barring his path, beyond a 5-mile stretch of rapids, was the French fort of Ticonderoga at the southern end of Lake Champlain, garrisoned by 4,000 troops under the Marquis de Montcalm. To make up for his numerical deficiency, Montcalm had cut down trees to clear his field of fire, and formed barriers from logs and sharpened stakes.

It was a daunting challenge, and one made more difficult still by the loss of Abercromby's right-hand man, the brilliant Brigadier-

General Lord Howe, in a skirmish as the army probed towards the fort on 6 July. Like Wolfe, Howe was a superb trainer and motivator of troops, a man who led by example; but he was also a born diplomat who could charm both Britons and colonials alike. Wolfe, on hearing rumours of his death, lamented: 'If this . . . be true, there is an end of the expedition, for he was the spirit of that army, and the very best officer in the King's service.'[15]

Wolfe was right. Lacking Howe's steadying influence, and fearful that French reinforcements were en route, Abercromby ordered a frontal attack on the fort on 8 July. Wave after wave was beaten back, until, in desperation, Abercromby committed his reserve of the 55th Foot and the 42nd Highlanders. Three times the men of the 42nd attacked, and three times they were repulsed, losing more than half their soldiers and two thirds of their officers in the process. In all, 314 officers and men were killed, and a further 333 wounded, a casualty rate so high that Pitt, after hearing of the Highlanders' heroism, announced to Parliament that henceforth the 42nd would be known as the Royal Highland Regiment, as a testimony of 'His Majesty's satisfaction and approbation of its extraordinary courage, loyalty and exemplary conduct'. In addition, the regiment was ordered to raise a second battalion, which would, Pitt assured his fellow MPs, 'conquer for you in every part of the world'.[16] The third expedition – Brigadier-General Forbes's attempt to capture Fort Duquesne – would also run into problems. The slow and methodical advance from eastern Pennsylvania, using a route to the north of General Braddock's, went smoothly enough, with Forbes's 7,000-strong force cutting a wagon road over the Allegheny Mountains (later known as Forbes Road) and building forts en route to serve as supply depots. But disaster struck on 15 September, when a reconnaissance force was surprised and defeated by French troops and their Indian allies in a mini rerun of Monongahela. So unnerved was Forbes that he postponed the expedition until the following spring, only to change his mind on hearing that the Indians of the Ohio Valley had agreed to abandon the French, thus causing the partial evacuation of Fort Duquesne. He ordered an immediate three-pronged assault on the weakened garrison. But when his lead troops arrived on 25 November, they found the French gone and the fort razed to the ground. Forbes ordered a new one to be built and renamed it Fort Pitt, in honour of the prime minister. He also named the nearby settlement Pittsborough (modern Pittsburgh), but it would be his final contribution to history. He fell ill soon after and was evacuated to Philadelphia, where he died in March 1759.

10.   Quebec

With no more operations planned that year, Wolfe returned to Britain on leave in November 1758, much to the irritation of Lord Barrington, the secretary at war, who felt he had acted without authority. Wolfe's defence was typically forthright, telling the secretary that his offer to take reinforcements to Abercromby had not been taken up, and as the alternative was languishing at Halifax under an officer recently promoted over his head (Brigadier-General Lawrence), he had thought it 'much better to get into the way of service, and out of the way of being insulted'.[1] The service he had in mind was in Germany under Brunswick, whose British Contingent included his former regiment, the 20th Foot. But Lord Ligonier was adamant: there were no suitable vacancies and the king would not allow anyone to serve in Germany as a volunteer. So Wolfe switched his attention back to Canada, the only other major theatre, telling Ligonier he was ready to return 'upon the first order'.[2]

That order came in mid-December, when Pitt offered him the command of the forthcoming Quebec expedition with the temporary rank of major-general, while Amherst – who had recently replaced the demoralized Abercromby as commander-in-chief in Canada – mounted a simultaneous assault on Montreal via Lake George. Wolfe accepted, on condition that he could choose his senior officers, but not without having reservations. 'In short,' he told Amherst, 'they have put this heavy task upon my shoulders, and I find nothing encouraging in the undertaking.'[3]

From his experience of Louisbourg – which, on paper, was a more straightforward operation than Quebec, and yet it had come within an ace of disaster – Wolfe knew only too well the risk of failure. He may also have questioned his suitability for a task that, as his first independent command, required mastery not only of battlefield tactics but also of campaign strategy. 'I am to act a greater part in this business than I wished or desired,' he wrote candidly to his uncle. 'I shall do my best, and leave the rest to fortune, as perforce we must when there are not the most commanding abilities.'[4]

Given that it would take time for Wolfe to reach America, however, Lord Amherst was instructed by Pitt to do the necessary groundwork, ensuring that the troops, supplies and transport were concentrated at Louisbourg in time for the projected start date of 7 May. Wolfe was told his force would consist of 12,000 men: ten infantry battalions, a powerful train of siege and field artillery manned by 300 Royal Artillerymen, and 600 American Rangers. Amherst would have slightly more men – 14,000 – for his own simultaneous attack, though a significant proportion of them would be colonials. He was ordered to advance either via Crown Point, at the foot of Lake Champlain, or La Galette, on the St Lawrence opposite Lake Ontario, or by both routes at the same time if that was possible. His objective was Montreal or Quebec, 'or both of the said places successively', either by dividing his forces or using them in a single body. With further to go on foot, he would start on 1 May.[5]

The plan was for these two hammer blows to strike French Canada – or New France as it was known – simultaneously, so forcing the defenders to dissipate their strength. Wolfe knew that he might not be able to capture Quebec on his own; but what he could guarantee, he told Amherst in a letter of 29 December, was to 'find employment for a good part of the force of [French] Canada', so smoothing Amherst's advance on Montreal. If that happened, there was every chance they could 'meet and unite for [the enemy's] destruction'.[6]

Wolfe's request to appoint his senior staff officers had been granted. But of the three brigadier-generals he asked for, only two were confirmed: Robert Monckton, son of the 1st Viscount Galway, who was appointed senior brigadier and Wolfe's second-in-command; and James Murray, son of a Scottish peer. Both were, like Wolfe, in their thirties and hugely experienced in war. What Wolfe could not know, however, was that Murray, the brother of a notorious Jacobite, had asked to serve under Amherst, and was mortified when he was assigned to the Quebec expedition. The third brigadier, not on

Wolfe's list, was 34-year-old George Townshend, another aristocrat, but one whose only knowledge of combat was on the staff (he had served as Cumberland's aide-de-camp at Lauffeldt). A difficult, irascible character with a tendency to fall out with his superiors, he owed his appointment to his family's close political connection to Pitt. But if Wolfe was disappointed that his third choice – Colonel Ralph Burton – had not been confirmed, he did not show it, instead telling his uncle that all three brigadiers were 'men of great spirit'.[7]

Given the amphibious nature of the operation, however, the key to its success was Wolfe's relationship with its naval chief, Vice-Admiral Sir Charles Saunders. Modest but highly proficient, a man who had accompanied George Anson (now first lord of the Admiralty) on his epic circumnavigation of the globe in the 1740s, Saunders was the ideal partner for the talented but outspoken Wolfe, who described him, after sailing across the Atlantic in his flagship, as a 'brilliant, brave officer'.[8] He was less impressed by Saunders's second-in-command, Rear-Admiral Philip Durell, a veteran of the Louisbourg assault who he felt was too cautious for such a risky undertaking.

With ice barring their entry to Louisbourg, Wolfe and Saunders diverted to Halifax in Nova Scotia, arriving on 30 April. There Wolfe was dismayed to discover Durell's squadron still at anchor, though the rear-admiral had been ordered to waste no time pushing up the St Lawrence River as far as the Île-de-Bic. Durell's excuse was that he needed extra troops, and once these were provided he left on 3 May. But the incident did nothing to dissuade Wolfe that Durell lacked aggression. Nor was his hesitation inconsequential: while Durell dallied in Halifax, more than twenty French frigates and merchantmen navigated the broken ice in the Gulf of St Lawrence to reach Quebec with vital supplies and ammunition.

Wolfe finally reached Louisbourg on 15 May, though ice and fog continued to delay the operation. He used the time to familiarize himself with his troops, most of whom had served with him at Louisbourg. They included Private Richard Humphrys of the 28th Foot, one of four battalions left to garrison the shattered fort during the winter, who recorded in his journal the fatigue that he and his comrades felt as they repaired 'the breaches we had made with our cannon

and bombs'.[9] Humphrys's career shatters the myth that the lower
ranks of the mid-Georgian army could never aspire to be officers.
The keeper of a highly readable journal from when he first joined
the 28th in 1757, he would rise in just six years to the rank of sergeant. It would take a further thirteen years, and the outbreak of the
American War of Independence, for him to receive his commission as
an ensign. But by 1779 he had been promoted again to lieutenant in
the 28th, and his captaincy – in the Bengal Engineers – would follow
in 1786.[10]

Humphrys was far from unique, though a more typical route for
promotion from the ranks was bravery in the field. In March 1760, for
example, a Sergeant John Fraser of the 48th Foot was promoted to
ensign without purchase 'having distinguished himself' in the Quebec campaign. Like Humphrys, he also became a captain. Another
Sergeant Fraser, this time an Alexander of the Royal Regiment, was
appointed quartermaster of a newly raised troop of light dragoons
for being the first into the breach during the storming of the El
Morro fortress at Havana in 1762. Yet the pugnacious Fraser would
meet a grisly end a year later when he was hanged for running
through a corporal who was sleeping with his wife.[11]

Though most of Wolfe's regular soldiers were British, they included
a number of American volunteers. One in eight soldiers of the 47th
and 48th Foot, for example, had been born in America, thus giving
these regular battalions a familiarity with local conditions that would
serve them well. The 58th Foot was more homogeneously British,
but with men from a variety of civilian occupations, including agricultural labourers, weavers, tin miners and even a harpsichord-maker.
Even more remarkably it contained a corporal – John Johnson of
Huntingdon – who had been a 'writing-master' and whose vivid
memoir of the campaign would put many an officer's recollections to
shame.

Wolfe, meanwhile, was learning as much as he could about Quebec and its defences from his chief engineer, Major Patrick Mackellar,
who had been held captive in the town after his capture at Oswego
in 1756. The town itself was situated on a rocky prominence on the
left (or north) bank of the St Lawrence River, with its east flank

protected by a tributary, the Saint-Charles. Its river and landward defences, said Mackellar, were patchy and incomplete. Though the plan that accompanied his memorandum was based on an out-of-date French map, and failed to include a more recent wall studded with bastions, the overall logic was correct: the defences were inadequate and any besieging force that managed to establish itself upon the high ground to the south-west of the town – known as the Heights of Abraham – would be impossible to resist. The obvious move, there-fore, would be to land troops on the left bank, or 'town', side of the river, yet Mackellar doubted whether such an operation was possible above the Saint-Charles River because the St Lawrence was too shal-low. Much better, he said, to set up camp 4 miles downstream on a large island known as the Île-d'Orléans from where they could launch their attack. Wolfe accepted this, and outlined his strategy in a letter to his uncle of 19 May:

> The town of Quebec is poorly fortified, but the ground round about it is rocky. To invest the place, and cut off all communication with the colony [upstream to Montreal], it will be necessary to encamp with our right to the river St Lawrence, and our left to the river St Charles [on the Heights of Abraham] . . . It is the business of our navy to be masters of the river, both above and below the town. If I find the enemy is strong, audacious, and well commanded, I shall proceed with the utmost caution and circumspection, giving Mr Amherst time to use his superiority. If they are timid, weak, and ignorant, we shall push them with more vivacity, that we may be able before the summer is gone to assist the Commander-in-Chief. I reckon we shall have a smart action at the passage of the river St Charles unless we can steal a detachment up the river St Lawrence, and land them three, four, five miles, or more, above the town, and get time to entrench so strongly they won't care to attack.[12]

But this last move would be made only after he had landed on the Île-d'Orléans and assessed local conditions.

By now the French authorities had received word from the relief ships that Wolfe was on his way and were bickering over how best to defend Canada. The Marquis de Vaudreuil, the governor-general, wanted to occupy the many frontier outposts so that the British were forced to divide their forces and fight on ground that favoured the Canadian militia and their Indian allies; Montcalm, commander of the regular French forces and victor of Ticonderoga, preferred to concentrate his force in the St Lawrence Valley. Both petitioned the French king, but Montcalm won the day thanks to his excellent contacts at court and the prestige of his recent victory. So as Wolfe prepared to descend the St Lawrence, Montcalm was busy fortifying the Beauport shoreline that stretched 6 miles north of the Saint-Charles to the Montmorency Falls. As well as constructing a long chain of trenches and redoubts, his men built a fortified bridge-of-boats across the Saint-Charles, and blocked its mouth with a boom protected by two beached vessels bristling with cannon. They also converted some of the recently arrived vessels into fireships, and assembled small gunboats and floating batteries to protect the approaches to the town. Yet Montcalm failed to fortify the heights opposite Quebec, on the south side of the St Lawrence, a strong-point that would have prevented the British from passing above the town and threatening its weaker, landward defences. Why? Partly because it was vulnerable to a landing further downstream; and partly because the French had long believed that Quebec's best defence was the treacherous St Lawrence. It was felt to be particularly unnavigable for warships upstream of Quebec – Wolfe's preferred point of assault – where, in any case, the shoreline was for miles an unbroken line of cliffs.

To guard the town, Montcalm had a formidable force of 1,200 veteran regulars, 600 local professionals (from the Compagnies Franches de la Marine), 900 Indian warriors and 10,000 local militiamen. Though amateurs, and unlikely to stand against British redcoats in open battle, the last were mostly expert marksmen who would be hard to dislodge from a good defensive position. Montcalm's total force therefore, including naval gunners, was more than 14,000.

Wolfe, as he complained to his uncle, had even fewer troops than he had been promised. 'The fleet consists of twenty-two sail of the line and many frigates,' he wrote on 19 May, 'the army of 9,000; in England it is called 12,000. We have ten battalions, three companies of

Grenadiers, some Marines (if the Admiral can spare them), and six new-raised companies of North American Rangers – not complete and the worst soldiers in the universe; a great train of artillery, plenty of provisions, tools, and implements of all sorts.'

One of Wolfe's battalions was a corps of light infantry under Colonel William Howe, brother of the brigadier-general killed near Ticonderoga and a man who had served under Wolfe in the 20th Foot. The first unit of regular light infantry – known as the 80th Regiment of Light Armed Foot – had been raised in early 1758 at his own expense by Lieutenant-Colonel Thomas Gage of the 44th Foot to provide specialist troops who could cope with the particular demands of North American bush-fighting. Within months, Amherst had formed his own 'body of light infantry, from the different corps to act as irregulars'. Each regular battalion provided thirty or forty men: units with American service would supply 'such as have been most accustomed to the woods, and are good marksmen', while those recently arrived from Britain were to give 'active marchers, and men that are expert at firing ball'. Such was the success of this corps during the successful siege of Louisbourg that, once the campaign was over, light companies were formed in all regular battalions in North America. Modifications to their uniform included replacing the tricorne hat with a cap, shortening the tunic and removing regimental lace. It was these light companies that Howe had joined into a separate corps of light infantry for Wolfe's forthcoming Quebec campaign.[13]

It would be the only British operation in North America during the Seven Years War that was outnumbered by its foe, an ominous handicap of which Wolfe was blissfully unaware. He assumed the defending force would be of a similar size to his own, and that 'if no accident happens in the river, I hope we shall succeed.' As to his personal safety, he assured his uncle he would take 'all proper care' unless 'it becomes a duty to do otherwise'. He added ominously: 'I never put myself unnecessarily in the way of danger. [But] young troops need to be encouraged.'[14]

On 4 June, the great armada of 22 warships and 119 transport and supply vessels finally set sail from Louisbourg, reaching the Île-de-Bic,

150 miles downstream from Quebec, two weeks later. Rear-Admiral Durell, determined to prove Wolfe wrong, had already covered a further 100 miles to the Île-aux-Coudres, where he dispatched four of his ships even closer to Quebec. They were guided by James Cook, the son of a Yorkshire farm manager and master of the 64-gun *Pembroke* (a man who as Captain Cook would find fame and death exploring the Pacific), and a Dutch engineer called Samuel Holland who together – using existing French charts, plumb lines and Holland's 'plane table'* – surveyed a notoriously dangerous stretch of the river known as The Traverse. Beyond it was the Île-d'Orléans that, thanks to their laborious work, the lead division of the main fleet reached on 25 June. Two days later, the first troops landed on the south shore of this 20-mile-long island – described by one officer as 'a delightful country' with its stone farmhouses and well-cultivated land.[15] The initial phase of Wolfe's plan was complete.

That same day, accompanied by Mackellar and an escort of Rangers, Wolfe walked to the western end of the island, from where, through his telescope, he could see the clifftop fortress of Quebec, 4 miles across the bay. What particularly caught his attention, however, was the sight of Montcalm's formidable chain of redoubts and trenches that now extended the full 6 miles of the Beauport shore from the Saint-Charles River to the Montmorency Falls. This, as he had told his uncle, was where he had hoped to land before fighting a 'smart action at the passage of the river St Charles'. Now that that was no longer possible, the best he could hope for was to land below Montmorency and fight his way through the bulk of Montcalm's army just to reach the town's main defences. His first move, he decided, would be to capture Point Lévis on the south shore, from where he could bombard Quebec and, in turn, protect the fleet from a French barrage.

Brigadier-General Monckton duly occupied the point with four battalions and some light troops on 29 June, having crossed from the

---

* A surveying instrument for direct plotting in the field, consisting of a circular drawing-board mounted horizontally on a tripod, and with a sighting device pivoted over its centre.

island under the cover of darkness. But his fitness for command was called into question two days later when he responded to the arrival of French gunboats by parading his whole command on the beach, thus incurring needless casualties from the inevitable French bombardment. Wolfe responded by ordering new defensive redoubts and constructing a battery of cannon and mortars at Pointe-aux-Père less than a mile from Quebec.

From that vantage point, a British volunteer described Quebec's upper town in a letter to a friend as

> a fortress of vast strength, overlooking both the river, city, and adjacent country. At the foot of this mountain, to the N.E. stands the lower town, defended by several batteries, equal with the surface of the water, and so situated, that shipping in passing the town, must come within the distance of 4 or 500 yards; but these two or three ships might easily silence, were they not cover'd by formidable batteries from the upper town, of forty-two and twenty-four pounders, which, though scarcely more than point-blank from the middle of the river, enjoy so superior a situation, as to defy the cannon of our shipping.[16]

When the battery at Pointe-aux-Père was ready, on 13 July, Wolfe ordered a bombardment of the city that over the next six weeks would fire '3,000 bombs and 22,000 shot', destroying more than 500 houses and the 'whole eastern Part of the lower Town'.[17] But the barrage alone was never going to force the French to submit.

Wolfe knew he would have to take the town by direct assault, and on 3 July had consulted with Admiral Saunders as to the best means of doing this. They both agreed that a landing above the town was preferable, given the strength of the defences below it, and resolved to make the attempt. The plan was to land a force at Saint-Michel, 3 miles upstream of Quebec, while a heavy bombardment was opened from the Pointe-aux-Père and Townshend's brigade made a diversionary landing below the Montmorency Falls. But at the last moment Wolfe had second thoughts and cancelled the operation.

He later claimed the French had second-guessed him by bringing 'artillery and a mortar (which being so near to Quebec, they could

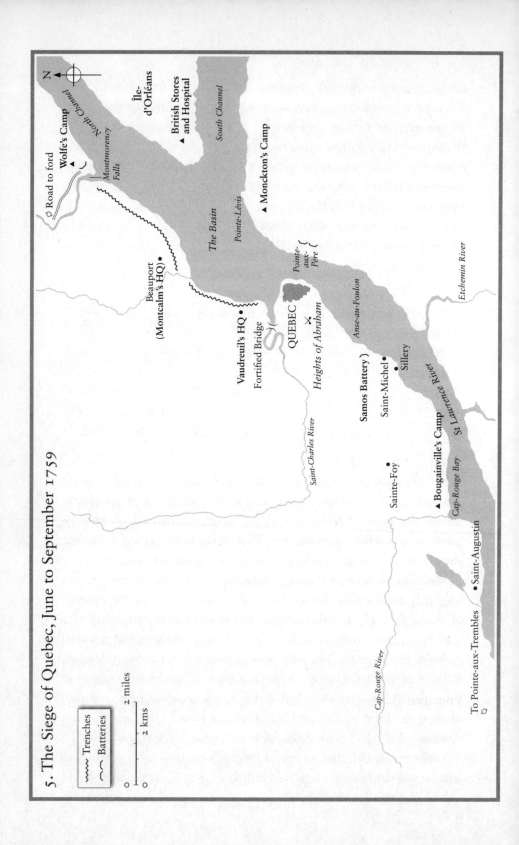

5. The Siege of Quebec, June to September 1759

Trenches
Batteries

0   2 kms
0   2 miles

N

Île-d'Orléans

British Stores and Hospital ▲

South Channel

▲ Monckton's Camp

Pointe-Lévis

The Basin

Pointe-aux-Père

North Channel

Wolfe's Camp ▲

Montmorency Falls

⚐ Road to ford

Beauport (Montcalm's HQ) ●

Vaudreuil's HQ ●

Fortified Bridge

QUEBEC

Heights of Abraham

Saint-Charles River

Anse-au-Foulon

Samos Battery

Saint-Michel ●

Sillery ●

Bougainville's Camp ▲

St Laurence River

Etchemin River

Cap-Rouge Bay

Sainte-Foy ●

Cap-Rouge River

Saint-Augustin ●

To Pointe-aux-Trembles ⚐

increase as they pleased) to play on the shipping'.[18] He also cited his poor communications, the poor seaworthiness of the rafts he hoped to use to ferry his men, and the lack of support he felt he was getting from the navy. Either way, this hesitancy was uncharacteristic of Wolfe and flew in the face of the views he had expressed so vehemently after the failure of the Rochefort expedition: namely that 'pushing on smartly is the road to success.' Was the responsibility of supreme command getting to him? It would seem so. Certainly his relationship with one of his brigadiers, probably Townshend, was showing signs of strain. On 7 July, for example, he recorded in his journal that a 'difference of opinion upon a point termed slight and insignificant' had led to Wolfe being threatened with a 'parliamentary inquiry into his conduct for not consulting an inferior officer and seeming to disregard his sentiment!'[19]

Two days later, with his attention now firmly fixed on the north shore downstream of Quebec, he landed with Townshend's brigade to the right of the Montmorency Falls. He knew the ground was higher there than on the French side of the Montmorency, he reported to Pitt, and that there was a 'ford below the fall, which may be passed for some hours in the latter part of the ebb'. He also had hopes of crossing higher up the Montmorency, 'so as to fight the Marquis de Montcalm upon terms of less disadvantage than directly attacking his entrenchments'. But he shelved that idea when his scouts reported that the opposite bank of the ford in question, 3 miles upriver, was 'entrenched, and so steep and so woody, that it was to no purpose to attempt a passage there'.[20]

Instead the French brought the fight to Wolfe by sending Indians across the Montmorency to harass British working parties in the woods above the falls. Only a day after the landing, a company of Rangers was surprised in the thick undergrowth and 'had so many killed and wounded as to be disabled for the rest of the campaign'. Fourteen Rangers were killed and scalped before the Indians were 'driven off by the nearest troops'.[21] Such bloody encounters were commonplace in the weeks ahead, and Corporal John Johnson of the 58th Foot reckoned that service at Montmorency was the hardest and most dangerous of the campaign, with many 'sharp skirmishes'.[22]

While his men camped in tents, Wolfe set up his headquarters in a small house where – according to the provisions of a will he made en route to Quebec – he must have lived in some style. Among the items he bequeathed to Admiral Saunders and his successor in command were a 'light service of plate', 'camp equipage, kitchen furniture, table linen, wine and provisions'. To his personal servant François he left 'half of my clothes and linen here', while his three footmen were to 'divide the rest between them'.[23] Hardship on campaign was clearly not to Wolfe's liking.

Yet he never lost sight of his mission and, as early as 12 July, was determined to attack the French position at Beauport with all three of his brigades. Once the floating batteries and rafts had been constructed, the Montmorency camp properly fortified and the artillery made ready, he told Monckton, 'wind and tide permitting we will attack them.'[24] This did not prevent him, however, from exploring all possibilities. On the night of 18/19 July he sent a 50-gun warship and three smaller vessels upriver of Quebec. The following day, accompanied by the engineer Samuel Holland, he made a personal reconnaissance of the upper river on one of these boats as far as the Chaudière inlet on the south shore, 2 miles upstream of Saint-Michel. It convinced him that he had been wrong to postpone the Saint-Michel operation, which at the time would 'probably have succeeded', and that an unguarded smaller cove on the north shore closer to Quebec, known as the Anse-au-Foulon, was a potential landing point of 'last resort' if all other plans failed. In the meantime Holland was to conceal his intentions from 'each and everyone', and to encourage the belief that a landing at Foulon was not feasible.[25]

Although the reconnaissance led to a temporary resurrection of the Saint-Michel scheme, it was postponed a second time when Admiral Saunders warned that it would be difficult to get enough flat-bottomed boats for the operation past Quebec in one piece. 'It seemed to me so hazardous,' wrote Wolfe to Pitt, 'that I thought it best to desist.'[26] But he did authorize a force under Colonel Guy Carleton, his adjutant-general, to gather intelligence from the village of Pointe-aux-Trembles on the north shore, a good 20 miles upstream of Quebec, on 20 July. He reported: 'The Colonel was fired upon by a body of Indians the moment he landed; but they were soon dispersed and driven into the woods; he searched for magazines but to no purpose; brought off some prisoners and returned with little loss.'[27] All the civilian prisoners – chiefly women and children – were delivered safely to Quebec under a flag of truce.

Still Wolfe was no closer to achieving his objective and, in desperation, he authorized an assault on the extreme left of the main French position at Beauport. He explained to Pitt:

> I now resolved to take the first opportunity which presented itself of attacking the enemy, though posted to great advantage, and everywhere prepared to receive us. As the men of war cannot for sufficient depth of water come near enough to the enemy's entrenchments [at Beauport] to annoy them in the least, the Admiral had prepared two transports, drawing but little water, which upon occasion could be run aground to favour a descent. With the help of these vessels, which I understood could be carried by the tide close in shore, I proposed to make myself master of a detached redoubt near to the water's edge, and whose situation appeared to be out of musket shot of the entrenchments upon the hill; if the enemy supported this detached piece it would necessarily bring on an engagement, what we most wished for; and if not, I should have it in my power to examine their situation as to be able to determine where best to attack them.[28]

In the above report, written for Pitt after the event, Wolfe deliberately underplayed the scale of the operation that was, in its final form, a full-blown assault on the main enemy position. The plan, as he relayed it to his senior officers on the eve of the assault, was for the initial assault on the French redoubt closest to the falls to be made by all thirteen companies of grenadiers, backed by 200 Royal Americans. If it went well, they would be supported by the rest of Monckton's brigade, waiting offshore in boats, and the two brigades at Montmorency – Townshend's and Murray's – who would cross the ford below the falls at low tide. The combined army would then storm the French trenches. Meanwhile troops would be sent on foot to the ford higher up the Montmorency

River, and in boats towards Saint-Michel, in the hope of dispersing the defending forces while the batteries at Montmorency opened fire on the French camp.

The operation began at 10 a.m. on 31 July, a burning hot day with a light wind, when the British batteries at Montmorency, supported by the 50-gun *Centurion* in the Basin, opened fire on the left of the French position, including the westernmost redoubt. But the attack soon ran into problems: the two armed transports – one of which contained Wolfe himself – grounded much further offshore than intended, so that their covering fire could not reach both the redoubt and the trenches beyond; and from there Wolfe could see that the redoubt was within effective musket range of the trenches above it, and was thus 'too much commanded to be kept without very great loss'.[29] Meanwhile Wolfe's transport came under cannon fire so heavy that he was 'no less than three times struck with splinters' and 'had my stick knocked out of my hand'.[30]

A cautious – indeed sensible – commander would have cancelled the operation then and there. But Wolfe had already postponed a number of previous assaults and, with his senior commanders beginning to lose confidence in him, was determined to press on. 'As the enemy seemed in confusion' from the Montmorency bombardment, he explained to Pitt, 'and we were prepared for action, I thought it a proper time to make an attempt upon their entrenchment.'[31]

But first he had to wait for the tide to ebb sufficiently for the troops to land, and it was not until 4 p.m. that the assault boats were ordered to make their final approach. As they did so, they grounded on a sandbar, causing Wolfe to halt Townshend's and Murray's advance over the ford while the boats were refloated and Wolfe himself led a reconnaissance of the beach to find an alternative place to land. 'We took one flat-bottomed boat with us to make the experiment,' he recalled, 'and as soon as we had found a fit part of the shore, the troops were ordered to embark, thinking it not too late for the attempt.'[32]

The grenadiers and Royal Americans had been ordered to form themselves into four 'distinct bodies', but not to attack the trenches until their supports from Monckton's brigade had landed and Townshend's and Murray's troops had crossed the ford. Instead, according to Private Richard Humphrys of the 28th Foot, they at once 'began to push up the banks, not waiting for the battalions that was crossing the fall, to come to their assistance, thinking they themselves would drive all before them'.[33]

One explanation for this impetuous advance is that two officers – one from the Royal Americans, one a grenadier, who had duelled the previous day – were competing to be first into the French trenches.[34] Whatever the truth, the Canadian militamen took full advantage, waiting until the exhausted Britons and Americans were in range before opening fire with musketry and canister. A sergeant-major of grenadiers recalled: 'As soon as we landed we fixed our bayonets and beat our Grenadier's March, and so advanced on; during all this time their cannon play'd very briskly on us; but their small-arms, in their trenches, lay cool 'till they were sure of their mark; then they pour'd their small-shot like showers of hail, which caus'd our brave Grenadiers to fall very fast.'[35]

Wolfe explained to Pitt what happened next:

The Grenadiers were checked by the enemy's first fire, and obliged to shelter themselves in or about the redoubt, which the French abandoned upon their approach. In this situation they continued for some time, unable to form under so hot a fire and having many gallant officers wounded, who, careless of their persons, had been solely intent upon their duty. I saw the absolute necessity of calling them off that they might form themselves behind Brigadier Monckton's corps, which was now landed, and drawn up on the beach, in extreme good order.[36]

Townshend, too, had crossed the ford and was in a position to attack. But Wolfe chose to cancel the whole operation. 'It was near night,' he explained to Pitt, 'and a sudden storm came on, and the tide began to make, so I thought it most advisable not to persevere in so difficult an attack, lest, in case of a repulse, the retreat of Brigadier Townshend's corps might be hazardous and uncertain.' Had the various setbacks not happened, he added, he felt certain that Townshend's men would have gained the trenches, not least because the British artillery 'had a great effect upon the enemy's left'. As it was, they were forced to leave a number of wounded men, who were later murdered and scalped by Indians. The rest got away safely by boat and on foot, with Wolfe accompanying the troops back across the ford. In his dispatch to Pitt, Wolfe tried hard to excuse his failure: 'The beach upon which the troops were drawn up was of deep mud, with holes, and cut by several gullies; the hill to be ascended was very steep, and not everywhere practicable; the enemy numerous in their entrenchments and their fire hot.'[37]

What Wolfe could not admit to Pitt was that he had launched a badly planned attack against an almost impregnable position; and one that, even had it succeeded, would have been only the first step on the long road to capturing Quebec. It had cost him almost 450 casualties. French losses, by contrast, were just 60 killed and wounded, most caused by the British bombardment. The greatest damage, however, was to Wolfe's reputation, with his 'enemies and rivals' – notably Brigadier-Generals Townshend and Murray – now castigating his 'impetuosity'.[38]

Determined to regain the initiative, and to separate his disaffected brigadiers, Wolfe now sent Murray and 1,200 men up the river on flat boats to destroy enemy shipping and harass the settlements on both shores. Two attempts to land were driven off, while a third succeeded in burning stores and a magazine at the village of Dechambault, 40 miles upriver of Quebec, on 19 August. But the bulk of French shipping remained beyond Murray's reach and, as each day passed, Wolfe began to accept the possibility of failure. On 11 August, for example, he told the commander at Louisbourg that, though he was still determined to seek 'a battle when occasion offers', he was also considering a withdrawal to the Île-aux-Coudres, where the army could sit out the winter.[39]

It did not help that there had recently been a serious outbreak of dysentery, or 'flux', in the British camp at Montmorency. Spread by unsanitary water, the disease caused severe diarrhoea and vomiting, and could lead to death by dehydration. At Quebec the unit worst affected was the marines – possibly because they were less used to camp life than regular infantry – with 150 of its 1,000 men sick by

9 August. Wolfe had already issued orders for battalions to dig new latrines every three days, and for earth to be thrown into them daily. Now, as the camp grew dirtier and dysentery spread, he ordered all offal to be buried, tents to be floored with spruce boughs and wood from nearby houses, and the men to make every effort to keep themselves clean and swim regularly. Despite these measures, by late August the hospital on the Île-d'Orléans was full to overflowing with sick and wounded, and female camp followers were pressed into service as emergency nurses. Any who refused, or left the hospital 'without being regularly dismissed by order of the director', announced Wolfe, 'shall be struck off the provision roll; and if found afterwards in any of the camps, shall be turned out immediately'.[40]

He was referring, of course, to 'soldiers' wives', a term used in its widest sense for the small number of women – some legitimately married to redcoats, some not – who were permitted to accompany British armies in the field and were therefore included on the ration roll. There was, at this stage, no fixed quota: when, for example, drafts were ordered to America from regiments in Britain and Ireland in 1757, it was suggested to the secretary at war that it was 'proper, and for the good of His Majesty's Service, that five or six women for every hundred Men be permitted to Embark'. The following autumn, an expedition to the West Indies was allowed to take ten women per company, which meant a total of 540 women or one for every ten soldiers.[41] This number did not include the unofficial camp followers, many of whom were prostitutes and not on the ration roll. Women accompanying Braddock's ill-fated march to Monongahela, for example, were obliged to undergo a medical examination to prevent the spread of venereal disease. The lucky ones found a husband in the ranks and went legitimate, like the 'Road Island whore' who in October 1758 married a 'Lobster Corperel' ('Lobster' being a synonym for redcoat).[42]

Only occasionally, when a campaign was either particularly arduous or of short duration, would the local commander forbid the presence of women. This happened on both the expeditions to Lake George in 1758 and 1759, and for the gruelling pursuit of Cherokee Indians in 1761. When women were permitted, they were often

caught up in the fighting. 'An Indian shot one of ours,' wrote a survivor of Monongahela, 'and began to scalp her', but she was saved by
her husband, who killed the warrior. Some wives became veterans.
'I have been a Wife 22 years,' wrote Mrs Martha May, who had been
confined for abusing her husband's commanding officer, 'and have
traveled with my husband every place or county the company marcht
too and have workt very hard ever since I was in the Army.' She
hoped to be pardoned 'that I may go with my poor husband, one
more time to carry him and my good officers water in yet hottest battle as I have done before.'[43]

Women were typically occupied as laundresses, charging a penny
for each item. But some of the more enterprising set themselves up as
sutlers (a civilian merchant who sells provisions to an army) or
money-changers, and made sizeable fortunes as a result. Not that the
authorities approved when the sale of rum caused widespread drunkenness, as it did during the siege of Louisbourg. 'I wish that pernicious
liquor banished from your camp,' wrote Admiral Boscawen to General Amherst. 'I know the women of the Highlanders, & the Royals
to be notorious sutlers.'[44]

And while it was not unusual for women to be dragooned as
nurses, as they were at Quebec, their skills were rudimentary at best,
and they could do little to halt the spread of disease. So weakened
were all three of Wolfe's brigades by late August that, according to
Corporal John Johnson of the 58th Foot, they had only a 'very small'
chance of becoming 'masters of Quebec'.[45]

Murray finally returned from his mission on 25 August, bringing
with him the welcome news – from prisoners and captured correspondence – that General Amherst had captured Ticonderoga, Crown
Point and Fort Niagara. Nevertheless there was, as yet, no firm intelligence as to whether Amherst had begun his advance upon Montreal,
an operation that would, inevitably, have forced Montcalm to divide
his army. None the wiser, and prostrated by nervous exhaustion
(explained at the time as a 'fever'),[46] Wolfe dictated a memorandum
to his brigadiers on 27 August, requesting them to 'meet and consult
for the public utility and advantage, and consider of the best method
to attack the enemy'. He told them he preferred to attack Montcalm's

army at Beauport, rather than the town itself, and suggested three options: the first, Wolfe's favourite, was for a night march to Beauport via the upper ford of the Montmorency; the remaining two were variations of the original attack, and differed only in the direction of the main assault, option two preferring an advance below the falls, and option three a landing by boat.[47]

None of these suggestions was either original or likely to succeed, and the brigadiers said as much in their reply to Wolfe's memorandum, written after they had met on 29 August and then consulted Admiral Saunders. 'The natural strength of the enemy's situation between the rivers St Charles and Montmorenci,' they wrote, 'now improved by all the art of their engineers, makes the defeat of their army, if attacked there, very doubtful.' Their preference, therefore, was to 'bring the troops to the south shore, and to carry the operations above the town'. They added:

> If we can establish ourselves on the north shore . . . we are between [Montcalm] and his provisions, and between him and the army opposing General Amherst. If he gives us battle and we defeat him, Quebec, and probably all Canada, will be our own, which is beyond any advantage we can expect from the Beauport side; and should the enemy pass over the river St Charles with force sufficient to oppose this operation, we may still, with more ease and probability of success, execute the General's third proposition (which is, in our opinion, the most eligible).[48]

In an attached 'Plan of Operations', the brigadiers suggested moving the bulk of the army to a point above the Etchemin River, opposite Saint-Michel, from where it could effect a night landing anywhere within a 12-mile stretch of the north shore from the 'heights of St John' to the Cap-Rouge River. The army would land in two waves – 2,000 to 2,500 men in the first, a further 1,500 in the second – so that a total of 4,000 men could get ashore in a single tide with the enemy none the wiser.[49]

Wolfe was surprised and disappointed by this summary rejection of his favoured plan. Yet he was still not well enough to lead it in person and felt, as he told Saunders, that it was 'of too desperate a nature to order others to execute'.[50] So he gave in to the brigadiers' recommendation to land above Quebec – an option that he had earlier preferred – but covered himself by leaving Pitt in no doubt that it was their idea and not his. '*They are all of opinion,*' he wrote in his final dispatch of 2 September, 'that, as more ships and provisions are now got above the town, they should try, by conveying a corps of four or five thousand men, which is nearly the whole strength of the army, after the Points of Levi and Orleans are left in a proper state of defense, to draw the enemy from their present situation, and bring them to an action. *I have acquiesced in* their proposal, and we are preparing to put it into execution.'[51]

Wolfe's lack of confidence in the scheme is evident in the final paragraph of his dispatch: 'In this situation there is such a choice of difficulties, that I own myself at a loss how to determine. The affairs of great Britain, I know, require the most vigorous measures; however, you may be assured that the small part of the campaign which remains shall be employed (as far as I am able) for the honour of His Majesty, and the interest of the nation.'[52]

With the die now cast, Wolfe's first move was to evacuate the camp at Montmorency, a tricky operation completed without loss of life in the early hours of 3 September, though the French bombarded the troops as they were rowed across the river. A day later an officer and three Rangers, exhausted from their long trek from Boston, arrived at Pointe-Lévis with dispatches from Amherst. They confirmed what Wolfe already knew: that Ticonderoga, Crown Point and Niagara were all in British hands – and ended with the rousing cry: 'Now is the time!'[53] From this, Wolfe must have surmised that Amherst was bearing down on Montreal, a move that would have made his own task easier. The truth, however, was that Amherst was still at the southern end of Lake Champlain, waiting for the construction of a freshwater fleet, while his subordinate Brigadier Gage had stalled at Niagara and Oswego. Unbeknown to Wolfe, the original three-pronged offensive had been reduced to one. He was on his own – and in more ways than one. Brigadier Townshend, who had long been critical of Wolfe, wrote to his wife on 6 September: 'General Wolf's health is but very bad. His generalship in my poor opinion – is not a bit better, this only between us. He never consulted any of us until the latter end of August, so that we have nothing to answer for I hope as to the success of the Campaign.'[54] It was hardly a ringing endorsement of either his commander or the plan that he, Townshend, had helped to formulate.

That evening, Wolfe joined his brigadiers and the bulk of the army – seven battalions – on board the warships and transports that Rear-Admiral Holmes had concentrated upriver of Quebec. They travelled up the river on the flood tide as far as the mouth of the Cap-Rouge, where, despite the presence of floating batteries and a strong breastwork, they intended to land the following evening. Once again the operation was cancelled at the last minute, chiefly because the turning tide had prevented the naval frigates from engaging the batteries and bombarding the shore. Two days later – 9 September – a new landing was planned at a point between Cap-Rouge and Pointe-aux-Trembles, near Saint-Augustin. But it, too, was called off – this time because of heavy rain. Had it gone ahead, and been successful, Townshend and his fellow brigadiers would have won the plaudits for capturing Quebec, while Wolfe would have been remembered not as the great might-have-been, but as just another talented battalion commander who had been promoted beyond his abilities.

11.   The Heights of Abraham

In the afternoon of 9 September 1759, following the cancellation of the Saint-Augustin operation, Wolfe made yet another reconnaissance of the shore above Quebec. As he passed the Anse-au-Foulon, the narrow cove that he and Holland had identified as a possible landing place in early July, he decided that now was the time to activate the plan of 'last resort'. Next day he returned to the cove with his senior officers: Admiral Holmes, Brigadiers Monckton and Townshend, and Major Mackellar, his chief engineer. Mackellar noted that the 'bank', or cliff, above the cove was so steep and wooded that the French had left only around a hundred men and some barricades to guard the narrow path up from the beach; and yet, 200 yards to the right, 'there appeared to be a slope in the bank' that looked scalable and would provide an alternative route on to the heights. 'These circumstances,' wrote Mackellar, 'and the distance of the place from succours seemed to promise a fair chance of success.'[1]

Wolfe was further influenced by intelligence he received from French deserters on 10 September that part of Montcalm's army had left to reinforce Montreal. The news was, in fact, a month old; but Wolfe did not know this and, in consequence, was doubly resolved to assist what he could only assume was Amherst's continued advance. Few of Wolfe's senior officers were supportive. According to Admiral Holmes, 'the alteration of the Plan of Operations was not, I believe, approved of by many, beside himself'. Holmes himself felt it should have been executed two months earlier, when the place was unguarded, and not revived at a time when it was 'highly improbable he should succeed'.[2]

Wolfe, however, had recovered his self-confidence and would brook no dissent. His plan, he told Colonel Burton (his original choice as third brigadier), was to sail the troops upriver on the 11th, 'as if intending to land above upon the north shore', before returning to Foulon a day later under the cover of darkness and disembarking at 4 a.m. on the 13th.[3] The night of 12/13 September was chosen because an ebb current, and the position of the moon, would give him the best chance of taking troops downriver and landing them undetected before daylight.

Detailed instructions were issued on the 11th. The first wave of 1,700 men, commanded by Monckton and Murray, would embark at 9 p.m. on the 12th, 'or when it is pretty near high water', and would be carried by the thirty flat-bottomed boats, each containing fifty men, as well as *The Terror of France* schooner and five longboats and cutters. The soldiers were to take nothing with them but their arms, seventy rounds of ammunition and two days' rations. As they would be in open boats for some time, they were to be issued with an extra gill of rum that they could mix with water in their canteens to make 'grog'.[4] Silence was imperative and on no account were the men to fire from the boats. They would be spearheaded by 400 of the elite light infantry, under Colonel Howe, with the rest following according to regimental seniority. Once the first wave was on shore, the boats would return to the fleet to collect the remaining 1,900 troops and artillerymen, under Brigadier Townshend. Finally, the two battalions that had been left to guard the Île-d'Orléans and Pointe-Lévis would be rowed across from the opposite bank.

During the evening of the 12th – having just received the welcome news from a French deserter that Montcalm was still at Beauport, his deputy en route to Montreal, and a third force under Colonel Bougainville were expecting an attack on the upper river – Wolfe issued a final rallying call to his men:

> The enemy's force is now divided; great scarcity of provisions is in their camp, and universal discontent among the Canadians. The second officer in command is gone to Montreal, or St John's, which gives reason to think that General Amherst is advancing into the colony. A vigorous blow struck by the army at this juncture may determine the fate of Canada . . .
>
> The first body that gets on shore is to march directly to the enemy, and drive them from any little post they may occupy . . . The battalions

must form on the upper ground with expedition, and be ready to charge whatever presents itself. When the artillery and troops are landed, a corps will be left to secure the landing-place, while the rest march on, and endeavour to bring the French and Canadians to battle. The officers and men will remember what their country expects from them, and what a determined body of soldiers, inured to war, is capable of doing against five weak French battalions mingled with disorderly peasantry.[5]

This rousing call to arms – almost a precursor to Nelson's pre-battle signal at Trafalgar – had the desired effect on Wolfe's men, with Corporal Johnson of the 58th noting that it was 'couched in such tender and expressive terms, as was sufficient to inspire the most frozen constitution with the thirst for glory'.[6]

His three brigadiers were less impressed, and at once sent him a joint letter complaining that they did not think themselves 'sufficiently informed of the several facts which may fall to our share in the execution of the descent you intend to-morrow', and requesting 'distinct orders', particularly the 'place or places we are to attack' which they could not 'learn from the public orders'.[7] Wolfe's response, addressed to Monckton and written at 8.30 p.m., just half an hour before the troops were to board their landing craft, betrayed his exasperation but little else. Having first reminded Monckton that he had the day before pointed out the landing spot from the opposite bank, he added: 'It is not a usual thing to point out in the public orders the direct spot of our attack, nor for any inferior Officers not charged with a particular duty to ask instructions upon that point. I had the honour to inform you to-day, that it is my duty to attack the French Army. To the best of my knowledge and abilities I have fixed upon the spot where we can act with the most force and are most likely to succeed. If I am mistaken I am sorry for it and must be answerable to his Majesty and the public for the consequences.' A second, briefer letter to Townshend simply confirmed his role as commander of the second wave and stressed the need for him to land his men with the 'utmost expedition'.[8]

An hour or so later the men of the first wave – Howe's Light Infantry, the 28th, 43rd, 47th, 58th, part of Fraser's Highlanders and fifty grenadiers of the Royal Americans – began to descend to the boats. The first boat included a Forlorn Hope of twenty-four handpicked light infantrymen, commanded by Captain William De Laune,* whose task was to be first up the cliff face. Wolfe and two of his staff officers were in another lead boat. At 2 a.m., as the flood began to ebb, two lanterns signalled the order to cast loose and the boats began to descend the river. With the tide running at 2½ knots it would take them two hours to cover the 9 miles to Foulon. They were able to navigate thanks to the position of the moon in its last quarter in the eastern sky, thus outlining the northern shore to the men in the boats; but for sentries looking up the river it would provide little assistance.

It was just before 4 a.m. when De Laune's lead boat neared the shore at Foulon. One of its occupants recalled:

> When we came pretty close to the heights we rowed close in with the north shore, which made the *Hunter* sloop-of-war, who lay off, suspect us to be an enemy, not being apprised of our coming down. However, we passed two sentries on the beach without being asked any questions. The third sentry challenged, 'Who is there?' Was answered by Capt. Fraser in the French tongue, 'French,' saying, 'we are the provision boats from Montreal', cautioning the sentry to be silent, otherwise he would expose us to the fire of the English man-of-war.[9]

The sentry waved them on and, minutes later, they grounded on Foulon's narrow shingle beach. Colonel Howe at once ordered De Laune and his Forlorn Hope to ascend the barricaded path that zig-zagged its way up the 200-yard-high cliff, while he led the rest of his light infantrymen – three companies – directly up the sheer face to the right of the path that Major Mackellar had identified as an alternative route to the top. Lieutenant John Knox of the 43rd, part of the first wave, described it as 'one of the steepest precipices that can be conceived, being almost a perpendicular, and of an incredible height'.[10] Yet somehow Howe and his men managed to struggle their way up it, their feet sliding on the loose shale, their hands clutching

---

* Seconded from Wolfe's own regiment, the 67th.

at the bushes that covered its surface. At the top they swung to the left and, assisted by De Laune and his men who had ascended the path, engaged and quickly overwhelmed the French picket, wounding its commander and driving the survivors into a neighbouring field of corn.

By now the support battalions had landed and were hurrying up the path and slope. 'As soon as we gained the summit,' recalled Knox, 'all was quiet, and not a shot was heard, owing to the excellent conduct of the light infantry under Colonel Howe; it was by this time clear day-light.'[11] Wolfe was jubilant at Howe's success, but for some reason – possibly a failure of nerve – decided to halt the disembarkation of the second wave until he knew more of the enemy's strength. But when Major Isaac Barré, Wolfe's quartermaster-general, reached the shore with the order, he saw that most of the boats were already alongside the transports and full of troops waiting to land. He therefore cancelled the order and the disembarkation continued.

A number of British casualties were inflicted by cannon-fire from the nearby Samos Battery of four guns, and from stray musket shots from the cliffs. But most of the second wave landed safely, as did the two battalions rowed across from the south shore and some artillery pieces, notably two light 6-pounder cannon that would play a crucial role in the battle to come.

At 5.30 a.m., whilst Brigadier Murray took the 58th Foot and Howe's Light Infantry to tackle the nearby Samos Battery, Wolfe marched the rest of the first wave north-east towards Quebec across gently rising ground – chiefly cornfields and scrub – known as the Heights or Plains of Abraham. 'Weather showery,' recorded Knox. 'About six o'clock the enemy first made their appearance upon the heights, between us and the town; whereupon we halted, and wheeled to the right, thereby forming the line of battle.'[12]

On hearing of the landing, Montcalm had at once sent a single regular battalion, the Guyenne, across the Saint-Charles River and up to the heights, following soon after with the bulk of his army and leaving just 1,500 militiamen to guard Beauport. But it would take a couple of hours for all his men to reach the heights, and in the meantime the French position on the low ridge known as the

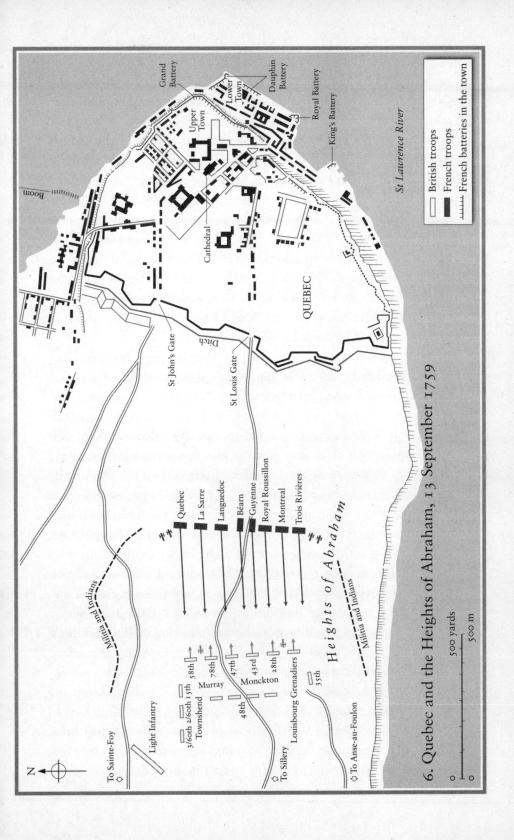

6. Quebec and the Heights of Abraham, 13 September 1759

Buttes-à-Neveu, 600 yards to Wolfe's front, was held only by the Guyenne. To disguise their relative weakness, skirmishers and Indians were sent forward to snipe the British line from a cornfield opposite Wolfe's right wing. These 'skulkers' annoyed the British considerably, and were forced to retire only when Colonel John Hale sent forward three platoons of his grenadiers. Next a French battery opened with round- and canister-shot, prompting Wolfe to order his men to lie down.

Wolfe has been criticized for not sweeping the Guyenne off the Buttes-à-Neveu while he had the chance. But if he had done so, he would have exposed his army to the powerful guns mounted on Quebec's walls. By remaining in the dead ground beyond the ridge, he protected his army until such time as Montcalm came to meet him in open battle. He did not have long to wait.

By 8 a.m. Wolfe had been joined by Murray's men, the battalions of the second and third waves, and the two 6-pounder cannon manned by Royal Artillerymen, giving him a grand total of 4,500 men. He at once formed up his men for battle: on the extreme right he placed the 35th Foot, with its right inclined to face the bushy bank of the St Lawrence, where enemy skirmishers were congregating; next, from right to left, came the Louisbourg Grenadiers, the 28th, 43rd, 47th, 78th (Fraser's Highlanders) and 58th Foot. To protect his open left flank, where the Canadian irregulars were particularly numerous, he sited the 15th Foot and two battalions of the Royal Americans (2/60th and 3/60th), facing north at right angles to the main line. Howe's Light Infantry, recently returned from their mission to silence the Samos Battery (which they managed without losing a man), was covering the rear of the position as, wrote an NCO, 'there was a body of enemy' in that direction; he was referring to Bougainville's force of 3,000 men, which Wolfe feared might appear at any moment.[13] The only reserve, stationed in four subdivisions behind Wolfe's centre, was Webb's 48th Foot. Both cannon, manned by Royal Artillerymen, were in the front line.

Wolfe's men, like all British troops in North America, had been trained that summer to fight in two ranks rather than three; this was because they were opposed chiefly by militia and Indians, who were not thought capable of facing regular troops in the open. Not that Wolfe had any option but to spread his force thin at Quebec thanks to, as Corporal Johnson of the 58th put it, the 'smallness of our number, as well as the quantity of ground we had to cover to secure our flanks'. Even then his men were placed in open order, with a gap of three feet between files, and 40 yards between battalions: a formation that would become famous in the nineteenth century as the 'Thin Red Line'.[14] Wolfe himself was stationed on a small knoll to the right of his main line, behind the Louisbourg Grenadiers. Monckton, the senior brigadier, commanded the right of the line; Murray the centre; and Townshend the left flank.

Facing them was an army of similar size – 4,500 men – but only the five battalions in the centre, clad in greyish-white coats, were regular French troops. The rest, clustered on both flanks, were part-time militiamen and Indians; and even the regulars had been bolstered by drafts of militiamen. Moreover, Montcalm's best troops, his grenadiers, were absent with Bougainville upriver. Under the circumstances, it made sense for Montcalm to avoid battle that day by withdrawing behind Quebec's defences and waiting for Bougainville's reinforcements; or at the very least to hold the high ground and let Wolfe attack him. Yet he chose to advance like the Duc de Gramont at Dettingen, and with similarly disastrous results.

Why did Montcalm do it? We will never know for certain, but his knowledge that Quebec could not survive a siege for long must have played its part in his decision. He may also have underestimated both the strength and effectiveness of Wolfe's force, his overconfidence a result of the easy victory at Beauport a month earlier. Or he may have been misled by the apparent weakness of the British line facing Quebec, which was only 1,800 muskets strong, because the majority of Wolfe's troops were on flanking, rearguard and reserve duty.[15] Whatever the reason, he played directly into Wolfe's hands.

Shortly after ten, Montcalm signalled his regulars forward down the gentle slope with a wave of his sword. They came on at a brisk pace, waving their hats and shouting 'Vive le Roi!' and advancing in what appeared to be three dense bodies. Montcalm had ordered only the two centre battalions – Béarn and Guyenne – to advance in column with companies ranged behind each other, but various obstacles caused the other battalions to shorten their frontage and they looked to the sergeant-major of the Louisbourg Grenadiers to be 'at least six deep'.[16] Lieutenant Knox, stationed with the 43rd in the very centre of the British line, recalled: 'The enemy began to advance briskly in three columns, with loud shouts and recovered arms, two of them inclining to the left of our army, and the third towards our right, firing obliquely at the two extremities of our line, from the distance of one hundred and thirty yards.'[17]

Though many of the shots flew high, this initial fusillade caused a number of casualties. Wolfe himself was shot in the wrist, the bullet severing his tendons, but he simply bound it up with a handkerchief before exhorting the men near him to stand firm. He had given the whole army strict instructions not to fire until the French were at point-blank range and, despite the provocation, its two fragile ranks maintained perfect discipline. Nearer came the French, firing all the while, yet still the redcoats stood immobile, their double-shotted muskets shouldered, waiting for the order to fire. Knox was struck by the 'intrepidity and firmness' with which the troops withstood the enemy's bullets, 'reserving their fire, and paying the strictest obedience to their officers'.[18]

As the French got ever closer – 100 yards, 90, 80 – it seemed as if the weight of their columns was bound to punch a hole through the thin British line. But already the French ranks were beginning to lose their cohesion as the rough ground prevented them from redeploying from column into line, skirmishers got mixed up with the advancing troops, and the drafts of militiamen reverted to type by taking cover, Indian fashion, once they had fired. The French were unnerved too, thought Knox, by the 'uncommon steadiness' of the British ranks facing them and this, 'together with the havoc which the grape-shot from our field pieces made among them, threw them into some disorder'.[19]

Still they advanced, 'firing by platoons',[20] until they were just 40 yards from the British line, at which point Wolfe's company officers barked out a succession of orders. 'Make ready.' 'Present.' 'Fire!'

That summer Wolfe had drilled his whole army in the Prussian 'alternate-fire' system, and the effect of these company volleys at such close range, one after the other, was to stop the French in their tracks. 'We poured in such a discharge', remembered Corporal Johnson of the 58th, and they continued it 'with such a regular briskness' that the 'good effect' was 'visible to all'.[21] Nowhere was this counter-fire more destructive than at the very centre of the British line, where the 43rd and 47th regiments of foot were facing the dense column of the Béarn and Guyenne regiments. Following the same advice that Wolfe had given to the 20th Foot in 1755, these two battalions inclined their fire inwards against the flanks of the advancing column, and then unleashed a double-shotted volley on its front. Knox of the 43rd was struck by the 'great calmness' with which his men fired 'as remarkable a close and heavy discharge, as I ever saw performed at a field of exercise, insomuch that better troops than we encountered could not possibly withstand it'.[22] This 'well-timed' and 'regular' discharge forced the French to give way and flee 'with precipitation', recalled Knox, 'so that by the time the cloud of smoke was vanished, our men were again loaded, and profiting by the advantage we had over them'.[23]

More company volleys were fired, and then a final destructive discharge from the whole line, before Monckton and Murray ordered their men to fix bayonets and, in the case of Fraser's Highlanders, draw their fearsome broadswords. With cheers and war cries, this thin red line tipped with steel began to advance over a carpet of dead and wounded French, few of whom were allowed to live. Private Humphrys of the 28th remembered the Highlanders falling on the broken French centre 'with irresistible impetuosity' and driving part of them 'with great slaughter into the town'.[24] Those who could not escape their flashing blades were left with fearsome wounds, as witnessed after the battle by a British volunteer:

Happy in escaping unhurt, I travers'd the field of battle, while strewed with bleeding carcasses, and covered with unemployed arms. A neat silver-mounted hangar, fastened to the side of an apparently headless trunk, and which consequently was useless to its original French possessor, attracted my attention. When the body was turned over, in order to unbuckle the belt, my astonishment was indeed great: his head lay underneath his breast, one stroke upon the back of his neck, having cut thro' the whole, except a small part of the skin of the throat, by which it remained connected with the body.[25]

One Highlander sergeant, James Thompson, remembered looking back and seeing the casualties lying 'on the field as thick as a flock of sheep and just as they had fallen, for the main body had been completely routed off the ground and had no opportunity of carrying away their dead and wounded'. It was 'horrid', he added, 'to see the effect of blood and dust on their white coats'.[26]

This charge of Fraser's 78th, and the heroic performance of the 42nd at Ticonderoga, would transform the image of the Highlanders in the popular consciousness from that of dangerous savages who posed a threat to the security of the state to loyal and hardy shock troops of empire. From this point on, the Highlanders joined the Guardsmen as the elite of the British Army, and both would win laurels in virtually every major conflict they fought, often – as was the case at Waterloo, the Alma, Tel-el-Kebir, Loos and Alamein – fighting almost side by side.

Meanwhile Wolfe, sword in hand, led the Louisbourg Grenadiers and 28th Foot forward on the right. For the hundreds of irregulars still hiding in the bushes above the St Lawrence, this tall officer in his open redcoat was an inviting target and Wolfe had not gone far when he was wounded a second time by a ball in the side of his 'belly'; fortunately it was a flesh wound and, ignoring it, he carried on. Moments later his luck ran out when he was struck in the breast by two musket-balls, or possibly a piece of grape from a gun, causing him to stagger. 'His principle care,' wrote Private Humphrys of the 28th, 'that he should not be seen to fall. "Support me," said he to such as were near him, "let not my brave soldiers see me drop, the day is ours, oh, keep it." He was immediately carried behind the ranks.'[27]

The men helping him to the rear were James Henderson, a volunteer, and two Louisbourg Grenadiers, Lieutenant Henry Browne and an unnamed private. Having reached a position of relative safety, they laid him on the ground with one of them supporting his head.

Asked if he needed a surgeon, the dying Wolfe replied: 'It is needless, it is all over with me.'

Moments later, one of his helpers glanced back at the mêlée and cried: 'They run, see how they run!'

'*Who* runs?' asked a semi-conscious Wolfe, almost forgetting where he was.

'The enemy, sir. Egad, they give way everywhere.'

The words returned Wolfe to the moment, and his response was typically professional. 'Go one of you, my lads, to Colonel Burton,' he gasped. 'Tell him to march Webb's regiment [48th Foot] with all speed to Charles's River, to cut off the retreat of the fugitives from the bridge.'

Then, certain in the belief that the battle was won and his reputation secure, he turned on his side and uttered: 'Now, God be praised, I will die in peace.'[28]

He expired soon after with, according to one account, a smile on his face.[29]

The battle, however, was far from over. Though the French regulars were no longer capable of resistance, the Canadian militiamen were fighting a stubborn rearguard action in the scrub that lined the escarpment above the Saint-Charles River, enabling many of their fleeing comrades to reach the relative safety of either Beauport, via the bridge that Wolfe had intended Webb's Regiment to secure, or Quebec. The first British battalion to be repulsed by the Canadians' fire was Fraser's Highlanders, their swords still bloody from the massacre of the regulars. 'They killed and wounded a great many of our men, and killed two Officers,' recalled a young subaltern called Malcolm Fraser, the son of a Jacobite who had died at Culloden, 'which obliged us to retire a little, and form again.'[30]

But it was only when the 58th Foot and a battalion of the Royal Americans arrived that the bush was finally cleared, and not before the Highlanders had lost 170 of their 500 men, prompting Malcolm Fraser to question the sense of attacking with cold steel. 'I dare say [the Highlanders' charge] increased [the French] panic,' he wrote, 'but saved many of their lives, whereas if the artillery had been allowed to play, and the army advanced regularly there would have been more of the enemy killed and wounded.'[31]

With Wolfe *hors de combat*, Monckton took command. But within minutes he was shot through the lungs and carried from the field, the command now devolving on Brigadier Townshend. 'He immediately quitted the Left Wing,' recorded Corporal Johnson of the 58th, 'and hastened to the centre of the Line, where Brigadier General Murray commanded; and finding the Centre pursuing the Enemy, in a confused and disorderly manner, he Rallyed them again with all haste. For at this very juncture Monsieur Bougainville arrived with a Body of Two Thousand men, in the Rear of our Army.'[32]

The time was now well after midday and, as Wolfe had feared, Colonel Bougainville had marched from Cap-Rouge to the sound of battle with the bulk of his command, including his formidable grenadiers. Hastily forming his men for action, the colonel seemed determined to snatch victory from the jaws of defeat or perish in the attempt. But, fortunately for his men, he let discretion be the better part of valour and chose not to attack, put off by the presence of Howe's Light Infantry and a battalion of the Royal Americans that were guarding the British rear, and the imminent arrival of two more battalions – the 35th and 48th – and two cannon that had been sent by Townshend. 'Bougainville immediately retired at their approach,' remembered Johnson, 'and very prudently declined attacking a Conquering Army.'[33] He withdrew the way he had come, and Townshend chose not to follow, later explaining to Pitt that he did not want to 'risk the fruit of so decisive a day'.[34] As darkness fell, the British victory was confirmed.

Compared to previous British successes (and defeats for that matter), the casualties sustained by Wolfe's force at Quebec were relatively light. It suffered 664 killed and wounded out of a total force of 4,500 – or slightly less than 15 per cent; at Blenheim, by contrast, Allied casualties were closer to one in four. French losses of around 1,500 killed, wounded and taken prisoner out of a similar-sized force as the British were also proportionately much lighter than the 57 per cent casualties they had sustained at Blenheim. What sets Quebec apart, however, is the unprecedented loss of senior officers on both sides. The French commander, the Marquis de Montcalm, was mortally wounded during the retreat of his regular troops, struck by a shell fragment as he tried to negotiate the unruly mob at the Saint-Louis Gate to the city, and died in Quebec a day later. His second-in-command was also killed during the battle, as was the commander of the Canadian militia on the right wing. Senior British casualties included Wolfe, killed, and Monckton, Isaac Barré (quartermaster-general), Guy Carleton (adjutant-general) and Hervey Smyth (Wolfe's aide-de-camp) all wounded. Barré lost an eye and later the sight in the other.

The news of Wolfe's death was received by British troops with universal sadness and regret. Private Humphrys of the 28th described it as 'an irreparable loss'.[35] Lieutenant Browne, who had comforted Wolfe in his final moments, told his father that 'even the soldiers dropped tears, who were but the minute before driving their bayonets through the French.' He added: 'I can't compare it to anything better, than to a family in tears and sorrow which had just lost their father, their friend and their whole dependence.'[36] Another officer wrote: 'Our joy at this success is inexpressibly damped by the loss we sustain of one of the greatest heroes that this or any other age can boast of.'[37]

It was not only professional soldiers who mourned his death. 'Thus fell a noble, a much loved, a much lamented officer,' wrote the British volunteer to a friend. 'Britain must regret the loss, but in the day of danger, may she never want a commander with the qualities of a *Wolfe*, to support her rights, and fight the battles of honour and liberty.'[38]

Less effusive was the mention of Wolfe in the General Orders issued by Townshend and Murray, the two unscathed generals (and Wolfe's biggest critics in the lead-up to the battle), the following day. Having congratulated the troops for their 'conduct and bravery', they added a lukewarm and not entirely genuine 'wish that the person who lately commanded them had survived so glorious a day, and had this day been able to give the troops their just encomiums'.[39]

A day earlier, with the fighting over, Townshend had ordered his exhausted men to fortify their position in case the French tried to counter-attack. They slept that night at their improvised barricades, muskets in hand, amidst the detritus of battle, their nostrils assailed by the stench of gunpowder and death. Most of the British wounded had been evacuated to the field hospital on the Île-d'Orléans – where medical treatment had changed little since Blenheim, and amputation without anaesthetic was still the norm for mangled limbs – but many French casualties were left to die overnight among the piles of bloodied corpses and heaps of discarded equipment.

The feared counter-attack never came, but it was certainly debated. When asked by Governor-General Vaudreuil for his advice that afternoon, the dying Montcalm gave him three options: surrender the colony; retire to the Jacques Cartier River, closer to Montreal; or attack the following day, using Bougainville's men and the survivors of the battle. Vaudreuil opted for the last course, and argued strongly for it at a council of war in Quebec during the evening of the 13th. But he could not persuade the surviving senior officers, who, according to one witness, were 'exaggerating somewhat the loss we had suffered' and 'all voted unanimously that the army should retreat.'[40] At 9 p.m. the remnants of Montcalm's army fled east along the Saint-Charles River, abandoning most of its supplies, ammunition and guns at Beauport. 'It was not a retreat,' recorded Montcalm's aide-de-camp, 'but an abominable flight.'[41]

Vaudreuil went with them, leaving instructions for the city commandant, Chevalier de Ramezay, to defend Quebec until he ran out of supplies. But Townshend soon forced the issue by preparing siege batteries for an assault, using naval guns dragged up the cliff at Anse-au-Foulon. 'We got up 12 heavy 24 Pounders,' recalled the sergeant-major of the Louisbourg Grenadiers, 'six heavy Twelve Pounders, some large mortars, and the 48 inch Howitzers to play upon the Town, and had been employed three days, intending to make the breach, and storm the City sword in hand, but were prevented by their beating a parley, and sending out a Flag of Truce with Articles of Capitulation.'[42]

Menaced both by Townshend's batteries and seven of Admiral Saunders's biggest warships that, during the morning of the 17th, were sailed close to the Lower Town, de Ramezay asked for terms.

Most had been granted by the time de Ramezay received new instructions from Vaudreuil to hold on because a relief army was rapidly approaching. He ignored them, and the terms were duly signed on the 18th. In return for surrendering the city, de Ramezay and the garrison of 600 men were given passage to France with the honours of war, while the inhabitants kept their property and their freedom to practise as Roman Catholics. That evening, British troops took possession of the city and its formidable arsenal of weapons, including no fewer than '250 Pieces of Cannon, a Number of mortars, from 9 to fifteen inches, Field-Pieces, Howitzers, etc., with a large Quantity of Artillery-Stores'.[43]

News of Wolfe's victory and the subsequent fall of Quebec were received in London on 16 October with a mixture of delight and relief, for on that very day the *London Gazette* had published Wolfe's despondent dispatch of 2 September. On reading the dispatch, Pitt had convinced himself that Quebec would not fall to British arms that year, and that his appointment of Wolfe had been a mistake. Others, like Horace Walpole, thought the expedition was bound to end in bloody failure. Pitt's relief was palpable as he wrote to the Duke of Newcastle of 'the joyful news, that Quebec is taken, after a signal and compleat Victory over the French army'.[44]

Next day, the *London Gazette* trumpeted this rapid change of fortune in Canada and, as the news spread through the country, celebrations erupted on a scale not seen since Blenheim: bonfires blazed, cannon boomed, bells rang out and toasts were drunk, including one in Bradford-upon-Avon to 'our brave countrymen in America, and the immortal memory of their late brave commander General Wolfe'.[45]

It is easy to see why 1759 is remembered as the 'Year of Victories'. First there was the capture of Fort Duquesne by Brigadier-General Forbes; then followed conquests at Gorée in Africa, Guadeloupe in the West Indies, and Niagara, Ticonderoga and Crown Point in North America; and finally there were triumphs over the French on land and sea in Europe, the former at Minden in Germany, on 1 August, when an unsupported force of British infantry set the tone by defeating the cream of the enemy horse (though the victory would

have been even more complete if Lord George Sackville, commanding the British cavalry, had not three times refused an order to charge
the beaten enemy), and the latter at Quiberon Bay, on 20 November,
when Admiral Hawke destroyed the remnants of French sea power.

Yet none of these victories captured the public's imagination like
Wolfe's triumph at Quebec. This was partly because the success was
so unexpected, partly because of the bold and dramatic nature of the
operation, but mainly because both commanders were mortally
wounded during the battle, Wolfe dying as victory was all but certain. 'For Britons still facing the prospect of French invasion,' writes
a recent biographer, 'Wolfe epitomized a new mood of patriotic defiance, and a revival of national pride. His prominence in the *annus
mirabilis* of 1759, which saw British victories on three continents, was
only reinforced by the exploits of his old regiment, the 20th Foot,
that August at the Battle of Minden.'[46]

Wolfe's hero status was at once confirmed in print, and later in verse
and on canvas. Two hastily produced articles for the *London Magazine*
set the victory in context, emphasizing Wolfe's excellent conduct during the War of the Austrian Succession, particularly at Lauffeldt, and
later speculating what he *would* have done at Rochefort if given the
chance, and what he *did* do at Louisbourg. His experience and professionalism as a soldier, they concluded, had equipped him to meet and
overcome the difficulties of his greatest challenge, where 'his abilities
shone out in their brightest lustre'.[47]

Wolfe's obvious attraction for the public at large was that he was
young, hard-working and talented, and had, to outward appearances
at least, risen in the army thanks to merit rather than interest (the
truth, of course, was that he had risen thanks to both). He was also
free of any overt political affiliation and had in recent years, more
thanks to luck than design, distanced himself from his old and now
disgraced patron, the Duke of Cumberland. As the years passed, his
popularity grew. In 1763 the Marsden Street Theatre in Manchester
performed an 'Emblematical Scene' with the 'General expiring in the
arms of Minerva . . . And Fame, triumphing over Death, with this
Motto: He can never be lost, who saves His Country'.[48] The following year the artist Edward Penny produced a fairly accurate if

unremarkable painting of Wolfe's death, with the two grenadiers in their mitre caps, and a deathly pale Wolfe being tended by a surgeon, just yards from the British firing line. But it was easily eclipsed by a more romantic depiction of Wolfe's last moments by the Anglo-American Benjamin West, first exhibited in 1771. In it, Wolfe is lying in a posture deliberately reminiscent of Christ taken down from the cross. He is surrounded by officers, including members of his staff, who were nowhere near when he died; and in the foreground sits a Native American, though Wolfe despised them as savages and let none serve in his ranks. It is, nevertheless, a magnificent work of art and became the most reproduced painting of the eighteenth century, sealing Wolfe's reputation as an imperial martyr in the process, and inspiring the young Horatio Nelson to emulate his deeds. Years later, the then Admiral Lord Nelson asked West why he had done no more like it. 'Because, my Lord,' replied West, 'there are no more subjects.'

'Damn it,' said Nelson. 'I didn't think of that.'

'My Lord, I fear your intrepidity may yet furnish me with another such scene, and if it should, I shall certainly avail myself of it.'

'*Will* you, Mr West?' said a delighted Nelson. 'Then I hope I shall die in the next battle.'[49]

The question is: did Wolfe deserve this adulation? Many at the time thought so, including the Marquess of Granby, the British commander at Minden, who told Pitt that had Wolfe lived he 'would have done the greater honour to his country, as he would have been of the utmost service to it, nature having endow'd him with activity, resolution and perseverance, qualities absolutely necessary for executing great plans of operations, all of which he had taken care to improve by great application'.[50] As a soldier of distinction in his own right, and a future commander-in-chief of the British Army, Granby's opinion matters. And there is no doubt that, prior to the Quebec operation, Wolfe was generally recognized as an officer of outstanding talent, a brilliant motivator of men and a tactical innovator ahead of his time. Nonetheless, he was still a young and relatively inexperienced general when he was given the onerous task of capturing Quebec, and the pressure seems to have got to him. He displayed, in particular, a shaky grasp of strategy and proved incapable of getting the best out of his three brigadier-generals, who all, at one time or another, lost confidence in him.

And yet he managed to put all this behind him by launching a bold, if extremely risky, operation that succeeded partly because of French failings, and partly because of the novel battle tactics used by his own highly trained and motivated foot soldiers, tactics that he had introduced. If he had lived, might he have emulated Marlborough? We will never know. Certainly the Quebec operation revealed some deficiencies in his generalship that might have become, in the words of one biographer, 'even more apparent had he lived to serve in the American War of Independence, particularly in the light of his robust attitude towards civilians in general and his often unguarded antipathy towards Americans'.[51]

This last judgement is perhaps a little harsh. Wolfe undoubtedly made mistakes during the Quebec operation – some of them serious – but he also showed a steely resolve to overcome his many difficulties. Nor should it be forgotten that it was his first experience of independent command, and that he was ever willing to learn from his own and others' failings. He was certainly a huge inspiration to his men on 13 September 1759 when they performed one of the great feats of arms of the eighteenth century; and if he was not yet a great general, he might in time have become one.

He left, moreover, an important legacy: the simple but effective battle tactic – a close-quarter musket volley, followed by a bayonet charge – that British infantrymen would use to sweep all (or almost all) before them for much of the next hundred years.

Wolfe is remembered today as the Conqueror of Canada; but at the time of his death there was still much to be done to extinguish French political power in North America. On 18 October, Townshend returned to Britain, leaving Murray in command at Quebec. A week earlier Amherst had launched his long-awaited naval operation to destroy the French flotilla on Lake Champlain, the precursor to a surprise assault on Montreal. But the operation was only partially successful – with three French sloops destroyed – and once again Amherst returned to Crown Point, justifying this backward step by claiming that Quebec's fall would cause the remnants of Montcalm's army to make for Montreal. With Brigadier-General Gage still at Oswego, and no more operations planned until the following spring, this left the British at Quebec dangerously isolated.

The Chevalier de Lévis, Montcalm's successor, was determined to take advantage, and in the spring of 1760 he marched his revitalized army of 7,000 men – including ten regular battalions – back to Quebec, camping close to the city on 27 April. The following day, though he had fewer than 4,000 redcoats fit for action, Murray led his entire force out of the city in an attempt to deny the French the high ground of the Buttes-à-Neveu. But instead of digging in and using his superior artillery, Murray, like Montcalm before him, chose to attack – with similar results. His men fought well, but they were outflanked and almost cut off from their retreat to Quebec. British casualties that day were over a thousand killed and wounded.

De Lévis at once put the city under siege, but was forced to raise it in May when melting ice enabled British warships to reach Quebec with men and supplies. Thus was Wolfe's triumph at Quebec confirmed not by another success on land, but by the naval victory at Quiberon Bay that had destroyed France's sea power and left its colonies, particularly Canada, at the mercy of the British. The final embers of French resistance in Canada were extinguished that summer by Amherst's slow but methodical three-pronged advance on Montreal (with one prong led by Murray from Quebec), culminating in the city's fall on 8 September. Wolfe's dream of an English-speaking North America – and one his victories at Louisbourg and Quebec had gone so far to achieving – was now a reality.

The fall of Canada, however, was far from the only British success against the French in 1760. First there was Sir Eyre Coote's decisive victory over the Comte de Lally at the small-scale but momentous Battle of Wandiwash in southern India on 22 January, a clash that established Britain as the dominant colonial power in the Subcontinent for almost the next 200 years. Then on 31 July, at the Battle of Warburg in Germany, Ferdinand of Brunswick's Allied army defeated the advance guard of a much larger French force under Marshal Victor de Broglie. The decisive action was a charge by the Marquess

of Granby's British cavalry that routed the French horse and drove it
back across the Diemel River, thus redeeming the disgrace of Lord
George Sackville's inaction at Minden.*

Further gains in 1761 included Pondicherry, the key French base in
southern India, while 1762 saw the capture of the sugar island of
Martinique, as well as victories over the Spanish, who had recently
entered the war on the side of the French, at Manila and Havana.

Despite these triumphs, Britain was tiring of the length and cost
of the war. During the eighteenth century the incremental price of
war rose from 74 per cent of the annual budget for the War of the
Spanish Succession, to 79 per cent for the War of the Austrian Succession, to 100 per cent for the Seven Years War. In other words the
British government had had to double its expenditure to pay for the
recent war, and the only way it could do this was by taking out ever
more long-term loans in the form of perpetual annuities† and bonds.
This, in turn, led to a massive increase in the National Debt from
£74.6 million in 1756 to £132.6 million by the end of the Seven Years
War in 1763, a financial time bomb that would explode in 1775.

Two royal deaths also helped to bring about peace. The first was
that of George II, on 25 October 1760, resulting in the accession of
his 22-year-old grandson, who became George III. The new king
had long favoured the Tories over the incumbent Whigs, and in May
1762 he felt confident enough to replace the Duke of Newcastle's
pro-war Whig ministry with one led by the pro-peace Scottish Tory
Lord Bute. In Russia, meanwhile, the death of the Empress Elizabeth in January 1762 meant that Prussia was rid of its most implacable
foe; the new Tsar Peter III, by contrast, was a great admirer of
Frederick II and moved quickly to end the war. The Treaty of
St Petersburg was signed on 5 May 1762, not a moment too soon for

---

* Granby is said to have lost his hat and wig during the charge, prompting the
expression 'to go bald-headed' at something. There are still many pubs today
named in his honour.
† A financial product that offered funded interest payments (at 5 per cent), but gave
the holder no right to demand repayment of the principal; the Treasury, on the
other hand, could redeem at will and so offer cheaper issues if the interest rate fell.

Frederick the Great, as Britain had recently stopped paying his annual war subsidy of £670,000, and his enemies were beginning to close in.

Though fighting continued for much of 1762, principally between Britain and Spain, and Prussia and Austria (with victories for the former at Burkersdorf in July and Reichenbach in August), the end was in sight. On 10 February 1763 Britain, France and Spain signed the Treaty of Paris (with Portugal in agreement). As with previous treaties, this one ensured that the majority of conquered territories were restored to their former owners: in the Caribbean, Spain recovered Cuba and Manila, and France got back Guadeloupe, Martinique and St Lucia, though Britain was allowed to keep the less important sugar islands of Dominica, Grenada, St Vincent, the Grenadines and Tobago; in India, the French were given back their 'factories', or trading posts, but in return they agreed to support the British client governments and not to base troops in Bengal; in the Far East, Spain and Britain recovered the Philippines and Sumatra respectively; in Africa, Britain returned the slave station on the isle of Gorée to the French, but kept the Senegal River and other conquests in West Africa; and in the Mediterranean, the island of Minorca reverted to Britain and Almeida to the Portuguese.

Only Britain was ceded large tracts of new territory, chiefly in North America, where it received Canada and Louisiana east of the Mississippi (not including New Orleans) from the French, and Florida from the Spanish. Britain, in return, promised her new Catholic subjects freedom of worship. But the confirmation of these territorial acquisitions did not satisfy many Whig MPs, who felt that Bute's government had betrayed its people by returning so many other hard-won gains. Pitt – who had been forced to resign in late 1761 when his cabinet refused to back a pre-emptive strike against a Spain that was about to enter the war on the French side – was particularly dismissive of the treaty. On 9 December 1762, in a passionate three-and-a-half-hour speech to Parliament that condemned the preliminary articles of the treaty, he concluded: 'The peace was insecure, because it restored the enemy to her former greatness. The peace was inadequate, because the places gained were no equivalent for the places surrendered.'[52]

This was Pitt playing politics. The peace, after all, had left Britain the master of North America, the possessor of lucrative new sugar islands and slave stations, and France all but finished as a commercial and political power in India. What Pitt could not acknowledge was that the war had gone as well for his country since his departure as before it, and that the North American terms, which he downplayed while railing against the loss of Guadeloupe and Martinique, were better than those he had earlier been willing to accept. Nevertheless, he was not alone in his criticism of the treaty, and it had the desired effect when Bute resigned as prime minister in April 1763 and was replaced by George Grenville.

A man with a more genuine cause for complaint was Frederick the Great of Prussia, who, like the Austrian rulers in 1713 and 1748, had been abandoned by his chief ally, Britain, and was forced to make a separate peace known as the Treaty of Hubertusburg on 15 February 1763. Yet its terms were far from unfavourable for Frederick, because, by returning all three signatories – Austria, Saxony and Prussia – to the *status quo ante bellum*, they confirmed Prussia's conquest of Silesia from the previous conflict. It was now established as a great power and the dominant force inside Germany, reducing still further the influence of the Holy Roman Empire and Habsburg Austria.

The chief beneficiary of the Seven Years War, however, was indisputably Britain. Most historians have attributed that success to her naval supremacy, particularly after the victory at Quiberon Bay. In truth, France's defeat was a joint effort by both the army and the navy – with the two services enjoying at Quebec, for example, a 'perfect good understanding'[53] – and a vindication of the government's strategy that the war had to be fought both on the Continent, at sea and in colonies across the world. A maritime strategy alone would have enabled France to bring to bear its superior military might, and would probably have cost Britain its growing empire. The war, in any event, was a close-run thing, particularly in Canada and Germany, where British soldiers, after early setbacks, were able to re-establish the reputation they enjoyed in Marlborough's day as the finest in Europe.

12. The Blunted Sword

Within twenty years of Wolfe's great victory at Quebec, and barely a decade after the successful conclusion of the Seven Years War, the British Army was plunged into another major conflict in North America, this time against its former colonial allies, who had played such a key role in helping Wolfe and Amherst overcome the French in Canada. It was a war that, in its first three years in particular, offered the British numerous opportunities for outright victory. Yet they were all spurned, and the man responsible was none other than General Sir William Howe, who, as a tough and intrepid thirty-year-old colonel of light infantry, had led Wolfe's army up the cliffs of the Anse-au-Foulon. Many of Howe's men at Quebec were Americans and, as we shall see, it was his affinity with the colonists and his sympathy for their cause – particularly during the crucial second and third years of the conflict, 1776–7, when he was in command of British troops in America – that discouraged him from prosecuting the war with the ruthless and single-minded determination necessary to subdue the rebels.

But even if Howe had been keener to strike the rebellion a mortal blow, the edge of the weapon in his hand was far blunter than the one available to British commanders in 1763. This was chiefly because of the drastic defence cuts that were introduced in the wake of the Seven Years War in an attempt to save money and help reduce the unprecedented National Debt of £133 million (or £13 billion today). Inevitably the service worst affected was the army, and with good reason. At its height, in 1760, it had numbered 203,000 soldiers (including German mercenaries) and over 100 regular infantry battalions. Four years later its peacetime establishment was fixed by Parliament at 45,000 men: 17,000 in Great Britain; 10,000 for the greatly increased colonial empire; 4,000 for Gibraltar and Minorca; 1,800 artillerymen; and 12,000 on the Irish establishment.

Not that a penny was saved, far from it. The intention was to return peacetime defence spending to the level it had been between 1750 and 1754, when the annual cost of the army, navy and ordnance had averaged £2.5 million. In the event the average spend from 1764 to 1775 was over £4 million a year. Much of the army's expenditure went on overseas garrisons, with no fewer than 15 battalions needed to police America, rising to 17 in 1774, 26 in 1775 and 42 in 1776.[1]

Even so, more than thirty infantry battalions were disbanded after 1763, while those that remained and had served in North America lost their light infantry companies, thus depriving the army of experienced wilderness fighters who would have proved invaluable during the early years of the coming conflict. At the same time the army adopted Wolfe's alternate-firing and bayonet drill for all battalions in its regulations of 1764, and all peacetime manoeuvres were organized on the model of the classic European battle between two regular opponents fighting in massed ranks. Similar battle tactics – multi-battalion volleys followed by an immediate bayonet charge – had worked for the British at Quebec and Minden, but would not fare so well against American irregulars in the mid-1770s.

Not that all the lessons of the earlier fighting in North America had been forgotten. In 1770 – partly in response to the Falkland Islands war scare of that summer, when a Spanish invasion of the British-controlled eastern island almost led to a full-scale conflict between Britain on the one hand, and the Bourbon powers of Spain and France on the other – light companies were reintroduced to all battalions. Moreover, several British Army officers brought out books that discussed the tactics of irregular warfare, including Robert Rogers's *Journals* (1765), Robert Stevenson's *Instructions for Officers Detached* (1770) and Major Robert Donkin's *Military Collections and Remarks* (1777).[2] One of the chief enthusiasts, not surprisingly, was William Howe. In 1774, by then a major-general, Howe supervised the intensive training of seven companies of light infantry during a six-week summer camp on Salisbury Plain, and then gave a special demonstration for George III at Richmond. The favourable impression that Howe made upon the king on this occasion was a key factor in his appointment as second-in-command of the forces tasked with suppressing the American rebellion that erupted in 1775. But, when it came to it, Howe's knowledge of both American warfare and the need to deploy light troops when faced with irregulars was more than counterbalanced by his sympathy for his opponent and his determination to secure a negotiated peace rather than outright victory.

There were, in any case, other structural problems with the British Army that the Seven Years War had failed to solve. Boredom and sickness were the chief enemies of a battalion stationed overseas in peacetime, and training was never as effective as it was at home. To remedy this, a system of rotation had been introduced in 1748 to bring battalions back from Gibraltar and Minorca, and something similar was tried in North America from 1765. But many units still spent far too long abroad: the 8th Foot, for example, remained in Canada from 1768 to 1785, while the 16th Foot was in America for almost as long. They were more fortunate than the 31st Foot, who arrived in West Florida, recently acquired from the Spanish, in the summer of 1767. Camped on a beach in fierce heat, with no sustenance 'but Salt Provisions and Water', the battalion was quickly decimated by sunstroke, fever and dysentery. 'In less than Six Weeks,' wrote its colonel, 'a Captain, Lieutenant, Surgeon, two Volunteers, five Officers Wives out of six, ninety-five Men, and above forty Women and Children were swept away.'[3]

The movement and supply of the army was still run on an ad hoc basis, with beasts and wagons hired from civilians, and commissaries appointed only during war. Even then, the local commander had no formal control over supply, as the commissaries were civilians responsible to the Treasury. Part of the reason for this division of responsibility was to prevent the concentration of too much power in military hands. But the end result was a tangled, inefficient and corrupt supply system, as Ferdinand of Brunswick discovered to his cost in 1760. 'I have a monster of a commissariat independent in some respects of me,' he complained, 'and composed of several heads, independent of each other, each with its own chief or protector in England, but together as ignorant and as incapable, as they are avid to line their own pockets.'[4] Prompted by Pitt, Lord Ligonier tried to solve the difficulties in Germany by militarizing the commissariat under an intendant-general on Ferdinand's staff. But the choice of officer was unfortunate and there were few improvements.

In Britain the military organization was no less inefficient, with the secretaries of state, secretary-at-war, master-general of the Ordnance, Treasury and commander-in-chief all operating within their own spheres of interest. It had somehow worked during the Seven Years War because an able soldier – Lord Ligonier – had served as both master-general and commander-in-chief, giving advice to Pitt and drafting instructions for theatre commanders. His responsibilities were similar to a modern chief of the general staff. But Ligonier was a one-off, and in the next war these divided responsibilities would not work in the local commander's favour.

The seeds of the conflict between Britain and her American colonies were largely sown during the Seven Years War, when the cost of defeating the French in North America was borne chiefly by the mother country. Of course the Americans had played their part: during the six years of the French and Indian War (as it was known in North America) they had raised armies totalling 75,000 men; and during Amherst's two-pronged campaign of 1759, the decisive engagement of the war, the troops provided by the six northern colonies had far exceeded the number of British regulars.[5] As well as their sacrifice on the battlefield, colonists had supplied the armies, built ships and paid exorbitant war taxes.

After the fall of Quebec, Americans in the northern provinces had celebrated every bit as rapturously as Britons, with bonfires, bell ringing and sermons of thanksgiving. Their patriotism knew no bounds. 'I am a BRITON,' proclaimed Benjamin Franklin, the distinguished scientist, diplomat and man of letters, and many Americans shared his enthusiasm. Some even contributed to memorials for fallen British heroes – including one in Westminster Abbey for Brigadier-General Lord Howe, paid for by the people of Massachusetts – in recognition of the role the British Army had played in the victory over the hated Roman Catholic French.

Peace in 1763 promised a new era of Anglo-American cooperation; but it lasted barely a year. For not only was Britain deeply in debt, it was also committed to keeping 8,500 troops in newly won Canada and the trans-Appalachian West, populated by unruly Indian tribes and some 9,000 French-Canadian Catholics. To raise the additional revenue required, Grenville's government increased taxes at home and abroad, levying duties on the colonists for the first time in an attempt to raise some of the £220,000 annual cost of policing North America's new frontier. Many MPs thought the new duties were justified: the colonies had been founded with British help, they argued, and it was only right that the inhabitants should contribute to the cost of their security. What was not discussed in Parliament was the government's hidden agenda to use old trade laws and new taxes to strengthen its control over the colonies.

For their part, the American colonies had never before been subjected to Metropolitan taxation, with funds for local government voted by the colonists' own assemblies. While acknowledging allegiance to the crown, they considered themselves independent of Parliament and their assemblies coequal to it. They therefore refused to pay the new levies, and grounded their resistance on the principle that a Briton was liable to be taxed only by his own representatives, whereas they had no London MPs.

The first direct tax, and by far the most controversial, was the Stamp Act of 1765, which required all printed materials in the colonies – including legal documents, magazines and newspapers – to be produced on paper embossed with a revenue stamp that had to be paid for in British currency. Among the few British MPs who opposed its introduction was Colonel Isaac Barré, Wolfe's adjutant-general who had lost an eye at Quebec. It was untrue, he told the House of Commons, that the colonies had been planted and nurtured by Britain. Rather the Americans had faced the 'Cruelties of a Savage foe' without any help from London. And yet, he continued, had it not been for the sacrifices of these 'Sons of Liberty' who had 'nobly taken up Arms in your defence', France would not have been defeated in Canada.[6]

Barré's rhetoric fell largely on stony ground in Parliament, but Americans, not surprisingly, were more receptive. Anti-tax protesters setup Sons of Liberty chapters, while Benjamin Franklin, by now regretting his earlier enthusiasm for Britain, expanded upon Barré's arguments in the evidence he gave to the House of Commons in 1766. The colonies had, he said, 'raised, cloathed and paid during the last war, near 25,000 men [annually], and spent many millions'. They had also paid taxes 'far beyond their abilities, and beyond their [fair] proportion, [and] they went deeply into debt doing this'. He even questioned the need for an armed British presence on the frontier. The colonists had 'defended themselves when they were but a handful, and the Indians much more numerous', and had eventually 'driven the Indians over the mountains, without any troops sent to their assistance from this country'. There was, he insisted, 'not the least occasion' to keep a British army in America; any military force sent there 'will not find a rebellion [but] they may indeed make one'.[7]

Franklin's evidence, along with widespread protests in America, helped to bring about the repeal of the Stamp Act after barely a year. At the same time Parliament asserted its right to tax the colonies – a right that Franklin and many Americans rejected with the cry 'No Taxation without [political] representation' – by passing the Declaratory Act, which insisted it had the power to legislate for the colonies 'in all cases whatsoever'. The following year, by which time Pitt (now the Earl of Chatham) was back in power, Parliament put this theory into practice by passing a series of Acts – named after Charles Townshend, the chancellor of the Exchequer – that were designed to reassert Metropolitan control. The two most controversial were the Revenue Act, which imposed new duties on paper, lead, paint, glass and tea (all items that were not produced in America and could be bought only from Britain), and gave customs officials broad powers to search for smuggled goods, and the Commissioners of Customs Act, which established the American Customs Board in Boston to enforce trade regulations.

Townshend had assumed the colonists' objection was only to direct, or 'internal', taxes like the Stamp Act, and not to indirect, or 'external', taxes on imports. He was mistaken. They regarded *any* tax imposed by the British Parliament as unconstitutional, and their opposition to these new duties was every bit as fierce as it had been to the Stamp Act. The government responded to the growing unrest by moving troops from the Western frontier to the population centres of the East Coast, chiefly New York City and Boston, a move interpreted by the more radical American newspapers, and not without some justification, as an attempt to 'dragoon' the colonists into submission. When London bolstered the military presence still further in 1768 by ordering a regiment to sail from Britain to Boston, zealots in the city talked of resisting the landing of these troops by force. Fortunately cooler heads prevailed; but not for long.

On 5 March 1770 British soldiers guarding the Customs House in Boston fired into a threatening mob, killing five and wounding many more. The radicals at once dubbed it the Boston Massacre and held an annual service of commemoration at which fiery orators condemned the presence of British troops as a military occupation. Ironically, on the same day as the 'massacre', Lord North, the new prime minister, proposed a partial repeal of the Revenue Act for all items bar tea, a piece of legislation that received the royal assent a month later. But, in truth, little had changed. North had retained the lucrative duty on tea to assert Parliament's right to tax the Americans; and he had also retained the hated American Board of Customs and the principle of making governors and magistrates independent of local control.

The discontent rumbled on, with Rhode Islanders burning the British customs schooner *Gaspée* in 1772. But it was the passing of the Tea Act the following year that brought Anglo-American relations to boiling point. To evade the tea duty, Americans had been smuggling Dutch tea, and so reducing the import of legitimate tea from the British-owned East India Company by almost two thirds. The Act was an attempt to shore up the company's profits by allowing it to sell tea directly to America, thereby skipping England and its customs duty of 2s.6d. per pound. Even with the Townshend duty of 3d. per pound still applicable, the Act would have enabled the East India Company to undercut the smugglers and make tea cheaper in America. But the colonists were not prepared to pay the duty on principle – nor were they happy to give the East India Company a monopoly on the tea trade – and they refused to allow the tea to land. At New York and Philadelphia, the tea ships were forced to return to Britain. At Charleston, the tea was left to rot on the docks. But in Boston the governor stood his ground and refused to let the ships leave without paying the duty. So the 'Sons of Liberty' took matters into their own hands during the evening of 16 December 1773, the deadline for paying the tax, by boarding the three Boston ships, disguised as Native Americans, and dumping all 342 chests of tea in the harbour.

The so-called 'Boston Tea Party' provoked a furious response in Britain, with even pro-American MPs agreeing that the colonists had gone too far and should be punished. A few cautioned against too severe a reaction, warning it might lead to war. But most members of North's government thought the colonists would back down before it came to that; and even if they did take up arms, the received opinion was that they would pose no serious military threat. This was, in part, a reflection of the low opinion many British officers – Wolfe included – had of American soldiers during the Seven Years War. In one letter, Wolfe had written: 'The Americans are in general the dirtiest most contemptible cowardly dogs you can conceive . . . rather an encumbrance than any real strength to an army.' His successor, General James Murray, was just as scathing, describing the colonials as 'very unfit for and very impatient of war'.[8]

These views were widespread. One colonel told the House of Commons that he 'knew the Americans well, was certain they would not fight. They would never dare face an English army, and did not possess any of the qualifications necessary to make a good soldier.'[9] General Thomas Clarke, aide-de-camp to the king, was even more dismissive, saying in Benjamin Franklin's hearing that 'with a Thousand British grenadiers, he would undertake to go from one end of America to the other, and geld all the males, partly by force and partly by a little Coaxing'.[10]

Small wonder that legislators were unconcerned. One lamented the fate of military officers 'who would have nothing to do but burn, sink and destroy'; another said it was 'romantic' to think the

Americans would fight, and that there 'was more military prowess in a militia drummer'.[11] Even Lord North, a relative moderate in his cabinet, assured the House of Commons that the 'militia of Boston were no match for the force of this country'.[12] His intention, therefore, was to single out Boston for punishment by passing a series of laws – known as the Coercive Acts – that applied chiefly to Massachusetts. Together they closed the port of Boston until the East India Company had been repaid in full and order restored; placed the local government of Massachusetts under the direct control of the crown; gave royal officials the right to a trial outside Massachusetts; and enabled British troops to be billeted in unoccupied buildings if suitable quarters were not made available by the colonial legislatures.

North justified the harsh legislation with the words: 'The Americans . . . have plundered your merchants, burnt your ships, denied all obedience to your laws and authority; yet so clement and so long forbearing has our conduct been that it is incumbent on us now to take a different course. Whatever may be the consequences, we must risk something; if we do not, all is over.'[13]

But if his intention was to isolate the Boston radicals it failed. Many colonies rallied behind Massachusetts by sending money and provisions, and that autumn of 1774 the First Continental Congress met in Philadelphia to formulate a response to the Coercive Acts. Its delegates came from twelve of the thirteen colonies – Georgia declined to send any because it was seeking help from London to pacify its Indian frontier – and included a 42-year-old colonel of Virginia militia and veteran of the Monongahela massacre called George Washington. For Washington, the Acts were part of a 'regular systematic plan [to] fix the shackles of slavery upon us'.[14]

Most of his fellow delegates were of a similar mind, and they resolved to boycott British imports until all laws concerning the colonies since 1763 were repealed; if this did not happen within a year, they vowed, all exports to Britain would be blocked. They also adopted ten resolutions on the rights of self-government, including self-taxation by their own legislatures, and gave in to the radicals' demand to endorse the 'Resolves' taken by Suffolk County in Massachusetts, which declared the Coercive Acts to be unconstitutional and invalid, authorized no obedience until they were repealed, and advised citizens to arm and form militia for defence if attacked. But fearful of alienating the conservatives among them, they stopped short of a call for independence, preferring to acknowledge their allegiance to the crown, yet at the same time underlining their status as a 'dominion' not subject to Parliament. All these grievances were contained in a petition to King George III. Had they not been redressed within a year, Congress would reconvene.[15]

In the meantime, aware of the corner they were painting themselves into, the colonies prepared for war. Even before Congress had met, the extralegal legislature of Massachusetts had directed each town to organize its militia, stipulating that 'one-third of the men of their respective towns, between sixteen and sixty years of age, be ready to act at a minute's warning'. Moreover these 'minutemen' should be 'immediately equipped with an effective firearm, bayonet, pouch, knapsack, thirty rounds of cartridges and balls, and that they be disciplined [drilled] three times a week, and oftener, as opportunity may offer'. Now the other colonies followed suit, and by early 1775 militiamen were also drilling in Rhode Island, New Hampshire, Maryland, South Carolina and Virginia (where, in Fairfax County, the training was personally supervised by Colonel George Washington).

In Britain, meanwhile, the response to Congress's resolutions – which reached London shortly before Christmas 1774 – was ambiguous. George III refused to receive Congress's petition and was keen for his government to take a hard line. 'I do not want to drive them to despair but to Submission,' he told Lord North on 15 December, 'which nothing but feeling the inconvenience of their situation can bring their pride to submit to.'[16] The hawks in the cabinet, particularly Lord Suffolk, the home secretary, shared the king's preference for coercion. But North himself and his colonial secretary, Lord Dartmouth, were more circumspect, preferring to seek an accommodation with the colonists that would achieve both parliamentary supremacy and peace.

However, the news that reached Britain from America in the New Year of 1775 was uniformly bad: the colonies were in open rebellion and, according to General Thomas Gage, the commander of British troops in America (based in Boston), an army of 20,000 was needed to restore order. This enabled Suffolk and the hawks in the cabinet to persuade their colleagues to send reinforcements – though not as many as Gage had requested – and to order the restriction of America's overseas trade (in two pieces of legislation, passed in March and April 1775, known as the Restraining Acts). At the same time the cabinet rejected Lord Dartmouth's proposal for sending peace commissioners to America, though Lord North continued to authorize secret negotiations with Benjamin Franklin, who was then in London.

During the talks, which had begun in early December 1774, Franklin maintained Congress's line that Parliament had to disavow all right to interfere in the domestic affairs of the colonies and to give up taxation for revenue. He also urged the repeal of the Coercive Acts and the tax on tea, the removal of British troops from Boston and the satisfaction of Congress's other grievances. In return he would ask Congress to vote revenue to pay for administration and imperial security, and to provide reparations to the East India Company. North and Dartmouth were able to satisfy Franklin on the question of taxation, saying that Parliament would give up taxing the colonies if they supported their own governments and contributed to imperial defence in wartime. But neither was prepared to concede parliamentary supremacy, or to repeal those Acts that had become symbolic of Parliament's right to legislate for the colonies, and it was here, on the issue of sovereignty, that the talks finally broke down in mid-February.[17]

Even before then North's government had ordered General Gage, whom it suspected of lacking resolve, 'to take a more active and determined Part' against the rebels. He was instructed by Dartmouth on 27 January to use the reinforcements from England to secure Boston and Salem, arrest leaders of the Massachusetts Provincial Congress, and, if necessary, impose martial law in the colony. But even as it attempted to stiffen Gage's backbone, the cabinet was seeking to replace him with Jeffery Amherst, the conqueror of Canada and the favoured candidate of George III. When the 58-year-old Amherst refused the offer – partly on the grounds that he had fought alongside many of the leading rebels, including George Washington – the government decided to keep Gage and send three able major-generals to assist him. One of them was William Howe.

In many ways, Howe was an obvious choice. Like Amherst, he had first-hand knowledge of American warfare and, in addition, was one of the most respected officers in the British Army. His recent work with light infantry – which had so impressed George III – implied he had lost none of the skills he had learned in Canada. No politician did more to ensure his appointment than Lord George Germain (formerly Sackville), the cavalry commander disgraced at Minden who had since become a respected MP and leader of the Whig Opposition. Germain particularly valued Howe's experience of irregular warfare, and was confident he was the right man to teach British soldiers how to fight from behind 'trees, walls, or Hedges'. The fact that Howe had many friends and admirers in America was not, as far as Germain was concerned, a disadvantage. On the contrary, he believed that Howe's 'name as well as his abilities would be instrumental to restore discipline and confidence'.[18]

But would Howe agree to go? Barely a year earlier, while campaigning for re-election as an independent MP for Nottingham, he had condemned the government's American policy as unnecessarily harsh. He had also doubted whether the whole British Army could enforce that policy, promised to vote for the repeal of the Coercive Acts and said he would refuse to serve in America. In January 1775 he was still saying much the same in public; but in private he told North and Dartmouth that he was willing to go out to Boston as second-in-command. He and his fellow major-generals – Henry Clinton and John Burgoyne – were duly appointed on 2 February.

Howe had agreed to go partly out of ambition: he knew that Gage was unpopular with the cabinet and that there was a good chance he would soon replace him as commander-in-chief. But he also wanted to play his part in any peace negotiations, and was convinced that a majority of colonists were loyal to the crown and would be satisfied with freedom from parliamentary taxation. He said as much when explaining his *volte-face* to a constituent:

I was ordered, and could not refuse, without incurring the odious name of backwardness to serve my country in distress . . . There are certainly those [in America] who do not agree with a taxation from hence, but who do not wish to sever themselves from the supremacy of this country. This last set of men, I should hope, by their being relieved of the grievance, will most readily return to all due obedience to the laws. With respect to the few, who, I am told, desire to separate themselves from the Mother Country, I trust, when they find they are not well supported . . . they will, from fear of punishment, subside to the laws.[19]

Like so many others, he was wrong. But his miscalculation was particularly costly, and would cause him to throw away his country's best chance to crush the rebellion and retain its American colonies.

Howe's endeavours were not helped by the relatively weak strength of the British Army in 1775. Despite a marginal augmentation since the low point of the mid-1760s, its strength was still under 50,000 men: 39,294 infantry, 6,896 cavalry and 2,484 gunners. As well as the Household Cavalry and the Brigade of Guards, who tended not to serve outside Europe, there were 25 cavalry regiments and 72 infantry battalions, the former made up of 231 men (divided into 6 troops) and the latter of 477 men (10 companies). Of the two infantry flank companies, the grenadiers no longer carried explosives but were typically the tallest men in the regiment and fought – when not detached – on the right of the battalion line; the men of the light company, on the other hand, acted almost as skirmishers and tended to be the fittest and most agile soldiers, and the best shots.

The standard infantry weapon was still the Brown Bess musket and bayonet – though a slightly more powerful version of earlier types, the Short Land Pattern Musket, had been introduced in 1768* – while sergeants continued to carry 7-foot-long halberds, and some officers preferred spontoons (a shorter version of the halberd) to swords. A small number of rifles – so called because their barrels had

---

* With the same 42-inch barrel as its predecessor, but a bigger bore of .78 inch.

rifled grooves to impart spin on their cone-shaped bullets to give them greater range and accuracy – had been used by certain corps during the Seven Years War and recently an improved form of breech-loading rifle had been demonstrated to the adjutant-general and other senior officers at Woolwich. According to an eyewitness, the inventor first fired six shots a minute and

> then poured a bottle of water into the pan and barrel of the piece when loaded, so as to wet every grain of powder; and in less than half a minute, he fired with her, as well as ever . . . Lastly, he hit the bull's eye lying on his back on the ground. Incredible as it may seem, considering the variation of the wind, and the wetness of the weather, he only missed the target three times during the whole course of the experiment.[20]

But, despite the success of this test, the breech-loading rifle was regarded as less robust than a musket and too expensive to produce en masse; it was felt, moreover, that it would hinder tactical aggression by encouraging troops to fire at long range and not close with the bayonet. So although a number of these breech-loading rifles were manufactured and a small corps of riflemen was raised for service in America, the flintlock musket was still the infantry weapon of choice (and would remain so until the percussion system of ignition was introduced in the 1830s). In addition to these personal arms, each battalion of foot was generally supported by two pieces of field artillery known as battalion guns.

Commissions for officers were still bought and sold, usually for sums far in excess of the official price recognized by the secretary-at-war. A lieutenant-colonelcy in the 1st Foot Guards, for example, might cost upwards of £20,000 (£2 million in today's money); a captaincy in a line battalion was a more modest £1,000. Prices were generally higher in the Guards than in ordinary foot battalions, and more in the cavalry than in the infantry. Those without money or patronage were promoted slowly – particularly in peacetime, when there was neither the possibility of battlefield casualties nor personal acts of gallantry to achieve a step in rank – and in some regiments there were grey-haired lieutenants serving under the young sons of

1. An officer and soldier of the 15th (East Riding) Regiment of Foot, c. 1685, one of nine infantry corps raised by James II during the Monmouth Rebellion.

2. Captain Robert Parker of the Royal Regiment of Ireland (later the 18th Foot), painted after his retirement in c. 1720. Promoted from the ranks, Parker fought in most of the great battles of the War of the Spanish Succession and left an absorbing memoir.

3. Equestrian portrait of the Duke of Marlborough in armour, with allegorical figure bestowing a wreath of victory, painted to commemorate his death in 1722.

4. The Battle of Blenheim, 13 August 1704, with a mounted Marlborough in the right foreground and the besieged village to the left. It was England's first major victory on the Continent for 300 years.

5. 'Blow Your Match'. A grenadier of the 1st Foot Guards keeps his match alight as he prepares to throw his grenade.

6. 'Throw Your Granade'.

7. 'The March of the Guards towards Scotland in the year 1745' by the satirist William Hogarth. George II was furious when he saw Hogarth's depiction of his personal guards as drunken womanizers.

8. 'The Battle of Culloden, 16 April 1746', showing the main attack by Bonnie Prince Charlie's Highland rebels on the left of the government line.

9. The Duke of Cumberland, favourite son of George II, who acquired the sobriquet 'Butcher' for his ruthless suppression of the Jacobite 'Forty-Five' rebellion.

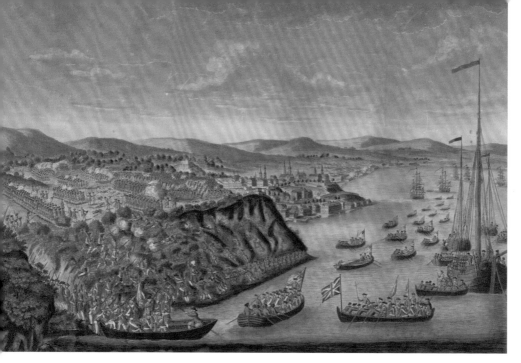

10. Perspective view of Wolfe's capture of Quebec on 13 September 1759, showing troops landing at the Anse-au-Foulon.

11. The most famous – yet wholly inaccurate – depiction of Wolfe's death at Quebec, by Benjamin West.

12. 'British Grenadier and Country Girl, *c.* 1760', underlining a soldier's enduring appeal for the opposite sex.

13. Recruiting parties would use all kinds of ruses to persuade men to enlist.

14. An etching by an unknown artist, *c.* 1773, emphasizing the contrasting fortunes of veteran officers and ordinary soldiers.

15. British soldiers retreat under fire from the village of Concord in Massachusetts on 19 April 1775, a skirmish that marked the start of the American War of Independence.

16. The Battle of Bunker Hill, 17 June 1775, a close-run and costly British victory.

17. General Sir William Howe, Commander-in-Chief of the British forces in America from 1775 to 1778.

18. One of the many depictions of George Washington's famous crossing of the Delaware River on 25 December 1776.

19. The Battle of Princeton, 3 January 1777. Washington, mounted, is leading rebel troops against the British right; in the foreground a British grenadier is bayoneting General Mercer.

20. Washington and his wife, visiting hungry and cold American troops in their camp at Valley Forge, Pennsylvania, during the winter of 1777/8.

21. The interior of a typical British cavalry barracks, complete with women and children, as seen by the caricaturist Thomas Rowlandson.

22. Rowlandson pokes more fun at the military with this chaotic depiction of a field day in Hyde Park.

23. 'Soldiers attending Divine Service', by Rowlandson.

rich and noble families. Rare indeed was the officer who, like Wolfe, had risen chiefly on merit.

The basic pay of a private soldier had not risen since the seventeenth century: 8*d*. a day, with money deducted for 'off-reckonings' and subsistence, and little left as a result. Inevitably recruits were hard to come by, though some were attracted by the smartness of the uniform with its thick red coat and buttoned-back lapels, stock, handsome gaiters and dashing tricorne hats. Yet the uniform was, in reality, tight fitting and uncomfortable, and the recruits were no more impressed by the greased, powdered and clubbed pigtails that army regulations required them to wear. A soldier of the late Georgian period, John Shipp of the 87th Foot, recalled his first acquaintance with the military 'queue':

> A large piece of candle-grease was applied, first to the sides of my head, then to the hind long hair; after this, the same kind of operation was performed with nasty stinking soap . . . [Next] a large pad, or bag filled with sand, was poked into the back of my head, round which the hair was gathered tight, and the whole tied round with a leather thong. When I was dressed for parade, I could scarcely get my eyelids to perform their office; the skin of my eyes and face drawn so tight by the plug that was struck in the back of my head, that I could not possibly shut my eyes; and to this, an enormous high stock was poked under my chin, so that, altogether, I felt as stiff as if I had swallowed a ramrod, or a sergeant's halberd.[21]

Discipline was as harsh as it had ever been, with offenders confined in dark, cramped cells for hours on end, beaten with sticks or belts, made to run the gauntlet of two rows of soldiers who struck them as they passed, or forced to sit on a wooden hump-backed horse with weights tied to their feet. Even minor offenders were flogged, and more serious crimes could still be punished by sentences of up to 2,000 lashes, though it was rare for more than 250 to be inflicted on any one day. A week would then elapse before the next flogging. Not for nothing did Americans call British soldiers 'bloody-backs' and 'lobsters'.

In 1775 the average recruit for the British Army was at least 5 feet

6½ inches tall, and certified by a surgeon as having 'no rupture nor ever troubled by Fits . . . and no way disabled by Lameness'. But, as the war progressed, and ever more recruits were required, standards were allowed to drop: recruits of 5 feet 3 inches were acceptable, and all convicted smugglers, 'all disorderly Persons who could not, upon Examination, prove themselves to exercise and industriously follow some lawful Trade or Employment' and 'incorrigible rogues . . . convicted of running from and leaving their Families chargeable upon the Parish' were liable to be forcibly enlisted by press-gangs.[22]

With officers and men drawn from such polar opposites of the social spectrum, it is hardly surprising that the attitude of civilians to the profession of soldiering was so ambivalent. It was summed up best in a 1776 conversation between Samuel Johnson – the great poet, critic, essayist and lexicographer – and his companion and biographer James Boswell:

> JOHNSON: The character of a soldier is high. They who stand forth the foremost in danger, for the community, have the respect of mankind. An officer is much more respected than any other man who has as little money. In a commercial country, money will always purchase respect. But you find, an officer, who has, properly speaking, no money, is every where well received and treated with attention . . .
>
> BOSWELL: Yet, Sir, I think that common soldiers are worse thought of than other men in the same rank of life; such as labourers.
>
> JOHNSON: Why, Sir, a common soldier is usually a very gross man, and any quality which procures respect may be overwhelmed by grossness . . . But when a common soldier is civil in his quarters, his red coat procures him a degree of respect.[23]

On a separate occasion in 1778, discussing war with Boswell, Johnson gave one of the best – and arguably the most quoted – explanations as to why so many males are drawn to the military life:

> Every man thinks meanly of himself for not having been a soldier, or not having been at sea . . . Were Socrates and [the great commander] Charles the Twelfth of Sweden both present in any company, and

Socrates to say, 'Follow me, and hear a lecture on philosophy,' and Charles, laying his hand on his sword, to say, 'Follow me, and dethrone the Czar,' a man would be ashamed to follow Socrates . . . The profession of soldiers and sailors has the dignity of danger. Mankind reverence those who have got over fear, which is so general a weakness.[24]

13.   First Shots

Even as William Howe and his fellow major-generals crossed the Atlantic, the British Army was fighting a running skirmish with Massachusetts rebels that would set the template for much of the war. It took place between Lexington and Concord, on 19 April 1775, and marks the start of what became the American War of Independence.

The immediate cause of the bloodletting was a second dispatch from Lord Dartmouth to General Gage, of 2 March, informing him that more reinforcements (including senior officers) were on the way, and ordering him to occupy or destroy all rebel fortifications, to seize their stores and to arrest leading rebels so that they could be tried for treason, either in Boston or London. Within days of receiving these orders, Gage had devised a plan of action. According to his latest intelligence, two of the principal Massachusetts rebels, John Hancock and Samuel Adams, were lodging at Lexington, a hamlet 12 miles north-west of Boston, while a rebel cache of arms and powder was located at Concord, a further 5 miles to the west. His plan, therefore, was for 700 of his best men – two flanking battalions of grenadiers and light infantry, formed of companies taken from the various corps at Boston[1] – to march through the night to Lexington and apprehend the rebel leaders, before continuing on to Concord, where they would destroy the rebel arsenal. Well aware that speed and surprise were essential if they were to avoid a serious confrontation with minutemen, Gage ordered his men to begin their march by midnight so that they could be safely back in Boston by noon the following day.

The British troops involved were delighted to have the opportunity to prove themselves against the rebels. Only three weeks earlier a column of British infantry had arrived at a bridge over the Charles River, near Boston, to be met by two loaded cannon. But a bloodbath was averted when the rebels chose discretion and ran off, leaving

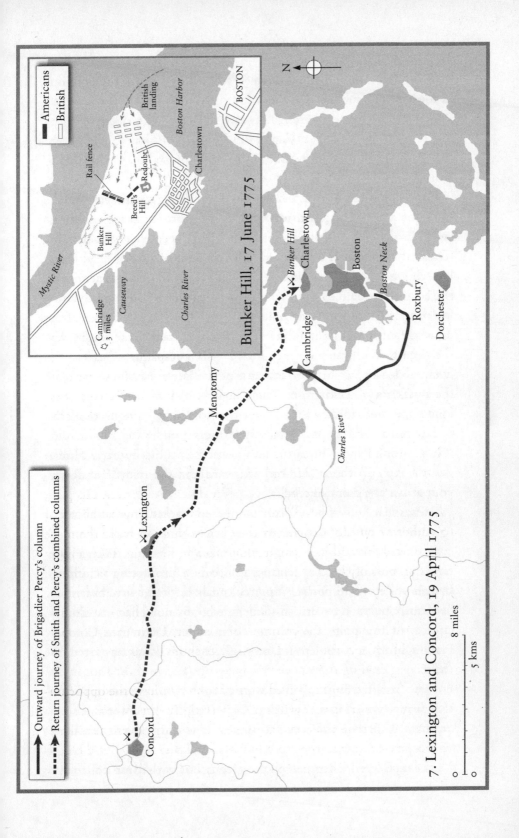

Americans

British

Rail fence

Redoubt

Breed's
Hill

Bunker
Hill

British
landing

Boston Harbor

Charlestown

BOSTON

Mystic River

Causeway

Charles River

Cambridge
3 miles

N

Bunker Hill, 17 June 1775

× Bunker Hill
Charlestown

Boston

Cambridge

Boston Neck

Roxbury

Dorchester

Charles River

Menotomy

× Lexington

× Concord

Outward journey of Brigadier Percy's column

Return journey of Smith and Percy's combined columns

7. Lexington and Concord, 19 April 1775

5 kms

8 miles

0

0

their unfired cannon behind them. It seemed to confirm the opinion of most British soldiers that the colonists were too cowardly to fight. 'Never did any nation so much deserve to be made an example of to future ages,' wrote one of Gage's subalterns to his father, 'and never [was] any set of men more anxious to be employed on so laudable a work.'[2]

Gage's plan for 19 April, however, soon began to unravel. Rebel spies got wind of his intentions and, even before the British column began its march, a dispatch rider named Paul Revere had left Boston to alert Lexington and Concord. The element of surprise had been lost, though the soldiers did not know it yet, and speed was next sacrificed at Boston's Back Bay, where the Royal Navy had provided too few boats to transport the column across the Charles River. The delay meant it was gone four in the morning, and already light, by the time the column's advance guard – six companies of 240 men, commanded by Major John Pitcairn of the Royal Marines – neared the outskirts of Lexington. Their quarry, alerted by Revere, was long gone. Instead they found their way barred by a single company of Lexington militia – mostly dairy farmers – under the 46-year-old Captain John Parker. Pitcairn, a no-nonsense Scot in his early fifties, saw them as no threat. He rode forward and shouted: 'Lay down your arms, you damned rebels!'[3]

Aware that he was heavily outnumbered, Parker ordered his men to withdraw but not disarm. As they began to move back, the red-coats moved forward menacingly, shouting and cheering. Then a shot rang out, possibly fired by a jittery militiaman, prompting a crashing British volley in response. Some colonials returned fire, but most fled, hotly pursued by British soldiers, who, by now, had lost all discipline. At this point the column commander, Lieutenant-Colonel Francis Smith, a corpulent infantry officer in his fifties, appeared on the scene. 'Finding the Rebels scamping off (except those shut up in houses),' recalled Smith, 'I endeavoured to the utmost to stop all further firing, which in a short time I effected.'[4] Eight militiamen lay dead and a further nine were wounded. The only British casualties were a private, shot in the leg, and Pitcairn's horse.

The men were re-formed on the green, 'but with some difficulty', recalled a subaltern, they 'were so wild they could hear no orders'. Some were shouting that the rebels were firing from houses, but Smith was loth to let them search Lexington's homes, 'knowing if the houses were once broken into, none within could well be saved'. He also knew, from the presence of the militia, that the rebel leaders must have received advance warning of the column's approach and left long ago. With more opposition inevitable, some of his officers advised him to abandon the march to Concord. Smith refused. He had his orders; but he did send Gage a request for reinforcements.

At 9 a.m. Smith continued his march to Concord, sending his light infantry into high ground to protect his right flank. Apart from one or two stray shots they entered Concord unopposed an hour later. The local militia had mustered, but they were unwilling to fire first and, unsure of British numbers, had gathered in hundreds on the slopes of Punkatasset Hill to the north of the village to await developments. Taking advantage of their absence, Smith used his grenadiers to search for arms, while two detachments of light infantry guarded bridges to the north and south of the town, and a third advanced a mile beyond the North Bridge to the home of the local colonel of militia, a 64-year-old miller called James Barrett. It was empty.

Soon after, the British lost a second man when a lone grenadier sentry was captured on the outskirts of the village; the minuteman responsible was Sylvanus Wood, a shoemaker by trade, who had followed the British from Lexington. 'I cocked my piece,' remembered Wood, 'and run up to him, seized his gun with my left hand. He surrendered his armor, one gun and bayonet, a large cutlash [cutlass] and brass fender, one box over the shoulder with twenty-two rounds, one round the waist with eighteen rounds. This was the first prisoner that was known to be taken that day.'[5]

In the village, meanwhile, the grenadiers found and spiked three cannon and burned their wooden gun carriages. They also uncovered some powder, which they dumped in the river, and cut down the village's Liberty Pole and flag. But an act not authorized by Smith, and one that triggered more bloodshed, was the burning of the Town House, the village's main public building. Accident or not, its flames were visible on Punkatasset Hill, where word quickly spread that the

British were burning the town. Barrett ordered his men to advance on the North Bridge, driving its defenders back across it and inflicting many casualties, including four out of eight officers. Inexplicably, the militiamen failed to secure the north end of the bridge, and so enabled the most advanced detachment of light infantry, hurrying back from Barrett's house, to withdraw across it to safety.

With his column now re-formed in a single body, Smith ordered a return to Lexington. But hundreds of militiamen now lay between them and safety, and Smith's men were forced to fight a running battle against an enemy they could barely see. 'They hardly ever fired but under cover of a stone wall, from behind a tree, or out of a house,' wrote an officer, 'and the moment they had fired they lay down out of sight until they had loaded again.'[6]

As before, the light infantry were used as flank protection while the grenadiers moved along the road. 'We at first kept our order and returned their fire as hot as we received it,' wrote Lieutenant Henry de Bernière of the 10th Foot's light company, 'but when we arrived within a mile of Lexington, our ammunition began to fail, and the light companies were so fatigued with flanking they were scarcely able to act.'[7]

With no sign of the long-expected reinforcement, Smith's men lost their discipline for the second time that day. 'We began to run,' recalled de Bernière, 'rather than retreat in good order.' At Lexington Green several officers tried to restore order by running ahead of their men and threatening them with death if they continued their flight. They were only partially successful, and just when it seemed that the whole column was about to dissolve into an unruly mob, the relief force appeared over the next ridge and quickly formed a line of battle on either side of the road. It consisted of 1,100 soldiers of four battalions, including the 23rd Royal Welch Fusiliers (the regiment that had fought so well at the battles of Dettingen and Minden), and was commanded by Brigadier-General Lord Percy, the 33-year-old son of the Duke of Northumberland.

The 23rd had arrived in America from England the previous July, 350 strong, and had since formed part of the Boston garrison with orders 'to rout anybody (that shall dare to attack them) with their bayonets'.[8] Their numbers included Lieutenant Frederick Mackenzie, the 44-year-old adjutant who had served in the same rank for more than twenty years, and whose wife Nancy ('Mrs Mac') was expecting their latest child; Corporal Jeffrey Grimes, promoted after less than five years with the 23rd; and Drummer Robert Mason, nineteen, the son of a fusilier and therefore a 'child of the regiment'. Despite its title, the 23rd was mostly made up of unskilled and illiterate Englishmen in their twenties, though a few had trades and could aspire to follow the example of Lieutenant Richard Baily, promoted from the ranks. Some had joined up to see the world. 'My chief intention,' claimed one soldier, 'being to travel and traverse the seas occasioned my enlisting.' But most did so out of financial necessity: to earn a wage or to escape creditors. A few could not adapt to the discipline and hardships of army life, and since arriving in America a sizeable number had deserted, some to join the rebels and fight against their former comrades.[9]

On the ridge above Lexington, on 19 April, Adjutant Mackenzie was impressed by the ease with which the brigade formed its line of battle, though 'by reason of the stone walls and other obstacles, it was not formed in so regular a manner as it should have been.'[10] Brigadier-General Percy had brought two cannon with him, and he now ordered these guns to open up on the militiamen pursuing Smith's exhausted light infantry and grenadiers. 'The shot from the cannon had the desired effect,' reported Percy to Gage, 'and stopped the rebels for a little time, who immediately dispersed and endeavoured to surround us, being very numerous.'[11]

It was now 2.30 p.m. and, to avoid being cut off, Percy ordered his expanded command to withdraw to Boston with Smith's men leading the way and the 23rd bringing up the rear. He also sent out strong flanking parties from his own fresh battalions, 'which were absolutely necessary, as there was not a stone wall or house tho' before in appearance evacuated, from whence the rebels did not fire upon us'.

A lieutenant of the 4th (King's Own) Foot remembered that 'almost every house in the road' had to be stormed, 'for the rebels had taken possession of them and galled us exceedingly, but they suffered for their temerity for all that we found in the houses were put to death'. A minuteman who entered one such house found bodies everywhere and 'the Blud . . . half over [my] Shoes'.[12]

The rearguard of the 23rd was, like most of the British Army, trained in Wolfe's tactics of a massed volley followed by a bayonet charge. Such methods were useless against an enemy that fired from behind obstacles, and Adjutant Mackenzie would later bemoan the fact that his men 'threw away their fire very inconsiderately, and without being certain of its effect'.[13] Pressed constantly by the pursuing militiamen and running out of ammunition, they were relieved as rearguard halfway to Boston. But they still had to run the gauntlet of Menotomy village (now Arlington), where hundreds of minutemen fired on the retreating column. It was here that Lieutenant-Colonel Benjamin Bernard of the 23rd became the highest-ranking British casualty when his thigh was shattered by a round-shot.

Two miles further on, as the column approached Cambridge, Percy made the wise decision to take the left fork to Charlestown, rather than retrace his steps back across the Charles River. It was just as well because the rebels had dismantled the planking on the bridge over the Charles and were lying in wait. But still the sniping continued, and it was well after seven, and already dark, when the column finally reached the safety of the British lines at Charlestown, 'very much fatigued with a march of above thirty miles, and having expended almost all our ammunition', reported Percy. He added: 'We had the misfortune in losing a good many men in the retreat, tho' nothing like the number which from many circumstances I have reason to believe were killed of the rebels.'[14]

This was wishful thinking. The British had lost 65 men and officers killed, and 207 wounded and missing; American losses were 94, with 40 to 45 of those killed. In private, Percy admitted he was stunned by the 'perseverance' of the citizen-soldiers. Anyone who expected a New England army to be 'an irregular mob', he added, 'will find himself much mistaken'.[15]

The following morning, grey and chilly, the British garrison at Boston woke to find themselves under siege by local militiamen. Over the next few days the siege army would grow to nearly 16,000 men as reinforcements arrived from New Hampshire, Rhode Island and Connecticut. It was nominally commanded by General Artemas Ward, forty-seven, the senior Massachusetts officer and a veteran of the French and Indian War, though political direction was provided by the Provincial Congress's Committee of Safety – headed by a young Boston physician and firebrand called Dr Joseph Warren – which set up its headquarters in Cambridge. The consequence of Gage's botched operation of 19 April, therefore, was that the rebellion had begun in earnest.

The first unofficial news of the fighting reached Britain on 28 May, two days after Parliament had begun its summer recess. George III was broadly pleased with the outcome, and congratulated Gage for accomplishing his goal (the destruction of the stores at Concord) with fewer casualties than the rebels. Even the arrival of Gage's official dispatches on 10 June – including details of the siege – failed to dent either the king's or his government's confidence. George III, for one, was convinced the size of the rebel force was exaggerated. But as more dispatches came in, the full extent of the rebellion became clear: New York, long considered the most loyal of the American cities, had expelled British officials, voted to support Congress and sent 2,000 men to Boston; at Philadelphia, and all along the Chesapeake, rebels had broken into royal magazines and armed themselves; the governors of New Hampshire, Pennsylvania, Virginia and the Carolinas were no longer in control. 'From what can be learned,' reported Gage in mid-May (a dispatch received in London on 24 June), 'it is not found that one Province is in a better situation than another, the People called Friends of Government are few in all and . . . the opposite Party numerous, active and violent.'[16]

George III and most of his ministers were determined to restore royal authority by force. 'With firmness and perseverance America will be brought to submission,' the king told Dartmouth, the colonial secretary and one of the few doves in the cabinet. 'If not, old England . . . will be able to make her rebellious children rue the hour they cast off obedience . . . Distant possessions standing upon an equality with the superior State is more ruinous than being deprived of such connections.'[17]

These sentiments were shared by Lord George Germain, who, though not yet a minister, was a powerful voice in Parliament and a confidant of Lord Suffolk (the leading hawk in the cabinet). His advice to Suffolk was to reinforce the army and navy in America, adopt tactics suited to the terrain, replace Gage with General Howe, arm loyal colonists★ and begin the reconquest of America from New York. Many of these policies, Howe's promotion included, were soon adopted. But while Dartmouth remained colonial secretary there was always the possibility – however distant – of peace. On 1 July, for example, in the same dispatch in which he told Gage that the rebellion had to be subdued,† he also expressed a hope that the colonists would still consider the Conciliatory Resolution that Parliament had passed in February. (The resolution had stated that, if a colony agreed to support its own government and contribute to imperial defence, the only external taxes it would have to bear would be for the regulation of trade, and even then all revenue would be spent in the colony in which it had been collected.) Even more significant, however, was his implicit criticism of Gage for starting the war. He assumed, he wrote, that the decision to march to Concord 'was taken upon the fullest Consideration of the Advantage on one hand and Hazard on the other of such an Enterprize, and of all the probable Consequences that were to result from it'. Lastly, he told Gage not to expect any more reinforcements before 1776. Some had been ordered to Boston from Scotland, Ireland and the Mediterranean, but it would take time to find replacements, to prepare supplies and shipping, and to transport them across the Atlantic.[18]

In Boston, meanwhile, a second battle had been fought. It was precipitated by the arrival on 25 May of the three major-generals and the latest reinforcements, bringing the strength of the Boston garrison up to 10,000 men. These extra troops made it possible for Gage to take the offensive, and his first objective was to seize the high ground to the north of Boston at Charlestown, from where he feared the

---

★ Known as loyalists or Tories.
† His specific advice was for Gage to use the men he had been sent in the spring either to break the siege of Boston or to form a detachment to capture New York.

rebels might establish artillery that could dominate the city and its shipping. It was to Charlestown, separated from Boston proper by a thin stretch of the Charles River, that Percy had withdrawn his troops from Lexington on 19 April; but soon after Gage, fearful of a general rising in the city, had brought them back across the Charles. Now, with more troops available, he proposed to re-establish his men on the heights above Charlestown, as well as taking the high ground to the south of Boston at Dorchester. Once both strategic positions were in his grasp, he would launch a pincer attack on the rebel head-quarters at Cambridge, and thus raise the siege.

But even with more troops, the morale and discipline of the Boston garrison were suspect. Soon after his arrival Major-General John Burgoyne – a 52-year-old playwright, womanizer and notori-ous gambler who, with an only moderate record of army service, had risen from captain to brigadier-general in just six years thanks to his excellent political connections – observed 'men still lost in a sort of stupefaction which the events of the 19th of April had occasioned, and venting expressions of censure, anger, or despondency'.[19] Lieu-tenant John Barker of the 4th Foot, who had fought at Concord, was shocked by the lack of discipline: 'Our soldiers the other day showed no want of courage, yet were so wild and irregular, that there was no keeping them in any order . . . The plundering was shameful; many hardly thought of anything else; what was worse they were encour-aged by some officers.'[20] But others were eager for revenge, and the proposed offensive would give them the opportunity.

Gage fixed the date for the British occupation of the twin heights above Charlestown – Breed's and Bunker hills – for the night of 18 June. But with a few days to go, spies brought word of the oper-ation to General Ward, the rebel commander. He was reluctant to pre-empt Gage by fortifying the heights because he feared that such a move would weaken the centre of his lines, due west of Boston, and make it vulnerable to a British attack. He also worried that a garrison on the heights would be cut off if the British used an amphibious assault to capture the narrow neck of the Charlestown Peninsula. But he was overruled by his political masters on the Massachusetts Com-mittee of Safety, who insisted the heights be held. During the night of 16 June, therefore, using 800 spades and pickaxes that had been collected from nearby towns, the colonists began to construct a square redoubt on Breed's Hill. Though slightly lower than Bunker Hill, Breed's was closer to Boston and its harbour, and was more likely to provoke Gage into an attack, which is what the Committee of Safety wanted.

By the morning of 17 June the 1,200-strong garrison under Colonel William Prescott – a 49-year-old veteran of two previous wars who had risen from the ranks – had constructed a square redoubt, its sides 130 feet long, on the summit of Breed's Hill. It was, in effect, one long continuous trench with the earth piled on the outward side as a rampart. On the south-west side facing Charlestown, where they expected the main attack, they had added a redan, or angular protrusion, which increased the defenders' field of fire and made it possible to enfilade an assaulting force. They had also used some of the excavated earth to build a breastwork, 6 feet high, that extended 80 yards from the east side of the redoubt in an attempt to cover what remained of the hilltop.

Even as the work was under way, a British patrol had detected the sound of digging and warned Gage and his senior officers what was afoot. Howe and the other major-generals urged immediate preparations for a dawn assault. But Gage preferred to wait for daylight to assess the strength of the American defences. Soon after dawn, at a formal council of war, Major-General Henry Clinton – the son of a former governor of New York and a sensible, prudent but frequently quarrelsome officer – suggested an amphibious attack on Charlestown Neck; that and a naval bombardment of the heights would, he argued, ensure a relatively bloodless victory. Howe, and possibly Burgoyne, preferred a frontal attack on the main redoubt, and Gage agreed. It would give the British regulars an opportunity to storm the hill with the bayonet, and in doing so they would confirm their battlefield superiority over the part-time American militia. The benefit of such an attack would be as much moral as physical – convincing rebels across America that it was impossible to stand against professional soldiers – and no one, not even Clinton, was in any doubt that it would succeed. 'The general idea,' he wrote soon after, 'was the redoubt was only a redan, that the hill was open and easy of ascent and in short that it would be easily carried.'[21]

This assumption robbed the British assault of any urgency, and it was further delayed by the need to wait for high tide so that the longboats could clear the offshore sandbanks. Finally, at 2 p.m. in the afternoon, the first of the 1,550 assaulting troops – made up of two flank battalions of grenadiers and light infantry, four line battalions (the 5th, 38th, 43rd and 52nd Foot), and some field artillery – landed unopposed near the south-east corner of the pear-shaped peninsula. Each soldier was wearing a tricorne hat (or, in the case of the grenadiers, a bearskin) over his powdered wig, a long-skirted heavy woollen scarlet coat and white crossbelts. His equipment included a canvas knapsack filled with a three-day supply of food, a rolled blanket, a haversack for personal items (including a cup and tools for cleaning his weapon), a scabbard with a two-pound bayonet and a cartridge box. So heavy was all this equipment that one historian likened it to carrying a 'good-sized deer on their backs'. They also carried flintlock Brown Bess muskets that had changed little since the 1720s: the weapon was 4 feet 9 inches long, weighed 12 lb. and fired a .78-calibre ball that was effective at 200 yards, but accurate only at very close range. There was no rear sight and men were simply told to level their muskets and fire in a volley, following it with a bayonet charge.[22]

As Gage's deputy, and a man with experience of amphibious operations, Howe had asked for and been given command of the assault. No sooner had he landed with the first wave than he began to study the rebel defences. To his left, 2,000 yards down the beach, lay the town of Charlestown, many of whose houses had been set on fire by a naval bombardment to deny their use to the enemy. To the right of the settlement, and barely 500 yards from where Howe stood, was the redoubt and the breastwork on Breed's Hill, a shallow incline no more than a hundred feet above sea level, defended by 1,500 men from Massachusetts and Connecticut. But Howe could see that the 200-yard gap that separated the fort from the fenced gardens on the edge of Charlestown was encumbered by obstacles, and decided it was too narrow for his men to manoeuvre through. The alternative was either a direct attack on the redoubt up sloping, treeless farmland that was intersected by rail fences and stone walls; or a flanking manoeuvre to the right, between Breed's Hill and the Mystic River, a 300-yard stretch that was protected on its water flank by 500 men and two guns behind a rail fence bolstered with brushwood, earth and hay, and in the space in between by 70 men in V-shaped entrenchments known as flèches, sited parallel to the shore, which enabled their defenders to enfilade an attacking force.

As the flèches were partly obscured by Breed's Hill, it is possible that Howe did not see them; or he might simply have discounted their worth. Either way he decided on a staggered two-pronged attack: he would lead the first assault on the right flank; and if it was successful he would attack the rear of the redoubt on Breed's Hill while his subordinate, Brigadier-General Robert Pigot, advanced on its front. But he could see ever more defenders pouring into the peninsula, and decided not to move until he had reinforcements. It took an hour for the extra troops – 700 men from the 47th Foot, 1st Marine Battalion and the last of the flank companies – to arrive. Once they had, he placed them in reserve behind Pigot's brigade, the 38th and 43rd Foot, which was facing the redoubt. Then he advanced with the remaining troops.

His plan was for the light infantry to move up the beach in column, while the grenadiers formed two lines and attacked the rail fence. Though the light infantry would have to operate in a confined space, he trusted them to break through the makeshift defences and take the rebels in the flank. The breakthrough could then be exploited by the two support battalions, the 5th and 52nd, who were following the grenadiers in line formation.

'We began the attack,' Howe informed his brother, 'by a sharp cannonade from our field pieces and two Howitzers, the lines advancing slowly, and frequently halting to give time for the artillery to fire.'[23] However, the grenadiers were impatient to be at the enemy and pushed on ahead – an eerie echo of the precipitous attack at Beauport in 1759 – kicking down the flimsier fences and clambering over others. As they neared the rail fence, the odd rebel bullet whistled overhead. But most of the defenders – men from Connecticut and New Hampshire – obeyed the order from their commander Colonel John Stark, a former Ranger, to hold their fire 'until they could see the enemy's half gaiters'.[24]

The attackers were not so disciplined and, according to Howe, both grenadiers and light infantry 'began firing, and by crowding fell into disorder'. It was now, with the British just 50 yards from the barrier, that the defenders fired a volley that, noted one of their officers, 'mowed down the whole front ranks'. As the grenadiers recoiled, they collided with the advancing 5th and 52nd Foot, causing yet more chaos.[25]

The attack on the beach had also stalled, prompting the fearless Howe to rush forward with his staff to see what was happening. It was far worse than he could have imagined: his favourite corps was retreating. 'The Light Infantry . . . being repulsed there,' he wrote, 'was a *moment that I never felt before.*' Howe and some of their officers managed to rally the light troops and form them up for a second attack to the right rear of the grenadiers. But disorientated by the smoke and noise of battle, not to mention the screams of their wounded comrades, they mistook the grenadiers for the enemy and opened fire on them, killing their commanding officer and many others.[26]

Even then, a few officers led their men forward; but they came on in clusters, rather than in an unbroken line, and were shot down before they reached the rail fence. The fire was particularly destructive from the flèches on the flanks, where militiamen who missed one target were bound to find another beyond. The British counter-fire, by contrast, was panicked and ineffective. 'The fire of the enemy was so badly directed,' recalled a New Hampshire defender, 'I should presume that forty-nine balls out of fifty passed from one to six feet over our heads.'[27]

With two of his aides hit, and his plan to outflank the redoubt in tatters, Howe pulled his men back and sent word to Brigadier-General Pigot to prepare for a joint attack on the hill. This time, Howe would lead the remainder of the grenadiers, 5th and 52nd Foot against the point where the flèches met the breastwork on the hill, while Pigot attacked the redoubt with the burning houses of

Charlestown to his left. Pigot had already lost a number of men to snipers, and many more fell to artillery fire as they attacked in earnest. But, as with the first attack, Colonel Prescott told his men on the hill to conserve their fire until the last moment. 'Finding our ammunition was almost spent,' he wrote, 'I commanded a cessation till the enemy advanced within 30 yards when we gave them such a hot fire, that they were obliged to retire nearly 150 yards before they could rally and come again to the attack.'[28]

Lieutenant Waller of the 1st Marines recalled: 'We were now in confusion, after being broke several times in getting over the rails, etc. I did all I could to form the two companies on our right, which at last I effected, losing many of them while it was performing. Major Picairn was killed close by me, with a captain and a subaltern, also a serjeant, and many of the privates, and had we stopped there much longer, the enemy would have picked us all off. I saw this, and begged Colonel Nesbitt of the 47th to form on our left, in order that we might advance with our bayonets to the parapet.'[29]

Howe's attack on the right, meanwhile, had reached the point where the flèches met the breastwork; but it could not break through. Instead, the men huddled beneath the entrenchments, where, wrote an officer of the 52nd, 'we were not nearly so much exposed to their fire as we were then in some degree covered.' Some tried to urge their men over the earth bank, and were shot as they exposed themselves. But eventually Lord Rawdon, a lieutenant in the 5th Foot, got some of his men to follow him, and as they scrambled over the bank the defences began to collapse. For the previous hour or so a steady trickle of defenders had been making for the safety of the neck, often encouraged by their officers; now, with most of them out of ammunition, the trickle became a flood.[30]

At the redoubt, too, the defenders knew the game was up, though many stayed to fight it out, using their muskets like cudgels. It was an unequal clash, now, and the marines and the 47th – the first British battalions to enter the redoubt – gave no quarter with their bayonets and swords. 'I cannot pretend to describe the horror of the scene within the redoubt when we entered it,' wrote Lieutenant Waller of the marines, ''twas streaming with blood and strewed with dead and dying men, the soldiers stabbing some and dashing out the brains of others.'[31] In a separate letter, he added: 'Nothing could be more shocking than the carnage that followed the storming of this work. We tumbled over the dead to get at the living, who were crowding out of the gorge of the redoubt, in order to form under the defences which they had prepared to cover their retreat.'[32]

Many were shot down as they fled, including Dr Warren, the leader of the Massachusetts Committee of Safety, who had spent at least part of the battle in the redoubt. Colonels Prescott and Stark, on the other hand, lived to fight another day.

With the battle over and the peninsula in British hands, the survivors dug in, carried their wounded to the boats below and buried their dead. They had won a victory of sorts – but at a terrible cost. Of the 3,000 or so British troops involved, 226 had been killed and a further 928 wounded, a casualty rate of just under 40 per cent, which was comparable to the appalling loss of Allied troops at the Schellenberg in 1704. Almost one in 12 of the casualties was an officer, an attrition rate also similar to the 1704 battle. But back then the Franco-Bavarians had lost even more troops than the Allies. This was not the case at Bunker Hill – as the battle was named after the larger of the two heights – where American casualties were 160 killed and 271 wounded.[33]

Dorothea Gamsby, ten, watched the battle from the house of her loyalist uncle, Sir George Nutting, and later recalled the aftermath: 'Uncle came home and said the rebels had retreated . . . Then came the loads of wounded men attended by long lines of soldiers, the gay banners torn and soiled, a sight to be remembered a lifetime. I have read many times of the glory of war but this one battle taught me, however it be painted by poet or novelist, there is nothing but woe and sorrow and shame to be found in the reality.'[34]

Howe was later criticized for not pursuing the fleeing Americans to Cambridge. He responded in a letter to his brother: 'The soldiers were so much harassed, and there were so many officers lost, that the pursuit was not followed with all the vigour that might be expected.'[35] He might have added that an advance upon Cambridge was not part of the original plan, and that it would have left his exhausted troops extremely vulnerable to a counter-attack or an ambush.

No one at Boston, however, was in any doubt that the objective had been gained at too high a cost. 'The loss we have sustained,' acknowledged Gage, 'is greater than we can bear.' Clinton, who had taken part in the final assault on the redoubt (having just arrived on the peninsula with the last of the reinforcements), described it as a 'dear bought victory, another such would have ruined us'.[36] Howe wrote home to his brother: 'The general's returns will give you the particulars of what I call this unhappy day – I freely confess to you, when I look to the consequences of it, in the loss of so many brave officers, I do it with horror.'[37]

Most officers blamed the indiscipline of the men for the heavy casualties. 'Our confidence in our own troops,' noted Lord Rawdon, 'is much lessened since the 17th of June. Some of them did, indeed, behave with infinite courage, but others behaved as remarkably ill.' General Burgoyne, who talked to many of his friends after the battle, came to the same conclusion. 'The zeal and intrepidity of the officers, which was without exception exemplary, was ill seconded by the private men. Discipline, not to say courage, was wanting. In the critical moment of carrying the redoubt, the officers of some corps were almost alone.'[38]

Some condemned the generals, who had, wrote one young officer, as good as 'murdered' the fallen redcoats with an ill-conceived plan that grew from 'gross ignorance'.[39] But another British officer, wounded at Bunker Hill, preferred to praise his foe. 'We have learnt one melancholy truth,' he wrote from his sickbed, 'which is, that the Americans, if they are equally well commanded, are full as good soldiers as ours, and, as it is, are very little inferior to us even in discipline and countenance.'[40]

News of Bunker Hill reached Britain in late July, hard on the heels of reports that a rebel force under Colonel Benedict Arnold had taken the forts of Ticonderoga and Crown Point in the Champlain Valley, capturing in the process a huge haul of munitions, including 78 cannon, 6 mortars, 3 howitzers, thousands of cannonballs, 18,000 lb. of musket-balls and 30,000 flints. Ministers were at once called back from their country homes, where most were spending the summer recess, to discuss the emergency. The official line put out by North's cabinet was that Bunker Hill was a notable victory. In private, ministers were less sanguine, acknowledging – as one under-secretary of state put it – that if 'we have eight more such victories there will be nobody left to bring home the news of them'. North himself now saw the need to treat the conflict not as a minor rebellion but 'as a foreign war'.[41]

Prior to receiving the news from Lexington–Concord, most ministers had assumed that the Americans would back down in the face of British force, and if they did not they would be soundly thrashed by regular troops. Bunker Hill removed the last scales from their eyes. Apart from Lord Dartmouth (who would shortly be replaced as colonial secretary by Lord George Germain), the cabinet was now united in its belief that hostilities were necessary and victory was possible, but it would probably take a second year of fighting to achieve. To that end, ministers voted over the coming weeks to send more reinforcements to America, expand further the size of the army and navy, hire foreign mercenaries and ask Parliament for new taxes to finance the war. They also acknowledged the danger of France, and possibly also Spain, intervening on the side of the colonists (a fear that was realized in 1778). Their only major miscalculation was to ignore all evidence to the contrary and assume that the great majority of Americans remained loyal to the crown, and that there was little support for the rebellion outside New England.

This had important consequences, not least the cabinet's fixation with killing the beast by severing its head. In practical terms, this meant concentrating its resources against New England, a strategy that even before Bunker Hill had been recommended by General Howe in a private letter to his brother, Rear-Admiral Lord Howe. In it, Howe rejected Gage's strategy of subduing Massachusetts as too hazardous, and instead proposed to strangle the rebellion at birth by holding Boston, blockading the New England ports, and launching attacks up the Hudson and Connecticut river valleys. Howe wrote this letter knowing that his brother would forward it to Lord George Germain, who, in turn, would make it known to the cabinet. It was a naked attempt by Howe to supplant Gage as commander-in-chief and, eventually, it succeeded. But first he had to deflect criticism of his conduct at Bunker Hill, and he did this by sending a second letter to his brother, giving his own private version of events and exculpating himself of any blame for the high number of casualties. His brother, who was lobbying for his own appointment as naval commander-in-chief in America, duly sent the letter on to Germain, adding his own belief that a vigorous prosecution of the war was necessary, and his fears that the government would not act decisively. 'I suspect,' wrote Lord Howe to Germain, 'that instead of the active measures your Lordship may think the Crisis demands, a languid idea of withdrawing the troops from Boston may prevail; on the principle of difficulty to furnish Recruits in the required Extent, for the proposed Reinforcement suggested in my Brother's former letter.'[42]

The letter had the desired effect. Shortly after receiving it, Germain told William Eden, under-secretary at the Home Office, that Britain could defeat the rebels only by launching offensive operations from New York, the same strategy that General Howe was urging. Within days the cabinet had agreed to all the measures that Germain and Suffolk had been urging since June: these included sending 2,000 men to Boston immediately, and having an army of 20,000 regulars in America by the following spring. It also decided to replace Gage with Howe, a move that Germain had long advocated. Dartmouth tried to sugar the pill for Gage by informing him, in a letter of 2 August, that his recall was temporary so that he could brief the cabinet in person, and that Howe would command in his absence. The charade was maintained until the following April, when Gage was formally removed from his post.

Gage left Boston for England in mid-October 1775, having relinquished command to Howe a few days earlier. Now was Howe's opportunity to put his new strategy into effect. As recently as August he had modified his earlier suggestion for two campaigns along the Hudson and Connecticut rivers to one that concentrated solely on the former river: one force of 15,000 men would advance from New York, and be met by a second, 4,000 strong, from Canada; a third force of 5,000 men would hold Boston. If the necessary troops could not be found, he recommended withdrawing all the king's forces from America so that time and anarchy might cure the colonists' desire for independence. Either way, he did not envisage a move from Boston until 1776 at the earliest.[43]

In early November, however, Howe received an order from Dartmouth to evacuate Boston and move all his troops to New York. He refused, arguing that the onset of winter and the scarcity of transport made such an enterprise too dangerous. 'I should be . . . dependent upon the return of transports,' he informed Dartmouth on 26 November, 'at a season when the navigation on this coast, from the violence of the north winds, is so very precarious.'[44] This disobedience produced no rebuke because, by the time Howe's letter reached London, Dartmouth was no longer colonial secretary. He had been moved to the Privy Seal and replaced by Howe's supporter Germain, who, though a hawk, was sensible enough to realize that it was too late in the year to launch a new campaign.

By now Lord North's government had decided to pursue a dual strategy: on the one hand it would prosecute the war as vigorously as possible; and on the other it would appoint a peace commission to try to find a political settlement that stopped short of conceding parliamentary sovereignty. In mid-October, with this in mind, North urged George III to approve an expedition to the southern colonies, arguing that the proposed peace commission would not be acceptable to Parliament 'unless they see that we are trying every possible method of collecting a large force, and unless they think we are determined to use it'.[45]

This opening up of a southern front was designed to exploit the strong loyalist sentiment that had been reported by the governors of Virginia and North Carolina. The king approved, and preliminary orders were given on 22 October for a small force of regulars to leave Ireland in December and rendezvous with one of Howe's generals off Cape Fear, before landing in North Carolina; once the loyalists had been re-established in the southern colonies, it would join the main army at New York.

Four days later, at the reopening of Parliament, an uncompromising King's Speech declared that the American colonies were in open rebellion to establish an independent empire. Compromise had failed, and now only force could protect the loyal colonists from their oppressors, and preserve the huge economic investment that Britain had made in America. To suppress the rebellion, the government had expanded the size of its army and navy, and had employed Hanoverian troops to release the garrisons of Minorca and Gibraltar. But Britain was not vindictive. If the colonists renounced rebellion, they would be received with tenderness and mercy; and to hasten reconciliation the king was prepared to send peace commissioners to grant pardons, receive submission and restore imperial commerce. The speech was passed by 278 votes to 108.

North, however, was keen to give the peace commission wider-ranging powers to remove restraints on trade and to discuss colonial grievances. So on 20 November he introduced a bill to prohibit all trade with the rebellious provinces, repeal as superfluous the Restraining Acts and the Boston Port Act (one of the Coercive Acts), and authorize the king to appoint a peace commission. The Prohibitory Act, which was approved on 22 December (and became effective on 1 March 1776), banned all American commerce and gave the peace commission the power to issue pardons, declare peace, suspend the Prohibitory Act and 'inquire into the State and condition of the colonies, and . . . confer with the proper persons upon such points as may be necessary for effecting the Restoration of the public Tranquility'.[46] The only outstanding matter was the identity of the peace commissioner, and that was settled in February 1776 with the appointment of the newly promoted Vice-Admiral Lord Howe, General Howe's brother, who was also given command of naval forces in America.

Like his brother, Admiral Howe was pro-American and a passionate believer that lasting peace could be achieved only by a negotiated settlement. Aged forty-eight, a hero of the Seven Years War whose heavy brows, swarthy expression and bravery in battle had earned him the soubriquet 'Black Dick', he had long insisted that kind words and a willingness to listen to grievances would go far towards ending the conflict. He had no wish to surrender parliamentary supremacy in the colonies, but like Dartmouth saw no gain in insisting that the colonists acknowledge that supremacy. By agreeing to become the naval chief as well as a peace commissioner, he would be able to wield both carrot and stick. 'In a dual commission,' writes one recent biographer, 'he saw his best prospect for saving the empire.'[47]

It is the ultimate irony that two brothers who doubted the wisdom of coercive measures had become the senior commanders in America under a government that was determined to crush by force its rebellious colonies. 'They had done so,' writes their biographer, 'by obscuring their own intentions, by exploiting the conflicting wishes of various members of the government, and by satisfying the ministry's need for able commanders.'[48] They had, in effect, talked of war so that ministers would give them the chance to make peace. Now that they had the opportunity, would they take it?

14.   The Lost Opportunity

One man who felt that General Howe had already missed a golden opportunity to strike the rebellion a fatal blow was George Washington, the recently appointed commander of the rebel troops at Boston. Tall, thin and muscular, the younger son of a wealthy Virginia estate owner, Washington had begun his career as a surveyor. But after inheriting the 2,500-acre estate of Mount Vernon and a number of slaves on the death of his elder brother, he switched to soldiering and made his name at Monongahela, where, as an aide to the ill-fated General Braddock, he led the survivors to safety. Still only twenty-three, he was rewarded with the command of all Virginia troops and by 1759, when he resigned his commission to marry a wealthy widow (whose dowry brought him yet more land and slaves), he had reached the rank of brigadier-general.

As a former brother-in-arms to the British, Washington did not enter the rebel ranks without qualms; nor did he, at first, seek independence from Britain. Yet he was determined to fight for rights and privileges that, he believed, were 'essential to the happiness of every free state'. Hence his appearance in uniform at the First Continental Congress in the autumn of 1774, where he impressed his fellow delegates by his sincerity and common sense, if not his powers of oratory. By the time the Second Congress – convened in Philadelphia after the first shots of the war were fired at Lexington–Concord – voted in mid-June to form the Continental Army out of the militia units surrounding Boston, Washington was an obvious choice to take command. But many delegates thought a Massachusetts man should be given the post, and it was John Adams, the influential delegate from Boston, who persuaded them that the choice of a Virginian would encourage support for the war in the south.[1]

No one was more surprised than Washington himself. 'So far from seeking this appointment,' he told his wife Patsy, 'I have used every endeavor in my power to avoid it, not only from my unwillingness to part with you and the family, but from a consciousness of its being a trust too great for my capacity . . . But as it has been a kind of destiny that has thrown me upon this service, I shall hope that my undertaking it is designed to answer some good purpose.'[2]

Washington arrived at Cambridge to take command of the siege of Boston a fortnight after Bunker Hill. He found the 16,000-strong army in disarray: discipline was lax, with drunkenness and malingering commonplace, little respect for officers and sentries regularly abandoning their posts; the camps were filthy, provisions meagre and ammunition so low that for a time no man had more than three rounds. Many had already voted with their feet, prompting some officers to offer rewards of $2 for their discovery. 'Deserted from Colonel Brewer's regiment . . . one John Daby,' read one advert, 'a long, hump-shouldered fellow, drawls his words, and for "comfortable" says "comfabel", had on a green coat, thick leather breeches, slim legs, lost some of his fore teeth.'[3]

Some of the officers were little better, refusing to cooperate with men from different colonies and even advising their men not to re-enlist. Washington was horrified: 'I have already broke one colonel and five captains for cowardice and drawing more pay and provisions than they had men in their companies . . . In short they are by no means such troops as you are led to believe of them from the accounts which are published . . . I daresay the men would fight very well (if properly officered) although they are exceedingly dirty and nasty people.'[4]

In Washington's opinion, Bunker Hill would not have been lost if the officers had done their duty. The chief problem, he felt, was that many of the officers were from 'the lower class of the people' and 'nearly of the same Kidney with the Privates'. They seemed incapable of giving, or enforcing, orders and were often seen fraternizing with their men, shaving them and repairing their shoes. Some men had even been given unofficial leave to work on their officers' farms.[5] To put a stop to all this, Washington had eight more officers court-martialled and one flogged. He persuaded Congress to recruit suitable officers from outside New England, and promoted those from the ranks who had shown 'spirited behaviour and good conduct' at Bunker Hill.[6] And finally he got permission from Congress to hang deserters, and issued a succession of orders designed to improve camp cleanliness and discipline. He was only partially successful. One visitor recorded:

> Notwithstanding the indefatigable endeavours of Mr Washington and the other generals, and particularly of Adjutant-General [Horatio] Gates, to arrange and discipline the army, yet any tolerable degree of order and subordination is what they are totally unacquainted with in the rebel camp. And the doctrines of independence and levellism have been so effectively sown throughout the country, and so universally imbibed by all ranks of men, that I apprehend it will be with the greatest difficulty that the inferior officers and soldiers will be ever brought to any tolerable degree of subjection to the commands of their superiors.[7]

Slowly but surely, however, Washington did impose order. 'The strictest government is taking place, and great distinction is made between officers and soldiers,' noted one army chaplain. 'Everyone is made to know his place, and keep in it, or be tied up and receive forty or fifty lashes according to his crime.'[8] After three months in the job Washington was able to relax. On taking command he had feared a British attack, but by September his defensive lines were completed and he concluded – correctly – that the 'Enemy have no Intention to come out, until they are re-inforced.' Only a few weeks earlier, he remarked to his brother Samuel, London had believed 'that the Americans were such poltroons & Cowards that they would not fight', but now their generals have 'no Inclination to pay us a visit'.[9]

Yet there was a greater threat to his army's existence than that from the British. Most of his men had signed on to serve until the end of the year, and unless they re-enlisted his army would disintegrate. So he appealed to their honour and patriotism, offered furloughs and additional supplies to those who stayed, and even promised them $2 and a blanket. Not even a cash bonus of one month's pay, which Congress offered late in 1775, made much difference. The farmers, in particular, were loth to be away from home for a second growing season.

When the Connecticut volunteers departed en masse in late November, Washington raged at the 'dearth of Public Spirit, & want of virtue', and added that had he known what he was to face 'no consideration on Earth should have induced me to accept this Command'.[10] Fortunately the losses were counterbalanced by much needed reinforcements from Pennsylvania, Maryland and Virginia, and by February 1776, despite many desertions, the Continental Army had increased in size to 17,000 men with 43 cannon and 16 mortars. But the ordeal of having 'one Army disbanded and another to raise' within sight of British regulars had caused him many sleepless nights, he told his aide Colonel Joseph Reed. That he got through it was thanks to the 'finger of Providence'.[11]

Washington would later criticize Howe for not attacking him while his army was in disarray. 'Search the volumes of history,' he wrote, 'and I much question whether a case similar to ours is to be found, to wit, to maintain a post against the flower of the British troops for six months altogether, without powder, and at the end of them to have one army disbanded and another to raise within the same distance of a reinforced enemy.'[12] But Howe had his reasons, not least a dearth of reliable military intelligence after the unravelling of his predecessor's network of informers. He also had fewer troops than the Americans, and Bunker Hill had demonstrated the tenacity with which the colonists were prepared to defend fixed positions.

So Howe and his 10,000 men sat tight, determined to wait until the spring. The price to pay for this inactivity, however, was an acute shortage of supplies. While the soldiers always had enough to eat, it was rarely fresh meat or vegetables. Howe complained to London that he was 'in great Pain from the small quantity of Provisions', and sent convoys to forage for hay and oats in the Bay of Fundy and the province of Quebec, and for rice and other cereals near Savannah. But the success of these missions was mixed, and Howe was forced to rely on what had been stored in Boston before 19 April, and on the occasional relief ship from Britain (though some brought only spoiled provisions). One officer asked his family to send him beef, butter and peas, explaining that 'any of them would be extremely acceptable in these hard times.'[13]

The best account of the siege by an ordinary soldier is the journal of Irishman Thomas Sullivan of the 49th Foot, a corps that arrived shortly before Bunker Hill. Not much is known of Sullivan's early years, beyond the fact that he was 'in my 20th year of age' when he enlisted in the 49th in Dublin in February 1775. After some cursory training, he joined his battalion on a transport for America in late April, arriving at Boston on the same day as the Battle of Bunker Hill.[14] Sullivan recorded the price of provisions in June 1775 as 'very cheap', with 'very good beef' at 2*d*. a pound, West Indian rum at 2*s*. a gallon and 'Spruce Beer' at a halfpenny a quart. But as the siege continued it all became 'very expensive' and the water 'very brackish, which was very destructive to the troops, giving them (it was supposed) the Flux, and a good many of the Inhabitants as well'. Sullivan also reveals the worsening relationship between the troops and Boston's residents:

> After the first engagement [Lexington–Concord] the troops grew more cruel against the Inhabitants, so that they began in most parts of the town to pull down the fences . . . around the houses [which] are about two-thirds built of wood; and one third of Brick, notwithstanding the repeated orders of the Commander-in-Chief issued to the contrary. After the Battle of Bunker's Hill they were so inveterate against the Rebels on account of the dreadful spectacles that presented themselves after that action, they destroyed everything they could come at without Scruple. When the troops went into winter Quarters the General gave Orders that all the Old houses in every part of the town should be pulled down for firing [burning] for the Army, the river being (that time) almost frozen so that the Shipping could not get out of the Harbour to bring timber from other Parts . . . The one-fourth part of the town was either pulled down for firing in that manner or otherwise destroyed in making Batteries.[15]

Even Boston's Liberty Tree, an ancient elm, was sacrificed for firewood. Looting became so prevalent that Howe ordered floggings and even executions, warning soldiers that the provost marshal would 'hang upon the spot the first man he should detect in the act without waiting for further proof by trial'.[16] The poor diet, cold weather and tainted water left many soldiers prey to smallpox, scurvy and dysentery, and at one stage more than thirty were dying every day. Not surprisingly, Bostonians left the city in droves, and by the spring of 1776 only 5,000 (mainly loyalists) were still in residence.

On 4 March 1776, while Howe waited for the ice to melt so that he could evacuate his army, Washington occupied Dorchester Heights to the south of Boston with 2,000 soldiers and 20 cannon. As the heights commanded both the southern part of the city and its sea approaches, Howe knew he had to respond. So the following day he ordered a night attack on the rebels' makeshift defences – the ground was too frozen for them to dig trenches – but it was postponed because of a violent storm and eventually cancelled. Instead Howe brought forward the date of his evacuation to 17 March, when 10,000 soldiers and 1,000 loyalists were crammed aboard the ships in the bay, and all surplus equipment and military stores were destroyed. After a delay of several days, the convoy finally set sail for Halifax, Nova Scotia, where Howe planned to reorganize his troops before launching his operation to recapture New York. He explained to the cabinet:

> I am justly sensible how much more conducive it would be to His Majesty's service if the army was in a situation to proceed immediately to New York; but the present condition of the troops, crowded in the transports, without regard to conveniences, the inevitable dissortment of stores, and all the incumbrances with which I am clogged, effectually disable me from the exertion of this force in any offensive operations.[17]

Howe's strategy for the summer of 1776 – outlined in a letter to Lord George Germain of 8 June – was to land at New York and seek an opportunity to destroy the Continental Army in battle. If none offered itself, he would wait until his army was strong enough to take both Manhattan and Rhode Island further north, and finally to advance up the Hudson River to precipitate the decisive action he sought. Germain approved because he could see no better way to force the colonists to accept Parliament's supremacy; Howe, on the other hand, saw a military victory as the only way to bring the rebels to the negotiating table where, inevitably, some concessions would have to be made.[18]

At this stage Howe was the more bullish, telling Germain that he was determined to attack New York before the rebels had properly entrenched themselves, and with the forces then available to him. Germain wanted him to wait for reinforcements, fearing that Howe might lose a battle if he launched the campaign with too few troops. Still, he bowed to Howe's local knowledge, and did all he could to support him by sending more troops than had been asked for – a total of 23,800 men for New York and 10,000 for Canada.[19]

Howe was also appointed a peace commissioner, alongside his brother, though neither had the power to discuss Parliament's right to tax the colonists or its general power to pass laws. As commanders-in-chief, the Howes were expected to subdue the rebellion, destroy the Continental Army, sweep American ships from the sea and strangle New England; as peace commissioners they would dictate Britain's terms of surrender. But neither Howe regarded total victory as a prerequisite for negotiation, and it was this unwillingness to prosecute the war as ruthlessly as they could have that undermined Britain's hope of victory.

By the time Admiral Howe reached Halifax aboard the 64-gun *Eagle* on 23 June, his brother had long since moved his army of 9,000 to Staten Island, just south of New York City at the mouth of the Hudson River. When the admiral joined him there on 12 July, the news was far from encouraging: not only was a rebel force, estimated to number anything from 20,000 to 35,000 men and 100 guns, well entrenched on Long Island and Manhattan; but word had just reached General Howe of Congress's Declaration of Independence. Drafted by Thomas Jefferson, a Virginian delegate who had already published his *Summary View of the Rights of British America* (in which he had argued there was no reason why '160,000 electors in the island of Great Britain should give law to four millions in the states of America'), and signed by his fellow congressmen on 4 July, the declaration contained the immortal lines:

> We hold these truths to be self-evident: that all men are created equal;
> that they are endowed by their Creator with certain inalienable rights;

that among these are life, liberty, and the pursuit of happiness; that to secure these rights, governments are instituted among men, deriving their just powers from the consent of the governed; that whenever any form of government becomes destructive of those ends, it is the right of the people to alter or to abolish it, and to institute new government.[20]

It was a point of no return, Howe told his sailor brother, and made it extremely unlikely that Congress would be amenable to talk of peace and reunion until its armies had been destroyed. Nonetheless, Admiral Howe was determined to show 'the people of America that the Door was yet open for Reconciliation', and the day after his arrival at Staten Island he sent word of his peace commission to various rebel assemblies, including Congress itself. He also sent a letter under a flag of truce to George Washington, now commanding the defence of New York, suggesting they meet to discuss an accommodation. Washington refused, insisting he had no authority to make peace. The reply from the radicals controlling Congress came via Benjamin Franklin, who told Howe that, as he could only pardon those who had first submitted, he had come in vain. [21]

Admiral Howe was forced to conclude that the rebels would only negotiate if they had first been defeated, and possibly not even then. 'As things now are,' he informed Germain on 11 August, 'the whole seems to depend upon Military and Naval Operations. The ensuing Campaign may possibly be decisive. Success (of which there are the greatest hopes) will naturally make room for negotiation and Peace. But the infatuated Expectations, and Perseverance of the present Rulers of America, appear so much beyond Reason, and Nature, that no common Powers of Penetration can determine the Effect of even the completest Victory.'[22] That victory could not be won, however, until the last of General Howe's extra troops and equipment had arrived on ships from Europe, South Carolina and the West Indies.

Among the reinforcements from Britain was John Peebles, thirty-six, a keen diarist and lieutenant in the 42nd Black Watch. He was far from a typical Scottish officer. Born in the Lowlands of Ayrshire, and older than most men of his rank, he had served as a surgeon's mate in both local and British regiments in America for much of the Seven Years War. During that time he had met a number of leading colonists – including Nathaniel Gist and Robert Magaw, both of whom had since become colonels in the Continental Army – and even acquired 500 acres of land in Nova Scotia. With the war over, and still just twenty-three, he joined the 42nd as an ensign. But, despite his military experience and good education – he was an avid reader, familiar with the works of Montesquieu, Hume and Gibbon – he lacked the funds to purchase promotion and had since gained just one step in rank (bought for him in 1770 by an Ayrshire grandee, the Earl of Eglintoun). For Peebles the rebellion was a heaven-sent opportunity to make something of his career – albeit in a war against former friends and colleagues – and, having landed at Staten Island on 5 August after a gruelling sixteen-week voyage, he and his company of grenadiers were eager for action. They would not have long to wait.[23]

By mid-August Howe had 30,000 troops, a quarter of them Germans (mostly Hessians), and was at last ready to strike. He had often declared his intention to destroy the Continental Army in the field, but now he changed his mind. Ignoring his subordinates, who were urging him to cut off the rebel army by using the Hudson to land troops above Manhattan, he chose instead to occupy territory: first Long Island, and then Manhattan and eastern New Jersey; while detachments captured Rhode Island and linked up with General Burgoyne, who was advancing down the Hudson from Canada.

Why, just when it seemed his plans for destroying the Continental Army might succeed, did he alter his strategy? The answer seems to lie in his and his brother's hope that the empire could be reunited. Determined to preserve his army, 'the stock upon which the national force in America must in future be grafted', and aware that his subordinates thought that time alone would defeat the Continental Army, he seems to have concluded that his best course was to avoid a decisive action and instead to apply steady pressure from New York and Canada in the hope that it would force the rebels to seek terms. Certainly Admiral Howe would have approved of – and may have argued for – such a change in his brother's plans. He had long feared that too

devastating a British victory would permanently alienate the colonists and make them ungovernable. 'A steady advance,' writes the
Howes' most recent biographer, 'creating the impression of British
invincibility without causing widespread loss of lives and property,
probably seemed to [Lord Howe] the only way of persuading the
colonists to negotiate on Britain's terms, the only way of achieving a
satisfactory reunion with the powers he then possessed.'[24]

General Howe's change of strategy was doubly unfortunate
in that, unbeknown to him, Washington was planning to hold
New York at all costs. It would have made much more sense for the
American commander to withdraw before Howe's superior force,
and thereafter to conduct a guerrilla campaign against the lengthen-
ing British lines of supply, or at the very least to offer battle only on
the most favourable terms. But instead Washington chose to risk his
whole army by making a stand at New York because he was convinced that his possession of Manhattan Island was the key to the
Hudson River and the defence of the colonies. 'Should they get that
Town and the Command of the North River,' he wrote on 6 August,
'they can stop the intercourse between the northern and southern
Colonies, upon which depends the safety of America.'[25]

Washington's strategy was flawed on a number of levels. His subordinate, Major-General Charles Lee, had already warned that the
gun batteries on Manhattan did not have sufficient range to prevent
the Royal Navy from sailing ships up the Hudson (a feat they had
first managed on 12 July). Even more importantly, New York City
was commanded by Brooklyn Heights on Long Island, and to defend
the latter required the possession of Governor's Island at the entrance
to the East River. In other words, Washington could hold New York
only if he divided his forces before a markedly superior fleet and
army. Realizing this, some of his officers urged him to withdraw,
arguing that the survival of his army was more important than the
psychological value of retaining Manhattan. Washington refused to
budge and, had Howe stuck to his initial strategy, the rebels might
have lost their main army and, possibly, the war.

Fortunately for Washington, Howe's new strategy was much more
limited in aim. During the morning of 22 August, after a night of

'thunder, lightning, and prodigious heavy rain',[26] 15,000 British soldiers were rowed across the Narrows between Staten Island and Long Island, landing unopposed at Gravesend. They were joined there, over the next three days, by 5,000 Hessians, giving Howe a numerical advantage over the American defenders of Long Island of two to one. Yet the Americans had concentrated their strength at each of the three passes that gave immediate access to the densely wooded hills of Brooklyn Heights – Gowanus, Flatbush and Bedford – and a direct attack on these well-dug-in positions was bound to be costly. That became unnecessary when Howe's subordinate Clinton discovered a fourth, unguarded pass, 2 miles east of Bedford, which enabled the British to outflank the entire rebel position.

The attack, for once, went entirely to plan. While two detachments of his army pinned the Americans at the Gowanus and Flatbush passes, Howe and Clinton led the remaining 10,000 men and 30 guns on a night march through the unguarded pass. The following morning, 27 August, they attacked the defenders from front and rear, inflicting 3,300 casualties (including 1,000 prisoners). Many of the rebels drowned as they retreated through a swamp to their main defensive position at Brooklyn. One survivor recalled:

> It is impossible for me to describe the confusion and horror of the scene: the artillery flying with the chains over the horses' backs, our men running in almost every direction, and run which way they would, they were almost sure to meet the British or Hessians. And the enemy huzzahing when they took prisoners made it truly a day of distress to the Americans. I escaped . . . and entered a swamp or marsh through which a great many of our men were retreating. Some of them were mired and crying to the fellows for God's sake to help them out; but every man was intent on his own safety and no assistance was rendered . . . Out of the eight men in our company who were on guard the day before . . . I only escaped. The others were either killed or taken prisoners.[27]

A number of wounded rebels were killed out of hand, with Hessian troops the chief culprits. 'We took care,' explained an officer of the 71st Highlanders, 'to tell the Hessians that the Rebels had resolved to give no quarter – to them in particular – which made them fight desperately, and put all to death that fell into their hands . . . it was fine to see with what alacrity they [and our brave Highlanders] dispatched the Rebels with their bayonets after we had surrounded them so that they could not resist.'[28]

British losses were fewer than 400 killed and wounded – among the dead was the young and recently promoted Sergeant Jeffrey Grimes of the 23rd Fusiliers – and Howe rightly considered the operation an unmitigated success. Yet he had held back an immediate pursuit with the intention of putting the main rebel position at Brooklyn under siege, trusting that time would deliver him both the Heights and New York City. It did, but only after Washington had used the cover of a storm and fog on the night of 29 August to remove his entire force from Long Island to Manhattan. Although New York was now within range of Howe's guns, and the first part of his strategy had been achieved sooner and with less cost than he had expected, he had still missed a great opportunity to destroy a large part of the Continental Army – and his critics, Clinton among them, were not impressed. 'Had our Troops followed them close up, they must have thrown down their arms and surrendered,' wrote one officer. 'Or had our Ships attacked the Batteries, which we have been in constant Expectation of being ordered to do, not a Man could have escaped from Long Island.'[29]

There were signs, however, that Howe's strategy was working. Spies and deserters brought word that the rebel army was in disarray, that thousands had voted with their feet, and that the rest were fearful of being trapped between the British on Long Island and the troops advancing from Canada. There was much truth in this: the Connecticut Militia had suffered the most casualties on Long Island and, after the evacuation, 6,000 of its disgusted soldiers returned to their homes; this was the start of the colony's gradual alienation from the rebel cause, which would culminate, by the end of the war, with its coastal area freely providing the British Army with forage and supplies.

It now seemed to some of Howe's brigadiers that the capture of Manhattan might even end the war. James Grant did 'not look for

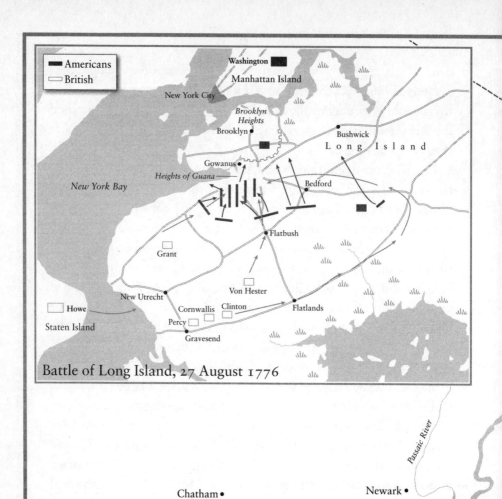

Americans
British

Washington

Manhattan Island

New York City

Brooklyn Heights

Brooklyn

Bushwick

L o n g   I s l a n d

Gowanus

Heights of Guana

Bedford

New York Bay

Flatbush

Grant

Von Hester

New Utrecht

Cornwallis   Clinton

Flatlands

Howe

Percy

Staten Island

Gravesend

Battle of Long Island, 27 August 1776

Chatham •

Newark •

Passaic River

N E W   J E R S E Y

Elizabeth •

Staten
Island

8. New York and Environs, August to October 1776

0		10 miles
0		15 kms

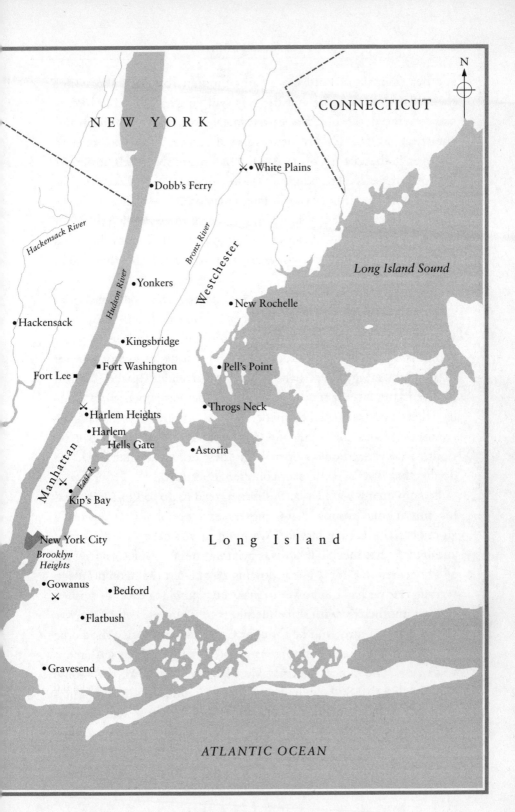

N

CONNECTICUT

NEW YORK

✕•White Plains

•Dobb's Ferry

Hackensack River

Bronx River

Long Island Sound

Westchester

Hudson River

•Yonkers

•Hackensack

•New Rochelle

•Kingsbridge

Fort Lee ■   ■ Fort Washington

•Pell's Point

✕•Harlem Heights

•Throgs Neck

•Harlem
Hells Gate

•Astoria

Manhattan

East R.

Kip's Bay

New York City

Long Island

Brooklyn Heights

•Gowanus
✕

•Bedford

•Flatbush

•Gravesend

ATLANTIC OCEAN

another campaign'; Lord Cornwallis thought that 'in a short time their army will disperse and the war will be over'; and Lord Percy was convinced 'this business is pretty near over.' Howe was more circumspect, as was his brother, Admiral Howe, who was keen to discover if the victory of 27 August had made the rebels any more desirous of peace. The admiral was in a quandary: he knew that he did not have the authority to discuss a plan of reconciliation until the rebels had surrendered; yet he also knew that the rebels would never surrender before all of America had been conquered unless he could find an unofficial way of letting them know what terms they might expect.

After the battle Admiral Howe invited two captured rebel generals, John Sullivan and Lord Stirling, to dine with him aboard his warship *Eagle*. During the meal he assured his guests that his peace commission had been misunderstood, and that his authority was not limited to issuing pardons and receiving surrender. Rather, he had received assurances from the government that Parliament would ratify whatever agreements he made. He went on to stress his family's connection with New England, his belief that Parliament had no right to tax the colonists or manage their domestic affairs, and his doubts that Britain could ever conquer America.[30]

So convincing was he that Sullivan agreed to go to Philadelphia as his emissary and propose that Congress send several of its delegates to an unofficial peace conference. Washington was happy to cooperate, and by 2 September Sullivan was briefing members of Congress on all Howe had told him. The following day he put the main points in writing: Howe had full power to make an equitable peace; he wished to treat unofficially with some members of Congress before the war took a decisive turn; and he thought Congress's authority should be recognized and many concessions granted before a final settlement was made. The radical majority were highly suspicious, with some complaining that Sullivan had been sent to 'seduce us into a renunciation of our independence' and to divert their efforts to win the war. Unwilling to alienate the moderates, however, they agreed on a compromise. A committee of three – two radicals, Benjamin Franklin and John Adams, and a moderate, Edward Rutledge – would meet with Howe to ask if he was able to negotiate officially with Congress, and to learn exactly what powers he did possess. This tactic, the radicals were convinced, would 'unmask' Howe, who could not negotiate with Congress without recognizing American independence, and who would never be able to offer terms as attractive as Sullivan had suggested.

They were right. At the meeting on Staten Island on 11 September, Admiral Howe told them that they could be received only as private gentlemen, rather than as representatives of Congress, and that if the colonies returned to their allegiance, he could declare them at peace, grant pardons and recommend changes in the imperial system to satisfy their grievances. When they asked him to be more specific, he was deliberately evasive. He did have the power to suspend the Prohibitory Act (which denied the colonists the right to trade), and also to replace parliamentary taxation with fixed colonial contributions to imperial defence, but he was under strict instructions to mention neither until the rebels had surrendered. The committee of three was unimpressed with vague promises of satisfactory terms upon surrender, not least because Congress had no intention of making peace until North's government had recognized American independence. And this, they knew, it would never do by choice. So the talks ended in failure. 'They met, they talked, they parted,' commented one British official. 'And now nothing remains but to fight it out.'[31]

General Howe, meanwhile, had been planning the capture of New York City. On 2 September he and Clinton had reconnoitred the shores of Manhattan and Westchester at the entrance to Long Island Sound. Clinton urged Howe to move the army to Westchester so that it could advance to the high ground to the north and sever all land communications to the rebel army on Manhattan. Howe refused, preferring instead to land at Kip's Bay on the lower-east side of Manhattan. Again it was a cautious plan that would force the rebels to give up New York without the need for a major engagement. All Clinton's protests – that a landing at Kip's Bay would simply drive the rebels to stronger positions at the north end of Manhattan, and that a landing at Westchester would trap the entire Continental Army – were in vain.

The assault at Kip's Bay finally took place on 15 September, after the negotiations had failed. But by then Washington, aware of the danger, had moved the bulk of his troops further north (including a detachment at Kingsbridge, to cover his retreat into Westchester), leaving fewer than 5,000 men to defend lower Manhattan and Kip's Bay itself. Among the assaulting troops was Lord Rawdon, the lieutenant in the 5th Foot who had fought so heroically at Bunker Hill. He recalled:

> As we approached [Kip's Bay] we saw the breastwork filled with men and two or three large columns marching down in great parade to support them . . . The ships had not as yet fired a shot but upon a signal from us they began the most tremendous peal I ever heard. The breastworks were blown to pieces in a few minutes, and those who were to have defended them were happy to escape as quick as possible through the ravines. The columns broke instantly, and betook themselves to the nearest woods for shelter. We pressed to shore, landed, and formed without losing a single man. As we were without artillery, upon an island where the enemy might attack us with five times our number . . . it was necessary to attain some post where we might maintain ourselves till we were reinforced . . . We accordingly attacked and forced a party of the rebels from the Inchenberg, a very commanding height, taking from them a new brass howitzer, some wagons of ammunition, and the tents of three or four battalions who were encamped on it.[32]

Around 300 rebels were taken prisoner, but the remainder of the force in New York City escaped up the east side of the island to Washington's new defensive position on Harlem Heights. More than once that day, Clinton had appealed to Howe to let him march his 1st Division to the Hudson, a distance of barely 2 miles, to sever the rebels' line of retreat. But Howe refused. The underlying reason may have been his brother's determination to renew negotiations once New York was in British hands. On 19 September the Howes issued a joint declaration, inviting all colonists to discuss with them the means of restoring peace and reuniting the empire, but also insisting that George III was prepared to revise any objectionable Acts of

Parliament. Though it, too, fell on deaf ears, the Howes seemed unconcerned that they were missing repeated opportunities to win a decisive victory. 'Temporarily,' writes Ira Gruber, 'they were willing to subordinate all else to their hopes of finding a permanent reconciliation – to their dreams of a triumphal return to England as the saviours of the Empire.'[33]

On 21 September, five days after Howe's men had first entered New York City to the delight of cheering loyalists, a deserter from the 23rd Fusiliers was caught and handed over to the provost for trial. His name was Private Thomas Watson, a former miner and ladies' man who had left his unit at Boston in early March 1775. He was suspected of having served in the rebel army, an offence for which the penalty was death by hanging.

At his court martial in early October, Watson insisted that he had been kidnapped by a colleague in the 23rd and his brother, a civilian living near Boston, and had tried many times to return to his battalion without success. But his story began to unravel when a Mary Smith, the daughter-in-law of a New York loyalist who had given Watson refuge, told the court that she had seen him in rebel uniform. Under cross-examination by Watson himself, she said that he had told her after the British had entered New York that, if he were to be returned to his unit, he wished immediately 'to be engaged with the rebels that he might have satisfaction of them'. She and other witnesses could not confirm that they had ever seen him armed, a crucial distinction that would have triggered the death sentence. But they testified to his desertion from the rebel army when it evacuated New York, and to his attempts since to rejoin the British Army.[34]

He was found guilty of desertion and joining the rebel army, but not of bearing arms against his own side, and was therefore spared the gallows. Instead he received a sentence of 700 lashes. But such punishments were rarely inflicted in full in America, and it is likely he escaped with only a partial chastisement. Clearly Watson did not learn his lesson because in early 1778 he would again desert the 23rd, and this time evade recapture. The motivation on both occasions – and hinted at during his court martial – was almost certainly a relationship with a local woman. It was a problem not confined to the 23rd Fusiliers and would ultimately cost the British Army in America the services of hundreds of men.[35]

Howe resumed his offensive in early October. His plan was to complete the conquest of Manhattan before turning his attention to Rhode Island; a junction with Burgoyne's Canadian Army on the Hudson and an incursion into New Jersey would have to wait until the New Year. While his goals had become more modest, his overall strategy had not altered. Occupying territory was still his priority, and to that end his plan for capturing upper Manhattan was designed to minimize casualties. A covering force would be left in front of the rebel position at Harlem Heights, while the rest of the army crossed to Westchester, thus turning Washington's flank and threatening his communications with New England. The rebels' only option would be to withdraw up the Hudson, leaving Manhattan in British hands. Much to Clinton's fury, it was still not Howe's intention to cut off the rebels' route of escape.

The first landing at Throgs Neck was accomplished with the loss of just one boat on 12 October, though for a time thick fog had threatened disaster. But the rebels were found in possession of the narrow causeway that linked the neck to the mainland, and it was thought advisable to reland the troops further up the Long Island Sound. Delayed by bad weather and the need to reprovision, this new landing at Pell's Point took place on the 18th. This gave Washington time to construct a series of defensive positions on the high ground from Kingsbridge in the south to White Plains in the north, with his front protected by the deep and swift-flowing Bronx River.

Howe's next move was to march his 13,000 men − half of them Hessians − to New Rochelle, a settlement north of Pell's Point, where he waited for a newly arrived division of 8,000 Hessians to join him. During this pause, he received intelligence that Washington intended to evacuate all of Manhattan except Fort Washington, a strongly fortified position on the Hudson north of Harlem. He was now convinced that Washington would flee north without risking a battle, and so intended to follow him as far as White Plains, where the road from Manhattan became two separate routes to New England. On 25 October, by which time the Hessian reinforcements had arrived, he marched to within 4 miles of White Plains and again halted to give Washington the opportunity to escape.

But the American commander preferred to make a stand, hoping that the British would make a frontal attack on his formidable defensive position. It was a two-tier system: the first line of fortifications, commanded by Lord Stirling (lately exchanged for British prisoners), ran along the headwaters of the Bronx and Mamaroneck rivers; the second, much stronger line under Washington was on high ground to the rear. On 28 October, realizing the rebels were determined to fight, Howe ordered the bulk of his army to make a feint attack against the centre and left of the rebel front line, while his left wing attacked an isolated outpost called Chatterton Hill. An American officer remembered the attacking Hessians were 'scattered like leaves in a whirlwind, and retreated so far' that his own men had time to collect the arms and equipment of the men who had fallen, and to drink their rum, before the attack was resumed:

> They advanced in solid columns ... The scene was grand and solemn; all the adjacent hills smoked as if on fire, and bellowed and trembled with a perpetual cannonade and fire of field pieces, howitzers and mortars. The air groaned with streams of cannon and musket-shot. The hills smoked and echoed terribly with the bursting of shells; the fences and walls were knocked down and torn to pieces, and men's legs, arms and bodies, mangled with cannon and grapeshot, all around us.[36]

One defender from Connecticut was appalled by the carnage caused by a single British round-shot. It 'first took off the head of Smith, a stout heavy man, and dashed it open,' he noted, 'then took Taylor across the bowels. It then struck Sergeant Garrett of our company on the hip [and] took off the point of the hip bone ... he died the same day ... Oh! What a sight it was to see within a distance of six rods those men with their legs and arms and guns and packs all in a heap.'[37]

Slowly but surely the British pressure on the hill began to tell. 'The steadiness and intrepidity of our troops,' noted the diarist Lieutenant

Peebles, 'beat them from their strong grounds where they had taken the advantage of fences and stone walls, and made them retire back on the remaining body that was posted on the hill, who immediately turned tail with the fugitives and ran off in the greatest confusion to their works on the other hill [in front of White Plains] . . . The Rebels suffered considerably both from our Cannon and Musketry and exhibited to our whole army (who were looking on) a recent proof of their inferiority in courage and discipline.'[38]

Next morning, having discovered that Washington had withdrawn all his troops to his more formidable second line, Howe again paused while his assault batteries were moved forward and more reinforcements arrived from Manhattan. On 1 November he was ready to attack, but heavy rain caused a 24-hour postponement. It was enough time for Washington to withdraw 5 miles across the Croton River to another strong position further north. Howe chose not to pursue. He had gained most of his limited strategic goals for 1776, and it only remained to capture Fort Washington, the last rebel stronghold on Manhattan, and Rhode Island. The former he achieved on 15 November by launching an attack from four separate directions that, for the loss of 350 men, gained him 2,800 prisoners and a huge store of guns and ammunition. Watching from Fort Lee across the Hudson, Washington was mortified. 'I had given it as my opinion to General [Nathanael] Greene,' he wrote, 'under whose care it was, that it would be best to evacuate the place; but, as the order was discretionary, and his opinion differed from mine, it was unhappily delayed too long, to my great grief.'[39]

Emboldened by this success, and the unseasonably fine weather, Howe decided to capture Fort Lee in neighbouring New Jersey before sending an expedition to Newport on Rhode Island. Both were in his hands by the end of the year, and so successful had the former operation been that Howe authorized its commander, Lord Cornwallis, to continue his pursuit of Washington's demoralized army through New Jersey as far as the Delaware River. On 6 December he joined Cornwallis at New Brunswick, and at once authorized him to keep up the chase with an advanced guard. Next day Cornwallis entered Princeton shortly after the rebel army had abandoned some of its weapons and marched for Trenton. On the 8th the British general reached Trenton as the rebels were leaving, and only narrowly failed to prevent Washington and his remaining 3,000 men from crossing the nearby Delaware into Pennsylvania. Cornwallis wanted to follow, but the rebels had removed all boats and placed cannon on the far bank.

Not that all of Washington's troops were safely across the river. Having trekked south to protect Fort Lee, Washington had left General Charles Lee (for whom the fort had been named) in command of the force above New York. As Washington began his withdrawal through New Jersey, he ordered Lee to bring his 7,000 men across the Hudson and meet him at New Brunswick. But Lee dawdled. A former lieutenant-colonel in the British Army and veteran of the Seven Years War who later settled in America, Lee had never forgiven Washington for accepting the supreme command of the Continental Army in 1775, an appointment he felt should have been his. Yet Lee, for all his experience, was not an obvious choice as commander-in-chief. He was not American and his eccentricities – including a slovenly appearance, coarse language and an unwillingness to keep his opinions to himself – meant that he lacked the personal skills required of a supreme commander. Nor could he hide his professional jealousy of Washington, telling Brigadier-General Gates in a letter of 13 December that he deplored the 'ingenious manoeuvre' at Fort Washington, and that 'a certain great man is damnably deficient.'[40]

Lee wrote that letter in a soiled dressing gown and bedroom slippers, having unwisely spent the previous night in a tavern that doubled as a whorehouse in Basking Ridge, New Jersey, some 3 miles distant from his army. He was still writing when an aide spotted riders approaching. They were British light dragoons, led by a young cornet called Banastre Tarleton who would end the war with a not entirely undeserved reputation for gratuitous butchery. The aide exclaimed:

'Here, Sir, are the British cavalry!'
  'Where?' replied the General who had signed the letter in the instant.
  'Around the house.'

General Lee appeared alarmed yet collected, and his second observation marked his self-possession: 'Where is the guard? – damn the
guard, why don't they fire?' and after a momentary pause, turned to
me and said, 'Do see what has become of the guard.'

The woman of the house at this moment entered the room and
proposed to him to conceal himself in a bed, which he rejected with
evident disgust. I caught up with my pistols which lay on the table,
thrust the letter he had been writing into my pocket, and passed into
a room at the opposite end of the house, where I had seen the guard
in the morning. Here I discovered their arms, but the men were
absent. I stepped out of the door and perceived the dragoons chasing
them in different directions.[41]

The aide prepared for a shoot-out, but Lee decided to give himself
up when a typically ruthless Tarleton threatened to set the tavern on
fire. 'The unfortunate Lee,' recalled his aide, 'mounted on my horse,
which stood ready at the door, was hurried off in triumph, bareheaded,
in his slippers and coat, his collar open and his shirt very much soiled
from several days' use.'[42]

With one general in the bag[43] and the rest of the Continental Army
in Pennsylvania, Howe wanted to end the campaign and put his men
into winter quarters along the south bank of the Raritan River; but
it was Cornwallis who persuaded him to leave a chain of outposts as
far as the Delaware, with the largest garrisons of 3,000 or so men at
New Brunswick, Princeton and Burlington. Howe then returned to
New York City, where he received the welcome news that Newport
on Rhode Island had been captured and that, as a reward for his
victory at Long Island, he was now *Sir* William. There were also
signs – in the wake of his brother's proclamation of 30 November,
offering a pardon and a release from all 'forfeitures, attainders, and
penalties' to anyone who submitted within sixty days – that popular
support for the rebellion was beginning to wane.[44] Thousands came
forward in New Jersey, and on Long Island alone more than 1,600
militiamen were pardoned. For a few days, at least, Howe must have
imagined that his strategy was working and that one more campaign
in 1777 really would bring an end to the war.

That was the belief of most of his men, including 26-year-old Captain the Honourable William Leslie, second son of the sixth Earl of Leven, who was garrisoned with the 17th Foot at Hillsborough in New Jersey. 'It is the general opinion,' he wrote to his mother on Christmas Day, 'that as soon as the river [Delaware] is froze up, we shall proceed to Phil[adelphia]: the object of our wishes, and for all the lateness and coldness of the season, I believe there is not an officer or soldier who is not sorry, and much disappointed, at not passing the Delaware. We are quartered here for Winter Quarters, but hope we shall pass part of the Winter there . . . The desolation that this unhappy country has suffered must distress every feeling heart, altho' the inhabitants deserve it as much as any set of people who ever rebelled against their Sovereign. They lived in plenty, even in luxury, every man was equal to his neighbour & not one beggar in the whole country; but now too late they feel the ravages of war.'⁴⁵

Washington, meanwhile, had been joined across the Delaware by volunteers from Philadelphia, a regiment of German immigrants, the remnants of General Lee's command and 500 men under General Gates, giving him a total force of around 6,000 men. But he feared even this modest army was on the verge of collapse. If he did not take the initiative, he was warned by some of his officers on 22 December, he ran the risk of his militiamen either going home or accepting Lord Howe's offer of a pardon. Many congressmen had fled Philadelphia in panic, they added, Congress itself was on the verge of bankruptcy and something had to be done to raise morale. Washington was persuaded.

At 8 a.m. on Boxing Day, having ferried 2,400 men back across the near-frozen Delaware in open boats the night before (a feat immortalized by many an American artist), the American commander stood poised outside the town of Trenton, which was garrisoned by 1,550 Hessians. He had deliberately chosen that day because the Hessians were known to 'make a great deal of Christmas in Germany'. They would have drunk and caroused the night before, he was assured, and would be sleeping off hangovers. It helped that their commander, Colonel Johann Rall, had refused to dig an entrenchment, exclaiming: 'Let them come! We want no trenches; we'll have at them with bayonets!'⁴⁶

In the event, Rall was mortally wounded in the hand-to-hand fighting that lasted barely an hour, and all but 500 of his command were killed or captured. Henry Knox, Washington's artillery chief, recorded:

> About half a mile from the town was an advanced guard on each road [which] we forced, and entered the town with them pell-mell; and there succeeded a scene of war of which I had often conceived, but never saw before . . . They endeavoured to form in the streets, the heads of which we had previously the possession of with cannon and howitzers; these, in the twinkling of an eye, cleared the streets . . . Measures were taken for putting an entire stop to their retreat by posting troops and cannon in such passes and roads as it was possible for them to get away by.[47]

Washington knew at once the significance of the victory, telling a young officer: 'This is a glorious day for our country.' As well as 900 prisoners, he had captured 6 guns, 40 horses, 1,000 muskets and bayonets, huge quantities of ammunition and 40 hogsheads* of rum. His own losses were in single figures (though one or two more would later die from exposure).[48]

Aware that a British relief force would not be long in coming, Washington wasted no time withdrawing across the Delaware with his prisoners and booty. But when he received word that the Hessians at Burlington and Bordentown, the remaining posts on the Delaware, had retreated towards the coast, he decided to risk a second crossing to 'pursue the Enemy in their retreat' and strike at vulnerable detachments before they reached safety. A council of war endorsed this decision – with one officer suggesting that a second victory might liberate much of New Jersey – and agreed to act immediately. Bad weather delayed the operation, however, and all the troops were not across until 31 December, just hours before his 1,000 or so most experienced men were, with their term of service up, at liberty to return home. The majority were persuaded to stay on an extra six weeks by the offer of a $10 bounty.[49]

---

* A hogshead was a large cask of liquid that varied in size, according to the commodity, from 52 gallons to 54.

Much had changed since the decision to recross the Delaware. The Hessians had rallied and were part of a force of 8,000 men that Cornwallis had gathered at the college town of Princeton, just 10 miles from where Washington's 5,000 men were assembled at Trenton, while a further 1,800 rebel militiamen were under Colonel Lambert Cadwalader near Bordentown, 7 miles to the east. Uncertain of his next move, Washington convened another council of war at his headquarters in Trenton on 1 January 1777. After much heated discussion, the council agreed that the main force, reinforced by Cadwalader, would make a stand at Trenton. Though slightly outnumbered, the rebels would have the advantage of an entrenched position and more than thirty artillery pieces, some of heavy calibre.

Next day Major-General the Earl Cornwallis began his advance from Princeton. A rich and extremely well-connected officer with an estate in Suffolk, Cornwallis had joined the 1st Foot Guards as an ensign in 1757, later seeing service at Minden as aide-de-camp to Lord Granby, and at the Battle of Villinghausen in 1761, where he commanded the 12th Foot and was commended for his gallantry. Like the Howes, he had strong sympathies for the colonists and was one of only five peers to vote against the Stamp Act in 1766; but he too had put his professional duty first by agreeing to serve against the rebels. A solid, conscientious officer who was well liked by his men, Cornwallis's first action in America was under Clinton during the failed siege of Charleston in early 1776. But since arriving at New York he had made his mark as an intrepid divisional commander, particularly at the Battle of Long Island and during the rapid pursuit of Washington through New Jersey. With the campaign seemingly over, he was about to depart for Britain to visit his ailing wife when word reached him of the defeat at Trenton.

His leave cancelled, Cornwallis received clear orders from Howe: find the Continental Army and destroy it. The quickest route to Trenton was via Maidenhead (now Lawrenceville); but because this meant an advance along a single axis, which in turn would allow Washington to slip away to the east, some of Cornwallis's officers suggested a parallel march towards Crosswicks, near Bordentown. Cornwallis refused. After the surprise at Trenton, he had no intention of dividing his force. So he marched his entire force – 8,000 men, guns and wagons – along a single road turned into a quagmire by the thaw, and was harassed at every turn by an advance party of 1,000 rebel riflemen who fired from the cover of thick woodland before melting away to take up new positions. There was, as a result, barely an hour of daylight left when Cornwallis's vanguard finally approached the main rebel position at Trenton, on rising ground behind the swollen Assunpink Creek.

Apart from the lateness of the hour, there were other compelling reasons for Cornwallis to postpone his assault to the following day: it would have enabled him to seal off the rebels' routes of escape and, more importantly, to have concentrated his full force for the attack. But, goaded by the Hessians, who were desperate to avenge the humiliation of their comrades in the first Trenton battle, he decided not to wait. The main focus of the assault was the only bridge over the Assunpink. Repeated attempts were made to storm it by heavily laden British and Hessian troops; all were repulsed, until the bridge, according to one New England defender, 'looked red as blood, with their killed and wounded, and their red coats'. When nightfall brought an end to the day's fighting, the British had lost 500 men (most of them at the bridge) and the rebels just over a hundred.[50]

Cornwallis, though, was not downhearted. He now knew the rebels' position was a strong one, with its left wing anchored on the Delaware; but he had identified the other wing as the weak point and intended to outflank it the following day. He never got his chance. That night, as the British slept, Washington's army slipped away to the east to attack the small force left at Princeton. To complete the deception, the rebels observed absolute silence during the move, muffled all wagon wheels with cloth and left their campfires burning. They were also helped by thick cloud, a cold wind from the north-west (carrying sounds away from the British), and freezing temperatures that hardened the ground and made marching easier. A young ensign from Virginia would later insist that had Cornwallis cut the rebels' sole escape route 'the war would have ended'.[51]

Early next morning Washington's vanguard was still 2 miles from Princeton when it was spotted by a British column advancing down the road. Commanded by Lieutenant-Colonel Charles Mawhood of the 17th Foot, whose eccentricities included riding into battle with two spaniels, it consisted of 700 men of the Princeton garrison (Mawhood's own battalion and men of the 55th Foot) who had been ordered to join Cornwallis at Trenton. A third battalion, the 40th Foot, was due to follow with the baggage. Had Mawhood left earlier, he would have missed the rebels altogether and left Princeton virtually defenceless; any later and Washington would have found the town defended by three alert regiments. As it was, Mawhood ordered an immediate counter-march and intercepted the rebel vanguard at a slight rise still known as Mercer's Heights, after the rebel Brigadier-General Hugh Mercer, who had fought for Bonnie Prince Charlie during the Forty-Five. Using classic Wolfe tactics, the British closed to within 40 yards, where they exchanged volley fire and, ignoring their inferior numbers and heavy casualties, charged with the bayonet. 'I never saw men [who] looked so furious as they did,' recorded one rebel, who, like most of his comrades, had broken and run at the sight of cold steel. In trying to rally his men, Mercer was clubbed from his horse and bayoneted.[52]

Among the British fatalities was Captain the Honourable William Leslie of the 17th, who, just over a week before, had boasted to his mother of how well the campaign was going. Leslie was shot twice through the body as he charged the crest. 'He no sooner received the shot,' recorded his brother-in-law, who had the story from the regimental surgeon, 'than he instantly expired without a groan, the only motion he made was to give his watch to his servant, who put the body in a baggage cart & conducted it for a considerable time in spite of a very heavy fire from the Enemy but at last he was obliged to abandon it* & follow the regt or must have given himself up as prisoner.'[53]

With the 55th Foot lagging behind, Mawhood led his 17th down

---

* Leslie's body was recognized by Dr Benjamin Rush, one of the signatories of the Declaration of Independence, who, as a young medical student, had stayed with the Leslie family in Edinburgh. Rush arranged for it to be buried in the village of Pluckemin with full military honours.

the hill after the fleeing rebels, but by now Cadwalader's Pennsylvanian Militia had entered the fray. It drove the 17th back on the 55th, which at this point was holding the hill; but there the British made their stand, using disciplined volleys to stop the militiamen in their tracks. It was the arrival of Washington's main force that tipped the balance. Directing the battle from the saddle of his distinctive grey horse, often at a distance from the British of no more than a few yards (so close, in fact, that an American colonel pulled his hat over his eyes so that he would not witness his chief's inevitable death), Washington was able to use his vast superiority in numbers to outflank Mawhood's rapidly diminishing command. At last the men of the 17th and 55th broke and ran for the Stony Brook Bridge, hotly pursued by the victorious rebels.

Some of the survivors formed on the 40th Foot at a stream just south of Princeton, giving the remnants of the garrison the opportunity to withdraw to New Brunswick with arms and supplies. But the 40th was eventually outflanked and forced back into Princeton itself, where 200 men made a final stand at the huge Nassau Hall. They capitulated after a brief artillery barrage, bringing the day's vicious fighting to a close. British casualties in the Battle of Princeton were appalling: 450 officers and men were killed, wounded or captured, almost half of their total force. American losses were again a fraction of those of their foes, though the 37 dead included one brigadier-general and a colonel. A rebel sergeant remembered the British prisoners as a 'haughty, crabbed set of men, as they fully exhibited on their march to the country'. He added: 'The Army retreated to the Pluckemin mountains. The weather was extremely cold, and we suffered from its severity . . . The inhabitants manifested very different feelings towards us from those exhibited a few weeks before, and were now ready to take up arms against the British.'[54]

This surge of support for the rebel cause was not confined to New Jersey, and underlines the vital importance of Washington's two victories at Trenton and Princeton. In just ten days the British had lost 2,000 men; the rebels fewer than 250. Thoroughly outwitted, Cornwallis withdrew his demoralized troops back to New Brunswick, while Washington wintered at Morristown, secure in the knowledge that the rebellion had been re-energized. Pennsylvania militiamen, who had been so loath to come forward before Christmas, now volunteered in droves; while in New Jersey, Virginia and Delaware whole companies of men were enlisted.

The consequences were not lost on General Howe, who acknowledged that the rebels would 'no doubt be much elated by their Success', that he would have to withdraw from western New Jersey, and that the war would probably continue through 1777. The governor of New York agreed: 'The moment was Critical and I believe the Rebel Chiefs were conscious if some stroke was not struck that would give life to their sinking cause, they should not raise another Army.'[55] Many Britons believed – General Clinton included – that Trenton alone had saved the rebellion.

It certainly put an end to the Howes' delicate balancing act. Since mid-August their secret strategy had been to advance inexorably on the military front, but not to risk a general engagement or to alienate the civilian population by devastating the countryside; this, they hoped, would destroy the colonists' faith in the Continental Army and make possible a lasting reconciliation with Britain. With this end in mind, they had ignored repeated opportunities to trap the Continental Army and to mount an effective blockade, while at the same time proffering an olive branch to Congress. And, but for Trenton and Princeton, it might have worked. By mid-December there were signs that the colonists were beginning to accept the inevitability of a British triumph.

Washington's victories – though relatively small in scale – changed everything. Howe acknowledged this in a letter to Germain of 20 January 1777: 'I do not see a prospect of terminating the war but by a general action, and I am aware of the difficulties in our way to obtain it, as the Enemy moves with so much more celerity than we possibly can with our foreign troops who are too much attached to their baggage.'[56] Having tried to end the war by a combination of force and persuasion, he now returned to the strategy he had favoured before his brother's arrival at New York. But it was too late. Washington had learned his lesson: never again would he expose his whole army to destruction as he had at New York; experience had taught him and his generals the importance of strategic withdrawals and the futility of clinging to any one position. Not that Howe's lost opportunities in August and September 1776 would have mattered had the rebellion collapsed, as he fully expected, during the winter of 1776/7. But Trenton and Princeton ensured that it would not, and thereafter Britain's likelihood of winning the war and retaining its colonies was very much reduced.

15.   Brandywine and Saratoga

Most of the British troops in New Jersey sat out the bitter winter of 1777 in fortified cantonments at New Brunswick and Perth Amboy, while the rebels were barely 25 miles distant in quarters at Elizabeth and Morristown. This proximity made it difficult for the British to obtain supplies as every forage party was liable to be ambushed. Though relatively small scale, these encounters sometimes cost the British up to fifty wounded and killed, and cumulatively they took their toll on manpower and morale.

The camps themselves were secure, but very cramped, officers even sleeping on the floor of huts, six or seven to a room. Cold and frequently hungry, the men had also to endure a long and tedious day of fatigue duties. It began at daybreak, with the drummers beating reveille through the principal streets of the camps, and ended at 8 p.m., when the evening drumbeat known as the tattoo* ordered everyone to quarters. In between, the soldiers were expected to carry out a variety of menial jobs: as part of a sanitary detail, burning or burying old meat, refuse or rubbish; loading and unloading provisions; collecting and transporting wood and other fuel; shovelling snow; and making fascines.

The least welcome chore was guard duty. In peacetime a soldier mounted guard every three or four days; in war, when it was necessary to guard against a surprise attack, much more frequently. After the main guard had paraded, detachments were sent to man posts at the military hospitals, magazines, prisons and commissaries. Others were assigned to protect the tents or quarters of senior officers, or to

---

* The name 'tattoo' dates from the seventeenth century, when British soldiers serving in the Low Countries were summoned back to their camps by drummers playing the 'tap toe', an instruction in old Dutch for innkeepers to 'turn off the tap', or stop serving beer.

man the numerous sentry posts that barred entry to garrisons and camps. Only the most trusted soldiers were assigned to the provost guard, 'whose regular police functions included the constraint of war prisoners, spies, and deserters, the control of camp disorders, the regulation of markets that formed in camps, the prevention of illegal sales of alcohol by unlicensed sutlers, and the execution of capital punishment'.[1]

But soldiers spent most of their time preparing for battle, and even veterans were expected to participate. There were three daily drill sessions, each of two hours. The first session was devoted to fitness, with all soldiers in America, even artillerymen, expected to be able to march up to 30 miles a day. A second drill period was spent practising the many complicated manoeuvres that made up both infantry and cavalry exercises. The third, known as parade exercise, put these various motions into practice at company and troop level. Such complicated movements by large numbers of troops required a high level of precision, and to achieve it the British Army concentrated first on marching. Using a stiff-kneed gait not unlike the Prussian goose-step, infantrymen would march at a steady 75 paces a minute, the time kept by fife and drum. Only in an emergency would this speed be increased to 120 paces a minute.

Once the requisite competence in marching had been reached, the troops were instructed in the tactical aspect of drill, such as how to wheel and how to change front. These were standard manoeuvres for all infantry, but others more suited to the American theatre of war were also taught to Howe's men, and to those under Burgoyne's command in Canada. At a review in Montreal, a lieutenant in the 29th Foot reported the men performing 'common manoeuvres' as well as 'several new ones, calculated for defence in this woody country'.[2] Once on campaign, in the broken country between Montreal and Saratoga, Burgoyne's men travelled most of the way by water and became, according to another witness, 'expert at rowing, having been ordered to practise frequently'.[3]

Because the process of loading and firing a musket was so laborious – there were no fewer than twenty-four separate motions, starting with opening the pan, removing the cartridge from a pouch worn at the waist, biting the top off the cartridge, pouring a little powder into the pan, shutting the pan, pulling the hammer back, etc., etc. – it was customary for British soldiers (and most other European armies, for that matter) to fire in volleys in the general direction of the enemy and not to aim at a specific target. But in America, where volley fire was far less effective, marksmanship was actively encouraged: even in bad weather regiments were encouraged to 'get any places in their barracks or elsewhere under cover [where] young and inexpert soldiers may be there perfected in the manual [arms]'; regimental competitions were frequent and prizes given to the best marksmen.[4]

The bayonet, however, remained the generals' weapon of choice. Before his Long Island campaign in August 1776, General Howe reminded his men of their proficiency with the weapon, 'even in woods where [the rebels] thought themselves invincible'. Burgoyne made the same point to his officers when he warned them that any success in the Canadian wilderness 'must greatly rest on the bayonet', and that they were to 'inculcate that idea into the minds of the men'.[5]

But battlefield performance in America was adversely affected by a number of factors, including long marches, exposure, hunger, thirst, lack of sleep and the weight of equipment. The musket alone – with ramrod and sling – weighed 16 lb. 7 oz.; the tin or wooden ammunition box, with cartridges, bayonet and scabbard, flints and cleaning materials, another 11 lb. 8 oz. On his back the soldier carried a pack topped by his greatcoat and blanket roll, a canteen, camp kettle, and a haversack filled with leather and tools for repairing shoes, a hatchet, and a three-day supply of beef and ship biscuit. Thus encumbered with more than 60 lb. of equipment, the soldier was, according to one veteran, 'half-beaten before he came to the scratch'.[6]

On 30 November 1776, when all was going to plan, General Howe had outlined his latest strategy for ending the war in a letter to Lord George Germain. Assuming that the army from Canada would not reach Albany in the Hudson Valley until September 1777 at the earliest, Howe proposed starting the new campaign with offensives against Boston and Albany. Both forces would number 10,000 men, leaving 5,000 to cover New York and 8,000 in New Jersey. Having linked hands with the Canadian Army at Albany, he would turn his attention to Philadelphia and Virginia, and in the winter conquer South Carolina and Georgia. It was a hugely ambitious plan and one, Howe felt, that required an extra 15,000 troops to bring his 'effective' (rather than his nominal) strength up to 35,000. He also asked for eight more warships, a battalion of artillery, more officers and 300 horses. Only with such a force could he promise victory over the Continental Army of 50,000 that Congress had authorized for 1777.[7]

Germain, however, mindful of the escalating cost of war, was wary of sending more troops. So when Howe's dispatch arrived on 30 December 1776, he deliberately confused the effective and nominal strength by telling the cabinet that 5,000 Germans and 3,000 recruits would 'very nearly' give the general the 35,000 men he had asked for.[8] The Earl of Sandwich, first lord of the Admiralty (the equivalent to secretary of state for the navy), was no more forthcoming, informing Lord Howe on 6 January that he could not order any more ships to America until he had considered the effect this would have on the strength of the home fleet.[9]

But then came the shocking news of Trenton and Princeton, which reached London in mid-February, followed soon after by Howe's revised plan for 1777. Now, thanks to reports of a loyalist groundswell in Pennsylvania, he intended to launch his first attack on Philadelphia. The assault on Boston would be postponed until he had enough troops simultaneously to invade Massachusetts and to leave a corps 'to act defensively upon the lower Part of Hudson's River to cover Jersey on that side, as well as to facilitate in some Degree the Approach of the army from Canada'. At first Howe was content to launch this new strategy before reinforcements had arrived. But, as the effect of Washington's victories became clear – particularly the upsurge of support for the rebels in eastern New Jersey – Howe returned to his demand for at least 15,000 more troops, though 20,000 would be preferable. With such a force, he told Germain in a letter that reached London in early March, he would be able to advance on Pennsylvania by land and sea, and also leave enough troops at Rhode Island to make simultaneous attacks on New England. Germain was so determined not to ask Parliament for any more money for reinforcements – beyond the 8,000 that he had already promised – that he agreed to Howe's new strategy to concentrate first on Philadelphia without ensuring that it was compatible with General Burgoyne's separate plan for an advance down the Hudson from Canada. Of the six ships of the line that Lord Howe had asked for, only four had reached New York by late summer. The Howes, therefore, were given neither the strategic direction nor the reinforcements that they now felt they needed to have any chance of winning the war.

Instead, left largely to their own devices, they made two last attempts to reconcile the rebels. The first took the form of a letter to Congress from the captured General Charles Lee, who, at their instigation, was offering to meet delegates to discuss terms. But Congress knew that the Howes had nothing new to offer and promptly rejected Lee's offer. The second attempt, however, was more successful. It took the form of a proclamation, issued on 15 March, that offered money, a pardon and security of property to anyone serving in the Continental Army who, by 1 May, had agreed to switch sides and join either a provincial corps or the British Army, or return home to England. By mid-April rebels were being recruited at the rate of forty a day.

Buoyed by this news, two successful raids on rebel stores in New York and Connecticut, and an improvement in the weather, General Howe at last opened his 1777 campaign in June. Part of the delay, which mystified many of his subordinates, was down to a lack of tents and stores; but the main reason was indecision. 'It seemed that the memory of Trenton – Sir William's sense of responsibility for that disaster – immobilized him' and 'kept him from taking the very measures which promised his vindication'.[10]

His first move in June was to advance his army in two columns west to Middlebush and Hillsborough, in the hope of tempting Washington to fight in New Jersey. But after two weeks of marching and counter-marching, and with nothing to show for his efforts bar a minor skirmish with the rebels' advance guard, he embarked his men for Staten Island to prepare for the amphibious invasion of Pennsylvania.

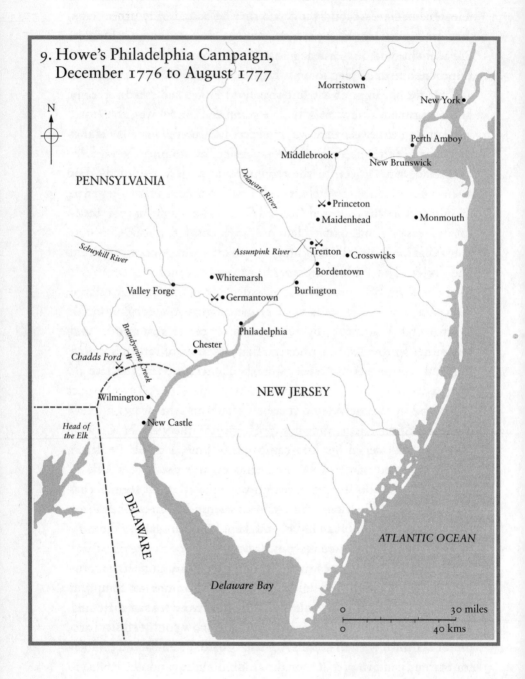

9. Howe's Philadelphia Campaign, December 1776 to August 1777

N

PENNSYLVANIA

Morristown

New York

Perth Amboy

Middlebrook

New Brunswick

Delaware River

Princeton

Maidenhead

Monmouth

Schuylkill River

Assunpink River

Trenton

Crosswicks

Whitemarsh

Bordentown

Valley Forge

Germantown

Burlington

Brandywine Creek

Philadelphia

Chester

Chadds Ford

NEW JERSEY

Wilmington

Head of
the Elk

New Castle

DELAWARE

ATLANTIC OCEAN

Delaware Bay

0   30 miles
0   40 kms

It was during the hiatus on the island that Howe was reminded by Lieutenant-General Sir Henry Clinton – recently returned from Britain, where he had been knighted for his part in the capture of New York – that in the coming campaign Lord North's government expected him to cooperate with Burgoyne, who was advancing down from Canada. Howe's testy response was that he had already received the government's sanction for him to capture Philadelphia. But would not such an expedition by sea, countered Clinton, enable Washington to concentrate his forces against either Burgoyne or New York? No, said Howe, he did not foresee such a danger. The furthest he would go was to concur with Clinton's observation that Burgoyne would have to be supplied from New York once he had advanced beyond Albany. But as for doing anything about this – like opening the Hudson to British shipping, or reducing the rebel forts in the Highlands of the river – he was silent.

On 7 July, fully aware that London wanted him to join up with the Canadian army so that they could campaign together, Howe told Germain that he doubted such a junction could be made in 1777 because Burgoyne would 'find full Employment for his Army against that of the Rebels opposed to him'. Clinton, meanwhile, would remain at New York 'to be upon the Defensive with Power to act otherwise according to concurrent Circumstances, without losing sight of the principal object in the Security of this Place'.[11]

Howe had convinced himself that the loyalists in the Delaware Valley were waiting to greet him with open arms. In mid-July he received word from Burgoyne that the latter had captured Fort Ticonderoga, the rebel fort guarding the southern end of Lake Champlain, 'that his army was in good health, and that Ticonderoga would be garrisoned from Canada, which would leave his force complete for further operations'.[12] Even the news that Washington had responded by moving his army towards the Highlands of the Hudson was not enough to persuade Howe to postpone his Pennsylvania expedition. He did, however, promise Burgoyne that 'if, contrary to my expectations', Washington continued to move north, 'I should soon be after him';[13] and he decided to go to Philadelphia via the Delaware, rather than the Chesapeake, so that he could remain as close as possible to the Hudson.

Of Howe's senior officers, only Earl Cornwallis supported the Pennsylvania expedition. The juniors were, if anything, even less enthusiastic. Captain Duncan Drummond, aide to Clinton, feared that if Howe went to Philadelphia he would ruin his army and leave Burgoyne to be 'cut up alive'; whereas if they joined forces along the Hudson, they would soon cut off New England from the other colonies and end the rebellion.[14]

But Howe would not be dissuaded and on 23 July, after yet more delays because of adverse weather, his fleet of 267 ships (carrying an army of 16,000 men) finally set sail. The plan now was to follow the Delaware to Philadelphia; it altered en route, however, after Howe had received intelligence that Washington was returning to the Delaware. Worried, too, that the rebels would use fire rafts, floating batteries and warships to oppose his landing – and ignoring the assurances of a Royal Navy captain that the transports could be safely unloaded below Philadelphia – he reverted to his original plan to sail further south for the Chesapeake. Informing Clinton of this change on 30 July, he suggested a diversion to help Burgoyne and promised reinforcements. None were ever sent.

Stalled by contrary winds, intermittent calms and uncharted waters, the huge fleet took a further three and a half weeks to reach its landing place at the head of the Chesapeake Bay, close to the Elk River. During that time, men and horses suffered terribly in the hot, airless compartments of the transports: 27 men and 170 horses died; a further 150 horses were destroyed on arrival, and so weakened was Howe's only cavalry regiment, the 16th Light Dragoons, that it could barely muster two squadrons. And yet the news that greeted the seasick British redcoats, desperate to be off the ships, was encouraging. 'Ticonderoga taken by Genl. Burgoyne, 6th July,' recorded Lieutenant John Peebles (now of the 2nd Grenadiers) in his diary on 22 August, adding a day later that 'there were no people in arms in this part of the country tho' many ill affected.' The disembarkation began on 25 August and was unopposed. Peebles wrote: 'We landed about 9 o'clock a little above the ferry & marched about 3 miles up the west side of the river. The inhabitants almost all gone off & carried everything with them they could. A pretty country, and plentiful crops – the day exceedingly hot, & in the night a thunder gust with a great deal of rain. I believe the whole army are landed.'[15]

On 28 August, the advance guard of the army reached the small town of Head of Elk.* 'The inhabitants fled before we reached Town,' noted the recently promoted Sergeant Thomas Sullivan of the 49th, 'leaving great quantities of stores in it, and on board several sloops that were in the river about a mile from the town; being informed or rather persuaded, that our Army would kill and destroy them and their families.'[16] Lieutenant Peebles told a similar story: 'Got to the Head of Elk (a pretty village) about 9, most of the inhabitants fled. Some of the Rebel troops had been there the night before, but went off in haste. General Washington had been there 2 days before, they say he has taken post with his Army about 9 or 10 miles from here towards the Delaware.'[17]

This was bittersweet news for Howe. All along the march to Head of Elk he had seen flourishing but empty farms, cattle and corn standing untended in the fields. Nowhere was there evidence of the strong loyalist sentiment he had been told to expect, and without it he knew that he would not have enough manpower to garrison his conquests: in short, his strategy of driving the rebels to the negotiating table by conquering America in stages was doomed to failure. But the intelligence that Washington was in the vicinity, and might well commit his army to a general action to save Philadelphia, gave Howe the option of reverting to his earlier strategy of destroying the rebellion in a single, decisive battle. He was eager to take it.

While at the Head of Elk, Howe replied to Germain's latest dispatch (dated 18 May) that had approved his plans for invading Pennsylvania by sea, while urging him to cooperate with Burgoyne before the end of the campaign; it also made clear that the government expected him to end the rebellion in 1777 by using loyalists in lieu of reinforcements. Howe's response was that he would not be able to link up with Burgoyne because the Continental Army, bolstered by the unexpectedly hostile colonists, would delay the

---

* Head of Elk was in Maryland, but not far from the Delaware and Pennsylvania borders. It is known as Elkton today.

reconquest of Pennsylvania for longer than he had anticipated; nor could he hope to end the rebellion that year without substantial reinforcements. Moreover, though he now knew that Washington was behind the Brandywine Creek on the road to Philadelphia, he told Germain that he doubted he could manoeuvre the Continental Army into a decisive engagement.[18] Howe was, of course, hedging his bets; but there was now little doubt in his own mind that he would need to destroy Washington's army at Brandywine Creek if he was to have any chance of ending the war.

Washington would give him that chance. Having reached Wilmington on Brandywine Creek on 25 August, the same day Howe's army disembarked at the Elk River, the American commander quickly decided to stand and fight. With fewer troops than Howe – 14,000 to the British general's 16,000 – he knew it was a fearful risk; but he also knew that if he abandoned Philadelphia, and forced the Continental Congress to flee, it would damage rebel morale and possibly cost him his job (not all congressmen approved of his hit-and-run tactics). An additional factor was the news that Major-General Horatio Gates had rebuffed an attempt by Burgoyne to capture the rebel supply depot of Bennington in the upper Hudson Valley, costing the British 900 men. Gates was a former British soldier who had served with the 20th Foot in the War of the Austrian Succession, and briefly under James Wolfe when the latter took command of the 20th in 1749. He had also fought in the Americas during the Seven Years War – acting as brigade major during the capture of Martinique – and later settled in Virginia after retiring from the British Army as a major in 1769. His experience of British staff work made him an obvious choice as the Continental Army's first adjutant-general, and his success in this post had given him the opportunity to lobby for the Canadian Command. Certainly Washington felt threatened by Gates's rising popularity, particularly after his success at Bennington, and was anxious for a victory of his own. He therefore 'made a sacrifice of his own excellent judgment', complained one of his young officers, 'upon the altar of public opinion'.[19]

Howe delayed his advance while he waited for his ships to sail to

New Castle on the Delaware, from where he could be resupplied; and this gave Washington time to call up 2,000 reinforcements – making the opposing forces equal in number – and build a system of defensive works behind the Red Clay Creek. They were never tested because Howe outflanked the works on 8 September, forcing Washington back to the heights that commanded Chadds Ford on Brandywine Creek, the direct route to Philadelphia. It was here that Washington's tactical inexperience was exposed. Having failed to reconnoitre properly the crossing points upstream, he had come to the conclusion that there were no fords 'within twelve miles to cross' above Buffington's Ford, and it was a 'long circuit through a very bad road' to reach that ford.[20] So he posted three divisions on his right to guard the crossings as far as Buffington's, two more divisions and the bulk of the artillery to protect Chadds Ford, and a further two brigades of Pennsylvania militia on his left, where a chain of steep knolls made a crossing unlikely. A single corps of riflemen, under Brigadier-General William Maxwell, was left west of the Brandywine to harass Howe's advance.

As far as it went, Washington's defensive system was a good one. But it had failed to identify another ford called Jeffries, 2 miles above Buffington's, that would enable Howe to outflank the whole American position. Howe had been told about Jeffries, and the fact that it was undefended, by local farmers in the pay of a Philadelphia loyalist, Joseph Galloway. It was Long Island all over again, and the plan that Howe devised was remarkably similar. General Knyphausen would launch a diversionary attack on the rebel centre at Chadds Ford with 6,800 Germans and Britons, while Howe took the remaining 8,500 men across Jeffries Ford. Once this flanking movement was complete, the two arms of Howe's army would crush the rebel centre in a pincer attack. It was an ambitious plan that depended upon the element of surprise and perfect timing; but it was also risky in that it divided Howe's army and put it in danger of being destroyed in detail.

With further to go, Howe's men began their 17-mile march in thick fog at dawn on 11 September. They moved through wooded terrain to avoid detection, guided by a local loyalist. An hour later

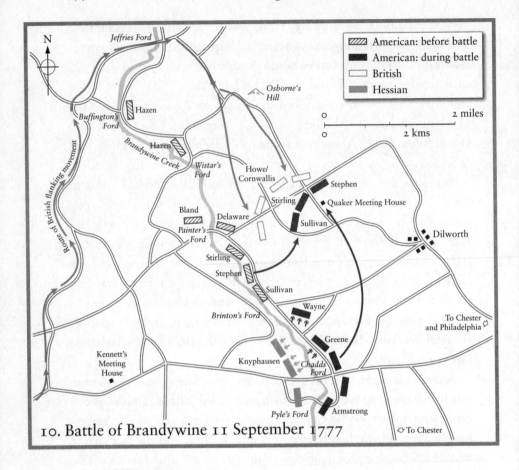

10. Battle of Brandywine 11 September 1777

Knyphausen set off from Kennett's Meeting House, 7 miles from Chadds Ford, and almost at once the greencoated men of his vanguard – Ferguson's Riflemen and the Queen's American Rangers – were skirmishing with Maxwell's light troops in the woods on either side of the road. Sergeant Sullivan of the 49th, whose corps was part of Knyphausen's 1st Brigade, remembered the rebels 'kept up a running fire, mixed with regular volleys for 5 miles, and they still retreating to their main posts, until they got almost in gun shot of the Ford'.[21]

These delaying tactics – with the rebels firing from the cover of trees, fences and rocks, before withdrawing to a new position further down the road – were hugely effective: it took Knyphausen more than five hours to reach Chadds Ford, and cost his vanguard 50 per cent casualties. A number were deceived when some rebels, hiding behind a fence, offered to surrender. 'But upon advancing,' wrote Sullivan,

> they fired a volley upon our men, and took to their heels, killed and wounded about thirty . . . By that and preceding skirmishes [the light troops] were much disabled, which occasioned our Brigade i.e. 1st to advance to the front, being separated (when we formed upon a little hill) by a small Creek, which ran between that and the opposite hill on which the enemy took post. We played upon them with two 6 pounders for half an hour, and drove them out of the breastworks, which was made of loose wood, upon the declivity of the hill . . . They crossed the Brandywine and took post on that side; leaving a few men killed and a few more wounded behind. 'Twas then about 10 o'clock, and the 2nd Brigade with all the Hessians and Artillery joined us.[22]

As his artillery engaged the rebel guns across the Brandywine, Knyphausen paused for news of Howe's flanking manoeuvre. It had not gone entirely to plan. On more than one occasion Howe's huge column had been spotted by American picquets, who at once informed their commander in his headquarters above Chadds Ford; other patrols had nothing to report. But so convinced was Washington that Knyphausen's advance was the enemy's principal assault that he actually ordered General John Sullivan to move a division from the right wing to the centre, from where it could counter-attack. He would later explain his blunder to Congress as follows: 'Unfortunately the intelligence received of the enemy's advancing up the Brandywine, and crossing at a ford about six miles above us, was uncertain and contradictory, notwithstanding all my pains to get the best. This prevented my making a disposition, adequate to the force with which the Enemy attacked us on the right.'[23]

Howe's redcoats crossed the Jeffries Ford unopposed at midday, having taken nearly seven hours to struggle through 12 miles of broken, wooded country. They were hot, tired and thirsty, and Howe gave them an hour and a half to rest and refresh themselves. At 1.30 they were off again, astonished that the rebels had left unguarded the long defile through which they were marching. They would not,

however, escape detection for much longer. Shortly after 2 p.m.
Washington received definite news of an enemy column on his right
so huge that it caused 'dust [to] rise back in the country for above an
hour'.[24] Still not convinced that Howe's force was the main threat,
the American commander sent only Sullivan's division back to his
right wing; but he did postpone the planned counter-attack in the
centre while he awaited developments.

Not until 4 p.m. were Howe's troops ready to attack the improvised rebel positions near the Quaker Meeting House on Birmingham
Hill, 3 miles to the north of Chadds Ford. After a brief bombardment, remembered Lieutenant Peebles (whose 2nd Grenadiers was
on the right of the three-brigade attack), Howe's elite troops 'form'd
their respective Corps & moved up to the Enemy under a heavy fire
mostly from behind fences'.[25] One redcoat recalled 'trees crackling
over one's head' and 'leaves falling as in autumn'. A French volunteer
with the rebels, meanwhile, had 'never witnessed so close & severe a
fire' on a European battlefield. 'Bombshells and shot fell round me
like hail,' wrote a militiaman, 'cutting down my comrades on every
side, and tearing off the limbs of the trees like a whirlwind.'[26]

Despite being outnumbered in this sector two to one, the rebels
fought with desperate savagery. Though part of their left wing broke
under pressure from the guards and both battalions of grenadiers, the
rest of the line fought on as the battle ebbed and flowed. Four times
the rebels were driven off the hill, and four times they retook it. 'We
broke and rallied and rallied & broke,' was how one American put
it.[27] But when they retreated for the fifth time, after ninety minutes
of bloody close-quarter fighting, there would be no counter-attack.
'After giving them a few rounds,' wrote Peebles, '[we] charged them
with such spirit that they immediately fled in confusion leaving several pieces of cannon in the field & playing those that were more
distant. [We] pursued the fugitives thro' the woods & over fences for
about 3 miles, when [we] came upon a second & more extensive line
of the Enemy's best troops drawn up & posted to great advantage.'[28]

Peebles was guilty of a little exaggeration. The second line he was
referring to was not 3 miles back but barely a mile, and it was composed of the remnants of the first line and a division under Nathanael

Greene that Washington, at last realizing the seriousness of the flank attack, had sent an hour earlier to bolster his crumbling defences. Greene's men covered the 4 miles in forty-five minutes, and once in position fought stoutly, heartened by the presence of Washington, who had ridden over with his staff to take command of the sector in person.

Meanwhile Knyphausen, observing Greene's departure, ordered his men to attack across the Brandywine so as to close the trap. Sergeant Sullivan recalled:

> As the 4th Battalion (being the first) forded the River under a heavy fire of Musquetry, the enemy's cannon [missed] fire in the Battery as they crossed, and before the gunners could fire them off, the men of that Battalion put them to the bayonet, and forced the enemy from the entrenchment, who drawing up in the field and orchard just by, rallied afresh and fought bayonet to bayonet. But the rest of the two Brigades . . . coming up, [they] were obliged to retreat in the greatest confusion, leaving their artillery and ammunition in the field.[29]

By now Washington and the right wing had conducted a fighting retreat to the village of Dilworth, closely pursued by Howe's grenadiers and guardsmen, who became entangled and lost in thick woodland. They emerged to see Major-General Anthony Wayne's division withdrawing invitingly across their front, along a road to the south of Dilworth. But with the light failing they were unable to take advantage. 'The weariness of the troops,' wrote Peebles, '& the night coming on prevented any further pursuit & saved thousands of the Rebels.'[30]

Washington ordered his men back to Chester, a retreat that was almost as gruesome as the battle itself. 'Our way was over the dead and dying,' recalled one American soldier, 'and I saw many bodies crushed to pieces beneath the wagons, and we were bespattered with blood.'[31] It was a humiliating defeat for the rebels, who, unusually for well-dug-in defenders, had suffered more casualties than the attacking force: 1,100 killed, wounded and taken prisoner; British losses, by contrast, were 89 killed and 488 wounded.[32]

This time, at least, Howe had outwitted Washington and forced him to abandon the field. But, crucially, the main rebel force was still intact. 'The enemy's army escaped a total overthrow,' Howe informed Germain, 'that must have been the consequence of an hour's more daylight.'[33] Was this intentional? One of Howe's Hessian Jäger officers thought so, claiming that the advance was deliberately slow 'so that the American army should not be destroyed to pay a fresh compliment to the Opposition Party [in London] and to bring forth a new [peace] proposal'.[34] But this is probably going too far. On the one hand, Howe was still hopeful of forcing a negotiated peace; on the other he knew he needed a crushing victory to make that possible. Brandywine was a victory; but it had left Washington far from crushed. 'Though we fought under many disadvantages,' he informed Congress that night,

> and . . . were obliged to retire, yet our loss of men is not, I am persuaded, very considerable, I believe much less than the enemy's. We have also lost about seven or eight pieces of cannon, according to the best information I can at present obtain. The baggage, having previously moved off, is all secure, saving the men's Blankets, which being at their backs, many of them doubtless are lost.
>
> I have directed all the Troops to assemble behind Chester, where they are now arranging for the night. Notwithstanding the misfortune of the day, I am happy to find the troops in good spirits; and I hope another time we shall compensate for the losses now sustained.[35]

True to form, Howe was in no hurry to exploit his victory. For three days the bulk of his army remained at Brandywine while supplies were brought up and his wounded were taken down to Wilmington on the Delaware. During the hiatus, Sergeant Thomas Sullivan of the 49th Foot was demoted to private and 'abused very grossly' by his colonel for failing to explain the provenance of 'some mutton that was roasting in camp' (it had almost certainly been looted from a nearby farm).[36] This was the start of Sullivan's disaffection. The following June, noting that the rebels were 'striving to throw off the Yoke, under which my native country sunk for many years', he deserted from his regiment and became a steward to General Nathanael Greene, then quartermaster-general to the Continental Army.

Sullivan's diary ends abruptly on 28 July 1778 and his fate is unknown.[37]

In the days after the battle Washington moved his army to the Warren Tavern in the hope of intercepting Howe as he advanced towards the fords on the upper Schuykill River, the last major obstacle before Philadelphia. When Howe discovered this on 16 September, he began a rapid march to confront Washington; but a battle never took place because a violent rainstorm made it impossible for either side to use their firearms. 'I wish I could give you a description of the downpour,' wrote one of Howe's Hessians. 'It came so hard that in a few minutes we were drenched and sank in mud up to our calves.'[38]

With his entire ammunition supply – more than 400,000 cartridges – ruined by the rain, Washington marched the bulk of his army north to a depot at Reading Furnace. Only Wayne's division of 1,500 men, hurriedly resupplied with cartridges, was left to shadow Howe's advance. Wayne's orders were to take any opportunity to fall on Howe's rearguard or baggage, but also to be wary of 'ambuscades'.[39] He ignored that advice.

For two nights in succession Wayne camped near an inn called the Paoli Tavern as his scouts kept track of Howe's movements. On the third, 20 September, he was attacked after dark by a column of 2,000 men under the command of Major-General Charles Grey, sent by Howe after loyalists had reported Wayne's whereabouts. Grey had ordered his men not to load their muskets, for fear of accidents, and the assault with bayonets and swords took the unsuspecting rebels completely by surprise. The enemy, wrote one of Grey's officers,

some with arms, others without, [ran] in all directions with the greatest confusion. The light infantry bayoneted every man they came up with. The camp was immediately set on fire, and this, with the cries of the wounded, formed altogether one of the most dreadful scenes I ever beheld. Every man that fired was instantly put to death. Captain Wolfe was killed, and I received a shot in my right hand, soon after we entered the camp. I saw the fellow present at me, as I was running up to him when he fired. He was immediately killed. The

enemy were pursued for two miles. I kept up till I grew faint from
[loss] of blood and was obliged to sit down . . . Four hundred and
sixty of the enemy were counted the next morning, lying dead, and
not one shot was fired by us – all done with the bayonet. We had only
twenty killed and wounded.[40]

Six days after the attack (dubbed by the rebels the Paoli Massacre),
having crossed the Schuykill on the 22nd, Howe's vanguard entered
Philadelphia. 'The streets crowded with inhabitants who seem to
rejoice on the occasion,' noted Lieutenant Peebles, 'tho' by all accounts
many of them were publickly on the other side before our arrival.
The Congress went off the day before yesterday in great haste to
Trenton & that way; the Rebels busy these two or three days past in
removing every thing they could over to [New] Jersey, whether public stores or Tory [loyalist] property.'[41]

A month before, while still at the Head of Elk, Howe had issued
a proclamation offering protection to all colonists who remained at
home or surrendered with their arms within a month. Now, having
reached Philadelphia, he tried to recruit loyalist troops by offering
grants of land to those who agreed to serve for two years. But neither
initiative met with much success, making a mockery of his assumption that British troops would be welcomed with open arms; nor did
it help that his men, despite the threat of draconian punishments,[*]
looted and stole at will. The Hessians were particularly ill-disciplined,
prompting a German-American resident of Philadelphia to ask one
soldier: 'What harm have we people done to you, that you Germans
come over here to suck us dry and drive us out of house and home.'[42]

Howe's chief preoccupation, now, was to clear the Delaware as far as
Philadelphia so he could supply his army by sea. This meant removing
obstacles and reducing forts on the New Jersey side of the river, a task
he began on 1 October when a force of two battalions captured the
strongpoint of Billingsport, 5 miles north of Chester. Three days later,

---

[*] Two men were executed and another two sentenced to 500 lashes for plundering
on the march to Philadelphia.

as he was about to launch the next assault, Howe was himself attacked in his main camp at Germantown, 10 miles north of Philadelphia.

Bolstered by reinforcements from New Jersey and Maryland (bringing his total strength up to 11,000), and encouraged by reports that Howe had split his force to protect Philadelphia, reduce the Delaware forts and escort supplies up from Chester, Washington was attempting a repeat of Trenton. Once again he was making a dawn attack on a garrison that was not entrenched; but this time little went to plan. Only Sullivan's column was in place to begin the assault at 5 a.m., the men screaming 'Revenge Wayne's affair!' as they charged.

They were up against a battalion of light infantry that fired a volley and charged in turn. 'They gave way on all sides,' remembered a British lieutenant, 'but again and again

> renewed the attack with fresh troops and greater force. We charged them twice, till the battalion was so reduced by killed and wounded, that the bugle was sounded to retreat . . . This was the first time we had retreated before the Americans, and it was with great difficulty to get our men to obey our orders. By this time, General Howe had come up, and seeing the battalion retreating, all broken, he got into a passion and exclaimed, 'For shame, light infantry! I never saw you retreat before. Form! Form! It's only a scouting party.' However he was soon convinced it was more . . . as the heads of the enemy's columns soon appeared. One, with three pieces of cannon in their front, immediately fired at the crowd that was standing with General Howe under a large chestnut tree. I think I never saw people enjoy a charge of grape before, but we really all felt pleased to see the enemy make such an appearance and to hear the grape rattle about the commander-in-chief's ears, after he had accused us of having run away from a scouting party. He rode off immediately at full speed.[43]

This attack came close to turning the British left flank and winning the battle; but the light infantry held on until they could be reinforced. Elsewhere events conspired to wreck Washington's battle plan: one column lost its way and never reached Germantown; the others arrived too late to tip the balance. But the biggest blunder was made by Washington himself, who threw battalion after battalion against a two-storey stone house that was occupied by just 120 men of the 40th Foot. It was never taken, the tiny garrison accounting for more than a third of rebel casualties at a cost of just four men.

After a fight lasting three hours, Washington was persuaded to withdraw with his wounded before British reinforcements arrived from Philadelphia. He departed not a moment too soon, leaving a battlefield strewn with corpses 'as thick as the stones in a stony plowfield'. He had come within an ace of replicating his success at Trenton – but on a much larger scale – and only a combination of bad luck and tactical naivety had cost him the victory. Later he tried to downplay the reverse by describing it as more 'unfortunate than injurious'. But a butcher's bill of 1,200 rebels and only 500 British said it all; and this setback, coming soon after the defeat at Brandywine, brought the inevitable recriminations. 'Our miscarriage,' railed one congressman, 'sprung from the usual source – want of abilities in our senior officers.' A scapegoat was needed and Brigadier-General Adam Stephen, who had clashed with Washington before, was the man chosen. Not only had he lost his way and arrived late for the battle; he then ordered a withdrawal, without authority, that left neighbouring units exposed. An unproven rumour went round that he was drunk on the day of the fight, and he was duly cashiered by a court martial for dereliction of duty. [44]

Howe, meanwhile, spooked by the near-run thing at Germantown, had asked Clinton to send 4,000 reinforcements from New York, knowing full well that such a diminution of his force would make it impossible for Clinton to assist Burgoyne (who, according to the latest reports, was encountering heavy opposition north of Albany). The extra men would take several weeks to reach Philadelphia, and in the meantime Howe continued the operation to clear the Delaware, but with limited success.

On 17 October, while Howe and his brother were still trying to win control of the river, a bombshell exploded in the form of dispatches from New York. They included letters from Germain, dated early August, which indirectly censured Howe for starting the campaign so late in the year, for declining to raid the coasts of New

England and for waging a half-hearted war. While accepting that Howe was a better judge of military strategy than the public, Germain felt it necessary to stress that the London mob was 'looking for bold and enterprising measures, and I shall be happy in seeing you meet with the Applause and Admiration of the Ignorant, as well as the abler judges of military merit'.[45] A separate letter to Lord Howe was no less critical, chiding him for allowing the colonists to continue subsistence fishing while the waters around Britain swarmed with American privateers. Taken together, Germain's dispatches were a less than subtle attempt to provoke the Howes either to resign or to wage war more ruthlessly, and both felt the implied criticism keenly.

But there was worse to come for General Howe in a letter from Burgoyne to Clinton, dated 28 September. In it, Burgoyne claimed that his army was surrounded by a vastly superior foe; and that he was contemplating a withdrawal to Canada, provided he was able and Clinton did not object. Burgoyne went on to suggest that Howe, by not providing him with assistance or specific instructions, was responsible for his predicament.[46]

Howe's furious response was to offer Germain his resignation. Though he would not admit it, his campaign in Pennsylvania had not justified his refusal to coordinate with Burgoyne: most Pennsylvanians had refused his offer of clemency; the Continental Army, though bruised from recent setbacks, was still in the field; Philadelphia was not yet securely held; and Burgoyne's army was in mortal danger. His conduct of the recent campaign, moreover, had brought him yet more criticism from officers and loyalists alike. It must have been obvious, even to him, that his attempt to atone for Trenton and Princeton – by proving that Pennsylvanians were basically loyal – had failed. Hence his offer to resign, an offer he must have hoped the government would not accept. It all now hinged on events further north.

Five months earlier, after forty days aboard the frigate *Apollo*, Lieutenant-General John Burgoyne had disembarked at Quebec with a spring in his step and an absolute conviction that he, a famous playwright, was about to bring the final curtain down on the American rebellion. The previous winter he had served as second-in-command to Sir Guy Carleton during the first, partially successful thrust from Canada into the colonies in the winter of 1776.* Now he was back to supersede Carleton and launch his own invasion.

His campaign plan – agreed with Germain in the early part of the year – was to leave 3,700 men with Carleton to defend Canada, send another 700 or so regulars with Colonel Barry St Leger on an expedition down the Mohawk Valley, and use the remaining 7,250 redcoats in Canada to advance along the Hudson Valley. This was, however, a thousand men fewer than he had hoped for, and instead of finding an additional 2,000 loyalists and Canadians under arms, he got barely 300. Undaunted, Burgoyne began to prepare for the forthcoming invasion with a thoroughness that belied his reputation as a womanizer and rake. A huge armada of canoes, boats and bateaux was gathered to transport his army, its supplies and camp followers (including six women per battalion) across Lake Champlain.[47] Burgoyne also enlisted 500 Indians scouts, warning their chiefs not to harm noncombatants or prisoners with either hatchet or knife. 'You shall receive compensation for the prisoners you take,' he told them, 'but you shall be called to account for the scalps.'[48]

In late June, on the eve of his departure, he issued a rousing call to arms:

> The Army embarks tomorrow to approach the Enemy [he wrote in General Orders]. We are to contend for the King and the Constitution of Great Britain, to vindicate the Law and to relieve the Oppressed . . . The Services required on this particular Expedition are critical and conspicuous. During our progress occasions may occur in which neither difficulty, nor labour, nor Life are to be regarded. THIS ARMY MUST NOT RETREAT.[49]

At first, he made good progress. Having landed his army on the southern shores of Lake Champlain on 30 June, Burgoyne took barely a week to capture the formidable Fort Ticonderoga by hauling guns up a nearby hill. The 3,000-strong rebel garrison withdrew

---

* Having captured Crown Point at the southern end of Lake Champlain, Carleton decided he could go no further and withdrew into Canada.

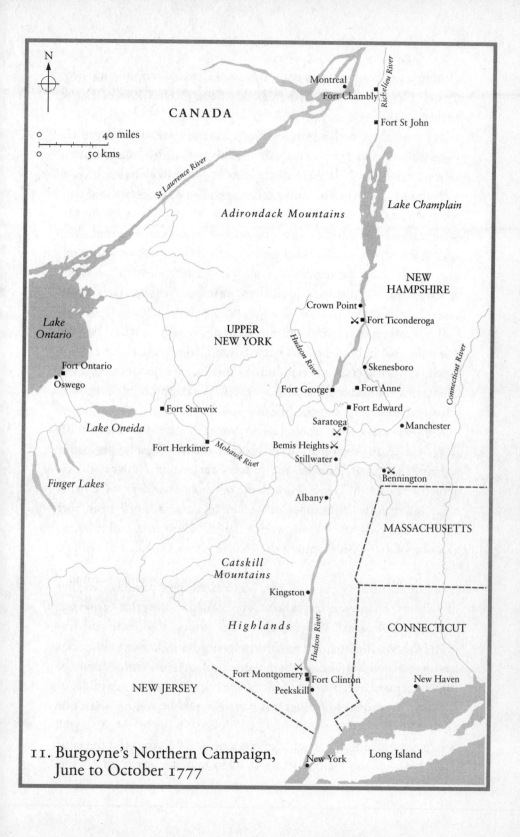

N

| | 40 miles |
| | 50 kms |

CANADA

Montreal

Fort Chambly

Richelieu River

Fort St John

St Lawrence River

Adirondack Mountains

Lake Champlain

NEW
HAMPSHIRE

Crown Point •

✕ ■ Fort Ticonderoga

*Lake
Ontario*

UPPER
NEW YORK

Hudson River

Skenesboro

Fort Ontario
■
Oswego

Fort George ■ ■ Fort Anne

Connecticut River

■ Fort Stanwix

■ Fort Edward

Lake Oneida

Saratoga

• Manchester

Fort Herkimer ■ *Mohawk River*

Bemis Heights ✕

Finger Lakes

Stillwater •

Bennington ✕

Albany •

MASSACHUSETTS

*Catskill
Mountains*

Kingston •

Highlands

CONNECTICUT

Hudson River

Fort Montgomery ✕
Peekskill • ■ Fort Clinton

New Haven •

NEW JERSEY

New York • Long Island

11. Burgoyne's Northern Campaign,
June to October 1777

without a fight and, within days, Burgoyne had reached Skenesboro, just 40 miles from Albany, where he hoped to receive news of Howe further south.

But from there on his progress slowed as the retreating Americans felled hundreds of trees to impede the progress of his huge artillery train of 138 guns. 'The face of the country was likewise so broken with creeks and marshes,' recorded Roger Lamb, a 22-year-old corporal of the 9th Foot, 'that there were no less than forty bridges to construct, one of which was over a morass two miles in extent. The difficulties of the march through this wilderness were encountered and overcome by the army with a spirit and alacrity which could not be exceeded.'[50] Burgoyne could have taken the easier water route down Lake George to Fort George, before marching south-east to Fort Edward on the upper Hudson; but he chose to go overland because it would enable him, he had been assured, to recruit thousands of loyalists. Instead only a few hundred came in. 'The great bulk of the country is undoubtedly with Congress,' a disappointed Burgoyne informed Germain, 'in principle and zeal.'[51]

Even waverers were discouraged from throwing their lot in with Burgoyne by the depredations of his Indian allies. Despite his earlier warning, scalpings, murder and pillage were commonplace. A surgeon on the staff of General Gates, the rebel commander, noted in his diary on 27 July: 'A number of Indians went to a house near Fort Edward and took two white women and a Negro man and woman, and one of the white women they killed upon the hill and scalped her.'[52]

The unfortunate victim was Jane McCrea, the pretty young daughter of a Presbyterian minister, who was betrothed to a loyalist lieutenant in Burgoyne's army. Worried about her safety, the lieutenant had promised two Indians a barrel of rum if they brought her to him. But having rescued her and another woman of loyalist sympathies, the Indians argued over who should receive the reward. 'In the midst of the fray,' according to a rebel prisoner who said he was present, 'one of the Chiefs in a rage shot Jenny [*sic*] McCrea in the breast, & she fell & expired immediately. Her hair was long and flowing, and the same chief took off the scalp, cutting so as to unbrace nearly the whole part of the head on which the hair grew. He then sprang up, tossed the scalp in the face of a young Indian standing by, brandished it in the air, and uttered a savage yell of exultation.'[53]

When General Gates learned of the outrage, he wrote Burgoyne a letter of protest, accusing him of paying blood money to the Indians for scalps. Burgoyne denied the charge, insisting that he had only agreed to pay for prisoners to 'prevent cruelty'. He 'abhorred' what had happened, but had decided to pardon the Iroquois chief involved. Had he executed the chief, he explained, the Indians would have deserted to a man and caused havoc on their way home.

More setbacks followed for Burgoyne. First a British expedition to capture the rebel supply depot of Bennington was easily repulsed by General Gates on 9 August (a defeat that cost Burgoyne 900 men and four cannon; and one that, conversely, prompted a jealous Washington to give battle at Brandywine); then came the news that Colonel St Leger had called off his expedition after failing to take Fort Stanwix at the head of the Mohawk River, and would not now be joining Burgoyne at Albany. At this point, having reached a deserted Fort Miller on the Hudson (8 miles south of Fort Edward), Burgoyne was tempted to fall back. His force and supplies were dwindling, and he was being criticized for spending too much time carousing and not enough planning the campaign. 'It was only too true,' wrote Baroness von Riedesel, the wife of a German officer, who had accompanied the army with her children, 'that General Burgoyne liked to make himself easy, and that he spent half his nights in singing and drinking, and diverting himself with . . . his mistress who was as fond of champaign as himself.'[54]

On 20 August he poured out his worries in a letter to Germain, asserting that upper New York, contrary to his expectations, abounded 'in the most active and rebellious' of people. Awaiting him, moreover, was an American army not only 'superior to mine in [Continental] troops', but its commander could have 'as many militia as he pleases'. His afflictions, he added, hang 'like a gathering storm'.[55]

His instinct was to pull back to Fort Edward and wait out the winter. But he still held out hope that Clinton would assist him from New York; and he probably knew that if he retreated it would be his last chance of an independent command. So he pushed on down the west side of the Hudson, reaching the settlement of Saratoga in mid-September. Four days later, on the 19th, he attempted to outflank General Gates's well-entrenched position at Bemis Heights, near Stillwater on the Hudson. After a brutal slugging match, Burgoyne remained in possession of the field at Freeman's Farm; but it was a hollow victory because his 600 casualties were twice those of the Americans and, more importantly, he had failed to unhinge Gates's defensive position.

That evening his hopes were raised by a message from Clinton, who promised to 'make a push' up the Hudson with 2,000 men on 22 September. This encouraged Burgoyne to dig in and wait. But, as the days passed with no sign of Clinton, the temperature plummeted and supplies dwindled. On 3 October Burgoyne ordered the daily ration to be cut by a third; two days later he called a council of war and proposed another attack. His senior commanders were not enthusiastic (preferring to retreat towards Saratoga), but Burgoyne got his way, describing the new operation as a reconnaissance in force, though its object was the same as before: to gain the high ground that dominated Gates's position at Bemis Heights, making it untenable.[56]

The outcome of the Battle of Bemis Heights, fought on 7 October, was never in doubt. After three hours of trying and failing to fight his way through a wheat field, bounded on two sides by woods, Burgoyne called off the attack. He had directed the fighting with great coolness and courage – losing a horse and having his hat and waistcoat riddled with bullet holes – but it was not enough. Among his 900 casualties were 40 officers and 2 generals (one of whom, Brigadier-General Simon Fraser, had played a key role in the victory at Quebec in 1759 by hoodwinking the French sentry at the base of the cliff); rebel losses were fewer than 130.

The wounded British officers included a Major Acland of the grena-diers, whose pregnant wife, Lady Harriet (the daughter of an earl), had accompanied him on campaign. On hearing that her badly injured hus-band was in rebel hands, she at once asked for and was given permission to cross the lines and nurse him. She duly made her way to the rebel camp by traversing the Hudson River in a canoe, an act of devotion later depicted in a famous painting by Robert Pollard. 'There is scarcely an instance,' wrote Roger Lamb of the 9th Foot, 'either in ancient or modern history, that more finely depicts the resolution, affection, and fortitude of woman toward the husband of her heart and vows than this. If war sometimes in bad men, calls forth all the viler passions of our nature, in women it is otherwise.' Sadly Lady Harriet's story did not have a happy ending. Having nursed her husband back to health, the Aclands rejoined Burgoyne's column. But Acland quarrelled with a fellow officer and was killed fighting a duel.[57]

A day after the Battle of Bemis Heights, many miles to the south, Clinton wrote to inform Burgoyne that he had just captured the last of the highland strongholds: '*Nous y voilà*, and nothing now between us but Gates. I sincerely hope this *little* success of ours may facilitate your operations.' The letter was hidden inside a small silver bullet and entrusted to a loyalist courier, Daniel Taylor. But Taylor was intercepted by rebels en route and, before he could be searched, was seen to swallow the bullet. Twice Taylor was forced to take a powerful emetic. The first time he snatched the bullet out of his faeces and swallowed it again; the second it was seized, the message extracted and shown to the governor of New York, George Clinton, who ordered Taylor to be shot as a spy. Burgoyne never learned, therefore, that help was on its way.[58]

Not that it would have made a difference. Fort Montgomery was more than 120 miles downstream of Bemis Heights, a distance that would have taken Clinton's force weeks to cover; and Burgoyne did not have weeks to wait. During the night of 9 October his battered army withdrew to Saratoga, leaving its fires burning and its tents standing. But it could go no further because, by 11 October, it was surrounded. Conditions inside the rain-lashed camp quickly deteriorated as supplies ran out and dead cattle lay putrefying on the hillside. And all the while the rebels kept up a constant bombardment of cannon and rifle fire, causing many of the British non-combatants to seek refuge in a cellar. Baroness von Riedesel recalled:

> My children lay down on the earth with their heads in my lap, and in
> this manner we passed the entire night . . . A horrible stench, the cries

of the children prevented me from closing my eyes. On the following morning the cannonade began again, but from a different side. I advised all to go out of the cellar for a little while, during which time I would have it cleaned . . . for the women and children, being afraid to venture forth, had soiled the whole cellar.

I had just given the cellars a good sweeping, and fumigated them by sprinkling vinegar on burning coals, and each had found his place prepared for him – when a fresh and terrible cannonade threw us all once more into alarm . . . Eleven cannon balls went through the house, and we could plainly hear them rolling over our heads. One poor soldier, whose leg they were about to amputate, having been laid upon a table for this purpose, had the other leg taken off by another cannon ball, in the very middle of the operation. His comrades all ran off, and when they again came back they found him in one corner of the room, where he had rolled in anguish, scarcely breathing.[59]

On 13 July, Burgoyne invited all his officers of captain and above to a council of war. His preference, he told them, was for the army to try to escape in small groups to Ticonderoga. But the majority knew this would lead to many unnecessary deaths, not to mention the abandonment of the non-combatants, and insisted instead on capitulation. Bowing to their will, Burgoyne drafted the terms of the surrender document and sent it to Gates under a white flag the following morning. The response was uncompromising: unconditional surrender.

At sunset, more in hope than expectation, Burgoyne made a new proposal. He would surrender if his men were allowed to march out with the honours of war, the regulars to be transported to Boston (and from there to England) while the loyalists and Canadians were given safe passage over the border; in return his men would pledge not to serve again in America for the rest of the war. Burgoyne had little expectation that Gates would agree to such generous terms. But the following morning he did, causing the British general to suspect that Clinton's relief force was on its way (it was). For almost two days Burgoyne stalled for time by querying the terms of a document he himself had drafted. Eventually Gates ran out of patience and sent him an ultimatum: sign within an hour or the bombardment would resume. Burgoyne signed at 9 a.m. on 17 October 1777, little knowing that his surrender was the beginning of the end for Britain's American Empire.[60]

An hour later, with many officers openly weeping, the 5,895 survivors of Burgoyne's army left their camp, one battalion after the other, and marched down a muddy road between two lines of rebel soldiers to a field where they piled their arms. Apart from the odd shout of triumph, the rebels appeared more sympathetic than exultant. They showed, recalled one British officer, 'not the least disrespect or even a taunting look but all was mute astonishment and pity';[61] another was impressed by the rebels' military bearing, standing 'so still that we were greatly amazed'. He added: 'Not one of them was properly uniformed but each man had on the clothes in which he goes to the field, the church, or to the tavern . . . The officers wore very few uniforms and those they did wear were of their own invention.'[62]

Even Gates was dressed simply for his meeting with Burgoyne in the dark blue frock coat favoured by generals of the Continental Army. The beaten Burgoyne, by contrast, was wearing the elaborate full-dress uniform of a British general, his immaculate scarlet coat topped by two huge gold epaulettes. 'The fortunes of war, General,' he said to Gates, 'have made me your prisoner.'

Gates's reply was typically generous: 'I shall always be ready to bear testimony that it has not been through any fault of Your Excellency.'[63]

The rebel commander then invited Burgoyne and his senior officers to join him and his staff for lunch in a nearby marquee, an offer that was eagerly accepted. A witness to this jovial repast of ham, goose, beef, boiled mutton and assorted side dishes, all washed down with cider mixed with rum, was Baroness von Riedesel, who arrived with her children as the meal was under way. She was shocked by the laughter coming from the marquee and, when refused admittance, was grateful to be taken in by one of Gates's deputies, General Philip Schuyler, who took her and her children to his tent and gave them a hot meal.[64]

As Burgoyne proposed a toast of 'George Washington!' and his

gallant host responded with 'King George III', the beaten army
was beginning its long march to Boston. 'From the outset,' recalled
Corporal Lamb of the 9th Foot, 'we experienced much hardship,
sleeping in barns, and having but bad clothing, and scanty provisions.
The way before and about us presented an uncheering appearance,
mountainous and barren, with little of pleasing scenery to amuse the
traveller.'[65] Despite the terms of the 'Convention', it would be many
years before Lamb and his fellow captives saw the shores of Britain.*

A few days after the surrender, General Gates wrote a heartfelt
appeal to his former friend and Opposition politician, the Marquess
of Rockingham:

> Born & Bred an Englishman, I cannot help feeling for the misfortunes
> brought upon my country by the wickedness of that Administration
> who begun & have continued this most unjust, unpolitic and unnat-
> ural War . . . The United States of America are willing to be Friends
> but will never submit to be the Slaves of the Parent Country. They
> are by Consanguinity, by Commerce, by Language & by the Affec-
> tion which naturally flow from these more attached to England than
> any country under the sun. Therefore, spurn not the Blessings which
> yet remain. Instantly withdraw your Fleets and Armies, cultivate the
> Friendship and commerce of America. Thus, and thus only can Eng-
> land hope to be Great and Happy.[66]

It was sound advice, but not likely to be heeded when word of the
disaster reached London on 2 December. Though warned by Howe's
resignation letter (which arrived a day earlier) that all was not well,
the government was profoundly shocked that a whole army had surrendered, leaving Canada virtually defenceless. They were in 'a great
state of distraction', confided one of Germain's secretaries to the

---

* Regarding the terms of the 'Convention' too lenient, Congress refused to ratify
it and the captive army spent the winter in huts near Boston. Only Burgoyne was
given permission to return home. In the summer of 1778 the prisoners were moved
to a stockade 50 miles south of Boston, and given wood and nails to build shelters.
It was from here that Lamb escaped to join the 23rd Fusiliers. He was later captured
with the 23rd at Yorktown, the defeat that effectively ended the war.

Opposition MP and chief opponent of the war, Edmund Burke, and knew not 'what to do, or which way to turn themselves'.[67]

Burke knew, of course, and that was to 'turn themselves out' of government. This was the Opposition's chance to bring down the North government for its pitiful handling of the war and it took it with both hands. The most devastating attack, however – and one that put the near-hopelessness of the army's task into context – was launched in the House of Lords by the 69-year-old William Pitt the Elder (now the Earl of Chatham), an elder statesman with no personal following:

> No man thinks more highly than I of the virtue and valour of British troops; I know they can achieve anything except impossibilities; and the conquest of America is an impossibility. You cannot, I venture to say it, *you cannot conquer America* . . . What is your present situation there? We do not know the worst, but we know that in three campaigns we have done nothing, and suffered much . . . Conquest is impossible: you may swell every expense and every effort still more extravagantly; pile and accumulate every assistance you can buy or borrow; traffic and barter with every pitiful German prince that sells his subjects to the shambles of a foreign power; your efforts are forever vain and impotent . . . If I were an American, as I am an Englishman, while a foreign troop was in my country, I never would lay down my arms, never – never – never![68]

So shaken was Lord North by this and other Opposition speeches – notably one by Charles James Fox on 2 February 1778 in favour of not sending any more troops to America (a motion defeated by the less than convincing majority of 259 votes to 165) – that he offered to resign, recommending the Earl of Chatham as his replacement. George III would not hear of it. 'I would rather lose the crown I now wear than bear the ignominy of possessing it under their shackles . . . No consideration in life will make me stoop to Opposition.'[69]

Reluctantly North agreed to remain in office. But he knew that someone had to bear responsibility for Saratoga and, when told by the king to choose between Lord George Germain and Sir William Howe, he opted for the latter – not least because Howe's resignation letter was already on the table. On 4 February, Germain informed Howe by letter that he could soon come home.[70]

The ministry's favoured strategy now was to resume the carrot-and-stick approach: continuing a vigorous prosecution of the war on the one hand (albeit with the emphasis on the Royal Navy attacking rebel ports rather than on land-based operations); and offering political concessions on the other. But all hope that such a strategy might succeed was dashed on 13 March when the French government announced that it had signed a treaty of amity and commerce with the United States, thereby recognizing the latter's independence. It was tantamount to a declaration of war and North's government responded by ordering its commanders in America (Sir Henry Clinton and Lord Howe, though the latter would soon follow his brother home) to concentrate on defeating the French: troops were to be withdrawn from Philadelphia (and New York, if necessary) to mount attacks on the French West Indies and to protect other loyal British colonies in America, particularly Canada; and ships were to be sent home to bolster the Channel fleet.

Under the circumstances, Sir William Howe was almost relieved to hand over his command to General Clinton and depart from Philadelphia in late May 1778. A week earlier Howe's staff had shown their appreciation of his and his brother's efforts during the previous three years by organizing an extravagant farewell party known as a Mischianza, or medley of festivities. Many of his senior officers felt that such elaborate celebrations were inappropriate. But Howe and his brother joined in with gusto, taking part in the grand waterborne procession down the Delaware, the tournament below the city, where knights contested for the honour of ladies dressed in Turkish gowns, and the entertainments at Sir Harry Calder's house, which included fireworks and a 100-piece orchestra. 'About 11,' noted Lieutenant Peebles,

> the Company went into the long room where Supper was laid, a room built for the occasion 100 feet long, painted & decorated in a very showy manner with numbers of lights & looking glasses. Here they sat down to a very Elegant Supper & a variety of the best wines. After

supper they danced & drank till day light when the Company retired to their respective homes highly pleased with the Entertainment.[71]

It was a bizarre way for General Howe to take his leave of America; and yet in keeping with his inability to see that he had let slip through his fingers Britain's best opportunity to crush the rebellion and save its colonies while such an outcome was still possible. Before France intervened (and even after), Americans were far from united in their opposition to British rule, with many, like the people of New Jersey in 1776, liable to join what appeared to be the winning side. Congress was not always united in its opposition to a negotiated settlement and, moreover, it lacked many of the centralized functions (not least a civil service) required for prosecuting a war. George Washington, meanwhile, was all too willing to risk his army in a set-piece battle, sometimes at a disadvantage: he sent reinforcements to Long Island both before and after the battle of 27 August 1776; delayed his departure from Manhattan until it was almost too late; recrossed the Delaware after defeating the Hessians at Trenton; and attacked Howe at Germantown after his mauling at Brandywine. All things considered, it seems fair to conclude that the Howes could have crushed the rebellion in 1776 or 1777.

That they failed to do so was, say some historians, entirely deliberate: either to serve their political allies at home or because of their sympathy for the colonists' predicament. That is going too far. Neither would have allowed such considerations to outweigh their utter conviction – shared by almost all MPs – that Parliament had a right to rule its colonies. But, as their most recent biographer Ira Gruber concedes, 'Lord Howe and – to a lesser degree – his brother did repeatedly allow conciliatory efforts to obstruct military operations; they did try to minimize fighting in the interests of an armistice and of a lasting reconciliation.'[72]

It was a classic case of two military commanders allowing their political preferences – a firmly held belief that 'by ignoring challenges to its constitutional authority and by relying on adroit diplomacy, the British government might recover both the obedience and affection of the colonies without yielding any of its authority'[73] – to influence their strategic and tactical decisions. By crossing that invisible line into politics – a line that Monck had drawn so assertively more than a century before – they not only cost Britain its best hope of recovering its American colonies, but tarnished the hard-won reputation of the British redcoat as a fighting soldier without equal. It was a reputation that would take almost forty years, and the talents of another outstanding British general, to re-establish.

'Oh God!' cried Lord North on hearing the news that General Cornwallis's army of 7,000 men had capitulated at Yorktown in Virginia on 18 October 1781. 'It is all over.'[74]

North was right, though in truth the war in America was lost as soon as France signed an alliance with the rebels in early 1778. This act transformed what had begun as a rebellion by Britain's American subjects into a general conflict, and one moreover that Britain was forced to fight without a Continental ally to divide French resources. Never was the importance of opening a 'Continental' theatre in a war against a major European power better demonstrated. 'England till this time,' noted the Admiralty, 'was never engaged in a sea war with the House of Bourbon thoroughly united, their naval force unbroken, and having no other war or object to draw off their attention and resources.'[75]

Not only was France able to bring the full weight of its naval and military capacity to bear against Britain, it was joined in 1779 by Spain and the Dutch Republic, and together their navies were able to wrest maritime supremacy from the British for the first time in more than a century. This was to prove decisive, and enabled men and arms to flow from France to America at a time when the Continental Army was in danger of disintegration. During the winter of 1777/8, even after the morale-boosting news from Saratoga, Washington's force had shrunk to a few thousand starving and ill-equipped men at Valley Forge, north-west of Philadelphia. But he held out and in 1778, with the help of Friedrich Steuben, a Prussian veteran, he put in place a uniform training system and administrative reforms that helped to turn the Continental Army into a regular, well-disciplined force on the European model.

France's entry into the war also caused a major shift in British strategy. Aware of the need to protect the sugar islands of the Caribbean, and convinced that the southern states of America were more loyal than those in the north (a conviction not borne out by events), Germain persuaded General Clinton, the new commander-in-chief, to move the weight of his operations to the south. The campaign began auspiciously with Colonel Archibald Campbell's brilliant capture of Savannah, following the invasion of Georgia, in December 1778; a second British incursion into North Carolina, led by Clinton himself, eventually resulted in the fall of Charleston in South Carolina in May 1780. But thereafter the southern strategy began to unravel.

Taking over from Clinton (who returned to New York), General Cornwallis conducted a series of marches and fights in up-country North Carolina that – despite notable victories at Camden and Guilford – steadily depleted his forces. In South Carolina, meanwhile, the rebels recovered all the ground they had lost. It was now that Cornwallis, relying on reinforcements from New York and British control of the sea, marched into Virginia and established a base at Yorktown, near the mouth of the Chesapeake River. Trapped there by rebel and French forces under the Marquis de Lafayette, he pinned his hopes on Clinton's arrival with a British fleet. But when a superior French fleet under the Comte de Grasse forced Rear-Admiral Graves's squadron to withdraw from Chesapeake Bay on 5 September, and soon after Washington's army arrived at Yorktown from the north, after feinting an attack on New York, Cornwallis was doomed. He surrendered on 18 October, the day after the fourth anniversary of Burgoyne's capitulation at Saratoga.

Bullish as ever, George III wanted to fight on; and for a time, though he knew the war was lost, Lord North agreed to do so. But on 20 March 1782, exactly a month after the government had narrowly survived a vote of no confidence in the way the naval war was being conducted, North resigned. 'Remember, my Lord, it is you that desert me, not I you,' said a bitter king, now at the mercy of his political enemies the Whigs.[76]

The Whig-negotiated Treaty of Paris was eventually signed in September 1783. It confirmed the independence of the new American

Republic, including the Trans-Appalachian West to the Mississippi River, and the contested southern states of Georgia and South Carolina; but not Canada, which remained under British rule. The only other consolations for Britain, after eight years of bitter war, were clauses requiring Americans to honour their pre-war debts to British citizens (and vice-versa), and forbidding the future persecution of loyalists.

Separate treaties were also signed with France, Spain and Holland that led to the return of all possessions conquered during the war, though Britain was also forced to relinquish territory in Africa and India to France, and Minorca and Florida to Spain. The terms of the treaty with France would undoubtedly have been worse had not Britain, in the form of Admiral Samuel Hood, defeated de Grasse's French fleet at the Battle of the Saintes in April 1782, a victory that prevented a Franco-Spanish invasion of Jamaica and re-established Britain's naval supremacy.

And yet the war, as a whole, was a national humiliation that had cost Britain its valuable North American colonies and reduced the country, in the eyes of some European rulers, to the rank of a second-rate power like Denmark and Sweden. The loss in manpower alone was horrific. Of the 42,000 British regulars sent to fight in North America during the war, just under a quarter perished (the majority, about 65 per cent, from disease). A further 7,500 Germans and 4,000 loyalists also lost their lives, giving a grand total of 21,000 deaths among the 85,000 soldiers who had fought for the British. Rebel fatalities were even higher, with around 30,000 deaths among the 100,000 men who bore arms (giving a total fatality rate of one man in sixteen of military age*).[77]

Never popular at the best of times, the defeated redcoats of the British Army who returned to Britain from America in 1783 and 1784 were looked upon as pariahs. Did they deserve this opprobrium? Mistakes were made and opportunities lost by their generals, particularly Howe, but the battlefield performance of the ordinary redcoat

---

* By comparison, one man in ten of military age died during the American Civil War, and one American male in seventy-five in the Second World War.

was, for the most part, barely less impressive than it had been during the Seven Years War. They had learned to adapt to the peculiar circumstances and difficulties of North American warfare by adopting a much looser, open order – with light infantry and grenadiers to the fore – than would have been used on a European battlefield. And the fact that not a single major set-piece battle was lost by the British – as opposed to smaller-scale engagements and skirmishes such as Lexington–Concord, Trenton and Princeton – is proof enough that the redcoats had not lost their ability to fight.

The inevitable reduction in the size of the British Army after the long and costly American war would have been more drastic still had it not been for the recent expansion of a new British Empire in India that, in time, would help to compensate for the loss of the Thirteen Colonies. In 1784, for example, more than 6,000 regular British troops were stationed in the Indian provinces administered by the East India Company, with a further 15,000 at Gibraltar and other parts of the empire. When added to the 17,000 on the home establishment and the 12,000 in Ireland, this gave a total standing army of 50,000 men, the same size it had been before the war. Thanks to India, therefore, only those extra units raised during the war were disbanded.

And it was also because of India, or rather the need to regulate its government, that William Pitt the Younger became prime minister at the age of twenty-four. In 1773, alarmed by the growth of the East India Company's private 'empire within an empire', not to mention the venality of Company officials (many of whom, including Robert Clive, had returned home with huge fortunes), Parliament passed the Regulating Act, which established the principle by which the British government could interfere in the affairs of India, as well as creating the framework for Company rule. But by the early 1780s, with the finances of the Company in turmoil, it was generally accepted that Parliament would have to have more of a say in the government of the Company's growing territories. The question was: how much more?

The India Bill proposed by the ruling Whigs in late 1783 was ingenious: it aimed to strengthen domestic control over the Company without increasing the power of the king's government by appointing a seven-member commission with executive authority. But the Tories opposed it – with their new star William Pitt the Younger, the exceptionally gifted son of the late Earl of Chatham, arguing that it combined 'absolute despotism' with 'gross corruption', and was 'one of the boldest and most alarming attempts at the exercise of tyranny that ever disgraced the annals of this or any other country' – and though it passed the House of Commons it was twice defeated in the Lords.[78] The Whigs resigned on 18 December 1783, after the second defeat, and a day later Pitt kissed hands as first lord of the Treasury and chancellor of the Exchequer (the youngest prime minister in history). Having strengthened his position by calling and winning a general election in the spring of 1784, Pitt was able to pass his own East India Bill. It gave executive control of Indian affairs to the newly created Board of Control in London, and made the board's president a cabinet minister and therefore answerable to Parliament. But the Company's Court of Directors retained their monopoly of patronage, and officials in India still enjoyed considerable freedom of action.

Pitt's greatest service to his country during his first term in office, however, was to put the country's finances back on a stable footing. When he became prime minister, the National Debt stood at a crippling £243 million, and to pay its interest required more than a third (£8.5 million) of the annual government budget of £24 million. Pitt at once set about reducing the debt by forcing through Parliament a host of new taxes on items of consumption. At the same time he boosted his popularity and undermined smuggling by slashing the duty on tea; and he reversed 'years of backstairs financial dealings' by ensuring 'that a loan of £6 million was subscribed through sealed bids, opened before witnesses, rather than channelled at discount rates to political connections'.[79] In 1786 he went further by passing legislation that placed the administration of the government's 'sinking fund' – a device that used budget surpluses to reduce the National Debt by accumulating compound interest – in the hands of independent commissioners. So successful was this fund that by 1792 the National Debt had shrunk to £170 million.

Much of this budget surplus came from tax revenue on exports that, partly thanks to a favourable commercial treaty with Bourbon France, were soaring by 1792. When Pitt gave his ninth budget speech in February 1792, he was able to announce the twin boons of a booming economy and international stability (which, in turn, had enabled him to make a cut in the military budget of £200,000). 'There never was a time in the history of this country,' he declared, 'when, from the situation of Europe, we might more reasonably expect fifteen years of peace, than we may at the present moment.'[80]

He could not have been more wrong; nor did it help that for much of the 1780s the British Army, having just lost the American War of Independence, was in a trough. 'For want of recruits,' writes a historian of the army, 'the regiments became skeletons. The worst of eighteenth-century military abuses flourished: promotion by favouritism, all kinds of military ignorance and negligence.'[81] And yet it was during this inauspicious time that a young Irish aristocrat joined the British Army who, like Marlborough and Wolfe before him, would transform his country's fortunes in a long war against France. His name was the Honourable Arthur Wellesley;* but he is better known by the title he was awarded for his unbroken success on the battlefield in a career spanning almost thirty years: the first Duke of Wellington.

---

* Until 1798 the family spelled their name 'Wesley'; it was Arthur's elder brother Richard who, in anticipation of his elevation in the peerage from earl to marquess, changed it back to the grander seventeenth-century spelling of Wellesley. I have used the more familiar Wellesley throughout.

16.   The Honourable Arthur Wellesley

Arthur Wellesley was the scion of a prominent Anglo-Norman family* who had lived in Ireland since the fourteenth century, steadily increasing their land and influence by marriage and public office. Along with most of the other leading Anglo-Irish families, they had converted to Anglicanism during or shortly after the Reformation and were part of the Protestant Ascendancy that had long ruled Ireland on behalf of the British crown.

Wealthy and influential, they lacked a hereditary title until 1746, when Arthur's grandfather, Richard Wellesley, became the first Baron Mornington, an Irish peerage that precluded him from sitting in the House of Lords. Arthur's father, Gerald (or Garrett as the Irish have it), was just twenty-three when he succeeded his father as the second Baron in 1758, by which time the Wellesley fortune, though diminished, was still a substantial £8,000 a year (or £2 million in today's money). An outstanding musician and scholar – who excelled at the violin and was composing music from the age of thirteen – Gerald became the first Earl of Mornington and professor of music at Trinity College, Dublin.

Of his five surviving sons – all of whom would have distinguished careers – four were brilliant scholars like their father. The exception was Arthur. Born on 1 May 1769, exactly halfway between the end of the Seven Years War and the start of the American War of Independence, Arthur did little work during his time at prep school in London, later describing himself as 'a dreamy, idle and shy lad'.[1] But nor would he participate in playground games – the consequence of indifferent health, according to a contemporary – and instead observed them from the shade of a large walnut tree, pointing out those who cheated.[2]

* One of Arthur's twelfth-century antecedents was said to have been Henry II's standard-bearer.

Arthur's chief love was music, though his skill at playing the violin never matched his father's. Nor did it help his modest standing in the family when his musical father died in May 1781, having squandered much of his fortune on funding an orchestra. So tight had money become that Arthur's eldest brother, Richard, was forced to leave Oxford without a degree; now, having succeeded his father as the second Earl of Mornington, Richard doubted whether it made financial sense to send a duffer like Arthur to Eton. But he was sent anyway, in the autumn of 1781, shortly before news of Cornwallis's capitulation at Yorktown reached London.

Was the twelve-year-old Arthur aware how close the British Army was to losing the war in America? He must have been, not least because the fathers of many of his contemporaries were serving officers. Whether this knowledge did more than stir up vague patriotic sympathy for his countrymen-in-arms, however, is another matter. He came from a family with no military tradition, far from it, and at this stage in his life had expressed no interest in joining the army. His time at Eton – during the closing years of a lost war – did nothing to change that. Arthur was later quoted as saying that his most famous battlefield success at Waterloo 'was won on the playing-fields of Eton'.[3] But this does not fit the facts. At Eton, as at prep school, Arthur avoided sport and kept his own company, playing by himself in the garden of his boarding house by repeatedly jumping over a broad ditch. He referred to these activities during a visit to Eton in 1818: 'I really believe I owe my spirit of enterprise to the tricks I used to play in the garden.'[4] It is almost certainly this remark that was later misquoted as 'playing-fields'.

Like many a loner, Arthur did not shy from a fight. After pelting a pupil named Smith with stones, Arthur 'soundly' thrashed him in the ensuing fist fight (a formal contest that closely resembled the popular sport of prize-fighting). On another occasion, after a game of marbles, Arthur came off worst in a contest with a young blacksmith, but bore his victorious opponent 'not a pin's worth of ill-will'.[5]

In class, however, he still struggled, showing little aptitude for the classics that made up the core of the Eton curriculum. After three largely fruitless years, therefore, he was taken out of school by his mother – on the advice of his elder brother, who felt the school fees would be better spent on his more academically gifted younger brothers – and sent to a tutor in Brighton. Then followed a year with his mother in lodgings in Brussels, the favourite refuge of the cash-strapped British aristocrat, during which time he still had no thought of a military career. According to a fellow lodger his wishes, 'if he had any', were for a civilian life.[6]

His family had other plans. No sooner had he left Eton than his brother Richard wrote to the lord lieutenant of Ireland about a pos-sible commission for Arthur in the British Army. Clearly Richard and his mother had decided that, having shown little intellectual promise, Arthur might as well become a soldier. Given the lack of a martial tradition in the Wellesley clan, and the fact that the British Army was then at its lowest ebb, this says everything about the low esteem in which Arthur was held. And, though nothing came of this first inquiry, his mother's mind was fixed. Her 'awkward son Arthur', she told her daughter-in-law, was 'food for powder and nothing more'.[7]

Though no commission had yet been secured, and without the funds to pay for one, the dowager Lady Mornington was confident that Richard would find a way. So to prepare her unenthusiastic son for a life in the army, she sent him to the Royal Academy of Equita-tion at Angers in France. For two centuries the ruling classes of Europe had been sent to Angers to learn the art of horsemanship, fencing, mathematics and the humanities. The late Earl of Chatham had been a pupil. Now it was the turn of 'awkward' sixteen-year-old Arthur Wellesley – along with another 107 Britons out of a total class of 334 – and the transformation after a year at Angers was impressive. He learned French, became an expert (if not a graceful) rider, and gained in both self-confidence and stature. His mother was impressed. 'I do believe,' she exclaimed on seeing the taller, smarter version of her son in late 1786, 'there is my ugly boy Arthur.'[8]

His brother Richard, rising quickly in the cut-throat world of London politics, wasted no time in pressing the Duke of Rutland, lord lieutenant of Ireland, to secure Arthur a commission without purchase. 'Let me remind you,' he wrote, 'of a younger brother of mine you were so kind as to take into consideration for a commission in the army. He is here at this moment, and perfectly idle. It is a matter of indifference to me what commission he gets, provided he gets it soon.'[9]

This time the request was listened to and on 17 March 1787, shortly before his eighteenth birthday, Arthur was gazetted an ensign in the 73rd (Highland) Regiment of Foot. It was not the career he would have chosen but 'since I have undertaken a profession', he declared, 'I had better try to understand it.'[10] This comment was later quoted in the memoirs of his friend John Wilson Croker, MP, and bears more than a hint of hindsight. In truth, Arthur seems to have spent most of the first six years of his military service avoiding the business of soldiering. He never actually joined the 73rd that, at the time, was stationed in India. Instead, in November 1787, thanks to fresh promptings from his brother Richard, he was appointed an aide-de-camp to the new lord lieutenant of Ireland, Lord Buckingham, on 10s. a day (almost double the pay of an ensign). He had, in addition, a modest but far from insignificant private income of £125 a year.

On Christmas Day, 1787, Buckingham's patronage secured Arthur a promotion to lieutenant in the 76th Foot, a corps newly raised by the East India Company for service in India. But Arthur was determined not to accompany his new unit to the unhealthy East Indies, not least because it would have meant the loss of his extra staff pay, and so in January 1788 he exchanged into another corps, the 41st Foot, that was conveniently garrisoned in Ireland. His early military education in Dublin, therefore, was confined to ordering supper for Lady Buckingham and flirting with society beauties.

A year on, momentous events in France would ensure that – sooner or later – Arthur would have to take his profession more seriously. They began on 5 May 1789 with the first meeting of the Estates-General, the French equivalent of the English Parliament, since 1614. A response to financial crisis and civil unrest that dated, in the short term at least, from the huge cost of supporting the rebels in the American War of Independence, the meeting exposed the deep fissures within French society and politics. Unlike George III – who could rule only with the cooperation of Parliament and the government of the day – France's King Louis XVI was still a virtual autocrat who presided over an *ancien régime* that virtually excluded the growing *bourgeoisie* (middle classes) and left the peasantry landless and increasingly hungry.

The issue on 5 May was whether the three orders of the Estates-General – the Clergy, Nobility and Third Estate (Commoners) – should sit in one assembly, and vote by head, or in three separate assemblies, each with one vote. As the members of the Third Estate outnumbered the other two put together, they naturally wanted a single chamber that they could dominate. The majority of the Nobility, on the other hand, were determined to consign them to a separate chamber and – they hoped – a minority of one to two. The outcome depended upon the Clergy. As many were representative of minor clerics, whose grievances were as numerous as those of the Third Estate, they backed the non-privileged order and were gradually joined by a number of abbots and bishops.

On 23 June, with the victory of the Third Estate guaranteed, the king tried to intervene by ordering the doors of the Estates-General's meeting-place to be locked and the members to sit in separate chambers. Refusing to comply, the majority met in a nearby indoor tennis-court and took an oath not to disperse until their demands for reform were met. Henceforth they would call themselves the National Assembly (renamed the Constituent Assembly in early July). The Revolution had begun.

Extremists, however, would soon force the pace of political change. On 14 July the workers of the Faubourg St Antoine district stormed the Bastille, the royal fortress on the east side of Paris that had gained exaggerated notoriety as a state prison by the circulation of revolutionary pamphlets. Having butchered the garrison (the governor was beheaded), released the prisoners and secured the arms stored there, the mob razed the fortress to the ground. Within days, the red and blue colours of the city of Paris had been merged with the white of the Bourbons to form the tricolour flag of the new France.

In Britain the reaction to this initial stage of the Revolution was generally sympathetic, particularly among the Opposition Whigs.

Charles James Fox, for example, compared it to Britain's own revolution – the Glorious Revolution of 1688 – that had so effectively limited monarchical power. How apt, he thought, that the French were following in their footsteps. The fall of the Bastille was, wrote Fox, 'the greatest event . . . that has ever happened in the history of the world'.[11] But not all his colleagues agreed. To Edmund Burke, another leading Whig who had supported the American War of Independence, the Constituent Assembly did not appear to have 'one jot more power than the King'; how could its members exercise 'any function of decided authority', he wrote, 'with a mob of constituents ready to hang them if they should deviate into moderation'.[12]

Burke was soon proved right. As the summer wore on, the Constituent Assembly issued a number of revolutionary decrees, including the Abolition of Feudalism in early August and the Declaration of the Rights of Man (the preface to the new Constitution) in September. Partly modelled on the American Bill of Rights, and heavily influenced by Rousseauian political philosophy, the Declaration was extremely radical for its time. It declared:

> Men are born free and equal in rights. The aim of every political association is the preservation of the natural and undoubted rights of man. These rights are liberty, property, security, and resistance to oppression. The principle of all sovereignty resides essentially in the nation.[13]

But such fine words could not prevent the price of bread from rising ever higher. Food riots and fears of a royalist counter-revolutionary plot culminated in the 'Bread March of the Women' to Versailles on 5 October to demand the return of the king to Paris. He went, followed by the Constituent Assembly a week later.

For a time it seemed as if a constitutional monarchy like Britain's was the most likely political settlement. But all this changed with the death of the Comte de Mirabeau, the moderate whose oratory had dominated the Assembly, in April 1791. With Mirabeau gone, extremist groups like the Jacobins and the Girondins began to gain ground. This in turn prompted the royal family's disastrous attempt to flee Paris and seek refuge with the still largely royalist army on the eastern frontier of France in June. Intercepted at Varennes and brought back to the capital in disgrace, the king's credibility as a constitutional ruler was destroyed.

With the support of the army, Louis XVI might still have retrieved the situation. But widespread mutinies in 1790 and 1791 (particularly after news of the king's betrayal reached the outlying garrisons) made it impossible to launch a counter-revolution. 'Civilians often provided encouragement to the soldiers,' writes a historian of the French Army, 'and the [Jacobin] clubs sometimes offered a forum for them to voice their complaints. But it was conditions in the army that created the complaints, and it was not the Revolution, but its overthrow of traditional authority, that allowed them to be expressed as they were.'[14]

French privates were poorly paid, badly housed and had little contact with their aristocratic superiors. 'The common soldier was scorned by his officers, and sometimes by the bourgeoisie, many of whom shut their doors and fastened their shutters on hearing of the approach of the military.' There was also no outlet for ambition: between 1781 and 1789, for example, only forty-six men were commissioned from the ranks; commoners were rarely promoted beyond lieutenant.[15] The Revolution was an opportunity to redress these past iniquities and led to an outburst of complaints against 'the monopolization of high ranks by nobles, harsh and sometimes inequitable discipline, the disdain with which they were treated by their superiors, and peculation [on] the part of their officers'.[16]

Chief among the rebels were non-commissioned officers or those officers who had already been promoted from the ranks. The latter came from the same lower-class background as the NCOs and had had similar, if slightly more successful, careers. 'Their frustration and resentment at never being fully accepted as officers made them at least as hostile to the Old Regime as were the sergeants.'[17]

But not all aristocratic officers were purged. Among those who welcomed the Revolution – for reasons of pragmatism as much as political conviction – was a handsome young Corsican nobleman, barely 5 foot 6 inches tall, called Napoleon Bonaparte. Born in Ajaccio in August 1769, just three months after Arthur Wellesley, Napoleon was trained at the military school of Brienne, the lowest ranked of the mainland's ten military colleges. Morning lessons of Latin, history, mathematics and geography were followed, after a two-hour lunch break, by fencing, dancing, music and handwriting. A prize-winning mathematician, Napoleon excelled academically at Brienne, but was in constant fights on account of his sallow skin and 'Italian' heritage.★ He was also a vociferous Corsican nationalist, telling his classmates that he would one day lead his homeland to independence. These nationalist ambitions – and his 'outsider' status generally – were significant factors in his later decision to embrace the Revolution.

Unlike Arthur Wellesley, Napoleon learned the rudiments of his profession with his regiment. He completed ten weeks of basic training, drilling progressively as a private, corporal and sergeant, and later attributed his famous 'common touch' to this ground-up method of instruction. Once a fully fledged officer, he undertook duties that included mounting guard, attending classes on mathematics, fortification and science, and looking after the men (a responsibility that few of his fellow officers took seriously). His income was a fairly generous 1,120 livres a year, but much of it he sent to his cash-strapped family in Corsica. He read widely – including works by Plutarch, Cicero, Tacitus, Racine, Voltaire and, above all, Rousseau – but not deeply. 'His knowledge of Rousseau was superficial and he was ignorant of much of Voltaire; he knew little of Montesquieu and less of Diderot; most surprising of all, he had not heard of Pierre Laclos's *Les Liaisons dangereuses*, published four years earlier and significant both because it was heavily influenced by Rousseau and because Laclos, like Napoleon, was an artilleryman.'[18]

When the Revolution began in 1789, Napoleon was garrisoned with his regiment at Auxonne in Burgundy. Though sympathetic to the Revolution's ideals, he did not approve of the breakdown of discipline in his regiment – particularly when the men marched to the garrison commander's house and demanded money with menaces – and later insisted that he would have fired on the mutineers if he had been ordered to. Shortly after he took an oath of fidelity to Nation, King and the Law. But a further long period of leave in Corsica, during

---

★ The Buonapartes were descended from Italian mercenaries in Genoese pay who settled in Corsica in the early sixteenth century.

which time he actively supported republican politicians and became a founder member of the Ajaccio Jacobin Club, saw him divested of any remaining loyalty to the king.

Now unashamedly pro-Revolution, he quarrelled with his mainly royalist fellow officers after returning to his regiment in early 1791; after one particularly acrimonious exchange they tried to throw him in the Saône. In June, partly to ease the tension, he was promoted to lieutenant and transferred to a separate artillery regiment, the 4th.★ Four days after Napoleon joined his new unit, the king made his abortive attempt to flee to Varennes. It was the beginning of the end for both the monarchy and the old army. Following the Varennes fiasco, all officers were compelled to take a new oath to maintain the Constitution against all enemies internal and external, to resist invasion and to obey no orders except those validated by the National Assembly's decrees. Thousands of royalist officers refused – including thirty-two from the 4th Regiment of Artillery – and were forced to resign, many to join the *émigrés* abroad. Napoleon was not among them; he took the oath on 6 July.

By now support for the beleaguered King Louis XVI and Queen Marie Antoinette was gathering beyond France's borders. In late August 1791 Holy Roman Emperor Leopold II (brother of Marie Antoinette) and King Frederick William II of Prussia issued the Declaration of Pillnitz, appealing for all European rulers to help restore monarchical government in France. This had the unintended effect of making that ever less likely because, hopeful of foreign intervention, Louis XVI saw no need to be trammelled by the new Constitution that he had sworn to maintain. Instead, urged on by his queen, he played a double game, saying the right things in public while secretly negotiating with the foreign powers.

When the Girondin faction took over the reins of power in March 1792, Louis XVI even encouraged their policy of war against Austria in the hope that military disaster would lead to the restoration of his

★ Earlier that year, to break down old allegiances, the National Assembly had abolished the names of artillery regiments and replaced them with numbers. The La Fère Régiment became the 1st.

autocratic power. The Girondins, for their part, were keen to attack the absolutist monarchies of Europe before France itself was attacked. On 20 April 1792, therefore, they declared war on Austria (and, by default, her allies Prussia and the League of German Princes).

The command of the Allied German army was given to the Duke of Brunswick, an experienced general who had just turned down a similar offer from the French. In late July he issued his famous manifesto, threatening the use of force unless Louis XVI's legal authority was re-established. The effect was not to divide the people of France, but to unite them against the German invader. Louis then made matters worse by dismissing his remaining Girondin ministers. Their reaction was to join with the Jacobins in inciting the Paris mob – already furious at the publication of the Brunswick manifesto – to invade the Tuileries, the royal palace, on 10 August.

Napoleon had spent much of the previous year on attachment to a battalion of Corsican volunteers, dabbling once again in local politics; but he was in Paris on 10 August, having just been promoted to captain, and witnessed the attack on the Tuileries that caused the royal family to flee to the nearby Legislative Assembly (so named since the passing of the Constitution). The 2,000 royal troops guarding the Tuileries were not so lucky. Overwhelmed by superior numbers, they were butchered to a man. Six hundred were shot and clubbed to death in the palace courtyard, before women stripped and mutilated their bodies. Napoleon wrote later: 'The sight of the dead Swiss Guards gave me an idea of the meaning of death such as I have never had since, on any of my battlefields. Perhaps it was that the smallness of the area made the number of corpses appear larger, or perhaps it was because this was the first time I had undergone such an experience. I saw well dressed women committing acts of the grossest indecency on the corpses of the Swiss Guards.'[19] It seems likely that Napoleon's hatred of the mob, and his conviction that only a bourgeois republic could hold in check the destructive forces of anarchy, dates from this grim experience.

Louis XVI had escaped from the Tuileries with his life, but all semblance of monarchical power ended when the Legislative Assembly suspended the king's authority and imprisoned him and his family in the Temple. Their hopes were briefly raised when the Duke of Brunswick captured the eastern French fortress of Verdun in late August. But the news prompted fresh massacres in Paris of thousands of people associated with the *ancien régime* and was, in any event, a false dawn. On 20 September, at Valmy to the west of Verdun, Brunswick's 35,000-strong army was defeated by a numerically superior French force. The invasion was over.

Meanwhile, the Girondins and Jacobins had transformed the Legislative Assembly into a Revolutionary Convention that met for the first time on 21 September. Emboldened by news of the great victory at Valmy, it abolished the monarchy and proclaimed the first French Republic. A week or so later it ordered its troops to invade the Austrian Netherlands and followed this up, in November, by issuing the Compulsory Liberty Decree, which offered military support to all nations who wanted to overthrow their rulers and become republics. The revolution was about to be exported.

In Britain, where moderate political opinion had turned firmly against the Revolution, the news of the massacres and the invasion of the Austrian Netherlands made war with France increasingly likely. As with the last two major wars in Europe, Britain was bound to participate if Hanover's territorial integrity was threatened; and, in any case, George III was obliged as the elector of Hanover to support the Holy Roman Emperor (who was also the Austrian Emperor). Britain would also fight if France invaded its ally Holland, a situation that seemed increasingly likely after the French took Antwerp and opened the Scheldt River to their warships.

What set this new conflict apart, however, was the likelihood that a victorious France would spread its dangerous political contagion across Europe. It had, therefore, to be stopped – and the final straw for Britain was the execution of Louis XVI by guillotine in the Place de la Révolution on 21 January 1793, two days after the Convention had found him guilty of treason by 380 votes to 310. His fate had been sealed by the discovery of letters in a strongbox in the Tuileries confirming his secret negotiations with foreign powers the previous November.

Pitt's government – bolstered by the recent addition of right-wing Whigs – was outraged when word reached London on 23 January of the king's demise and at once expelled the French ambassador. When word of this reached Paris, there was an explosion of anti-British feeling. The ruling Executive Council at once rescinded France's commercial treaty with Britain (signed in 1787), imposed an embargo on British and Dutch shipping, and ordered the invasion of Holland. The Convention confirmed these decisions on 1 February by voting to declare war on Britain and Holland; it also issued a fraternal decree calling on the people of Britain to rise up against their rulers. So began the war between Britain and Republican (later Imperial) France that, apart from a brief hiatus from 1802 to 1804, would last for more than twenty years.

The problem for Britain's soldiers – Arthur Wellesley included – is that in 1793 they were in no condition to fight. 'The nine years of peace between the American war and the wars of the French Revolution and Empire,' writes a historian of the British Army, 'were a time of rigid economy, financial reorganization and reform under the younger Pitt. The result was a decline in the efficiency of the army more rapid and complete than under [Sir Robert] Walpole.'[20] In size alone the army had recently shrunk to a nominal strength of just under 44,000, though its true effective strength – thanks to the difficulties of recruitment – was more like 36,500.[21] In December 1792, with war ever more likely, Parliament had authorized an expansion in the size of the army to 50,992 men (chiefly by augmenting corps of cavalry and infantry by 60 and 100 men respectively). But not all units were affected by this augmentation and, in reality, 'all Parliament did was to restore the original 1792 establishment with only a slight increase for 1793.'[22] Even in February 1793, after France had declared war, the secretary at war only asked Parliament for an additional 15,000 men to be added to the British and Irish establishments. This was easier said than done. In practice, regiments 'could hardly reach their authorized strengths let alone try to raise the additional men granted in any augmentation'. The 14th Foot, for example, ordered on active service on 1 March 1793, was still 186 men short of its then establishment of 499 men.[23]

Numbers were not the only problem. The internal organization of the army was still in disarray, with different authorities in charge of the component parts: the commander-in-chief (when he was appointed, and there had not been one since 1784) had control only over the line cavalry and infantry; the monarch was responsible for the Household troops; the Board of Ordnance, through its master general, for the engineers and artillery; and the Home Office for the militia, via the lord lieutenants of the counties. All land transport was hired from civilian sources, while movement by sea had to be arranged through the Transport Board, an offshoot of the Admiralty.

There was no permanent or even ad hoc division or brigade structure, and no large camps of instruction had been held since the end of the American War of Independence. The only recent military reform was on the tactical level, and even that appeared to be a backward step. In 1788 Colonel (later General Sir David) Dundas had published his *Principles of Military Movements*, affirming his belief that the loose formation and tactics of the recent war would prove ineffective against trained European troops. Like Wolfe, Dundas was convinced that the British Army needed to imitate the even pace and exact evolutions of the Prussian model. The War Office agreed and in 1792 introduced an abridgement of Dundas's book as the first official drill manual for the British Army, entitled *Rules and Regulations for the Formations, Field-Exercise, and Movements of His Majesty's Forces*. A small camp was held in the summer of 1792 to introduce the new Prussian Drill, but it would take time before the whole army was familiar with it. Even then many observers ridiculed it as too mechanical and inflexible. It certainly had its weaknesses, not the least of which was its neglect of light infantry, an arm that the French Army in particular was expanding; but it also had its uses, especially on a European battlefield, and many of Britain's greatest victories in the long wars to come were won by Dundas's 'steady' infantry.

They were helped by key improvements in British weapons. In the American War of Independence, for example, cannon were still largely the same weapons that had been used by Marlborough: smooth-bore, muzzle-loading and mounted on heavy two-wheeled carriages, and firing round-shot, canister and shell. But in 1785

Colonel Shrapnel invented a new shell for howitzers* that took his name and gave British artillery a crucial edge on the battlefield. It consisted of the same hollow cast-iron sphere and fuse as a common shell, but filled with gunpowder *and* lead balls that would burst over an enemy position with lethal consequences. Another important development was the replacement of heavy twin-bracketed gun carriages with a much lighter single block-trail carriage, introduced by General Sir William Congreve in 1792. Now the gun could be traversed (aimed) by the commander alone, whereas before it had required two men under his instruction to do this, and fewer horses (usually six) were needed to draw it.[24]

By 1793, however, these improvements in drill and weapons were undermined by the venality and lack of professionalism at the heart of the British Army's officer corps. Both abuses were much in evidence during the brief but eventful military career of William Cobbett, the future essayist, radical MP and author of *Rural Rides* (1821–6). The son of a Hampshire yeoman farmer, Cobbett was twenty and working as a clerk in Gray's Inn when he inadvertently enlisted as a private in the 54th Foot in early 1784. Seduced by a poster for the Royal Marines, he had travelled to Chatham to join the navy. 'But the next morning,' he recalled, 'I found myself before a Captain of a marching regiment. There was no retreating. I had taken a shilling to drink his Majesty's health, and his further bounty was ready for my reception.'[25]

The 54th Foot was then stationed in Nova Scotia, Canada. But Cobbett did not join it for another year because the commandant of Chatham, Colonel Debbieg, impressed by the young soldier's literacy and numeracy, promptly employed him as a secretary and copyist. It was Debbieg who encouraged Cobbett to purchase a Lowth's *Grammar*[26] to improve his written English. Cobbett learned it by heart. All his spare time was spent reading and writing. 'The edge of my berth,' he wrote, 'or that of the guard-bed, was my seat to study in; my knapsack was my bookcase; a bit of board lying on my lap was my writing table; and the task did not demand any thing like a year of my life.'[27]

---

* British field batteries of the period usually consisted of five guns (usually 6- or 9-pounders) and one howitzer (with a bore of 5½ inches).

The greatest hardship for Cobbett was surviving on a shilling a day: 'Of my sixpence, nothing like fivepence was left to purchase food for the day. Indeed not fourpence. For there was washing, mending, soap, flour for hair-powder, shoes, stockings, shirts, stocks and gaiters, pipe-clay and several other things to come out of the miserable sixpence! Judge then the quantity of food to sustain life in a lad of sixteen, and to enable him to exercise with a musket (weighing fourteen pounds) six to eight hours a day . . . We had several recruits from Norfolk and many of them deserted from sheer hunger.'[28]

Cobbett was lucky in that his education gained him, before the year was out, a promotion to corporal and an extra twopence a day. But he was still keen to join his regiment in Nova Scotia and did so in early 1785. He would spend the next six years in Canada, chiefly in New Brunswick, and soon became indispensable as the regimental clerk, drawing up the returns, reports and other official papers. 'Neither adjutant, paymaster or quarter-master,' he recalled, 'could move an inch without my assistance.'[29]

Then, in 1786, after barely two years in the army, he was promoted from corporal to sergeant-major, the senior non-commissioned rank, over the heads of thirty longer-serving sergeants. Aware that such rapid, almost unprecedented promotion was likely to make him many enemies, he took to rising early and working incessantly, so that 'every one felt that what I did he had never done and never could do'.[30] But his appointment to sergeant-major also brought him into regular contact with the officers 'whose profound and surprising ignorance I discovered in a twinkling'.[31] So ignorant were they of their military duties that he had to instruct them what to say on parade and give them crib cards of the regiment's movements. He recalled, with evident disgust:

> There was I, at the review, upon the flank of the grenadier company, with my worsted shoulder-knot and my great, high, coarse, hairy cap; confounded in the ranks among other men, while those who commanded me to move my hands or my feet, thus or thus, were, in fact, uttering words which I had taught them and were, in everything except authority, my inferiors.[32]

Cobbett loathed his officers 'for their gross ignorance and their vanity' and 'for their drunkenness and rapacity', but realized he could do nothing about it while he was still a soldier. One false step, he knew, might see him 'broken and flogged for fifty different offences'.[33] So in December 1791, shortly after the return of the 54th Foot to Britain, Cobbett asked for and was granted a discharge. The reason was soon apparent. On 5 February 1792, the day Cobbett married the daughter of an artillery sergeant he had met in New Brunswick, Captain Richard Powell of the 54th wrote to the Judge Advocate-General: 'I understand that an accusation of seventeen charges, preferred by the late Serjeant-Major of the 54th regiment, against me as Commanding Officer of the regiment while in America, has been laid before the Secretary of War, and by him presented to his Majesty.'[34]

Powell's fears were soon confirmed. But it was not only him that Cobbett had accused of 'false and improper musters'; two lieutenants were also implicated, and all three officers were duly court-martialled at Horse Guards in London in March 1792. For an Other Rank to lay charges against his own officers was highly unusual in the eighteenth century. For them to be acted upon was rarer still; but then Cobbett, as his later career makes clear, was no ordinary soldier. For him, the lack of professionalism among officers was bad enough; but what particularly outraged him was their greedy desire to enrich themselves at the army's expense. The charge he had made against his own officers – that of making 'false and improper musters' – was a prime example of this. The substance of the charge was that the officers had exaggerated the number of men under their command – either through invention or by including the names of those 'who were employed in the capacity of servants in the regiment, or who were permitted by him [Captain Powell] to hire themselves as servants to the inhabitants of New Brunswick' – so that they could profit by selling the excess rations and firewood for the non-existent soldiers,* and by making fraudulent claims for their clothing entitlement.[35]

To back up his accusations, Cobbett and a Corporal Bestland in his

---

* Known, in the parlance of the time, as 'widow's men'.

office – 'the only sober man in the whole regiment' – had put together comprehensive and duplicate records of the officers' systematic abuse. 'If my accusation is without foundation,' he had assured the Judge Advocate-General, 'the authors of cruelty have not yet devised the tortures I ought to endure.' But he was sufficiently aware of the danger in which he was placing serving members of the 54th to add: 'The names of the witnesses from the regiment, Sir, I shall send to you as soon as I know the date of the trial; and my reason for not doing it now, is, that I shall perhaps thereby expose the poor fellows to the most unmerciful of treatment.'[36]

In the event, the case against the officers stood little chance of success because they had possession of the regimental books – and were therefore able to amend them before they were submitted to the court martial – and Cobbett felt unable to call his key witness, Corporal Bestland, for fear of reprisals. He discovered, moreover, a conspiracy in which witnesses were prepared to swear he had 'downed a drink to the destruction of the house of Brunswick' at his party on leaving the regiment.[37]

Fearing repercussions, he and his wife fled to France two days before the trial was due to begin. Without its star witness, the prosecution could offer no evidence and the case collapsed, prompting the court martial to conclude that 'the several charges against those officers are, and every part thereof is, totally unfounded.' Cobbett responded with an anonymous 22-page pamphlet, *The Soldier's Friend*, which denounced generally the practices he had accused his officers of. He eventually left France for New York in September 1792, convinced 'that a war with England was inevitable, and it was not difficult to foresee what would be the fate of Englishmen, in that country, where the rulers had laid aside even the appearance of justice and mercy'.[38]

Cobbett spent seven years in the United States, where he became a prominent pamphleteer and political writer. In 1802, two years after returning to Britain, he founded the weekly *Political Register*. He became increasingly radical in his politics and campaigned for parliamentary reform, the abolition of flogging, and free speech. He was finally elected to Parliament at the fifth attempt in 1832, three years before his death. And yet he 'remained devoted to the army, to every soldier in it' and would happily attest to the maxim 'Once a soldier, always a soldier'.[39]

In early 1793 Arthur Wellesley was exactly the type of British officer that Cobbett despised: high-born, well connected, ignorant of his duties and absent from his unit, which, since his most recent exchange a year earlier (his fifth in five years), was a cavalry corps – the 18th Light Dragoons – stationed in Ireland.* Though still aide-de-camp to the lord lieutenant, he had spent much of the previous two years in the Dublin parliament as MP for the family seat of Trim. A silent supporter of the government for most of this time – part of a clique condemned by the Irish nationalist Wolfe Tone as 'the common prostitutes of the Treasury Bench' – Wellesley spoke for the first time in January 1793 when he seconded the Address from the Throne, deploring the imprisonment of Louis XVI and the French invasion of the Netherlands.[40]

The turning point for Wellesley was the outbreak of war between Britain and France on 1 February. Now, with active service inevitable, he was forced to learn his profession (an additional incentive was the recent rejection of his proposed marriage to Lady Kitty Pakenham by her brother, Lord Longford). He did so by burning his violins and asking his brother Richard to lobby for him to join one of the flank battalions of light infantry and grenadiers that were being formed in Ireland that summer to, it was rumoured, support the Dutch. That initiative did not come off – fortunately for Wellesley, as the flank battalions were sent to Martinique, where many died of yellow fever – but he had better luck in persuading Richard to buy him successive promotions in the 33rd (West Riding) Regiment of Foot, a unit first raised to fight in the War of the Spanish Succession. He thus became, at the age of twenty-four, the lieutenant-colonel of

---

* In June 1789 Wellesley had exchanged from the 41st Foot into the 12th Light Dragoons, also stationed in Ireland. Two years later he became a captain in the 58th Foot, thus achieving two steps in promotion in just four years, none of which had been spent with his various parent corps.

an infantry corps that was bound, sooner or later, to be sent to fight in Europe. Wholly unqualified as he was for such a responsibility, he worked hard to master the internal workings of the battalion, 'immersing himself in the minutiae of its accounts and preparing standing orders that became a model of their kind'.[41] But it says everything about the parlous state of the army in 1793 that he had gained the command of a battalion without any formal training.

Wellesley was keen to serve on the Continent but the strategic focus of Pitt's government was, like his father's, not on Europe but on French possessions elsewhere, particularly in the Caribbean. Between 1793 and 1796 the British Army lost 80,000 men – half killed or died of disease, the rest rendered unfit for service – capturing the French sugar islands. The British Contingent in the Low Countries, on the other hand, never accounted for more than 10,000 men. Thus, while Revolutionary France's colonies were conquered, her position in Europe became ever more formidable.[42]

In 1793 such an outcome had looked unlikely as the early campaigns in Europe went the way of the British-engineered First Coalition (a catch-all term for the separate alliances that Britain concluded with Russia, Sardinia-Piedmont, Spain, Naples and Sicily, Prussia, Austria and Portugal). In March an Austrian army, under Prince Frederick of Saxe-Coburg, won a series of victories over the French in Flanders. The Prussians, too, had reached French soil; while even the poorly equipped British and Hanoverian troops in the Low Countries – led by HRH the Duke of York, the second son of George III* – enjoyed some early success when they captured Valenciennes in July and went on to besiege Dunkirk. In southern France, too, the Allies won a major coup in late August when counter-revolutionaries took control of Toulon, the main French naval base in the Mediterranean, and invited an Anglo-Spanish fleet to garrison the town. 'I am much mistaken,' wrote Lord Grenville, 'if the business at Toulon is not decisive of the war.'[43]

The capture of Toulon, however, was a false dawn. Within weeks,

---

* Born Prince Frederick in 1763. At Dunkirk, York had 6,500 British, 13,000 Hanoverian and 15,000 Dutch troops under his command.

Saxe-Coburg had been defeated at Wattignies in northern France by General Jourdan and, as part of the Allies' general retirement, York was forced to raise the siege of Dunkirk and withdraw to Ostend. In December, Toulon was retaken by a revolutionary army, with the newly promoted Major Napoleon Bonaparte playing a prominent role as commander of the assault force's artillery. Because of Pitt's preoccupation with the West Indies, the Allied defenders of Toulon had numbered just 7,000 poor-quality Neapolitans, 6,000 lacklustre Spaniards and only 2,000 British troops. With defeat certain, they burned as many French ships as they could and evacuated the port a week before Christmas. Napoleon was rewarded with promotion to brigadier-general and a ringing endorsement from his immediate superior, who reported to the Ministry of War: 'I lack words to convey Bonaparte's merit to you; much knowledge, equal intelligence and too much bravery; that is but a feeble sketch of this rare officer's virtues.'[44]

Arthur Wellesley, meanwhile, had yet to hear a shot fired in anger. But that was about to change. In June 1794 he sailed with the 33rd from Cork to Ostend as part of a division sent to reinforce York's battered army in Flanders. Then just twenty-nine years old, York was an inexperienced and mediocre commander who owed his appointment to his royal connections. 'He was not at this time popular with his men,' wrote Sir John Fortescue, the author of a classic thirteen-volume history of the British Army, 'while his officers, who had been taught to look for preferment from politicians,

> resented his authority whether for good or ill . . . He had the cool personal bravery which belongs to his race, but not the higher moral courage which gives constancy and patience in difficulty or misfortune; and hence he was at once sanguine and easily discouraged. He had learned his work, so far as it could be acquired by the industry of a mediocre intellect, but he was slow of apprehension, without sagacity, penetration or width of view, and with so little imagination or resource that an unforeseen emergency confounded him. On the other hand, his dutiful loyalty and submission, in most trying circumstances, towards Coburg on the one hand, and the Cabinet on the other, were beyond all praise.[45]

A more forceful commander would have persuaded Prince Frederick of Saxe-Coburg to march on Paris in the spring of 1793 when he had the chance. 'The opportunity was favourable,' noted Fortescue, 'and the hazard was slight compared with the certain danger of delay.'[46] But instead York had meekly followed Saxe-Coburg's lead in attempting to reduce the frontier fortresses, and the moment passed.

In May 1794 the tide began to turn even more forcefully against York and his Austrian allies when, despite a slight superiority in numbers, they were defeated by the French at Tourcoing, north of Lille. French skirmishers had played a vital role in the victory, with one British officer describing them 'as sharp-sighted as ferrets, as active as squirrels'.[47]

York had eight British infantry battalions and six cavalry squadrons at Tourcoing, a modest force given that at least 30,000 men were enlisted in the British Army between November 1793 and March 1794.[48] As part of this expansion, the army created its first transport unit, the Corps of Royal Waggoners, known from the colour of its uniform and the supposedly 'criminal' origin of its men as 'The Newgate Blues'. A 'greater set of scoundrels', complained a member of York's staff, 'never disgraced an army'.[49]

Other problems facing York in 1794 were inadequate supplies of equipment (including muskets and uniforms), battalions composed chiefly of raw recruits, and poorly trained officers and men. Private William Surtees of the 56th Foot was honoured to be made 'light bob' – a member of his battalion's light company – but was given no proper instruction and, when he came up against specialist French light infantry, found they had 'greatly the advantage over us in point of shooting'.[50] Sir John Fortescue wrote:

> The regiments despatched to Holland contained only a very few old soldiers mixed with great numbers of recruits, who were utterly without training and discipline. 'Many of them do not know one end of a fire-lock from the other,' wrote Craig [one of York's staff officers], 'and will never know it.' Six of the battalions had been deprived of their best men, to make up General Grey's force in the West Indies; and no sooner did the new levies find themselves released from the

crimping-house and the gaol for active service, than they fell to plundering in all directions.[51]

Too many officers had, like Wellesley, reached high rank thanks to money and influence, rather than merit and experience. 'The commanders of the new battalions,' wrote Fortescue, 'who had been

> juggled into seniority by the Government and the army-brokers, were not fit to command a company, much less a brigade. Some of them were boys of twenty-one who knew nothing of their simplest duties. Though they went cheerfully into action, they looked upon the whole campaign as an elaborate picnic, for which they did not fail to provide themselves with abundance of comforts; and thus the baggage-columns were filled with private wagons under the charge of insubordinate drivers . . . Thrust into the army to satisfy the claims of dependants, constituents, importunate creditors, and discarded concubines, many of [the junior officers] were at once a disgrace and an encumbrance to the force . . . It was no uncommon thing for regiments to start on the march under charge of the Adjutant and Sergeant-Major only, while the officers stayed behind, to come galloping up several hours later, full of wine, careless where they rode, careless of the confusion into which they threw the columns.[52]

In Fortescue's opinion, the man chiefly responsible for allowing such a poorly led, trained and provisioned British force to take the field was Henry Dundas, recently appointed as the first secretary of state for war, the cabinet minister with responsibility for military affairs. 'Dundas's idea of putting an army in the field,' wrote Fortescue, 'was to land raw men on a foreign shore, and to expect discipline, arms, ammunition, clothing, victuals, medical stores, and medical treatment to descend on them from Heaven. Some kind of medical staff was improvised out of drunken apothecaries, broken-down practitioners, and rogues of every description, who were provided under some cheap contract; the charges of respectable members of the medical profession being deemed exorbitant.'[53]

On 26 June, the day after Wellesley and the 33rd arrived at Ostend, the Allies suffered another serious defeat at Fleurus, near Charleroi,

when, after fifteen hours of brutal close-quarter fighting, Prince
Frederick of Saxe-Coburg lost his nerve and ordered the remnants of his
Austro-Dutch army to quit the field, thus gifting the French an unexpected victory. Thereafter the Austrians withdrew across the Rhine,
while the British and Hanoverians moved back towards Holland.

It was not a propitious moment for Wellesley to go to war. He and
his men were poorly trained, there was no adequate food supply, and
the Allies were in retreat. Yet, as he told a friend many years later, the
lessons of the campaign were useful: 'Why – I learnt what one ought
not to do, and that is always something.'[54] Given command of a brigade at Ostend – his own battalion, and two others, the 8th and
44th – he moved it by sea to Antwerp, where he joined the Duke
of York. In mid-September, near Breda in Holland, he received his
baptism of fire when his battalion helped to check a French attack, an
action for which York commended the 33rd for its 'good conduct'.[55]
The praise was deserved as the battalion had coolly obeyed Wellesley's orders to hold its fire until the French column was almost upon
it; thus, from the time of his first action, was Wellesley convinced of
the superiority that a line formation had over a column.

The retreat continued as the temperature plummeted and, on
reaching the River Waal in October, Wellesley assumed the army
would go into winter quarters. But the French kept attacking. 'We
turn out once, sometimes twice every night,' he wrote to his brother
Richard. 'The officers and men are harassed to death . . . I have not
had the clothes off my back for a long time, and generally spend the
greater part of the night upon the bank of the river.'[56] York took the
blame for the failure of the campaign and was recalled in December
and replaced by Lord Cathcart. The public's lack of confidence in
York's abilities as a commander was evident in the popular ditty 'The
noble Duke of York/He had ten thousand men,/He marched them
up to the top of the hill,/and he marched them down again.'

Wellesley, who had been suffering from an 'aguish complaint'
since July, also hoped to return to Britain on sick leave. Instead he
remained on the Waal in Holland until January 1794, a three-month
stint that passed without a single visit from the commander-in-chief.
When he, in turn, visited British headquarters, 30 miles to the rear,

he found it a 'scene of jollifications', with dispatches from their allies not allowed to interrupt the passing of port after dinner.[57]

The ordinary soldiers, meanwhile, were suffering appalling privations, with thousands perishing in the overcrowded field hospital at Rhenen on the north bank of the Leck. The diary entry for 7 January of Robert Brown, a highly literate corporal in the 2nd (Coldstream) Guards, reads:

> Part of the church, and a large building resembling a monastery adjoining, has been converted into a hospital since August last, for the whole of the British Army. The hospital, as well as every other place, [is] filled with soldiers, and no trade of any kind appears. Several large temporary hospitals have been erected in the fields adjoining. The great mortality which has lately pervaded this army, added to the shameful abuse and neglect in several of the hospital departments, has made it a perfect Golgotha. Upwards of four thousand men having been buried here within the last three months. At this time near half the army are sick, and the other half much fatigued with hard duty. This is now the tenth day since any of us has had a night's rest, or had time to undress.[58]

In mid-January 1795, as the withdrawal resumed, Brown recorded one particularly dispiriting march that lasted from four in the morning to ten at night, with the last 15 miles spent crossing 'a bare sandy desert with a tuft of withered grass, or solitary shrub, here and there: the wind was excessive high, and drifted the snow and sand together so strong, that we could hardly wrestle against it; to which was added, a severity of cold almost insufferable'. He added:

> Night fast approaching, a great number, both men and women, began to linger behind, their spirits being quite exhausted, and without hopes of reaching their destination; and if they once lost sight of the column of march, though but a few minutes, it being dark, and no track to follow, there was no chance of finding it again. In this state numbers were induced to sit down, or creep under the shelter of bushes; where, weary, spiritless, and without hope, a few moments consigned them to sleep; but alas! Whoever slept awaked no more.[59]

So bad had conditions become that to survive the frozen and hungry Allied soldiers were forced to loot their own supplies. 'Marauders from the regiments of all nations swarmed round the columns,' wrote Fortescue, 'the drivers of the wagons freed themselves from all control, and the line of march was disorderly beyond description. When the day was ended, the troops of different nations fought for such scanty comforts as were to be found; and there was a pitched battle between the Guards and the Hessians, who had been on bad terms with each other from the beginning of the campaign.' Fortescue added:

> Day after day the cold steadily increased; and those of the army that woke on the morning of 17th of January saw about them such a sight as they never forgot. Far as the eye could reach over the whitened plain were scattered gun-limbers, wagons full of baggage, stores, or sick men, sutlers' carts and private carriages. Beside them lay the horses, dead; around them scores or hundreds of soldiers, dead; here a straggler who had staggered on to the bivouac, and dropped to sleep in the arms of the frost; there a group of British and Germans round an empty rum cask; here forty English Guardsmen huddled together about a plundered wagon; there a pack-horse with a woman lying beside it, and a baby, swaddled in rags, peeping out of the pack, with its mother's milk turned to ice upon its lips – one and all stark, frozen, dead. Had the retreat lasted but three or four days longer, not a man would have escaped.[60]

Corporal Brown was shocked by the hostility of the Dutch. 'The inhabitants,' he wrote on 19 January, 'are our most inveterate enemies, and where the opportunity offers, will rather murder a poor, lost, distressed Englishman, than direct him the right way, several instances of which we have already known. It is reported that in the several columns of the army about 700 are missing, since we left the river Leck.'[61]

His most severe criticism, however, was reserved for the British medical staff. He recorded on 21 January:

> The shameful neglect that prevails through all [the medical] department, makes our hospitals mere slaughter-houses. Without covering,

without attendance and even without clean straw and sufficient shelter from the weather, they are thrown together in heaps, unpitied, and unprotected, to perish from contagion; while legions of vultures, down to the stewards, nurses, and their numberless dependants, pamper their bodies and fill their coffers with the nation's treasure, and like beasts of prey fatten on the blood and carcases of their unhappy fellow creatures . . . For the truth of what I say, I appeal to every man in the army who has only for a few hours observed with an attentive eye the general rule of conduct in our hospitals of late, and witness here the scene before me while I now write. A number of men laying on a scanty allowance of dirty wet straw, which from the heat of their bodies, sends up a visible steam, unable to help themselves; and though a sufficient number of men are liberally paid for their attendance, none has been near for several hours, even to help them to a drink of water.[62]

Soon after Brown wrote this, the Duke of York, snug in London, was informed by one of his former German subordinates that his army was no more. 'The officers, their carriages, and a large train are safe,' wrote General Walmoden on 3 February, 'but the men are destroyed. The army has now more than six thousand fighting men, but it has all the drawbacks of thirty-three battalions, and consumes a vast quantity of forage.'[63]

By now the army had crossed the frontier into Germany, where, by and large, the locals were friendlier. And yet, as Corporal Brown noted, despite the 'kindness of the inhabitants, outrages and depredations have been already committed here; a proof that no treatment, however kind, will prevent irregularities in the army, if the reins of discipline are slackened. A woman has been ravished and almost murdered by four of our men, who are discovered and in confinement.'[64]

Lieutenant-Colonel Wellesley was fortunate to receive permission to return to Britain from the Prussian port of Bremen in early March. The bulk of the army – the 33rd included – was not evacuated until mid-April. 'The number embarked was nearly fifteen thousand,' wrote Fortescue, 'some proportion of the sick having been recovered;

so that the losses after the retreat from the Leck [in mid-January] must have amounted to about six thousand men, of which not a tithe were killed or wounded in action. Thus disgracefully ended the first expedition of Pitt and Dundas to the Low Countries.'[65]

If Wellesley felt guilty for abandoning his men he never let on. Instead, years later, he put the blame for the army's disintegration squarely on the senior officers. 'Many of the regiments were excellent,' he confided to Lord Stanhope, but the man in authority was generally 'quite an imposter; in fact no one knew anything of the management of an army . . . The real reason why I succeeded in my own campaigns is because I was always on the spot – I saw everything, and did everything myself.'[66]

It was a useful lesson to learn. But though Wellesley had done well in his first campaign, he was still very much an amateur in the business of war who, for a time, seemed to have had his fill of active service. No sooner had he returned to Ireland in the spring of 1795 than he resumed his place in Parliament and as aide-de-camp to the lord lieutenant, and began to lobby for a permanent post in the Irish government: first as secretary at war and then, when that did not transpire, at either of the Revenue or Treasury boards. All were denied him though he was offered, thanks to his brother, the post of surveyor-general of the Ordnance. He refused it, not least because the incumbent (who would have to be turned out) was his old flame Kitty Pakenham's uncle. Only once his political hopes had been dashed did Wellesley turn his mind back to soldiering.

History in general, and the outcome of Britain's long war against France in particular, might have been very different had the recently promoted Colonel the Honourable Arthur Wellesley died like so many other soldiers of a tropical fever in the West Indies. That is where he and the 33rd Foot were heading in early 1796 when a violent, but ultimately propitious, storm blew their transports back to a British port. By the time they were ready to resume their voyage, the 33rd's posting had been changed to India. They finally arrived at Calcutta, after a torturous five-month voyage from the Cape, in February 1797.

Wellesley had passed the time at sea by reading from his large trunk of books. They included histories, dictionaries, grammars and maps of India; but also several works of military history, notably Julius Caesar's *Commentaries* (in Latin), fifteen volumes on Frederick the Great and Major-General Henry Lloyd's *Reflections on the Principles of the Art of War*. There were works by Voltaire, Rousseau, Locke and Adam Smith, and, for lighter reading, ten volumes of Louvet de Couvray's erotic *Les Aventures du Chevalier de Faublas*.[1] Wellesley's library mirrored the contrasting sides of his character, a contradiction not lost on the governor-general of India, Sir John Shore, when they met shortly after the 33rd's arrival. Shore found in Wellesley 'a union of strong sense and boyish playfulness', and thought he would distinguish himself if he had the chance.[2]

That opportunity did not come quickly, though Wellesley and the 33rd were part of an expedition to the Spanish colony of Manila in the Philippines – Spain and Holland having recently re-entered the war on France's side – that got as far as Penang before it was recalled. But the arrival of a new governor-general in May 1798, following Shore's resignation, changed everything; for the latest ruler of British India was none other than Wellesley's brother Richard, the second

Earl of Mornington. The total extent of territories controlled by the East India Company at this time was relatively modest: the Bengal Presidency was made up of just Bengal, Bihar and Benares (the last two provinces acquired in 1775 and 1781 respectively); the Bombay Presidency was confined to a relatively small area around the city of Bombay; while the Madras Confederacy was little more than 'a few scattered districts'.[3] And yet within seven years, by means of treaty and conquest, Mornington (or Marquess Wellesley as he became) had added huge tracts of land to each presidency, bringing British control to roughly half the Subcontinent. He achieved this by means of conquest *and* diplomacy, but particularly the former, and no soldier played a more prominent role than his brother Arthur.

Mornington arrived in India with a fixed determination to expand British rule – partly for the benefit of British trade, and partly to deny other European powers, particularly France, the chance to re-establish their own influence in the region. His main opponents were those powerful Indian princes who had been 'driven by the imminent threat to their own independence to revitalize their administrations and create more effective military forces partly on European lines'.[4] None was more obstinate than the pro-French Sultan of Mysore in southern India.

After Coote's victory at Wandiwash in 1760, French influence in southern India had been reduced to a few trading posts; yet the desire to check British power and maintain useful alliances remained. 'French agents, in some cases merchants and in others military officers on more or less unofficial reconnaissance missions,' writes David Andress in *1789: The Revolutions That Shook the World*, 'visited the princely courts of southern India in the late 1760s and early 1770s, reporting back on British ambitions and the potential for their defeat.'[5] French 'volunteer' officers also served as commanders and advisers to the armies of various Indian allies, notably Mysore, a huge territory located between British-influenced Hyderabad to the north and the smaller spice-producing states at the tip of India.

In the 1760s the Muslim general Hyder Ali had wrested control of Mysore from its weak Hindu prince, who remained as an ineffective figurehead. Having reorganized its army, Hyder took on the British at nearby Madras in the first Anglo-Mysore War, which ended in 1769, after a number of Mysore victories, in a peace treaty that provided for the restoration of all land seized, and for mutual aid and alliance in a defensive war. But when the agreement was tested in 1772, with the attack on Mysore from the north by the Hindu Maratha Confederacy, the British failed to provide military assistance and Hyder never forgave them. Thereafter he was a prime candidate for an alliance with the French, which was duly secured as France entered the American War of Independence in 1778. A year later he launched the second Anglo-Mysore War with French army and naval support, and, after yet more battlefield victories over the British, narrowly failed to capture Madras in 1780. 'Only the frantic rallying of British forces from across the subcontinent,' writes Andress, 'along with a successful naval campaign to prevent the landing of French reinforcements, prevented a total defeat.'[6]

Three successive victories by Sir Eyre Coote, the hero of Wandiwash in 1760, helped convince Hyder that he could never completely defeat an enemy that had command of the sea. He died in December 1782 and was succeeded by his son Tipu Sultan, the 'Tiger' of Mysore, who was no less formidable a soldier and who already had victories over the British to his name. With the support of French engineers and artillery, Tipu was making good progress in his siege of the British fortress of Mangalore in 1783 when news of the Anglo-French ceasefire arrived, forcing him to break off the attack and make a separate peace that restored the *status quo ante*.

Tipu was prepared to bide his time. A more devout Muslim than his father, he came to see war against the British as a holy *jihad*, a fanaticism that caused Lord Cornwallis, the then governor-general, to condemn him in 1789 as having a 'general character of bigotry . . . jealousy and hatred of Europeans'.[7] What particularly alarmed Cornwallis was the dynamism and sophistication of Mysore's army and economy, and Tipu's continued – albeit unofficial – links with France. He continued to employ French soldiers, engineers and artillerymen, while his own craftsmen and ironsmiths produced modern artillery, including 1-lb. iron rockets that could travel 1,000 yards.* It was to curb this growing threat, therefore, that Cornwallis fought the third Anglo-Mysore War of 1790–92, deploying tens of thousands of British and Indian troops, and a huge siege train of hundreds of guns, to bring Tipu to heel.

Defeated and forced to sue for peace, Tipu agreed to surrender two of his sons as hostages and to cede almost half of his territory. But by the time Lord Mornington arrived in India in 1798, Tipu had revitalized both his army and his economy, and had begun to seek allies in India, the Ottoman Empire and the French Republic. While the last had no battalions to spare, it did provide moral support and expertise (in the form of military advisers), prompting Tipu to plant a 'liberty tree' in his fortress capital of Seringapatam.[8] The alliance became official in January 1798 when the French governor of Mauritius published Tipu's proclamation that he only awaited 'the moment when the French shall come to his assistance to declare a war against the English who he ardently desires to expel from India'.[9]

Determined to break Tipu's power for good, Mornington asked his brother Arthur to prepare the ground. But at first Colonel Wellesley was not convinced that war was necessary. 'In my opinion,' he wrote to Mornington from Madras on 28 June, 'if it be possible to adopt a line of conduct which would not inevitably lead to war, provided it can be done with honour, which I think indispensable in this Government, it ought to be adopted in preference to that proposed.'[10]

Gradually, however, as more evidence of Tipu's bad faith was discovered, Wellesley came to see the war as inevitable. As a preliminary measure, he advised the disarming of the neighbouring princely state of Hyderabad, whose 14,000-strong army was officered by Frenchmen. Mornington agreed and 6,000 Company troops were sent into Hyderabad in October. They arrived to discover that the local sepoys had already risen against their French officers, who were promptly handed over to the British. The elderly ruler (or nizam, as he was

---

* European rockets at this time were not iron-cased and were therefore incapable of taking the larger chamber pressures that were needed to propel them over such a distance.

known) also agreed to a new treaty: under its terms his troops would henceforth be reorganized under British officers, and the 6,000 Company troops would remain in Hyderabad to guarantee the nizam's security. The final piece of the jigsaw was put in place when Mornington concluded a separate treaty with the peshwa of the powerful Maratha Confederacy – an alliance of Hindu states that stretched from the border of Mysore to Delhi in northern India, and then the dominant Indian polity – who agreed not to side with Tipu in the event of a war between Britain and Mysore.

The question of who would command the invasion of Mysore, however, was still undecided, and the most that Colonel Wellesley could have hoped for at this juncture, given his relative inexperience, was a brigade. But fortune smiled on him when the more senior Colonel Henry Aston of the 12th Foot, the man chosen to prepare the Madras Army for the invasion, was mortally wounded in a duel with one of his officers in December 1798. Named as Aston's replacement, Wellesley's first task was to travel to neighbouring Hyderabad to prepare the nizam's troops for war.

The trademark of all Wellesley's campaigns was his thorough logistical preparations, and Mysore was no different. Aware that the invading army had to cross more than 250 miles of jungle and hill terrain to reach Tipu's capital, and would not be able to live off the land, he encouraged merchants to bring in their produce from a wide area, and arranged for them to accompany the columns. He also assembled a siege train of two 24-pounders, thirty 18-pounders and eight long 9-pounders, with 1,200 rounds a gun, for the final assault; and he drilled the battalions in brigade formation with live firing exercises. So impressed was Lieutenant-General Sir George Harris, the commander-in-chief of Madras, that he congratulated Wellesley in a general order for bringing the invasion force to such an admirable state of organization and discipline.[11]

On 13 February 1799, with the preparations complete, the advance began. The plan was for a pincer attack on Seringapatam, with Harris advancing from Vellore in the east with an army of 21,000 men (including 1,000 cavalry and 4,300 Europeans), while a smaller force of 6,000 men from the Bombay Army, under Lieutenant-General

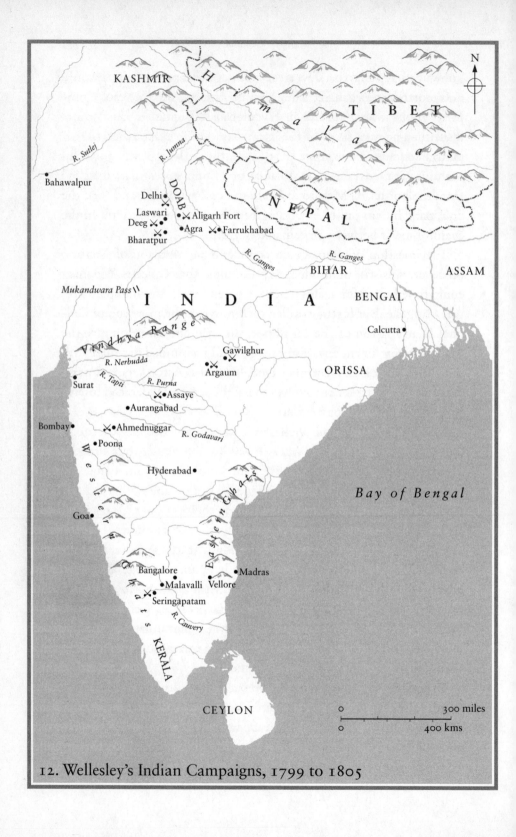

N

KASHMIR

HIMALAYAS

TIBET

R. Sutlej

R. Jumna

NEPAL

Bahawalpur

DOAB

Delhi
Laswari ✕
Deeg ✕✕ ✕ Aligarh Fort
Bharatpur ● Agra ✕ Farrukhabad

R. Ganges

R. Ganges

BIHAR

ASSAM

BENGAL

Calcutta ●

Mukandwara Pass ⦚

I N D I A

Vindhya Range

R. Nerbudda

Gawilghur
✕
Argaum

ORISSA

R. Tapti
Surat ●

R. Purna

✕ Assaye

● Aurangabad

Bombay ●

✕ ● Ahmednuggar

R. Godavari

● Poona

Hyderabad ●

Bay of Bengal

Goa ●

Western Ghats

Eastern Ghats

Bangalore ●
● Malavalli
Seringapatam

✕ ● Madras
Vellore

R. Cauvery

KERALA

CEYLON

0 ——————— 300 miles
0 ——————— 400 kms

12. Wellesley's Indian Campaigns, 1799 to 1805

James Stuart, marched from the western coast. Harris reached Amboor on 18 February; here he linked up with the 16,000 troops from Hyderabad. Many of Harris's senior officers – four of whom were major-generals – were anxious for the Hyderabad command. But Harris preferred to give it to Wellesley, in addition to the command of the 33rd Foot. Not yet thirty, Wellesley would hold the local rank of brigadier-general and be in charge of a force equivalent to a British division. Not surprisingly, there were protests from the major-generals, but Harris was unmoved. No doubt he was influenced by Wellesley's kinship to the governor-general; but he had also seen enough of the young colonel's organizational ability to trust him with such a vital role.

On 6 March the huge Madras column – trailed by more than 100,000 camp followers – entered Mysore territory. Eight years earlier, when Cornwallis had invaded by the same route, Tipu had defended Bangalore. This time Tipu destroyed its defences and withdrew to the west, burning crops as he went. It was a wise move. In 1792 the failure of his army's supplies had forced Cornwallis to abandon his march on Seringapatam and make peace on terms that, though harsh, left Tipu on his throne. The 'Tiger' clearly hoped for a similar outcome.

The first serious test for Harris's force was near the village of Malavalli, barely 30 miles from Seringapatam, on 27 March. The column had just completed a 6-mile march when scouts reported a large enemy force on a low ridge to the west, blocking the main road to Tipu's capital. Harris decided to give battle immediately, and advanced with his Madras force to the north of the road and Wellesley's Hyderabad Contingent to the south. As he neared the enemy position, Wellesley ordered his battalions to form from column into a two-deep line, with the battalions echeloned from the right, 200 yards between each, and the 33rd in the van.

Expecting the Mysore troops to hold fast, Wellesley was astonished to see 2,000 of Tipu's French-trained infantry advancing in column on the 33rd 'with the utmost steadiness'.[12] He responded by ordering the 33rd to halt and fire repeated volleys that eventually broke up the attack, though Tipu's men 'behaved better than they have ever been known to behave'.[13] Some of them even stood up to the 33rd's bayonet charge, but others fled and, before long, the whole force was streaming back up the hill. On the far side of the road, Tipu's cavalry attacked the forward Madras brigade, under Major-General David Baird, but it was only to buy time while the rest of the infantry withdrew. Even then, the retreating sepoys were badly cut up by pursuing horsemen from the 19th Light Dragoons and two units of Indian horse.

The road to Seringapatam was now open, but so exhausted and reduced in number were his bullocks that it took Harris more than a week to cover the 28 miles to the capital. He finally arrived 2 miles to the west of Seringapatam's defences on 5 April, having made a wide detour to the south; Tipu, meanwhile, had withdrawn into the fortress itself, which was sited on the western end of an island in the River Cauvery, with its northern and western walls flanked by branches of the river. In the rainy season the river was a formidable barrier: too deep to ford and too fast-flowing to cross in boats. But it was still the dry season and the river was little more than a trickle; the walls flanked by the Cauvery, moreover, were less formidable than those open to the rest of the island. For both these reasons, Harris had chosen to breach the fortress's western wall. But first Harris had to clear a number of enemy outposts in front of the river, notably a strong position in a tope, or thicket, of trees that was enclosed within a drainage canal known as The Aqueduct.

Wellesley was given the job of clearing the tope and the neighbouring village of Sultanpettah, while a Colonel Shaw made a simultaneous attack on an outpost to the north. Both operations would take place after dark on the 5th. So confident was Wellesley that he wrote to assure his brother that 'we shall be masters of this place before much time passes over our Heads.'[14] But he had badly underestimated the fighting quality of the Mysore troops and the difficulty of the terrain. That afternoon, unsure of his objective, he had asked Harris to ride out in front of the lines and point out the exact place. 'Upon looking at the tope as I came in just now,' he observed to Harris, 'it appeared to me that when you get possession of the bank of [The Aqueduct], you have the tope as a matter of course, as

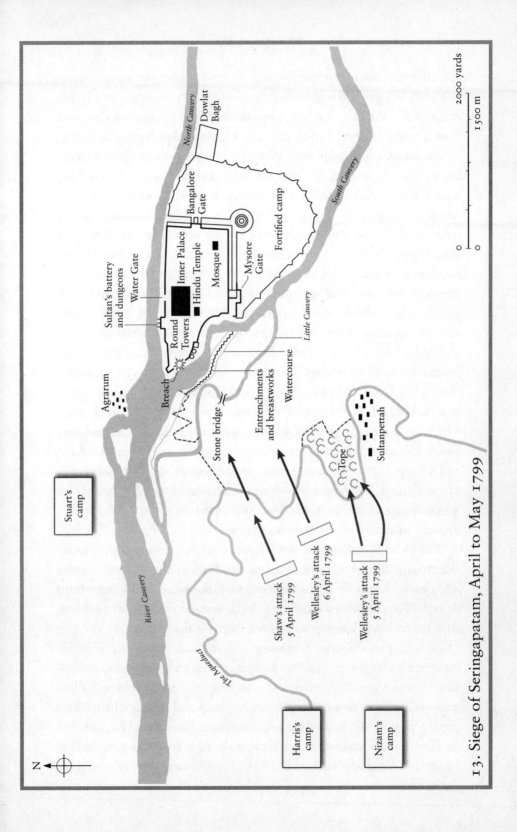

13. Siege of Seringapatam, April to May 1799

the latter is in the rear of the former.'[15] Harris, however, was too busy to survey the ground and Wellesley also failed to reconnoitre. He did not realize that the tope was criss-crossed with irrigation channels from 4 to 6 feet deep, and almost impossible to negotiate in the dark.

The attack began well, with Wellesley ignoring musket- and rocket-fire to lead the two flank companies of the 33rd across the nullah, with the rest of the battalion following. But, as it advanced blindly down the slope into the tope, the 33rd was counter-attacked by an enemy it could not see, and in fierce hand-to-hand fighting Lieutenant Fitzgerald, the brother of one of Wellesley's closest friends, was killed and twelve soldiers taken prisoner (later to be executed, on Tipu's orders, by both strangulation and the barbarous method of having nails driven into their skulls). The survivors retired back across the nullah, where Wellesley, lightly wounded in the knee by a spent musket-ball, tried and failed to restore order. Crushed by his defeat, he rode to Harris's headquarters. 'Near twelve,' recorded Harris, 'Colonel Wellesley came to my tent in a good deal of agitation, to say he had not carried the tope. It proved that the 33rd, with which he attacked, got into confusion, and could not be formed, which was a great pity, as it must be particularly unpleasant to him.'[16]

This was one of the few reverses of Wellesley's military career and its lesson stayed with him. Never again, he told his brother, would he 'suffer an attack to be made by night upon an enemy who is . . . strongly posted, and whose posts have not been reconnoitred by daylight'.[17] Next morning, he was given an immediate opportunity to redeem himself when he was ordered to lead a second attack on the tope, with a larger force. This time the attack succeeded without loss; though Wellesley almost forfeited the command when he arrived late on the start line, claiming he had not received the original order.

On 14 April, Lieutenant-General Stuart and his detachment of the Bombay Army reached Seringapatam and camped to the north-west of the city. Thereafter the two armies pushed forward their siege-works — batteries, parallels (trenches) and zigzags (interconnecting trenches) — until their big guns were close enough to silence the enemy's and make a breach in the wall. The latter was achieved on 3 May and the assault scheduled for the following day. It would be made by a combined Madras–Bombay force of 4,000 men, and commanded by Major-General Baird, who had a score to settle: he had been captured by Tipu during the previous war and kept chained for three years in Seringapatam's dungeon. Wellesley – possibly as a result of his poor showing on the 5th – was given the less glamorous task of commanding the reserve, which would be committed only if the original attacking force was held up.

In the event, the attack went entirely to plan, though the resistance was fierce, and the most that was required of Wellesley was to provide a battalion to guard the breach. Inside the walls the fighting continued for a further hour, but the result was never in doubt. Tipu's body was later found in a carpet of dead near the northern Water Gate of the city. He seems to have lived up to his name of the 'Tiger of Mysore', with British witnesses claiming to have seen a short, fat officer of the same description playing a gallant role in the defence, firing muskets that were handed to him by his retainers. He was hit several times and killed by a shot to the head that was fired at close range, according to one report, by a British soldier who wanted the jewel in his turban.[18]

For the rest of the day, the victorious attackers plundered, raped and murdered their way through the town. Some put their bloodlust down to their relatively heavy loss of 8 officers and 75 men killed, and a further 300 wounded; others to the discovery of the murdered soldiers taken a month earlier. But, in truth, it was a scene that had been acted out on many previous occasions when towns were held to the last; and it would be again, the inevitable consequence of a hard-fought victory that the fastidious Wellesley found hard to stomach.

The following day, by which time he had replaced Baird as temporary governor of Seringapatam, Wellesley used harsh punishments to bring the troops into line. He wrote to his brother:

> It was impossible to expect that after the labour which the troops had
> undergone in working up to the place, and the various successes they
> had had in six different affairs with Tippoo's troops, in all of which
> they had come to the bayonet with them, they should not have looked
> to the plunder of this place. Nothing, therefore, can have exceeded

what was done on the night of the 4th. Scarcely a house was left unplundered, and I understand that in camp jewels of the greatest value, bars of gold, etc., etc., have been offered for sale in the bazaars of the army by our soldiers, sepoys, and foreigners. I came in to take command on the 5th, and by the greatest exertion, by hanging, flogging, etc., etc., in the course of that day I restored order among the troops, and I hope I have gained the confidence of the people. They are returning to their houses, and beginning again to follow their occupations, but the property of every one is gone.[19]

Part of Wellesley's fury was the knowledge that unofficial plunder was not shared. The British prize agents, however, still amassed a sizeable fortune of £1,143,000 which was distributed among the troops according to rank: Harris received £150,000, Wellesley and the other full colonels £4,000, a British soldier £7 and a sepoy £5. For Wellesley, a man almost always in debt, it was a hugely welcome windfall and one that made it possible to repay the money his brother had spent buying him a lieutenant-colonelcy. But his offer to do so was graciously refused. 'I am not in want of money and probably never shall be,' replied his brother, 'when I am, it will be time enough to call upon you.'[20]

To ensure that it would never again challenge British supremacy, Mysore was broken up – with the bulk of its territory given to the Madras Presidency and its ally Hyderabad, and a smaller portion to the Marathas – and the rump left in the hands of the new five-year-old raja, a descendant of the Hindu rulers whom Hyder had usurped. Until the raja reached his majority, a chief minister would rule with the help of a British resident. It was by using this system of 'advisers' that the East India Company was able to influence the policy – particularly the foreign policy – of Indian states like Mysore that it did not directly rule.

With his coffers replenished and his reputation as an officer of promise largely enhanced, Arthur Wellesley could be forgiven a feeling of quiet self-satisfaction at the close of the Mysore campaign. Certainly his brother Richard had a high regard for his ability, telling General

Harris that 'my opinion, or rather knowledge and experience, of [Arthur's] discretion, judgment, temper, and integrity are such, that if you had not placed him in [command of] Seringapatam, I would have done so of my own authority, because I think him in every point of view the most proper for that service.'[21]

And yet, as 1799 gave way to a new century, Wellesley still held the substantive rank of colonel in the British Army; meanwhile Napoleon Bonaparte, the Corsican officer born in the same year as him, had enjoyed a rise so meteoric that by December 1799 he was both a full general and First Consul of France, dictator in all but name. He had managed this thanks to his unusual mix of qualities: his military talent, his willingness to take risks, his facility for self-publicity and, above all, his political opportunism.

The first quality had enabled him to play the leading role in the recapture of Toulon in 1793 when he went from being an obscure major of artillery to a celebrated brigadier-general, the saviour of the Republic, in the space of a few months. The 'Thermidor' coup of 27 July 1794 – that saw the Jacobin government replaced by more moderate republicans under Lazare Carnot – was a time of great danger for Napoleon because of his close links to the ousted Jacobin leader, Maximilien Robespierre. He was unjustly accused of plotting a counter-stroke and held for a time under house arrest. But eventually his value as a soldier was seen to outweigh his questionable political leanings, and he was released and confirmed in his role as general of Artillery.

Carnot, however, was not supportive of Napoleon's military schemes – including a plan to win control of the Alpine passes – and his career seemed to be heading nowhere, when he was given an infantry brigade in the army sent to fight a royalist rising in the western French province of the Vendée in the spring of 1795. Regarding the appointment as a demotion, Napoleon protested to the Ministry of War in Paris and was put on half-pay for his pains. In late August, Napoleon received a second order to join the Army of the West in the Vendée. Again he refused, sending in a bogus doctor's certificate that said he was unfit for duty. The War Office did not believe him and repeated the order. In desperation he appealed to Paul Barras, formerly a political commissar at the retaking of Toulon, and now a member of the five-man Directory that had ruled France since June. 'A deeply unpleasant man, even by the not very elevated standards of the Thermidorian regime, he was corrupt, amoral, cynical, venal, sardonic and opportunistic.'[22] He was also an admirer of Napoleon's military talents and, just when it seemed they would be wasted in the Vendée, he got the young general a posting to the Topographical Bureau of the Committee of Public Safety (the equivalent of a modern General Staff).

Yet another setback occurred in September when Napoleon was sacked from the Bureau, ostensibly for refusing to serve in the Vendée. Once again he was plunged into depression, but redemption was not long in coming. On 3 October (12 Vendémiaire), an unholy alliance of royalists and disgruntled National Guardsmen tried to overthrow the new regime. Napoleon later admitted that, on first hearing of the coup, he was unsure which side to take and was leaning towards the royalists when Barras sent for him. Barras's own version is that, having finally tracked Napoleon down, he offered him the command of the Paris garrison's artillery on condition that he accepted within three minutes. Napoleon did so.[23]

Next morning Napoleon made a count of government troops at the Tuilieries. There were no more than 6,000 effectives, with minimal ammunition and no artillery. Surrounding them were 20,000 well-equipped royalists, moving steadily in from the suburbs. With time running out, and the gruesome lessons of 10 August 1792 still fresh in his mind, he knew that only artillery could save the government. So he ordered the squadron commander of the 21st Chasseurs to seize the National Guard's guns in the Place de Sablons at midnight on the 4th. The officer in question was Joachim Murat, a huge and coarse 28-year-old Gascon 'whose courage always outran his intelligence'. He was the perfect man for the job. Accompanied by 260 men, he reached the Place de Sablons at the same time as a company of National Guardsmen on the same errand. Warned they would be cut to pieces if they tried to intervene, the guardsmen backed down and Murat returned to the Tuilieries with the guns.[24]

Next day, at 4 p.m., their advance delayed by a rainstorm, the royalists attacked the Tuilieries and were cut to pieces by the guns

under Napoleon's personal command. More than 1,400 royalists were
mown down in an action later described by Napoleon as a 'whiff of
grapeshot'. The coup had failed and Napoleon, the hero of the hour,
was eventually rewarded with promotion to major-general and the
plum job of commander-in-chief of the Army of the Interior: which,
on top of an annual salary of 48,000 francs, made Napoleon the de
facto governor of Paris and head of police and secret service. But for
the inadequacies of the rebels – who had fatally delayed their attack
on the Tuileries until the guns were in position – Napoleon would
have been put up against a wall and shot, just another casualty of the
Revolution.[25]

Napoleon was now rich, famous and powerful; and yet he han-
kered for a proper command in the field and, after bombarding the
Directory with various schemes for achieving victory over Austria,
he eventually got his way in March 1796 – a week before his marriage
to Josephine de Beauharnais, the Martinique-born widow of an
aristocrat executed during the Terror – when he was appointed
commander-in-chief of the Army of Italy. His task in the spring of
1796 was to coordinate with Generals Jourdan and Moreau in a three-
pronged attack on Austria: Jourdan would advance along the Mainz
Valley into Franconia; Moreau into Swabia and the Danube Valley;
and Napoleon would engage the Austrians in the Po Valley and,
if successful, move up the Adige Valley to the Tyrol, where he and
Moreau would apply the *coup de grâce*.

The army at Napoleon's disposal was far from adequate. On reaching his headquarters in Nice, he found 37,000 demoralized and poorly
supplied troops with which to take on 52,000 Austrians and Piedmontese. Yet he soon whipped his men into shape and told them, so
he claimed on Saint Helena, that he wanted to lead them 'into the most
fertile plains in the world'. Under Napoleon's inspired leadership –
and that of his talented deputies, Masséna, Augereau and Sérurier – this
small army won a series of rapid victories in the Alpine passes, split-
ting the forces of its opponents and forcing the Piedmontese to
request an armistice. 'Soldiers!' he proclaimed, with only a little
exaggeration. 'In fifteen days you have gained six victories, taken
twenty-one colours and 55 pieces of artillery, seized several fortresses

and conquered the richest parts of Piedmont. You have taken 15,000 prisoners and killed and wounded more than 10,000.'[26]

Nor did the victories end there. On 10 May, at Lodi near Milan, he defeated 12,000 Austrians and captured a vital bridge over the River Adda by sending his cavalry on a wide flank attack, though the initial frontal assault cost him 200 dead. Milan fell a week later. The completion of Napoleon's conquest of northern Italy, however, would take another year, during which time the Austrians counter-attacked down the Adige Valley and, for a time, forced him to raise the siege of Mantua. But the new Austrian commander, Count Wurmser, was well beaten at Castiglione in August and at Bassano a month later. Moreau, meanwhile, had not replicated Napoleon's successes and by October was back on the Rhine. This released Austrian troops for a second counter-offensive in Italy, which again made early inroads, defeating General Vaubois at Trent and Napoleon himself at Caldiero, near Verona, in early November (the first setback of Napoleon's military career). He redeemed himself a few days later with a narrow victory over the Austrians at Arcole in a three-day slugging match for possession of the bridge over the Adige.

A final Austrian offensive was defeated by Napoleon in January 1797, with victories at Rivoli and La Favorita inflicting 21,000 casualties. Mantua finally surrendered on 2 February. At this juncture there was little to prevent Napoleon from invading Austria itself through the Brenner Pass. But first the Directory wanted him to defeat the armies of the Pope – which he managed in barely a week – and the assault on Austria did not begin until early March. By the end of the month he had crossed the Brenner and taken Klagenfurt. Moreau, on the other hand, had not advanced from the Rhine, and Napoleon knew that he could not take Vienna unaided. So instead, and without consulting the Directory, he offered a full set of peace terms, giving the Austrians until 18 April to accept. It was a high-risk strategy: if the Austrians turned him down and Moreau did not begin his offensive, his bluff would have been called. Nor were the terms particularly generous: Austria was being asked to cede the Austrian Netherlands (modern Belgium) to France, allow the French to occupy the west bank of the Rhine and the Ionian Islands, and also recognize the new Cisalpine Republic that Napoleon had set up in Milan, Bologna and Modena; in return Austria was allowed to keep a foothold in Italy and the Adriatic by retaining the territories of Istria, Dalmatia and Frioul.

The Austrians caved in with a day to go and the preliminaries of peace were signed on 18 April (and confirmed by the Treaty of Campo Formio in October). Moreau had finally crossed the Rhine but it was too late. 'I was playing vingt-et-un,' a rueful Napoleon wrote later, 'and I stopped at twenty.' At the time he was apoplectic and blamed the Directory for this lost opportunity to destroy Austria's power for a generation.[27] Yet his astonishing achievements during the Italian campaign of 1796–7 could not be ignored, and that October the Directory presented the Army of Italy with a flag commemorating its eighteen victories, 150,000 prisoners and booty that included 540 cannon, 170 standards, 5 pontoon trains, 9 ships of the line and 12 frigates.

Napoleon's victories in Italy were not just down to him. Even before the Revolution, the French Army had experienced a renaissance in military organization, tactics and equipment: there were improvements in the pay, clothing and recruitment of regiments; in the calibre, accuracy and mobility of artillery; and there was a shift in attack from the column to the line (though the former could still be used when the situation demanded a rapid series of assaults on a given objective) and a liberal use of tirailleurs (skirmishers) to screen the main force. After the Revolution the citizen nature of the French Army, and its meritocratic system of promotion, gave it a spirit and patriotism not present, for example, in the peasant-recruited polyglot army of the Austrian Empire. Morale was also boosted in Italy by Napoleon's practice of letting his men keep whatever booty they could get their hands on. And the fact that his army carried just three days' rations and otherwise lived off the land, whereas the Austrians carried nine, meant that he could march faster and further, appearing where least expected.

But the key factor in the successes of 1796–7 was Napoleon's military genius. 'He was a painstaking, mathematical planner; a master of deception; a supremely talented improviser; he had an amazing, special and geographical imagination; and he had a phenomenal memory for facts and minute detail . . . By carefully calculating the odds he knew the likely outcome of his own moves and his opponent's.' From the Italian campaign he developed certain principles that never altered: always to keep open the army's lines of communication; to have a clear primary objective; to attack, and never remain on the defensive; to have more artillery than the enemy, and never fewer than four cannon per one thousand men; to remember the moral factor is three times as important as the material. 'Above all,' writes the biographer Frank McLynn, 'Napoleon emphasized the importance of concentration of force, speed and the factor of time, and the cardinal principle of outflanking.'[28]

If he had a weakness as a general, it was his willingness to take excessive risks: like at Arcole, when his army could and should have been trapped in the swamps as he fought obstinately for the bridge. He was, in modern parlance, a 'maxi-max' general, prepared to take maximum risk for maximum gain. But if theorists such as Sun-Tzu and Clausewitz have one thing in common, it is a belief that, all things being equal, a high-risk-taking general will always be beaten by a low-risk-taking general; that a 'maxi-max' will lose to a 'mini-max' (minimum risk, maximum gain). Napoleon's final and most spectacular defeat is evidence of that.

Napoleon's ambition was not confined to the military arena, and during the night of 3/4 September 1797 his political influence in Paris was strengthened when his deputy, Augereau – in concert with Barras and the other two moderate members of the Directory – surrounded the Tuileries with troops and arrested the two most right-wing members of the government, Barthélemy and Carnot, as well as a number of other suspected monarchists (a coup known to history as 'Fructidor', after the revolutionary month in which it took place).

On returning to Paris in December 1797, Napoleon was asked by the reconstituted Directory to plan an invasion of Britain. A year earlier a 15,000-strong force under Hoche had come within an ace of landing in Ireland, and the Directory wanted Napoleon to succeed where Hoche, now dead, had failed. But Napoleon knew that without naval supremacy such an operation could not succeed, and that the Royal Navy's recent victory over a numerically superior Spanish fleet at Cape St Vincent (a battle won by Admiral Jervis, but one in which the brilliant Commodore Horatio Nelson played the key role) had made attaining that edge increasingly unlikely. So he turned instead to Egypt.

While still in Italy, he had written: 'The time is not far distant when we shall feel that, in order to destroy England once and for all we must occupy Egypt. The approaching death of the vast Ottoman Empire forces us to think ahead about our trade in the Levant.'[29] In late February, Napoleon submitted a memorandum to the Directory, in which he suggested that Egypt might one day take the place of Santo Domingo and the sugar islands of the West Indies, and would provide France with both raw materials and a market for its manufactures. It could also, he claimed, be used as a springboard for reinforcing France's allies in India, including Tipu Sultan of Mysore, and ultimately for expelling the British from the Subcontinent. Such a threat would, at the very least, encourage Pitt to sue for peace.

In March 1798 the Directory gave its consent to the expedition, partly to remove the powerful and popular figure of Napoleon from Paris, and it was duly launched from Toulon and other Mediterranean ports in mid-May. It included 38,000 troops and more than 150 eminent scientists, engineers and orientalists who had answered Napoleon's call to 'civilize' Egypt. His chief motive, of course, was conquest and for a time he was successful. Having evaded Nelson's Mediterranean squadron and captured Malta, he landed near Alexandria on 1 July and stormed the great port a day later. Three weeks later Cairo fell, after Napoleon had destroyed the army of the ruling Mamelukes at the Battle of the Pyramids (an engagement so one-sided that the French lost just 29 killed and 260 wounded to the Mamelukes' 10,000 casualties).

But no sooner had Napoleon announced the advent of French rule, with each of the country's fourteen provinces run by a committee of nine Egyptians and one French adviser, than disaster struck. On 1 August the French fleet that had escorted Napoleon's troopships to Egypt was surprised at anchor in Aboukir Bay near Alexandria by Nelson's Mediterranean squadron and, in a brief but furious action that lasted barely three hours, all but two of its thirteen ships of the line were taken or destroyed. Not only had the so-called Battle of the Nile destroyed France's naval presence in the Mediterranean and left Napoleon marooned in Egypt, largely cut off from French reinforcement or resupply, but it also persuaded other European states that French power was waning. Turkey, which had been negotiating an alliance with France, at once suspended the talks and turned instead to the Allies. When the Second Coalition was formed against France in February 1799, it contained the Ottoman Empire, Naples and Portugal, as well as Britain, Austria and Russia.

Egyptian opposition to French rule found its expression in random attacks on military outposts and, more seriously, a rising in Cairo in October that cost the lives of 300 of Napoleon's countrymen before it was crushed. By February 1799 the threat was external, as Napoleon received word that two Ottoman armies were advancing on Egypt. His plan was to march into Palestine and seize the fortress of Acre, before beating the two armies one after the other. But delays, disease, the loss of his crucial siege guns and a spirited Ottoman defence of Acre – supervised by the British naval officer Sir Sidney Smith – left Napoleon's strategy in tatters and, having sustained 4,500 casualties out of an army of 13,000, he finally raised the 63-day siege and withdrew to Egypt.

After one final victory in Egypt in July, when he destroyed a Turkish army twice his size that had landed at Aboukir Bay (the enemy dead alone numbered 5,000), he made plans to return to a France that, once again, was threatened by enemies on all sides: an Anglo-Russian army had invaded Holland; a Turco-Russian fleet had captured Corfu; and one Austro-Russian army was in control of Switzerland while another had swept into northern Italy and, in a matter of weeks, reduced Napoleon's achievements there to rubble. France, moreover, was said to be on the verge of economic collapse, with royalist sentiment running high. Fearing a coup was imminent, he left Egypt by frigate on 23 August – accompanied by only a handful of his favourite generals, including Berthier, Lannes, Murat and Marmont – and finally landed in France, after a brief stopover in Corsica, on 9 October, reaching Paris a week later.

The news from the front was more optimistic. In September 1799 General André Masséna had won the second battle of Zurich, routing the Russians, while General Aleksandr Suvorov was transferring from the Italian front to the Swiss. The Russians blamed the Austrians for switching commanders – the previously successful Archduke Charles had, at the same time, been moved from Switzerland to Germany – and would withdraw from the coalition in January 1800. Other recent French successes included General Michel Ney's defeat of the Austrians on the Rhine, and General Guillaume Brune's victory over the Duke of York at Castricum on 6 October, which was soon followed by the evacuation of all British forces from the Low Countries. Napoleon's return to Paris, therefore, coincided with an upturn in French military fortunes. On the one hand, this made a coup less likely; on the other hand, the stunning military victories of Masséna and Brune, in particular, threatened to eclipse Napoleon's vaunted military reputation. He was, therefore, quite willing to act as the 'sword' in the scheme by the new rising star of the Directory, the Abbé Sieyès, to purge a government infamous for unrestrained corruption, rampant inflation and high taxes.

The coup was launched on 9 November (18 Brumaire). The key players were Sieyès, Roger Ducos (both members of the Directory), Joseph Fouché (Paris chief of police), Charles-Maurice de Talleyrand (the foreign minister) and Napoleon, whose job it was to arrest the other three members of the Directory (including his former mentor, Paul Barras) and force the two chambers of the Legislature to dissolve themselves. The plan almost backfired the following day, when Napoleon, flanked by two grenadiers, strode confidently into the Council of 500 to announce the resignation of the Directory. Instead of meekly succumbing to the inevitable, the enraged deputies grabbed Napoleon and almost lynched him before he was rescued by his soldiers, his face scratched and bleeding. But a bloodbath was avoided when the National Guardsmen at Saint-Cloud, anxious to avoid the fate of the Swiss Guardsmen in 1792, agreed to clear the chamber of hostile deputies. The few that remained were soon persuaded to wind up the Directory and swear an oath of loyalty to the new government, headed by three provisional consuls: Napoleon,

Sieyès and Ducos. Their equal status would not last long. On 12
December, Napoleon presented his draft constitution: a First Consul
with executive powers would be appointed for ten years, and flanked
by two other consuls with advisory powers; there would, in addition, be four assemblies to assist the executive, though in reality
these bodies cancelled each other out and left the First Consul with
virtually untrammelled power. He was, of course, Napoleon. 'By
excluding Jacobins and royalists from national representation,' writes
McLynn, 'Napoleon seemed merely to be consolidating the bourgeois revolution and to represent continuity rather than change.'[30]

But new government or not, France desperately needed peace,
and towards the end of 1799 made overtures to Britain. They were
rejected because Pitt's administration refused to make peace while the
Low Countries were in French hands. So Napoleon turned his attention to Austria, his most inveterate opponent in mainland Europe,
and in June 1800, having crossed the St Bernard Pass with 40,000 men,
narrowly and fortuitously defeated an Austrian army at Marengo.
After another French victory in December – by Moreau at Hohen-
linden, opening the route to Vienna – the Austrians agreed to a new
peace treaty at Lunéville in February 1801, which, in effect, reaffirmed
the terms of Campo Formio.

That same month, Pitt resigned as first minister (because George III
would not sanction Catholic Emancipation) and was replaced by the
unexceptional Henry Addington, who, unlike his predecessor, recognized a compelling argument for peace. Following the collapse of
the Second Coalition, the Northern League of Denmark, Sweden,
Prussia and Russia had imposed an embargo on trade with Britain.
The huge cost of the war – particularly the large subsidies needed to
keep foreign armies in the field – had all but bankrupted the country.
Peace was essential, though it would take many months of negotiations before an agreement was finally reached at Amiens in March
1802.

Of its recent imperial conquests, Britain kept only Ceylon and
Trinidad and Tobago. Cochin, the Cape and the Spice Islands were
returned to Holland (now the Batavian Republic); the captured Indian
and African stations to France, as well as a number of Caribbean

24. The young Arthur Wellesley (later Duke of Wellington) with his tutor at the Royal Academy of Equitation in Angers, France.

25. A miniature of Major-General Sir Arthur Wellesley, painted shortly before his first departure for Portugal in 1808.

26. 'The Storming of Seringapatam, 4 May 1799'. Wellesley was in command of the reserve – a punishment for his earlier failure to take an outlying village.

27. The Battle of Corunna, 16 January 1809, a defensive victory that enabled the bulk of the British Army to escape from Spain but cost its commander, Sir John Moore, his life.

28. 'Royal Artillery Drivers', from Charles Hamilton Smith's *Costumes of the Army of the British Empire, according to the Last Regulations 1812.*

29. 'British Riflemen', from the same source.

30. Wellington – shown directing troops in the left foreground – at the Battle of Salamanca on 22 July 1812.

31. George Cruikshank's caricature of the aftermath of the Battle of Vitoria on 21 June 1813, the culmination of a brilliant two-month campaign by Wellington that saw King Joseph and Marshal Jourdan's army pushed back to the French border.

32. 'Camp Scenes' by W. H. Pyne. Baggage, women and carts following soldiers on a march, 1811.

33. Thomas Rowlandson's caricature of the 3rd Regiment of Foot (The Buffs) and assorted camp followers fording a stream. Three women are carrying children; another an officer.

34. 'Napoleon as First Consul,' *c.* 1801. After a meteoric rise, and a string of impressive victories over the Austrians, the former artillery officer had become the leading citizen of revolutionary France.

35. In March 1815, having just escaped from his first exile on Elba, Napoleon re-enters Paris to begin his second term as French emperor.

BONAPARTE Entering PARIS. *March 20th was attended by Gen. Bertrand and another Officer, Escorted by Only 20 Dragoons. Louis 18 precipitably fled at his approach. Napoleon left Elba to invade France & traversed upwards of 300 Miles in that Country without encountering the smallest opposition from the Kings Troops, but on the contrary was every where greeted by the Military with unanimous acclamations of Vive l'Empereur.*

36. Prince Blücher, the Prussian commander, is unhorsed and narrowly avoids capture during his defeat by Napoleon at the Battle of Ligny on 16 June 1815.

37. Wellington and his senior officers at the Battle of Waterloo, 18 June 1815.

38. The fierce struggle for the burning Chateau of Hougoumont, one of the keystones of Wellington's defensive position at Waterloo.

39. The Life Guards, part of the Household Brigade, attacking French lancers at Waterloo.

40. Prussian (*right*) and French infantry clash at the village of Plancenoit during the evening of 18 June 1815.

41. The village of Waterloo on the day after the battle, 19 June 1815.

42. Chelsea Pensioners reading Wellington's Waterloo dispatch.

islands; Minorca to Spain; Malta to the Knights of St John; and Egypt (which had been captured by the British from Napoleon's successors in 1801) to Turkey. In return, France agreed to compensate the House of Orange – exiled from Holland – and to evacuate Naples and the Papal States. It was a treaty very much in France's favour, and one that was followed in August 1802 by a plebiscite confirming Napoleon's appointment as First Consul, or dictator, for life.

In India, meanwhile, Arthur Wellesley's post-Mysore military career had not thrived in the way he might have hoped. The early signs were positive when his brother assigned him to command a British expedition against the French island of Mauritius. But when this was cancelled in January 1801, in favour of a larger-scale mission to assist the reconquest of Egypt, Wellesley was incensed to learn that the more senior Major-General Sir David Baird would command. 'I was at the top of the tree in this country,' he wrote indignantly to his younger brother Henry, Lord Wellesley's private secretary. 'But this supersession has ruined all my prospects . . . However, I have lost neither my health, spirits, nor temper in consequence thereof.'[31]

He was offered partial recompense in April 1802 with promotion to major-general (though solely on the India list). But he knew that only a victory in battle would remove the stigma of his supersession, and the chance came in 1803 after one Maratha chief, Holkar of Indore, had turned on two others, the Peshwa of Poona and Scindia of Gwalior, and soundly defeated them. Having signed a treaty with the peshwa, Lord Wellesley declared war on Holkar and gave command of the Anglo-Indian field army of 10,000 men to his brother Arthur, who only months earlier, anticipating a war with the Marathas, had made a detailed study of the terrain and the supplies needed to cross it. They included 90,000 lb. of salted meat, 'packed in kegs well fortified, 54 lb. in each keg, besides pickle, etc; and the same quantity of biscuits in round baskets, containing 60 lb. each'.[32]

Such careful planning, a highly efficient bullock-train and rigid discipline enabled General Wellesley to enter Poona with his cavalry on 19 April 1803, having covered the 600 miles from Madras territory in a matter of weeks. Holkar had wisely chosen not to defend Poona;

but no sooner had he withdrawn from the fray than two other Maratha chiefs, Scindia and the Raja of Berar, entered it by threatening Britain's ally Hyderabad. Lord Wellesley responded in early August by ordering General Lake to invade Scindia's territory from the north while General Wellesley did the same further south with an army of 11,000.

The first obstacle in Wellesley's way was Scindia's hill-fortress at Ahmednuggar, defended by a garrison of 2,000. The assault began on 8 August with the capture of the outer walls, and was completed four days later when siege guns battered the citadel into submission. It was an easy victory that, a few years later in the Peninsular War, he would struggle to replicate with fortresses held by determined Frenchmen.

Having mopped up most of Scindia's possessions south of the River Godavari, Wellesley crossed the river and linked up with Colonel James Stevenson and the 9,500 men of the Hyderabad Contingent at Budnapur on 21 September. Wellesley's plan was for the two armies to move separately to make it easier to feed them and harder for Scindia to escape. So on 22 September they separated, with Stevenson's line of march 14 miles to the west of Wellesley's. The intention was to reunite in the vicinity of Borkardan, where they hoped to trap Scindia's army. But on 23 September, as his troops completed their morning march, Wellesley received intelligence that Scindia's infantry was in camp near the village of Assaye, just 6 miles distant.

Riding forward with a cavalry escort to reconnoitre, Wellesley was shocked to discover the whole Maratha army spread over 7 miles of plain. Scindia's 30,000 horsemen were to the left of the enemy position, near Borkardan, while 20,000 infantry and 128 guns were in the centre and round the village of Assaye on the right. The River Kaitna protected the Marathas' front, and another stream, the Juah, their left flank and rear. It was an immensely strong position, and the safest option for Wellesley would have been to withdraw towards Stevenson and attack the following day. He had barely 7,000 troops and 22 guns, most of them light calibre, at his immediate disposal; and of the soldiers, only 1,800 were British – men from the 19th Light Dragoons, 74th and 78th Highlanders, and 160 artillerymen – and all were tired from the morning march of 24 miles. Yet Wellesley

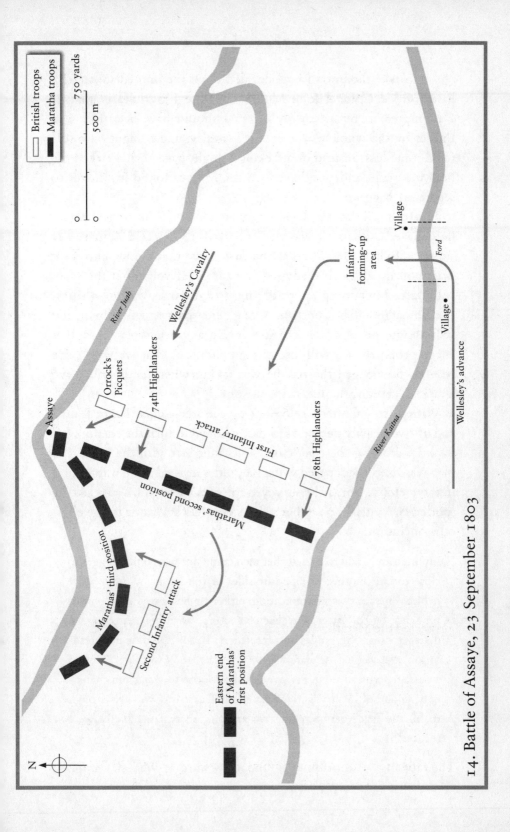

14. Battle of Assaye, 23 September 1803

chose to take the initiative. 'I decided upon the immediate attack,' he informed Colonel John Munro, 'because I saw clearly that, if I attempted to return to my camp, I should have been followed thither by the whole of the enemy's cavalry, and I might have suffered some loss; instead of attacking I might have been attacked the next morning; and, at all events, I might have found it difficult to secure my baggage.'[33]

In truth, Wellesley decided to attack at all hazards because he believed aggression was the only way to defeat a numerically superior Indian foe. 'Dash at the first party that comes into your neighbourhood,' he had advised Stevenson. 'If you adopt this plan, and succeed in cutting up, or driving to a distance, one good party, the campaign will be our own. A long defensive war will ruin us, and will answer no purpose whatsoever. By any other plan than that above proposed, we will lose our supplies, do what we will.'[34] He later acknowledged the risk he was taking when he described the attack as 'certainly a most desperate one'.[35]

With a frontal attack ruled out by the steep-sided River Kaitna and its two heavily defended fords, he hoped to turn the enemy's left flank by crossing the river close to its junction with the Juah. The plan was almost scuppered when his guides insisted there was no ford in the vicinity. But, as he surveyed the area through his spyglass, he spotted two villages on either side of the river and came to the obvious conclusion:

> I immediately said to myself that men could not have built villages so close to one another on opposite sides of the stream without some habitual means of communication, either by boats or a ford – most probably by the latter. On that conjecture, or rather reasoning, in defiance of all my guides and informers, I took the desperate resolution, as it seemed, of marching for the river, and I was right. I found a passage, crossed my army over, had no more to fear from the enemy's cloud of cavalry, and my army, small as it was, was just enough to fill the space between the two streams, so that my flanks were secure.[36]

The crossing was not quite as straightforward as Wellesley implies.

'No sooner . . . did the head of the column [of infantry] begin to ascend the opposite bank,' wrote an officer of the Madras Engineers, 'than it was met by a shower of shot

> from a battery advanced near the bank for that purpose, which, continuing without intermission, caused us severe loss. At this time the General's orderly dragoon had the top of his head carried off by a cannon ball, but the body being kept in its seat by the valise, holsters, and other appendages of a cavalry saddle, it was some time before the terrified horse could rid himself of the ghastly burden, in the endeavour to effect which he kicked and plunged, and dashed the poor man's brains in our faces, to our no small danger and annoyance . . . Being ordered forward to examine the ground in the direction of the enemy . . . I observed, on gaining the top of the high ground between the two rivers, the enemy's infantry in the act of changing their front, and taking up a new position, with their right to the river Kaitna and their left on the village of Assaye. On returning to the General, I found that not supposing the enemy to be capable of such a manoeuvre in the face of an attacking force, he had, in conformity with his original intention of attacking them in flank, already formed the infantry in two lines, while the cavalry . . . was drawn up as a reserve in the rear.[37]

Wellesley had intended to outflank the Marathas' line by marching his right wing past Assaye. But the enemy's well-drilled change of front – made possible by years of French-supervised training – made him alter his point of attack away from Assaye, which was well defended and bristling with cannon, to his left wing near the River Kaitna. He knew, he wrote later, 'that the village of Assaye must fall when the right should be beat'. So he instructed Lieutenant-Colonel William Orrock, commanding the picquets on the right, not to stray too close to the village. But for some reason Orrock ignored the order and attacked Assaye with his picquets and the supports from the 74th Foot. 'There was a large break in our line,' recalled Wellesley, 'between these corps and those on our left. They were exposed to a most terrible cannonade from Assaye, and were charged by the [enemy] cavalry; consequently, in the picquets and the 74th regiment we sustained the greatest part of our loss.'[38]

For a time, thanks to Orrock's incompetence, the battle hung in the balance. If the main attack on the left had also been repulsed, Wellesley and his small army would have been doomed. But, though the Marathas in that sector fought well and inflicted many casualties, they could not hold their line. 'I cannot write in too strong terms of the conduct of the troops,' wrote Wellesley to the governor-general a day later. 'They advanced in the best order, and with the greatest steadiness, under a most destructive fire, against a body of infantry far superior in number, who appeared determined to contend with them to the last, and who were driven from the guns only with the bayonet; and notwithstanding the numbers of the enemy's cavalry, and the repeated demonstrations they made of an intention to charge, they were kept at a distance by our infantry.'[39]

On the right, too, the position was stabilized when Wellesley sent the 19th Light Dragoons and the 4th Native Cavalry to support the battered 74th. Their charge took them 'through the enemy's left like a torrent that had burst its banks, bearing along the broken and scattered materials which had opposed it'. The Maratha centre, meanwhile, had reformed a little further back on the Juah, from where they repulsed a second charge by the British cavalry, killing the colonel of the 19th Light Dragoons in the process. But already the Maratha horse had left the field and, with the 78th Highlanders moving up to attack, the infantry fled across the Juah, leaving the 'whole country strewn with killed and wounded, both European and natives, ours as well as the enemy's'.[40] Among the weapons abandoned by the Marathas were more than 90 cannon.

Appalled by the carnage, and no doubt shocked by how close he had come to disaster, Wellesley sank to the ground and sat with his head between his knees. His small army of 7,000 had suffered a crippling 1,584 casualties, 650 of them British; the enemy dead and wounded were more than 6,000. 'I should not like to see again such loss as I sustained on the 23rd September,' he wrote to Stevenson a month later, 'even if attended by such a gain.'[41]

That night he would have a recurring nightmare that all his men had been killed. When asked, years later, what was the 'best thing' he ever did in the way of fighting, he replied with one word: 'Assaye.'[42]

He knew he had taken a fearful risk and only narrowly come through it. During the fighting, one charger was killed under him and another piked. Yet, when faced with each new setback, he had refused to panic. 'I never saw a man so cool and collected as he was,' wrote Colin Campbell of the 78th, 'though I can assure you, till our troops got the orders to advance the fate of the day seemed doubtful.'[43]

In the flush of victory, and no doubt mindful of his own frailties that day, Wellesley could afford to be generous to Colonel Orrock, who, incredibly, had survived his attack on Assaye. 'I lament the consequences of his mistake,' he wrote, 'but I must acknowledge that it was not possible for a man to lead a body into a hotter fire than he did the picquets on that day.'[44]

After Assaye, Wellesley was hopeful that Scindia would sue for peace. But preliminary talks foundered in mid-November – on Scindia's refusal to move his troops away from the Deccan Plateau south of the Narmada River – and by the end of the month Wellesley was once again in the field, wearing a uniform that would become familiar throughout Europe: white pantaloons tucked into Hessian boots, scarlet tunic, black cocked hat and a curved Indian sword, or *tulwar*, hanging from his waist.

At 3 p.m. on 29 November, having just linked up with Colonel Stevenson's Hyderabad Contingent (giving him a combined force of 11,000 men) after an exhausting march of nine hours, Wellesley spotted Scindia's 30,000-strong army 5 miles to the north, on a flat plain to the front of the village of Argaum. It was Assaye all over again – though this time the Marathas' numerical superiority was slightly less marked – and, though his troops were tired from their long march, Wellesley gave orders for an immediate attack. It began badly, as the fierce Maratha bombardment caused the bullock-drawn guns of Wellesley's advance guard to flee in panic, taking three battalions of native infantry with them. Wellesley tried to rally them by waving his sword and shouting. When they failed to respond, he followed them to the rear and, once they had regained their composure, led them back to the firing line. He wrote later: 'What do you think of nearly three entire battalions, who behaved so admirably in the battle of Assaye, being broke and running off, when the cannonade commenced at Argaum, which was not to be compared with that at Assaye? Luckily, I happened to be at no great distance from them, and I was able to rally them and to re-establish the battle. If I had not been there, I am convinced we should have lost the day.'[45]

It was 4.30 p.m. before Wellesley's army was ready to attack. 'I formed the army into two lines,' he reported, 'the infantry in the first, the cavalry in the second.'

> When formed, the whole advanced in the greatest order . . . Their whole line retired in disorder before our troops, leaving in our hands thirty-eight pieces of cannon and all their ammunition. The British cavalry then pursued them for several miles, destroyed great numbers, took many elephants and camels and much baggage. The Mogul and Mysore cavalry also pursued the fugitives, and did them great mischief.[46]

Wellesley added, in a separate letter: 'If we had had daylight an hour more, not a man would have escaped . . . The troops were under arms, and I was in the saddle, from six in the morning until twelve at night.'[47] He had routed Scindia's troops a second time at a cost of just 360 casualties, of whom less than half were British.

Further north, Scindia's European-led forces had suffered three more defeats at the hands of General Gerard Lake at Aligarh Fort (1 September), Delhi (11 September) and Laswari (1 November). Yet still Scindia and his allies refused to submit, so Wellesley pursued the remnant of the Maratha infantry from Argaum to the mountain fortress of Gawilghur, between the headwaters of the Tapti and Purna rivers. A brief siege culminated in the place being taken by assault on 15 December, though in truth the defenders gave up after their outer works were captured. It did not save the Marathas caught on the battlements, fit and wounded, who were hurled to their deaths on the rocks below.

With his military power destroyed, Scindia finally agreed to terms that deprived him of Gujarat in western India, which became part of the Bombay Presidency, and all his lands north of the Jumna River, including Agra, Delhi and Meerut. But that still left Holkar of

Indore, the original aggressor, to be dealt with. Wellesley's orders were to move up from the south while General Lake's army advanced from the north, but the strategy began to unravel when a famine in the Deccan delayed Wellesley's departure. Holkar took advantage by falling on and heavily defeating a wing of Lake's army, under Colonel William Monson, at the Mukandwara Pass in Rajputana in July 1804. Wellesley thought Monson's defeat a 'disgrace' and attributed it to three factors: no attention to supplies, no boats (to aid Monson's retreat) and a failure to 'make a good dash at Holkar'.[48] He added, in a letter to John Malcolm: 'Would to God I had come round here in March, and Holkar would have been in the tomb of all the Capulets!'[49]

Holkar's forces went on to besiege Delhi in October, and withdrew only when Lake's relieving army arrived on the 19th. Barely a month later, Holkar was routed by Lake at Farrukhabad, the last major set-piece battle of the war. There were, however, two more sieges of Maratha forts: that of Deeg, which fell to Lake after a month-long operation, in late December; and that of Bharatpur, which resisted four separate attempts by Lake to storm it in January 1805. The war, overall, had been a great success for Generals Wellesley and Lake, and had added great swathes of territory to British India. But it had not been popular with the directors of the East India Company, who resented both Lord Wellesley's pro-consular style of government and the huge cost of both the Mysore and Maratha wars. The setbacks at Mukandwara and Bharatpur were just the excuse they needed to persuade the government to recall Governor-General Earl Wellesley in late 1805.

His brother Arthur had already left, sailing on HMS *Trident* in March 1805. He had been awarded a knighthood (KCB) for his victories over the Marathas, and would return home with a fortune of £42,000 – chiefly his share of prize money – that made him 'independent of all office or employment'.[50] Since arriving in India eight years earlier, he had risen in rank to major-general, fought in two successful campaigns and personally won two major battlefield victories at Assaye and Argaum over vastly superior enemy forces. A historian of his generalship wrote:

On both occasions [he] stumbled across the enemy army at the end of a tiring march, made a rapid personal reconnaissance and then determined that an immediate attack was preferable to an overnight delay. On both occasions he brought up his troops in echelons to one flank in a manner very reminiscent of Frederick the Great's 'oblique order' . . . In both battles – especially Assaye – there was some hard fighting and some errors by subordinate commanders; but in both cases the British bayonet was ultimately triumphant.[51]

In a tactical sense, therefore, India taught Wellesley that aggression and risk were the keys to winning battles. He would learn soon enough that veteran French troops did not buckle quite as easily as Indian sepoys, and would have to adapt his tactics accordingly. But one area of his Indian experience required no fine-tuning, and that was his expertise in matters of logistics. 'He was a logistician *par excellence*, and he repeatedly overturned accepted wisdoms by the speed with which he could bring together a moving bazaar – actually a sort of free-enterprise "rolling magazine" – to keep his forces fed while they operated far from their base. His campaigns were therefore notable for their range and cross-country mobility, even in near-desert conditions.'[52]

18. Retreat to Corunna

On 12 September 1805, shortly after his return from India, Major-General Sir Arthur Wellesley walked into the anteroom of the Colonial Office in Downing Street to find a diminutive one-armed admiral who, like him, was waiting to see Lord Castlereagh, the newly appointed secretary of state for War and the Colonies. Wellesley instantly recognized the sailor as Admiral Lord Nelson, commander-in-chief of the Royal Navy's Mediterranean Fleet, whose victory in the Battle of the Nile in 1798 had made him a national hero (a status merely enhanced by his later success at Copenhagen in 1803). Nelson, by contrast, had no idea who the tall, sunburnt general was and proceeded to 'talk about himself', recalled Wellesley, 'in a style so vain and silly as to surprise and almost disgust me'. The soldier added:

> I suppose something that I happened to say may have made him guess that I was *somebody*, and he went out of the room for a moment, I have no doubt to ask the office-keeper who I was, for when he came back he was altogether a different man, both in manner and matter. All that I had thought a charlatan style had vanished, and he talked of the state of this country, and of the aspect and probability of affairs on the Continent with a good sense, and a knowledge of subjects at home and abroad that surprised me . . . in fact he talked like an officer and a statesman. The Secretary of State kept us long waiting, and certainly, for the last half or three-quarters of an hour, I don't know that I ever had a conversation that interested me more.[1]

During their brief conversation, Wellesley was brought fully up to date with the military and political situation in Europe, since Addington's government, outraged that Napoleon Bonaparte was defying the spirit if not the letter of the Treaty of Amiens,* had ended the

* In 1802, having negotiated with Spain to acquire Louisiana, the isle of Elba and

brief outbreak of peace by declaring war on France in May 1803. For much of that year, and the next, Britain had fought a largely defensive war, with Nelson's Mediterranean squadron countering the threat of invasion by blockading the main French fleet in Toulon. All the while the French Grand Army at Boulogne had grown in strength to 160,000, waiting for the Franco-Spanish fleet to escort it across the Channel in transports. The chance seemed to have come in March 1805, when Admiral Villeneuve took advantage of westerly gales to leave Toulon with twenty men-of-war. Initially wrong-footed, Nelson gambled that Villeneuve was bound for Jamaica and set off in pursuit. 'If they are not gone to the West Indies,' declared the one-eyed, one-armed admiral (he had lost the sight of his right eye during the siege of Calvi in 1794, and his right limb at Tenerife three years later), 'I shall be blamed: to be burnt in effigy, or Westminster Abbey is my alternative.'[2]

Fortunately for Britain, Nelson's gamble paid off and the Channel was not left undefended. Once Villeneuve realized Nelson was in pursuit (he took thirty-four days to cross the Atlantic, to Nelson's twenty-four), he ignored his instructions to wait until all French naval forces had joined him and returned to Europe. Bound for Brest, he was intercepted off Cape Finisterre by Vice-Admiral Sir Robert Calder's Atlantic squadron of fifteen ships and, during a confused action in fog on 22 July, lost two of his ships and withdrew to Ferrol. Calder, however, was court-martialled for not pressing home his attack and his command transferred to Nelson, who, following this action, had returned to Britain on leave for the first time in two years. Wellesley referred to the Cape Finisterre battle in his conversation with Nelson, contrasting Calder's feeble performance with the decisive victories that Nelson had 'taught the public to expect'. Nelson returned the compliment by expressing a hope that Wellesley

---

the Duchy of Parma, Napoleon then accepted the presidency of the Cisalpine Republic. By the end of the year he had annexed Piedmont and invaded the Helvetic Republic, while Spain, France's client state, had confiscated the property of the Knights of St John. Britain had responded by postponing the restitution of Malta and France's settlements in India.

would be given command of an expedition to attack the French in Sardinia, a strategy that in his opinion made much more sense than the landing in northern Germany that Pitt – reinstated as prime minister since May 1804 – was actually planning.[3]

In August 1805 Pitt had finally persuaded Austria to re-enter the fight against France. The final straw for Austria was when Napoleon (emperor of France since May 1804) had himself crowned king of Italy in May. Austria could accept the loss of its influence in Germany or Italy, but not both at the same time. In the interests of self-preservation, therefore, it had joined Britain, Russia and Portugal in what became known as the Third Coalition. Napoleon's response was to postpone indefinitely the invasion of Britain so that he could march against Austria, and by early September the camps at Boulogne were deserted.

The news that Britain was safe from invasion would take some time to reach London, and meanwhile Nelson's orders, when he returned to active service the day after his chance meeting with Wellesley, were to destroy the Franco-Spanish fleet (now at Cadiz) by any means at his disposal. On 20 October 1805, in a final throw of the dice, Villeneuve sailed out of Cadiz with thirty-three warships. A day later, Nelson's fleet of twenty-seven ships attacked him off Cape Trafalgar. Advancing in two divisions, Nelson pierced Villeneuve's crescent-shaped line in two places so that his vanguard of ten ships took no real part in the action. Superior British tactics, gunnery and seamanship accounted for the rest. Eighteen of Villeneuve's ships were captured or destroyed, including his flagship *Bucentaure*, though many of the prizes foundered in the violent storm that followed the battle. French and Spanish casualties were 5,800 killed and wounded, and 20,000 captured (among them Admiral Villeneuve). British losses were just 1,690 – but they included Lord Nelson, who had been shot by a sniper from the mizzen mast of the French ship *Redoubtable* as he strode the quarterdeck of his flagship, HMS *Victory*, in the decorations of his four chivalric orders.

As Nelson lay dying in the surgeon's quarters below deck, Captain Hardy reported a 'brilliant victory', adding that at least 14 enemy ships had been taken. 'That is well,' replied Nelson, 'but I bargained for twenty.' His last words were: 'Thank God I have done my duty.'[4]

At 4.30 in the afternoon, three hours after receiving the fatal wound, Nelson died. When the news reached London, *The Times* remarked: 'We do not know whether we should mourn or rejoice. The country has gained the most splendid and decisive Victory that has ever graced the naval annals of England; but it has been dearly purchased. *The great and gallant* NELSON *is no more*.'[5] Brought back to London in a cask of brandy, he was given a state funeral in St Paul's Cathedral on 9 January 1806.

Two weeks later, the country mourned an even greater loss. Already weak from overwork and worry, Pitt's frail constitution had been dealt an additional blow by the news that Napoleon had destroyed an Austro-Russian army in arguably his finest battlefield victory at Austerlitz on 2 December 1805, resulting in the collapse of the Third Coalition. On 23 January 1806, at the age of just forty-six, Pitt died in Downing Street.

'Twenty-three years Minister of this country,' recorded the Tory MP Charles Abbott in his diary, 'founder of the only effectual sinking fund for the reduction of the debt; deliverer of this country from the horrors of the French Revolution and accomplisher of the Union with Ireland [in 1800]. His transcendent eloquence and talents gave him a complete and easy victory over all his rivals in Parliament, and a popularity throughout the nation which he never condescended to solicit.'[6]

Soon after his meeting with Nelson and his audience with Castlereagh, Wellesley had two discussions with Pitt. At the first, during a ride from Wimbledon Common to London, Wellesley defended his brother's policies in India, and Pitt seemed 'satisfied'.[7] At the second, barely three months before his death, Pitt made the extraordinary prophecy that Napoleon would be checked as soon as he faced 'a national resistance', that 'Spain was the place for it, and that then England would intervene'.[8]

It is doubly remarkable that Pitt made this prophecy to the very man who would see it fulfilled. Did he suspect that the brilliant 36-year-old sepoy general would adapt his talents to the European theatre? It seems likely. But first Wellesley had to overcome the hostility of HRH the Duke of York, commander-in-chief of the British

Army since 1795, who was not convinced that such a young officer deserved the rank of major-general. Given a minor command on the south coast by York, Wellesley turned his attention to politics and affairs of the heart, entering the Commons as MP for Rye on 1 April 1806 and marrying his old flame Lady Kitty Pakenham, now thirty-four, in London nine days later. He had not set eyes on her for more than ten years and was shocked by her appearance. 'She has grown ugly, by Jove!' he whispered to his brother Gerald at the ceremony. Many years later, he confessed to a friend: 'I married her because they asked me to do it & I did not know myself. I thought I should never care for anybody again, & that I sh[oul]d be with my army &, in short, I was a fool.'[9]

In Parliament he supported the Grenville–Fox 'Ministry of All the Talents' that had replaced Pitt's Tory administration in February 1806. But when that ministry fell over the issue of Catholic Emancipation in March 1807, and was replaced by the Duke of Portland's Tories (with Lord Castlereagh as war secretary, and George Canning as foreign secretary), Wellesley entered government for the first time as chief secretary for Ireland, the lord lieutenant's deputy. This initial taste of ministerial life did not last long. Word soon reached him in Dublin that the government was planning an expedition to Copenhagen to seize the Danish fleet, lest it fall into French hands, and he at once volunteered. York made sure he was given only a brigade, while his old sparring partner Sir David Baird got a division; but he still won the lion's share of the laurels by defeating a Danish attempt to raise the siege of Copenhagen on 26 August. Just over a week later the city surrendered and the powerful Danish fleet was safely in British hands. Wellesley was appointed one of three commissioners to arrange the terms of the capitulation – a task he accomplished, according to one of the Danish commissioners, with 'human and generous conduct'.[10]

The British Army that Wellesley returned to from India in late 1805, and commanded in Denmark in the summer of 1807, was much improved from the one he had left in 1796. The man chiefly responsible was Commander-in-Chief York, who had shown far more talent as an administrator and military reformer than as a battlefield general. His immediate advantage over his predecessor, the septuagenarian Lord Amherst of Seven Years War fame, was that he had witnessed at first hand the army's deficiencies in the Low Countries. It helped, too, that, as a member of the Royal Family and the favourite son of King George III, he was above politics.

His first general order of 14 February 1795 had set out his reforming agenda by announcing that 'all matters respecting His Majesty's Military Service, excepting what may relate to the Foot Guards, should pass through His Royal Highness' hands.'[11] He began by recruiting a proper headquarters staff of twenty officers and a dozen secretaries and clerks at the Horse Guards in London, including an adjutant-general (to deal with personnel and legal matters), a quartermaster-general (whose task was supply) and a military secretary (promotion and appointments). Realizing that radical structural reform was impossible during wartime, he concentrated on improving what already existed. He tried to ensure, for example, that despite the purchase system all officers were professionally competent to hold their rank. New candidates needed to be at least sixteen and required a written recommendation by an officer of field rank. No officer could purchase a captaincy until he had served for at least two years, nor could he buy a majority without six years' service. All officers were assessed by regular confidential reports, and York himself kept a list of talented but impecunious officers who were eligible for promotion without purchase. The founding in 1801 of the Senior Department of the Royal Military College at High Wycombe (now the Staff College, Camberley) to train officers in staff duties, and later the Junior Department for officer cadets (now the RMA Sandhurst) – both under the lieutenant-governorship of the inspirational Colonel John Le Marchant – owed much to York's determination to improve the army's professionalism.

The war required a huge expansion in the size of the armed services, particularly the army, and York helped this process by sponsoring a bill in 1799 that allowed volunteers to transfer from reserve forces like the militia and Fencibles into the regular army in return for a cash bounty. There was also an attempt to make military service more attractive by ending the practice of powdering hair, making uniforms more practical, building barracks and reducing stoppages of pay. As part of this process, York increased the basic pay of a private from 8*d*. a day to one shilling, the first rise since the days of the Commonwealth. But deductions for equipment and food (apart from bread, which was provided) left the soldier barely enough to feed himself, let alone support a family, and most soldiers still came from the agricultural and urban poor.

In 1806, in an effort to attract a better class of recruit, York reduced the term of enlistment from twenty-one years to seven, and increased the bounty to £18.12*s*. (over a year's pay). 'It was,' wrote a supporter of limited enlistment, 'repugnant to the principles of our constitution, that there should exist in it an army composed of men quite distinct from the rest of the community, and who have given up those liberties which are incompatible with military discipline, never to resume them.' But the measure failed either to improve enlistment rates or to change the general character of recruits, and from 1808 new soldiers were given the choice of signing on for either seven or twenty-one years, with the vast majority opting for the latter (and an extra £5.5*s*.). By 1812, thanks to these sizeable financial inducements, the army establishment was largely up to strength. The only significant change was in the number of Irish recruits: in 1783 they had totalled only 4.4 per cent of the army; by the Napoleonic War – thanks to a dearth of recruits in the traditional recruiting areas of England and Scotland, the rise in the Irish population and the emancipation of Irish Catholics – that proportion had increased to a third, most of them Catholics.[12]

Punishments were harsher than ever, with sentences of up to 1,000 lashes now administered in a single parade. Private William Surtees had not been long in the 95th Rifles, having joined the new corps from the 56th Foot in 1802, when he witnessed the punishment of a man found guilty of stealing the officers' plate. '[He was] sentenced to receive 800 lashes,' he recalled, 'all of which he took at one standing, and that without evincing much suffering; this was the most I ever saw inflicted at one time.'[13]

Wellesley and most officers were great believers in the deterrent effect of the lash; but many other ranks also approved. 'Philanthropists,' wrote Quartermaster-Sergeant James Anton of the 42nd Highlanders, 'who decry the lash ought to consider in what manner the good men – the deserving, exemplary soldiers – are to be protected; if no coercive measures are to be resorted to in purpose to prevent ruthless ruffians from insulting with immunity the temperate, the well-inclined, and the orderly disposed, the good must be left to the mercy of the worthless.'[14]

But if the Duke of York was unwilling to tamper with the draconian system of punishments, he could at least ensure that soldiers were properly trained. He insisted, therefore, on rigid compliance with Dundas's infantry drill manual, and the follow-up manual for the cavalry that appeared in 1795. It did not cover sword exercise, however, and that gap was filled by the distribution to all cavalry regiments of Colonel John Le Marchant's *Rules and Regulations for the Sword Exercise of the Cavalry*, printed by York's order in 1797.

Perhaps York's single greatest achievement in the field of training and tactics was his reform of light troops. In 1797, having seen at first hand the effectiveness of French tirailleurs in the Low Countries, he ordered commanding officers to give their light companies separate training exercises and shooting practice. A year later his assistant adjutant-general, Sir Harry Calvert, wrote a memorandum on the creation of special 'corps of Light Troops', and that summer a trial exercise of light infantry, light cavalry and horse artillery* was held in Essex.[15]

In 1800 York took the development of light troops a step further when he authorized the 'formation of a Corps of Riflemen by detachments to be returned to their Corps when properly trained'. This experimental corps, under the command of Major-General Coote Manningham, was composed of men selected from fourteen regiments as suitable for training in the use of the British Baker rifle, which, following competitive tests at Woolwich Arsenal, had been chosen ahead of other models from Britain, mainland Europe and

---

* Horse artillery had been created by Frederick the Great in the eighteenth century as a mobile reserve that could be rushed to any part of the battlefield more quickly than traditional field artillery; its chief role, however, was to support cavalry. The first British units of Royal Horse Artillery were formed in 1793.

America as giving the best balance of qualities for service in the field. The Baker's chief advantage was that its rifling twist rate – which imparted spin on the bullet, and therefore increased accuracy – was only one quarter of a turn. Its inventor, Ezekiel Baker, a Whitechapel gunsmith, explained:

> It was . . . remarked [after the trials], that the barrel was less liable to foul from frequent firing, than [those with] whole, three-quarters, or half-turns in angles of the rifle, which was considered of great advantage to the corps [of riflemen], particularly when engaged, as they would not require so often sponging out as the greater angles would, and yet possess every advantage of the other rifle in point of accuracy and strength of shooting at three hundred yards distance. For all these reasons the committee gave mine a preference, and recommended to the Honorable Board of Ordnance to have their rifles made upon a similar construction.[16]

The Baker rifle that was produced for the British Army was, at just under 4 feet long, shorter and lighter than a musket, and fired a smaller bullet of .625 calibre. However, it used the same flintlock firing system and was slower to load, because the ball, wrapped in a patch of oiled leather to ease its passage, had to be tight-fitting to engage with the rifling.

Equipped with Baker rifles, the new 'Corps of Riflemen' was first deployed as an ad hoc unit on the expedition to Ferrol in 1800. So successful was this deployment that, following its return to Britain, the corps ceased to be experimental and was gazetted as a permanent unit under its new title of the Rifle Corps. It gained its first battle honour in 1801, during Nelson's Copenhagen expedition, and a year later became part of the Infantry of the Line as the 95th (Rifles) Regiment of Foot. A second battalion was added in 1805 and a third in 1809. William Surtees, the well-educated son of a Northumberland tradesman who transferred to the regiment from the 56th Foot in 1802, recalled the training he received at Eastbourne:

> We immediately commenced our light drill, in which I took great delight; but most of all I liked the shooting at the target. As recruits,

we were first drilled at what is termed the horse, i.e. a machine to assist young riflemen in taking aim. At this I pleased my commanding-officer so much the first time I tried, that he ordered me to the front, and told me to load, and fire at the target. I did, and made a pretty good shot, hitting pretty near the bull's eye; on which he made me load again and fire, and hitting that also, he made me go on till I had fired ten rounds, all of which hit the target, and two of which had struck the bull's eye. The distance indeed was only fifty yards, but for a recruit, that is, a person unaccustomed to rifle-shooting, he called it a wonderful exhibition, and in consequence he gave me sixpence out of his pocket, and ordered me home.[17]

The following year, as the threat of a French invasion caused large formations to be concentrated on the south coast, the 95th was brigaded at Shorncliffe in Kent with two infantry units which had been designated as light infantry: the 43rd (Monmouthshire) and 52nd (Oxfordshire) Foot. All three were under the command of Major-General John Moore, who is generally credited with creating the body of light troops that became famous in the Pensinsular as first the Light Brigade and later the Light Division. Moore was unusual among officers of his generation in that he regarded soldiering as a profession. Born in Glasgow in 1761, the son of a highly regarded physician and writer, he first saw action with the newly raised 82nd Foot in the American War of Independence. But the greatest early influence on Moore's preference for light troops was his three-year stint as a major with the 60th Royal American Foot, a unit that practised a less rigid form of drill and movement than was normal in line regiments. As a battalion commander, he distinguished himself at the siege of Calvi in Corsica in 1794; and as a brigade commander, under Lieutenant-General Sir Ralph Abercromby, he was wounded in the Battle of Alexandria in Egypt in 1801. It was during his time at Minorca in 1800, however, that Moore was persuaded by Abercromby of the need for a light infantry corps to challenge the French tirailleurs.

Shorncliffe gave him the opportunity to create such a specialized formation, and the ideas he put into practice there on light-infantry training and tactics were derived chiefly from a book by a German

officer, Major-General Baron de Rottenburg, that had been translated into English in 1798 as *Regulations for the Exercise of Riflemen and
Light Infantry*. Moore acknowledged his use of de Rottenburg as 'the
groundwork, noting in the margin whatever changes we make from
him'.[18] The fruit of this period of training was a grand review of
Moore's 4,000 light troops by the Duke of York on 23 August 1804.
After the initial inspection, the brigade marched in slow time and
then with the faster pace prescribed for the light infantry. The redcoated 43rd and 52nd Foot then formed column and line, all the time
protected by a screen of green jackets, the uniform worn by the riflemen of the 95th. Finally the troops fought a mock battle, 'with the
sharpshooters seeking concealed positions in hedges, the artillery firing numerous blanks and the infantry of the line showing how they
could deliver a devastating volley'.[19] It was all 'conducted with the
greatest order', recorded an onlooker, 'no mistake occurred'.[20]

The Duke of York's highly successful first stint as commander-in-
chief would come to an abrupt end in early 1809, when he was accused
in Parliament of using the patronage at his disposal for the benefit
of his former mistress, Mary Anne Clarke. She had, his accusers
claimed, accepted money from officers seeking employment or promotion, and the duke had not only agreed to her recommendations
but shared in the profits. These were unsubstantiated allegations,
made by Mrs Clarke when the duke refused to pay her 'hush' money
of £2,000, and a lengthy House of Commons inquiry found him innocent of either personal corruption or connivance by 278 votes to 196.
But the relatively small size of the majority, coupled with the revelation that the commander-in-chief was in the habit of discussing official
business with his mistress, left the duke no option but to resign.[21]

Fortunately, for the sake of the British Army, most of his key
reforms had already borne fruit. 'I can say from my own knowledge,'
declared Sir Arthur Wellesley, in the House of Commons in
January 1809, 'as having been a lieutenant colonel in the army when
HRH was appointed to command it, that it is materially improved in
every respect; that the discipline of the soldiers is improved; that
under the establishments formed under the direction of HRH, the
officers are improved in knowledge; that the staff of the army is

much better than it was; and much more complete than it was; that the cavalry is improved . . . and everything that relates to the military discipline of the soldiers and the military efficiency of the army has been greatly improved since HRH was appointed Commander-in-Chief.'[22]

The Duke of York's reform of the British Army had created both a shield for Britain's defence and a sword to take the fight to Napoleon. In the autumn of 1807, as Wellesley returned in triumph from Copenhagen, the only questions that remained were where the main blow would fall and which general would deliver it.

In June 1808, two months after his promotion to lieutenant-general, Wellesley was offered the command of 9,000 troops who were being sent to South America to assist Venezuelan revolutionaries in their attempt to overthrow their Spanish overlords. An earlier attempt to harm Napoleon by attacking his Spanish ally's South American empire had produced decidedly mixed results: the cities of Montevideo and Buenos Aires were captured in 1806; but the latter was lost in 1807 to a Spanish counter-attack that cost the British, in one disastrous day of fighting, more than 2,800 casualties.[23] Moore's vaunted Light Brigade, now under the command of Brigadier-General Robert Craufurd, was part of the force that was repulsed from Buenos Aires in a defeat *The Times* described as 'perhaps the greatest which has been felt by this country since the commencement of the revolutionary war'. On his return to Britain in early 1808, the British commander General John Whitelocke was court-martialled, found guilty of conduct 'tending to the dishonour of his majesty's arms' and cashiered.[24]

Though Wellesley knew of Whitelocke's fate – his sentence having been read at the head of every British regiment – he also knew that independent commands were extremely rare, and that only a fool would turn one down. But he would never get the chance to test himself in South America, because, shortly before he was due to sail from Cork, his expedition was redirected to Portugal. The chain of events that caused this change of plan had begun in June 1807 when Napoleon defeated the Russians at the Battle of Friedland. The subsequent Treaty of Tilsit had caused Russia to close all her ports to British trade in return for a free hand in the Baltic and the Bosphorus, thus transforming Britain's last ally into an aggressive opponent. This, in turn, had left Napoleon free to begin the subjugation of the one area of Western Europe beyond his control: the Iberian Peninsula. In November 1807, with his ally Spain giving his troops free passage, he invaded Portugal and the regent, Prince John, was forced to escape with his government to Brazil. Portugal's fleet, meanwhile, sailed for Britain. At first some of the Portuguese welcomed the French soldiers as liberators. But the invading army's high-handed behaviour soon alienated its hosts and there were risings across Portugal, notably at Oporto, where a hastily elected junta appealed to the British for help. Before long, French rule was confined to Lisbon and a handful of fortresses.

In Spain, too, an economic crisis and the presence of foreign troops were causing an anti-French backlash. In March 1808 a mob of soldiers and peasants forced the corrupt and conservative pro-French king, Charles IV, to abdicate in favour of his son Ferdinand. Napoleon responded by luring the Spanish royal family to Bayonne, where, in early May, he intimidated Ferdinand by threats of execution into returning the throne to his father. The craven Charles then promptly handed the Spanish crown to Napoleon, who, in turn, gave it to his elder brother Joseph. But this time he had gone too far and, even before the official announcement was made, the outraged inhabitants of Madrid rose against the French garrison and their Spanish collaborators. The rising was quickly and brutally suppressed, but not before it had sparked off a general insurrection across the country. It was a conflict that would rage for five years and prove, ultimately, to be Napoleon's Achilles heel. 'That unlucky war ruined me,' he conceded later. 'It divided my resources, obliged me to multiply my efforts, and caused my principles to be assailed . . . it destroyed my moral power in Europe, rendered my embarrassments more complicated, and opened a school for the English soldiers.'[25]

In June 1808, even as Wellesley was preparing to embark for South America, a deputation of Spanish rebels reached London to request British military assistance; in July a Portuguese mission arrived with a similar request. It was too good an opportunity to miss, and Portland's government duly switched Wellesley's destination to Portugal, a change that the general himself fully supported. This was 'a crisis', he told the cabinet, 'in which a great effort might be made with advantage'.[26] Shortly before his departure, he confided his hopes and fears to his friend, the MP and diarist John Wilson Croker:

> I am thinking of the French that I am going to fight: I have not seen them since the campaign in Flanders, when they were capital soldiers, and a dozen years of victory under Bonaparte must have made them better still. They have besides, it seems, a new system of strategy which has out-manoeuvred and overwhelmed all the armies of Europe. 'Tis enough to make one thoughtful; but no matter: my die is cast, they may overwhelm me, but I don't think they will out-manoeuvre me. First, because I am not afraid of them, as everybody else seems to be; and secondly, because if what I hear of their system of manoeuvre is true, I think it a false one as against steady troops. I suspect all the continental armies were more than half beaten before the battle was begun – I, at least, will not be frightened beforehand.[27]

Wellesley sailed from Cork on 12 July 1808, landing first at Corunna in northern Spain and then at Oporto to confer with the Spanish and Portuguese juntas respectively. Informed that the local French commander, General Jean-Andoche Junot, had concentrated his troops near Lisbon, he decided to land his army 100 miles to the north at Mondego Bay. Before he did so, he outlined his strategy in a letter to his second-in-command, Major-General Sir Brent Spencer, who was joining him with troops from Gibraltar. Irrespective of how well the Spanish fared in their war, he wrote, 'nothing we can do can be so useful to them as to get possession of and organize a good army in Portugal . . . whether Spain is to continue or to fail, Portugal is an object, and your presence here is most necessary.'[28]

This was an understandably cautious strategy that acknowledged the relatively small size of Wellesley's army and the need to guarantee his maritime lines of communication. His plan, therefore, was to create a solid base in Portugal before venturing further afield. But even before he had established himself ashore, Wellesley's long-term aspirations were dashed when he received a letter from Lord Castlereagh, the war secretary, informing him that an additional 15,000 troops were being sent to Portugal (most from a recent expedition that Sir John Moore had led to Sweden), and that he was too junior to command such a large force. He would, therefore, be superseded by Sir Hew Dalrymple, with Sir Harry Burrard taking over as second-in-command, and Moore and three other lieutenant-generals joining as Wellesley's seniors. Wellesley masked his disappointment in a courteous reply that promised he would not try to win laurels before his superiors landed by rushing into battle. To his former boss, the Duke of Richmond, lord lieutenant of Ireland, he was more candid: 'I hope that I shall have beat Junot before any of them arrive, and then they may do as they please with me.'[29]

On 31 July, the day before the landings, Wellesley issued his first General Order of the Peninsular War. It reminded his soldiers that 'Portugal is a friendly country' and urged them to have respect for their hosts' devotion to the Roman Catholic religion. Officers were expected to remove their hats, soldiers to salute and sentries to present arms when the Host passed in the street. As for logistics, the troops would be accompanied by six women to every one hundred men (drawn by lot before embarkation); the men to have one pound of biscuits and one pound of meat every day, with wine added if the meat was salted, while the women would be on half-rations and no wine.[30]

With the landings completed by 8 August, Wellesley had a total force of 15,000 men on Portuguese soil. Convinced that Junot had only a thousand men more, he decided to take the initiative by advancing south on the Lisbon road, supported by 1,600 Portuguese troops. The first collision took place on 15 August at Brilos, near Óbidos, when a company of the 95th Rifles drove in a French outpost, but then pushed on too far and lost an officer and twenty-six men in a clash with the enemy rearguard. Among the wounded was Wellesley's young brother-in-law, Captain Hercules Pakenham.

Two days later, Wellesley attacked 4,300 French troops under General Henri-François Delaborde at the village of Roliça, 8 miles to the south of Óbidos. Using three columns to pin the French in front

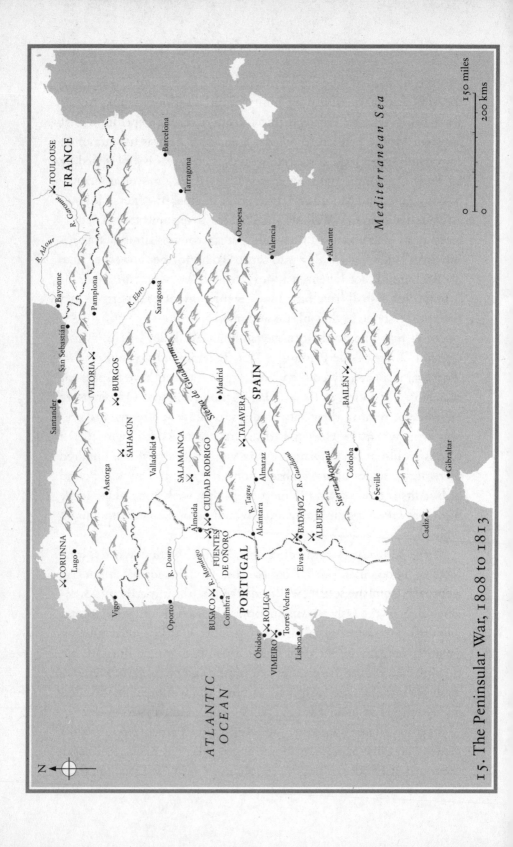

15. The Peninsular War, 1808 to 1813

of the village, Wellesley sent two more to turn the flanks. But Delaborde was too wily and withdrew to an even stronger position south of Roliça on a steep ridge cut by deep gullies. Wellesley tried his dual-flanking manoeuvre a second time, but it was upset when Colonel Lake of the 1/29th Foot advanced up a gully into the centre of the French position, where he was killed and his battalion decimated. This prompted Wellesley to launch a general attack before the flanking columns were in position, giving Delaborde the chance to extricate the majority of his command, if not his guns. Having lost 487 men to Delaborde's 700, Wellesley described the action as 'most desperate' and that he had never seen 'such fighting as in the pass'.[31] It was a solid if unspectacular start to his Portugal campaign, but an indication that he was hoping to use against the French the aggressive tactics that had served him so well in India.

From 18 to 20 August, the disembarkation of yet more reinforcements at the mouth of the Maceira River brought Wellesley's troop numbers up to 17,000. With such a force he was convinced he could defeat Junot's main army and recapture Lisbon. But the arrival offshore of Sir Harry Burrard on 20 August put paid to this plan. Aware that Junot's true strength was 30,000 men, including those on the Spanish frontier, Burrard ordered Wellesley not to advance until Sir John Moore had arrived with more men. By choosing not to disembark that day, however, Burrard gave Wellesley the opportunity to fight another battle.

It was Junot who forced the issue by marching north from Torres Vedras to take the British by surprise. Expecting the French to approach from the south, Wellesley had deployed his troops on two long ridges, with the village of Vimeiro to their front. Among his men was a young private of the 71st (Highland) Regiment of Foot who would pen one of the finest journals of the war. When it was published in 1819 he chose 'from motives of delicacy' to remain anonymous. He has since been identified as Thomas Pococke,[32] born in Edinburgh in 1790, the son of 'poor but respectable parents' who 'kept from themselves many comforts' that he 'might appear genteel and attend the best schools'. They hoped he would become a clergyman or a writer; instead, at the age of sixteen, he abandoned his studies to become an actor. But stage fright wrecked his debut – 'hisses began from the audience; I utterly failed' – and he fled 'unseen from the theatre, bewildered and in a state of despair'. Determined to leave Edinburgh, he met a party of recruits about to embark for the Isle of Wight and 'rashly offered to go with them'. Thus began his initial term of seven years in the 71st, for which he was paid a bounty of eleven guineas. 'Tall and well made, of a genteel appearance and address', he would soon discover that the life of a raw recruit was not to his liking.

> How different was my situation from what it had been [wrote Pococke in his journal]! Forced from bed at five o'clock each morning, to get all things ready for drill; then drilled for three hours with the most unfeeling rigour, and often beat by the sergeant for the faults of others. I who had never been crossed at home, I who never knew fatigue, was now fainting under it . . . I could not associate with the common soldiers; their habits made me shudder. I feared an oath – they never spoke without one; I could not drink – they loved liquor; they gamed – I knew nothing of play. Thus was I a solitary individual among hundreds.[33]

Only after he had fought and beat one 'particularly active' tormentor was he left alone. 'I became much esteemed among my fellow-soldiers, who before had despised me,' he wrote. 'Still, I could not associate with them. Their pleasures were repugnant to my feelings.'[34]

Pococke had been with the 71st Foot for barely two weeks when it was sent overseas, first to Cape Town and then South America, where it took part in Whitelocke's failed attempt to recapture Buenos Aires in the summer of 1807. Taken prisoner with most of his battalion, on his release he returned to Ireland in time to join Wellesley's expedition to Portugal. At Roliça he saw little action. 'We were manoeuvring all day to turn their flank,' he recorded, 'so that our fatigue was excessive, though our loss was but small.'[35]

At Vimeiro, however, Pococke and his battalion would play a key role. On Sunday, 21 August, having stood to arms for an hour before daybreak, he and his comrades were dismissed with orders to parade

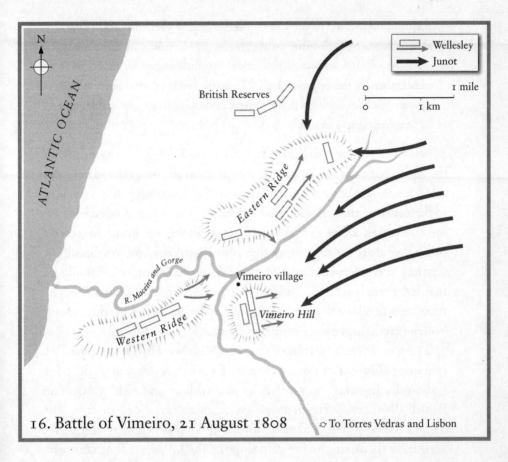

16. Battle of Vimeiro, 21 August 1808

again at ten o'clock in the morning. He recalled the calm before the storm:

> Vimeiro is situated in a lovely valley, through which the small River Maceira winds, adding beauty to one of the sweetest scenes, surrounded on all sides by mountains and the sea, from which the village is distant about three miles ... We were posted on these mountains and had a complete view of the valley below. I here, for a time, indulged in one of the most pleasing reveries I had enjoyed since I left home.
>
> Soon my daydream broke and vanished from sight. The bustle around was great. There was no trace of a day of rest. Many were

washing their linen in the river, others cleaning their firelocks; every man was engaged in some employment. In the midst of our preparation for divine service, the French columns began to make their appearance on the opposite hills. 'To arms, to arms!' was beat, at half past eight o'clock. Everything was packed up as soon as possible, and left on the camp ground.[36]

When word reached Wellesley that the French were coming not from the south but the east, he moved troops from the western ridge to the eastern, and pushed two brigades on to the flat-topped Vimeiro Hill to the south of the village. The battle saw the first use of what became his trademark defensive tactic: placing the main body of troops behind a ridge line to protect them from artillery, and putting light infantry and riflemen on the forward slopes to counter the tirailleurs that led French attacks. Unlike the French, who tended to concentrate their artillery in grand batteries, Wellesley spread his guns along his front to hamper the enemy approach.

The first French assault was against Vimeiro Hill. It consisted of two huge columns of infantry, each of 30 men broad and 42 deep (or 1,260 men in total), supported by skirmishers and field guns. The British defenders were deployed with three battalions of foot just behind the crest line, and two more to their rear as a tactical reserve. Screening them, on the forward slope of the hill, were four companies of the 2/95th and the whole of the 5/60th, all armed with rifles. Benjamin Harris of the 2/95th, a former shepherd from Blandford, was among the first to fire on the French and remembered how difficult it was to see the enemy through the smoke that quickly enveloped him. 'The French, in great numbers, came steadily upon us,' he recalled, 'and we pelted away upon them like a shower of leaden hail. Under any cover we found we lay, firing one moment, jumping up and running for it the next, and when we could see before us we observed the cannon balls making a lane through the enemy columns as they advanced, huzzaing and shouting like madmen.'[37]

The riflemen managed to stem the advance of the French skirmishers with accurate fire, and withdrew behind the crest only on the approach of the huge columns. The French tactic was to use the more manoeuvrable columns to approach an enemy position, and then deploy into line for greater firepower if they met stubborn resistance. But, like Marlborough and Wolfe before him, Wellesley had the answer to this. His infantry battalions were drawn up in two ranks and, before the French could deploy into line, would fire a close-range rolling volley, company by company, into the head and flanks of the column. Then they would let out a great cheer and charge the enemy with fixed bayonets. At Vimeiro Hill this tactic worked to perfection. Harris's company commander, Captain John Leach, recalled:

> On the pickets being driven in, I joined my own brigade, which was on the left of the Ninety-Seventh. Here the business was beginning to assume a serious aspect. Some heavy masses of infantry, preceded by a swarm of light troops, were advancing with great resolution . . . against the brigade on which our battalion was posted. In spite of the deadly fire which several hundred riflemen kept up on them, they continued to press forward . . . until the old Fiftieth Regiment received them with a destructive volley, following it instantly with a most brilliant . . . charge with the bayonet.[38]

Four separate columns attacked the hill, and each time they were repulsed. By now Sir Harry Burrard had arrived on the ridge; but, seeing that Wellesley had matters well in hand, he generously allowed his subordinate to direct the battle. It did not all go to plan. A determined French assault on the village of Vimeiro was stopped only after a 'desperate struggle' in which the light troops of the 43rd Foot suffered more casualties than any other British unit on that day.[39] Then, determined to take the initiative, Wellesley ordered the 20th Light Dragoons and some Portuguese cavalry to charge a body of enemy horse. Sergeant George Landsheit of the 20th recalled Wellesley shouting 'Now, Twentieth! Now!', while his staff 'clapped their hands and gave us a cheery',

> the sound of which was still in our ears when we put our horses to their speed. The Portuguese likewise pushed forward, but through the dust which entirely enveloped us, the enemy threw in a fire which

seemed to have the effect of paralysing altogether our handsome allies. Right and left they pulled up, as if by word of command, and we never saw more of them till the battle was over. But we went differently to work. In an instant we were in the heart of the French cavalry, cutting and hacking, and upsetting men and horses in the most extraordinary manner possible, till they broke and fled in every direction, and then we fell on the infantry.[40]

The 20th cut down the fleeing infantry, but pushed on too far – not for the last time in the Peninsular – and was faced with unbroken French infantry and two more regiments of cavalry. In minutes the 20th had lost its commanding officer and a quarter of its strength, the survivors fleeing back to the British lines.

On the ridge behind Vimeiro, meanwhile, successive French assaults were beaten back. Private Thomas Pococke recorded:

We marched out two miles, to meet the enemy, formed line, and lay under cover of a hill for about an hour, until they came to us. We gave them one volley and three cheers, three distinct cheers. Then all was still as death. They came upon us, crying and shouting, to the very point of our bayonets. Our awful silence and determined advance they could not stand. They put about and fled without much resistance. At this charge we took thirteen guns and one General.*

We advanced into a hollow, and formed again; then returned in file, from the right in companies, to the rear. The French came down upon us again. We gave them another specimen of a charge, as effectual as the first, and pursued them three miles.[41]

By noon the battle was won. The French had lost 2,000 men and 13 guns; Wellesley 720 soldiers. Now was the time to turn victory into rout and, turning to Burrard, Wellesley urged: 'Sir Harry, now is your chance. The French are completely beaten; we have a large body of troops that have not yet been in action. Let us move on Torres Vedras. You take the force here straight forward; I will bring

---

* General Antoine-François Brenier. His captor, Corporal Mackay of the 71st Foot, was rewarded with an ensign's commission.

round the left with the troops already there. We shall be in Lisbon in three days.'[42]

Burrard refused. Still wary of Junot's numerical superiority, he told Wellesley he would advance only when Moore had arrived with reinforcements. Wellesley withdrew in disgust, though later that day he wrote jubilant letters to his brother William and the Duke of Richmond, describing himself as 'the Child of Fortune' and 'the most fortunate man in the world'. Thanks to Junot's overconfidence, he had been able to prove what he had long imagined: that the vaunted French columns could be beaten by well-led, steady troops. Years later he told his friend John Wilson Croker that the French advanced with more confidence at Vimeiro – 'seeming less to *feel their way*' – than they ever would again.[43] Wellesley had not only won the first significant British land victory over French troops in Europe during the Napoleonic Wars, he had destroyed the aura of invincibility that the French Army had possessed since Bonaparte's success at Marengo in 1800.[44]

But victory at Vimeiro was not followed by a vigorous pursuit, and those British troops who had not fought in the battle were the most disappointed. Among them was James Hale, a former militiaman from Gloucestershire, who had joined the 9th Foot a year earlier. He recalled:

> Just in the midst of our glory, we were ordered to halt, and were not permitted to advance any more that day, which caused great murmuring among the army, in particular in such regiments as had not been engaged, for every soldier seemed anxious to push on as we could plainly see that a great part of the French army would have been our prisoners ... had we been permitted to continue the advance ... As Sir Arthur Wellesley was riding up and down in front of our brigade, the men loudly called out to him from one end of the line to the other, saying, 'Let us advance! Let us advance! The enemy is in great confusion!', but his answer was 'I have nothing to do with it: I have no command.'[45]

As ever, the wounded suffered most. One British surgeon witnessed a 'most distressing' scene at a small farmhouse in the battlefield.

'Around the building,' he recorded, 'whose interior was crowded with the wounded',

> lay a number of poor fellows in the greatest agony, not only from the anguish of their wounds, many of which were deplorable, but from the intense heat of the sun, which increased the parching fever induced by pain and loss of blood. Two fig trees afforded the scanty blessing of a sort of shade to the few who were huddled together beneath their almost leafless branches. Over the surrounding field lay scattered the fragments of arms and military equipment of every description – caps, muskets, swords, bayonets, belts and cartouche boxes covered the ground, on which were also stretched in many an awful group, the friend and foe, the dying and the dead.[46]

Next day Wellesley was supervising the evacuation of the wounded from the beach when Sir Hew Dalrymple arrived from Gibraltar to take command. Again Wellesley pressed for an 'immediate advance', but Dalrymple would not agree until he had first spoken with Burrard. At the meeting, to which Wellesley was belatedly invited, Burrard stressed the logistical difficulties of an advance. But no firm decision had been taken by 2 p.m. when Junot's deputy, General François Étienne de Kellermann, appeared under a flag of truce. He had come to offer an armistice.[47]

Convinced his long-term prospects were hopeless, Junot was keen to negotiate an evacuation of French troops from Portugal. All three British generals were happy to do so, not least because, in Wellesley's calculation, the opportunity to destroy Junot's army had gone. So they first discussed terms amongst themselves, and then with Kellermann. Dalrymple later claimed that Wellesley bore 'the prominent part in this discussion'.[48] Wellesley denied this, claiming he had criticized the proposed armistice terms that were then drafted by Dalrymple and Kellermann alone. What is not in doubt, however, is that Wellesley alone signed the document. He did so at Kellermann's request – the justification being that they were both of corresponding rank – and later excused himself on the grounds that he agreed with its terms in principle, if not in detail, and did not want to contradict the wishes of his superior officer. It was a decision he would soon regret.[49]

The formal treaty, the Convention of Cintra, was ratified on 31 August. It stated that all French troops in Portugal would be shipped home by the Royal Navy, and would take with them 'their arms and baggage, with their personal property of every kind' (which, in practice, meant booty that included a Bible from the royal library and two carriages belonging to the Duke of Sussex). Moreover the Russian naval squadron at Lisbon could sail away unmolested, and no reprisals would be taken against those Portuguese who had collaborated with the French. It was, in essence, a treaty that seemed to favour a beaten army, and when its terms were published in the *London Gazette* on 16 September they provoked an outcry. Viscount Sidmouth (formerly Henry Addington), who had himself come to terms with the French in 1802, felt 'every heart must sicken at this break-down of the country's honour.' Wordsworth agreed, proclaiming in a sonnet that 'selfish interest' had led a brave army astray; while Byron devoted no fewer than three stanzas of *Childe Harold's Pilgrimage* to the 'shame' of Cintra.[50] Portland, the prime minister, thought the terms so disadvantageous that it was hard to believe any English officer 'could have sanctioned them'.[51]

Even Wellesley, sensing too late the public's anger, tried to deny responsibility in a letter to Castlereagh. He insisted that the treaty had been negotiated not by him but by Dalrymple; and, though he agreed in principle with the evacuation, he regarded the terms as too generous. This was, in essence, the truth. Yet if Wellesley really had objected to the terms as much as he later claimed, he should have made his feelings known more forcefully at the time. He did not, claimed his biographer Elizabeth Longford, because he was eager to please and had been since childhood. 'It was a weakness of character, perhaps,' wrote Longford, 'though an endearing one.'[52]

For a time, not surprisingly, Wellesley was tarred with the same brush as Dalrymple and Burrard. He returned home in early October to defend himself from attacks in Parliament and the press – by, among others, the former soldier William Cobbett* – and was soon

---

* Cobbett believed that Wellesley was the 'prime cause' of 'all the mischief, and that from the motive of thwarting everything *after he was superseded*' (Longford, *Wellington*, Vol. I, p. 161).

followed by his superiors, both of whom were recalled by government. The subsequent Board of Inquiry, headed by seven generals, was convened in the Royal Hospital at Chelsea on 14 November. Having examined a mass of written and verbal evidence, the board approved the Convention by six votes to one, and its terms by four to three. It was by no means a ringing endorsement of the decisions taken by the three generals, though Wellesley was congratulated for operations that were 'highly honourable and successful', and no blame was attached to him for not following up his victory at Vimeiro. He had just about escaped with his reputation intact. Dalrymple and Burrard were not so fortunate, and would never again command troops in the field.

In Portugal, meanwhile, Lieutenant-General Sir John Moore had taken command of the enlarged British field army of 30,000 troops. With the country now free of French troops, the British government ordered him to cooperate with the Spanish rebels, who had recently inflicted upon Napoleon's armies a string of defeats. The most demoralizing was at Bailén, near the foot of the Sierra Morena in southern Spain, where General Dupont's corps of 17,500 inexperienced men was forced to surrender to the junta forces under General Castaños on 22 July. The terms were similar to Cintra in that they allowed for Dupont's men to be shipped back to France. But the junta shamelessly reneged on the agreement – saying there was no need to play by the rules of war when dealing with a 'captain of bandits' – and instead sent the prisoners to the desolate Isla de Cabrera, south of Mallorca, where 10,000 of them perished.[53]

The Spanish, to be fair, had good reason to resent Dupont's men: Córdoba had been sacked only a few weeks before Bailén. Already the war was assuming the savage nature for which it would become infamous, with mass executions, rapes, and deaths by mutilation, crucifixion, being boiled in oil and buried alive. Yet, in the autumn of 1808 at least, the war was in the balance, and the British government hoped that Moore's arrival in Spain would tip it decisively against Napoleon.

In late October 1808, leaving 10,000 men to garrison Portugal,

Moore set off from Lisbon with an army of 20,000. His intention was to rendezvous at Valladolid in Spain with Lieutenant-General Sir David Baird, who was bringing another 10,000 men from Britain, and a separate column of artillery and cavalry under Lieutenant-General the Honourable John Hope. He had also been promised additional Spanish support of 60,000–70,000 men. But, having reached Salamanca on 13 November, Moore learned that Napoleon himself had entered Spain with seven corps (160,000 men) and forced two Spanish armies to retreat. Moore soon realized that no Spanish help would be forthcoming, and on 28 November took the decision to withdraw to Lisbon, ordering Hope to join him and Baird, who was still 100 miles to the north, to fall back independently to Corunna. 'I conceive the British troops were sent in aid of the Spanish armies,' he wrote by way of explanation to Lord Castlereagh, 'but not singly to resist France, if the Spaniards made no efforts.'[54]

Within a week, responding to a plea from the Spaniards to help them protect Madrid, Moore had changed his mind. He decided to strike east against the French line of communication and ordered Baird to join him. Even when he discovered that he was too late, and that Madrid had fallen to Napoleon on 4 December, he chose to attack a detached French corps that was operating in northern Spain under Marshal Nicolas Soult. He duly crossed the River Douro on the 15th and linked up with Baird on the 20th. A day later his cavalry, under Lieutenant-General Lord Paget (later the second Earl of Uxbridge), brilliantly defeated a brigade of Soult's horsemen at Sahagún. But before he could engage Soult's main force he received word that the French emperor had left Madrid and was marching towards his rear. It was a classic Napoleonic manoeuvre that, but for the Sierra de Guadarrama lying between them, might have succeeded. The two days that Napoleon lost in the mountains, however, meant a forewarned Moore was able to reach Astorga first on 30 December. Already discipline in Moore's army was breaking down as his men – bitterly disappointed that they had not come to grips with the French, and forced to slog through mud-filled roads – were taking out their frustrations on the locals in an orgy of pillage, rape and murder. Moore responded with a General Order of 27 December, chastising his men for their 'extreme bad conduct' at a time when 'they are about to enter into contact with the Enemy, and when the greatest regularity and the best conduct are most requisite'. He added:

> The Spanish Forces have been overpower'd and until such time as they are reassembled and ready again to come forward the situation of this Army must be arduous – and such as to call for the exertion of qualities, the most rare and valuable in a military Body. These are not bravery alone, but patience and constancy under fatigue & Hardship – obedience to command, Sobriety and orderly conduct, firmness and resolution in every difficult situation in which they may be placed: it is by the display of such qualities alone that the Army can expect to deserve the name of Soldiers – that they may be able to withstand the Forces opposed to them, or to fulfil the expectation of their Country.[55]

With no hope of reaching Lisbon, Moore's only option was to withdraw 200 miles north-east to the ports of Corunna and Vigo, through mountainous terrain and in the depth of winter. In a journal entry for 24 December, he foresaw the rigours of the march in 'a country without fuel [where] it is impossible to bivouac; the villages are small, which obliges us to march thus by corps in succession. Our retreat, therefore, becomes much more difficult.'[56] Napoleon, meanwhile, saw little to be gained from a chase he assumed would be futile, and gave command of the pursuing force to Soult and Ney.

Less two brigades that were sent due west to Vigo, Moore's army left Astorga for Corunna on 1 January 1808. Private Thomas Pococke of the 71st Highlanders recorded the horrors of marching that day through a 9-mile snow-clogged mountain pass:

> The silence was only interrupted by the groans of the men, who, unable to proceed farther, laid themselves down in despair to perish in the snow, and where the report of a pistol told the death of a horse, which had fallen down, unable to proceed. I felt an unusual listlessness steal over me. Many times have I said, 'These men who have resigned themselves to their fate are happier than I. What have I to struggle for? Welcome death! Happy deliverer!' These thoughts

passed in my mind involuntarily . . . The rain poured in torrents; the melted snow was half knee-deep in places, and stained by the blood that flowed from our wounded and bruised feet. To add to our misery, we were forced by turns to drag the baggage. This was more than human nature could sustain. Many wagons were abandoned and much ammunition destroyed.[57]

At Villafranca, which the army reached that night, there was more indiscipline, as British soldiers fought Spanish troops for the precious resource of firewood. 'They said one to the other, "Kill him", and began to push me about,' recalled Corporal Benjamin Miller of the Royal Artillery. 'One of them luckily pushed me against the stairs. I immediately ran up,

and told the four men to be on their guard or we should all be killed. One placed himself behind the door and I and the other three stood with our swords drawn. In a few minutes up came three Spanish soldiers with large staves and knives. The man behind the door ran one of them through, and I cut down another and the third had three swords in on him. We left them all for dead . . . On our road to La Coruña we burned down a village because the people would not sell us anything.[58]

During the arduous march from Villafranca to Castro de Rei, Pococke of the 71st was close to giving up. He recalled:

There was nothing to sustain our famished bodies or shelter them from the rain or snow. We were either drenched with rain or crackling with ice. Fuel we could find none. The sick and wounded . . . were now left to perish in the snow . . . Donald McDonald, the hardy Highlander, began to fail. He, as well as myself, had long been barefooted and lame; he that had encouraged me to proceed, now himself lay down to die. For two days he had been almost blind, and unable, from a severe cold, to hold up his head. We sat down together; not a word escaped our lips. We looked around, then at each other, and closed our eyes. We felt there was no hope . . . We had not sat half an hour, sleep was stealing upon me, when I perceived a bustle around me. It was an advanced party of the French. Unconscious of the action, I started upon my feet, levelled my musket, which I had still retained, fired, and formed with the other stragglers. The French faced about and left us. There were more of them than of us. The action, and the approach of danger in a shape which we had it in our power to repel, roused our dormant feelings, and we joined at Castro.[59]

On 6 January, with his army close to disintegration, Moore paused at the town of Vigo to rest his exhausted troops and offer battle to his pursuers. But Soult made only a few probing attacks, easily repulsed by the British outposts, and the retreat continued in darkness on the 8th. Moore had issued general orders that exhorted his men to keep order. 'But, alas!' wrote Pococke. 'How could men observe order amidst such sufferings? . . . The officers, in many points, suffered as much as the men. I have seen officers of the Guards, and others, worth thousands, with pieces of old blankets wrapt round their feet and legs; the men pointing at them, with a malicious satisfaction, saying, "There goes three thousand a year." '[60] He remembered many soldiers drowning their sorrows in drink. 'They lay down intoxicated upon the snow and slept the sleep of death; or, staggering behind, were overtaken and cut down by the merciless French soldiers.'[61]

Also suffering were the hundreds of soldiers' wives and children – many of them unofficial – who always followed the British Army on campaign. Their 'agonies', thought Anthony Hamilton of the 43rd Light Infantry, were 'still more dreadful to behold' than those of the men. He added:

Of these, by some strange neglect, or by some mistaken sentiment of humanity, an unusually large proportion had been suffered to accompany the army. Some of these unhappy creatures were taken in labour on the road, and amidst the storms of sleet and snow gave birth to infants, which, with their mothers, perished as soon as they had seen the light . . . Others in the unconquerable energy of maternal love would toil on with one or two children on their backs; till on looking round, they perceived that the hapless objects of their affections were frozen to death.[62]

Finally, on 11 January 1809, Moore's depleted and exhausted force reached Corunna. It was, wrote Moore, 'completely disorganized' and its 'conduct during the late march has been infamous beyond belief'.[63] To the ordinary soldiers, however, the sight of the ocean promised deliverance. 'I felt all my former despondency drop from my mind,' wrote Pococke. 'My galled feet trod lighter on the icy road. Every face near me seemed to brighten up. Britain and the sea are two words which cannot be disunited. The sea and home appeared one and the same.'[64]

Moore could not begin the evacuation until the transports, delayed by contrary winds, arrived from Vigo on 14 January. The day before, in his last letter to Lord Castlereagh, he had promised to 'accept no terms that are in the least dishonourable to the Army, or to the Country'.[65] By then the French had arrived in force, and on the 14th began a 'cannonade' on the British position in the hills above the harbour. It did not prevent Moore from embarking the sick and the dismounted cavalry, and all but eight of his guns – seven 6-pounders and a howitzer – which were placed in line while four Spanish guns were kept in reserve. Having helped his sick friend Donald McDonald aboard one of the transports, Private Pococke was returning to camp when he witnessed a 'most moving' scene: 'The beach was covered with dead horses, and resounded with the reports of the pistols that were carrying this havoc amongst them. The animals, as if warned by the dead bodies of their fellows, appeared frantic, neighed and screamed in a most frightful manner. Many broke loose and galloped alongst the beach with their manes erect and their mouths wide open.'[66]

The main embarkation of the 15,000 infantrymen was scheduled for 4 p.m. on the 16th. Two and a half hours before it was due to begin, Soult began his attack on the right wing of Moore's defences along the Monte Mero ridge, 2 miles south of Corunna. The first attack by two 'very compact columns' was against Lord William Bentinck's brigade of the 4th, 42nd and 50th regiments of foot. A 23-year-old private in the 42nd Black Watch recalled:

Our artillery fired a few shots, and then retreated for want of ammunition. Our flankers were sent out to assist the pickets. The French soon formed line and advanced, driving the pickets and flankers before them, while their artillery kept up a close cannonade on our line with grape and round shot. A few of the Forty-Second were killed, and some were wounded . . . We had not then moved an inch in advance or retreat. Sir John came in front of the Forty-Second. He said, 'There is no use in making a long speech, but, Forty-Second, I hope you will do as you have done before.' With that he rode off the ground in front of us . . . Our colonel gave orders for us to lie on the ground at the back of the height our position was on, and, whenever the French were within a few yards of us, we were to start up and fire our muskets, and then give them the bayonet. They came up the hill cheering as if there were none to oppose them, we being out of sight. When they came to the top of the hill, all the word of command that was given was 'Forty-Second: charge!' In one moment, every man was up . . . and every shot did execution. They were so close upon us we gave them the bayonet the instant we fired . . . and many of us skewered pairs, front and rear rank. To the right about they went, and we after them . . . When we had driven them in upon their other columns, we ourselves retreated.[67]

The rest of Bentinck's brigade played its part, with Moore ordering the right-most battalion, the 4th, to refuse its flank so that it could fire into the side of the longer enemy line. At around the same time the 50th, 'climbing over an enclosure, got right in front of the French, charged and drove them out of the village of Elvina'.[68] Moore had already survived a number of near misses when, just as the Black Watch went into action, he was knocked from his horse by a cannon ball that, according to his aide-de-camp, Captain Henry Hardinge (a future commander-in-chief of the British Army), 'carried away his left shoulder and part of the collar-bone, leaving the arm hanging by the flesh'. Hardinge added:

The violence of the stroke threw him off the horse, on his back. Not a muscle of his face altered, nor did a sigh betray the least sensation of pain. I dismounted and, taking his hand, he pressed mine forcibly, casting his eyes very anxiously towards the Forty-Second Regiment, which was hotly engaged, and his countenance expressed satisfaction when I informed him that the regiment was advancing. Assisted by a soldier from the Forty-Second, he was removed a few yards behind the shelter of a wall . . . The blood flowed fast; but the attempt to stop it with my sash was useless from the size of the wound. Sir John assented to being removed in a blanket to the rear. In raising him for this purpose, his sword, hanging on the wounded side, touched his arm, and became entangled with his legs. I perceived the inconvenience, and was in the act of unbuckling it from his waist, when he said in his usual tone and manner, and in a very distinct voice, 'It is well as it is: I had rather it should go out of the field with me.'[69]

Observing the 'resolution and composure' of Moore's features, Hardinge expressed a hope that, once the wound had been dressed, his chief might recover. But Moore had no illusions. 'No, Hardinge,' he responded. 'I feel that to be impossible.'[70]

With Moore's deputy, Sir David Baird, also badly wounded, the command passed to Lieutenant-General the Honourable John Hope, who wrote later:

The Enemy, finding himself foiled in every attempt to force the right of the position, endeavoured by numbers to turn it. A judicious and well-timed movement which was made by Major-General Paget, with the reserve, which corps had moved out of its cantonments to support the right of the army, by a vigorous attack, defeated this intention [Further attacks on the centre and left of the British line were also pushed back, the latter by the 14th Foot] . . . Before five in the evening, we had not only successfully repelled every attack made upon the position, but had gained ground in almost all points, and occupied a more forward line than at the commencement of the action . . . At six the firing ceased.[71]

Moore, meanwhile, had been carried to his quarters in the town and laid on a mattress. On hearing that all French attacks had been repulsed, he exclaimed: 'I hope the people of England will be satisfied. I hope my country will do me justice.'[72]

He died shortly before 8 p.m. and, in accordance with his wishes, was buried the following morning in a grave dug within the landward bastion of the citadel of Corunna by the soldiers of the 9th Foot. Already the bulk of the army had been evacuated under the cover of darkness. It only remained for the reserve and rearguard to take ship. 'We were scarcely arrived on the beach,' recorded Pococke, 'ere the French began to fire upon the transports in the harbour.'[73] Several transports ran aground and had to be burned. But eventually the French guns were silenced by counter-fire from the Royal Navy and the rescue continued, with the last soldiers embarking at one in the morning of 18 January.

Nine days later the ships arrived at Portsmouth. 'Nothing,' wrote Benjamin Harris of the 95th Rifles, 'could exceed the dreadful appearance we cut on the occasion of the disembarkation from La Coruña, and the inhabitants of Portsmouth, who had assembled in some numbers to see us land, were horror-stricken with the sight of their countrymen . . . with feet swathed in bloody rags, clothing that hardly covered their nakedness, accoutrements in shreds, beards covering their faces, eyes dimmed with toil (for some were even blind), arms nearly useless to those who had them left, the rifles being encrusted with rust and the swords glued to the scabbard.'[74]

Some, like the men of the 71st Highlanders, were not allowed to land until they had been given new uniforms to look more respectable. Once on shore, the people showed them 'all manner of kindness, carrying the lame and leading the blind'. Private Pococke recalled: 'We were received into every house as if we had been their own relations. How proud did I feel to belong to such a people!'[75]

The 5,000–6,000 wounded or sick – around a fifth of the 28,000 British troops evacuated from Corunna – presented a particularly formidable logistical problem, because many of the south-coast general hospitals had been closed to save money and the ones that remained were quickly overwhelmed. Fortunately the local deputy inspector of hospitals, James McGrigor, was a highly motivated doctor who would become a very effective senior medical officer in the Peninsula. He set up temporary hospitals in barracks, ships and hulks, and recruited extra doctors in the form of military surgeons from the Household Brigade in London, medical students and civilian volunteers. Among the last was Charles Bell, thirty-four, a brilliant

Edinburgh-born surgeon and anatomist who at the time was lecturing in medicine in London. Determined to help, Bell hurried down to the Haslar Hospital in Portsmouth – put at the disposal of the army by the Royal Navy – and, for the future instruction of his students, produced annotated sketches of his cases that were later completed in oils. Perhaps the most grotesque is of a soldier wounded in the scrotum, the ball passing 'through both testicles without touching the thighs'.[76] The scrotum is depicted as grotesquely swollen thanks to bruising, inflammation and sepsis. Bell does not mention the unfortunate soldier's fate, though it is likely that he succumbed to Fournier's Gangrene, a bacterial infection of the scrotum that was often fatal. Another patient died from 'loss of blood' after his badly wounded arm was amputated at the shoulder, prompting Bell to comment that the method of operating 'followed by our army surgeons was too bold, and not suited to common practice, and especially in the case like this, when the patient was reduced by a complication in the wound'.[77] Many more recovered from wounds and illnesses, including a patient of Bell's who had been shot through the chest, the ball narrowly missing his liver.[78] But the overall mortality rate at Portsmouth – where 405 (or 17 per cent) of the 2,427 sick and wounded did not survive – was higher than average for general military hospitals at the time, and Bell put it down partly to the relatively poor quality of army surgeons compared to civil doctors.[79]

Overall the Corunna campaign had been a strategic disaster: 6,000 British troops were lost during the retreat (at least a third of them taken prisoner), and Spain abandoned to the French. Moore, inevitably, was the focus of much criticism from the government for marching deeper into Spain when the odds were so heavily stacked against him. The issue quickly became politicized when the Whig Opposition defended him and attacked the government for its handling of the campaign. Yet no one could deny that Moore's march to Corunna, and stubborn repulse of Soult outside the port, had both saved the bulk of the British Army in the Peninsula and diverted the French to north-west Spain, thus preventing Napoleon from immediately occupying either the south of the country or Portugal. He had, in other words, made it possible to continue the war in the Peninsula.

The Duke of York, preoccupied with his former mistress's accusation of corruption, still found time to praise the dead Moore in a General Order of 1 February: 'During the seasons of repose, his time was devoted to the care and instruction of the officers and soldiers. In war he courted service in every quarter of the globe . . . his virtues live in the recollection of his associates, and his fame remains the strongest incentive to great and glorious action.'[80]

An even more effusive tribute was written by one of Moore's senior officers. 'Like the immortal Wolfe,' wrote Hope to Baird on 18 January, 'he is snatched from his Country at an early period of life spent in her service; like Wolfe, his last moments were guided by the prospect of success, and cheered by the acclamation of victory; like Wolfe also, his memory will for ever remain sacred in that Country which he sincerely loved, and which he had so faithfully served.'[81]

This is, perhaps, going a little too far. Corunna, for all its saving graces, was hardly a victory to set alongside Wolfe's at Quebec. Yet Moore's development of light troops did leave a significant military legacy, and his opponent Marshal Soult would later pay generous tribute to his military skill in the Peninsular.

Perhaps the greatest short-term impact of Moore's death, and Baird's loss of an arm, is that it made possible the rehabilitation of the semi-disgraced Sir Arthur Wellesley, now back in Ireland as chief secretary. Before his death, Moore had claimed that if Spain fell to the French, Portugal could not survive. Many in government were of the same mind, and there was little support for a second expeditionary force to shore up the 10,000 British troops still in Portugal under Sir John 'Beau' Cradock. But Wellesley did not agree, and set out his argument in a memorandum of 7 March 1809 to Lord Castlereagh. 'I have,' he wrote, 'always been of opinion that Portugal might be defended whatever the result of the contest in Spain.' But to do so, he added, would require a British force of 30,000 men, including 4,000 cavalry; a Portuguese Army restructured under British command; and the Spaniards to keep at least some of the French pinned down in their country.[82]

Castlereagh was persuaded and, thanks to his strong advocacy, so were his cabinet colleagues. It remained only to convince George III, who, until now, had not been Wellesley's keenest advocate. Yet he had accepted the verdict of the Board of Officers on the Cintra issue and, with Moore no longer available, was prepared to sanction Wellesley's appointment. It helped, too, that the hostile Duke of York was in the process of stepping down as commander-in-chief. Wellesley's instructions were to consider the defence of Portugal 'as the first and most immediate object of your attention'. He was to use his discretion on when and how to cooperate with the Spanish, but only after receiving the sanction of the British government.[83]

This suited Wellesley. Having studied the Corunna campaign in detail, he had come to the conclusion that the Spanish armies were too disorganized, and the British too few in number, to take on the French in open battle on the great plains of the Peninsula. He felt, on the other hand, the rugged mountainous terrain, especially in Portugal, offered good opportunities for defence. He thus conceived what he would later describe as his 'cautious system', building up British troop strength in Portugal, nurturing the infant Portuguese Army and striking at the French from a secure base. The war, he believed, would be ended not by a single brilliant campaign but by a long process of attrition.[84]

19.   The 'Cautious System'

On 22 April 1809, barely six months since his unhappy departure, Sir Arthur Wellesley stepped ashore in Lisbon to a hero's welcome. He had been appointed marshal-general of all forces in Portugal and, with Cintra now forgotten, the famous Black Horse Square was packed with 'groups dancing to castanets and drums, plump ladies in painted litters', gentlemen with tricorne hats bearing the motto 'Conquer or Die', 'peasants in long straw cloaks, white shirts, blue drawers and black shovel hats', and 'ballad singers thumping out future triumphs for Arthur Wellesley on guitars'.[1]

For all this public rejoicing, the strategic outlook was far from encouraging: Soult had overrun northern Portugal and was at Oporto with 20,000 men; a similar force, under Ney, was in neighbouring Galicia, while Marshal Claude Victor stood poised at Mérida to invade central Portugal with an even larger army. A lesser general would have waited on events. Not least because the twenty-five British infantry battalions available to Wellesley were mostly under-strength home-service formations, and of poorer quality than those Moore had commanded. Only five, for example, had fought with Wellesley at Vimeiro. He had, in addition, just four cavalry regiments and lacked money, experienced commissaries and artillery horses. Nonetheless, he chose to take the initiative by gathering oxen, mules and horses to transport the bulk of his army north to Oporto, leaving smaller forces – one under Lieutenant-General Sir William Beresford, the new commander of the Portuguese Army – to watch Victor and prevent a junction with Soult.

The Oporto campaign was a model of daring leadership. Having crossed the River Douro under fire on 12 May, Wellesley drove Soult first out of Oporto and then out of northern Portugal, inflicting 4,000 casualties at a cost of only 500 men. The one cloud on Wellesley's horizon was the continued indiscipline of the ordinary soldiers, who, he told Castlereagh on 31 May, 'cannot bear success any more than Sir J. Moore's army could bear failure'. It was, he added on 17 June, 'impossible to describe the irregularities and outrages committed by the troops'. In his opinion, the men would do their duty only if they feared punishment or hoped for reward. Yet he had 'not the power of rewarding, or promising a reward to a single officer in the army', and his ability to punish was also too limited: the sentences handed down by regimental courts martial were not severe enough, and he needed more provost staff to keep order.[2]

A graphic example of British indiscipline on the march was provided by John Cooper, a 23-year-old private in the 7th Fusiliers, who remembered his whole battalion, after one particularly long and wet march, being 'turned like bullocks into a damp church'. The men promptly tore apart the priests' stalls to provide wood for a fire. Cooper recorded:

> The crashing of wood, the bawling and swearing of hundreds in the building [and] the choking smoke that completely filled the edifice were awful, and when darkness set in the place was a perfect pandemonium. During the uproar a large box of wax candles was found [and many lighted], and the scene was complete and fit for Hogarth's pencil . . . At this period the English troops made sad work of Portugal by plundering the inhabitants. No sooner was the day's march ended than the men turned out to steal pigs, poultry, wine, etc.[3]

Castlereagh could not solve the problem of discipline, but he could free Wellesley's hands in terms of strategy, and on 11 June, having heard that Portugal was clear of French troops, he gave the forty-year-old general permission to operate inside Spain. Wellesley's plan was to cross the border near the Spanish fortress of Badajoz and, with help from a Spanish army under General Gregorio de la Cuesta, defeat Marshal Victor before liberating Madrid. It was, perhaps, an overly ambitious strategy, relying as it did on Spanish promises to supply his army and tie down any other French forces so they could not intervene. Wellesley had yet to experience defeat in a major action, and his early success at Oporto may have imbued him with a sense of overconfidence.

The operation started promisingly when Wellesley's army of 20,000 men linked up with 35,000 Spaniards under General Cuesta at Oropesa, 30 miles west of Victor's position at Talavera, on 21 July. A day later the Allies pushed Victor's advanced posts back through Talavera to the River Alberche. But the planned attack on the 23rd – with the Spaniards assaulting across the river, while the British attempted to turn Victor's position from the north – never took place because the Spanish troops, according to the 68-year-old Cuesta, were too tired to fight that day. Cuesta agreed to advance on the 24th, but by then Victor had slipped away. Wellesley was running out of supplies and could march no further, so Cuesta pursued Victor towards Toledo alone. En route he discovered that Victor had been reinforced by troops from both Madrid and further south, and that a combined French army of 40,000 veterans, under the personal command of King Joseph, was heading his way. Cuesta promptly fell back towards Wellesley, with the French in hot pursuit.

The Allies decided to make their stand behind the shallow Portina Stream that bisected a mile-wide plain that ran north from the walled town of Talavera: the Spanish holding the stronger southern sector, protected by a redoubt and breastworks, from the town walls to a hill called the Pajar de Vergara; and the British defending the open country from the base of the Pajar to another hill known as the Cerro de Medellin. On 27 July, Wellesley moved two divisions forward to cover the withdrawal of the Spanish to the Portina, and was looking through his telescope from the tower of a strongly built farmhouse when he noticed French light troops approaching. With only seconds to spare, he and his staff clattered down the stone steps and escaped on horseback, pursued by musket-shots. It was the closest he came to capture during the Peninsular War. 'If the French had been cool,' he confided later, 'they might have taken us all.'[4] The French did, however, manage to surprise one of his brigades that had stopped for an impromptu siesta, inflicting more than 440 casualties at a cost to the enemy of just one hundred.

That evening, the French launched another surprise attack across the Portina and briefly seized from the King's German Legion* the

---

* A first-rate formation of exiles from the French-occupied Kingdom of Hanover.

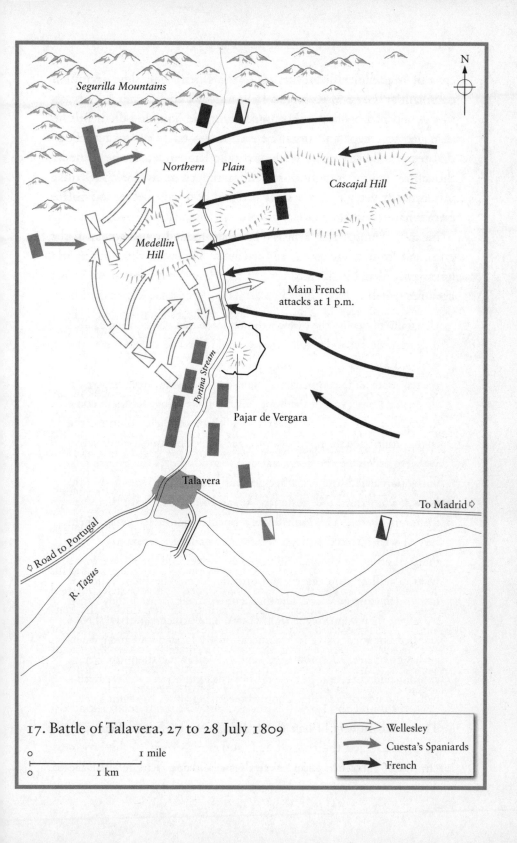

Segurilla Mountains

Northern Plain

Cascajal Hill

Medellin Hill

Main French attacks at 1 p.m.

Portina Stream

Pajar de Vergara

Talavera

To Madrid ◇

◇ Road to Portugal

R. Tagus

N

17. Battle of Talavera, 27 to 28 July 1809

0   1 mile

0   1 km

Wellesley

Cuesta's Spaniards

French

crest of Medellin Hill on the left of the British line. The divisional commander, General Rowland Hill, mistook the French for British troops and had his horse shot under him and an aide killed. But he managed to escape and organize a counter-attack by the 29th Foot that recaptured the crest. Wellesley, who had ridden to the scene of the action, slept that night on the hill, wrapped in his cloak. He could not know it yet, but both sides had lost 300 men before the battle proper had even begun.

Next morning, after a heavy bombardment by more than sixty guns, the French again attacked Medellin Hill with three huge columns preceded by skirmishers. Ensign Charles Leslie of the 29th Foot recorded:

> General Hill, seeing the overwhelming force that was coming against us, gave orders that the light troops should be recalled, and the bugles sounded accordingly. The skirmishers were closing in and filing to the rear with all the regularity of field-day and parade exercise, which the general observing, called out, 'Damn their filing; let them come in anyhow.' In order to cover the advance of their columns, the enemy continued the terrific cannonade, which became so destructive we were ordered to lie down flat on the ground. [As the French column approached, the brigadier-general] said 'Now, Twenty-Ninth! Now is your time!' We instantly sprang to our feet, gave three tremendous cheers, and immediately opened our fire, giving them several well-directed volleys, which they gallantly returned . . . We then got orders to charge, which was no sooner said than done. In we went, a wall of stout hearts and bristling steel. The French did not fancy such close quarters. The moment we made the rush they began to waver, then went to the right about. The principal portion broke and fled but some brave fellows occasionally faced about and gave us an irregular fire. We, however, kept . . . following them up, firing, running and cheering. In the midst of the exultation . . . I received a ball in the side of my thigh about three inches above the right knee.[5]

There was now a lull in the fighting, as the French and British infantry recovered their wounded, and went down to the brook to fetch water. Around noon Wellesley could see a huge dust cloud ahead, heralding the arrival of an extra 15,000 French troops – the corps of Generals Horace Sébastiani and Pierre Lapisse – giving Joseph an army of 55,000 men, most of whom were concentrated against the northern sector of the Anglo-Spanish line held by the British. Fearing he might be outflanked, he asked Cuesta for reinforcements and sent them to the northern end of his line, between the Medellin and the Segurilla mountains, from where he suspected a new attack might come.

Instead, at around 1 p.m., eighty French guns concentrated their fire on the centre of the line between the Pajar and the Medellin, while 30,000 infantrymen advanced in huge columns. Sergeant Andrew Pearson of the 61st Foot recalled:

> They advanced, the front ranks firing from the hip, and, when within fifty yards of the [stream], they halted and opened a murderous fire on our columns. Sir Arthur Wellesley immediately saw that were the divisions allowed to stand they could be cut down, and he accordingly ordered them to lie down ... The French, gaining courage from our apparent cowardice, advanced across the [stream] and moved up the opposite bank. It was too much for us to lie any longer, and, leaping up, we gave the well-known British cheer and charged. This was a movement for which they were not prepared, and we soon broke their front ranks, when they immediately fell back on the dense columns in the rear.[6]

This success was replicated all along the front: British musketry fire[7] and bayonet charges broke up the French columns as they tried to deploy into line. Most of the British troops then returned to their former positions. But one division – General John Sherbrooke's, which was posted just north of the Pajar – did not. 'The whole division,' recalled Anthony Hamilton of the 1st Battalion of Detachments (a unit cobbled together from invalids and stragglers from Moore's army), 'as if moved by one powerful and undivided impulse, advanced to meet [the French], and, pouring in a most galling and destructive fire, their ranks were speedily broken and they gave way.'[8] Soon after, Hamilton's skull was fractured by a piece of shell. But his comrades in the division continued their pursuit of the

French over the brook. One brigade, Campbell's, managed to re-form on the other side; but the remaining three, including the Guards' Brigade, carried on until they were counter-attacked and driven back with huge losses by the French reserves. The 2nd (Coldstream) Guards alone lost twelve officers and 300 men killed and wounded.[9]

There was now a gaping hole in the centre of Wellesley's line that the French tried to exploit by sending forward 10,000 infantrymen in columns, supported by dragoons and artillery. Fortunately Wellesley had observed Sherbrooke's unauthorized advance – one he would describe later as 'nearly fatal to us' – and at once ordered reserves from the Medellin and further south to seal the gap. First on the scene was the 1/48th Foot, the biggest battalion in the army, which wheeled its companies to allow the survivors of Sherbrooke's div-ision to pass through, and then re-formed its two-rank line to halt and push the French back over the stream. The battle was won when the southernmost French column was charged and routed by General Stapleton Cotton's cavalry brigade.[10]

The only other cavalry charge that day was against French col-umns advancing north of the Medellin. Most historians treat it as a postscript to the main battle, and assume it took place after the decisive action in the centre of the British line; Wellesley, on the other hand, thought it took place *before* Sherbrooke's advance. Either way, it was only partially successful, and cost the 23rd Light Drag-oons almost half its officers and men, the victims of a concealed chasm, French infantry squares★ and a regiment of Polish lancers. For once, Wellesley was magnanimous, noting in his dispatch that the charge 'had the effect of preventing the execution of that part of the enemy's plan'.[11]

By late afternoon the battle was won, though the French waited until nightfall to withdraw back across the River Alberche. They had lost 20 guns and 7,000 men, killed and wounded. British casualties were 5,365 men, almost a third of those engaged. So numerous were the dead that Wellesley ordered the bodies to be burned rather than

---

★ An infantry square was formed of multiple ranks in each face, hollow in the centre, and was the approved tactic in most European armies for repelling horsemen.

buried. 'This was certainly a more convenient,' wrote Sergeant Andrew Pearson of the 61st, 'though to not a few a more revolting way of disposing of our comrades.' Appointed orderly sergeant to Wellesley himself, Pearson made his way to the British headquarters in Talavera, where a 'most appalling sight presented itself'.

> The streets [he wrote] were lined with the dead and dying, indis-criminately heaped in piles, a narrow passage to enable us to pass along being the only space unoccupied by the carcasses of the sol-diers. The first man that caught my eye was a corporal of my company, who was dragging himself along, carrying his bowels in his clasped hands. He had been cut across the abdomen by grape shot, but he did not go far till, from pain and exhaustion, he fell down and died . . . The groanings of the wounded were the only sounds that greeted the ear, and painful they were, while each man, as he passed along the piles of dead and dying, seemed borne down with grief and horror.[12]

John Timewell, a private in the 43rd Light Infantry who reached Talavera the day after the battle, was shocked at the number of corpses 'gathered in great heaps and Burned for the smell was so great that no soldier could stand it'.[13]

Though sickened by the carnage, Wellesley put the 'great loss' of 'valuable Officers and Soldiers' in perspective when he noted that his opponents had 'more than double our numbers'.[14] This was true, in so far as the French had concentrated their efforts against the more vulnerable British sector of the line, leaving most of the Spanish troops to cope with nothing more severe than an artillery bombard-ment. For some this was enough. 'The Spaniards,' noted a German commissary, 'unaccustomed to the endurance of the English, and losing heart at the sight [of the main French attack] . . . dashed head-long in masses through the town, and, mixed up with vast quantities of baggage, blocked the street . . . I watched this amazing tumult with amazement.'[15]

Back home, Talavera was lauded as another glorious victory over the French and Wellesley was rewarded with a viscountcy. With no time to consult him over the title, his brother William chose 'Vis-count Wellington of Talavera and Wellington, and Baron Douro of

Welleslie in the county of Somerset'. The town of Wellington was near Welleslie, explained William, and he hoped his brother would not find 'anything unpleasant or trifling' in his choice of title. Wellesley did not, and used his new name for the first time on 16 September 1809 when he signed a letter about 'biscuits and cash balances' to John Villiers, the British envoy in Lisbon.[16]

Wellington later described the Battle of Talavera as 'the hardest fought of modern days'. He added: 'The fire at Assaye was heavier while it lasted; but the battle of Talavera lasted for two days and a night.'[17] It was, moreoever, the closest he had yet come to defeat, and undoubtedly shook his confidence. 'If Vimeiro had been a near run thing,' wrote Paddy Griffith in his study of Wellesley's generalship, 'Talavera was much, much nearer . . . The whole episode was so laden with disappointments and narrow escapes that it stamped a new prudence onto his hitherto recklessly aggressive style of operations. After Talavera, Wellington at last started to believe that his army might be beaten unless it was very carefully husbanded, and for a short time he even seemed to think that an evacuation of the whole Peninsula would eventually be necessary.'[18]

The despondency would not last; but the caution did, and it was justified by two serious setbacks to Allied arms in 1809 that tipped the balance in the Peninsular War still further towards the French. In March, hoping to take advantage of French distractions in the Peninsular, the Austrians had re-entered the war as part of a Fifth Coalition* and, two months later, the Archduke Charles defeated Napoleon's Grand Army of Germany as it attempted to cross the Danube at Aspern-Essling. It was the first time that the emperor had been bested in battle since Caldiero in 1796, and encouraged Portland's government to send an expeditionary force to the Scheldt Estuary to capture the vital port of Antwerp. But even as the campaign got under way

---

* The short-lived Fourth Coalition of Prussia, Russia, Saxony, Sweden and the United Kingdom had ended after France defeated the Prussians at Jena-Auerstädt and the Russians at Friedland in October 1806 and June 1807 respectively. The Fifth Coalition was formed in 1809 by Austria, the United Kingdom, Spain, Sicily and Sardinia.

in early July, Napoleon was gaining revenge for Aspern by narrowly defeating Archduke Charles at Wagram in a brutal two-day struggle that left the field strewn with more than 50,000 killed and wounded, and soon caused the Emperor Francis I to sue for peace. Undeterred, the British expeditionary force invested Flushing, taking it after a two-week siege. But this gave the French time to strengthen Antwerp's defences, and by the time the majority of troops had been landed on the islands of Walcheren and South Beveland, preparatory to an assault, the British commanders were united in their belief that their main objective could no longer be taken. Most of the men were re-embarked in mid-September, though a strong force was left on Walcheren to keep the Scheldt open to British trade. It, too, was evacuated in December after fever on the marshy island had decimated its ranks.

The political fallout from the Scheldt fiasco was a duel between Lord Castlereagh and George Canning, the foreign secretary, which ended with the latter wounded, both resigning and the collapse of Portland's government. It was replaced in October 1809 by another Tory administration, led by Spencer Perceval, with Lords Bathurst and Liverpool as foreign and war secretaries respectively. The newly ennobled Lord Wellington was thereby deprived of his most influential government supporter, Castlereagh, and became even more cautious in his military operations as a result.

He had wanted to take advantage of victory at Talavera by recapturing Madrid. But Cuesta's troops were 'not in a state of discipline' to attempt such a manoeuvre, he wrote in a private memorandum, and word soon reached him that Soult was approaching from the north.[19] He therefore agreed with Cuesta that he would march to Oropesa to intercept Soult, while the Spaniards remained in Talavera to watch King Joseph and guard the British wounded. But, having reached Oropesa on 3 August, Wellington heard two disastrous pieces of news: the Austrians had made peace with Napoleon, thereby freeing up more French troops for the Peninsula; and Cuesta had gone back on his word by abandoning Talavera, and the 1,500 British wounded, to the French.

Wellington was incandescent with rage, and this betrayal, coupled with the junta's failure to supply his army with food and transport, caused him to withdraw into Portugal to prepare for the inevitable French onslaught. The retreat to Badajoz on the frontier, through a 'desolate region' with 'nothing but rugged mountains on all sides', was a harrowing experience to compare with Corunna. Private John Cooper of the 7th Fusiliers wrote:

> Notwithstanding our weak state through want of food, we had to drag the artillery by ropes up some steep mountains, as horses could not keep on their feet. Great numbers of these animals died. Stores and cannon were buried. Men looked like skeletons. Our clothing was in rags; shirts, shoes and stockings were worn out and there was no bread . . . Tents during this campaign we had none, nor yet blankets. We slept in the open air, and this was the mode: the greatcoat was inverted and our legs thrust into the sleeves.[20]

The pillaging of Spanish settlements was inevitable, and the chief culprits were often women. Even when they paid for food, the soldiers' wives managed to provoke Wellington's fury by ranging ahead of the columns and leaving nothing for the commissariat to buy for the troops. Wellington's response was to have them beaten with the cat-o'-nine-tails. On one occasion, a dozen women were given 'sax and thirty lashes a piece on the bare doup', according to a Highland soldier who witnessed the punishment, 'and it was lang afore it was forgotten on 'em'.[21] Years later, responding to criticism of these harsh measures, Wellington declared: 'It is well known that in all armies the Women are at least as bad, if not worse, than the men, as Plunderers! And the exemption of the Ladies would have encouraged Plunder!' The flogging of women would not be outlawed in England until 1817.[22]

On 20 October, having carried out a personal reconnaissance of the Lisbon Peninsula, he set out his strategy in a memorandum to his chief engineer, Lieutenant-Colonel Richard Fletcher. He tasked Fletcher with creating three lines of fortification across the peninsula: the first from Alhandra on the Tagus, via the town of Torres Vedras, and on to the coast; the second, 6 miles further south; and the third, centred on Forte de São Julião at the entrance to the Tagus, to cover an embarkation. Rivers were to be dammed and roads broken up to disrupt the French advance, while forts were built on high ground, and connected by trenches and ramparts. Wellington also set about strengthening the Portuguese Army by incorporating a brigade into each of his divisions, and by reorganizing the local militia. 'The whole of Portugal was converted into a gigantic trap for the French,' wrote Paddy Griffith, 'who were to be allowed free access into a countryside denuded of food supplies – but denied either a decisive battle or access to Lisbon and its essential harbour.'[23]

For the next two years Wellington pursued this essentially cautious strategy with great success. He won defensive battles against the vaunted Marshal Masséna at Busaco Ridge in September 1810 and, more narrowly, at Fuentes de Oñoro the following May. The climax of the latter battle was a bitter fight for the town of Fuentes, with Thomas Pococke's 71st Highlanders in the thick of the action:

> We advanced as quick as we could [wrote Pococke] and met the light companies retreating as fast as they could. We continued to advance, at double quick time, our firelocks at the trail, our bonnets in our hands. They called to us, 'Seventy-First, you will come back quicker than you advance.' We soon came full in front of the enemy. The Colonel cries, 'Here is food, my lads, cut away.' Thrice we waved our bonnets, and thrice we cheered; brought our firelocks to the charge, and forced them back through the town . . .
>
> During our first advance, a bayonet went between my side and clothes, to my knapsack, which stopped its progress. The Frenchman to whom the bayonet belonged fell, pierced by a musket ball from my rear-rank man. Whilst freeing myself from the bayonet, a ball took off part of my right shoulder wing and killed my rear-rank man, who fell upon me. Narrow as this escape was, I felt no uneasiness.[24]

Having cleared the town, the 71st unwisely continued their pursuit of the beaten French and were counter-attacked by cavalry. They retreated to the town and, during one halt 'to check the enemy', Pococke remembered standing 'with a foot upon each side of a wounded man, who . . . pierced my heart with his cries to be lifted out of the way of the cavalry'. That night, Pococke's shoulder 'was as black as a coal' from the recoil of his musket; he had fired 107 rounds of ball-cartridge.[25]

At Fuentes, in particular, Wellington's new defensive tactics – the clever use of ground and outposts in depth to protect his main line from enemy fire until the last possible moment – worked beautifully and in 'four days on an indifferent position' he 'lost scarcely more men than he had in a morning at Busaco on the strongest position in Portugal; some 1,600 as against 1,200, or less than a third of the casualties suffered at Talavera'.[26]

Wellington has been criticized by some historians for being too passive during this period, and for letting pass 'many excellent opportunities' for destroying French armies in battle. At Busaco Ridge, for example, he repulsed several attacks 'in a most convincing manner but failed once again to finish the business with a decisive counterstroke; and at Fuentes, too, he 'decided against a counter-offensive' both 'because the French remained too strong' and because such a move 'might uncover the siege of Almeida'.[27]

However, Wellington had good reason to be circumspect. Strung out on lengthy lines of communication that stretched by sea back to Britain, and without the reserves of manpower available to the French, he could not afford to risk a decisive defeat. And a measure of how the alliance would have fared without Wellington was given on 16 May 1811, barely a week after Fuentes, when Marshal Soult came within an ace of trouncing Beresford's Anglo-Portuguese-Spanish army at Albuera. The situation was saved when a bright staff officer, Major Henry Hardinge, persuaded the commander of the reserve, General Lowry Cole, to move his two weak brigades forward without orders to retake the height that had just been lost by the 2nd Division. A member of the Fusilier Brigade that led the charge was Lieutenant John Harrison of the 1/23rd. He wrote to his mother:

> Some Cavalry arriving on our right to divert the attention of the Enemy's Cavalry, our Brigade advanced at a steady pace reserving our fire and leaving the Portuguese brigade to join our second line. The French Infantry were formed on an eminence and we had every dis-

advantage of the ground. They soon opened fire. We returned it handsomely, came down to the charge, and cheered. They faced about after a few paces and others coming to their assistance the contest soon became general and a most determined fire kept up on both sides, so near almost *muzzle to muzzle*. They again drew us on by showing us their backs, and we twice repeated the former treatment. This work lasted some time, they continuing to bring up fresh regiments, our brigade being much broken by its loss, *not above one third of our men were standing* . . . I had a close shave when we first went into action, a ball passed through the centre of my cap, taking the point of my hair and went through several folds of my pocket handkerchief which was in my cap.[28]

Harrison's battalion alone lost 14 officers and 319 men killed and wounded out of a total of 540, an almost unprecedented casualty rate for an unbeaten unit of 62 per cent (and even greater than the Black Watch losses at Ticonderoga).[29]

It was a victory of sorts – as Soult eventually withdrew – but so severe were Beresford's 6,000 casualties (two thirds of them British infantrymen), and so violent was the criticism of his handling of the battle, that the government felt it had no option but to relieve him of his command on 27 May. 'The Marshal is confin'd to his bed by a *severe fever*,' wrote an English correspondent from Lisbon two days later. 'Poor man, he has not philosophy to bear up against the Buffets of Military Critics who attack on all quarters. You know not the severity with which he is treated.'[30]

Before Albuera, Beresford had been conducting the siege of the frontier fortress of Badajoz. Wellington now arrived to take personal command, bringing reinforcements from the north. But two attempts to storm the outlying fort of San Cristóbal, to the north of the town, were easily beaten off and, with French armies concentrating against him, Wellington raised the siege in mid-June and withdrew to a strong position on the River Caia. Though slightly outnumbered – with 54,000 troops to the French Army's 60,000 – Wellington was hoping to fight and win another defensive battle. But the French commanders, Soult and Marshal Auguste Marmont (Masséna's replacement), were now wary of attacking him at a place of his choosing, and the stand-off ended when they dispersed to find supplies. Wellington, by contrast, was able to keep his army concentrated thanks to his mastery of logistics.

In September he turned his attention to the more northerly fortress of Ciudad Rodrigo, but was again forced to retire when the French concentrated two of their armies. As before, Marmont chose not to risk an attack and soon withdrew. The only significant action of late 1811 was at Arroyo dos Molinos, where an isolated French division was surprised and routed by a detached force of 16,000 men under General 'Daddy' Hill.

Portugal was now reasonably secure, but Wellington could make little headway in Spain because the French armies near Ciudad Rodrigo and Badajoz were too strong. The stalemate was broken, unwittingly, by two of Napoleon's decisions: the first was to send part of Marmont's Army of the North to help Marshal Louis Suchet complete the conquest of Valencia from the Spanish; the second was to prepare, in early 1812, a Grand Army of 500,000 men for an invasion of Russia, with 27,000 men taken from the armies in Spain. These decisions weakened Marmont – who would receive no more replacements and reinforcements – and gave Wellington the opportunity to strike a fatal blow.

Before venturing deeper into Spain, however, he needed to secure his rear by taking the two frontier fortresses. He decided to concentrate on Ciudad Rodrigo – the weaker of the two, defended by barely 2,000 men – and resumed his siege with heavy guns on 8 January 1812. The weather was bitterly cold and, recorded Private John Timewell of the 1/43rd Light Infantry, 'we had to cross a river every morning up to our middle – the ice fit to cut us in two and remain working in that condition for 12 hours under heavy shot from the town where many a brave soldier was killed.'[31] Two breaches were made in the walls and on 19 January, at nine in the evening, the storming parties from the 3rd and Light divisions attacked. Among the Light Division's forlorn hope was Private Edward Costello of the 95th Rifles:

Calling out, 'Now, lads, for the breach!', General Craufurd led the way. We started off in double-quick time, and got under fire in turning the left corner of the [convent] wall. As we neared the breach, canister, grape, round-shot and shell, with fire-balls to show our ground, came pouring . . . around us, with a regular hailstorm of bullets. General Craufurd fell almost immediately, mortally wounded. Without a pause, however, we dashed onwards to the town, and precipitated ourselves into the ditch before the walls . . . At length, one or two ladders having been procured, they were instantly placed against the scarp of the trench, and up we mounted to attack the breach. The fire kept up there was most deadly, and our men, for some minutes, as they appeared in small bodies, were swept away. However, they still persevered, and gradually formed a lodgement.[32]

Once in the town, the men went on the rampage, pillaging houses, stealing alcohol and firing at random. The men 'committed shameful excesses disgraceful to the whole army', wrote an officer of the Royal Artillery, and 'the dead were scarcely cold when they were inhumanly stripped'.[33] General Thomas Picton, commanding the 3rd Division, tried to restore order by shouting 'Damnation' and hitting drunken soldiers with a broken musket.[34] But it was exhaustion that finally brought the plunder to an end.

Next morning, as he rode into the town, Wellington failed to recognize the battalion marching in the opposite direction. One of their officers, Lieutenant Johnny Kindaid, wrote, 'There was scarcely a vestige of uniform among the men, some of whom were dressed in Frenchmen's coats, some in white breeches and huge jackboots, some with cocked hats and queues. Most of their swords [bayonets] were fixed on their rifles, and stuck full of hams, tongues and loaves of bread, and not a few were carrying bird cages.' On inquiring their identity, he was told they were the 1/95th Rifles.[35]

Robert Craufurd, the intrepid commander of the Light Division, died a week later from his wound. He had been one of Wellington's sternest critics, believing his defensive strategy to be too cautious. But as he lay dying he begged Wellington's forgiveness for the intrigues he had carried on with General Charles Stewart and the other 'croakers'.

He 'talked to me', remembered Wellington, 'as they do in a novel'. He was buried in the breach that he and his men had assaulted, lamented by soldiers who had found him too severe at first; now, in honour of his insistence that time was not wasted on detours, they marched from the funeral back to camp through an icy pond.[36] 'We lost our noble Craufurd,' noted Private Timewell in his diary, 'who was afraid of no French man.'[37]

Wellington's reward for taking Ciudad Rodrigo was his elevation from viscount to earl and an increased pension of £4,000 a year (it had been half that). The grateful Spanish made him a duke. But, though gratified, he quickly turned his attention to Badajoz, 140 miles to the south. Protected to the north and east by the River Guardiana and the flooded Rivillas Brook respectively, and everywhere else by squat modern bastions that allowed interlocking fields of fire, it was garrisoned by 4,000 determined men. Wellington knew it was a tougher nut to crack than Ciudad Rodrigo – having failed the previous September – and began his siege works on 17 March. It took almost three weeks to make three practicable breaches in the south wall, and even then Wellington would have liked more time to widen them. But with Marmont and Soult on the march, he felt compelled to order the assault for the night of 6 April. The Light and 4th divisions would concentrate on the breaches, while secondary attacks were made by the 3rd and 5th divisions, on the castle in the north-east corner of the city and the San Vincente Bastion in the north-west respectively.

When the attack began at the breaches at 10 p.m., the French were waiting with extra muskets, grenades and fused shells. They had lined the slopes of rubble with spiked planks and placed a *cheval de frise* – made of sword blades hammered into stout timbers – at the top. To even get to the breach, the British had to drop into a steep ditch and climb out the other side. Private William Lawrence of the 40th Foot, a member of a ladder party, recalled the moment he reached the ditch: 'A shower of shot, canister and grape, together with fire-balls, was hurled . . . among us. Poor Pig [Harding] received his death wound immediately.' Lawrence himself was shot in the left knee and side, but still he held on to his ladder and made it over the ditch. 'Numbers had by this time fallen,' he wrote, but 'we hastened to the breach. There, to our great discouragement, we found a *cheval de frise* had been fixed . . . Vain attempts were made to remove this fearful obstacle, during which my left hand was fearfully cut by one of the blades, but, finding no success in that quarter, we were forced to retire for a time.'[38]

At all three breaches the story was the same. Lieutenant John Harrison of the 23rd Fusiliers was 'halfway up the breach when', he informed his mother, 'I was shot through the right arm nearly above an inch of the elbow. I had scarcely time to thank them for this, before they gave me another in the right shoulder.'[39] Harry Smith, a lieutenant in the 95th (and a future general), remembered the fire as so 'murderous' that as he and his men rushed the breach 'we were broken, and carried no weight with us, though every soldier was a hero.' He added: 'A rifleman stood amongst the sword blades on the top of one of the chevaux de frises. We made a glorious rush to follow, but alas! in vain. He was knocked over. My old captain, O'Hare, who commanded the storming party, was killed. All were awfully wounded except, I do believe, myself and little Freer of the 43rd.'[40]

Watching in tense anticipation from a small rise near the main breach was Lord Wellington and various members of his staff, including Dr James McGrigor, the former deputy inspector of hospitals and now Wellington's senior medical officer. McGrigor was shocked by the intensity of the defensive fire. 'Blue lights were frequently thrown out by the Garrison,' he wrote, 'which clearly showed the red masses of troops in the ditch advancing to the breach and illuminated all around.' But then an officer arrived with the news that Lieutenant-Colonel Charles McLeod of the 43rd Light Infantry and 'several officers had been killed, and heaps of the dead and wounded choked the approach to the breach.' McGrigor added:

> At this time the group was so near the ramparts we could distinctly hear the shouts of the combatants in the momentary intervals of the firing; and were distressed to find, that the sounds from the assailants became fainter and those from the ramparts, louder every moment mixed with oaths and execrations . . . In a short time another officer

came up with a still more unfavourable report. At this moment I cast
my eyes on the countenance of Lord Wellington with the light of the
torch held by Lord March [aide-de-camp] upon it. I never can forget
it to the last moment of my life, and I could now sketch it. The jaw
had fallen, and the face was of unusual length, whilst the torch cast
over it a lurid colouring – more shade than light, still the expression
was very firm.[41]

So shaken was Wellington by the news that the attack on the breaches
had failed that he turned to McGrigor and, mistaking him for one of
his staff, told him: 'Go immediately to Picton and tell him he must
succeed at the Castle.'

'My Lord, I have no horse,' replied the doctor, 'but will go on foot
as fast as I can; and I know the way.'

Only then did Wellington realize his mistake and send someone
else. 'This moment appears to have been the crisis of the great Commander's agony during this awful night,' wrote the doctor. 'After
a short but dreadful suspense, a horseman was heard approaching,
who shouted, "Where is Lord Wellington?" "Here, here," everyone
exclaimed. Then when he had come up, he cried out, "My Lord, the
Castle is your own." '[42]

Not that Picton's men had had it easy. 'When the ladders were
placed,' wrote Private Joseph Donaldson of the 94th Foot, 'eager to
mount, [the soldiers] crowded them in such a way that many of them
broke, and poor fellows who had nearly reached the top were precipitated a height of thirty to forty feet and impaled on the bayonets
of their comrades below. Other ladders were pushed aside by the
enemy on the walls, and fell with a crash on those in the ditch, while
[men] who got to the top without accident were shot on reaching the
parapet, and, tumbling headlong, brought down those beneath them.
This continued for some time, until at length, a few having made a
landing . . . [they] enabled others to follow.'[43]

Soon after, men of the 5th Division entered the bastion of San
Vicente on the opposite side of the town. With his defences crumbling, the French governor ordered a counter-attack; when it failed,
he escaped across the bridge to the San Cristóbal Fort and surrendered

the following morning. The town, meanwhile, was subjected to an even more brutal sacking than Ciudad Rodrigo had faced. 'There was no safety for women even in churches,' wrote Ensign Robert Blakeney of the 28th Foot, 'and any who interfered or offered resistance was sure to get shot. Every house presented a scene of plunder, debauchery and bloodshed committed with wanton cruelty . . . by our soldiery, and in many instances I saw the savages tear the rings from the ears of beautiful women.' Men, women and children 'were shot', according to Blakeney, 'for no other reason than pastime'.[44]

Among the perpetrators was Edward Costello of the 95th Rifles, who helped men of the 3rd Division to rob the house of an old Spanish man, and received 27 dollars as his share. Eventually his drunken comrades 'discovered the two daughters of the old *patron*, who had concealed themselves upstairs'. Costello wrote: 'They were both young and very pretty. The mother, too, was shortly afterwards dragged from her hiding place. Without dwelling on the frightful scene that followed, it may be sufficient to add that our men, more infuriated by drink than before, again seized the old man, and insisted on a fresh supply of liquor.'[45]

Men were not the only looters. An officer of the King's German Legion witnessed around 200 soldiers' wives swarm into the town after it had fallen, and was 'sickened' when he saw them 'coolly step over the dying, indifferent to their cries for a drop of water, and deliberately search the pockets of the dead for money, or even divest them of their bloody coats'.[46]

More than 250 Spanish civilians were killed in the assault and sack of Badajoz. Wellington was so furious that he could hardly bring himself to thank the troops for their gallant efforts in taking the town. Instead he issued a General Order for the looting to stop, and had a gallows erected in the town square as a warning. In the event, no one was hanged, though Lieutenant William Grattan of the 88th Connaught Rangers felt 'hundreds deserved it'.[47] Wellington knew that it was customary for troops who had stormed a town to enjoy its plunder. He had turned a blind eye before, and would do so again. What he could not condone, however, was rape and murder.

He had, on the other hand, only admiration and pity for the 5,000 men he had lost during the siege. Standing among the fallen at one of the breaches, he broke down and wept. 'Good God,' exclaimed the wounded Picton, unnerved by this uncharacteristic show of emotion, 'what is the matter?' Wellington's response was to curse the government for not giving him enough sappers and miners (a preoccupation that would lead to the creation of a separate corps of siege specialists, the Royal Sappers and Miners, in 1813). 'The capture of Badajoz,' he wrote later to Lord Liverpool, 'affords as strong an instance of the gallantry of our troops as has ever been displayed. But I greatly hope that I shall never again be the instrument of putting them to such a test.'[48]

It was only after the battle that the hopelessness of the Light Division's task became clear. 'If our men had stormed the breaches they never would have taken the town,' wrote a lieutenant of the Royal Horse Artillery,

> as the French had dug a deep & wide ditch inside, which entirely cut off the breaches from the Town, over which ditch the French had placed Boards for them to pass over, which they would have pulled away as they had passed; they had built a low wall on the side of the ditch to fire over, & had cut loop holes in the House near for musquetry; they had turned every gun they could on the breaches, & had constructed a Battery in the entrance of the Town on a rising ground, of 8 guns 24 pounders that commanded the part of ground that our troops would have been on had they driven the French from the top of the breaches. But the French were so numerous . . . that our brave soldiers could not get up & were in consequence killed by hundreds in the ditch of the place.[49]

Many of the 2,200 wounded were left to suffer for hours, and in some cases days, before they were collected and taken in sprung wagons to military hospitals in Elvas and Estremoz. An Irish sergeant of the 43rd, shot in the thigh, recorded:

> On alighting from our vehicles at Elvas, we were at first placed in a dark, uncomfortable apartment adjoining the fortifications. The roof was of arched masonry and so damp on the inner side that water fell

on us in large drops. Our attendants were also nothing to boast of, for, under the pretence of bringing our haversacks with provisions, they walked away with them altogether, an evil against which we knew no remedy, being unable, through weakness, to search for the depredators or procure more food . . . On our arrival at Estremoz, we found accommodation more suited to the exigencies of the invalided guests: a convent, sufficiently spacious, had been fitted up as a military hospital and was well adapted for the purpose . . . Having an excellent constitution, I soon recovered my health and in the course of a few weeks was pronounced convalescent.[50]

Another wounded soldier, Lieutenant Grattan of the 88th, was carried back to the cot in his tent on the day of the battle to find it occupied by his batman's wife, Nelly Carsons, who had collapsed there having drunk too much rum. One of his stretcher-bearers tried to waken her, remembered Grattan, but to no avail:

A battery of a dozen guns might have been fired close to her ear without danger of disturbing her repose! 'Why then sir,' said he, 'the bed's big enough for yees both, and she'll keep you nate and warm, for, be the powers, you're kilt with the cold and the loss ov blood.' I was in no mood to stand on ceremony, or indeed, to stand at all. I allowed myself to be placed beside my partner, without any further persuasion . . . Weakness from loss of blood soon caused me to fall asleep.[51]

Grattan was eventually woken by a loud grunt from Nelly, who, mistaking the lieutenant for her husband, put her hand on his leg and exclaimed: 'Arrah! Dan jewel. What makes you so stiff this morning?' Grattan laughed so hard he reopened his wound and might have died had not the surgeon appeared. Nelly hid her embarrassment by making tea.[52]

With the frontier now secure, Wellington's strategy was to advance cautiously into Spain with the intention of bringing either Marmont or Soult to battle. The French still had 230,000 troops in Spain, but they were divided between five armies and most had their hands full with guerrillas and Spanish regulars. This, and the knowledge that all available French reinforcements were being sent east for Napoleon's imminent invasion of Russia, gave Wellington the confidence to seek a general engagement. 'The certainty of the loss in every action,' he wrote on 26 May, 'and the risk which always attends such an operation, ought not, therefore, in my opinion, to prevent its being tried at present.'[53]

The news that Wellington's troops had successfully stormed the Spanish fortress of Badajoz provoked a bout of wild rejoicing when it reached London in late April 1812. But the capital's celebrations were soon given over to mourning. In the early evening of 11 May, Spencer Perceval became the only British prime minister to be assassinated in office when he was shot and killed in the lobby of the House of Commons by a failed businessman named John Bellingham. When Wellington heard the news he feared that the prince regent – standing in as monarch since his father's mental incapacity a year earlier – might summon the Whig Opposition and agree to peace with Napoleon. In fact Wellington's recent run of success in the Peninsula – culminating in the capture of Ciudad Rodrigo and Badajoz – had convinced the regent that the war had to be supported to its conclusion. Thus the regent chose to retain the pro-war Tory government, with Lord Liverpool as the new prime minister and Earl Bathurst as war secretary.[54] Wellington was mightily relieved, telling Liverpool that he was 'perfectly satisfied' with Bathurst's appointment, and regretted only that no place could be found in government for his brother Richard.[55]

Wellington could now concentrate on bringing the French in Spain to a decisive battle and, having entered Salamanca to a rapturous welcome on 17 June, he pursued Marmont as far as the Douro River, 50 miles to the north-east. But, on hearing that Marmont had been reinforced to 50,000 men, Wellington let discretion be the better part of valour and withdrew with his own army of 52,000 to Salamanca. Marmont followed, and so began a week of shadow boxing as the French marshal sought to cut his line of retreat to Portugal. 'Marmont will certainly not risk an action unless he should have an advantage,' Wellington told Sir Thomas Graham on 21 July, 'and I shall certainly not risk one unless I should have an advantage, and matters therefore do not appear to be brought to that criterion very soon.'[56]

A campaign that had begun with such high hopes was about to end with a timorous withdrawal to the safety of Portugal. 'He is no longer the reckless gambler of Assaye,' writes Paddy Griffith, 'but neither is he entirely the timid actuary of Torres Vedras. Instead, he is visibly wrestling to find some middle course by which he can win the triumph that has eluded him so long, without falling into the near disaster of some new Corunna or Talavera.'[57]

Wellington did, however, have one ace up his sleeve. His assistant quartermaster-general, Major George Scovell, had recently cracked the main French code – known as the 'Great Paris Cipher' – which meant the British could read captured enemy correspondence. One message in particular, found hidden in a riding crop, contained vital information from King Joseph to Marmont. Written on 9 July, intercepted a week later and decoded by the 20th, it made clear that Joseph's Army of the Centre was marching to unite with Marmont, and that if Wellington was to have any hope of beating the latter's Army of Portugal he had to give battle before 24 July at the latest.[58]

Thus Wellington actively sought an action on 21 July by taking up a strong position on the San Christoval Ridge to the north of Salamanca. But Marmont refused to take the bait and, just when it seemed that the opportunity for a decisive engagement was slipping away, Wellington was the recipient of an extraordinary piece of good fortune. It came at midday on 22 July, as the two armies were marching, parallel to each other, across a plain 5 miles south-east of Salamanca. Fearing that the faster-moving French might attempt to turn his right, Wellington had ordered his divisions to line the ridge that separated the two armies. But instead of also changing front, Marmont's men continued their march in division-sized blocks to the west. Wellington was munching on a chicken leg when he spotted this cardinal error through his telescope. 'By God,' he exclaimed, 'that will do!'[59]

Tossing aside the half-eaten chicken leg, he spurred up a nearby rise to get a better view. The sight that greeted him was beyond belief; not only were the French trudging onwards, but a dangerous gap had opened between their leading divisions and their centre.

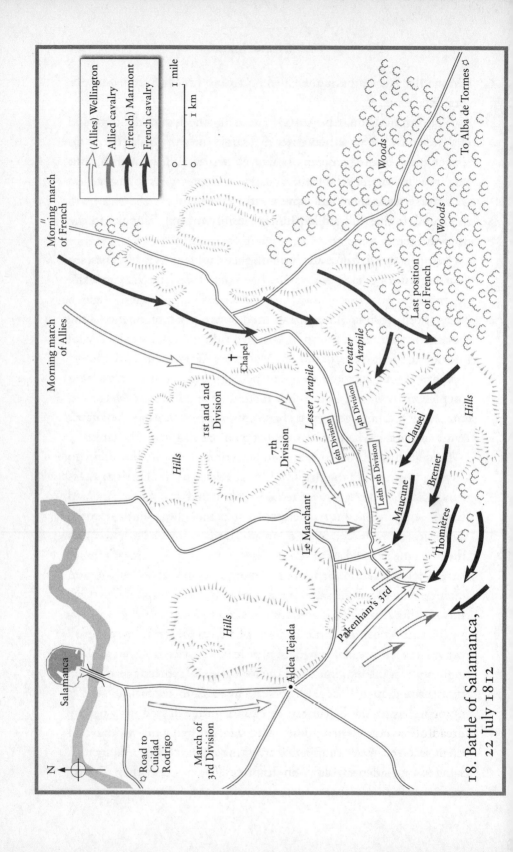

Morning march of French

Morning march of Allies

+ Chapel

To Alba de Tormes

Woods

Woods

Last position of French

Greater Arapile

Lesser Arapile

4th Division

6th Division

Leith 5th Division

1st and 2nd Division

7th Division

Hills

Hills

Clausel

Brenier

Maucune

Thomières

Hills

Le Marchant

Pakenham's 3rd

Salamanca

Hills

Aldea Tejada

⟲ Road to Cuidad Rodrigo

March of 3rd Division

N

18. Battle of Salamanca, 22 July 1812

'Mon cher Álava,' exclaimed Wellington to his Spanish liaison officer, 'Marmont est perdu!'[60]

Wasting no time, he galloped ahead to find his leading division, the 3rd, now under the command of his brother-in-law, Sir Edward Pakenham. 'Ned, d'ye see those fellows on the hill?' he asked, pointing to the foremost French column. 'Throw your division into column, have at them and drive them to the devil.'

'I will, my Lord,' said Pakenham, visibly moved, 'if you will give me your hand.'[61]

The pair shook hands and, while Pakenham put his men in motion, Wellington rode back the way he had come to launch his remaining divisions in a succession of attacks from west to east against the flank of the strung-out French army. The first blow was struck by the leading battalions of 3rd Division and a brigade of Portuguese cavalry – nearly 6,000 veterans in all – against the unsuspecting head and flank of Marmont's advance guard, under General Jean Thomières. 'The crash was magnificent!' wrote Pakenham, having witnessed Wallace's brigade of the 45th, 74th and 88th Foot destroy half of Thomières's formation with musketry fire and a bayonet charge.[62] But the rear French battalions, slightly forewarned, put up a better fight. The 5th Fusiliers, for example, were repulsed in their first attack up a hill 'on whose crest masses of the enemy were stationed'. After words of encouragement from General Pakenham himself, they attacked a second time and, according to Sergeant Stephen Morley of the 5th Fusiliers, 'awful was the retribution we exacted for our former repulse'.[63]

With Thomières killed, his surviving men fled east towards General Antoine Maucune's division, pursued by cavalry and infantry. 'In this manner driving in their left,' recalled Private Joseph Donaldson of the 94th Foot, 'we came in front of where our artillery was playing on the enemy, but no time was lost; we marched past in open column, while they continued to fire without interruption, sending their shot through the intervals between each company, without doing us any injury . . . The enemy's shot and shell were now making dreadful havoc. A Portuguese cadet who was attached to our regiment received a shell in the centre of his body, which, bursting at the same instant, literally blew him to pieces.'[64]

Maucune's division was under threat not only from Pakenham's men, but also General James Leith's 5th Division and a brigade of heavy British cavalry under Major-General John Le Marchant (who had recently relinquished the lieutenant-governorship of the Royal Military College at High Wycombe that he had helped to found). With Leith's infantry was an unidentified soldier of the 38th Foot:

> We then ran in double quick time for a great distance by the side of a hill so that we were covered from the enemy's fire. As soon as we got to the end of the hill we were ordered to drop down instantly. We did so, and in a few seconds General Leith came up, waving his hat, and shouting, 'Now my Lads, this is the day for [Old] England! They would play at long ball with us from morning until night, but we will soon give them something else.' So as soon as he got to the right of the line, the bugle sounded to stand to our arms and to charge them immediately.[65]

They did so, driving the French back through a village and over a ridge. 'As soon as we got to the top,' wrote the soldier of the 38th, 'the French were in a square not more than 200 yards from us.'

Spotting the heavy cavalry of Le Marchant's brigade to his left, Maucune had ordered his infantry units to form hollow squares. They now had to contend with Leith's infantry to their front and Le Marchant's horsemen, who had torn through the remnants of Thomières's division, to their flank and rear. William Bragge of the 3rd Dragoons recalled:

> The cavalry advanced upon the banks of the infantry. Our brigade literally rode over the regiments in their front and dashed through the wood at a gallop, the infantry cheering us in all directions. We quickly came up with the French columns and charged their rear. Hundreds threw down their arms, their cavalry ran away, and most of the artillery jumped upon their horses and followed their cavalry. One or two charges mixed up the whole brigade it being impossible to see for dust and smoke.[66]

Having watched Le Marchant's glorious charge, Wellington turned to his cavalry commander, Sir Stapleton Cotton, and exclaimed: 'By God, Cotton, I never saw anything so beautiful in my life; the day is *yours*.'[67]

Wellington had every reason to assume the battle was over. In just forty minutes he had destroyed two divisions and part of a third, General Antoine Brenier's. But not everything was going his way: Le Marchant was shot and killed as he led his horsemen against Maucune's squares; an attack by a Portuguese brigade on a strong position in the centre of the French line was beaten off with heavy losses; and though Marmont himself was disabled at the start of the action by a piece of shell, as was his deputy Jean Bonnet, their successor General Bertrand Clausel had reacted brilliantly to the destruction of the French left by launching a two-division counter-attack against the British centre that almost succeeded. The blow fell on the two British brigades of General Cole's 4th Division – badly under-strength since Badajoz – which had just driven part of Clausel's original division off the ridge, a fight in which Cole had been wounded. John Burgoyne, son of the defeated general at Saratoga and a member of Cole's staff, recorded the calm and precision of the French counter-attack:

> The French regiment came up the hill with a brisk and regular step and their drums beating the *pas-de-charge*. Our men fired wildly . . . among them; the French never returned a shot but continued their steady advance. The English fired again . . . but men in such confusion had no chance against the perfect order of the enemy, and when the French were close upon them, they wavered and gave way. The officers all advanced in a line in front, waving their swords and cheering their men to come on, but the confusion became a panic, and there was a regular *sauve qui peut* down the hill.[68]

Fortunately Wellington had prepared for such an eventuality by supporting the 5th and 4th divisions with the 7th and 6th respectively. The men of Henry Clinton's 6th Division, therefore, were on hand to plug the gap in the British line, until, as evening drew on, they were ordered forward to attack part of the French rearguard under General Claude-François Ferey. Henry Ross-Lewin of the 32nd Foot remembered:

> The ground over which we had to pass was a remarkably clear slope, like the glacis of a fortification – most favourable for the defensive fire

of the enemy and disadvantageous for the assailants – but the division advanced towards the position with perfect steadiness and confidence. A craggy ridge on which the French infantry were drawn up rose so abruptly that they could fire four or five deep . . . [The fire of musketry] was by far the heaviest I have ever experienced, and was accompanied by constant discharges of grape.[69]

In danger of being surrounded, Ferey's men fell back to a wood on the eastern edge of the battlefield, where they fought off one attack by Portuguese troops, and looked like they might do the same to a second by British troops when, according to Captain Lemonnier-Delafosse of the 31st Regiment, 'our left wing ceased fire and broke and ran'. He added: 'The Seventieth Line had been enveloped by cavalry and swept away the Twenty-Sixth and Forty-Seventh Line in its flight. Yet the Thirty-First Léger [Light Regiment], for all that it mustered only two battalions and was now all on its own, stood firm and checked the enemy . . . Only when the sun had finally set did our gallant [commander] evacuate the position.'[70]

This gallant rearguard action by Ferey's division – during which their commander was cut in two by a round-shot – helped Clausel to withdraw the shattered remnants of the French army to the southeast. They might have been stopped at Alba de Tormes; but the Spanish commander had withdrawn the garrison, contrary to Wellington's orders, and the French were able to cross the bridge unimpeded. 'If I had known there was no garrison at Alba,' commented Wellington, 'I should have marched there, and probably had the whole.'[71]

The fall of darkness, moreover, prevented any effective pursuit, and Wellington had to be content with a decisive victory, but not an annihilation. The French had lost 14,000 men; the Anglo-Portuguese 4,700, or slightly less than 10 per cent of all the Allied troops present that day. The French wounded, according to one British officer, 'suffered horribly, for, three days after, I saw a great many still lying who had received no assistance nor were likely to till next day, and had lain scorching in the sun without a drop of water or the least shade. It was a most dreadful sight.'[72]

All the casualties were fair game for the women – many of them

British soldiers' wives – who habitually scoured the battlefields for clothes and money. Captain Browne of the 1/23rd Fusiliers remembered them 'stripping and plundering friend & foe alike' at Salamanca. He added: 'It is not doubted that they gave the finishing blow to many an Officer who was struggling with a mortal wound; and Major Offley of the 23rd Regiment, who lay on the ground, unable to move, but not dead, is said to have fallen a victim to this unheard of barbarity.'[73]

One military historian has described the victory at Salamanca as the British Army's greatest 'since the Battle of Blenheim in 1704'.[74] It is an opinion that was probably shared by one of Wellington's opponents that day, the French divisional commander Maximilien Foy, who thought the battle raised the British general's reputation 'almost to the level of Marlborough'. Foy added: 'Hitherto we have been aware of his prudence, his eye for choosing a position, and his skill in utilising it. At Salamanca he has shown himself a great and able master of manoeuvres. He kept his dispositions concealed for almost the whole day; he waited till we were committed to our movements before he developed his own; he played a safe game; he fought in the oblique order – it was a battle in the style of Frederick the Great.'[75]

This is high praise, and much of it deserved. Though not anticipating a battle, Wellington took full advantage of his opponent's error to destroy a marginally superior force, delivering most of his key orders in person, and moving across the battlefield without thought for his own safety. 'Our Chief was everywhere,' wrote Pakenham, 'and sadly exposed himself; in his preservation our little prayers were heard most surely.'[76] Another officer wrote: 'The great novelty of the day was the keeping [of] the troops so well in hand, and stopping their headlong impetuosity after each succeeding attack. The 3 divisions [3rd, 4th and 5th] wheel'd round as a single company would, & the long lines were preserved most beautifully.'[77]

Not all assigned the victory to Wellington's genius. John Mills, a young ensign in the Coldstream Guards, described the 'whole business' in a letter home as 'truly lucky'. He explained: 'Lord Wellington did not mean to fight but to retire into Portugal. Luckily for us they bullied and that brought it on. They fought very ill and seem at last to have been panic struck . . . Yesterday I saw them running through cornfields like a pack of hounds.'[78]

A more recent commentator regards Wellington's performance at Salamanca as a return to the risk-taking style of his India days: 'Taking his courage in both hands, and reminding us vividly of the man of Assaye, he seized upon the first slight mistake which he detected in the French deployment. He launched his whole army impatiently forward into the sort of wild charge that had by this time been all but forgotten in the sedate military transactions of the Peninsula. Fortunately it surprised the French rather more than it surprised Wellington's own associates, and led to almost complete victory.'[79]

In the wake of his success at Salamanca – for which he was made a marquess and voted £100,000 by Parliament to buy a suitably grand country estate – Wellington was able to liberate Madrid for the first time in more than three years. 'Nothing could equal the joy of the inhabitants on seeing us enter Madrid,' wrote Lieutenant John McDonald of the 1/23rd Fusiliers to his father, 'in fact no language that I can use can convey the least Idea of it. They surrounded us in immense crowds, embracing the soldiers, pulling the officers very nearly off their horses, & every body exclaiming, "Viva los Inglezos." Any unconcerned spectator would have thought them mad, the Young and Old dancing about all parts of the City, the church Bells all ringing, the Bands of the Different Regiments playing, the houses all beautifully decorated with tapestry, & at night illuminated.'[80]

Perhaps the victory and this rapturous welcome went to Wellington's head; perhaps he felt that, with good news coming in from elsewhere in Spain (particularly the south, where Soult had given up his siege of Cadiz), he had the French on the run. Either way a sense of overconfidence made him divide his precious resources and, leaving half his army to cover Madrid, take the rest in pursuit of Clausel towards the French border. With only the 2,200-strong garrison at Burgos, capital of Old Castile, standing in his way, he tried to take the fortress by storm. But repeated attempts were beaten off – not least because Wellington lacked siege guns and, as ever, miners and engineers – and the month-long siege ended in failure on 21 October. That day he learned that Soult and King Joseph had united their

60,000 men and were advancing towards General Hill, who had only 35,000 to defend the capital. Hill, moreover, was 150 miles south of Burgos and could expect no immediate help from his chief. For the third time since 1808 (and the second time for Wellington personally), a British army had ventured too far into Spain for its own safety and was forced to withdraw to Portugal.

The two halves of the army were reunited at Salamanca, but still Wellington was heavily outnumbered and the retreat continued. For some the appalling weather, lack of supplies and constant pressure from the French – who, at one point, defeated two brigades of British cavalry – was an unwelcome reminder of the horrors of the Corunna campaign. Lieutenant John McDonald of the 23rd Fusiliers wrote home:

> For the last month we have been constantly moving, always without any covering, & so often without any baggage in the worst weather possible & roads as deep as any part of the moss at Bunecairing. It is the first time I have been in a serious retreat & I hope it shall be the last as the scenes of misery we must every day [see] exceed any thing I could form an idea of. Animals of all descriptions and even men, women and children lying on all sides, starving of hunger & cold, without a possibility of affording the least succour. Marching almost constantly, our commissariat badly supplied and a superior enemy pressing us in rear, with all this you may conceive the state we have been in for the last six weeks . . . Our Regiment is merely a skeleton, not more than two hundred men, but have a strong draft just landed at Lisbon from the [2]nd Battalion which will make us respectable again. We lost one officer & between forty and fifty men in this retreat from fatigue and hunger.[81]

The mood of most soldiers had turned from triumph to despair, and Wellington did not escape their ire. 'Our want of success at Burgos,' wrote Ensign John Mills of the Coldstream Guards, 'and the subsequent retreat . . . has turned the tide of affairs here and Spain I think is lost. If ever a man ruined himself the Marquis has done it; for the last two months he has acted like a madman. The reputation he has acquired will not bear him out – such is the opinion here.'[82]

It was not only officers who were critical of their chief. Private Joseph Donaldson of the 94th recorded:

> I never saw troops in such bad humour. Retreating before the enemy at any time was a grievous business, but in such weather it was doubly so. The rain, now pouring down in torrents, drenched us to the skin, and the road, composed of clay soil, stuck to our shoes so fast, that they were torn off our feet . . . Few words were spoken, and, as if ashamed to complain of the hardships we suffered, execrating the retreat and blaming Lord Wellington for not having sufficient confidence in us to hazard a battle with the enemy . . . were the only topics discussed.[83]

Wellington described the retreat as 'the worst scrape I ever was in'. Yet he accepted full responsibility, telling Lord Liverpool: 'The Government had nothing to say to the siege [of Burgos]. It was entirely my own act.' Years later he explained to friends: 'It was all my own fault; I had got, with small means, into the forts near Salamanca. The Castle [in Burgos] was not unlike a hill-fort in India, and I had got into a good many of those. I could not get into this.'[84]

By late November, Wellington's army had reached its winter quarters at Freneida in north-east Portugal, where, at last, it could rest and recuperate. The outlook, though bleak, was far from hopeless. The French had, it is true, retaken Madrid and forced Wellington to relinquish all his gains in central and northern Spain. But elsewhere, hard-pressed by resurgent Spanish forces, they had lost control of much of southern and western Spain.

Worse still for the French in the Peninsula, Napoleon's invasion of Russia had met with utter disaster. Crossing the River Niemen in late June with a polyglot Grande Armée of 450,000 troops, he had hugely underestimated the problem of resupply and from the outset lost men at the rate of 5,000 a day to desertion, disease and suicide. The Russians, meanwhile, refused to give battle and destroyed crops and supplies as they withdrew, luring Napoleon ever further across forests, marshes and steppes. There were only two significant battles: at Smolensk, where the Russians were defeated, and at Borodino, near Moscow, a bloody and inconclusive contest that resulted in combined casualties of 80,000 men (44,000 Russian). As the with-drawal continued, Napoleon entered Moscow in mid-September. But the Tsar's refusal to sue for peace, and the problems of supply caused by his 'scorched earth' policy, gave Napoleon little option but to retreat. Assailed by hunger, the cold and Russian cavalry, the Grande Armée wasted away. By the time Napoleon abandoned it to its fate in Poland – arriving back in Paris on 5 December – it numbered fewer than 10,000 effectives.

Napoleon would spend much of 1813 in Germany, building up his broken army and fighting off the resurgent armies of Russia, Prussia, Austria and Sweden. There were, as a result, no reinforcements available for Spain, where King Joseph and his marshals had to remain on the defensive. Wellington was well aware of this, and, with the new campaigning season in mind, he spent the winter of 1812/13 bringing his battalions up to full strength, re-establishing discipline and improving his men's equipment (including lighter camp-kettles and tents that housed twenty-five soldiers). Finally, on 22 May 1813, having arranged a number of diversionary operations, he crossed back into Spain with the prescient words: 'Farewell Portugal! I shall never see you again.'[85]

Wellington's strategy was to drive the French out of the Peninsula altogether by inflicting upon them a major defeat. This was easier said than done. His army had swelled to 81,000 men – roughly two thirds British to one third Portuguese – while a further 25,000 Spaniards were willing to cooperate. But there were still 200,000 French troops south of the Pyrenees and to overcome them he needed to keep them apart. So when his excellent intelligence network informed him that the main French army, under King Joseph and Marshal Jean-Baptiste Jourdan, had left Madrid and was marching north to join Clausel – a union that, if he allowed it to happen, would produce a total force of 125,000 men – he knew he had to intercept it at all costs.

He won the race by a brilliant piece of deception. He convinced the French that he was going to advance up the Ciudad Rodrigo–Salamanca road – as he had the previous year – and once again they tried to block him on the Douro north of Salamanca. But he took

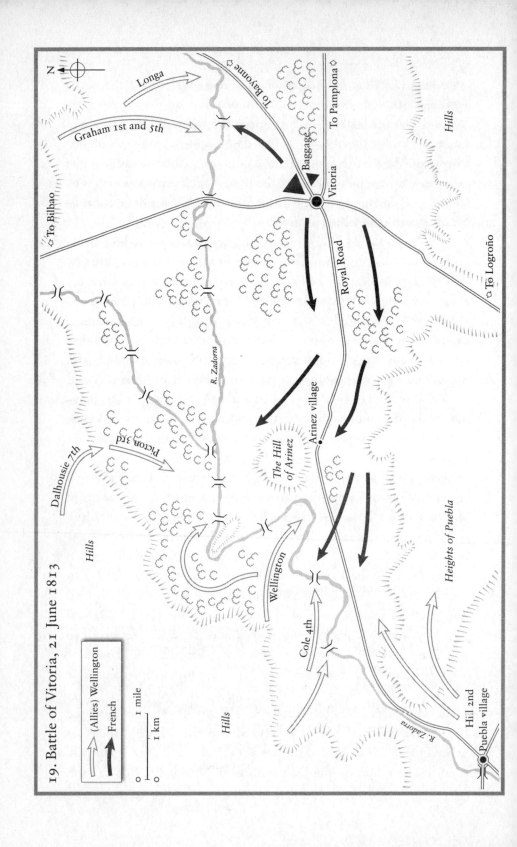

19. Battle of Vitoria, 21 June 1813

(Allies) Wellington
French

1 mile
1 km

Hills

Hills

Hills

Dalhousie 7th

Picton 3rd

R. Zadorra

To Bilbao

Longa

Graham 1st and 5th

To Bayonne

Baggage

Vitoria

To Pamplona

Royal Road

To Logroño

Hills

The Hill
of Arinez

Arinez village

Heights of Puebla

Wellington

Cole 4th

R. Zadorra

Hill 2nd

Puebla village

N

only a third of his army – mainly cavalry and a small force of infantry – by that route, and moved the rest through the mountains of northern Portugal to outflank King Joseph's position and force him to retire to the north-east. Thereafter the pursuit followed a similar pattern: every time the French stopped to make a stand, Wellington's reunited army would march round their right flank. On 21 June, having blown up the castle at Burgos a week earlier, the French army of 66,000 men was camped round the town of Vitoria in the Zadorra Valley, just 60 miles from France. Aware that Wellington was approaching, King Joseph and Jourdan assumed he would try his usual flanking manoeuvre; but instead he attacked, using four columns to try to trap them in a valley that was enclosed on three sides by mountains.

Wellington's plan was to pin the French in position with an initial assault from the west, before his three flanking columns attacked in succession from the north and north-east. The fourth column, under General Sir Thomas Graham, had the longest march and was scheduled to fall on the French rear to the west of Vitoria and cut off the army's line of retreat. It was an extremely ambitious and somewhat risky plan, and one that required near perfect timing to succeed.

It began well, with an attack on the Puebla Pass by Spanish and British troops at 8 a.m. that gradually sucked in French reinforcements and weakened their position in the valley. Thomas Pococke recorded the ebb and flow of this first phase of the battle:

> We charged up the hill, the pipes playing 'Hey Johnny Cope'. The French had possession of the top, but we soon forced them back and drew up in column on the height, sending out four companies to our left to skirmish. The remainder moved on to the opposite height. As we advanced, driving them before us, a French officer, a pretty fellow, was pricking his men to stand. They heeded him not . . . and down he fell, pierced by more than one ball.
>
> Scarce were we upon the height when a heavy column, dressed in greatcoats, with white covers on their hats, exactly resembling the Spanish, gave us a volley, which put us to the right about at double quick time down the hill, the French close behind, through the whins. The four companies got the word the French were on them. They

likewise thought them Spaniards, until they got a volley that killed or wounded almost every one of them. We retired to the height, covered by the 50th, who gave the pursuing column a volley which checked their speed.[86]

Meanwhile the second and third columns had crossed the Zadorra River to attack the northern flank of the French position. Major John Duffy of the 43rd Light Infantry was with the second column:

> As soon as the 3rd Division had crossed [the Zadorra River] about 11 o'clock we moved on and the battle became general . . . The enemy allowed us to gain the high ground without opposition but opened a tremendous fire from behind a village [Arinez] on the top of it which brought a temporary check. The village however was carried by part of the Rifle Regiment and some of the 3rd Division and we then moved on without a halt for the remainder of the day.[87]

So far so good; but Wellington's plan could work only if his fourth column – 20,000 men under Graham – was able to cut the two roads out of Vitoria before the French were able to retreat down them. It was certainly in a position to do so, having reached the River Zadorra well before the main exodus began. But to get across the river his men had to storm three enemy-held villages and their adjacent bridges, and only an attack on the easternmost crossing by a brigade of Spanish infantry under Colonel Francisco Longa was successful. When two brigades of the British 5th Division tried to repeat the trick at the middle bridge, they were cut to pieces by a ferocious defence and were unable to cross until the French had pulled back. By then, of course, the bulk of the French army had escaped down the second, smaller, road to Pamplona.

The outcome might have been very different if Graham had assaulted the westernmost bridge. He had another whole British division, the 1st, at his disposal and yet chose to use only a part of it to capture the village but not the bridge after Wellington had ordered him to press his attack with more vigour at 2 p.m. 'The rest of the 1st Division did not fire a shot,' wrote a disgruntled brigade commander of the 5th Division, 'nor could I even see them.'[88]

Both cavalry and light infantry were sent after the French as they fled down the Pamplona road; but the pursuit was not as vigorous as it might have been because many horsemen stopped to plunder the huge baggage trains the French had abandoned to the east of Vitoria. '[King] Joseph had a body guard of about one Hundred Hussars,' recalled Lieutenant Woodberry of the 18th Hussars, 'and I think Kennedy's troop would have taken him had they kept together but they run after a set of fellows and Plunder and did not support their Captain who was very near being taken prisoner.'[89]

Also taking part in the sack of the French transport were soldiers' wives, who, according to a Captain Thomas Browne of the 1/23rd Fusiliers, 'were seen for weeks after the action in muslins, three or four gowns one over the other, trimmed with fine lace, several pairs of earrings dangling from their ears, reticules, watches & fans as part of their costume. The contrast of these decorations with their brazen tanned faces and brawny arms was ludicrous enough.'[90]

The pursuing infantry, on the other hand, kept to their duty. 'The quantity of baggage taken is enormous,' wrote Lieutenant John McDonald of the 1/23rd to his father, '& though our division [the 4th] were the first that passed over it,

> yet from having his Lordship [Wellington] along with us, & the quick-
> ness with which we followed them we had no time for plunder. We
> repeatedly saw on each side of us carts & wagons loaded with plates &
> silver, without a man falling out of his ranks to lay his hands on it. The
> Division in our rear got an immense quantity, some officers having got
> from eight to ten thousand dollars, & even our band who had charge
> of the officers' horses came up next morning loaded with dollars &
> plate. Our camp next morning more resembled a Fair, than a regular
> encampment, every man selling or buying some article of plunder.[91]

A fellow officer in the 1/23rd Fusiliers noted: 'I am sure we passed ten elegant carriages. They were filled with women and musicians and poodle dogs and I understand they were the property of Joseph. I am sorry to say that this baggage impeded the progress of some of our cavalry but as Lord Wellington has threatened to dismount them, they will probably get on better next time.'[92]

Wellington's fury at this latest instance of military lawlessness –
more serious, in this instance, as it hampered his pursuit of the
enemy – is evident in his complaint to Lord Bathurst that the battle
had 'totally annihilated all order and discipline'. He added: 'This is the
consequence of the state of discipline of the British army. We may
gain the greatest victories, but we shall do no good, until we shall so
far alter our system, as to force all ranks to perform their duty.'[93]

Wellington was being a little harsh. The British redcoat rarely
shirked his duty when a fight was at its hottest; once it was won, however, he felt it was his right to loot. Wellington's failure to destroy
Joseph's army at Vitoria was, in any case, not chiefly due to soldierly
indiscipline but rather to General Graham's failure to cut the French
line of retreat. Nevertheless, Wellington had comprehensively out-
generalled both Joseph and Jourdan with a brilliantly fought campaign
that in just over two months had driven the bulk of the French forces
in Spain to the very borders of France, where, at Vitoria, he had
inflicted another stinging defeat. Not that victory had come cheap.
He had lost almost 5,000 men; the French 7,000, all but two of their
153 guns and all of their baggage. But this time Wellington's success
on the field of battle would not be followed by a strategic retreat. The
French had no more reinforcements to send to Spain and defeat at
Vitoria marked the end of Napoleon's long, costly and ultimately
futile campaign to conquer the Iberian Peninsula.

All Europe acknowledged the significance of the battle, with
Beethoven composing 'Wellington's Victory' in its honour. The prince
regent went further by promoting Wellington to the new rank of field
marshal. 'You have sent me, among the trophies of your unrivalled
fame, the staff of a French Marshal,' wrote the regent on 3 July, referring to Marshal Jourdan's baton, which had been salvaged from the
baggage train, 'and I send you in return that of England.' He had personally designed Wellington's baton, the first of its kind, adorning it
with lions rather than eagles. 'I can evince my gratitude for your Royal
Highness's repeated favours,' replied Wellington a trifle unctuously,
'only by devoting my life to your service.'[94]

There was more hard fighting to come in Spain – notably at the
border town of San Sebastián, where the French garrison held out for

more than two months – but by October 1813 Wellington had forced the defences on the River Bidassoa and entered France. The following spring, after another hard fight in which his army suffered 4,500 casualties, he captured the city of Toulouse. That afternoon, 12 April 1814, he was dressing for a celebration dinner in the Toulouse prefecture when one of his officers brought the extraordinary news that the Prussians had entered Paris and Napoleon had abdicated. 'You don't say so, upon my honour!' exclaimed Wellington, snapping his fingers in delight. 'Hurrah!'[95]

The official confirmation of Napoleon's abdication – on 6 April, meaning the Battle of Toulouse need not have been fought – and the restoration of the Bourbons arrived during the celebration dinner. Wellington proposed a toast to the new French king, Louis XVIII;* and General Álava responded with one to the 'Liberator of Spain'. At once the room was on its feet, acclaiming Wellington in five languages and cheering him for a full ten minutes. His typically understated response was to call for coffee.

Private Thomas Pococke of the 71st, who had fought in the Peninsula since 1808, was with his battalion north of Toulouse when General Soult came in under a flag of truce. 'We then got word that Bonaparte was deposed,' wrote Pococke, 'and we were soon to have peace. Joy beamed on every face, and made every tongue eloquent. We sung and drank that whole night and talked of home.'[96] Pococke was one of seventy-five survivors from the original 650 men of the 71st who had returned to Portugal in 1810.

On 24 April, Louis XVIII returned to Paris; four days later, Napoleon was exiled to the tiny Mediterranean island of Elba with a pension of two million francs. The subsequent Treaty of Paris confined France to her pre-1792 frontiers (with the addition of a piece of Savoy), and gave the Austrian Netherlands (later Belgium) to Holland. After more than two decades of war, Europe was finally at

---

* Brother of the executed Louis XVI. The missing 'Louis XVII' was the former monarch's son, Louis-Charles. He was never crowned king and was just ten years old when he died in the Temple Prison in Paris in June 1795, two years after his father's death.

peace. The Allies owed their victory in no small part to Wellington and the soldiers of the British Army, who for almost six years – and for much of that time unsupported by any other great power – had fought and beaten French armies in the Peninsula. Not only had the campaign drained French strength in terms of soldiers and treasure, it also damaged Napoleon's prestige. Wellington's victories at Roliça and Vimeiro in 1808 were the first significant defeats inflicted upon Napoleon's armies in Europe. These and subsequent French setbacks in the Peninsula encouraged other Continental powers to re-enter the fray. This is not to suggest that Napoleon's fate was decided in Spain and Portugal, rather than in Russia and central Europe; it was not. Yet the emperor's decision to invade Russia while as many as 250,000 men were still tied down in the Peninsula was a key factor in his ultimate downfall. And much of the credit for this must go to Wellington, who, in late April, was made a duke and appointed the new British ambassador to France. At last he had emulated the social rank of that other great soldier, the Duke of Marlborough; but many of his redcoats thought this scant reward, with one sergeant commenting that 'he ought to be made a Prince of the Blood for he was sure he had shed enough of it.'[97]

For his part, Wellington used his final General Order of 14 June to congratulate his troops 'upon the recent events which have restored peace to their country and the world'. He added: 'The share which the British army has had in producing these events, and the high character with which the army will quit this country, must be equally satisfactory to every individual belonging to it, as it is to the Commander of the Forces . . . [He] assures them that he shall never cease to feel the warmest interest in their welfare and honour, and that he will at all times be happy to be of service to those whose conduct, discipline and gallantry, their country is much indebted.'[98]

He and they had come a long way from the broken, dispirited British force that was driven out of Holland by the victorious French Revolutionary Army during the bitter winter of 1794/5. The reforms of the Duke of York had helped to create a more efficient, meritocratic army; and the long years of almost constant combat in the Peninsula had turned Wellington's soldiers into battle-hardened veterans to compare with any in history. Certainly Wellington felt that by 1814 no task, however difficult, was beyond them. 'They will do for me,' he declared, 'what perhaps no one else can make them do.'[99]

But with the war over, this formidable fighting force was broken up, some to be sent to North America and the East and West Indies, others to Britain and Ireland. As for the Portuguese and Spanish women camp followers who had marched, cooked, washed, slept with and plundered for the soldiers, they were to be ruthlessly discarded. The last sound that Wellington's men remember as their transports weighed anchor at Bordeaux was the wailing of the women left behind.[100]

In Paris, meanwhile, Wellington was asked if he had any regrets that he was never opposed by Napoleon in person. 'No, and I am very glad I never was,' he replied with disarming humility. 'I would at any time rather have heard that a reinforcement of forty thousand men had joined the French army, than that he had arrived to take command.'[101]

20. Escape from Elba

On 1 March 1815 an armed brig and six smaller vessels dropped anchor off Golfe-Juan, near the French fort of Antibes on the Côte d'Azur. Within minutes, cutters packed with soldiers were heading for the rocky shoreline. The first to disembark and approach the fort were arrested. But the soldiers kept coming, and soon more than a thousand grenadiers, a troop of Polish lancers and two guns had been landed. As the light began to fail, a familiar short stocky figure came ashore, walking along an improvised gangway held up by soldiers waist-deep in the water. This time an officer was dispatched to the fort to inform the commandant that the ex-Emperor Napoleon, after ten months' exile on Elba, had returned to reclaim his throne.

News of Napoleon's escape reached Paris on 4 March, and three days later Vienna, where the Duke of Wellington was sitting as Britain's plenipotentiary to the Congress tasked with redrawing Europe's boundaries. Many of the delegates thought the news a joke and burst out laughing. But confirmation soon arrived, and on 12 March Wellington informed Lord Castlereagh, the foreign secretary, that the Allies planned to raise three armies to oppose Napoleon: an Austrian army in northern Italy; an Austro-German army on the upper Rhine; and a Prussian army on the lower Rhine that would advance into the Netherlands to link up with the British and Hanoverian army of occupation. A slower-moving Russian army, meanwhile, would constitute a reserve.

Castlereagh's response was to offer Wellington a choice: remain in Vienna as the British plenipotentiary or take command of the Anglo-Hanoverian troops in Flanders. Preferring to 'carry a musket', he opted for the latter. Before leaving Vienna, he was left in no doubt of his responsibility. 'It is for you,' said Tsar Alexander, laying a hand on his shoulder, 'to save the world again.'[1] By now the Congress had declared Napoleon an outlaw subject to 'vindicte publique' (though there was much debate as to whether this authorized summary punishment or the need for a trial).[2]

Back in London, the government and the public anxiously awaited the outcome of Napoleon's audacious move. On 12 March dispatches arrived from Colonel FitzRoy Somerset in Paris to the effect that 'Bonaparte had not advanced further than Gap, and had not received any assistance.' Four days later Somerset corrected himself: 'Bonaparte had been joined by all the troops which had been sent against him, and . . . had entered Grenoble, and afterwards Lyon on the 10th.'[3]

Somerset was more optimistic on the 18th. Napoleon, whose 'whole force did not amount to 9,000 men', had not advanced beyond Lyons, Paris was 'quite quiet' and the marshals 'were all firm in their allegiance' to Louis XVIII. Two days later came an unofficial report that Napoleon's rearguard 'had been defeated with great loss by Marshal Ney'. A more accurate picture emerged on the 22nd, when a King's Messenger confirmed that the French king had left Paris for Abbeville. The following day, word was received that Napoleon had made a triumphal entry into Paris on the 20th. 'No . . . dispatches have arrived,' recorded the diarist Charles Greville, 'but it appears that the Troops everywhere joined him, and that he marched to the capital without the slightest opposition, or a shot having been fired since his landing at Cannes [*sic*].'[4]

Once in Paris, Napoleon wrote personally to all the sovereigns of Europe, assuring them that he desired only peace and renouncing all claims to the territories that had belonged to France at the height of his empire. The monarchs did not even deign to respond, though in Britain the reaction from senior politicians was surprisingly mixed. Earl Grey and a significant proportion of the Whig Opposition wanted to recognize Bonaparte's new regime as a lesser evil than Louis XVIII's corrupt government. So, too, did Lord Wellesley, Wellington's elder brother. But Liverpool's government, backed by a sizeable parliamentary majority – all the Tories, most of the Independent MPs and Lord Grenville's Whigs – was determined to crush Napoleon once and for all. Britain's three European allies – Prussia, Austria and Russia – were similarly resolute, with each country pledging 150,000 men and Britain an additional £6 million in subsidies to make up for its shortfall in troops. With the government short of cash, it was left to the Rothschild brothers to raise the money.

Wellington reached Brussels on 4 April to find the French royal family in residence. He had little time for the king and his brother, the Comte d'Artois, having witnessed at first hand the failings of the restored monarchy during his time as ambassador in Paris from June 1814 to February 1815. He therefore proposed to his government a compromise 'third term' monarch in the person of the Duc d'Orléans, son of Philippe Égalité and head of a junior branch of the Bourbons. But Castlereagh was unimpressed, informing Wellington on 16 April that Louis XVIII must be supported 'for the present'.[5]

With his political initiative rebuffed, Wellington concentrated on what he knew best: preparing an army for war. He was helped immeasurably by the decision of King William I of the Netherlands to make him commander-in-chief of all Dutch–Belgian forces on 3 May. This allowed him to mix Dutch–Belgian and German troops with his more reliable British and King's German Legion (KGL) units, as he had done so successfully with Portuguese troops in the Peninsula. His three corps – I, II and a Reserve Corps commanded by him in person – were each composed of two British divisions and two of other nationalities. Yet still he was concerned. 'I have got an infamous army,' he complained in mid-May, 'very weak and ill-equipped, and a very inexperienced staff. In my opinion they are doing nothing in England.'[6]

Wellington was right to complain. Many of his Peninsular veterans had been disbanded or dispatched overseas – some to America, where the insufficiently named War of 1812 with the United States had just ended with a British victory and a measure of revenge for the army's humiliation in the War of Independence – and even those garrisoned in the British Isles were arriving in dribs and drabs. One of the first battalions to reach the Netherlands from England was the 1/23rd Fusiliers, once more a single-unit regiment since the disbandment of its 2nd Battalion in October 1814. It was in barracks at Gosport on the south coast when it was warned of its move on 23 March. 'We are all in the highest spirits,' wrote Lieutenant John McDonald to his father that day.

Quite delighted for we received our order for embarkation this morning. Destination of course not mentioned but must be either France
or Holland. Every person quite astonished at the progress Bonaparte
has made. A messenger passed this morning who said he's at Fontain-
bleu [near Paris], also that all the troops refuse to act against him, but
we do not believe every thing we hear this way for we have had so
many sharpers [conmen] that pretend to be government agents and
have taken in the good people of Portsmouth for large sums. We
embark tomorrow morning at nine o'clock about seven hundred as
fine men as ever fixed bayonets.[7]

Contrary winds prevented McDonald's battalion from landing in
Ostend until 30 March, and from there it moved by barge to Bruges,
and on foot to its billets in Ghent, arriving on 2 April. McDonald
wrote a day later:

Tell the Girls [his sisters] I saw Louis the Eighteenth yesterday and
was even at his dinner table! . . . The King and Royal Family always dine
in Public, at last allowing all Ladies to enter, and yesterday he included
all British officers in uniform. [Marshals] Victor, Augereau, Marmont, Clarke and a number of other French officers of distinction
were at his table.[8]

Another of Wellington's Peninsular veterans who arrived in Flanders
at this time was Private Thomas Pococke of the 71st Highlanders.
His battalion had been due to sail from Cork for America; but
unfavourable winds delayed its departure for six weeks, long enough
for the transports to be diverted to Antwerp. 'Next morning,' wrote
Pococke, 'we were marched to Leuze, where we lay, quartered in different villages around, until the 16th of June, 1815. We used to be
drilled every day.'[9] The 71st was – with the 52nd Light Infantry and
the 2nd/95th Rifles – part of the crack Light Brigade under Major-
General Frederick Adam.

Private Charles Stanley of the 1st King's Dragoon Guards, who had
not fought in Spain, had landed at Ostend in April and by mid-May
was billeted with his regiment to the west of Brussels as part of the
Household Brigade of Heavy Cavalry. He could not wait to get to

grips with Bonaparte's Army of the North, part of which was stationed on the French frontier, just 15 miles south of Brussels. 'We have the most cavalry of the English that ever was at one time,' he wrote to his cousin in May, 'and in good condition and good spirits. There is no doubt of us beating the confounded rascal. It may cost me my life, and many more, [but] that will only be the fortune of war. My life I set no store by at all . . . I hope you will never think of being a soldier. It is a very rough concern.'[10]

An officer in the same regiment, Lieutenant John Hibbert, was pleasantly surprised by the reception they received from the locals as they marched through Flanders. He wrote to his father on 15 May:

> The country we have hitherto passed through is most beautiful; from Ostend to Ghent the road is paved and as level as a bowling green the whole way, but the country on each side is a perfect garden, the cottages and gardens far surpass England and the inhabitants are uncommonly civil especially to English men who are much liked in Flanders. They detest the Prussians; they gave us to understand that it was impossible to satisfy them in any particular, and the common men would generally plunder them of everything they had before they departed from their billets. They said we behaved like gentlemen, and therefore tried to anticipate our wishes in everything they could.[11]

As ever, the number of soldiers' wives that were allowed to follow the troops on campaign was tightly restricted. When the Scots Greys embarked from Gravesend, for example, 'many a man left behind him a wife and children unprotected and unprovided for', according to the diary of a quartermaster-sergeant. He added: 'On going ashore [before departure] we had the opportunity of witnessing the most distressing scenes of women parting from their husbands, their faces covered with tears, and some of them with a child on their back and one in each hand, calling out from the shore to their husbands on board the transports, many of whom would never meet again.'[12]

Some of those following the 42nd Highlanders got as far as Ostend before they were separated from their protectors and told to fend for themselves. Two days later, recorded Quartermaster-Sergeant James Anton, 'they found their way to the regiment' at Ghent, but were recognized and taken back to Ostend. Undeterred, 'they eluded the vigilance of the sentries, and joined their husbands once more, and as no official reports were made to their prejudice, they followed the fortunes of their husbands during the campaign, along with those who boasted the privilege.'[13] Anton's own view was that no women should be allowed to accompany their husbands to war. 'If an exception is made in one single instance,' he wrote,

> it only gives room for pressing, and almost irresistible applications from others, and throws the performance of a very painful duty, namely, that of refusing permission, on the officers commanding the companies . . . Why should not the soldier contribute part of his pay towards the maintenance of his family at home? In fact, it ought to be stipulated that he should do so, before permission is given him to marry. If no women were permitted to accompany the army (I mean on a hostile campaign, for I see no objection that can be made to the women being permitted to follow their husbands in time of peace . . .), the married men might earn more than their daily pay, by washing for the officers and non-commissioned officers, and to any of the single men who are not inclined to wash their own linen, and thus be enabled to make the larger remittances.[14]

For those seemingly fortunate wives who made the quota, conditions on campaign were both harsh and dangerous, and would have been unbearable 'were it not that each sees her neighbour suffering as much as herself'. Anton explained: 'Her bed is generally the damp ground; her threadbare mantle, which envelops her bundle by day, serves for a sheet by night, and her husband's blanket for a coverlet.'[15]

By late May only a little over a third of Wellington's 114,000-strong army was made up of British soldiers. They were stiffened by units of cavalry and infantry from the KGL, a formation loyal to George III that in the Peninsula had proved itself equal to any British unit. 'It was,' concluded the Waterloo chronicler Ian Fletcher, 'a pale shadow of the old Peninsular army, but there were, nevertheless, some fine regiments present, and the British contingent was certainly not the inexperienced and raw army . . . that some historians would have us believe.'[16]

Regardless of his complaints, even Wellington was confident that he and the Prussians, under the sprightly 73-year-old Marshal Gebhard von Blücher, would be too strong for Napoleon. 'By God!' he told the diarist Thomas Creevey in a Brussels park, 'I think Blücher and myself can do the thing.' He then pointed to a British private admiring the park's statues: 'It all depends upon that article whether we do the business or not. Give me enough of it, and I am sure.'[17]

What Wellington was not expecting was for Napoleon to take the initiative. 'Blücher and I are so well united, and so strong,' he told Charles Stewart, Castlereagh's brother, on 8 May, that he did not believe they would be attacked.[18] His intention, instead, was to wait for the other Allied armies to reach the frontiers of France before he and Blücher advanced side by side. But he was also acutely aware that his army, as ever, depended upon maritime lines of communication – both for resupply and, in the event of a reverse in battle, possible evacuation – and it was for that reason that he fortified and left sizeable garrisons in Antwerp and Ostend to guard these two potential lines of retreat.

On 3 May, Wellington and Blücher met at Tirlemont, 25 miles east of Brussels, to discuss strategy. Neither left a detailed record of the meeting, but we do know they agreed that the old Roman road from Ligny to Maastricht would be their line of demarcation, with Wellington's army keeping to the west of the line and the Prussians to the east. It seems likely they also decided, in the event of Napoleon advancing through either Charleroi or Mons to threaten their line of junction, to concentrate their respective armies at Nivelles (Wellington) and Sombreffe (Blücher), either side of the strategic crossroads at Quatre Bras so that they could support each other. They had already exchanged liaison officers, with Colonel Henry Hardinge (the hero of Albuera) accompanying Blücher and Major-General Baron Carl von Müffling joining Wellington's staff.

Efforts were made to gather intelligence, with Lieutenant-Colonel Colquhoun Grant running a spy ring inside France for Wellington, and Major-General Sir William Dörnberg, commanding a Hanoverian cavalry brigade near Mons on the frontier, also sending reports back to headquarters. But their efforts were hampered by the fact that, as Wellington put it on 11 May, they were 'neither at war nor at peace, unable on that account to patrole up to the enemy and ascertain his position by view'; moreover Dörnberg was not privy to Grant's mission and failed to forward a message from him on 14 June that would have given Wellington advance warning of French movements.[19]

Napoleon, meanwhile, was busily expanding the army he had inherited from the Bourbons by recalling the previous year's conscripts, mobilizing the National Guard, mass producing muskets and buying or confiscating all available horses. By early June he had assembled a field army – the Army of the North – of 124,000 men and 344 guns. Commanded by him in person, it was made up of the Imperial Guard, a cavalry army and five infantry corps, and contained a mixture of veterans and untried conscripts, staunch Bonapartists and resentful royalists. 'It lacked,' wrote Richard Holmes, 'the innate cohesion and staying power of the armies that Napoleon had once commanded.'[20]

The emperor himself was not at his best during the campaign, with historians suggesting a myriad of illnesses from a tumour on the pituitary gland to piles. Perhaps the best assessment was given by David Chandler, the Napoleonic scholar, who described his performance in the campaign as 'obstinate, arrogant and overconfident', and although 'the decline in his mental and physical powers have been overrated, there are yet some undeniable indications of deterioration in his overall ability'.[21] His biographer Frank McLynn agrees: 'Throughout the short Belgian campaign he was fatigued, needed lots of sleep, was lethargic and indecisive and generally prone to inertia.'[22] It certainly did not help that many of his best marshals – Marmont, Victor, Augereau and Berthier, his indispensable chief of staff (killed in a fall from a window on 1 June) – remained loyal to Louis XVIII, and that he chose to rely instead on the decidedly second-rate Honoré Reille, Georges Lobau, Jean-Baptiste d'Erlon, Étienne Gérard, Emmanuel de Grouchy and Ney as his senior commanders, while Soult, one of the few marshals of genuine talent still available to him, was wasted as Berthier's replacement, and Louis-Nicolas Davout was left in Paris as minister of war.

Napoleon knew that he could not defeat the Allied armies once they had concentrated against him, so he decided to deal with the British and Prussians before the others could intervene. Neither was a particularly formidable force: Wellington's army of 114,000, as we have seen, was polyglot, with troops from Britain, the Low Countries and various German principalities, including Hanover, Brunswick and Nassau; Blücher's slightly larger force of 116,000 men contained a slight majority of Landwehr (militia), with many recruited from outside Prussia, though the regulars it did contain were tough and hardy.

Another advantage for Napoleon was that, until operations began, the two Allied armies would remain quartered with civilians over a huge area – much of modern Belgium – one (Wellington's) largely to the west of Brussels and the other (Blücher's) to the east. Assuming that each of his opponents would take at least two or three days to concentrate his forces, Napoleon planned to advance between them and attack the first one he came across. Having defeated it, he would then deal with the other one. It all hinged on the element of surprise, and to give himself the best chance he closed the borders of France in early June, forbidding either a man or a letter to leave the country. At the same time he swiftly concentrated his Army of the North close to the Netherlands border between Mauberge and Philippeville, and himself left Paris to join it on 12 June.

Wellington received word of this the following day from a variety of sources, including a remarkably accurate report from Dörnberg that named Mauberge as the concentration area and said Napoleon was 'hourly expected'. The duke was unconvinced. 'There is nothing new here,' he wrote to his former comrade Sir Thomas Graham (now Lord Lynedoch) on 13 June. 'We have reports of Buonaparte's joining the army and attacking us; but I have accounts from Paris of the 10th, on which day he was still there; and I judge from his speech to the Legislature [on the 7th] that his departure was not likely to be imminent. I think we are now too strong for him here.'[23]

In truth, his force was dangerously spread out, with his II Corps (under General 'Daddy' Hill) forward on the right covering the roads to Ghent and Ostend, his I Corps (under HRH the Prince of Orange) forward on the left protecting the roads to Brussels and Antwerp, and the Reserve Corps with him in and around Brussels. This wide deployment did, however, enable him to meet any of Napoleon's three most likely thrusts: through Tournai, aimed at cutting his communications; through Mons, with Brussels as its objective; and through Charleroi, towards the junction of the two armies. He regarded the third option through Charleroi as the least likely. Inevitably it was the one that Napoleon chose.

At dawn on Thursday, 15 June, French cavalrymen crossed the Netherlands border near Philippeville and advanced up the road towards Charleroi, followed by dense columns of infantry. By noon Napoleon's Imperial Guard had driven the Prussians out of Charleroi and the French were soon pouring across the Sambre. In the early afternoon Napoleon split his army: Marshal Ney was sent up the Brussels road with two infantry corps and a large force of cavalry to capture Quatre Bras before Wellington could reinforce it, thus keeping Napoleon's strategic options open; while Marshal Grouchy was given command of the French right wing and told to push the Prussians east towards Sombreffe near Ligny, where, as it happened, Blücher had planned to concentrate his army in the event of a surprise attack. Napoleon would bring up the centre of the army and destroy whichever enemy appeared first.

This was likely to be the Prussians. Blücher knew this and, having sent Wellington word of the French attack on the 15th, he assumed that his ally would move his own army to assist him, as they had agreed at Tirlemont. But Wellington – who received a number of warning messages that day – remained cautious. The first dispatch arrived at nine in the morning. It was from General Hans Joachim von Ziethen, commanding the Prussian I Corps at Charleroi, and stated that his outposts had been attacked and driven in at Thuin near the border. Wellington's reaction was to wait for more news; and when, according to his friend and biographer G. R. Gleig, this was not immediately forthcoming, 'the Duke naturally assumed that [the attack] was a feint to cover some serious operations elsewhere.'[24]

A second dispatch arrived from Ziethen in the afternoon and was delivered to Wellington by his Prussian liaison, General Müffling, at 'half past four'. [25] But it was not until the receipt of a message at 5 p.m. from the Prince of Orange – to the effect that the Prussians had been pushed out of the village of Binche, and that the prince had heard gunfire around Charleroi with his own ears – that Wellington finally decided to act.[26] He told Colonel William De Lancey, his quartermaster-general, to order all units of the Reserve Corps to assemble at their divisional headquarters and be ready to march at a moment's notice. Colonel Somerset, his military secretary, remembered returning to headquarters to find 'the Duke in the Park giving

> necessary orders to those around him. He wished everything to be in
> readiness to move on an instant; but was waiting for further informa-
> tion before he made a decided movement with any part of his army, it
> being of the utmost consequence first to ascertain the point to which
> Bonaparte directed his operations.[27]

Concerned that Wellington had given no definite order to march, Somerset looked for reassurance. 'No doubt,' he remarked later to his chief, 'we shall be able to manage those Fellows.'

'There is little doubt,' replied Wellington with more confidence than he could have felt, 'provided I do not make a false Movement.'[28]

Wellington's cautious reaction was potentially fatal for the Prussians. Müffling was well aware of this when he delivered a third message to Wellington – this time from General Neidhardt von Gneisenau, Blücher's chief of staff – at around 9.30 p.m., confirming that Blücher had concentrated his army at Sombreffe as agreed. What was Wellington going to do to support him? asked Müffling. Nothing, replied Wellington, until he knew for certain that the main attack was not coming through Mons. 'For this reason,' he added, 'I must wait for my advice from Mons before I fix my rendezvous.'[29]

That advice arrived shortly after in the form of a message from General Dörnberg at Mons: Napoleon had moved on Charleroi with 'all his force, and that he . . . has nothing in his front'.[30] Only now would Wellington issue new orders for his troops to concentrate on Nivelles. In the meantime, he told his staff, it was vital that they continued with their plan to attend the Duchess of Richmond's ball to prevent panic and to mislead French spies as to their intentions. Wellington arrived at the ball – held in a coach-house on the ground floor of the Richmonds' Brussels residence – at 10.30 and stayed until shortly after midnight. He did his best to conceal his understandable worry at what the morrow would bring, but one female guest who sat beside him on a sofa was not fooled. 'Although the duke affected great gaiety and cheefulness,' recalled Lady Hamilton-Dalrymple, 'it struck me that I had never seen him have such an expression of care and anxiety on his countenance.'[31] She added: 'Frequently in the middle of a sentence he stopped abruptly and called to some officer, giving him directions, in particular to the Duke of Brunswick and Prince of Orange, who both left the ball before supper.'[32]

Shortly after midnight, the Prince of Orange returned and gave Wellington a message he had just received from his corps headquarters at Braine-le-Comte on the road to Mons. It was from the prince's chief of staff, General Jean Rebecque, and stated that the French had tried to take Quatre Bras but had been repulsed by a brigade of General Hendrik Perponcher's Netherlands Division, and that Rebecque had on his own initiative ordered up a second brigade in support.[33] (But for Ney's hesitation, fearing a larger force than he was actually opposed to, the crossroads would already have been in French hands.) Now Wellington knew for certain that Napoleon was advancing up two separate axes, and that his own left flank at Quatre Bras was in danger of being overwhelmed unless it was reinforced. He at once rose and asked his host, the Duke of Richmond, if he had a good map. Richmond showed him one in his study, causing Wellington to exclaim: 'Napoleon has humbugged me, by God! He has gained twenty-four hours' march on me.'

'What do you intend doing?' asked Richmond.

'I have ordered the army to concentrate at Quatre Bras; but we shall not stop him there, and if so, I must fight him *here*,' said Wellington, placing his thumb on the ridge before the village of Waterloo, on the road between Quatre Bras and Brussels.[34]

It is a wonderfully vivid anecdote that, not surprisingly, has been repeated by most chroniclers of the battle, certainly those wishing to exculpate Wellington's potentially disastrous hesitation on 15 June.

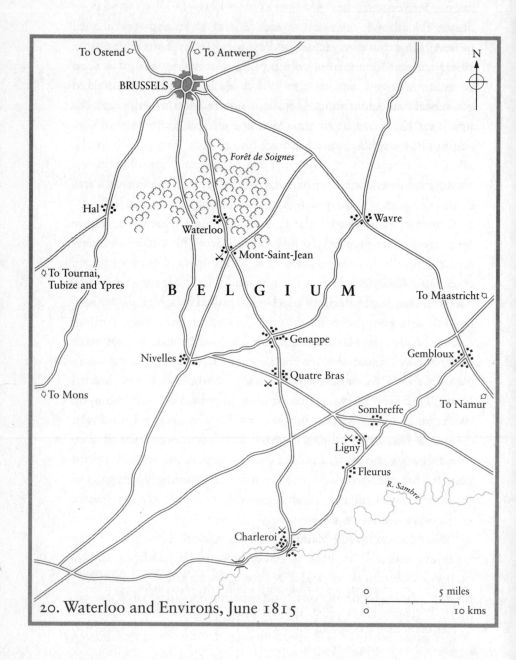

N

To Ostend

To Antwerp

BRUSSELS

Forêt de Soignes

Hal

Wavre

Waterloo

Mont-Saint-Jean

To Tournai,
Tubize and Ypres

B E L G I U M

To Maastricht

Genappe

Gembloux

Nivelles

Quatre Bras

To Mons

To Namur

Sombreffe

Ligny

Fleurus

R. Sambre

Charleroi

5 miles

10 kms

20. Waterloo and Environs, June 1815

Yet its veracity is to be doubted on two grounds: first, its original source, Richmond's aide-de-camp, Captain Bowles, was not present during the alleged conversation; and second Wellington had not yet ordered the army to concentrate at Quatre Bras, though he would shortly do so. What is not in doubt, however, is that Wellington had been 'humbugged' and that he now knew, beyond question, that Napoleon was attempting to drive a wedge between him and the Prussians. He also knew he had to move fast to prevent this from happening. But was he already too late?

Wellington rose at 5.30 a.m. on the 16th, after little more than three hours' sleep, and by seven was riding south to Quatre Bras, followed by the slower-moving infantry of Picton's 5th Division. Private Dixon Vallance of the 79th Highlanders, billeted in a Brussels public house with three others, remembered the call to arms: 'Drums, trumpets, bugles, all kicking up the finest discord that ever was heard. The inhabitants all rose from their beds and the soldiers were collecting in the streets, such shouting, swearing, crying, arms rattling, dragoons and officers galloping about, in short I think the confusion at Babel was a fool to it.'[35]

An officer in the same brigade, Lieutenant Johnny Kincaid of the 1/95th Rifles, recalled trying to snatch an hour's sleep on the pavement while all the battalions were assembled in the Place Royale. 'But we were every instant disturbed, by ladies as well as gentlemen; some stumbling over us in the dark – some shaking us out of our sleep, to be told the news – and not a few, conceiving their immediate safety depending upon our standing in place of lying.'[36] Finally, at around 8 a.m., they were on their way. Corporal Edward Costello of the 1/95th, who like Kincaid had stormed the breach at Ciudad Rodrigo, wrote:

> All things arranged, we passed the gates of Brussels, and descended the wood of Soignes, that leads to the little village of Waterloo. It was the 16th – a beautiful summer morning – the sun slowly rising above the horizon and peeping through the trees, while our men were as merry as crickets, laughing and joking with each other, and at times

pondered in their minds what all this fuss, as they called it, could be about: for even the old soldiers could not believe the enemy were so near.[37]

Riding ahead, Wellington and his staff reached Quatre Bras at 10 a.m., where he found the two Netherlands brigades in a defensive position. There was no sign of Ney. Wellington dashed off a quick note to Blücher, noting the position of his army as much further south-east than it actually was (though, to be fair, it was moving in that direction), and declaring that 'I await news from Your Highness and the arrival of troops to decide my operations for the day.'[38] He then rode over to Sombreffe to talk to Blücher in person, noting while he was there that the Prussian marshal had posted three of his four corps around the village of Ligny and would shortly be attacked. When Blücher asked for assistance, Wellington said he would provide it in the afternoon, but only if he was 'not attacked' first.[39] Before leaving, he advised Blücher to withdraw his exposed men behind reverse slopes for protection. Blücher's chief of staff, Gneisenau, responded dismissively: 'My men like to see the enemy.'[40]

Wellington arrived back at Quatre Bras to find the battle under way and Perponcher's Netherlands Division giving ground to Ney's 20,000-strong II Corps, with another corps of the same strength in reserve. Napoleon's intention had been for Ney to take the crossroads and then support his attack on the Prussians at Ligny. But Ney's orders from Soult were less than clear: 'The intention of his Majesty is that you attack whatever is before you and after vigorously throwing them back, join us to envelop this corps.'[41] Soult's error was a failure to emphasize that the action at Ligny had priority, and that Ney should not commit himself to a battle that would prevent him from turning on the Prussians. Even so, Ney could easily have taken Quatre Bras and sent most of his men back to Ligny if he had started his main attack earlier. But he delayed until almost 2 p.m. and, just as he was making progress by capturing the hill and farm at Quatre Bras, the first battalions of Picton's 5th Division arrived to shore up the creaking Netherlanders' defence of the Bossu Wood. It now became a race between Wellington's reinforcements, marching up the road from Brussels in stifling heat, and Ney's increasingly bold attackers. Fortunately, the imperturbable Wellington was on hand to direct the British troops to their defensive positions. Among the first to reach the battlefield was Sergeant James Anton of the kilted 42nd Highlanders:

> We were all ready and in line. 'Forward!' was the word of command, and forward we hastened, though we saw no enemy in front. The stalks of rye, like the reeds that grow on the margin of some swamp, opposed our advance . . . By the time we reached a field of clover on the other side, we were very much straggled; however, we united in line as time and our speedy advance would permit. The Belgic skirmishers retired through our ranks, and in an instant we were on their victorious pursuers. Our sudden appearance seemed to paralyse their advance. The singular appearance of our dress, combined no doubt with our sudden debut, tended to stagger their resolution: we were on them, our pieces were loaded, and our bayonets glittered . . . Those who had so proudly driven the Belgians before them, turned now to fly, whilst our loud cheers made the fields echo to our wild hurrahs.[42]

Picton's Brunswick Contingent was the next to reach Quatre Bras and, led by the Duke of Brunswick himself, its cavalry charged the retreating French infantry. But they were swiftly counter-attacked and driven back by French chasseurs, who mortally wounded the Duke of Brunswick and caused Wellington to seek refuge in the square of the 92nd Highlanders.

Two regiments of French lancers were the next to charge and, mistaking them for Brunswickers, the 42nd was caught with its square only half formed. Anton recalled:

> We stood with too much confidence, gazing towards them as if they had been our friends . . . making no preparative movement to receive them as enemies, further than the reloading of the muskets, until a German orderly dragoon galloped up, exclaiming, 'Franchee! Franchee!', and wheeling about, galloped off. We instantly formed a rallying square. Every man's piece was loaded, and our enemies

approached at full charge; the feet of their horses seemed to tear up the ground. Our skirmishers having been impressed with the same opinion, that these were Brunswick cavalry, fell beneath their lances, and few escaped death or wounds. Our brave colonel fell at this time, pierced through the chin until the point of the lance reached the brain.[43]

In a matter of minutes the 42nd lost three successive commanding officers to wounds and death. Fortunately a brigade of the 3rd Division had now arrived and Wellington at once sent it forward. The brigade commander, Sir Colin Halkett, ordered his battalions to form squares; but he was overruled by his corps commander, the Prince of Orange, who, seeing no more French cavalry, told Halkett to form his men into line. No sooner had he done so than the brigade was charged by French cuirassiers – heavy cavalry with armoured breast-plates – and badly mauled. The 2/69th was almost destroyed; the 2/73rd forced to take cover in a wood; and the 33rd, though it managed to form a square in time, was severely cut up by artillery fire. 'The superiority of the enemy in cavalry,' commented Sergeant Anton, 'afforded him a decided advantage on the open plain, for our British cavalry and artillery had not yet reached the field.'[44]

It was left, therefore, to successive battalions of British infantry to hold the ground. Ensign Nevill Macready of the 2/30th, the fourth of Halkett's battalions, arrived late with a detachment and was directed towards his unit. He wrote:

The roaring of great guns and musquetry, the bursting of shells and shouts of the combatants raised an infernal and indescribable din, while the galloping of horses, the mingled crowds of wounded and fugitives (Belgians), the volumes of smoke and flashing of fire struck out a scene which accorded admirably with the music. As we passed a spot where the 44th our old chums had suffered considerably the poor wounded fellows raised themselves up and welcomed us with faint shouts 'push on old Thirtieth – pay 'em off for the poor 44th you're much wanted my boys . . .' We reached [our battalion] just as a body of Lancers and Cuirassiers had enveloped two faces of its square. We formed up to the left and fired away. The tremendous volley which our square . . . gave them, sent off these fellows with the loss of a number of men and their commanding officer . . . On our repulse of the Cavalry, Sir Thomas Picton rode up and thanked us warmly as this body had cut up two or three regiments.[45]

Out on Wellington's left flank, meanwhile, the 1/95th had been pushed forward to keep open the road to Ligny. But, having easily taken a wood from light French troops – during which operation Corporal Costello was wounded – they were eventually forced back by weight of numbers. 'The Adjutant [Lieutenant Kincaid] came with an order for us to retire,' recalled Lieutenant James Gairdner, 'and occupy some houses on a ridge in our rear. There was no order for the Brunswickers to retire. However they came away with us. The consequence was that the French crowded into the wood when they saw us leave it . . . We were obliged to halt on a bare ridge above it and there make a stand. I there received a wound in the foot and went to the rear, and afterwards heard that three attempts were made to Retake the wood that night but the French kept it after all.'[46]

Elsewhere the French were making little headway, and Ney sent infantry columns forward as his last throw of the dice. But they were repulsed by fresh reinforcements from the 1st Division and a gallant charge by the 92nd Highlanders. At around 9 p.m. Ney admitted defeat and withdrew. He had lost slightly fewer troops than Wellington – 4,000 to 4,800 – but the real significance of his repulse is that it deprived Napoleon of reinforcements at Ligny that might have turned victory over the Prussians into a rout.

The battle had begun well for Napoleon, with his massed artillery batteries tearing great holes in the exposed Prussian infantry. If Ney had appeared on the Prussians' right flank, as planned, the result would have been a crushing French victory. But he did not appear. In desperation, Napoleon ordered the commander of Ney's uncommitted reserve, General d'Erlon, to march to Ligny with his 20,000 men. D'Erlon duly turned his men around and reached Ligny at around 6 p.m. while the battle was still raging. But he arrived not on the flank of the Prussians but of the French, causing a momentary panic in Napoleon's army as it assumed they were enemy troops. By the time the confusion was sorted out, and d'Erlon's men redirected to the Prussian flank, Ney had countermanded Napoleon's order and recalled d'Erlon to Quatre Bras on pain of court martial. D'Erlon obeyed, and his troops took no part in either battle, thus ensuring that neither engagement ended in a complete victory for Napoleon.

Still, Ligny came close, because at 8 p.m, an hour and a half later than planned, Napoleon's Imperial Guard smashed through the centre of the Prussian position. In desperation Blücher led a cavalry counter-attack; but it was easily beaten off and, in the mêlée, the Prussian commander was unhorsed and ridden over. He would have been captured but for the quick thinking of his aide-de-camp, Count Nostitz, who threw a cloak over his chief's medals and helped him to a nearby cottage. Only the onset of darkness saved the Prussian army from an overwhelming defeat. It had lost 16,000 men at Ligny – 4,000 more than the French – and a further 9,000 deserted as the survivors withdrew in the night. Its centre had been destroyed but not its two wings, thanks to Ney, and it was still a force to be reckoned with if it could maintain contact with Wellington's army.

At first that seemed unlikely, as Gneisenau, commander in Blücher's temporary absence, gave orders for the army to fall back on its line of communications to the east, thus swinging it away from Wellington. He did this, at least in part, because he felt the British had reneged on their pledge to support the Prussians that day, telling the King of Prussia that they had agreed to fight at Ligny only because 'the Duke of Wellington promised to be at Quatre Bras at 10am with 20,000 men'.[47] But he was overruled by Blücher – who had eventually arrived bruised and bloodied at the farmhouse that was serving as Prussian headquarters – and the army was redirected north to Wavre, from where it could maintain contact with the British and move back on its lines of communication if necessary.

Back at Quatre Bras, meanwhile, Wellington's troops were still arriving on the field of battle. Among them was Captain Cavalié Mercer, commanding G Troop of the Royal Horse Artillery, who had marched that day with the cavalry from west of Brussels, a distance of more than 30 miles. On entering Nivelles, he and his men could hear the sound of firing, and see smoke rising, from nearby

Quatre Bras. 'The whole population of Nivelle[s] was in the streets,' he recorded in his journal, 'doors and windows all wide open, whilst the inmates of the houses, male and female, stood huddled together in little groups like frightened sheep, or were hurrying along with the distracted air of people uncertain where they are going, or what they are doing.' Some cheered the British troops; others 'stood apart, with gloomy discontented looks, eyeing their fellow-citizens with evident contempt, and us with scowls, not unmixed with derision, as they marked our dusty and jaded apperance'.[48]

Beyond the town, wrote Mercer, the 'road was covered with soldiers, many of them wounded, but also many apparently untouched'. Each wounded soldier had 'six, eight, ten, and even more attendants', and when asked why they had left the battle, they answered, 'Monsieur, tout est perdu!' They were mostly Nassauers and Belgians, according to Mercer, who did not see one unwounded redcoat 'amongst this dastardly crew'. When he finally reached the field of Quatre Bras – 'our horses stumbling from time to time over the corpses of the slain' – the battle was over bar the firing of a few cannon and muskets. He wrote:

> Darks crowds of men moved in the increasing obscurity of evening, and the whole seemed alive with them. What a moment of excitement and anxiety as we proceeded amongst all this tumult, and amidst the dead and dying, ignorant as yet how the affair had terminated! Arrived at a mass of buildings, where four roads met (*les quatres bras*), Major McDonald again came up with orders for us to bivouac on an adjoining field, where, accordingly, we established ourselves amongst the remains of a wheat crop. Our men dismounted, and the horses tied to the wheels of the [gun] carriages, every one was despatched with canteens and water-buckets to a well at the farm, to procure water for themselves and horses.[49]

Wellington spent the night in the Roi d'Espagne inn at Genappe, 3 miles north of Quatre Bras, hopeful that Blücher had also held his ground. He had received one gloomy report from a young captain – brother of his liaison officer, Henry Hardinge, who had lost a hand at Ligny – to the effect that the Prussians had 'suffered severely'. But he was not aware of the scale of the Prussian defeat until seven the following morning, when a British cavalry patrol returned to Quatre Bras with the unwelcome news. A shocked Wellington turned to Captain Bowles and exclaimed: 'Old Blücher has had a damned good licking and gone back to Wavre, eighteen miles. As he has gone back we must go too. I suppose in England they will say that we have been licked. I can't help it.'[50]

For the next hour or so, Wellington and his staff worked on the orders for the retreat. The Royal Engineers had for some days been surveying the ridges to the south of the village of Waterloo, in case a battle needed to be fought there, and it was to this location that the army was ordered to retire during the morning of the 17th. De Lancey, Wellington's quartermaster-general, was sent in advance to mark out the ground, and it was his decision not to choose the more southerly and commanding of the two ridges, either side of La Belle Alliance inn, because the 'ground was too extended to be occupied by our Troops'.[51] Instead he selected the crossroads on the Mont-Saint-Jean Ridge, 1½ miles to the north, giving a potential battlefield of just 2½ miles across. Not only was it a very strong defensive position, it was also just 7 miles west of Wavre; and Wellington was happy to make a stand there, he told Müffling, if 'the Field-Marshal were inclined to come to his assistance even with one corps only'.[52]

The withdrawal to the ridge began at 11 a.m., much to the consternation of the troops at Quatre Bras, who, after the success of the previous day, were anticipating 'an immediate attack on the French position'.[53] Apart from some skirmishing between horsemen in Genappe, the move was uncontested and by evening the bulk of the troops were bivouacking in the rain on the reverse slope behind the ridge. The only troops forward of that were picquets and two picked garrisons that had been selected to hold two strongholds – the wood and Chateau of Hougoumont and, slightly to its left rear, the fortified farmhouse of La Haye-Sainte – in the valley between the two ridges. To Hougoumont he had assigned just 1,500 picked men: the light companies of the Foot Guards and a battalion of German riflemen. La Haye-Sainte was held by the 2nd Light Battalion of the KGL and, from a sandpit across the road, a detachment of the 1/95th.

Assuming that the Prussians would eventually bolster his left, it remained only to protect his right flank and his communications with the coast, and he did this by posting a strong force of 17,000 men – chiefly Colville's 4th Division and Prince Frederick's Netherlands Corps – at Hal and Tubize, 8 miles west of Hougoumont. That left him with about 73,000 men to defend Mont-Saint-Jean.

The 17th represented yet another missed opportunity for Napoleon. If he had ordered Ney to attack Wellington at Quatre Bras in the morning, he could have pinned him there while the rest of his men moved round the Anglo-Dutch army's exposed right flank. But he had assumed that both Allied armies would already be on the move – Wellington north to Brussels and Blücher east to Liège – and when he discovered the truth it was too late for Ney to attack. Wellington had already withdrawn. Napoleon decided to follow with the bulk of his army (77,000 men) while Grouchy pursued the Prussians with the remaining 33,000. The emperor dined that evening in the La Belle Alliance inn, fully expecting to attack and beat Wellington the following morning. At 11 p.m., however, he received the astounding news that Grouchy had stopped for the night at Gembloux, just 6 miles north of Ligny and 12 miles short of Wavre, and would not continue his pursuit until first light. It was at this point that Napoleon should have sent an express to Grouchy, ordering him to break off his pursuit and instead move his men north-west to a point between Wavre and Waterloo that would have prevented Blücher from marching to Wellington's assistance. But he failed to send this crucial message until 10 a.m. on 18 June. Even then Grouchy's late arrival at Waterloo might have made a difference had not Soult again mangled his chief's intentions with a typically unfathomable order. It read: 'His Majesty desires that you will head for Wavre in order to draw near to us, and to place yourself in touch with our operations, and to keep up your communications with us, pushing before you those positions of the Prussian army which have taken this direction and which have halted at Wavre; this place you ought to reach as soon as possible.'[54]

Given that Wavre was to the north of Grouchy, and the emperor to the north-west, the order made no sense; moreover 'pushing before you' the Prussians would simply have meant driving Blücher towards Waterloo, which is exactly what Napoleon did not want to happen. But, instead of seeking clarification, Grouchy latched on to the one part of the order that seemed clear – 'head for Wavre' – and ignored the rest.

Wellington, meanwhile, had spent the night of the 17th in a two-storey inn at Waterloo, a small village on the edge of the forest of Soignes, a mile below and to the north of the Mont-Saint-Jean Ridge. That evening, as he awaited confirmation that the Prussians would march to his assistance the following day, he was visited by his cavalry commander, Lord Uxbridge, a man who had eloped with his sister-in-law and who had been thrust upon him by the prince regent. Ignoring the tension between them, Uxbridge told Wellington that, as the next senior commander, he felt it only right that he knew something of the duke's plans in case the latter was incapacitated during the battle. Wellington's icy reply had much in common with the response Wolfe gave to a similar query by his brigadiers before Quebec. 'Who will attack first tomorrow, I or Bonaparte?' asked Wellington.

'Bonaparte.'

'Well, Bonaparte has not given me any idea of his projects: and as my plans will depend on his, how can you expect me to tell you what mine are?' Aware he had been too stern, the duke put his hand on his subordinate's shoulder and added: 'There is one thing certain, Uxbridge, that is, that whatever happens, you and I will do our duty.'[55]

In reality, there was much they could have discussed about Wellington's plan to hold the ridge by retaining forward strongpoints at the Chateau de Hougoumont and the fortified farm of La Haye-Sainte; of keeping his infantry protected behind the reverse slope until the last possible moment; and of his hopes for Prussian reinforcement. But Wellington chose to share none of this and, in the process, was seriously compromising Uxbridge's ability to take charge of the battle should that be required. It was ever Wellington's habit to devolve as little authority as possible to subordinates, and he was not about to change.

Having spoken to Uxbridge, Wellington turned in. But he was

woken at 3 a.m. on 18 June with the extremely welcome news that Blücher was sending von Bülow's unscathed IV Corps to his assistance at first light, 'immediately followed by the [IInd] Corps of Pirch'. The message added: 'The Ist and IIIrd Corps will also hold themselves in readiness to proceed towards you.'[56] Even so, Wellington knew the battle was still in the balance, not least because the Prussians might be prevented from reaching Waterloo; and even if they did make it, there was every chance Grouchy would be hard on their heels. So he made every contingency for a setback, ordering routes to be found for a possible retreat through the Forest of Soignes, and advising his lover Lady Frances Wedderburn-Webster (in a letter written that night) that she should make preparations 'to remove from Bruxelles to Antwerp in case such a measure should be necessary'. He added:

> We fought a desperate battle on Friday, in which I was successful, though I had but very few troops. The Prussians were very roughly handled, and retired in the night, which obliged me to do the same to this place yesterday. The course of my operations may oblige me to uncover Bruxelles for a moment, and may expose that town to the enemy . . . I will give you the earliest intimation of any danger that may come to my knowledge: at present I know of none.[57]

21. 'The nearest run thing'

At 6 a.m. on 18 June, after just a few hours' sleep, the Duke of Wellington rode out of Waterloo village on his chestnut thoroughbred, Copenhagen, the horse that had carried him safely through the battles of Vitoria and Toulouse, to check on his forward posts and exhort his men to stand firm. Lieutenant Gronow of the 1st Foot Guards was breakfasting with his colonel under 'a sort of gipsy-tent' made of 'blankets, a serjeant's halberd and a couple of muskets' when he spotted Wellington riding past, dressed in a 'gray great-coat with a cape, white cravat, leather pantaloons, Hessian boots and a large cocked hat'. He and his staff 'seemed as gay and unconcerned as if they were riding to meet the hounds in some quiet English county'.[1]

The bulk of Wellington's troops, having bivouacked in the open under their blankets, were trying to dry themselves by fires that had been lit using wood torn from fences, barns and even houses. Some were cleaning their weapons, others smoking, and here and there were groups of officers discussing the coming battle. Few had slept much the night before and most were cold, wet, tired and hungry. Their supply wagons had yet to catch up with them, and only the resourceful were able to rustle up something to eat. One such was a bombardier of Captain Mercer's troop of Royal Horse Artillery, who returned to the bivouac in the morning with 'a considerable quantity of beef, biscut, and oatmeal', as well as a canteen of rum, that he had picked up on the road to Langeveldt. 'The rum was divided on the spot,' wrote Mercer, 'and surely if ardent spirits are ever beneficial, it must be to men situated as ours were ... The oatmeal was converted speedily into a stirabout, and afforded our people a hearty meal, after which all hands set to work to prepare the beef, make soup.' But the troop was never able to finish the meal because the battle intervened.[2]

Corporal Dickson of the 2nd Dragoons (Scots Greys) was on picquet duty as the French army across the valley stirred into action:

There were great columns of infantry and squadron after squadron of Cuirassiers, red Dragoons, brown Hussars and green Lancers with little swallow tail flags at the end of their lances. The grandest sight was a regiment of Cuirassiers dashing at full gallop over the brow of the hill opposite me, with the sun shining on their steel breastplates. Every now and then the sun lit up the whole country. No one who saw it could ever forget it. Between eight and nine there was a sudden roll of drums along the whole of the enemy's lines and a burst of music from the bands of a hundred battalions came to me on the wind. I seemed to recognise the *Marseillaise* but the sounds got mixed and lost in the sudden uproar that arose. Then every regiment began to move. They were taking up position for the battle.[3]

The narrowness of the front that Wellington had chosen to defend – just 2½ miles – meant that he could fight in depth, with a thin front line and plenty of reserves behind. Yet his dispositions were strangely lopsided. To the left of the cobblestone road that bisected his position he initially placed just two weak infantry divisions, Picton's Anglo-Hanoverian 5th and Perponcher's Dutch–Belgians, both of which had been severely mauled at Quatre Bras two days earlier. Even when he supported Picton with three brigades of cavalry (3,000 sabres) and two brigades of Sir Lowry Cole's 6th Division, one of which only arrived during the morning of the battle, the total strength of the left wing of his army was just 19,000 men and 33 guns.

In the centre, to the right rear of La Haye-Sainte, were the 7,000 bayonets of Charles Alten's Anglo-Hanoverian 3rd Division, supported by the 2,500 men of August von Kruse's 1st Nassau Regiment, and with Lord Edward Somerset's Household Cavalry Brigade (1,000 sabres) and the entire Netherlands Cavalry Division (another 3,000 sabres) a little further back in reserve. The total frontage was just a few hundred yards, and yet 50 guns were in position, some in line and others in reserve.

The right wing was even stronger. Protecting Hougoumont and the ridge above were the 3,700 elite troops of Major-General George Cooke's 1st (Guards) Division and 1,000 German Jäger riflemen detached from Alten's and Perponcher's divisions. Further back, and partly in echelon to the right to prevent Napoleon from turning the Allied flank, were Mitchell's 4th British Brigade, Clinton's Anglo-Hanoverian 2nd Division and the Brunswick Contingent. Posted well behind the front line, near the village of Braine-l'Alleud, were the Dutch–Belgians of General David Chassé's 3rd Netherlands Division. All told, these reserve bayonets numbered 20,000, and in support were three cavalry brigades (3,700 sabres) and 74 guns, giving a total force of more than 28,000.

Wellington had unbalanced his defence – with a mighty right wing, a strong centre and a comparatively weak left wing – because he feared an attack on his right flank and/or an attempt to sever his lines of communication with the coast. He was much less concerned with his left because that was where he expected the Prussians to appear in support. But would they arrive in time; and would, moreover, the two keystones to his defensive system, the isolated strongholds of Hougoumont and La Haye-Sainte, hold out until then? Only time would tell, but not all of Wellington's subordinates were convinced by his dispositions. 'I never saw,' remarked Sir Thomas Picton, having ridden across the entire line, 'a worse position taken up by any army.'[4]

Fortunately for Wellington, his opponent knew little of his dispositions because most of the Allied troops were hidden behind the Mont-Saint-Jean Ridge. Instead, as he waited for the sun to come out and dry the ground so that he could site his grand battery of artillery, Napoleon rode along his front inspecting the troops. 'He looked to me to be in the best of health, extraordinarily active and intense,' recalled one young officer. 'Several times he doffed his hat to us.' The officer added: 'He seems to be deep in thought and seldom speaks, except when he gives some sudden terse order. As for his complexion, it's without colour, almost waxen, not yellow, but rather white, like a Pascal candle.'[5]

Unaware of Napoleon's ailments, most of his soldiers were delighted to see him in person and, brandishing their shakos on their bayonets and swords, roared, '*Vive l'Empereur!*' An officer in d'Erlon's corps wrote: 'Never had those words been shouted with more enthusiasm; we were practically delirious.'[6]

But they were also, like their opponents, wet, hungry and tired. 'Marching all night without rations,' recalled a French infantryman, 'sleeping in water, forbidden to light fires, and then preparing to face grape and canister took away any desire to sing. We were just glad to pull our shoes out of the holes they sunk into with every step . . . Even the bravest of us looked discontented. It's true that the regimental bands were playing marches, and that the cavalry's trumpets and the infantry's drums mingled their sounds to grandiose effect, but as for me, I never heard anyone sing at Waterloo.'

When all his troops were in position, Napoleon left Ney to coordinate the battle while he retired to a vantage point a mile to the rear, on high ground above the Rossomme farm, where his staff set up a camp chair and spread maps on a table. It was from here, at around 11 a.m., that he dictated his first General Order: Ney was to begin the attack at one o'clock with the intention of seizing the village of Mont-Saint-Jean, 'at the intersection of the Nivelles and Brussels road'. Napoleon's plan was to bombard Wellington's position and then launch two simultaneous assaults: one by Reille's 14,500-strong II Corps on Hougoumont and the ridge beyond; and one by d'Erlon's as yet untested I Corps of 16,000 men against the centre and left of Wellington's position. At first he intended d'Erlon to unroll his attack from right to left, with the final blow falling on Wellington's centre; but this was modified during the morning so that the left-hand division in d'Erlon's corps was the first to advance. 'Count d'Erlon will observe,' wrote Ney on the back of the order, 'that the attack is to commence from the left, not the right. Communicate this new disposition to General Reille.' Reille understood, and told his officers, that the main attack was to be made by d'Erlon's corps, and that II Corps' task was simply to occupy the woods at Hougoumont as a cover for the advance of the French right wing. One of his battalion commanders confirmed that their orders were 'to prevent the enemy from coming out on our left flank; for I had been well forewarned that the army was going to pivot on us, and consequently that it was imperative for us, at all costs, to hold our position.'[7]

That morning Soult told Napoleon that, in his experience, British infantry were hard to shift if attacked head on. Napoleon was

dismissive: 'Because you have been beaten by Wellington you consider him a great general. And now I will tell you that he is a bad
general, that the English are bad troops, and that this affair is nothing
more serious than eating one's breakfast.'[8]

If Napoleon's original battle plan had been adhered to, the weakness of Wellington's left wing would have been exposed. But it began
to unravel when Reille ordered a division forward at around midday
to take Hougoumont Wood, which, as far as he knew, was unoccupied by Allied soldiers. With tirailleurs leading the way, and supporting
artillery firing on the ridge beyond, the columns of the 1st Light
Infantry Regiment began the attack. But it was broken up by accurate
British artillery fire and, with the columns taking refuge in a sunken
road, it was left to the tirailleurs to discover the wood was held by a
battalion of greencoated Nassau Jägers. As more men from the main
French columns were fed into the wood, the Jägers were gradually
pushed back to the chateau and its walled garden. Many joined the
garrison there, but some slipped away; when Wellington, observing
their flight from the ridge above, tried to stop them he was shot at.
'Do you see those fellows run?' he remarked with disgust. 'Well, it is
with these that I must win the battle.'[9]

The French made it as far as the walled garden, where the combined
fire of the guardsmen and the surviving Germans drove them back into
the wood. It was at this point that Wellington directed a battery of
howitzers to fire shrapnel shells – fused to explode in mid-air in a hail
of musket-balls – over the wood. It was enough to clear the wood,
which was then reoccupied by guardsmen. But they, in turn, were
forced to retire when a second French brigade was deployed and the
fighting again reached the loopholed walls of the chateau and garden.
For a time the French attackers were pinned down by British artillery
fire, but this began to lift as battery commanders ignored Wellington's
orders to concentrate on infantry and cavalry targets, and instead targeted French guns. Captain Mercer, whose battery of horse artillery
was on the extreme right of the artillery line, wrote later:

> I ventured to disobey orders, and open a slow deliberate fire at the
> [French] battery, thinking with my 9-pounders soon to silence his

4-pounders. My astonishment was great, however, when our very first gun was responded to by at least half-a-dozen gentlemen of very superior calibre, whose presence I had not even suspected, and whose superiority we immediately recognized by their rushing noise and long reach, for they flew far beyond us. I instantly saw my folly, and ceased firing, and they did the same – the 4-pounders alone continuing the cannonade as before.[10]

With the Allied artillery distracted, the French again assaulted Hougoumont and some troops made their way round to the unbarricaded gate on the north wall that, only minutes earlier, had been opened to allow ammunition carts to enter. Hacking their way through the gate, the French entered the courtyard and a fierce mêlée ensued. It ended when a blood-spattered Lieutenant-Colonel Macdonell of the 2nd Foot Guards and eight others managed to close the gate and all the intruders were killed bar a drummer boy who was spared on account of his age. Wellington later maintained that the battle hinged on the closing of Hougoumont's north gate. Though the complex was attacked many more times that day – with more than 10,000 troops from both armies falling in the immediate vicinity, the vast majority of them French – it was never again in serious danger of falling.

In the centre, meanwhile, a Grande Batterie of 54 guns – mostly 6- and 12-pounders – had been bombarding the Allied line from halfway down the slope of La Belle Alliance since 1 p.m. Each 12-pounder required a crew of fifteen gunners to sponge, load, prime and fire it, with some shuttling back to ammunition wagons that, for safety, were sited at least 30 yards to the rear. The guns weighed a ton and, with no recoil mechanism, had to be hauled back into position after each shot. Napoleon's order to his artillery commander, General Jean-Charles Desale, was 'to astonish the enemy and shake his morale', and in that he was only partly successful, thanks to Wellington's tactic of protecting most of his infantry behind a reverse slope. But the need to deploy his infantry in columns of companies – one behind the other like rungs on a ladder, so that they could easily form either line or square – meant they were more vulnerable than usual to an artillery bombardment and many lives were lost before the main attack began. 'I slept sound for some time,' recalled Private Tom Pococke of the 71st, on the ridge behind Hougoumont, 'while the cannonballs, plunging in amongst us, killed a great many. I was suddenly awakened. A ball struck the ground a little below me, turned me heels-over-head, broke my musket in pieces and killed a lad at my side. I was stunned and confused and knew not whether I was wounded or not. I felt a numbness in my arm for some time. We lay thus, about an hour and a half, under a dreadful fire, which cost us about 60 men, while we had never fired a shot.'[11]

Only one of Perponcher's Dutch–Belgian brigades was in front of the ridge, to keep up communications with La Haye-Sainte, and it was this formation that took the most serious casualties from artillery fire until it withdrew to a more sheltered position. It helped that the ground was still soft from the rain the night before and capable of absorbing much of the French cannonballs' energy.

At 1.30, just as d'Erlon was about to launch his assault against the Allied centre and left, Napoleon's attention was drawn to movement on his far right – beyond the Allied left – where troops could be seen approaching Chapelle-Saint-Lambert, a village 5 miles distant. This meant they would be able to reach the extreme right of the French line, in the front of the village of Papelotte, in under three hours. Soult suggested, more in hope than expectation, that they were Grouchy's men; but Napoleon must have known that Grouchy could never have covered the ground from Gembloux in that time. Yet he sent only 2,000 light horsemen as far as the Fichermont Wood, near the River Lasnes, to protect that side of the battlefield. Had he sent infantry instead, they could have prevented enemy troops from crossing the river for many hours. The confirmation that they were indeed Prussians arrived soon after in the form of a courier, captured on his way to deliver a message to Wellington, who admitted to Napoleon that the troops in the distance were the vanguard of von Bülow's corps, that the entire Prussian army had spent the night at Wavre, and that it had not encountered a single Frenchman during its march.

Still Napoleon persisted in his belief that Grouchy would arrive in time to prevent the Prussians from tipping the balance. To encourage the marshal, he at once dispatched an order that read: 'A letter that has just been intercepted states that General Bülow is to attack our flank. We believe that we see this corps on the high ground at Saint-Lambert; therefore, do not lose an instant in drawing near to us, in order to join us and crush Bülow, who you will catch in flagrante delicto.'[12]

Napoleon then turned his attention to d'Erlon's attack, one he hoped would win the battle. The first assault was made on La Haye-Sainte by d'Erlon's left-most division, and before long its light troops had captured the orchard and cleared the sandpit on the far side of the road. With the farm in danger of being overwhelmed, General Kielmansegge, commanding the 1st Hanoverian Brigade on the ridge above, sent a battalion of light infantry down the slope in support. But they were taken in the flank by four squadrons of French cuirassiers who emerged over a rise to their right and cut the battalion to pieces, causing more than 200 casualties in a matter of minutes. Many of the KGL men guarding the farm also fled up the slope, though a hard core remained in the farmhouse and on the roof of the piggery.

By now, with the farm complex surrounded, d'Erlon's other three divisions had begun their advance to the east of the Brussels road, one after the other, from left to right in conformity with Napoleon's orders. Over a front of barely 1,000 yards marched a solid mass of 14,000 men, their 76 paces a minute tapped out by the battalion drums. Instead of advancing in their usual dense columns of nine deep and up to sixty wide – a formation that Napoleon and his senior commanders had decided that morning not to use against British infantry because it lessened French firepower and made it difficult to deploy into line – each battalion was already in a continuous line of three ranks, but positioned one behind the other, four to a brigade, with barely 5 or 6 paces between battalions. There were, as a result, a total of six brigade columns in echelon, each with a front of around 100 yards. Preceding them, as ever, was a cloud of 2,500 tirailleurs in open order, but close enough to the main body of troops to form an unbroken chain. It was a sight to chill the blood.

As the two leading brigades on the left neared the ridge, they passed through their skirmishers and prepared to attack. Facing them were two weak brigades of Perponcher's Netherlands Division, one of which was stationed in front of the sunken road known as the Chemin d'Ohain, fringed with thorn bushes and willow trees, that ran along the ridge. At the last moment the brigade was ordered to withdraw to the road and it did so with much disorder, many soldiers fleeing to the rear. Now all that was guarding the centre left of Wellington's position were the three battered brigades of Picton's 5th Division, barely 3,600 bayonets in all. As the French crossed the road, the lead battalions rose from their lying position 100 yards away, fired a volley and, cheered on by Picton – who moments later was shot in the temple and killed – charged with the bayonet. Sergeant Anton of the 42nd Highlanders – part of General Denis Pack's 9th Brigade – recalled:

> France now pushed forward on the line of our Belgic allies, drove them from their post and rolled them in one promiscuous mass of confusion through the ranks of our brigade, which instantly advanced to repel the pursuers . . . The foe beheld our front and paused; a sudden terror seized his flushed ranks. We were in the act of breaking through the hedge, when our general gave orders to open our ranks. In an instant our cavalry passed through, leaped both hedges, and plunged on the panic-stricken foe.[13]

It was at this key psychological moment, as the battle hung in the balance, that Lord Uxbridge ordered the Household and Union brigades of cavalry to charge d'Erlon's brigade columns. Corporal Dickson of the Scots Greys recorded:

> The General of the Union Brigade, Sir William Ponsonby, came riding up to us on a small bay hack. He ordered us forward to within fifty yards of the beech hedge by the roadside. From our new position we could descry the three regiments of Highlanders, only a thousand in all, bravely firing down on the advancing masses of Frenchmen. Then I saw the Brigadier, Sir Denis Pack, turn to the Gordons and shout with great energy 'Ninety Second, you must advance! All in front have given way!' The Highlanders instantly, with fixed bayonets, began to press forward through the beech and holly hedge to a

line of bushes that grew along the face of the slope in front. They uttered loud shouts as they ran forward and fired a volley at twenty yards into the French.

Luckily at this moment the long-awaited signal came, and immediately our Colonel, Inglis Hamilton, shouted out 'Now then Scots Greys, Charge' and waving his sword in the air he rode straight at the hedges in front, which he took in grand style. At once a great cheer rose from our ranks, and we too waved our swords and followed him. I dug my spurs into my brave old Rattler and we were off like the wind. We heard the Highland pipers playing among the smoke and firing below. Our Colonel went on before us, past our guns and down the slope, and we followed; we saw the Royals and Inniskillings clearing the road and hedges at full gallop away to the right. Before me rode young Armour, our rough rider from Mauchline . . . and Sergeant Ewart on the right, at the end of the line beside our cornet, Kinchant. We could make out the feather bonnets of the Highlanders and heard the officers crying out to them to wheel back by sections. A moment more and we were among them. Poor fellows! Some of them had not time to get clear of us and were knocked down. I remembered one lad crying out 'Eh! But I didna think ye wad hae hurt me sae.'[14]

Once past their own troops, the cavalrymen smashed into the French columns. 'What pen can describe the scene,' wrote Anton in typically florid prose. 'Horse's hooves sinking in men's breasts, breaking bones, riders' swords streaming in blood, waving over their heads and descending in deadly vengeance. Stroke follows stroke, like the turning of flail in the hands of a dexterous thresher.'[15]

Assailed by Picton's division and the two heavy brigades of cavalry, d'Erlon's columns disintegrated. A French officer confessed: 'Just as it is difficult for the best cavalry to break into infantry who are formed into squares and who defend themselves with coolness and daring, so it is true that once the ranks have been penetrated, then resistance is useless and nothing remains for the cavalry to do but to slaughter at almost no risk to themselves. This is what happened, in vain our poor fellows stood up and stretched out their arms; they could not reach far enough to bayonet these cavalrymen mounted on powerful horses, and the few shots fired in this chaotic mêlée were just as fatal to our own men as to the English.'[16]

Two thousand French prisoners were taken, many more were killed and wounded, and the rest fled down the slope, pursued by the victorious cavalry, who, in the process, captured two regimental Eagles★ (the equivalent of a British battalion's colours). One of the men responsible was Sergeant Ewart of the Scots Greys:

> I took the Eagle [of the 45th Regiment] from the enemy: he and I had a hard contest for it; he thrust for my groin – I parried it off, and I cut him through the head; after which I was attacked by one of their Lancers, who threw his lance at me, but missed the mark . . . Then I cut him from the chin upwards, which cut went through his teeth. Next I was attacked by a foot soldier, who, after firing at me, charged me with his bayonet; but he very soon lost the combat, for I parried it, and cut him down through the head; so that finished the combat for the Eagle.[17]

The second Eagle, property of the 105th Infantry Regiment, was captured by Captain Alexander Clark of the 1st Dragoons (Royals). 'When I first saw it,' he wrote later,

> it was perhaps about forty yards to my left and a little in my front. The officer who carried it, and his companions, were moving with their backs towards me, and endeavouring to force their way through the crowd. I gave the order to my squadron 'Right shoulders forward! Attack the colour!' . . . On reaching it, I ran my sword into the officer's right side, a little above the hip-joint. He was a little to my left side, and fell to that side, with the Eagle across my horse's head. I tried to catch it with my left hand, but could only touch the fringe of the flag, and it is probable it would have fallen to the ground had it not been prevented by the neck of Corporal Styles' horse . . . On taking up the Eagle, I endeavoured to break [it] from the pole with the intention of putting it into the breast of my coat; but I could not break it. Corporal

★ Each Eagle weighed 4 lb. and was fixed to a 6-foot-long wooden staff. The French troops called them 'cuckoos'.

Styles said, 'Pray, sir, do not break it,' on which I replied, 'Very well, carry it to the rear as fast as you can, it belongs to me.'[18]

Much of the Household Brigade and the right squadron of the Royals, meanwhile, had clashed with French cuirassiers on either side of La Haye-Sainte. Private Smithies of the Royals recalled:

> On we rushed at each other, and when we met the shock was terrific. We wedged ourselves between them as much as possible, to prevent them from cutting, and the noise of the horses, the clashing of swords against their steel armour, can be imagined only by those who have heard it. There were some riders who caught hold of each other's bodies – wrestling fashion – and fighting for life, but the superior physical strength of our regiment soon showed itself.[19]

At this point, having succeeded in their aim of breaking up the French infantry attack, the British cavalry should have reined in and trotted back over the ridge. But their blood was up and, egged on by their officers, horsemen of both brigades careered on down the slope and up the far side, a few scattered groups making it as far as Napoleon's Grande Batterie. Dickson recalled: 'Colonel Hamilton rode up to us crying "Charge, Charge the guns" and went off like the wind up the hill towards the terrible batteries. We got among the guns and had our revenge. Such slaughtering! We sabred the gunners, lamed their horses and cut their traces and harness. I can hear the Frenchmen yet crying "Diable" when I struck at them and the long hiss through their teeth as my sword went home.'[20]

The British cavalry had, however, overreached themselves. On blown horses, deep in the enemy position, they were counter-attacked by French lancers and few made it back to their own lines. A quartermaster-sergeant of the Scots Greys recorded: 'We were obliged to retreat, which was no sooner discovered by the Lancers than they made an oblique movement, and got round between us and the British lines, which led to a severe conflict, from which few indeed of the Greys returned . . . All that were left of the 400 Greys were about 60 rank and file.'[21]

Among the survivors were the quartermaster-sergeant and Corporal

Dickson, both aided by the timely arrival of a squadron of 16th Light Dragoons who saw off their pursuers. The dead included Colonel Hamilton, last seen with wounds in both arms and the reins in his teeth, and the brigade commander, Ponsonby, who was speared by a lancer as he tried to urge his exhausted horse up the slope. 'Ponsonby might have escaped if he had been better mounted,' wrote a contemporary historian, 'but the groom with his chestnut charger could not be found at the moment of the charge, and he was riding a small bay hack, which soon stuck fast in the heavy ground. Seeing he must be overtaken, he was handing over his watch and a miniature to his brigade major to deliver to his family, when the French lancers came up and killed them both.'[22]

Of the 2,500 sabres that charged, more than a thousand were killed or wounded, putting both brigades to all intents and purposes out of action. According to Gronow, Wellington was 'perfectly furious that this arm had been engaged without his orders and sent them to the rear'. Uxbridge was suitably chastened, admitting later: 'The pursuit had been continued without order and too far . . . After the overthrow of the Cuirassiers I had in vain attempted to stop my people by sounding the Rally, but neither voice nor trumpet availed; so I went back to seek the support of the 2nd line . . . I committed a great mistake in having led the attack. The *carrière* once begun, the leader is no better than any other man; whereas if I had placed myself at the head of the 2nd line, there is no saying what great advantages might not have accrued from it.'[23]

Yet Wellington had emerged from the first two serious crises of the day in a strong position: Hougoumont and La Haye-Sainte were still in his hands (he personally rode down to the latter to re-establish the 1/95th in the sandpit); a large proportion of two French corps had been badly mauled; and, most importantly, he now knew for certain that Prussian help was close at hand.

Following the repulse of d'Erlon's infantry, Ney ordered a mass cavalry attack of 5,000 horsemen — later reinforced by a similar number — through the gap between the two British strongpoints. Why he did this has never been properly explained: some have conjectured that he misread the withdrawal of some ambulance wagons as a sign that the Allies were wavering; others that he mistook a redeployment in Wellington's lines for a general retreat. It may be that he hoped to replicate the success of the British cavalry over his own infantry. Whatever the reason, the outcome was utterly predictable. As the cavalry approached the ridge, the British gunners abandoned their batteries and took refuge in the hollow infantry squares that were, as the French officer observed, almost impregnable to enemy horsemen. 'The first charge was magnificent,' recalled Ensign Macready of the 30th.

As soon as they quickened their trot into a gallop the Cuirassiers bent their heads so that the peak of their helmets looked like visors and they seemed cased in armour from the plume to the saddle. Not a shot was fired till they were within thirty yards when the word was given . . . The effect was magical. Thro' the smoke we could see helmets falling – cavaliers starting from their seats with convulsive springs as they received our balls, horses plunging & rearing in the agonies of fright and pain, and crowds of the soldiery dismounted; part of the squadrons in retreat, but the more daring remainder backing their horses to force them on our bayonets. Our fire soon disposed of these gentlemen. The main body reformed in our front were reinforced and rapidly and gallantly repeated their attacks. In fact from this time (about four o'clock) till near six we had a constant repetition of these brave but unavailing charges . . . The best cavalry is contemptible to a steady and well supplied Infantry regiment – even our men saw this and began to pity the useless perseverance of their assailants and as they advanced would growl out 'here come those damned fools again.'[24]

Not all the squares got off so lightly. Sergeant Tom Morris of the 73rd remembered some French horsemen bringing up gunners who turned an abandoned cannon on his square, its fire proving 'very destructive, making complete lanes through us'. Many squares were hit by French artillery fire as the cavalry attacks receded, and by late afternoon the situation for Morris's battalion was 'truly awful; our men were falling by dozens from enemy fire.' A single shell killed and wounded seventeen men.[25]

Lieutenant Gronow described the square of the 1st Foot Guards as a 'perfect hospital, being full of dead, dying and mutilated soldiers', and found the cavalry charges a 'great relief, as the artillery could no longer fire on us'. At one point Wellington took refuge in the guardsmen's square and Gronow thought him 'perfectly composed', but looking 'very thoughtful and pale'.[26] He could hear cannon-fire from beyond his left flank and knew that the Prussians must be near.

They were. At around 4.30 p.m., von Bülow's vanguard attacked the French posts in the village of Plancenoit, to the right rear of the main French battle line. Von Bülow's original intention had been to reinforce the weak left of Wellington's line at Smohain, but, seeing the latter under attack, he had swung further south to turn Napoleon's flank. The emperor had countered by sending Lobau's corps of 10,000 men – later reinforced by the 4,000-strong elite Young Guard Division – to stop him and, though outnumbered by more than three to one, this force managed to hold up von Bülow's advance at Plancenoit for more than two hours.

As von Bülow's men were entering the fray, Napoleon received the crushing news that Grouchy was heavily engaged with Johann von Thielmann's Prussian corps near Wavre and would not make it to Waterloo. The emperor's only hope now was to defeat Wellington before the Prussian presence could make itself felt, and to this end he ordered Ney to capture La Haye-Sainte at all costs. A fresh attack was launched by three battalions and some engineers; and finally, at around 6.30 p.m., with the defenders almost out of ammunition, the farm fell to the French after a heroic last stand by its KGL garrison, only 43 of whom escaped out of the original 400. Soon after a brave but suicidal attempt to retake the farm was made by Colonel Christian von Ompteda and the 5th KGL, at the request of General Alten; it ended with Ompteda's death, the destruction of his battalion and the loss of its standards to French cuirassiers, who were once again on the prowl.

Elated, Ney moved forward his horse artillery and blasted away at Wellington's centre, which, because of the lie of the land, was not as protected by the ridge as on both flanks. The 27th Inniskillings, for example, lost more than 400 men before firing a shot. So alarmed was Halkett by his casualties that he sent Wellington a message, begging 'that his brigade, which had lost two-thirds, should be relieved for a short time; but there was no reserve to take its place, and Wellington replied, "Tell him, what he asks is impossible: he and I, and every Englishman on the field, must die on the spot we now occupy." '[27]

To shore up his crumbling centre, however, Wellington moved troops across from the right, including Sir Hussey Vivian's brigade of cavalry and part of the Brunswick Contingent. He himself rode up and down the line, positioning cavalry reserves behind wavering infantry to discourage them from breaking. With French sharpshooters just 300 yards away, it was a time of great danger for Wellington; so many of his staff had already been killed or wounded – including William De Lancey, his quartermaster-general, who was talking to the duke when a round-shot struck him in the back, and Lord Fitz-Roy Somerset, his military secretary, whose elbow was shattered by a rifle-ball fired from La Haye-Sainte – that he was forced to use stray civilians to carry his orders. And all the time he glanced anxiously to the east for a sign that the Prussians were near. 'God bring me night or bring me Blücher,' he was heard to remark.[28] 'The time they occupied in approaching seemed interminable,' he wrote later. 'Both they and my watch seemed to have stuck fast.'

Recognizing that now was the time for a final effort to breach Wellington's line, Ney asked Napoleon for reinforcements. 'Troops!' responded the exasperated emperor. 'Where do you want me to get them from? Do you want me to make them?'[29] He had begun the day with a reserve of 37 battalions for just this moment; but the threat from the Prussians had caused him to send no fewer than 23 of these battalions to Plancenoit. That left him with just 14 battalions of the Imperial Guard, elite troops he would commit only when he was certain they could make a difference. Now was not that moment, because the Prussians had just driven the Young Guard out of Plancenoit, and Napoloen knew he had to stabilize his right flank before he committed his reserve. So he sent two battalions of the Old Guard to recapture Plancenoit and, when word came back they had been successful, released all but one battalion of the rest for Ney's final attack.

Napoleon himself led these 6,000 ferocious-looking soldiers – six battalions of the Middle Guard and five of the Old Guard (all moustachioed giants, veterans of at least ten campaigns, looking like pirates with their garish tattoos and gold earrings) – down the cobblestone road to the smoking ruin of La Haye-Sainte, where he handed them over to Ney. He also instructed his aides to spread the rumour that the troops approaching from the south-east were Grouchy's men. '*Vive l'Empereur!*' shouted Ney's adjutant as he galloped along the line. '*Soldats, voilà Grouchy!*' Thousands of soldiers took up the cry, convinced that victory was near.[30] But they had been deceived and, unbeknown even to Napoleon, the vanguard of von Ziethen's I Corps had by now reached the hamlet of Smohain on the extreme left of Wellington's defensive line, thus enabling the duke to move more troops across to his threatened centre.

At around 7.30 p.m., Ney led the first line of five battalions of the Middle Guard up the slope in person, flanked on both sides by the remnants of Reille's and d'Erlon's corps, as well as cuirassiers and horse artillery. Moving in open squares to protect them from a cavalry counter-attack, they brushed aside a Brunswick battalion and captured the guns of two field brigades. Then they engaged Halkett's badly mauled brigade, pressing back both the 2/30th and 2/73rd Foot, which had few officers left to rally them. 'I cannot conceive what the enemy was about during our confusion,' wrote Ensign Macready. 'Fifty cuirassiers would have annihilated our brigade.'[31] Fortunately the foremost battalion of the Middle Guard, the 1/3rd Grenadiers, paused after their long climb, giving Halkett's remaining officers the chance to rally their men; he himself had been taken to the rear after a bullet passed through both cheeks.

It was now that a Dutch–Belgian brigade, recalled from Braine-l'Alleud, made a decisive contribution by driving back the 1/3rd Grenadiers and the flanking troops of d'Erlon's corps with grapeshot from horse artillery guns and a bayonet charge. But the rest of the Middle Guard continued to advance and, supported by cannon, the 1/4th Grenadiers engaged Halkett's remaining two battalions, the 33rd and 2/69th Foot.

While this struggle was going on, two battalions of the Middle Guard's 3rd Chasseurs à pied approached the ridge to the right of Halkett's brigade, a sector defended by two units of the 1st Foot

Guards that Wellington had moved across from the right. It would be the first and only time these elite units faced each other in battle. The British guardsmen, part of Maitland's brigade, were lying on the reverse slope with Wellington a short way behind them. As the 3rd Chasseurs crested the ridge and stopped to deploy, Wellington cried out: 'Now, Maitland! Now's your time! Up Guards! Make ready! Fire!'[32]

Standing in four ranks, and at a distance of less than 60 yards, the volley of the 1st Foot Guards was devastating. 'Those who from a distance and more on the flank could see the affair,' wrote a guards' officer, 'tell us that the effect of our fire seemed to force the head of the Column bodily back.'[33] Maitland's men then advanced with fixed bayonets and were astonished to see the 3rd Chasseurs turn and flee. Gronow recorded:

> We rushed on with fixed bayonets and that hearty 'hurrah' peculiar to British soldiers. It appeared that our men, deliberately and with calculation, singled out their victims, for as they came upon the Imperial Guard our line broke, and the fighting became irregular. The impetuosity of our men seemed almost to paralyze their enemies. I witnessed several of the Imperial Guard who were run through the body apparently without any resistance on their parts. I observed a big Welshman by the name of Hughes, who was six feet seven inches in height, run through with his bayonet and knock down with the butt-end of his firelock, I should think a dozen at least of his opponents.[34]

In their haste to pursue, the 1st Foot Guards were almost outflanked by the last battalion of the Middle Guard, the 4th Chasseurs; but they managed to stop in time and retire to the ridge. There they held the 4th Chasseurs long enough for artillery and Adam's brigade to come to their assistance. Taken in flank by Colonel John Colborne's 52nd Light Infantry, the 4th Chasseurs broke and ran. 'Go on, Colborne!' shouted Wellington as he waved his hat for a general advance. 'Go on. They won't stand. Don't give them time to rally.'[35]

As Napoleon's praetorians fled down the slope, a cry rose from their astonished comrades: '*La Garde recule!*' ('The Guard is retreating!')[36] The shock of seeing the Imperial Guard, a unit that had swept

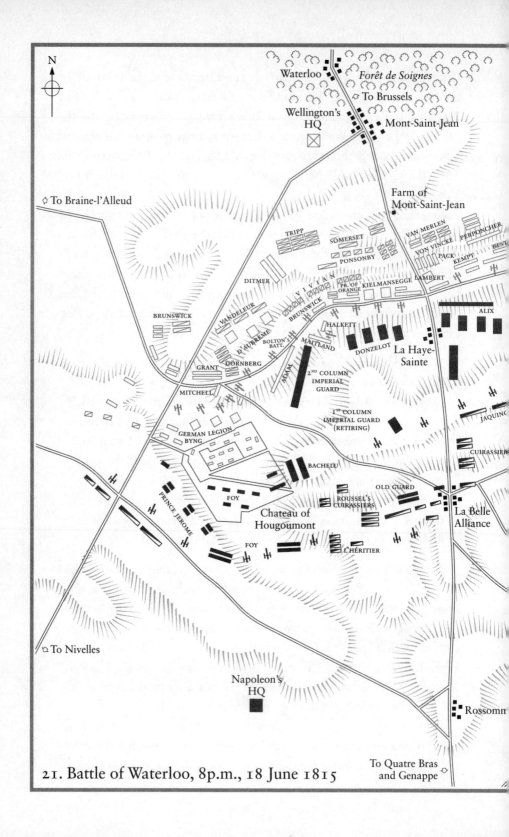

N

Waterloo
Forêt de Soignes
To Brussels
Wellington's
HQ
Mont-Saint-Jean

To Braine-l'Alleud

Farm of
Mont-Saint-Jean

TRIPP
SOMERSET
VAN MERLEN
PERPONCHER
VON VINCKE
PACK
PONSONBY
KEMPT
BEST
DITMER
PR. OF
KIELMANSEGGE
ORANGE
LAMBERT
BRUNSWICK
VIVIAN
VANDELEUR
BRUNSWICK
ALIX
D'AUBREME
HALKETT
BOLTON'S
BATT.
MAITLAND
GRANT
DÖRNBERG
DONZELOT
La Haye-
Sainte
MITCHELL
ADAM
2ᴺᴰ COLUMN
IMPERIAL
GUARD
JAQUINO
1ˢᵀ COLUMN
IMPERIAL GUARD
(RETIRING)
CUIRASSIER
GERMAN LEGION
BYNG
BACHELU
OLD GUARD
FOY
ROUSSEL'S
CUIRASSIERS
PRINCE JEROME
Chateau of
Hougoumont
La Belle
Alliance
FOY
L'HÉRITIER

To Nivelles

Napoleon's
HQ

Rossomn

21. Battle of Waterloo, 8p.m., 18 June 1815

To Quatre Bras
and Genappe

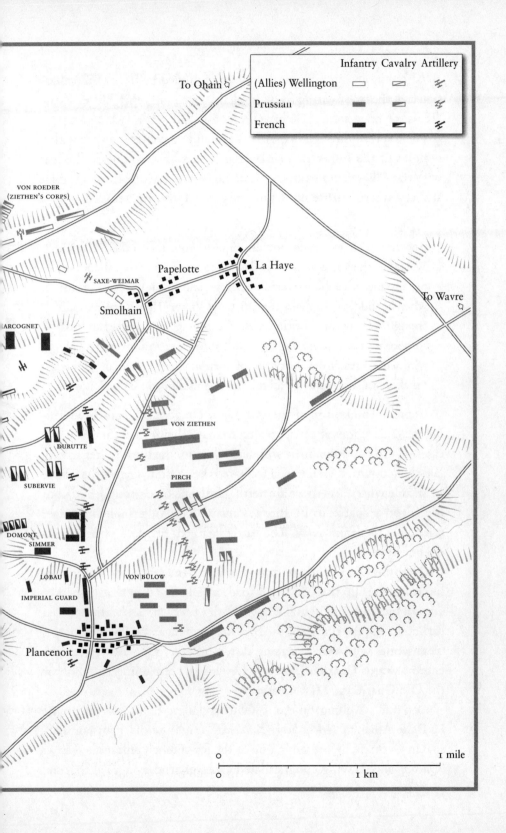

To Ohain

Infantry Cavalry Artillery

(Allies) Wellington

Prussian

French

VON ROEDER
(ZIETHEN'S CORPS)

Papelotte   La Haye

To Wavre

SAXE-WEIMAR

Smolhain

ARCOGNET

VON ZIETHEN

DURUTTE

PIRCH

SUBERVIE

DOMONT

SIMMER

LOBAU

VON BÜLOW

IMPERIAL GUARD

Plancenoit

0
1 mile

0
1 km

all before it, fleeing in disarray was compounded by the awful realization that the troops firing from Smohain were not French but Prussian. 'Treason!' cried some. 'We have been betrayed!'[37]

Panic spread through Napoleon's army like a contagion and, within minutes of the Imperial Guard's repulse, it was streaming to the rear with the Allies in close pursuit. Captain Mercer, whose troop of horse artillery was too shattered to join the general advance, recalled:

> We had ceased firing – the plain below being covered with masses of troops, which we could not distinguish from each other. Captain Walcot of the horse-artillery had come to us, and we were all looking out anxiously at the movements below, and on the opposite ridge, when he suddenly shouted out, 'Victory! Victory! They fly!' and sure enough we saw some of the masses dissolving, as it were, and those composing them streaming away in confused crowds over the field, whilst the already desultory fire of their artillery ceased altogether. I shall never forget this joyful moment! This moment of exaltation![38]

Captain Tomkinson of the 16th Light Dragoons remembered 'riding in all directions at parties trying to make their escape, and in many cases had to cut down men who had taken up their arms after having laid them down'.[39] Wellington followed the pursuit, against the advice of an aide who warned 'we are getting into enclosed ground, and your life is too valuable to be thrown away.' The duke replied: 'Never mind. Let them fire away. The battle's gained: my life's of no consequence now.'[40]

Only the Old Guard attempted to cover the retreat by withdrawing in squares up the Charleroi road, a gallant action that helped to save all but two regimental Eagles (both of which had been captured earlier during the charge of the British heavy cavalry). Their emperor, meanwhile, with tears coursing down his face, rode away from the battle towards Charleroi, escorted by his last remaining battalion of the Old Guard, the 1/1st Chasseurs.

At 9 p.m., Wellington met Blücher in failing light near the inn of La Belle Alliance. '*Mein lieber Kamerad!*' cried the old Prussian marshal in German, before using one of the few French phrases he knew. '*Quel affaire.*' Having congratulated each other, they agreed that the fresher Prussians would continue the pursuit alone (a task Blücher's men set about with single-minded ruthlessness, bayoneting the wounded and capturing almost all Napoleon's guns). Then Wellington rode back to his headquarters in Waterloo, looking 'sombre and dejected . . . The few individuals who attended him wore, too, rather the aspect of a little funeral train rather than that of victors in one of the most important battles ever fought.'[41]

The field of battle was strewn with a scarcely credible 47,000 bodies: the beaten French had suffered the worst with 25,000 killed and wounded, and a further 8,000 taken prisoner; next came Wellington's army with losses of 15,000, the highest of his career in a single battle; and finally the Prussians, who, though they had fought for only part of the battle, had 7,000 casualties. Many thousands of horses had also been killed or were lying with grievous wounds, their 'piteous neighing' the sole sound as darkness fell. Captain Mercer's G Troop had lost 140 of its 200 horses, and 'of the men, scarcely two-thirds of those necessary for four guns remained, and these so completely exhausted as to be totally incapable of further exertion.' Most of the troops bivouacked on the field, but Mercer could not sleep and rose to observe the scene by moonlight:

> Here and there some poor wretch, sitting up amidst the countless dead, busied himself in endeavours to staunch the flowing stream with which his life was fast ebbing away. Many whom I saw so employed that night were, when morning dawned, lying stiff and tranquil . . . From time to time a figure would half raise itself from the ground, and then, with a despairing groan, fall back again. Others, slowly and painfully rising, stronger, or having less deadly hurt, would stagger away with uncertain steps across the field in search of succour. Many of these I followed with my gaze until lost in the obscurity of the distance; but many, alas! after staggering a few paces, would sink again on the ground, probably to rise no more. It was heart-rending – and yet I gazed![42]

The day had been particularly nerve-racking for the large British community in Brussels. From 11.30 in the morning they could hear the thunder of cannon from the battlefield and many waited for news with their carriages prepared for instant flight. Curiosity got the better of the diarist Thomas Creevey, who walked 2 miles south of Brussels in search of information. 'A most curious, busy scene it was,' he wrote, 'with every kind of thing upon the road, the Sunday population of Brussels being all out in the suburbs out of the Porte Namur, sitting about tables drinking beer and smoking and making merry, as if races or other sports were going on, instead of the great pitched battle which was then fighting.'[43]

Creevey returned to Brussels none the wiser and was dressing for dinner when his stepdaughter ran into his room crying: 'The French are in town!' This false report, he soon discovered, had been caused by 'the flight of a German regiment of cavalry, the Cumberland Hussars, who had quitted the field of battle, galloping through the forest of Soignes, entering the Porte Namur, and going full speed down the Rue de Namur and thro' the Place Royale, crying out the French were at their heels'.[44]

The German horsemen, according to another British witness, were followed by their wives and girlfriends, who were also 'well mounted, riding astride on men's saddles'. He added: 'They had on boots and trousers like dragoons, and wore a gown over all, with small round bonnets on their heads . . . These women were amongst the first retreating party who entered Brussels screaming as they went.'[45]

True or not, the rumours caused hundreds if not thousands of civilians and soldiers to flee in panic up the road to Antwerp, swelling the number who had already chosen to leave. Juana, the Spanish-born wife of Major Harry Smith of the 95th Rifles, recalled being overtaken by five or six horsemen, including one of her own servants and a British officer of Hussars: 'I addressed myself to the Hussar, who appeared the oldest of the party. "Pray, sir, is there any danger?" "Danger, mum! When I left Brussels the French were in pursuit down the hill." "Oh, sir, what shall I do?" "Come to Antwerp with me." He never pulled up. During the whole conversation we were full gallop.'[46]

Eventually the rumours of French troops were proved to be false. But those reports that did arrive from the battlefield were far from optimistic – Creevey spoke to one wounded officer of the 1st Foot Guards who said he would not be staying long as the French would be in Brussels that night – and it was not until the early hours of 19 June that one of Wellington's ADCs brought definite news of an Allied victory.

Wellington returned to his quarters in Waterloo at 11 p.m. and, after a light supper with his Spanish liaison officer, General Álava (the only member of his staff to survive the battle unscathed), he fell into an exhausted sleep. He was woken at three by Dr Hume, his personal physician, and told that his favourite aide-de-camp, Alexander Gordon, had just died from his wounds. Hume then recited the long list of casualties that had come in since midnight. It contained so many familiar names that Wellington broke down in tears, exclaiming: 'Well, thank God, I don't know what it is to lose a battle; but certainly nothing can be more painful than to gain one with the loss of so many of one's friends.'[47]

Now awake, Wellington began to write the famous campaign dispatch for Lord Bathurst that would be published in *The Times* on 22 June. Covering the period from 15 to 18 June, and recorded entirely from memory by a man still reeling from the horrors of two battles, it is a document remarkable for its fluency and detail. The chief complaint of many soldiers was that it was far too scant in its praise, omitting to mention many of the officers and units that had performed so well at Waterloo. There was, for example, no reference to the Royal Horse Artillery, or to a single Hussar regiment, or to Colonel Colborne and his gallant 52nd. When it came to the chief reason for the victory, however, it could not have been more specific:

> I should not do justice to my own feelings, or to Marshal Blücher and the Prussian Army, if I did not attribute the successful result of this arduous day to the cordial and timely assistance I received from them. The operation of General Bülow upon the enemy's flank was a most decisive one; and, even if I had not found myself in a situation to make the attack which produced the final result, it would have forced the enemy to retire if his attacks should have failed, and would have prevented him from taking advantage of them if they should unfortunately have succeeded.[48]

The following day, having sent the dispatch from Brussels, Wellington wrote to his brother William:★ 'You'll see the account of our desperate battle and victory over Boney!! It was the most desperate business I ever was in; I never took so much trouble about any battle; and never was so near being beat. Our loss is immense particularly in that best of all instruments British Infantry. I never saw the Infantry behave so well. I am going immediately. Can we be reinforced in Cavalry or Infantry or both? We must have Lord Combermere as Lord Uxbridge has lost his leg.'[49]

He said something similar that morning to Thomas Creevey, depicting the fight as a 'damned nice thing – the nearest run thing you ever saw in your life'. Creevey recalled: 'Then, as he walked about, he praised greatly those Guards who kept the farm (meaning Hugomont [*sic*]) against the repeated attacks of the French; and he praised all our troops, uttering repeated expressions of astonishment at our men's courage . . . Then he said: "By God! I don't think it would have been done if I had not been there." '[50]

Within these two documents and the conversation with Creevey – either written or uttered while Wellington's memory was at its freshest – lies the essential truth of the battle: that he almost lost it, and certainly would have done but for two crucial factors – the timely arrival of the Prussians; and the fighting quality of his British redcoats, who, time and again, plugged gaps in his line and pushed the French back. Many historians regard the first point as irrelevant, insisting that he fought at Waterloo only because he knew the Prussians would come to his assistance. That may be true. But when we come to assess Wellington's skill as a general, it is hard to see the Waterloo campaign in general, and the final battle in particular, as strong evidence of his military genius. Yes, he was up against the finest captain of his

---

★ The addressee of this famous letter is often said by historians to have been Wellington's elder brother Richard. In fact it was his next eldest brother, the Honourable William Wellesley-Pole (later the third Earl of Mornington), who was father-in-law to Wellington's military secretary, Colonel Lord FitzRoy Somerset (later the first Lord Raglan). The letter is now in the possession of Henry van Moyland, nephew of the late fifth Lord Raglan.

era, and one of the greatest of all time; but had Napoleon and his marshals been on form they would surely have taken advantage of Wellington's early errors, particularly his failure to anticipate the direction of the initial French advance, and his unwarranted and prolonged conviction that it was only a feint and the true axis was further west at Mons. These errors allowed Napoleon to drive a wedge between the two Allied armies, and gave him the opportunity to defeat them one by one; but for Ney's interference on the 16th, recalling d'Erlon's corps in defiance of the emperor's express orders, the Prussian army would have been destroyed at Ligny and Napoleon free to turn on Wellington without fear of interruption.

There were further opportunities: for Napoleon to strike a decisive blow against Wellington at Quatre Bras on the 17th; and for Grouchy to prevent the Prussians from reaching Waterloo on the 18th. But neither was taken. 'The plain truth,' writes Frank McLynn, 'seems to be that Napoleon performed far below his best form, and that something happened to his martial talents in general during the lacklustre four-day Belgian campaign.'[51] And yet, by Wellington's own admission, the emperor almost pulled off an unlikely victory at Waterloo, fighting uphill against a general who was acknowledged as the master of the defensive battle. There is no doubt that Wellington performed well at Waterloo by criss-crossing the battlefield, inspiring his troops and moving reserves to threatened sectors. But against an opponent of similar strength this might not have been enough. His decision to leave 17,000 valuable troops at Hal and Tubize was yet another error that, fortunately for him, he was not made to pay for.

Where does this leave Wellington in the pantheon of great British generals? Close to the top, certainly. He was undoubtedly a brilliant organizer and unflappable in a crisis; he could even, on occasion, show flashes of brilliance in his strategic and tactical generalship. At Salamanca he took full advantage of Marmont's overextension of his army to launch a superbly coordinated attack that destroyed the French vanguard; during the Vitoria campaign, possibly his finest, he combined strategic finesse with a bold and imaginative battle plan that, but for General Graham's failings, would have trapped and overwhelmed a whole French army. But at other times he showed his

limitations as a general by either fighting recklessly offensive battles
that only just came off (Assaye), or by becoming overcautious and
not taking advantage of the opportunities that were presented to him
(Busaco and Fuentes). At Waterloo he seems to have regained his
gambler's instinct; but it almost cost him the battle, his reputation
and his life.

The prince regent was at a private party in St James's Square when
Major the Honourable Henry Percy, still bloodstained and dusty
from the battlefield, arrived with Wellington's dispatch. As it mentioned many of the officer casualties, the ladies were asked to leave
the room before it was read aloud by Lord Liverpool, the prime minister. When he had finished, the regent turned to Percy and said: 'I
congratulate you, *Colonel* Percy.'

But the regent's joy was mixed with sadness and, as he reflected
upon the huge number of killed and wounded, tears began to course
down his fleshy cheeks. 'It is a glorious victory, and we must rejoice
at it,' he said, 'but the loss of life has been fearful, and *I* have lost
many friends.'[52]

In a generous act of compassion, the regent put the royal yacht at
the disposal of Lady Uxbridge, whose husband had had his right
leg amputated after a piece of grapeshot had shattered his knee. One
of the last salvos fired by the French, the shot had narrowly missed
Wellington as it passed over the neck of his horse and struck
Uxbridge. 'By God, sir,' exclaimed the wounded cavalry chief, 'I've
lost my leg.'

'By God, sir,' replied Wellington, taking the telescope from his
eye, 'so you have!'[53]

Uxbridge's operation was on the kitchen table of the small white-
washed house that served as the cavalry headquarters in Waterloo.
There was no anaesthetic, and Uxbridge had to grit his teeth as a canvas tourniquet was applied around the top of his wounded leg to
prevent him from bleeding to death; then the flesh above his knee
was cut with a sharp surgical knife – leaving flaps of spare skin and
tissue to cover the stump – and retracted so that the exposed leg bone
could be separated with a small saw. Finally the arteries were ligated

with silk thread, the flaps closed over the stump and secured with sutures, and the line of the wound dressed with lint and covered by a 'Maltese cross' bandage.[54] All the while Uxbridge was held down by various helpers, including his aide-de-camp, Captain Thomas Wildman of the 7th Hussars,★ who remembered he bore the loss of his limb with fortitude and humour. 'He never moved or complained,' wrote Wildman, 'no one even held his hand. He said once perfectly calmly that he thought the instrument was not very sharp. When it was over, his nerves did not appear the least shaken and the surgeons said his pulse was not altered. He said smiling, "I have been a beau these forty-seven years and it would not be fair to cut the young men out any longer." '[55]

Having accompanied his wife back across the Channel in the royal yacht, the one-legged earl was greeted by joyous crowds when he reached London on 9 July. The regent visited Uxbridge the following day and told him 'that he *loved* him . . . that he was his best officer and subject', and that he was going to make him a marquess. (He duly became the Marquess of Anglesey.)[56]

Many of the wounded were treated by volunteer doctors like Charles Bell, who travelled out from England to assist the overwhelmed medical surgeons at six large hospitals in Brussels. Once again Bell sketched (and later painted) his patients' wounds, leaving a remarkable visual record of the treatment of early-nineteenth-century battle injuries. They included a soldier of the French 21st Régiment de Ligne, part of d'Erlon's corps, who had been stabbed through the oesophagus by the 'small-sword' of a British officer, causing saliva, liquids and food to exit from the wound site. He was lucky; had the sword penetrated his windpipe he would almost certainly have died.[57]

One of the most critically wounded of Bell's patients was an unidentified trooper of the 1st Dragoons (Royals), who had received multiple sabre wounds to his skull, chin and ear, probably from above

★ The bloodstained glove that Wildman wore that day is now on display at the National Army Museum in London, as is the saw that was used to sever Uxbridge's leg.

after his horse was killed and he lost his toughened leather helmet. Bell noted: 'A portion of the skull . . . completely detached by the sabre-cut; the corresponding part of the scalp remains connected by a small isthmus . . . On being urged to speak, he makes painful effort to speak but cannot. He can sit up in a chair without support, but stands languidly and with a vacant and indifferent expression of countenance.' Incredibly he recovered.[58]

Another unlikely survivor was an anonymous soldier – probably British – who had had his left arm taken off at the shoulder by a piece of howitzer shell. Bell shows him lying on his right side, his eyes closed and his hand clutching a rope so that he could change positions. His grotesque wound, with the main artery ligated, is clearly visible. Bell commented: 'Artery taken up [ligated] on the field. Eleven days and no haemorrhage. Wound healthy. This man will do well.'[59]

Less fortunate was James Alexander of the 1st (Royal) Dragoons who had 'received a deep perforating wound of the right lower half of the neck from grapeshot', probably while charging d'Erlon's corps. He survived the initial heavy loss of blood, but died later of an embolism as air entered the vein in his neck. Dr Collier, who took up Alexander's care after Bell★ departed Brussels, noted: 'He died as I have seen many, from the powers of life yielding to an injury they are unable to repair.'[60]

Wellington's reward for helping to save Europe from Napoleon was the Royal Hanoverian Guelphic Order – the regent had no other honours left to give him. A more fitting honour, given the scale and importance of the victory, was the title of Prince of Waterloo bestowed upon him by a grateful King William I of the Netherlands. Some of Wellington's senior officers were given peerages, knighthoods and made Companions of the Order of the Bath (CB). But, as ever, the ordinary redcoats – who, in Wellington's estimation, had 'never behaved so well' as they did at Waterloo – got nothing. Thomas

★ Bell was later knighted and appointed Professor of Anatomy and Surgery at the Royal College of Surgeons.

Pococke of the 71st did not care. Having survived both the Peninsular and Waterloo, his only concern was to be given a discharge and return home. He got his wish in the winter of 1815, by which time Napoleon, having abdicated for a second time in Paris on 22 June, was safely in exile on the British South Atlantic island of Saint Helena. 'I left my comrades with regret,' recalled Pococke, 'but the service with joy. I came down to the coast to embark, with light steps and a joyful heart, singing, "When wild war's deadly blast was blawn". I was poor as poor could be; but I had hope before me, and pleasing dreams of home.'[61]

Arriving in Edinburgh by ship, he went straight to his parents' home. They no longer lived there, nor did the new occupants know their address. Fortunately the landlord remembered Tom and took him to his mother for a tearful reunion, the first in nine years. Pococke spent the next two years completing an account of his time in the army and sent it to a friend in the hope that it might be published. It was in 1819. But by then his mother was dead and he, unable to find work even as a labourer, had disappeared. Having left the army sound of body and without the requisite twenty years' service, Pococke was not eligible for a pension. He was last heard of working as a road mender 'with a number of other poor labourers thrown out of general employment'.[62] Thus did Britain reward 'that best of all instruments British Infantry'.

Epilogue

On 24 July 1815, nine days after Napoleon had left France for the last time on the British warship *Bellerophon*, the triumphant Allied sovereigns held a grand review of Wellington's troops on the plains of Saint-Denis, north of Paris. Captain Cavalié Mercer recalled:

> First came the Emperor Alexander [of Russia] and the King of Prussia in their respective green and blue uniforms, riding together – the former, as usual, all smiles; the latter taciturn and melancholy. A little in the rear followed the Austrian Emperor, in a white uniform, turned up with red, but quite plain – a thin, dried-up, thread-paper of a man, not of the most distinguished bearing; his lean brown visage, however, bore an expression of kindliness and *bonhomie*, which folk say his true character in no way belies. They passed along, scanning our people with evident interest and curiosity; and in passing me (as they did to every commanding officer), pulled off their hats, and saluted me with most gracious smiles.[1]

Most of the foreign corps that Mercer had seen in Paris were 'uncommonly well dressed in new clothes, smartly made, setting the men off to the greatest advantage – add to which their *coiffure* of high broad-topped shakos, or enormous caps of bear-skin'. At the review he could not help noticing that the British redcoats, by contrast, were wearing the 'same clothes in which they had marched, slept, and fought for months'. He added:

> The colour had faded to a dusky brick-dust hue; their coats, originally not very smartly made, had acquired by constant wearing that loose easy set so characteristic of old clothes, comfortable to the wearer, but not calculated to add grace to his appearance. *Pour surcroît de laideur* (To make them even more unsightly), their cap is perhaps the meanest, ugliest thing every invented. From all these causes it

arose that our infantry appeared to the utmost disadvantage – dirty, shabby, mean, and very small. Some such impression was, I fear, made on the sovereigns, for a report has reached me this morning, that they remarked to the Duke what very small men the English were. 'Ay,' replied our noble chief [Wellington], 'they are small; but your Majesties will find none who fight so well.'[2]

Wellington confirmed his high opinion of the ordinary redcoat when fashionable British visitors to Paris suggested that the cavalry made the greatest contribution to victory at Waterloo. 'I have told them that the British infantry won the battle and all our battles,' he confided to William Napier, the future historian of the Peninsular War, 'but it has been intimated to me that I know nothing of the matter, and I expect soon to be told I was not there.'[3] Waterloo was Wellington's last battle. He would devote most of the remaining thirty-seven years of his long and illustrious career as a public servant to politics and military administration, reaching the pinnacle of both as prime minister (1828–30, and again briefly in 1834) and commander-in-chief of the British Army (1827–8 and 1842–52). His time in office was not particularly successful, as Wellington's natural conservatism had little sympathy with the growing public clamour for political, social and military reform.

Perhaps his most significant post-Waterloo military legacy was to coin the generic name of 'Tommy' for a British infantryman. He was in Paris, shortly after the battle, when he received a draft military paper with a suggested name for a private that would appear on the specimen page of all future pay-books. He is said to have crossed the name out and replaced it with 'Thomas Atkins', the name of a private in the 33rd Foot who had fallen as the battalion checked a French attack near Breda in 1794, an action for which the regiment had been commended by the Duke of York. The name stuck, and in its shortened form was still being used by the friends and foes of British soldiers in the Second World War.[4]

The Battle of Waterloo brought to a close a century and a quarter of war between Britain and France, a period known to historians as 'the long eighteenth century'. Only once, in America in 1783, had these conflicts ended in defeat and humiliation. The other three major contests – the War of the Spanish Succession, the Seven Years War and the Napoleonic Wars – had all resulted in emphatic British victories that laid the foundations for imperial expansion across the globe. By 1815 Britain was indisputably the paramount maritime and industrial power in the world, and would remain so for much of the nineteenth century.

This extraordinary run of martial success – recorded on the colours of countless regiments as honours for battles as far flung as Blenheim, Ramillies, Dettingen, Plassey, Minden, Quebec, Assaye, Corunna, Vimeiro, Talavera, Salamanca, Vitoria and Waterloo – was due in no small part to the talents of a succession of brilliant field commanders of whom the Duke of Marlborough was surely *primus inter pares*. But it was also down to the fighting qualities of the junior officers and the ever-dependable British redcoats, who – in spite of harsh service conditions that included low pay, poor housing, inadequate food and brutal discipline – rarely let their commanders down in battle.

After Waterloo, however, the primacy of Britain's world position, and the lack of any serious threat of a French invasion, meant the country 'enjoyed almost four decades of peace in Europe, and this in itself sapped the army's preparedness to fight a large-scale land war'.[5] It also gave the government the opportunity to make the usual post-conflict inroads into the budget and size of the army. Army expenditure declined from £43 million in 1815 to just £8 million at the time of Queen Victoria's accession in 1837; during the same period the army's manpower was reduced from 234,000 to 88,000, with more than half that number garrisoned abroad.[6] This policy was reversed in the 1840s and early 1850s, thanks to increased imperial commitments and constant sabre-rattling by the rejuvenated French, and by 1854 the army had grown to 153,000 men. Yet the modest expeditionary force that took the field against Russia in the Crimean War of 1854–6 – the only conflict that Britain fought against a European power for almost a century after Waterloo – was a pale shadow of the well-oiled veteran force that had overwhelmed the French at Vitoria in 1813. The future Field Marshal Viscount Wolseley wrote:

> Every ordnance storehouse in Great Britain was ransacked in order to collect guns and harness and ammunition wagons for the ten batteries of horse and field artillery sent to the East for the war. We had, however, some weak battalions of excellent foot soldiers, and a few attenuated regiments of cavalry, the men of both arms being dressed and accoutred for the show. We had no reserves of any kind, and in order to make up to their regulation field strength the thirty battalions of the Foot Guards and the Line . . . sent to Bulgaria in 1854, the few battalions left at home were drained of their best men.[7]

Crimea was the last major war fought by the redcoats before their distinctive tunics were gradually replaced by khaki from the 1880s onwards.* But even by the time of the Crimean War they had swapped their muskets for faster-firing and more accurate rifles, and the tried and tested infantry tactic of a close-range volley followed by a bayonet charge was no longer effective against a European foe with modern weapons. In other ways, too, the British Army was hopelessly outdated, a Napoleonic force in an industrial age with its unprofessional officer corps, chaotic administration, poor supply and unsuitable uniforms; and only the public scandal of tens of thousands of soldiers lost to disease, exposure and hunger would usher in the post-Crimea reforms that changed the British Army for ever.

It is fitting, perhaps, to close this book with a quote from a soldier whose Prussian (later German) Army would dominate Europe's battlefields from the mid-nineteenth to the mid-twentieth centuries in much the same way the British Army had for the century and a half prior to that. 'For a battle,' wrote Baron von Müffling, Wellington's former Prussian liaison officer, in 1816, 'there is not perhaps in Europe an army equal to the British, that is to say, none whose

---

* Defeat for Britain in the Anglo-Transvaal War of 1880–81, when redcoats were shot down like rabbits by Boers armed with modern breech-loading rifles, marked the beginning of the end for the famous scarlet tunic.

tuition, discipline, and whole military tendency, is so purely and exclusively calculated for giving battle.' He added:

> The British soldier is vigorous, well fed, by nature highly brave and intrepid, trained to the most vigorous discipline, and admirably well armed. The infantry resist the attacks of cavalry with great confidence, and when taken in the flank or rear, British troops are less disconcerted than any other European army. These circumstances in their favour will explain how this army, since the Duke of Wellington conducted it, has never yet been defeated in the open field.[8]

Notes

Prologue

1. John Tincey, *Sedgemoor 1685: Marlborough's First Victory* (2005), p. 92.
2. Richard Brooks, *Cassell's Battlefields of Britain and Ireland* (2005), p. 564.
3. Tincey, *Sedgemoor 1685*, p. 103.
4. Barney White-Spunner, *Horse Guards* (2006), p. 90.
5. Tincey, *Sedgemoor 1685*, p. 109.
6. Reverend Paschall, in ibid., p. 110.
7. Richard Holmes, *Marlborough: England's Fragile Genius* (2008), p. 124.
8. Tincey, *Sedgemoor 1685*, pp. 118–19.
9. Brooks, *Cassell's Battlefields*, p. 566.
10. Tincey, *Sedgemoor 1685*, p. 129.
11. Ibid., p. 130.
12. Brooks, *Cassell's Battlefields*, p. 566.
13. Ibid.
14. James II to William of Orange, in Tincey, *Sedgemoor 1685*, p. 138.
15. Holmes, *Marlborough*, p. 126.
16. Tincey, *Sedgemoor 1685*, p. 158.
17. N.A.M. Rodger, *The Command of the Ocean: A Naval History of Britain, 1649–1815* (2004), p. 576.

1. The Restoration Soldier

1. Holmes, *Marlborough*, pp. 45–8.
2. Austin Woolrych, *Britain's Revolution: 1625–1660* (2002), pp. 744–5.
3. *Pepys Diary*, 25 May 1660.
4. Ibid.
5. Duke of Albemarle [George Monck], *Observations upon Military and Political Affairs* (1671), p. 20.

6. John Childs, *The Army of Charles II* (1976), Appendix H, pp. 257–8; White-Spunner, *Horse Guards*, pp. 27–8.

7. Ibid., pp. 29–30.

8. Hew Strachan, *The Politics of the British Army* (1997), pp. 20–21.

9. Childs, *The Army of Charles II*, p. 24.

10. Ibid., p. 23.

11. Edward Chamberlayne, quoted in ibid., p. 24.

12. Norman Tucker (ed.), 'The Military Memoirs of John Gwyn' (1967), pp. 99–100.

13. White-Spunner, *Horse Guards*, p. 23.

14. Ibid., p. 83; Michael Blacklock, *The Royal Scots Greys* (1971), p. 2.

15. John Childs, 'The Restoration Army 1660–1702', in David Chandler (ed.), *The Oxford History of the British Army* (1994; this edition 1996), pp. 60–61; Childs, *The Army of Charles II*, p. 109.

16. Childs, 'The Restoration Army 1660–1702', p. 61.

17. White-Spunner, *Horse Guards*, pp. 31–3.

18. Childs, *The Army of Charles II*, p. 58.

19. John Childs, *The Army, James II, and the Glorious Revolution* (1980), p. 36.

20. Childs, *The Army of Charles II*, p. 71.

21. David Chandler, *Blenheim Preparation: The English Army on the March to the Danube* (2004), p. 78.

22. Childs, 'The Restoration Army 1660–1702', p. 62.

23. Annabel Venning, *Following the Drum: The Lives of Army Wives and Daughters, Past and Present* (2005), pp. 7–8.

24. Ibid., pp. 11–12.

2. The 'First' Churchill

1. Winston S. Churchill, *Marlborough: His Life and Times* (4 vols., 1933–8), Vol. I, p. 52.

2. Archbishop Coxe, quoted in Holmes, *Marlborough*, p. 59.

3. Childs, 'The Restoration Army 1660–1702', p. 48.

4. Sir Hugh Cholmly, quoted in Holmes, *Marlborough*, p. 60.

5. White-Spunner, *Horse Guards*, pp. 79–80.

6. Colonel Lord Alington, quoted in Holmes, *Marlborough*, p. 76.

7. Monmouth, quoted in ibid., p. 77.

8. C. T. Atkinson, *Marlborough and the Rise of the British Army* (1921), pp. 57–8.

9. Holmes, *Marlborough*, p. 105.

10. Churchill had been made a Scottish baron by Charles II in 1681.

11. Childs, 'The Restoration Army 1660–1702', p. 58. The horse later became the 1st–6th Dragoon Guards, the dragoons the 3rd (King's Own) and 4th Light Dragoons, and the infantry the 7th Royal Regiment of Fusiliers and the 8th–15th Regiments of Foot. An imitation of a French corps, the Fusiliers – or 'Fusileers' – was unique in that it had no pikemen, with all men armed with fusils and plug bayonets, instead of just the grenadier company. Its original task was to escort the Artillery on the march, but in practice it operated like any other infantry unit.

12. Childs, *The Army, James II, and the Glorious Revolution*, p. 204.

13. Childs, 'The Restoration Army 1660–1702', p. 58.

14. Holmes, *Marlborough*, pp. 138–9.

15. Quoted in Edward Vallance, *The Glorious Revolution: 1688 – Britain's Fight for Liberty* (2006), pp. 101–2.

16. Holmes, *Marlborough*, p. 137.

17. Childs, *The Army, James II, and the Glorious Revolution*, p. 206.

18. Colonel Clifford Walton, *History of the British Standing Army: 1660–1700* (1894), p. 180.

19. Vallance, *The Glorious Revolution*, pp. 175–6.

20. Ibid., p. 177.

21. Ibid., p. 178.

3. William's Wars

1. John Childs, *The British Army of William III* (1987), p. 25.

2. Ibid., p. 14.

3. Ibid., p. 13.

4. Ibid., p. 14.

5. David Chandler, *Marlborough as Military Commander* (1984), p. 31.

6. Holmes, *Marlborough*, p. 160.

7. Chandler, *Marlborough as Military Commander*, p. 33.

8. Holmes, *Marlborough*, p. 162.

9. Donald Macbean, quoted in Brooks, *Cassell's Battlefields of Britain and Ireland*, p. 570.

10. Walton, *History of the British Standing Army 1660–1700*, pp. 61–2.

11. Quoted in Vallance, *The Glorious Revolution*, pp. 216–17.

12. Holmes, *Marlborough*, p. 168.

13. [Anonymous], *A True Relation of the Battle of the Boyne in Ireland, fought by His Majesty King William, in the Year 1690, without Observation or Reflection* (1700).

14. Ibid.

15. 'A Jacobite Narrative of the War in Ireland', quoted in Brooks, *Cassell's Battlefields of Britain and Ireland*, p. 579.

16. Quoted in ibid., p. 581.

17. Ibid., p. 579.

18. [Anonymous], *A True Relation of the Battle of the Boyne in Ireland*.

19. 'Account by Rowland Davies, Chaplain to a Williamite Cavalry Regiment', quoted in John Lewis-Stempel, *The Autobiography of the British Soldier: From Agincourt to Basra, in His Own Words* (2007), pp. 55–6.

20. Ibid., p. 56.

21. Ibid.

22. Quoted in Vallance, *The Glorious Revolution*, p. 218.

23. Ibid., p. 219.

24. Quoted in Brooks, *Cassell's Battlefields of Britain and Ireland*, p. 585.

25. Quoted in Holmes, *Marlborough*, p. 72.

26. Ibid.

27. Ian Roy, 'Towards the Standing Army 1485–1660', in Chandler, *The Oxford History of the British Army*, pp. 28–30.

28. Chandler, *Marlborough as Military Commander*, p. 64; Chandler, *Blenheim Preparation*, p. 8.

29. Childs, 'The Restoration Army 1660–1702', p. 65.

30. Maréchal de Puységur, quoted in Chandler, *Blenheim Preparation*, p. 75.

31. Chandler, *Marlborough as Military Commander*, p. 64.

32. Childs, 'The Restoration Army 1660–1702', p. 66.

33. Blacklock, *The Royal Scots Greys*, p. 2.

34. Quoted in Holmes, *Marlborough*, p. 102.

35. Chandler, *Blenheim Preparation*, p. 110.

36. Ibid., p. 121.
37. Ibid., p. 122.

4. The War of the Spanish Succession

1. Chandler, *Blenheim Preparation*, p. 192.
2. Quoted in Chandler, *Marlborough as Military Commander*, p. 54.
3. Holmes, *Marlborough*, p. 208.
4. Ibid., p. 480.
5. Arthur Herman, *To Rule the Waves: How the British Navy Shaped the Modern World* (2005), p. 221.
6. Holmes, *Marlborough*, p. 189.
7. David Chandler, 'The Great Captain General 1702–1714', in Chandler, *The Oxford History of the British Army*, p. 69.
8. Quoted in Lewis-Stempel, *The Autobiography of the British Soldier*, p. 58.
9. Ibid, p. 75.
10. Chandler, 'The Great Captain General', p. 75.
11. Quoted in Lewis-Stempel, *The Autobiography of the British Soldier*, p. 57.
12. Quoted in Holmes, *Marlborough*, p. 225.
13. Ibid.
14. David Chandler (ed.), *Military Memoirs: Robert Parker and the Comte de Mérode-Westerloo* (1968), p. 20.
15. Ibid., p. 25.
16. Holmes, *Marlborough*, p. 233.

5. The March to the Danube

1. Holmes, *Marlborough*, p. 235.
2. Quoted in ibid., p. 253.
3. Ibid., p. 256.
4. Corelli Barnett, *Marlborough* (first published 1974; this edition 1999), p. 82.
5. Charles Spencer, *Blenheim: Battle for Europe* (2004), pp. 135–6.
6. Captain Richard Kane, quoted in Holmes, *Marlborough*, p. 258.

7. Chandler, *Military Memoirs: Robert Parker and the Comte de Mérode-Westerloo*, p. 31.

8. David Chandler (ed.), *Military Miscellany II: Manuscripts from Marlborough's Wars, the American War of Independence and the Boer War* (2005), p. 40.

9. David Chandler (ed.), *Journal of Marlborough's Campaigns . . . by John Marshall Deane* (1984), p. 5.

10. Marlborough to his brother, 18 June 1704, in *Marlborough Correspondence* (5 vols., 1845), Vol. I, p. 313.

11. Ibid., 8 June 1704, p. 301.

12. Ibid., 22 June 1704, p. 321.

13. Chandler, *Blenheim Preparation*, p. 226.

14. Dr Francis Hare, 'Detailed Account of the Action at the Schellenberg', quoted in *Marlborough Correspondence*, Vol. I, p. 352.

15. Walter Horsley (ed.), *The Chronicles of an Old Campaigner: M. de la Colonie 1692–1717* (1904), p. 176.

16. Ibid., p. 177.

17. Hare, 'Detailed Account of the Action at the Schellenberg', p. 332.

18. G. F. Bacon, 'Early History of the Scots Greys', *Navy and Army Illustrated*, 15 Jan. 1897.

19. Hare, 'Detailed Account of the Action at the Schellenberg', p. 333.

20. Horsley, *The Chronicles of an Old Campaigner*, p. 179.

21. Hare, 'Detailed Account of the Action at the Schellenberg', p. 334.

22. Horsley, *The Chronicles of an Old Campaigner*, p. 181.

23. Hare, 'Detailed Account of the Action at the Schellenberg', pp. 334–5.

24. Horsley, *The Chronicles of an Old Campaigner*, pp. 182–3.

25. Hare, 'Detailed Account of the Action at the Schellenberg', p. 335.

26. Ibid., p. 336.

27. Ibid.

28. Ibid., p. 337.

29. Horsley, *The Chronicles of an Old Campaigner*, pp. 184–5.

30. Hare, 'Detailed Account of the Action at the Schellenberg', p. 337.

31. Horsley, *The Chronicles of an Old Campaigner*, p. 187.

32. Hare, 'Detailed Account of the Action at the Schellenberg', p. 337.

33. Ibid., pp. 337–8.

34. Quoted in James Falkner, *Marlborough's Wars: Eyewitness Accounts 1702–1713* (2005), p. 49.

35. Horsley, *The Chronicles of an Old Campaigner*, pp. 192–4.

36. Hare, 'Detailed Account of the Action at the Schellenberg', p. 338.

37. Holmes, *Marlborough*, p. 274; Chandler, *Marlborough as Military Commander*, p. 137.

38. Spencer, *Blenheim*, p. 185.

39. John Hunter, an eighteenth-century medical officer and philosopher, quoted in ibid., pp. 185–6.

40. Venning, *Following the Drum*, pp. 307–8.

41. Holmes, *Marlborough*, p. 275.

42. Chandler, *Journal of Marlborough's Campaigns*, pp. 7–8.

43. Lieutenant Richard Pope of Schomberg's Regiment of Horse, quoted in James Falkner, *Great and Glorious Days: Marlborough's Battles 1704–1709* (2007), p. 44.

6. *Blenheim*

1. Holmes, *Marlborough*, p. 277.

2. Ibid., p. 278.

3. Spencer, *Blenheim*, p. 213.

4. Falkner, *Great and Glorious Days*, p. 53.

5. Holmes, *Marlborough*, p. 279.

6. Chandler, *Marlborough as Military Commander*, p. 140.

7. Chandler, *Military Memoirs: Robert Parker and the Comte de Mérode-Westerloo*, p. 41.

8. Sergeant John Millner, *Journal of All the Marches, Famous Battles, and Sieges* (1733), p. 111.

9. Marlborough's army was comprised of 66 infantry battalions and 160 cavalry squadrons. Only 14 battalions and 14 squadrons were British; the rest were from Holland, Prussia, Denmark, Hesse, Hanover, Switzerland, Austria, Lunenburg, Zell, Swabia, Franconia and Württemberg. See Dr Francis Hare, 'Account of the Battle of Blenheim', in *Marlborough Correspondence*, Vol. I, pp. 397–8.

10. Marlborough to Mr Secretary Harley, 14 Aug. 1704, in ibid., p. 391.

11. Sir Edward Seymour, quoted in Spencer, *Blenheim*, p. 171.

12. Josias Sandby, quoted in ibid., p. 225.

13. Chandler, *Military Memoirs: Robert Parker and the Comte de Mérode-Westerloo*, p. 166.

14. Ibid., p. 168.

15. Chandler, *Blenheim Preparations*, p. 260.

16. Hare, 'Account of the Battle of Blenheim', p. 400.

17. Falkner, *Marlborough's Wars*, p. 63.

18. Hare, 'Account of the Battle of Blenheim', p. 401.

19. Mérode-Westerloo, quoted in Chandler, *Military Memoirs: Robert Parker and the Comte de Mérode-Westerloo*, p. 164.

20. Chandler, *Blenheim Preparation*, p. 260.

21. Hare, 'Account of the Battle of Blenheim', p. 403.

22. Spencer, *Blenheim*, p. 247.

23. Chandler, *Military Memoirs: Robert Parker and the Comte de Mérode-Westerloo*, p. 169.

24. Spencer, *Blenheim*, p. 258.

25. Hare, 'Account of the Battle of Blenheim', p. 405.

26. Sergeant Millner, *Journal of All the Marches*, p. 117.

27. Chandler, *Military Memoirs: Robert Parker and the Comte de Mérode-Westerloo*, p. 172.

28. Spencer, *Blenheim*, p. 270.

29. Ibid., p. 271.

30. Hare, 'Account of the Battle of Blenheim', p. 405.

31. Sergeant Millner, *Journal of All the Marches*, pp. 118–19.

32. Spencer, *Blenheim*, p. 273.

33. Hare, 'Account of the Battle of Blenheim', pp. 405–6.

34. Chandler, *Military Memoirs: Robert Parker and the Comte de Mérode-Westerloo*, pp. 173–6.

35. Falkner, *Great and Glorious Days*, p. 76.

36. Spencer, *Blenheim*, p. 278.

37. Chandler, *Military Memoirs: Robert Parker and the Comte de Mérode-Westerloo*, p. 43.

38. Hare, 'Account of the Battle of Blenheim', p. 407.

39. Ibid., p. 408.

40. Chandler, *Blenheim Preparation*, pp. 260–61.

41. Hare, 'Account of the Battle of Blenheim', p. 408.

42. Chandler, *Blenheim Preparation*, p. 261.

43. Ibid., pp. 408–9.

44. Chandler, *Marlborough as Military Commander*, p. 148; Spencer, *Blenheim*, p. 295.

45. Falkner, *Marlborough's Wars*, p. 71.

46. Marlborough to Mr Secretary Harley, 14 Aug. 1704, in *Marlborough Correspondence*, Vol. I, pp. 392–3.

47. Chandler, *Marlborough as Military Commander*, p. 149.

48. Barnett, *Marlborough*, p. 127.

49. Allan Mallinson, *The Making of the British Army* (2010), p. 64.

50. Spencer, *Blenheim*, p. 312.

51. Barnett, *Marlborough*, p. 239.

52. Ibid., pp. 239–40.

53. Chandler, *Military Memoirs: Robert Parker and the Comte de Mérode-Westerloo*, p. 126.

54. Ibid., p. 262.

55. Holmes, *Marlborough*, p. 481.

7. *The Two Georges*

1. Anthony Clayton, *The British Officer: Leading the Army from 1660 to the Present* (2006), p. 38.

2. John Parker, *Black Watch: The Inside Story of the Oldest Highland Regiment in the British Army* (2006), p. 14.

3. Ibid., p. 482.

4. Chandler, *Military Memoirs: Robert Parker and the Comte de Mérode-Westerloo*, pp. 125–6.

5. Clayton, *The British Officer*, pp. 44–5.

6. White-Spunner, *Horse Guards*, p. 194.

7. Ibid., pp. 192–3.

8. Hew Strachan, *The Politics of the British Army* (1997), pp. 23–4.

9. White-Spunner, *Horse Guards*, p. 194.

10. Clayton, *The British Officer*, pp. 39–40.

11. John Prebble, *Culloden* (1961; this edition 1967), p. 19.

12. Ibid., pp. 22–3.

13. Ibid., p. 23.

14. Letter from Gunner James Hardcastle to his father, 25 Aug. 1743 (O.S.), NAM, 1976–07–40.

15. A. D. L. Cary and S. McCance, *Regimental Records of the Royal Welch Fusiliers. Vol. I: 1689–1815* (1920; this edition 2005), pp. 106–7.

16. Ibid., p. 107.

17. Corelli Barnett, *Britain and Her Army: A Military, Political and Social History of the British Army 1509–1970* (1970; this edition 1999), p. 184.

18. Cary and McCance, *Regimental Records of the Royal Welch Fusiliers. Vol. I*, p. 107.

8. James Wolfe

1. Wolfe to his father, 4 July 1743, in Beckles Willson, *The Life and Letters of James Wolfe* (1909), p. 37.

2. Ibid., pp. 37–8.

3. Prebble, *Culloden*, p. 33.

4. Ibid., p. 35.

5. Ibid., p. 38.

6. Willson, *Life and Letters of James Wolfe*, p. 53.

7. Ibid., p. 54.

8. Ibid.

9. Stephen Brumwell, *Paths of Glory: The Life and Death of General James Wolfe* (2006), p. 45.

10. Ibid., pp. 46–7.

11. Ibid., p. 47.

12. Ibid.

13. Ibid., p. 48.

14. Ibid.

15. Ibid.

16. Ibid., pp. 49–50.

17. Prebble, *Culloden*, p. 18.

18. Willson, *Life and Letters of James Wolfe*, p. 59.

19. Prebble, *Culloden*, p. 223.

20. Richard Holmes, *Redcoat: The British Soldier in the Age of Horse and Musket* (2001; this edition 2002), p. 295.

21. Prebble, Culloden, pp. 13, 23.

22. Ibid., p. 26.

23. Ibid., p. 28.

24. Willson, *Life and Letters of James Wolfe*, p. 61.

25. Prebble, *Culloden*, p. 31.

26. Ibid., p. 91.

27. Ibid., p. 92.

28. Ibid., p. 97.

29. Wolfe to Henry Delabene, 17 Apr. 1746, in Willson, *Life and Letters of James Wolfe*, p. 63.

30. Prebble, *Culloden*, p. 99.

31. Ibid., p. 104.

32. Ibid., p. 105.

33. Wolfe to Henry Delabane, 17 Apr. 1746, in Willson, *Life and Letters of James Wolfe*, p. 63.

34. Brumwell, *Paths of Glory*, p. 53.

35. Ibid., p. 54.

36. Wolfe to Henry Delabane, 17 Apr. 1746, in Willson, *Life and Letters of James Wolfe*, p. 63.

37. Wolfe to William Sotheron, 17 Apr. 1746, in Willson, *Life and Letters of James Wolfe*, p. 65.

38. Ibid.

39. Wolfe to Captain Hamilton, 19 May 1746, in Willson, *Life and Letters of James Wolfe*, p. 68.

40. Ibid., 22 July 1746, p. 69.

41. Prebble, *Culloden*, p. 169.

42. Ibid.

43. Brumwell, *Paths of Glory*, p. 59.

44. Willson, *Life and Letters of James Wolfe*, p. 77.

45. Brumwell, *Paths of Glory*, pp. 62–3.

46. Wolfe to his father, Oct. 1751, in Willson, *Life and Letters of James Wolfe*, p. 157.

47. Ibid., pp. 88–9.

48. Holmes, *Redcoat*, p. 293.

49. Brumwell, *Paths of Glory*, p. 107.

50. Ibid., p. 108.

51. Ibid., pp. 112–13.

52. Ibid., p. 113.

53. Ibid., p. 130.

54. Andrew Cormack and Alan Jones (eds.), *The Journal of Corporal Todd 1745–1762* (2001), p. xiii.

55. Ibid., pp. 1–2.

56. Ibid., pp. 2–3.

57. Ibid., pp. 3, 6–7.

58. Ibid., pp. 7, 10.

59. Ibid., pp. 16, 18.

9. The Seven Years War

1. Frank McLynn, *1759: The Year Britain Became Master of the World* (2004), p. 95.

2. Cormack and Jones, *The Journal of Corporal Todd*, pp. 33–4. Todd would later fight in Germany with the 30th and 12th regiments of foot. He survived the war, married and had a daughter, and died in the East Riding in 1791 at the age of sixty-seven.

3. Wolfe to Major Walter Wolfe, 18 Oct. 1757, in Willson, *Life and Letters of James Wolfe*, pp. 336–7.

4. Brumwell, *Paths of Glory*, p. 135.

5. Wolfe to Major Rickson, 5 Nov.1757, in Willson, *Life and Letters of James Wolfe*, p. 339.

6. Giles MacDonogh, *Frederick the Great* (1999), p. 264.

7. Ibid., p. 265.

8. Barnett, *Britain and Her Army*, p. 181.

9. Ibid., p. 183.

10. Brumwell, *Paths of Glory*, p. 141.

11. Ibid., p. 150.

12. Lieutenant Thomas Bell of the marines, quoted in ibid., p. 160.

13. Ibid., p. 161.

14. Ibid., p. 159.

15. Wolfe to Major Walter Wolfe, 27 July 1758, in Willson, *Life and Letters of James Wolfe*, p. 385.

16. Ibid., p. 49.

10. Quebec

1. Brumwell, *Paths of Glory*, p. 170.
2. Ibid., p. 172.
3. Ibid., p. 176.
4. Wolfe to Major Walter Wolfe, 29 Jan. 1759, in Willson, *Life and Letters of James Wolfe*, p. 385.
5. Pitt to Amherst, 29 Dec. 1758, in Brumwell, *Paths of Glory*, p. 178.
6. Ibid.
7. Wolfe to Major Walter Wolfe, 19 May 1759, in Willson, *Life and Letters of James Wolfe*, p. 427.
8. Ibid., p. 428.
9. Brumwell, *Paths of Glory*, p. 190.
10. Stephen Brumwell, *Redcoats: The British Soldier and War in the Americas 1755–1763* (2000; this edition 2006), p. 96.
11. Ibid., pp. 96–7.
12. Wolfe to Major Walter Wolfe, 19 May 1759, in Willson, *Life and Letters of James Wolfe*, p. 427.
13. Brumwell, *Redcoats*, pp. 229–30.
14. Wolfe to Major Walter Wolfe, 19 May 1759, in Willson, *Life and Letters of James Wolfe*, pp. 427–9.
15. Lieutenant John Knox, 43rd Foot, in Willson, *Life and Letters of James Wolfe*, p. 436.
16. 'Genuine Letters from a Volunteer in the British Service at Quebec', in A. Doughty and G. W. Parmelee, *The Siege of Quebec and the Battle of the Plains of Abraham*, (6 vols., 1901), Vol. V, p. 15.
17. 'Sergeant-Major's Journal', in ibid., p. 11.
18. Wolfe to Pitt, 2 Sept. 1759, in Willson, *Life and Letters of James Wolfe*, p. 455.
19. Brumwell, *Paths of Glory*, p. 202.
20. Wolfe to Pitt, 2 Sept. 1759, in Willson, *Life and Letters of James Wolfe*, p. 455.
21. Ibid.
22. Brumwell, *Paths of Glory*, p. 203.
23. Wolfe's Last Will and Testament, 8 June 1759, in Willson, *Life and Letters of James Wolfe*, p. 483.

24. Brumwell, *Paths of Glory*, p. 206.

25. Ibid., p. 210.

26. Willson, *Life and Letters of James Wolfe*, p. 456.

27. Brumwell, *Paths of Glory*, p. 210.

28. Ibid.

29. Willson, *Life and Letters of James Wolfe*, p. 457.

30. Wolfe to Admiral Saunders, 30 Aug. 1759, in Willson, *Life and Letters of James Wolfe*, p. 461.

31. Wolfe to Pitt, 2 Sept. 1759, in Willson, *Life and Letters of James Wolfe*, p. 457.

32. Ibid.

33. Humphrys's journal, British Library Add. MS 45662.

34. Brumwell, *Paths of Glory*, pp. 222–3.

35. 'A Journal of the Expedition up the River St Lawrence by the Serjeant-Major of Gen. Hopson's [Louisbourg] Grenadiers', in Doughty and Parmelee, *The Siege of Quebec*, Vol. V, p. 4.

36. Wolfe to Pitt, 2 Sept. 1759, in Willson, *Life and Letters of James Wolfe*, pp. 457–8.

37. Ibid., p. 458.

38. Captain Alexander Schomberg. R.N., in Brumwell, *Paths of Glory*, p. 225.

39. Brumwell, *Paths of Glory*, p. 234.

40. Dan Snow, *Death or Victory: The Battle of Quebec and the Birth of Empire* (2009), pp. 282–5.

41. Brumwell, *Redcoats*, p. 123.

42. Ibid., p. 122.

43. Ibid., p. 124.

44. Ibid., p. 125.

45. John Johnson, 'Memoirs of the Siege of Quebec', in Doughty and Parmelee, *The Siege of Quebec*, Vol. V, p. 99.

46. Ibid., p. 95.

47. Wolfe to his brigadiers, 27 Aug. 1759, in Willson, *Life and Letters of James Wolfe*, pp. 466–7.

48. Brigadiers to Wolfe, 29 Aug. 1759, in ibid., pp. 467–8.

49. Brumwell, *Paths of Glory*, pp. 250–51.

50. Ibid., p. 251.

51. Wolfe to Pitt, 2 Sept. 1759, in Willson, *Life and Letters of James Wolfe*, p. 470.

52. Ibid., p. 471.

53. Brumwell, *Paths of Glory*, p. 256.

54. Ibid., pp. 258–9.

11. The Heights of Abraham

1. Brumwell, *Paths of Glory*, p. 262.

2. Willson, *Life and Letters of James Wolfe*, pp. 478, 481.

3. Wolfe to Colonel Burton, 10 Sept. 1759, in Willson, *Life and Letters of James Wolfe*, p. 477.

4. Orders to the Army before Quebec, 11 Sept. 1759, in ibid., pp. 479–80.

5. Orders to the Army before Quebec, 12 Sept. 1759, in ibid., pp. 481–2.

6. Johnson, 'Memoirs of the Siege of Quebec', in Doughty and Parmelee, *The Siege of Quebec*, Vol. V, p. 102.

7. Brigadiers to Wolfe, 12 Sept. 1759, in Willson, *Life and Letters of James Wolfe*, p. 484.

8. Willson, *Life and Letters of James Wolfe*, pp. 485–6.

9. 'An NCO of Fraser's Regiment', in T. H. McGuffie (ed.), *Rank and File: The Common Soldier at Peace and War 1642–1914* (1964), p. 304.

10. Lewis-Stempel, *The Autobiography of the British Soldier*, p. 88.

11. Ibid.

12. Ibid.

13. 'An NCO of Fraser's Regiment', in McGuffie, *Rank and File*, p. 305.

14. Johnson, 'Memoirs of the Siege of Quebec', in Doughty and Parmelee, *The Siege of Quebec*, Vol. V, pp. 254–5.

15. Snow, *Death or Victory*, p. 350. This figure includes the battalions in the front line: the Louisbourg Grenadiers, and the 28th, 43rd, 47th, 78th and 58th of foot. But not the 35th, 48th and 15th foot, the two battalions of Royal Americans and the light infantry.

16. 'A Journal of the Expedition up the River St Lawrence', in Doughty and Parmelee, *The Siege of Quebec*, Vol. V, p. 9.

17. Lewis-Stempel, *The Autobiography of the British Soldier*, p. 89.

18. Ibid.

19. Ibid.

20. 'A Journal of the Expedition up the River St Lawrence', in Doughty and Parmelee, *The Siege of Quebec*, Vol. V, p. 10.

21. Johnson, 'Memoirs of the Siege of Quebec', in Doughty and Parmelee, *The Siege of Quebec*, Vol. V, p. 104.

22. Brumwell, *Paths of Glory*, p. 283.

23. Lieutenant John Knox, in Lewis-Stempel, *The Autobiography of the British Soldier*, p. 89.

24. Humphrys's journal, British Library Add. MS 45662.

25. 'Genuine Letters from a Volunteer', in Doughty and Parmelee, *The Siege of Quebec*, Vol. V, pp. 23–4.

26. Snow, *Death or Victory*, p. 377.

27. Humphrys's journal, British Library Add. MS 45662.

28. Lewis-Stempel, *The Autobiography of the British Soldier*, p. 89.

29. 'Genuine Letters from a Volunteer', in Doughty and Parmelee, *The Siege of Quebec*, Vol. V, p. 23.

30. Snow, *Death or Victory*, p. 379.

31. Ibid., p. 377.

32. Johnson, 'Memoirs of the Siege of Quebec', in Doughty and Parmelee, *The Siege of Quebec*, Vol. V, p. 106.

33. Ibid.

34. Snow, *Death or Victory*, p. 382.

35. Humphrys's journal, British Library Add. MS 45662.

36. Brumwell, *Paths of Glory*, p. 287.

37. Willson, *Life and Letters of James Wolfe*, p. 496.

38. 'Genuine Letters from a Volunteer', in Doughty and Parmelee, *The Siege of Quebec*, Vol. V, p. 23.

39. Willson, *Life and Letters of James Wolfe*, p. 497.

40. Snow, *Death or Victory*, p. 389.

41. Ibid.

42. 'A Journal of the Expedition up the River St Lawrence', in Doughty and Parmelee, *The Siege of Quebec*, Vol. V, pp. 10–11.

43. Ibid., p. 11.

44. Brumwell, *Paths of Glory*, p. 292.

45. Ibid., p. 293.

46. Stephen Brumwell, 'James Wolfe', in Andrew Roberts (ed.), *The Art of War: Great Commanders of the Modern World* (2008), p. 115.

47. Ibid., p. 294.

48. K. Wilson, 'Empire of Virtue: The Imperial Project and Hanoverian Culture *c.* 1720–1785', in L. Stone (ed.), *An Imperial State at War: Britain from 1689 to 1815* (1994), p. 150.

49. Christopher Hibbert, *Nelson: A Personal History* (1995), p. 384.

50. Brumwell, *Paths of Glory*, p. 297.

51. Stephen Reid, 'James Wolfe', in Brian Harrison and H. C. G. Matthew (eds.), *Oxford Dictionary of National Biography* (2004).

52. *Pitt Correspondence* (4 vols., 1838), Vol. II, pp. 198–9.

53. Admiral Saunders, in Rodger, *The Command of the Ocean*, p. 288.

12. The Blunted Sword

1. Tony Hayter, 'The Army and the First British Empire 1714–1783', in Chandler, *The Oxford History of the British Army*, p. 124.

2. Ibid., pp. 121–2.

3. Ibid., pp. 122–3.

4. Barnett, *Britain and Her Army*, p. 214.

5. John Ferling, *Almost a Miracle: The American Victory in the War of Independence* (Oxford, 2007), p. 21.

6. Ibid., p. 22.

7. Ibid., p. 23.

8. Barbara Tuchman, *The March of Folly* (1984; this edition 1990), p. 178.

9. T. S. Anderson, *The Command of the Howe Brothers during the American Revolution* (New York, 1936), p. 30.

10. Ferling, *Almost a Miracle*, p. 26.

11. Anderson, *The Command of the Howe Brothers*, p. 30.

12. Ibid., p. 31.

13. William Cobbett (ed.), *The Parliamentary History of England: From the Earliest Period to the Year 1803* (1813), Vol. XVII, pp. 1,280–81.

14. Tuchman, *The March of Folly*, p. 249.

15. Ibid., p. 250.

16. Ira D. Gruber, *The Howe Brothers and the American Revolution* (1974), p. 6.

17. Ibid., p. 17.

18. Ibid., p. 59.

19. Howe to Mr Kirk, 21 Feb. 1775, in Anderson, *The Command of the Howe Brothers*, p. 49.

20. Christopher Hibbert, *Redcoats and Rebels: The War for America 1770–1781* (1990; this edition 2008), p. 82.

21. McGuffie, *Rank and File*, pp. 42–3.

22. Ibid., p. 85.

23. James Boswell, *Life of Johnson. Vol. III: 1776–1780* (1934), p. 9.

24. Ibid., pp. 265–6.

13. First Shots

1. The Boston garrison in early 1775 was comprised of the 5th, 10th, 18th, 23rd, 38th, 43rd, 52nd and 59th foot.

2. Mark Urban, *Fusiliers: Eight Years with the Redcoats in America* (2007), p. 3.

3. Ferling, *Almost a Miracle*, p. 30.

4. Urban, *Fusiliers*, p. 20.

5. John C. Dann (ed.), *The Revolution Remembered: Eyewitness Accounts of the War of Independence* (1980), pp. 7–8.

6. Ibid., p. 24.

7. Ibid.

8. Cary and McCance, *Regimental Records of the Royal Welch Fusiliers*, p. 152.

9. Urban, *Fusiliers*, pp. 16–17.

10. Ibid., p. 17.

11. Cary and McCance, *Regimental Records of the Royal Welch Fusiliers*, p. 154.

12. Ferling, *Almost a Miracle*, p. 32.

13. Urban, *Fusiliers*, p. 25.

14. Cary and McCance, *Regimental Records of the Royal Welch Fusiliers*, p. 154.

15. Ferling, *Almost a Miracle*, pp. 32–3.

16. Gruber, *The Howe Brothers*, p. 22.

17. Ibid.

18. Ibid., p. 23.

19. Urban, *Fusiliers*, p. 31.

20. Ibid.

21. Anderson, *The Command of the Howe Brothers*, p. 76.

22. Ferling, *Almost a Miracle*, p. 54.

23. Howe to Admiral Lord Howe, 22 June 1775, in Harold Murdock, *Bunker Hill: Notes and Queries on a Famous Battle* (1927), p. 148.

24. Urban, *Fusiliers*, p. 38.

25. Ibid., p. 39.

26. Ibid.

27. Ibid.

28. Ibid., pp. 41–2.

29. Letter of Lieutenant J. Waller, 22 June 1775, in www.teachingamerican history.org/library

30. Urban, *Fusiliers*, p. 42.

31. Ibid.

32. Letter of Lieutenant J. Waller, 22 June 1775, in www.teachingamerican history.org/library

33. Ferling, *Almost a Miracle*, p. 59.

34. Dorothea Gamsby's account of the Battle of Bunker Hill: see www. grgordon.tripod.com/bunkerhi.htm

35. Howe to Admiral Lord Howe, 22 June 1775, in Murdock, *Bunker Hill*, p. 148.

36. Ferling, *Almost a Miracle*, p. 60.

37. Urban, *Fusiliers*, p. 43.

38. Both quoted in ibid., p. 44.

39. Ferling, *Almost a Miracle*, p. 60.

40. Anonymous officer, quoted in Urban, *Fusiliers*, p. 45.

41. Ferling, *Almost a Miracle*, pp. 61–2.

42. Gruber, *The Howe Brothers*, p. 61.

43. Ibid., p. 31.

44. Anderson, *The Command of the Howe Brothers*, p. 86.

45. Gruber, *The Howe Brothers*, p. 34.

46. Ibid., p. 37.

47. Ibid., p. 67.

48. Ibid., p. 70.

14. The Lost Opportunity

1. Hibbert, *Redcoats and Rebels*, p. 66.
2. Ibid., p. 67.
3. Ibid., pp. 67–8.
4. Ibid., p. 68.
5. Ferling, *Almost a Miracle*, p. 77.
6. Ibid.
7. Hibbert, *Redcoats and Rebels*, p. 71.
8. Ibid.
9. Ferling, *Almost a Miracle*, p. 79.
10. Ibid., pp. 79–80.
11. Ibid.
12. Mark Urban, *Generals: Ten British Commanders Who Shaped the World* (2005), pp. 75–6.
13. Ferling, *Almost a Miracle*, p. 101.
14. Joseph Lee Boyle (ed.), *From Redcoat to Rebel: The Thomas Sullivan Journal* (1997), p. iv.
15. Hibbert, *Redcoats and Rebels*, p. 73.
16. Ibid., p. 72.
17. Howe to Dartmouth, 21 Mar. 1776, in Anderson, *The Command of the Howe Brothers*, pp. 104–5.
18. Gruber, *The Howe Brothers*, pp. 83–4.
19. Ibid., pp. 84–5.
20. Hibbert, *Redcoats and Rebels*, p. 116.
21. Gruber, *The Howe Brothers*, pp. 94–5.
22. Ibid., p. 100.
23. Ira D. Gruber (ed.), *John Peebles' American War: The Diary of a Scottish Grenadier 1776–1782* (1997), pp. 2–3.
24. Gruber, *The Howe Brothers*, pp. 106–7.
25. Ibid., p. 107.
26. Ibid., p. 109.
27. Hibbert, *Redcoats and Rebels*, p. 123.
28. Hugh Bicheno, *Rebels and Redcoats: The American Revolutionary War* (2003; this edition 2004), p. 45.

29. Gruber, *The Howe Brothers*, p. 115.

30. Ibid., pp. 115–17.

31. Ibid., pp. 118–19.

32. Hibbert, *Redcoats and Rebels*, p. 126.

33. Gruber, *The Howe Brothers*, p. 126.

34. Urban, *Fusiliers*, pp. 90–91.

35. Ibid, pp. 148–9.

36. Hibbert, *Recoats and Rebels*, p. 129.

37. Ibid.

38. Gruber, *John Peebles' American War*, p. 59.

39. Bicheno, *Rebels and Redcoats*, p. 53.

40. Ferling, *Almost a Miracle*, p. 171.

41. Hibbert, *Redcoats and Rebels*, p. 146.

42. Ibid.

43. While a prisoner of the British, and possibly to save himself from execution (Germain was threatening to court-martial him for desertion even though he had long resigned from the British Army), General Lee agreed to draft a plan of operations against the rebels. In the spring of 1778 he was exchanged for a captured British general, but was later sacked from the Continental Army for disobeying Washington's orders at the Battle of Monmouth (June 1778). He died in 1782.

44. Gruber, *The Howe Brothers*, p. 146.

45. Marianne Gilchrist (ed.), 'Captain Hon. William Leslie: His Life, Letters and Commemoration', in Chandler, *Military Miscellany II*, pp. 163–4.

46. Hibbert, *Redcoats and Rebels*, p. 148.

47. Bicheno, *Rebels and Redcoats*, p. 66.

48. Ferling, *Almost a Miracle*, p. 178.

49. Ibid., p. 180.

50. Ibid., p. 183.

51. Ibid., p. 184.

52. Ibid., p. 185.

53. Gilchrist, 'Captain Hon. William Leslie: His Life, Letters and Commemoration', in Chandler, *Military Miscellany II*, pp. 171–2.

54. Hibbert, *Redcoats and Rebels*, pp. 150–51.

55. Both quoted in Gruber, *The Howe Brothers*, pp. 155–6, 177.

56. Ibid., pp. 156–7.

15. Brandywine and Saratoga

1. Sylvia R. Frey, *The British Soldier in America: A Social History of Military Life in the Revolutionary Period* (1982), pp. 95–6.

2. Thomas Anburey, *Travels through the Interior Parts of America, by an Officer* (2 vols., 1789), Vol. I, p. 205.

3. Frey, *The British Soldier in America*, p. 99.

4. Ibid., p. 101.

5. Ibid., pp. 101–2.

6. Anburey, *Travels through the Interior Parts of America, by an Officer*, Vol. I, p. 379.

7. Gruber, *The Howe Brothers*, p. 174.

8. Ibid., p. 175.

9. Ibid., p. 176.

10. Gruber, *The Howe Brothers*, p. 227.

11. Ibid., p. 231.

12. *The Narrative of Lieutenant-General Sir William Howe, in a Committee of the House of Commons* . . . (1780), p. 22.

13. Ibid.

14. Gruber, *The Howe Brothers*, pp. 233–4.

15. Gruber, *John Peebles' American War*, pp. 125–8.

16. Sullivan journal, in the *Pennsylvania Magazine of History and Biography*, 31, 4 (1907), p. 409.

17. Gruber, *John Peebles' American War*, p. 128.

18. Gruber, *The Howe Brothers*, p. 239.

19. Ferling, *Almost a Miracle*, p. 246.

20. Ibid., p. 247.

21. Sullivan journal, *Pennsylvania Magazine of History and Biography*, p. 413.

22. Ibid., pp. 413–14.

23. General George Washington to the Continental Congress, Midnight, Chester, 11 Sept. 1777, Washington Papers, Library of Congress.

24. Ferling, *Almost a Miracle*, p. 248.

25. Gruber, *John Peebles' American War*, p. 132.

26. Ferling, *Almost a Miracle*, p. 249.

27. Ibid.

28. Gruber, *John Peebles' American War*, p. 133.

29. Sullivan journal, *Pennsylvania Magazine of History and Biography*, pp. 416–17.

30. Gruber, *John Peebles' American War*, p. 133.

31. Ferling, *Almost a Miracle*, p. 250.

32. Ibid.

33. Bicheno, *Rebels and Redcoats*, p. 75.

34. Captain Ewald, quoted in ibid.

35. Washington to the Continental Congress, Midnight, Chester, 11 Sept. 1777, Washington Papers.

36. Sullivan journal, *Pennsylvania Magazine of History and Biography*, p. 418.

37. Ibid.

38. Ferling, *Almost a Miracle*, p. 251.

39. Ibid.

40. Hibbert, *Redcoats and Rebels*, p. 159.

41. Gruber, *John Peebles' American War*, p. 138.

42. Ferling, *Almost a Miracle*, p. 253.

43. Lieutenant Martin Hunter, quoted in Hibbert, *Redcoats and Rebels*, p. 161.

44. Ferling, *Almost a Miracle*, p. 256.

45. Gruber, *The Howe Brothers*, p. 221.

46. Ibid., p. 253.

47. Hibbert, *Redcoats and Rebels*, p. 166.

48. R. Lamb, *An Original and Authentic Journal of the Occurrences during the Late American War from Its Commencement to the Year 1783* (1809), p. 136.

49. Hibbert, *Redcoats and Rebels*, pp. 163–4.

50. Lamb, *Journal*, p. 144.

51. Hibbert, *Redcoats and Rebels*, p. 171.

52. Diary of Estes Howe, in ibid., p. 172.

53. Ibid., p. 173.

54. Hibbert, *Redcoats and Rebels*, p. 178.

55. Ferling, *Almost a Miracle*, p. 229.

56. Ibid., pp. 235–7.

57. Venning, *Following the Drum*, pp. 117–20.

58. Hibbert, *Redcoats and Rebels*, pp. 190–91.

59. Ibid., pp. 194–5.

60. Ferling, *Almost a Miracle*, pp. 239–40.

61. Lieutenant Thomas Anburey, quoted in Hibbert, *Redcoats and Rebels*, pp. 196–7.

62. Ibid., p. 197.

63. William Digby of the 53rd, quoted in ibid.

64. Ibid., p. 198.

65. McGuffie, *Rank and File*, p. 376.

66. Hibbert, *Redcoats and Rebels*, p. 200.

67. Ibid., p. 201.

68. Ibid., pp. 201–2.

69. Ibid., p. 204.

70. Gruber, *The Howe Brothers*, p. 275.

71. Gruber, *John Peebles' American War*, p. 183.

72. Gruber, *The Howe Brothers*, pp. 359–60.

73. Ibid., p. 362.

74. John Clarke, *The Life and Times of George III* (1972), p. 103.

75. Barnett, *Britain and Her Army*, p. 7.

76. Clarke, *George III*, p. 104.

77. Ferling, *Almost a Miracle*, pp. 558–9.

78. Stanley Ayling, *Fox: The Life of Charles James Fox* (1991), pp. 118–23.

79. David Andress, *1789: The Revolutions That Shook the World* (2008; this edition 2010), pp. 96–7.

80. Ibid., p. 375.

81. Barnett, *Britain and Her Army*, p. 226.

16. The Honourable Arthur Wellesley

1. Elizabeth Longford, *Wellington. Vol. I: Years of the Sword* (1969; this edition 1972), p. 14.

2. Ibid.

3. Sir Edward Creasy, *Eminent Etonians* (1876), p. 521.

4. Longford, *Wellington*, Vol. I, p. 16.

5. G. R. Gleig, *Life of Arthur, Duke of Wellington* (1889), p. 5.

6. Ibid., p. 6.

7. Longford, *Wellington*, Vol. I, p. 19.

8. Ibid., p. 21.

9. Ibid., p. 22.

10. Ibid.

11. Ayling, *Fox*, p. 167.

12. Ibid.

13. Saul David, *Prince of Pleasure: The Prince of Wales and the Making of the Regency* (1998; this edition 1999), p. 128.

14. Samuel F. Scott, *The Response of the Royal Army to the French Revolution* (1978), p. 100.

15. Jean-Paul Bertaud, *The Army and the French Revolution* (1979), pp. 17, 19–20.

16. Scott, *Response of the Royal Army to the French Revolution*, p. 111.

17. Ibid., p. 112.

18. Frank McLynn, *Napoleon: A Biography* (1997), pp. 27, 33–4.

19. Ibid., p. 56.

20. Barnett, *Britain and Her Army*, p. 226.

21. Ron McGuigan, 'The British Army: 1 February 1793', in *The Napoleon Series*, May 2003 (www.napoleon-series.org/military/organization/c_britarmy1793b.html). The number of effectives included 13,092 in Great Britain (including 1,513 in invalid artillery companies), 441 recruits for overseas regiments and 75 recruits for India, 13,818 in the colonies and 9,647 in India.

22. Ibid.

23. Ibid.

24. Graeme Rimer, 'The Weapons of Wellington's Army', in Paddy Griffith (ed.), *Wellington: Commander* (1986), pp. 176–8.

25. William Reitzel (ed.), *The Autobiography of William Cobbett: The Progress of a Plough-Boy to a Seat in Parliament* (1933), p. 24.

26. *A Short Introduction to English Grammar* by Robert Lowth, first published in 1762, was the standard work on the subject.

27. Jeremy Archer, *The Old West Country Regiments: From Plassey to the Somme* (2011), p. 55.

28. Ibid., p. 54.

29. Ibid., p. 55.

30. Reitzel, *Autobiography of William Cobbett*, p. 32.

31. Archer, *The Old West Country Regiments*, p. 57.

32. Reitzel, *Autobiography of William Cobbett*, p. 33.

33. Ibid.

34. Archer, *The Old West Country Regiments*, p. 56.

35. Ibid., p. 57.

36. Ibid.

37. Ibid., p. 58.

38. Ibid.

39. Reitzel, *Autobiography of William Cobbett*, p. 33.

40. Longford, *Wellington*, Vol. I, p. 33.

41. Richard Holmes, *Wellington: The Iron Duke* (2002; this edition 2003), p. 21.

42. Barnett, *Britain and Her Army*, p. 234.

43. Herman, *To Rule the Waves*, p. 334.

44. McLynn, *Napoleon*, p. 76.

45. Sir John Fortescue, *History of the British Army* (13 vols., 1899–1930), Vol. IV, Part I, pp. 96–7.

46. Ibid., p. 98.

47. Barnett, *Britain and Her Army*, p. 235.

48. Fortescue, *History of the British Army*, Vol. IV, Part I, pp. 210–11.

49. Ibid., p. 299.

50. William Surtees, *Twenty-Five Years in the Rifle Brigade* (1973), pp. 16–17.

51. Fortescue, *History of the British Army*, Vol. IV, Part I, p. 295.

52. Ibid., pp. 296–7.

53. Ibid., pp. 299–300.

54. Longford, *Wellington*, Vol. I, p. 37.

55. Holmes, *Wellington*, p. 31.

56. Ibid.

57. Ibid., pp. 31–2.

58. Robert Brown, *Corporal Brown's Campaigns in the Low Countries: Recollections of a Coldstream Guard in the Early Campaigns against Revolutionary France 1793–1795* (1795; this edition 2008), p. 153.

59. Ibid., p. 156 (diary entry for 16 Jan. 1795).

60. Fortescue, *History of the British Army*, Vol. IV, Part I, pp. 320–21.

61. Brown, *Corporal Brown's Campaigns*, p. 160.

62. Ibid., pp. 160–61.

63. Fortescue, *History of the British Army*, Vol. IV, Part I, p. 322.

64. Brown, *Corporal Brown's Campaigns*, p. 165.

65. Fortescue, *History of the British Army*, Vol. IV, Part I, pp. 323–4.

66. Lord Stanhope, *Notes of Conversations with the Duke of Wellington 1831–1852* (1888), p. 182.

17. Sepoy General

1. Longford, *Wellington*, Vol. I, pp. 43–4; Holmes, *Wellington*, p. 40.

2. Holmes, *Wellington*, p. 41.

3. George Chesney, *Indian Polity: A View of the System of Administration in India* (1868), p. 28.

4. C. A. Bayly, 'Wellesley, Richard, Marquess Wellesley (1760–1842)', *Oxford Dictionary of National Biography* (2004).

5. Andress, *1789*, p. 140.

6. Ibid., p. 141.

7. Ibid., p. 142.

8. Bayly, 'Wellesley, Richard, Marquess Wellesley (1760–1842)', *Oxford Dictionary of National Biography*.

9. Anthony S. Bennell (ed.), *The Maratha War Papers of Arthur Wellesley: January to December 1803* (1998), Introduction, p. 3.

10. Sir Herbert Maxwell, *The Life of Wellington* (2 vols., 1900), Vol. I, p. 25.

11. Ibid., p. 28.

12. Longford, *Wellington*, Vol. I, p. 62.

13. Holmes, *Wellington*, p. 53.

14. Longford, *Wellington*, Vol. I, p. 62.

15. Maxwell, *The Life of Wellington*, Vol. I, p. 33.

16. Ibid., p. 32.

17. Colonel Wellesley to Mornington, 18 Apr. 1799, in Longford, *Wellington*, Vol. I, p. 63.

18. Holmes, *Wellington*, p. 61.

19. Colonel Wellesley to Mornington, 8 May, in Maxwell, *The Life of Wellington*, Vol. I, p. 35.

20. Ibid., 19 June 1799, p. 38.

21. Mornington to General Harris, undated, in ibid., p. 36.

22. McLynn, *Napoleon*, pp. 90–91.

23. Ibid., p. 94.

24. Ibid., p. 95.

25. Ibid., p. 96.

26. Ibid., p. 111.

27. Ibid., pp. 131–2.

28. Ibid., p. 143.

29. Ibid., p. 167.

30. Ibid., p. 220.

31. Longford, *Wellington*, Vol. I, p. 75.

32. Holmes, *Wellington*, p. 69.

33. Michael Glover, *Wellington as Military Commander* (1968), p. 41.

34. Ibid.

35. Maxwell, *The Life of Wellington*, Vol. I, p. 56.

36. Glover, *Wellington as Military Commander*, p. 42.

37. John Blakiston, *Twelve Years' Military Adventure* . . . (2 vols., 1829; this edition 1840), Vol. I, pp. 160–62.

38. Glover, *Wellington as Military Commander*, p. 43.

39. Ibid.

40. Holmes, *Wellington*, p. 81.

41. Longford, *Wellington*, Vol. I, pp. 92–3.

42. Ibid., p. 93.

43. Ibid.

44. Glover, *Wellington as Military Commander*, p. 45.

45. Ibid.

46. Ibid., pp. 45–6.

47. Ibid., p. 46.

48. Longford, *Wellington*, Vol. I, p. 96.

49. Ibid.

50. Wellesley to Sir John Cradock, 15 Jan. 1805, in ibid., p. 97.

51. Paddy Griffith, 'Wellington – Commander', in Griffith (ed.), *Wellington: Commander*, pp. 27–8.

52. Ibid., p. 22.

18. Retreat to Corunna

1. John Wilson Croker, *The Croker Papers* (3 vols., 1884), Vol. II, p. 233.
2. J. Steven Watson, *The Reign of George III* (Oxford, 1960), pp. 428–30.
3. Longford, *Wellington*, Vol. I, p. 110.
4. Hibbert, *Nelson*, pp. 375–7.
5. *The Times*, 7 Nov. 1805.
6. Lord Colchester, *The Diary and Correspondence of Charles Abbott, Lord Colchester* (3 vols., 1861), Vol. II, p. 28.
7. Longford, *Wellington*, Vol. I, p. 112.
8. Ibid., p. 119.
9. Ibid., p. 122.
10. Ibid., p. 136.
11. Urban, *Generals*, p. 104.
12. Steven Schwamenfeld, 'The Foundation of British Strength: National Identity and the British Common Soldier', unpublished Ph.D. thesis (Florida State University, 2007), pp. 6–9.
13. Surtees, *Twenty-Five Years*, p. 43.
14. Barnett, *Britain and Her Army*, p. 242.
15. Ibid., p. 244.
16. Ezekiel Baker, quoted on www.home.vicnet.net.au/~rifles95/rifle.htm
17. Surtees, *Twenty-Five Years in the Rifle Brigade*, pp. 41–2.
18. Barnett, *Britain and Her Army*, p. 244.
19. Urban, *Generals*, p. 111.
20. Ibid.
21. Hansard's Parliamentary Debates, 1st Series, Vol. XII, pp. 663–708.
22. Urban, *Generals*, p. 118.
23. Ian Hernon, *The Savage Empire: Forgotten Wars of the Nineteenth Century* (2000), p. 17.
24. Ibid., pp. 18–19.
25. Holmes, *Wellington*, p. 104.
26. Ibid., p. 106.
27. Croker, *The Croker Papers*, Vol. I, pp. 12–13.
28. Holmes, *Wellington*, p. 108.

29. Ibid., p. 109.

30. Longford, *Wellington*, Vol. I, pp. 147–8.

31. Longford, *Wellington*, Vol. I, p. 152.

32. By, among others, the military historian Richard Holmes. See Holmes, *Wellington*, p. 149.

33. Christopher Hibbert (ed.), *A Soldier of the Seventy-First: The Journal of a Soldier of the Highland Light Infantry 1806–1815* (1975), pp. xii–xiii.

34. Ibid., p. xiv.

35. Ibid., p. 16.

36. Ibid., p. 17.

37. Christopher Hibbert (ed.), *The Recollections of Rifleman Harris as Told to Henry Curling* (1970), pp. 26–7.

38. Charles J. Esdaile, *Peninsular Eyewitnesses: The Experience of War in Spain and Portugal 1808–1813* (2008), p. 37.

39. Private Anthony Hamilton of the 43rd Foot, quoted in ibid.

40. Holmes, *Wellington*, p. 116.

41. Hibbert, *A Soldier of the Seventy-First*, pp. 17–18.

42. Holmes, *Wellington*, p. 118.

43. Longford, *Wellington*, Vol. I, pp. 155–6.

44. Vimeiro, in this respect, was a battle to rank alongside Montgomery's triumph at El Alamein in Oct. 1942.

45. Esdaile, *Peninsular Eyewitnesses*, pp. 39–40.

46. Surgeon Adam Neale, quoted in ibid., p. 41.

47. Holmes, *Wellington*, p. 120.

48. Ibid. p. 121.

49. Longford, *Wellington*, Vol. I, p. 157.

50. Ibid., p. 158.

51. Holmes, *Wellington*, p. 123.

52. Longford, *Wellington*, Vol. I, p. 157.

53. McLynn, *Napoleon*, pp. 399–400.

54. B. S. Brownrigg (ed.), *The Life and Letters of Sir John Moore* (1923), p. 221.

55. Andrew Uffindell, *The National Army Museum Book of Wellington's Armies* (2003; this edition 2005), p. 43.

56. Ibid., p. 237.

57. Hibbert, *A Soldier of the Seventy-First*, pp. 16–17.

58. Esdaile, *Peninsular Eyewitnesses*, pp. 68–9.

59. Hibbert, *A Soldier of the Seventy-First*, pp. 28–9.

60. Ibid., p. 33.

61. Ibid.

62. Holmes, *Redcoat*, p. 295.

63. Charles Oman, *Sir John Moore* (1953), p. 587.

64. Hibbert, *A Soldier of the Seventy-First*, p. 34.

65. *Moore Letters*, p. 260.

66. Hibbert, *A Soldier of the Seventy-First*, pp. 34–5.

67. Esdaile, *Peninsular Eyewitnesses*, pp. 70–71.

68. Hibbert, *A Soldier of the Seventy-First*, p. 35.

69. *Moore Letters*, pp. 220–21.

70. Ibid., p. 221.

71. Lieutenant-General the Honourable John Hope to Sir David Baird, 18 Jan. 1809, ibid., p. 233.

72. *Moore Letters*, p. 268.

73. Hibbert, *A Soldier of the Seventy-First*, p. 37.

74. Hibbert, *The Recollections of Rifleman Harris*, pp. 60–61.

75. Hibbert, *A Soldier of the Seventy-First*, pp. 38–9.

76. M. K. H. Crumplin and P. Starling, *A Surgical Artist at War* (2005), p. 19.

77. Ibid., p. 7.

78. Ibid., p. 15.

79. Ibid., pp. 3, 7.

80. *Moore Letters*, p. 271.

81. Ibid., p. 221.

82. Longford, *Wellington*, Vol. I, p. 172.

83. Ibid.

84. Griffith, *Wellington: Commander*, p. 31.

19. The 'Cautious System'

1. Longford, *Wellington*, Vol. I, p. 177.

2. Holmes, *Wellington*, p. 132.

3. Esdaile, *Peninsular Eyewitnesses*, p. 104.

4. Holmes, *Wellington*, p. 136.

5. Esdaile, *Peninsular Eyewitnesses*, p. 107.

6. Ibid., p. 109.

7. The most widely used British musket during the Napoleonic Wars was the cheap-to-produce 'India Pattern', with a bore of .75 inches and a barrel length of 39 inches. This was slightly smaller than the 1768 Short Land Pattern Musket (.78 calibre and a 42-inch barrel), which it replaced in 1797. Both used a socket bayonet with a 17-inch triangular blade.

8. Esdaile, *Peninsular Eyewitnesses*, p. 109.

9. Ensign William Walton of the Coldstream Guards, in Uffindell, *Wellington's Armies*, p. 65.

10. Holmes, *Wellington*, p. 139.

11. Ibid., p. 140.

12. Esdaile, *Peninsular Eyewitnesses*, p. 111.

13. Timewell Diary, Royal Greenjackets Museum, 0781/Box 1a/1.

14. Holmes, *Wellington*, p. 140.

15. August Schaumann, in Esdaile, *Peninsular Eyewitnesses*, p. 108.

16. Holmes, *Wellington*, p. 142.

17. Longford, *Wellington*, Vol. I, p. 197.

18. Griffith, *Wellington: Commander*, p. 32.

19. Longford, *Wellington*, Vol. I, p. 196.

20. Esdaile, *Peninsular Eyewitnesses*, p. 117.

21. Venning, *Following the Drum*, p. 139.

22. Ibid.

23. Griffith, *Wellington: Commander*, p. 33.

24. Hibbert, *A Soldier of the Seventy-First*, pp. 60–61.

25. Ibid., p. 61.

26. Ibid., p. 34.

27. Ibid., pp. 33–4.

28. Harrison to his mother, 24 May 1811, Harrison Letters, Royal Welch Fusiliers Museum.

29. Ibid.

30. Uffindell, *Wellington's Armies*, p. 106.

31. Timewell Diary, Royal Greenjackets Museum, 0781/Box 1a/1.

32. Edward Costello, *The Adventures of a Soldier* (1841), pp. 14–17.

33. William Swabey, in Esdaile, *Peninsular Eyewitnesses*, p. 204.

34. J. Kincaid, *Adventures in the Rifle Brigade in the Peninsula, France and the Netherlands from 1809 to 1815* (1830), pp. 115–16.

35. Ibid., pp. 116–17.

36. Longford, *Wellington*, Vol. I, p. 266.

37. Timewell Diary, Royal Greenjackets Museum, 0781/Box 1a/1.

38. Esdaile, *Peninsular Eyewitnesses*, pp. 207–8.

39. Harrison to his mother, 23 Apr. 1812, Harrison Letters, Royal Welch Fusiliers Museum.

40. Harry Smith, *The Autobiography of Lieutenant-General Sir Harry Smith* (2 vols., 1901), Vol. I, pp. 64–5.

41. Uffindell, *Wellington's Armies*, p. 118.

42. Ibid., pp. 118–19.

43. Esdaile, *Peninsular Eyewitnesses*, p. 209.

44. Ibid., p. 210.

45. Costello, *Adventures of a Soldier*, pp. 177–9.

46. Venning, *Following the Drum*, p. 138.

47. Holmes, *Wellington*, p. 161.

48. Longford, *Wellington*, Vol. I, p. 273.

49. Letter from Lieutenant William Bent to his sister, 26 Apr. 1812, Royal Artillery Museum, MD632.

50. Esdaile, *Peninsular Eyewitnesses*, p. 209.

51. Venning, *Following the Drum*, p. 134.

52. Ibid., pp. 134–5.

53. J. Gurwood (ed.), *Selections from the Dispatches and General Orders of Field Marshal the Duke of Wellington* (1841), p. 593.

54. David, *Prince of Pleasure*, pp. 325, 334–5.

55. Longford, *Wellington*, Vol. I, pp. 276–7.

56. Holmes, *Wellington*, p. 164.

57. Griffith, *Wellington: Commander*, p. 39.

58. Mark Urban, *The Man Who Broke Napoleon's Codes: The Story of George Scovell* (2001), pp. 198, 202–4.

59. Holmes, *Wellington*, p. 166.

60. Longford, *Wellington*, Vol. I, p. 285.

61. Holmes, *Wellington*, p. 166.

62. Longford, *Wellington*, Vol. I, p. 287.

63. Esdaile, *Peninsular Eyewitnesses*, p. 218.

64. Ibid., pp. 218–19.

65. Ibid., p. 219.

66. Ibid., p. 220.

67. Longford, *Wellington*, Vol. I, p. 287.

68. Esdaile, *Peninsular Eyewitnesses*, p. 221.

69. Ibid.

70. Ibid., p. 222.

71. Holmes, *Wellington*, p. 168.

72. William Warre, in Esdaile, *Peninsular Eyewitnesses*, p. 223.

73. Venning, *Following the Drum*, p. 142.

74. Uffindell, *Wellington's Armies*, p. 132.

75. Holmes, *Wellington*, p. 168.

76. Longford, *Wellington*, Vol. I, p. 288.

77. Uffindell, *Wellington's Armies*, p. 132.

78. Esdaile, *Peninsular Eyewitnesses*, p. 222.

79. Griffith, *Wellington: Commander*, p. 39.

80. Lieutenant McDonald to his father, 25 Aug. 1812, McDonald Letters, Royal Welch Fusiliers Museum.

81. Ibid., 26 Nov. 1812, Villa de Agia, Spain.

82. Holmes, *Wellington*, pp. 172–3.

83. Esdaile, *Peninsular Eyewitnesses*, p. 239.

84. Holmes, *Wellington*, pp. 171, 173.

85. Ibid., p. 185.

86. Hibbert, *A Soldier of the Seventy-First*, p. 87.

87. Uffindell, *Wellington's Armies*, p. 212.

88. Major-General Andrew Hay, in ibid., p. 216.

89. Lieutenant Woodberry, in ibid., p. 217.

90. Venning, *Following the Drum*, p. 140.

91. Lieutenant McDonald to his father, 1 July 1813, McDonald Letters, Royal Welch Fusiliers Museum.

92. Letter from Captain Gordon Booker to his father, 10 July 1813, Booker Letters, Royal Welch Fusiliers Museum.

93. Holmes, *Wellington*, p. 186.

94. Longford, *Wellington*, Vol. I, pp. 323–4.

95. Ibid., pp. 344–5.

96. Hibbert, *A Soldier of the Seventy-First*, p. 101.

97. Lieutenant-Colonel Murray of the 18th Hussars to his wife, 9 Aug. 1813, in Uffindell, *Wellington's Armies*, p. 260.

98. Holmes, *Wellington*, pp. 199–200.
99. Sir George Larpent (ed.), *The Private Journal of F. Seymour Larpent, Judge Advocate General* (2 vols., 1853), Vol. I, p. 285.
100. Longford, *Wellington*, Vol. I, p. 350.
101. Ibid., pp. 348–9.

20. Escape from Elba

1. Holmes, *Wellington*, p. 208.
2. Alessandro Barbero, *The Battle: A New History of the Battle of Waterloo* (2005), p. 2.
3. Lytton Strachey and Roger Fulford (eds.), *The Greville Memoirs 1814–1860* (3 vols., 1938), Vol. I, p. 29.
4. Ibid., pp. 30–34.
5. Longford, *Wellington*, Vol. I, p. 397.
6. Andrew Roberts, *Waterloo: Napoleon's Last Gamble* (2005), p. 22.
7. Lieutenant McDonald to his father, 23 Mar. 1815, McDonald Letters, Royal Welch Fusiliers Museum.
8. Ibid., 3 Apr. 1815.
9. Hibbert, *A Soldier of the Seventy-First*, p. 105.
10. Michael Mann, *The Regimental History of 1st The Queen's Dragoon Guards* (1993), pp. 172–3.
11. Hibbert Letters, 1st Queen's Dragoon Guards Museum, CARDG: 1988.1764.
12. Quartermaster-Sergeant's Diary, Royal Scots Dragoon Guards Museum, GB46/G167.
13. Parker, *Black Watch*, p. 100.
14. Ibid., pp. 100–102.
15. Ibid., p. 98.
16. Ian Fletcher, *A Desperate Business* (2001), p. 21.
17. Herbert Maxwell (ed.), *The Creevey Papers* (1903; this edition 1905), p. 228.
18. Holmes, *Wellington*, p. 214.
19. Ibid., pp. 218–19.
20. Ibid., p. 219.
21. David G. Chandler, *The Campaigns of Napoleon* (1967), p. 1,092.

22. McLynn, *Napoleon*, p. 613.

23. Peter Hofschröer, *1815: The Waterloo Campaign. Vol. I: Wellington, His German Allies and the Battles of Ligny and Quatre Bras* (1998), pp. 154–5.

24. Ibid., pp. 193–4.

25. Baron von Müffling, *History of the Campaign of the British, Dutch, Hanoverian, and Brunswick Armie . . . and of the Prussians . . . in the Year 1815* (1816), p. 1.

26. Longford, *Wellington*, Vol. I, pp. 413–14.

27. Holmes, *Wellington*, p. 222.

28. Longford, *Wellington*, Vol. I, p. 415.

29. Ibid.

30. Ibid.

31. Holmes, *Wellington*, p. 227.

32. Longford, *Wellington*, Vol. I, p. 418.

33. Ibid., p. 420.

34. Ibid., p. 421.

35. Nick Foulkes, *Dancing into Battle: A Social History of Waterloo* (2006), p. 149.

36. Kincaid, *Adventures*, p. 154.

37. Costello, *Adventures*, p. 150.

38. Holmes, *Wellington*, p. 228.

39. Ibid., p. 229.

40. Longford, *Wellington*, Vol. I, p. 425.

41. McLynn, *Napoleon*, p. 615.

42. Parker, *Black Watch*, pp. 141–2.

43. Ibid., pp. 142–3.

44. Ibid., p. 143.

45. Uffindell, *Wellington's Armies*, p. 280.

46. Ibid., p. 279.

47. Holmes, *Wellington*, p. 230.

48. General Cavalié Mercer, *Journal of the Waterloo Campaign* (1870; this edition 1985), pp. 136–7.

49. Ibid., pp. 137–9.

50. Holmes, *Wellington*, p. 233.

51. Lord FitzRoy Somerset, quoted in Longford, *Wellington*, Vol. I, p. 441.

52. Holmes, *Wellington*, p. 234.

53. Mercer, *Journal*, p. 143.

54. McLynn, *Napoleon*, p. 620.

55. Marquess of Anglesey, *One-Leg: The Life and Letters of Henry William Paget, First Marquess of Anglesey* (1961), p. 133.

56. Longford, *Wellington*, Vol. I, p. 443.

57. Foulkes, *Dancing into Battle*, p. 173.

21. 'The nearest run thing'

1. John Raymond (ed.), *The Reminiscences and Recollections of Captain Gronow* (1964), p. 141.

2. Mercer, *Journal*, pp. 159–61.

3. Blacklock, *The Royal Scots Greys*, pp. 47–51.

4. Barbero, *The Battle*, p. 64.

5. Ibid., p. 67.

6. Ibid., p. 68.

7. Ibid., pp. 74–5.

8. Holmes, *Wellington*, p. 239.

9. Barbero, *The Battle*, p. 89.

10. Mercer, *Journal*, pp. 164–5.

11. Hibbert, *A Soldier of the Seventy-First*, p. 107.

12. Barbero, *The Battle*, p. 111.

13. Parker, *Black Watch*, p. 147.

14. Blacklock, *The Royal Scots Greys*, pp. 51–2.

15. Parker, *Black Watch*, p. 147.

16. Holmes, *Wellington*, p. 242.

17. Roberts, *Waterloo*, p. 69.

18. White-Spunner, *Horse Guards*, p. 334; Christopher Summerville, *Who Was Who at Waterloo: A Biography of the Battle* (2007), pp. 76–7.

19. White-Spunner, *Horse Guards*, p. 333.

20. Blacklock, *The Royal Scots Greys*, p. 52.

21. Quartermaster-Sergeant's Diary, 18 June 1815, Royal Scots Dragoon Guards Museum, GB46/G167.

22. William Siborne, quoted in Summerville, *Who Was Who at Waterloo*, p. 330.

23. Anglesey, *One-Leg*, pp. 140–41.

24. Uffindell, *Wellington's Armies*, p. 298.

25. Holmes, *Wellington*, p. 244.

26. Raymond, *Gronow*, p. 45.

27. Holmes, *Wellington*, p. 246.

28. McLynn, *Napoleon*, p. 625.

29. Roberts, *Waterloo*, p. 94.

30. Barbero, *The Battle*, p. 255.

31. Ibid., p. 267.

32. Holmes, *Wellington*, p. 249.

33. Barbero, *The Battle*, p. 271.

34. Raymond, *Gronow*, p. 48.

35. Holmes, *Wellington*, p. 249.

36. Barbero, *The Battle*, p. 275.

37. McLynn, *Napoleon*, p. 626.

38. Mercer, *Journal*, p. 180.

39. Colonel Henry Graham, *History of the Sixteenth* (2 vols., 1912), Vol. I, p. 67.

40. Holmes, *Wellington*, p. 249.

41. Ibid., p. 250.

42. Mercer, *Journal*, pp. 182–3.

43. Foulkes, *Dancing into Battle*, p. 181.

44. Ibid., pp. 182–3.

45. Ibid., p. 183.

46. Ibid., p. 185.

47. Longford, *Wellington*, Vol. I, p. 485.

48. Waterloo dispatch, in Summerville, *Who Was Who at Waterloo*, p. 451.

49. Wellington to his brother William, Brussels, 19 June 1815, Raglan Papers, Family Papers.

50. Foulkes, *Dancing into Battle*, pp. 190–91.

51. McLynn, *Napoleon*, p. 627.

52. Christopher Hibbert, *George IV: Regent and King 1811–1830* (1973), p. 80.

53. Anglesey, *One-Leg*, p. 149.

54. Crumplin and Starling, *A Surgical Artist at War*, p. 8.

55. Anglesey, *One-Leg*, p. 150.

56. Ibid., pp. 151–2.

57. Crumplin and Starling, *A Surgical Artist at War*, p. 60.

58. Ibid., p. 43.

59. Ibid., p. 81.

60. Ibid., p. 63.

61. Hibbert, *A Soldier of the Seventy-First*, p. 111.

62. Ibid., pp. 112–13.

Epilogue

1. Mercer, *Journal*, pp. 298–9.

2. Ibid., p. 299.

3. Elizabeth Longford, *Wellington: Vol. II: Pillar of State* (1972), p. 11.

4. Ibid., pp. 12–13.

5. Peter Burroughs, 'An Unreformed Army? 1815–1868', in Chandler, *The Oxford History of the British Army*, p. 161.

6. Ibid., pp. 163–4.

7. Field Marshal Viscount Wolseley, *The Story of a Soldier's Life* (2 vols., 1903), Vol. I, pp. 82–3.

8. Von Müffling, *History of the Campaign*, p. 81.

Bibliography

All sources published in London unless otherwise indicated.

Primary Sources, Unpublished

British Library, London
Journal of Private Richard Humphrys

Family papers
Letter from the Duke of Wellington to William Wellesley-Pole, 19 June 1815 (part of
the Raglan Papers, courtesy of Henry van Moyland, Cefntilla, Monmouthshire)

Library of Congress, Washington, DC
Washington Papers: the papers of George Washington

National Army Museum (NAM)
Letter from Gunner James Hardcastle to his father, 25 August 1743 (O.S.)

National Museums of Liverpool
Nichol Memoirs: Memoirs of Colour-Sergeant W. Nichol, 8th (King's) Regiment
of Foot, 1790–1808

1st Queen's Dragoon Guards Museum, Cardiff Castle
Hibbert Letters: letters of Lieutenant John Hibbert, 1st King's Dragoon Guards
Diary of Captain James Naylor, 1st King's Dragoon Guards

Royal Artillery Museum (Firepower), Woolwich
Letter from Lieutenant William Bent to his sister, 26 April 1812, on the siege of
Badajoz

Royal Greenjackets Museum, Winchester
Diary of Private John Timewell, 1/43rd Light Infantry

Royal Scots Dragoon Guards Museum, Edinburgh
Letter from William Donaldson to Lord Braco, 23 June 1743, referring to the Scots
Greys at Dettingen
Diary of a quartermaster-sergeant of the 2nd Dragoons (Scots Greys)
Letter from Sergeant-Major Russell, 2nd Dragoons, to his wife, 24 June 1815

Royal Welch Fusiliers Museum, Carnarfon Castle
Letters of Captain Gordon Booker, 1/23rd (Royal Welch) Fusiliers
Letters of Lieutenant John Harrison, 1/23rd
Memoir by Private Thomas Jeremiah, 1/23rd
Letters of Lieutenant John McDonald, 1/23rd

Primary Sources, Published

Published Diaries, Letters and Memoirs

Anbury, Thomas, *Travels through the Interior Parts of America, by an Officer* (2 vols., 1789)

Anglesey, seventh Marquess of, *One-Leg: The Life and Letters of Henry William Paget, First Marquess of Anglesey, 1768–1854* (1961)

[Anonymous], *A True Relation of the Battle of the Boyne in Ireland, Fought by His Majesty King William, in the Year 1690, without Observation or Reflection* (1700)

Archer, Jeremy, *The Old West Country Regiments: From Plassey to the Somme* (2011)

Bennell, Anthony S. (ed.), *The Maratha War Papers of Arthur Wellesley: January to December 1803* (1998)

Blakiston, John, *Twelves Years Military Adventure in Three Quarters of the Globe: Or, Memoirs of an Officer Who Served in the Armies of His Majesty and of the East India Company . . .* (2 vols., 1840)

Boyle, Joseph Lee (ed.), *From Redcoat to Rebel: The Thomas Sullivan Journal* (1997)

Brown, Robert, *Corporal Brown's Campaigns in the Low Countries: Recollections of a Coldstream Guard in the Early Campaigns against Revolutionary France 1793–1795* (1795; this edition 2008)

Chandler, David G. (ed.), *Military Memoirs: Robert Parker and the Comte de Mérode-Westerloo* (1968)

— *Journal of Marlborough's Campaigns by John Marshall Deane* (1984)

— *Military Miscellany II: Manuscripts from Marlborough's Wars, the American War of Independence and the Boer War* (Stroud, 2005)

Colchester, Lord, *The Diary and Correspondence of Charles Abbott, Lord Colchester* (3 vols., 1861)

Cormack, Andrew, and Jones, Alan (eds.), *The Journal of Corporal Todd, 1745–1762* (2001)

Costello, Edward, *Adventures of a Soldier* (1841)

Creevey Papers: Maxwell, Sir Herbert (ed.), *The Creevey Papers: A Selection from the Correspondence and Diary of the Late Thomas Creevey, MP* (1903; this edition 1905)

Croker, John Wilson, *The Croker Papers* (3 vols., 1884)

Dann, John C. (ed.), *The Revolution Remembered: Eyewitness Accounts of the War of Independence* (Chicago, 1980)

Esdaile, Charles (ed.), *Peninsular Eyewitnesses: The Experience of War in Spain and Portugal 1808–1813* (2008)

Greville Memoirs: Strachey, Lytton, and Fulford, Roger (eds.), *The Greville Memoirs 1814–1860* (3 vols., 1938)

Hibbert, Christopher (ed.), *The Recollections of Rifleman Harris as Told to Henry Curling* (1970)

— *A Soldier of the Seventy-First: The Journal of a Soldier of the Highland Light Infantry 1806–1815* (1975)

Horsley, Walter (ed.), *The Chronicles of an Old Campaigner: M. de la Colonie 1692–1717* (1904)

Howe Narrative: The Narrative of Lieutenant-General Sir William Howe, in a Committee of the House of Commons, April 29 1779, relative to his conduct during his late command of the King's troops in North America (1780)

Kincaid, J., *Adventures in the Rifle Brigade in the Peninsula, France and the Netherlands from 1809 to 1815* (1830)

Lamb, R., *An Original and Authentic Journal of the Occurrences during the Late American War from Its Commencement to the Year 1783* (Dublin, 1809)

Larpent, Sir George (ed.), *The Private Journal of F. Seymour Larpent, Judge Advocate General* (2 vols., 1853)

Lewis-Stempel, John, *The Autobiography of the British Soldier: From Agincourt to Basra, In His Own Words* (2007; this edition 2008)

McGuffie, T. H. (ed.), *Rank and File: The Common Soldier at Peace and War 1642–1914* (1964)

Marlborough Correspondence: Murray, George (ed.), *The Letters and Dispatches of John Churchill, First Duke of Marlborough, from 1702–1712* (5 vols., 1845)

Mercer, General Cavalié, *Journal of the Waterloo Campaign* (first published in 1870; this edition 1985)

Millner, Sergeant John, *Journal of All the Marches, Famous Battles, and Sieges* (1733)

Moore Letters: Brownrigg, B. S. (ed.), *The Life and Letters of Sir John Moore* (1923)

Müffling, Baron Carl von, *History of the Campaign of the British, Dutch, Hanoverian, and Brunswick Armies . . . and of the Prussians . . . in the Year 1815* (1816)

— *The Memoirs of Baron von Müffling: A Prussian Officer in the Napoleonic Wars* (1997)

Pepys Diary: Latham Robert, and Matthews, William (eds.), *The Diary of Samuel Pepys* (11 vols., 1970–1983)

Pitt Correspondence: Taylor, W. S., and Pringle, Captain John, *Correspondence of William Pitt, Earl of Chatham* (4 vols., 1834–42)

Raymond, John (ed.), *The Reminiscences and Recollections of Captain Gronow* (1964)

Reitzel, William (ed.), *The Autobiography of William Cobbett: The Progress of a Plough-Boy to a Seat in Parliament* (1933)

Sabine, Major-General Edward, *Letters of Colonel Sir Augustus Simon Frazer, KCB, Commanding the Royal Horse Artillery in the Army under the Duke of Wellington* (1859; this edition 2001)

Smith, Harry, *The Autobiography of Lieutenant-General Sir Harry Smith* (2 vols., 1901)

Sullivan Journal: Thomas Sullivan, 'Before and after the Battle of Brandywine: Extracts from the Journal of Sergeant Thomas Sullivan of H.M. Forty-Ninth of Foot', *Pennsylvania Magazine of History and Biography*, 31, 4 (1907), p. 409

Surtees, William, *Twenty-Five Years in the Rifle Brigade* (1973)

Tucker, Norman (ed.), 'The Military Memoirs of John Gwyn' (1967)

Wellington Dispatches: Gurwood, J. (ed.), *Selections from the Dispatches and General Orders of Field Marshal the Duke of Wellington* (1841)

Willson, Beckles, *The Life and Letters of James Wolfe* (1909)

Wolseley, Field Marshal Viscount, *The Story of a Soldier's Life* (2 vols., 1903)

Wylly, Colonel H. C., *The Military Memoirs of Lieutieutenant-General Sir Joseph Thackwell: Arranged from Diaries and Correspondence* (1908)

Contemporary Publications

Albemarle, Duke of [George Monck], *Observations upon Military & Political Affairs* (1671)

Boswell, James, *Life of Johnson. Volume III: 1776–1780* (1934)

Cobbett, William (ed.), *The Parliamentary History of England: From the Earliest Period to the Year 1803* (36 vols., 1813)

Hansard's Parliamentary Debates (1st Series, 41 vols., 1803–20)

Moore, James, *A Narrative of the Campaign of the British Army in Spain, Authenticated by Official Papers and Original Letters* (1809)

Stanhope, Earl, *Notes of Conversations with the Duke of Wellington, 1831–1852* (1888)

Secondary Sources

Books and Articles

Anderson, T. S., *The Command of the Howe Brothers during the American Revolution* (New York, 1936)

Andress, David, *1789: The Revolutions That Shook the World* (2008; this edition 2010)

Ashley, M., *Marlborough* (1939)

Atkinson, C. T., *Marlborough and the Rise of the British Army* (New York, 1921)

Ayling, Stanley, *Fox: The Life of Charles James Fox* (1991)

Barbero, Alessandro, *The Battle: A New History of the Battle of Waterloo* (2005)

Barnett, Corelli, *Britain and Her Army: A Military, Political and Social History of the British Army 1509–1970* (1970; this edition 2000)

— *Marlborough* (1974; this edition 1999)

Beckett, Ian, *The Amateur Military Tradition 1558–1945* (1991)

Bertaud, Jean-Paul, *The Army and the French Revolution* (Princeton, 1979)

Bicheno, Hugh, *Rebels & Redcoats: The American Revolutionary War* (2003; this edition 2004)

Black, Jeremy, *Warfare in the Eighteenth Century* (1999)

Blacklock, Michael, *The Royal Scots Greys* (1971)

Brewer, John, *Sinews of Power: War, Money and the English State 1688–1783* (1989)

Brooks, Richard, *Cassell's Battlefields of Britain and Ireland* (2005)

Brumwell, Stephen, *Redcoats: The British Soldier and War in the Americas 1755–1763* (2000; this edition 2006)

— *Paths of Glory: The Life and Death of General James Wolfe* (2006)

Cary, A. D. L., and McCance, S., *Regimental Records of the Royal Welch Fusiliers. Volume I: 1689–1815* (1920; this edition 2005)

Carver, Michael, *Seven Ages of the British Army* (1986)

Chandler, David G., *The Campaigns of Napoleon* (1967)

— *Marlborough as Military Commander* (Staplehurst, 1984)

— *Blenheim Preparation: The English Army on the March to the Danube* (Staplehurst, 2004)

— and Beckett, Ian (eds.), *The Oxford History of the British Army* (Oxford, 1994; this edition 1996)

Chesney, George, *Indian Polity: A View of the System of Administration in India* (1868)

Childs, John, *The Army of Charles II* (1976)

— *The Army, James II, and the Glorious Revolution* (Manchester, 1980)

— *The British Army of William III 1689–1702* (Manchester, 1987)

— *Warfare in the Seventeenth Century* (2001)

Churchill, Winston S., *Marlborough: His Life and Times* (6 vols., New York, 1938)

Clarke, John, *The Life and Times of George III* (1972)

Clayton, Anthony, *The British Officer: Leading the Army from 1660 to the Present* (2006)

Corbett, Julian, *The Seven Years' War* (1907; this edition 2001)

Creasy, Sir Edward, *Eminent Etonians* (1876)

Crumplin, M. K. H., and Starling, P., *A Surgical Artist at War: The Paintings and Sketches of Sir Charles Bell 1809–1815* (2005)

David, Saul, *Prince of Pleasure: The Prince of Wales and the Making of the Regency* (1998; this edition 1999)

Doughty, A., and Parmelee, G. W., *The Siege of Quebec and the Battle of the Plains of Abraham*, Vol. V (Quebec, 1901)

Falkner, James, *Marlborough's Wars: Eyewitness Accounts 1702–1713* (2005)

— *Great and Glorious Days: Marlborough's Battles 1704–1709* (2007)

Ferling, John, *Almost a Miracle: The American Victory in the War of Independence* (Oxford, 2007)

Fletcher, Ian, *A Desperate Business: Wellington, the British Army and the Waterloo Campaign* (2001)

Foulkes, Nick, *Dancing into Battle: A Social History of Waterloo* (2006)

Fortescue, Sir John, *History of the British Army* (13 vols., 1899–1930)

French, David, *The British Way in Warfare 1688–2000* (1990)

Frey, Sylvia R., *The British Soldier in America: A Social History of Military Life in the Revolutionary Period* (Austin, 1982)

Gates, David, *The Spanish Ulcer: A History of the Peninsular War* (1986)

— *The British Light Infantry Arm c. 1790–1815* (1987)

Gleig, G. R., *Life of Arthur, Duke of Wellington* (1889)

Glover, Michael, *Wellington as Military Commander* (1968)

Glover, R. G., *Peninsular Preparation: The Reform of the British Army 1795–1809* (Cambridge, 1963)

Graham, Colonel Henry, *History of the Sixteenth, the Queen's, Light Dragoons (Lancers), 1759 to 1912* (1912)

Griffith, Paddy (ed.), *Wellington Commander: The Iron Duke's Generalship* (1986)

Gruber, Ira D., *The Howe Brothers and the American Revolution* (Chapel Hill, 1974)

— (ed.), *John Peebles' American War: The Diary of a Scottish Grenadier 1776–1782* (1997)

Guy, Alan, *Glorious Revolution? Fall and Rise of the British Army 1660–1704* (1988)

Harrison, Brian, and Matthew, H. C. G. (eds.), *Oxford Dictionary of National Biography: From the Earliest Times to the Year 2000* (Oxford, 2004)

Hernon, Ian, *The Savage Empire: Forgotten Wars of the Nineteenth Century* (2000)

Herman, Arthur, *To Rule the Waves: How the British Navy Shaped the Modern World* (2005)

Hibbert, Christopher, *George IV: Regent and King 1811–1830* (1973)

— *Redcoats & Rebels: The War for America 1770–1781* (1990; this edition 2008)

— *Nelson: A Personal History* (1995)

— *Wellington: A Personal History* (1997)

Hofschröer, Peter, *1815: The Waterloo Campaign. Volume I: Wellington, His German Allies and the Battles of Ligny and Quatre Bras* (1998)

Holmes, Richard, *Redcoat: The British Soldier in the Age of Horse and Musket* (2001; this edition 2002)

— *Wellington: The Iron Duke* (2002; this edition 2003)

— *Marlborough: England's Fragile Genius* (2008)

Houlding, J. A., *Fit for Service: The Training of the British Army 1715–1795* (Oxford, 1981)

Howard, Michael, *The British Way in Warfare: A Reappraisal* (1975)

Kitson, General Sir Frank, *Warfare as a Whole* (1987)

Kopperman, Paul, 'The British High Command and Soldiers' Wives in America 1755–1783', *Journal of the Society for Army Historical Research*, 60 (Spring 1982)

Lewis-Stempel, John, *Autobiography of the British Soldier* (2007)

Longford, Elizabeth, *Wellington* (2 vols., 1969 and 1972)

MacDonogh, Giles, *Frederick the Great* (1999)

Mackesy, P., *The War for America 1775–1783* (1964)

McLynn, Frank, *Napoleon: A Biography* (1997)

— *1759: The Year Britain Became Master of the World* (2004)

Mallinson, Allan, *The Making of the British Army: From the English Civil War to the War on Terror* (2009)

Mann, Michael, *The Regimental History of the 1st The Queen's Dragoon Guards* (1993)

Manning, Stephen, *Quebec: The Story of Three Sieges* (2009)

Maxwell, Sir Herbert, *The Life of Wellington* (2 vols., 1900)

Murdock, Harold, *Bunker Hill: Notes and Queries on a Famous Battle* (Boston, 1927)

Myatt, Frederick, *The Soldier's Trade: British Military Developments 1660–1914* (1974)

— *British Infantry 1660–1945: Evolution of a Fighting Force* (Blandford, 1983)

Parker, John, *Black Watch: The Inside Story of the Oldest Highland Regiment in the British Army* (2006)

Prebble, John, *Culloden* (1961; this edition 1967)

Roberts, Andrew (ed.), *Napoleon and Wellington: The Long Duel* (2001)

— *Waterloo: Napoleon's Last Gamble* (2005)

— *The Art of War: Great Commanders of the Modern World* (2008)

Rodger, N. A. M., *The Command of the Ocean: A Naval History of Britain 1649–1815* (2004)

Rogers, H. C. B., *The British Army of the Eighteenth Century* (1977)

Roy, Ian, 'The Profession of Arms', in W. Pest (ed.), *The Professions in Early Modern England* (1987), pp. 181–229

Savory, Reginald, *His Britannic Majesty's Army in Germany during the Seven Years' War* (Oxford, 1966)

Scott, Samuel F., *The Response of the Royal Army to the French Revolution* (Oxford, 1978)

Snow, Dan, *Death or Victory: The Battle of Quebec and the Birth of Empire* (2009)

Spencer, Charles, *Blenheim: Battle for Europe* (2004)

Stone, L. (ed.), *An Imperial State at War: Britain from 1689 to 1815* (1994)

Strachan, Hew, 'The British Way in Warfare Revisited', *Historical Journal*, 26 (1983), pp. 447–61

— *The Politics of the British Army* (1997)

Summerville, Christopher, *Who Was Who at Waterloo: A Biography of the Battle* (2007)

Tincey, John, *Sedgemoor 1685: Marlborough's First Victory* (Barnsley, 2005)

Tuchman, Barbara, *The March of Folly* (1984; this edition 1990)

Uffindell, Andrew, *The National Army Museum Book of Wellington's Armies* (2003; this edition 2005)

Urban, Mark, *The Man Who Broke Napoleon's Codes: The Story of George Scovell* (2001)

— *Rifles: Six Years with Wellington's Elite* (2003)

— *Generals: Ten British Commanders Who Shaped the World* (2005)

— *Fusiliers: Eight Years with the Redcoats in America* (2007)

Vallance, Edward, *The Glorious Revolution: 1688 – Britain's Fight for Liberty* (2006)

Venning, Annabel, *Following the Drum: The Lives of Army Wives and Daughters, Past and Present* (2005)

Walton, Colonel Clifford, *History of the British Standing Army 1660–1700* (1894)

Watson, J. Steven, *The Reign of George III* (Oxford, 1960)

White-Spunner, Barney, *Horse Guards* (2006)

Whitworth, R., *Field Marshal Lord Ligonier: A Story of the British Army 1702–1770* (Oxford, 1958)

Willcox, William B., *Portrait of a General: Sir Henry Clinton in the American War of Independence* (New York, 1964)

Woolrych, Austin, *Britain's Revolution 1625–1660* (Oxford, 2002)

Unpublished Theses

Steven Schwamenfeld, 'The Foundation of British Strength: National Identity and the British Common Soldier', unpublished Ph.D. thesis, Florida State University (2007)

Websites

www.grgordon.tripod.com/bunkerhi.htm

www.home.vicnet.net.au/~rifles95/rifle.htm

www.masshist.org/bh/accounts.html

www.napoleon-series.org/military/organization/c_britarmy1793b.html

www.teachingamericanhistory.org/library

Index

NOTE: Ranks and titles are generally the highest mentioned in the text